The Developing Person

Helen L. Bee
Sandra K. Mitchell

UNIVERSITY OF WASHINGTON

The Developing Person
A Life-Span Approach   SECOND EDITION

HARPER & ROW, PUBLISHERS, New York
Cambridge, Philadelphia, San Francisco,
London, Mexico City, São Paulo, Sydney

1817

To Sandy from Helen, and to Helen from Sandy, as a mututal toast to friendship that has increased our scholarship, broadened our thinking, nurtured our development, and enriched our selves.

Sponsoring Editor: Susan Mackey
Project Editor: Ronni Strell
Designer: Robert Sugar
Production Manager: Willie Lane
Photo Researcher: Mira Schachne
Compositor: ComCom Division of Haddon Craftsmen, Inc.
Printer and Binder: The Murray Printing Company
Art Studio: J&R Art Services, Inc.

THE DEVELOPING PERSON: A Life-Span Approach, Second Edition
Copyright © 1984 by Helen L. Bee and Sandra K. Mitchell

Library of Congress Cataloging in Publication Data

Bee, Helen L., 1939–
    The developing person.

    Bibliography: p.
    Includes index.
    1. Developmental psychology.   I. Mitchell, Sandra.
II. Title.
BF713.B43   1984   155   83–26510
ISBN 0–06–040578–3

Acknowledgments and Credits

We gratefully acknowledge the use of the following photographs:

Part I opener: Cole, Stock, Boston; Lejeune, Stock, Boston; (c) Marjorie Pickens, 1983; Zeiberg, Taurus; McKoy, Taurus; NYT Pictures.

Chapter 1: opener, (c) Morrow, Stock, Boston; 1.1, (c) Szasz, 1981, Photo Researchers; 1.3, FOR BETTER OR WORSE, Copyright, 1980, Universal Press Syndicate. Reprinted with permission. All rights reserved; 1.4, (c) Marjorie Pickens, 1983.

Chapter 2: opener, (c) Elizabeth Crews; 2.2A; Zeiberg, Taurus; 2.2B, Leo de Wys Inc., 2.2C, Merrim, Monkmeyer; 2.4, Landrum B. Shettles, M.D.; 2.5, Sybil Shelton–Monkmeyer; 2.6, Forsyth, Monkmeyer; 2.9, (c) Menzel, 1982, Stock, Boston; 2.10, (c) Arms, 1981, Jeroboam; 2.11, L. Johnston, *Hi Mom! Hi Dad! The first 12 months of parenthood.* Wazata, Minn.: Meadowbrook Press, p. 18.

Chapter 3: opener, Mazzachi, Stock, Boston; 3.11, William Vandivert; 3.12, J. E. Steiner, Human facial expressions in response to taste and smell stimulation, in H. W. Reese & L. P. Lipsitt (Eds.), *Advances in Child Development and Behavior,* vol. 13, Academic Press, New York, 1979.

Chapter 4: opener, Forsyth, Monkmeyer; 4.1, Shelton, Monkmeyer; 4.2A, Cole, Stock, Boston; 4.2B, Klutinis, Jeroboam; 4.3, Anderson, Monkmeyer; 4.4, Forsyth, Monkmeyer; 4.5, NYT Pictures; 4.7, Courtesy, Irving Sigel, Educational Testing Service; 4.8, Merrim, Monkmeyer.

Chapter 5: opener, (c) Elizabeth Crews.

Chapter 6: opener, Moon, Stock, Boston; 6.1, McKoy, Taurus; 6.5, Suzanne Szasz.

Chapter 7: opener, (c) Marjorie Pickens; 7.2, Traendly, Jeroboam; 7.5, Stroufe, 1978, pp. 52–53; 7.7A, Lejeune, Stock, Boston; 7.7B, Merrim, Monkmeyer.

Summary I: I.1, Zeiberg, Taurus; I.2, Holland, Stock, Boston; I.3, R. Davis/DPI; I.4, Zeiberg, Taurus; I.6, Holland, Stock, Boston.

Part II opener: Dietz, Stock, Boston; Siteman, Stock, Boston; Bodin, Stock, Boston; (c) Crews, Stock, Boston; Conklin, Monkmeyer.

Chapter 8: opener, (c) 1980, Dunn, Picture Group; 8.1A, (c) Crews, Stock, Boston; 8.1B, Siteman, Stock, Boston; 8.3, From Tanner, Fetus into Man, 1978, Harvard University Press; 8.5, Tanner, J.M., "Growth and endocrinology of the adolescent." In L. J. Gardner (Ed.), Endocrine and genetic diseases of childhood and adolescence, 2nd ed. (c) 1975 by the W.B. Saunders Co., Philadelphia, PA.

Chapter 9: opener, Dietz, Stock, Boston.

Chapter 10: opener, Druskis, Jeroboam; 10.1, (c) Bodin, Stock, Boston; 10.3, Forsyth, Monkmeyer; 10.7, Conklin, Monkmeyer.

Summary II: II.2, (c) Zeiberg, Taurus.

Part III opener: (c) Hankin, Stock, Boston; Herwig, Stock, Boston; Rogers, Monkmeyer; Arms/Jeroboam; Falk, Monkmeyer.

Chapter 11: opener, Dunn, DPI; 11.3, Dr. Leon Pastalan.

Chapter 12: opener, Herwig, Stock, Boston.

Chapter 13: opener, Reno, Jeroboam; 13.4, (c) Hankin, Stock, Boston; 13.8, DOONESBURY. Copyright 1980, G. B. Trudeau. Reprinted with permis-

Contents

Part II
The Developing Adolescent and Youth

Part III
The Developing Adult

Preface

This second edition of *The Developing Person* is a guidebook for students traveling in the wide territory defined by life-span developmental psychology. Most textbooks, in our view, take the form of an encyclopedia or a dictionary—lots of facts arranged in logical order. Volumes like that are very useful for some purposes (like preparing lectures) but not—in our experience—for helping students gain a "cognitive map" of the compelling and fascinating world of human development.

What do we mean by a *guidebook?* Well, a good guidebook divides a vast area (like a foreign country) into regions, describes each of them in general, points out some "four-star" attractions that ought not to be missed, and then directs you to your next destination. In this book, the "regions" are the topical areas of human development, such as physical growth, cognition, and social development. Each chapter is organized to describe the basic facts and theories about one area of development—the "lay of the land." In each chapter, we also try to point out the highlights—the ideas or experiments or theories that are especially clever or innovative or integrative. Finally, we try in every chapter to lead the reader on to the next topic or the next age, by making connections among ideas presented in different chapters.

Who is our guidebook designed for? The beginning undergraduate student of human development, whether taking a course in psychology, education, home economics, family life, nursing, or some other college department. While that means that most of our readers are young adults, we are certainly aware that students are an increasingly diverse group. So we have made a special effort to write in a way that will be meaningful for nontraditional students as well as traditional ones. For us, that means writing in a personal and informal style, the way we would explain things if we could talk individually with each student. It also means including a few personal anecdotes, so that the student can see real life examples of the concepts we are describing and so that she can see a real live person on the other side of the page.

And we are real people. Helen is 44 and has two children—Arwen, who is 14, and Rex, who is 22. Sandy is 37 and also has two children—Amanda, aged 10, and Colleen, who is 7. And we have parents and aunts and uncles—whole families of relatives who have taught us a great deal about development over the life span.

THE BOOK

If we needed to describe *The Developing Person* in a less poetic way, we'd have to say that it is a *topically* organized *developmental psycho-*

logical book about changes through the life span, based on *research and theory* with a strong emphasis on practical applications.

Let's take those one at a time! First of all, since the table of contents shows three separate sections (childhood, adolescence and youth, adulthood), how can this be a *topical* book? Well, the best answer is that we think about development topically, and we wrote the first draft of this book in a topical way (we'll talk about the order of the table of contents in a minute). That is, we worked on all of the chapters that are about one topic at one time. So all of the physical development chapters were written together, and all of the cognitive ones, and so forth. In this way, we think we have maximized the connection among the discussions of a single topic at different age periods. We have used similar terms and, wherever possible, parallel examples of research and theorizing. Instructors who prefer to use an entirely topical format for their courses, then, can easily make use of this second edition (the instructor's manual has suggestions for doing this).

Second, we wrote this book as *developmental psychologists*. This doesn't mean that all the data and theories we discuss come from developmental psychology—many of them don't. But most of our academic training (Helen Bee's at Stanford and Sandy Mitchell's at Illinois and Washington) centered on the first third of life and on traditional psychological research methods. As our professional (and personal) lives have progressed, we have become increasingly fascinated by those developmental processes that seem to continue over the whole of the life span—things like attachment and information processing and self-concept. We think that these concepts help to organize our thinking about development during the rest of the life span—and help us to interpret data from other disciplines as well.

Third, this is a book that is hard to categorize as a "research book" or a "theory book" or an "applied book." Our feeling is that both *data and theory* are needed to understand development—data to describe what happens as humans grow and change and theories to integrate this information and lead us to new ways of thinking about what we observe. Practical applications can be based either on data or on theory, but the best ones (in our estimation at least) are based on both.

WHAT'S NEW IN THIS EDITION

In some ways, this volume is a new book altogether, rather than a revision in the traditional sense. We did, of course, update our references and examples, write new boxes, and look for new and better suggested readings. But we also made some major changes.

The most obvious change is probably the length of the book. We have reduced the number of pages and the number of chapters, so that it will fit more reasonably into a one-term course on life-span development. Rather than just leaving out some material, we tried to tighten up the organization of the entire book. That is, we tried to combine material in a different way that would allow the number of chapters to be relatively small, but would still cover the most important topics in life-span development.

This need to reorganize led to the second major change in this book—the chapter order. The first edition was entirely topical—development through the life span in each domain was covered in one or two adjacent chapters. In this edition, the organization is topical *within broad age ranges*. This most emphatically does NOT mean that it is now an "ages and stages" book. What it does mean is that instructors may choose *either* a completely topical or an age-range–topical approach to presenting their courses. Our own view, after working on the book, tends to favor the age-range–topical approach.

The reason for our preference is based on another important change in this edition—the inclusion of three separate integrating *age-range summaries*. The purpose of these summaries is to help students weave together the various strands of development that are presented separately in the various chapters. We think these summaries are the most important sections of the book, and we hope that instructors will agree with us.

We also hope that instructors will agree with the shifts and additions we have made in the content of the book. From our own reading, and from the comments made by users of the first edition, we concluded that some areas needed new or different kinds of coverage. Although there are many examples of these, we'd like to call attention to just a few.

In the area of cognitive development we have increased our coverage of *information processing*. Rather than just tacking it on the end of the chapter, though, we have tried to use the concepts from this approach to integrate data and theory from the three approaches to the study of cognition—power, structure, and style.

Similarly, in the area of social development, we have included considerably more information about the results of *divorce,* both on children and on the adults involved. This material is included in the chapters on attachments—since divorce represents an occasion when an attachment relationship must be altered, often dramatically.

As a final example, we have increased our coverage of material related to *health* and psychological functioning, especially in youth and adulthood. Many human development texts limit their discussion of physical growth and change to the very early years of life, tracing motor development, height, and weight. We are convinced (perhaps because of our long academic association with a school of nursing) that changes in physical status and health continue to be important influences on psychological development throughout the life span. More-over, there is mounting evidence that changes in life-style (especially smoking, exercise, and diet) can make long-lasting changes in health, changes that are reflected in psychological processes as well.

WHAT'S STILL GREAT IN THIS EDITION?

The best things we've carried along from the first edition are our writing style and enthusiasm for the topic. After that, we hope that we have continued the pedagogical features that help students the most.

Chapter outlines—Every chapter begins with an outline of the important topics to be covered. This feature helps students identify the most important concepts and anticipate questions they may have as they read.

Chapter summaries—Each chapter ends with a summary of the most important data and theories presented. Students can use summaries to check their understanding, as well as for reviewing for tests.

Key terms—Each new technical term introduced is printed in boldface type, and each chapter includes a glossary of these new key terms.

Suggested readings—Annotated reading lists are included at the end of every chapter. We have tried to steer students to both classic works and popular ones—and to identify which is which.

Projects—The purpose of the projects, which are included for most chapters, is to encourage students to have real "hands-on" experience doing research in developmental psychology. Some can be done by individual students, while others are more successful if done in groups.

Boxes—The "boxes" in each chapter are our way of highlighting the practical applications of the research and theories we discuss. Some of them highlight atypical development, others everyday problems.

OTHER TEACHING AIDS

There are three related publications available from Harper & Row that you may want to use:

Study Guide—Prepared by Robert Deitchman, this is designed to help students study the text more effectively. It includes study and review questions, along with workbook assignments on key topics and new words.

Instructor's Manual—We wrote this manual to pass along to you some of our experience in teaching human development courses. It includes supplementary topics for lectures, information on atypical development, and in-class projects and exercises.

Test Manual—This separate booklet provides the instructor with factual and conceptual questions in both multiple-choice and essay format.

SOME THANK-YOU NOTES

We're grateful for the help of many of our friends and colleagues while we were working on this revision. First on the list are our editors at Harper & Row, Susan Mackey and Kathy Robinson. We suspect that they have saved us many hours of hassle by taking care of details that we didn't even know existed. Our production editor, Ronni Strell, has been tireless in her attention to detail, and her efforts are also much appreciated.

A number of excellent reviewers contributed to this volume: Harriett Amster, University of Texas at Arlington; David E. Borrebach, La Roche College; Lois Muir Byrd, University of Wisconsin—La Crosse; David Page, Nazareth College; John J. Rieser, Vanderbilt University; Brian Shaw, Massey University; Samuel S. Snyder, North Carolina State University; Kathleen M. White, Boston University; and Leonard Zusne, University of Tulsa. Their varying viewpoints and careful comments were extremely helpful.

Our local colleagues have been a source of innumerable key references, helpful ideas, and encouraging words. Kathy Barnard, Cathy Booth, Philip Dale, Nancy Jackson, and Nancy Woods all come to mind, but others have pitched in, too. Our thanks to them, especially for their patience when other work has been interrupted to finish something on "the book." Awards for patience also go to Terry, Amanda, and Colleen Mitchell, who put up with the sound of Ozzie the *& ^ $*@@ word processor for hours on end and provided support in all those ways known only to the families of textbook authors.

Finally, writing a book together can be hard on a relationship—professional schedules, personal lives, and editorial deadlines sometimes conspire to undermine even "secure attachments." So we are happy to report that this particular "development" in our lives has not undermined one of our most precious assets, our friendship.

Helen Bee
Sandy Mitchell

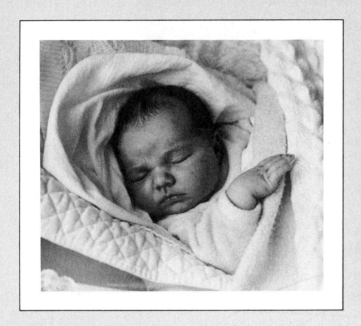

PART I
The Developing Child

Chapter 1
The Process of Development: Theories and Methods

We would like you to begin your journey through this book by taking an imaginary journey through time. Think back to your high school graduation. For many of you, that is not so long ago; for some, it has been many years. Try to remember your friends and acquaintances as clearly as you can. Was there a class "comic?" Were there some who were shy, others who were gregarious? Probably there were athletes and scholars, popular and unpopular students. Fix those people in your mind.

Now imagine your tenth class reunion. You're all about 27 or 28 years old, and you've come together in the old high school gym, all wearing name tags, with the inevitable crepe paper streamers hanging from the gym ceiling. Will you recognize your friends?

They certainly won't all look the way they did before. Some of the men will have begun to lose their hair; some men and women will have gained weight; others will be fitter than they were 10 years earlier.

Figure 1.1. These people at their twenty-fifth high school reunion are struggling to recognize each other. Once they get past the changes in appearance, will they recognize the same personality qualities in each other? Or will they have changed in important ways? Will the boy who was always the life of the party at 17 still be a bit of a show-off? Or is that something you see in teenagers but not in people in their forties? These are questions we will examine throughout the book.

Some of the people who used to wear only jeans and T-shirts will be wearing suits (and vice versa). But these are surface changes. Once you get past those alterations in appearance, the more interesting question is whether you will find the same people underneath. Will the class comic still be the life of the party? Will the shy ones still be standing on the edge of things?

What will you talk about with your 28-year-old friends? Will your conversations be different from the ones you had with these same people when you were 18? By the age of 28 most of your classmates will have married and many will have young children, so their lives are very different from what they were. You can probably expect the conversation to touch on families, on careers, maybe on a few anxieties about choices still to be faced.

Now if your imagination is still working, try to take yourself even further into the future, to your twenty-fifth reunion, or even your fortieth. Will you still recognize anyone? By now there are many more physical changes, which will make recognition harder. But again the real question is whether there are any stable characteristics, any persisting patterns of behavior that will allow you to recognize someone as the same person—as the Sally or Joe or John or Jane you knew in your teens. Even if the people have remained the same in some ways, you are likely to be talking about different things—about "midlife crises," or changing careers, or the triumphs and tragedies of your children.

You can see that there are two basic questions hidden in this imaginary trip—questions that are central to our discussion of development over the life span. Are there ways in which people *change* predictably as they age, and are there ways in which people are *consistent* over their lifetimes? Your friend Sally may still be the shyest person in your class 25 years later, which would show consistency, but you and Sally may both have changed in similar ways. You are now 25 years older; your bodies have aged, and you may have gone through similar experiences.

If we state these two questions more broadly, the two central issues for us to address in studying life-span development are these: (1) What are the *shared* patterns of development—sequences or trends that are characteristic of all children, all adults? For example, how are all 2-year-olds like one another, and how are they different from 12-year-olds or 28-year-olds or 80-year-olds? How does our physical strength or our relationships with other people or our ability to solve complex problems change as we move through childhood and through adulthood? (2) What are the *unique* elements of personal development that are special to each one of us? Superimposed on the shared developmental changes, are there individual differences in our reactions to the world or to the process of aging? If so, are those individual differences consistent over time? Does each of us have a "personality" or "temperament" that is visible in childhood and stays with us for the rest of our years? Or do our individual patterns, too, change over time? A quick thought about your classmates at your twenty-fifth or fortieth reunion will persuade you that the answer to both questions is "yes." If there were no consistencies of individual personality or style over time, you would have no way to recognize your classmates, except perhaps by noticing any remaining physical similarities. But it is also true that some of us modify those individual patterns more than others do—we change, we grow, we learn better ways to handle ourselves and our relationships. Our task in this book is to sort out these separate influences on life-span development.

Both questions are basically *what* questions. They involve *description* of developmental patterns or individual variations. A third fundamental question is *why* development occurs as it does, either collectively or individually. How can we explain the changes that we see?

Cast in the simplest possible terms, we will be asking whether developmental patterns and individual consistencies or inconsistencies arise primarily from *internal forces* such as genetic programming, from *external forces* such as major differences in life experiences, or from some combination or *interaction* of the two. Perhaps Sally is shy because she was born with a shy temperament, or perhaps her parents were less attentive and loving than other parents so that she learned to fear relationships or failed to learn how to be assertive with others. Her shy behavior could also result from a combination of these forces.

A fourth question we will return to repeatedly is, How do we find out the answers to the what or why questions? What techniques have developmental psychologists devised to describe and explain consistency and change over the life span?

A WORD ON INTERACTIONS

Most of us are well aware of the fact that our behavior is the result of a mixture of forces, all working together. The idea that there may be both internal and external causes at work at the same time is not a difficult one to accept. But often the relationship of the several causes is complex. It is not simply a question of adding the causes together; they may interact in complicated ways. This is an important concept, so it is worth an illustration or two.

Several decades ago Emmy Werner and her colleagues (Werner, Simonian, Bierman, & French, 1967) began a study of all the babies born in one year on the island of Kauai, in Hawaii. They kept track of any problems each mother had during her pregnancy, whether the baby was born prematurely, and so forth. They also noted the overall social-class level of the family rearing each child and later measured the children's intelligence. We might expect that infants whose mothers had some kind of problem during the pregnancy or who were born prematurely would be slower to develop or have more difficulties. Psychologists would describe this as a *main effect* of birth complications. We might also expect that children growing up in poverty would have a harder time than those in middle-class families, regardless of whether or not they had experienced any pregnancy or birth complications. In technical language, we are predicting a second main effect, in this case the effect of economic conditions on the child's development. So far this is pretty straightforward; we are looking for both an internal and an external influence. But if we look at each of these effects separately, we will not discover what happens when the two of them operate in combination. Do the effects of poor prenatal conditions and poor rearing conditions just add up or do they interact in some way?

Table 1.1, which gives one of the findings from Werner's study, shows all three elements. If you look along the bottom row of the table, you can see the average 2-year-old IQ scores for the children who experienced different levels of pregnancy or birth complications. As the complications increased, the children's IQs went down, illustrating a main effect of a biological condition. Now if you look at the right-hand column, you can see a main effect of environment (social class). The children growing up in poverty had lower IQ scores than did those in middle-class or upper-class families.

These findings are interesting; but if we look at only these two parts of the table, we miss the most fascinating result. Look at the numbers within the table and you will see that complications during pregnancy were associated with low IQ *only* when they were severe and when they were combined with poverty. Severe birth complications did not lead to substantially lower IQs if the children were reared in more advantaged families. The two elements, birth complications and family environment, did not just add—they interacted.

TABLE 1.1

One Interaction between a Biological and an Environmental Influence
Average IQ Scores at Age 2 for Different Groups

	LEVEL OF PRENATAL AND BIRTH COMPLICATIONS				Average IQ for each social-class group
	None	*Mild*	*Moderate*	*Severe*	
Social-class level					
High	102	100	104	95	101.3
Medium	100	100	98	91	99.6
Low	98	96	93	61	96.4
Average IQ for each birth-complication group	99.6	98.8	97.4	85.1	

SOURCE: Adapted from Werner, Simonian, Bierman, & French, 1967, Tables IV and VII.

Another example of an interaction, this time in a study of adults, comes from research on job satisfaction (U.S. Department of Labor, 1974). The main question these researchers were interested in was whether workers with young children were more or less satisfied with their jobs than those without young children. One might imagine that having children under the age of 6 would complicate an adult's life in a number of ways that might reduce job satisfaction to some extent. But would it have equal effects for men and for women? Figure 1.2 shows the main results.

Again we have two main effects and an interaction. Women were generally less satisfied with their jobs than were men (a main effect of gender), and both men and women who had young children were less satisfied than those without young children (a main effect of children). But again these two facts do not tell the whole story. The effect of young children was much greater for women than for men. Women's job-satisfaction ratings dropped twice as much when they had children as did men's—from −8 to −18 for women, from +3 to −2 for men.

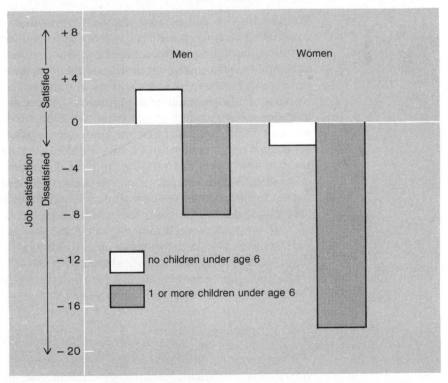

Figure 1.2. A second example of both main effects and interactions. Men like their jobs better than women do, and adults of both sexes like their jobs better if they do not have young children. However, the effect of young children at home is greater for women than it is for men—an interaction effect. (*Source:* U.S. Department of Labor, 1974.)

That is, gender and family status interacted to affect job satisfaction.

It is important to keep this concept of interaction in mind throughout the book. Many of us have a tendency to think that somehow the environment *happens* to a person, that the individual is some kind of blotter for experience. But he is not. The effect of any given experience depends on the age of the person, his intellectual level, his physical state, his gender, and many other factors.

One particular type of interaction effect, often called a **transaction,** is of special importance in developmental psychology. Not only does the environment influence the developing person, the individual also affects the environment. A cranky baby is treated differently from a placid one; an adult who smiles a lot gets smiled at more often than one who smiles less. The relationships that each of us creates with those around us are a process of mutual influence, with the end result more than merely the sum of the individual parts.

BACK TO THE BASIC QUESTIONS

Most of what we will say in this book is connected in one way or another to one of three basic issues. We will try to trace the basic developmental patterns, beginning with conception. But we will grapple constantly with the fact that not everyone goes through those developmental sequences in exactly the same way or at exactly the same rate. Finally, we will tackle the task of explanation. *Why* does development occur as it does? In exploring these issues, we hope we can convey to you the sense of excitement and fascination we have with the study of human development. It is very much like a detective story, but one in which the last few pages are missing. Individual pieces of research are the clues we can use to construct or select the best explanations of how humans develop. Each time new clues are added, we have to take another look at our old theories, our old guesses about "whodunit." Sometimes we find we must search for new suspects, new explanations.

Let us set the stage for our exploration by talking about some basic theories of development. You also need a working knowledge of the major techniques developmental psychologists have devised to answer the kinds of questions we have raised.

THEORIES OF DEVELOPMENT

Within developmental psychology there are four distinctive theoretical viewpoints: biological, learning, psychoanalytic, and cognitive developmental. Each of the four offers different descriptions and explanations of development. To this traditional set of four, we have added a fifth view, role theory, which emerges from sociology rather than from psychology, and which may offer insights particularly into the developmental patterns of adults. Since we will use these five theoretical views throughout the book as a basis for many discussions, we need to describe them at least briefly.

Biological Theories

The most basic proposition of biological theories of development is that both our common patterns of development and our unique individual behavioral tendencies are programmed in the genetic code. This does not mean that biological theorists think that behavior is not influenced by experience. No one takes such an extreme position. But genetic programming is seen by many psychologists as a powerful framework affecting both shared and individual patterns of development.

As you know from earlier courses in biology or psychology, each of us inherits from our parents a set of 46 **chromosomes.** Each chromosome, in turn, is made up of thousands of **genes.** It is the genes that contain the "instructions" for development and for individual characteristics.

Arnold Gesell (1925), perhaps more than any other theorist, has used a biological theory to explain why we all develop in similar sequences. The central concept in his theory is **maturation,** which we may define as internally determined patterns of change that unfold with age and are relatively independent of external influences. The transition from crawling to walking to running in a young child is a good example of a maturational change. The hormonal changes at adolescence that trigger the body changes of puberty are part of a long chain of signals that appear to be programmed in the genes. Maturational patterns are not immune from environmental influence. At the least, some minimal level of environmental support is necessary. In the case of pubertal changes, for example, an adequate diet is essential. But you don't have to *practice* growing hair under your arms.

It is important to understand several points about maturational theory. First, not all changes that happen with age are necessarily maturational. The term is not synonymous with growth. Growth normally refers to some step-by-step change in quantity or quality, such as the growth of the child's vocabulary or the growth of his body. Such changes may be the result of maturation, but not necessarily. A change in height might occur because the child's diet had improved—which would not be maturational—or because internally programmed signals led to the release of growth hormones—which would be a maturational change.

A second group of theorists has used genetic mechanisms to explain differences among children (or adults) in speed or pattern of development. Many of the thousands of genes we each possess are the same for all of us, which is why we all mature in similar ways. But many of the genes vary from one person to the next. Whether you have prematurely gray hair or not, are tall or short, have blue eyes or brown is controlled by your own unique combination of genes.

Some developmental psychologists have argued that we can use the same kind of genetic explanation for differences in performance on IQ tests or for differences in those characteristic patterns of response to individuals and objects that we call **temperament** or **personality.** For example, Alexander Thomas and Stella Chess (1977) have emphasized such qualities as activity rate, general mood, rhythmicity, adaptability to new experiences, and intensity of response as basic properties of inherited temperament. Arnold Buss and Robert Plomin (1975) describe somewhat different temperamental dimensions: active versus lethargic, emotional versus impassive, gregarious versus detached, and impulsive versus deliberate. Both pairs of theorists argue that these temperamental qualities are inherited and that they persist throughout the individual's lifetime.

Biological theories of development have been enjoying something of a revival in recent years, so we will see a number of variations on these themes in the chapters to come. The basic propositions of biological theory are summarized in Table 1.2.

Learning Theories

A very different emphasis is apparent in learning theories of development. A leading theorist, Albert Bandura, puts the basic proposition flatly:

TABLE 1.2
The Basic Propositions of Biological Theories of Development

Proposition 1:	Each individual is born with genetically programmed "instructions" that govern both sequences of development shared by all humans (maturational patterns) and unique individual patterns.
Proposition 2:	The expression of these genetic codes is not immune from environmental influence: A minimum supportive environment is required for normal unfolding of maturational sequences, and individual genetic patterns may be influenced by specific experience. But the genetic code is normally a powerful template for behavior.
Proposition 3:	The unique individual patterns, such as temperament or other qualities, not only influence the way a child or adult approaches people and objects, but they also affect other people's response to that child or adult (for example, a temperamentally gregarious child may draw more smiles than a withdrawn one). Thus the genetic pattern influences the environment, as well as the reverse.

> Except for elementary reflexes, people are not equipped with inborn repertoires of behavior. They must learn them. (Bandura, 1977, p. 16)

Bandura and other learning theorists are not rejecting biology. He goes on to say that biological factors such as hormones or inherited propensities can affect behavior. But he clearly comes down hard on the side of the environment as the major cause of the behavior we observe. Many other psychologists would agree with him.

Two important subvarieties of learning approaches to development have been influential in recent decades. The first of these, which we might call the *traditional* learning view, is wonderfully exemplified by Donald Baer's "age irrelevant concept of development" (Baer, 1966). Baer argues that development can be best understood as a long sequence of individual learning experiences. Since he assumes that the basic principles of learning are the same for infants as they are for children or adults, what is needed to explain any particular development, in this view, is a description of the sequence of experiences necessary to produce it. This is an *age-irrelevant* view because Baer argues that there is really no such thing as 2-year-old behavior or 20-year-old behavior. If one could merely devise the right sequence of learning experiences, 2-year-olds could perform tasks we normally think of as 10- or 20-year-old tasks.

Few developmental psychologists today would agree with such an extreme learning position. But there is certainly agreement on the importance of the two basic learning processes that are central to this approach: **classical conditioning** and **operant conditioning.**

Classical Conditioning.   Classical conditioning is a process by which reflexive responses can come to be triggered by new cues. For example, if you touch a baby on the cheek, he will turn toward the touch and begin to suck. In the technical terminology of classical conditioning, the touch on the cheek is the **unconditioned stimulus** and the turning and sucking are **unconditioned responses.** In the infant's normal experience the touches on the cheek are usually immediately preceded or accompanied by a series of sounds and other touches: the mother's footsteps approaching, the feeling of being picked up, perhaps the sound of the mother's voice, and so on. If any or all of these stimuli are paired often enough with the unconditioned stimulus of the touch on the cheek, they can become **conditioned stimuli.** That is, the sound of the mother's voice or the sensations of being picked up can trigger the response of turning and sucking. As a result, the infant may begin to show some form of nipple seeking before being touched on the cheek. Eventually, the child may begin sucking movements at the *sight* of breast or bottle.

This may seem to be a relatively minor type of learning, but it is particularly important for the establishment of emotional responses in both children and adults. Things or people that are present when you feel good come to be associated with feeling good. Those that are associated with uncomfortable feelings may later trigger fear or anxiety or embarrassment. Since a child's mother is present so often when nice things happen—when the child feels warm, comfortable, and cuddled—mother usually comes to be a conditioned stimulus for pleasant feelings. A tormenting older sibling or an unkind teacher, however, may come to be a conditioned stimulus for fearful or angry feelings.

Operant Conditioning.   A second type of learning involves the use of rewards and punishments to change a person's behavior. This is most often called **operant conditioning,** but it is also referred to as **instrumental conditioning.** The basic principles are these:

1. Any behavior that is reinforced will be more likely to occur again in the same or similar situations. There are two types of reinforcements. **Positive reinforcements** are pleasant consequences such as praise, a smile, food, a hug, or attention. Any time one of these occurs, the person is likely to try to repeat whatever it was that produced the goodies.

   Negative reinforcements, in contrast, are unpleasant events that, when *removed,* tend to strengthen whatever you did to remove them. This is a confusing concept, so an example will help. If your child is whining to be picked up (an unpleasant event) and then stops whining when you finally do pick him up, your picking-up behavior has been negatively reinforced by the ending (removal) of whining. In the same sequence, your child's whining has been *positively* reinforced, since being picked up is presumably a pleasurable outcome for him.

   A third concept is that of **punishment.** Many people assume that punishments are the same as negative reinforcements, but the terms are used differently by most psychologists. While a negative reinforcer *strengthens* behavior by its *removal,* a punishment is normally intended to *weaken* some behavior by its *application.* If you spank your son after he throws his glass of milk at you or frown at your spouse after he or she leaves the cap off the toothpaste tube for the thirty-fourth time, you are applying punishment in the hope that the undesired behavior will be eliminated. In fact, punishment rarely has this desired weakening effect.

2. When you reinforce someone part of the time but not all the time—a procedure called **partial reinforcement**—not only is his behavior strengthened, but it is also harder to get rid of. If you only smile at your daughter every fifth or sixth time she brings a picture to show

Figure 1.3.   Lynn Johnston has captured some of the frustrations of misunderstanding (or misusing) learning principles in this comic. These moms may think they are punishing their sons for misbehaving, but they are actually providing positive reinforcement, in the form of treats and special attention, for all the bad behavior. (*Source:* Johnston, Lynn. For Better or Worse. c 1980 Universal Press Syndicate.)

you, she will keep on bringing pictures for a long stretch, even after you quit smiling altogether. In the technical words of learning theory, a partially reinforced response is highly *resistant to extinction*.

3. Reinforcements do not have to be from the outside. There are also internal reinforcements, called *intrinsic rewards* or *intrinsic reinforcements,* including such things as the pleasure a child feels when he finally figures out how to draw a star or the sense of satisfaction you may experience after strenuous exercise. Pride, discovery, that *aha* experience are all powerful intrinsic reinforcements.

Social Learning Theory and Observational Learning.   A second type of theory, within the family of learning theories but with a quite different emphasis, is usually called **social learning theory.** This approach differs in at least two critical respects from Baer's age-irrelevant view: It places central emphasis on a different basic learning process, namely observational learning, and in its present form social learning theory is an age-*relevant* theory. There are a great many current developmental psychologists who base their thinking on this approach, but Albert Bandura (1977) is undoubtedly the most thorough and eloquent spokesman.

Bandura does not reject classical and operant conditioning. He agrees that reinforcements affect behavior. But he argues that reinforcement is not necessary for learning to occur. Learning can also occur merely as a result of watching someone else perform some action, a process called observational learning, or **modeling.** Children and adults learn methods of aggression by watching violent television programs; we learn generous behavior by observing others making donations of money or goods; we learn physical skills such as bike riding or skiing partly from watching other people demonstrate them.

Observational learning is not automatic. Bandura suggests that what we learn from observing someone else is influenced by what we pay attention to, by our ability to make sense out of what we see and to remember it, and by our actual capacity to repeat the observed action. It is precisely this aspect of the theory that makes it an age-relevant approach: You could demonstrate bike riding to a 2-year-old till you were red in the face without the child learning the appropriate actions. The 2-year-old does not yet have the motor skills to ride a bike nor the mental skills to analyze your actions and remember them. In other words, what is learned from observation may well change in systematic ways over development as the child's cognitive and motor skills develop.

The basic propositions of each of these two varieties of learning theory of development are listed in Table 1.3.

Psychoanalytic Theories

The psychoanalytic approach stands in sharp contrast to both traditional and social learning views: Psychoanalytic theories are strongly developmental in emphasis and assume that internal processes are as important as external experiences in shaping behavior.

Sigmund Freud (1905, 1920) was the originator of the psychoanalytic approach, and his theory of development continues to be of some importance. But theories in this same tradition, such as those proposed by Erik Erikson (1950, 1959, 1980) and Jane Loevinger (1976), are probably more influential in current thinking.

Freud's interest in development arose from his desire to explain the origins of deviant behavior among adults. Since he was mostly observing disorders of personality in adults, it was the process of personality development that he focused on. The development of perception, lan-

TABLE 1.3
The Basic Propositions
of Traditional and Social Learning Theories of Development

Traditional operant theories

Proposition 1:	The pattern of behaviors shown by each child or adult is primarily a result of the reinforcement history of that individual.
Proposition 2:	Changes with age that we normally describe as development can better be understood as the product of specific sequences of stimuli and reinforcements. If those same sequences were available to children or adults of other ages, they would show the same developmental changes.
Proposition 3:	Similarities in the behavior of individuals in any particular age group thus largely reflect common reinforcement patterns in our culture. For example, nearly all 2-year-olds are taught not to touch stoves; 6-year-olds are taught to read; 16-year-olds learn to drive a car, and so forth.

Social learning theories

Proposition 1:	The same as in proposition 1 above.
Proposition 2:	New behaviors are learned primarily through observation of the behavior of others—a process called observational learning or modeling.
Proposition 3:	What is learned through observation, however, is affected by the motor skills and cognitive capacity of the observer. Thus children of different ages, or adults, may learn different things from viewing the same model.
Proposition 4:	Similarities in the behavior of individuals in any particular age group result both from common models and reinforcement patterns and from shared cognitive and motor skills.

guage, or cognition were side issues. That is less true of some of the current psychoanalytic theorists. Erikson and Loevinger, for example, are much more centrally interested in cognition. But Freud's emphasis on personality is still a prominent characteristic of this theoretical approach.

Freud saw personality as emerging from important *instinctive* biological roots. Each individual, in his view, is basically focused on gratification of a set of instincts, of which the sexual instinct is the most central. The specific form of gratification sought and the strategies used to obtain it change with age, but the inner push to obtain gratification remains constant over the life span.

All the major psychoanalytic theorists agree that development of the personality occurs in a series of steps or stages. Freud described five **psychosexual** stages. At each stage, sexual energy (which Freud called the **libido**) is invested in a single part of the body, called an **erogenous zone.** Freud believed that the order in which the erogenous zones become paramount is governed by maturation. The infant first focuses stimulation on the mouth because that is the most sensitive part of the body. Later when neurological development has progressed, other parts of the anatomy become more sensitive and the child's focus of sexual energy shifts—first to the anus and then to the genitals.

Erikson, too, proposes a series of stages, which he calls **psychosocial** stages. Unlike Freud, Erikson emphasizes the conscious self as much as unconscious instincts. He sees development over the life span as a prolonged search for a mature *sense of identity.* In the process, Erikson thinks each person moves through a fixed sequence of tasks or dilemmas, each centered on the development of a particular facet of identity. For example, the first task or dilemma Erikson proposes, which he thought was central in the first 12 to 18 months of life, is the development of a sense of *basic trust.* If, however, the child's caregivers are not responsive and loving, the child may instead develop a sense of *mistrust,* which will affect his responses to all the later stages.

We have summarized the stages proposed by Freud and by Erikson in Table 1.4, which shows the parallels and the differences. One of the most obvious differences is that Erikson suggests that development continues over the entire life span—which is one reason his theory has been particularly influential in current thinking about adult development.

Despite the differences, however, Freud and Erikson share some important assumptions. They both see development as resulting from the interaction of the child's instincts and patterns with the responses of those around her. Basic trust cannot be developed unless the parents (or other caregivers) respond to the infant in a loving, consistent manner. The oral stage cannot be fully completed unless the infant is given sufficient gratification of the desire for oral stimulation.

Freud and Erikson also agree that leftover or unresolved issues from early stages will be carried forward and will affect the person's ability to deal with subsequent stages. Thus a young adult who has not successfully resolved the dilemma of identity versus role confusion during adolescence would have a more difficult time establishing a satisfying intimate relationship in his twenties. Since either the maturation of erogenous zones or the demands of culture push the child and the

TABLE 1.4
A Brief Sketch of the Stages Proposed by Freud and Erikson

Age	Freud's psychosexual stages	Erikson's psychosocial stages
0–1	*Oral stage:* Mouth is the major focus of stimulation; weaning is key task.	*Basic trust versus mistrust:* Infant forms first trusting relationship with caregiver.
2–3	*Anal stage:* Anus is focus of stimulation; toilet training is key task.	*Autonomy versus shame, doubt:* Toddler begins to push for independence.
4–5	*Phallic stage:* Genitals are focus of stimulation; identification with same-sex parent is key task.	*Initiative versus guilt:* Child becomes more assertive, resulting conflict may lead to guilt.
6–12	*Latency stage:* Sexual energy is quiescent.	*Industry versus inferiority:* Child must learn basic cultural skills, such as school skills.
13–18	*Genital stage:* Genitals are again focus of stimulation; formation of mature sexual relationship is key task.	*Identity versus role confusion:* Teenager must figure out who he or she is and who he or she will be.
19–25	(No new stage)	*Intimacy versus isolation:* Adult must form at least one truly intimate relationship.
26–50	(No new stage)	*Generativity versus stagnation:* Adult must rear children or perform some other creative act.
50+	(No new stage)	*Ego integrity versus despair:* Adult must integrate earlier stages and achieve sense of integrity.

adult forward to new stages, like it or not, an individual may carry with him an entire collection of unfinished or unresolved tasks and issues. It is this collection of "excess baggage" (which Roger Gould, 1978, calls "childhood consciousness") that leads to abnormal or deviant personality patterns in the child or the adult.

As usual, we have summarized psychoanalytic theory in a series of propositions (in Table 1.5).

Cognitive Developmental Theories

All the psychoanalytic explanations of development place greater emphasis on relationships with people than interactions with objects, and on the development of personality than thinking. Cognitive developmental theorists reverse this order of dominance and place greatest emphasis on the development of thinking. The central figure in cognitive developmental theory is Jean Piaget (1952, 1976, 1977; Inhelder

TABLE 1.5
Basic Propositions of Psychoanalytic Theory

Proposition 1:	The individual is fundamentally focused throughout life on the gratification of basic instincts. This proposition is more characteristic of Freud's theory than of Erikson's, but it is clearly a basic tenet of the psychoanalytic approach.
Proposition 2:	Each individual passes through a series of distinct stages in the course of development. Freud believes these stages are dictated by maturation of the nervous system; Erikson emphasizes the changes in cultural demands as well as physical changes. Erikson's stages cover the entire life span while Freud's cover only the period of childhood and adolescence.
Proposition 3:	Whether the demands of a particular stage are fully met or the tasks completed will depend on the responses of the people around the individual at that time.
Proposition 4:	Any stage that is incomplete will leave a residue of unfinished business that will interfere with the completion of later tasks or stages.

& Piaget, 1969), a Swiss psychologist whose theories have shaped the thinking of an entire generation of developmental psychologists.

Piaget, like other cognitive theorists such as Lev Vygotsky (1962) and Heinz Werner (1948), was struck by the great regularities in the development of children's thinking. He noticed that all children seemed to go through the same kind of sequential discoveries about their world, making the same types of mistakes and arriving at the same solutions. Nearly all 3- and 4-year-olds seem to think that if you pour water from a short, fat glass into a tall, thin one, there is now more water because the water level is higher in the thin glass than it was in the fat glass. But most 7-year-olds realize that there is still the same amount of water in either case. If a 2-year-old loses her shoe, she may look for it briefly and haphazardly, but she is unable to undertake a systematic search. A 10-year-old, in contrast, might use such good strategies as retracing her steps or looking in one room after another.

These changes in the abstractness and complexity of the child's thinking intrigued Piaget and persuaded him that there were powerful developmental forces at work. Perhaps because his early training was in biology, Piaget's theories about those developmental forces have a distinctly biological flavor.

Piaget assumed, first of all, that the nature of the human organism is to *adapt* to its environment. This is an active process, not a passive one. In contrast to the social learning view, Piaget does not think that the environment *shapes* the child. Rather, the child (and the adult) actively seeks to understand the environment. In the process, she explores, manipulates, and examines the objects and people in her world.

The process of adaptation, in turn, is made up of three *functional invariants*—**assimilation, accommodation,** and **equilibration.** (These terms may be unfamiliar, but the concepts are not inherently any more difficult than ideas such as reinforcement or classical conditioning.) Each time we encounter some object, some person, some experience, we assimilate it in some way. We notice it, recognize it, take it in, and hook it up with earlier experiences or categories. If someone serves you wine from a bottle shaped differently from the usual wine bottle, you will still recognize that it is a wine bottle. In Piaget's language, you have assimilated the container to your wine bottle mental category. If you are trying to learn how to bake bread and you watch a friend kneading dough, you will assimilate parts of what he is doing—those parts that you notice and understand.

Accommodation is the second process, the process of changing your concepts or your strategies because of the new information you have assimilated. Your wine bottle category has accommodated to the new shape, so the next time you see such a bottle, you will recognize it immediately. Your bread kneading strategy has accommodated, too, and is now closer to that of the instructor. Piaget calls the strategies and mental categories **schemes**—a concept we will discuss further in Chapter 4.

Equilibration is a broader concept. It is the basic self-regulatory process resulting from a fundamental motive to stay "in balance." The child is always striving to achieve an overall mental structure that fits all the experience he has had, all the assimilations and accommodations of the past. A scientist shows a kind of equilibration when she tries to make sense out of all the facts she has learned. She tries to fit the facts into her theory (assimilate them) and makes adjustments in the theory so that the facts fit better (accommodation). But sometimes the accumulation of facts just cannot be made to fit, and a new theory is needed.

The process of changing the basic assumptions, the basic theory, is what Piaget has in mind with the concept of equilibration. He sees the child as constructing a series of "theories" about the world. Each "theory" seems adequate initially but is eventually given up in the face of new experiences and new information, until at adolescence the child finally arrives at a "theory" that works for nearly all experiences.

Because all infants begin at the same point, because the processes of assimilation and accommodation and equilibration are the same for all children, and because the environments children encounter are highly similar, the sequence of "theories" they develop are likewise similar. Piaget identified four major stages in this developmental process, which are listed briefly in Table 1.6.

To help you contrast this theoretical view with the other three, we have listed several major propositions of Piaget's theory in Table 1.7. Note that the emphasis is almost entirely on explaining the ways in which children develop similarly. Piaget had little interest in individual differences in rate of development or in any possible differences in the sequence or pattern of development. American researchers have focused more attention on such differences, as well as on the application of Piaget's basic ideas to the development of relationships with others. But these expansions of the theory are variations on the themes originally suggested by Piaget.

Role Theories

A fifth view of development we have borrowed from sociology (Mead, 1934; Cottrell, 1942). The key concept is that of a **role.** Any social system can be thought of as being made up of a series of interlocking *positions,* such as employer and worker, supervisor or teacher. A *role* is the content of a position or the behavioral implications of occupy-

TABLE 1.6
Stages of Development in Piaget's Cognitive Developmental Theory

Age	Stage
0–2	*Sensorimotor stage.* The infant interacts with the world primarily through his senses and the actions he can perform on objects. He does not yet have the capacity to represent objects or people to himself mentally.
2–6	*Preoperational stage.* The child can now represent things to himself internally, but he is still focusing his attention on such external characteristics of objects or people as size, shape, color, clothing. Still, he uses these features for classifying objects into groups.
6–12	*Concrete operations stage.* The child makes a major step forward in the abstractness of thought. He discovers an entire set of basic rules about objects, such as the fact that they can be arrayed in various orders (from small to large or fat to thin, for example) or that aspects of them remain constant even in the face of external change (which Piaget calls conservation). He also develops the ability to use complex mental operations—such as addition, subtraction, or simultaneous classification of one object into two or more categories (a chair is both a piece of furniture and a wooden object, for example).
12+	*Formal operations stage.* As a final step, the teenager becomes able to think still more abstractly, using deductive as well as inductive logic and approaching decisions and problems in a systematic fashion. He can now think about ideas as well as objects and imagine objects or events that he has never actually experienced himself.

TABLE 1.7
Basic Propositions of Piaget's Theory of Development

Proposition 1:	Every child is born with certain strategies for interacting with the environment. These primitive strategies are the beginning point in the development of thinking.
Proposition 2:	Changes in the primitive strategies gradually occur as the child assimilates new experiences and accommodates the original strategies. Active interaction with the environment is an essential ingredient of this progression.
Proposition 3:	Over the years of childhood and adolescence, the child develops a series of "theories" or "models" of the world based on the level of understanding she has achieved thus far. These stages build upon one another so that, for example, concrete operations cannot be developed until the child has moved through the steps of preoperational thought.
Proposition 4:	While learning of specific skills and maturation of the body are ingredients in this developmental progression, the critical ingredient is the child's own *construction* of reality, which comes about through active exploration and experimentation with the environment.

ing that position. There are certain things we expect from a teacher, for example. He should be knowledgeable, able to communicate, a good role model for others, prepared, well organized, clear, and so forth. This set of expected behaviors or qualities defines the *role* of teacher.

For our purposes, there are several important properties of roles. First, they are at least partially culture specific. *Teacher* may be a different role (a different set of expected behaviors) in different cultures or in the same culture at different times. A hundred years ago in the United States, women teachers were generally expected to be unmarried and were certainly expected to demonstrate the ultimate in moral rectitude. Nowadays, it is illegal even to ask a prospective teacher if he (or she) is married. Thus roles change within a culture.

A second important point about roles is that they nearly always occur in complementary pairs. For there to be a teacher role, there has to be a role of student. The role of parent requires there be a role of child, while the role of husband requires the role of wife. Roles thus frequently imply relationships with others.

A third point is that most of us occupy many roles at the same time. As an example, one of us occupies at least nine roles: wife, mother, researcher, teacher, coauthor, child (of her own parents), daughter-in-law, girl scout leader, and friend. Whenever someone occupies many different roles, there is the potential for *role conflict*. The demands of the different roles may not always fit together perfectly. This is true in the physical sense that there may not be enough hours in the day to meet the demands of all the roles. It is also true the psychological sense that the several roles may require different or partially incompatible behaviors or characteristics. The role of parent requires nurturance; the roles of researcher and coauthor call for competence, critical insight, and assertiveness. Switching back and forth can cause confusion or conflict within the individual.

Sociologists also talk about *role strain,* which occurs when an individual finds it difficult to live up to the demands of some role he is occupying. A parent who feels incompetent because he just cannot figure out how to keep his 2-year-old from drawing on the walls is experiencing role strain. A newly minted PhD in her first professional job, who feels anxious about her ability to do high quality research, is also experiencing role strain.

The concept of role is an important one for our understanding of development over the life span for one central reason: The set of roles each of us occupies changes systematically from childhood through adulthood and into old age.

We can think of four categories of roles that change systematically over the life span: family roles, work roles, gender roles, and age roles. The most visible changes are probably in *family roles.* Any adult who marries and has children moves through a distinct set of roles in a specific order. A number of authors (for example, Duvall, 1962; and Rollins & Feldman, 1970) have suggested specific *family life-cycle* stages, which we have listed in Table 1.8. Each of these stages can be described as a set of family roles. Obviously adults who do not marry or those who marry but do not have children will not experience this set of age-related roles. But for the great majority of adults, this sequence shapes many aspects of life experiences over a 30-to-40-year period.

Changes in *work roles* represent another age-related sequence. The role of worker itself is age related. Most of us occupy this role beginning in our late teens or early twenties and continue to occupy it until retirement, when we take up the role of retired worker. But within the years when we are workers, there are also role changes. Many people move from novice worker to some kind of middle-level worker. Many of us then move on to levels of still further responsibility. The older worker is not only expected to be more skillful, she is also expected to serve as mentor to younger workers, training them and initiating them into the various special expectations of that type of work. There is thus something of the student in the role of younger worker and something of the teacher in the role of older worker.

A third set of role changes over the life span is in *sex roles.* You may think that once a child figures out that she is a girl or he is a boy and learns the basic cultural expectations (the role) for his or her gen-

TABLE 1.8
Eight Proposed Stages in the Family Life Cycle

Stage	Characteristics
1	Newly married with no children. Major new role is that of spouse.
2	New parents. First child is still an infant. New role of parent has been added.
3	Families with preschool children. Oldest child is not yet in school. The parental role is changing as the child gets older.
4	Oldest child in school. Again the role shifts as the parent must deal with the child's new characteristics and with the school system.
5	Oldest child a teenager. As the teenager goes through puberty and begins to push for independence, the parents' role shifts again.
6	Oldest child has left home. Some authors describe the family during this period as a *launching center.*
7	All children gone from home. This involves the loss of a good portion of the role of parent, although other elements remain. Often described as the *postparental* period.
8	Aging families. This may include the role of grandparent and of retired person.

der, there are no further changes in the sex roles. But recently researchers have shown that over the adult years there are some shifts in the "job descriptions" for men and women. Among older adults (those past 40 or 50), for example, the male and female roles appear to be much more alike than they are among younger adults.

Finally, there are *age roles.* In all cultures we know of there are certain specific expectations for people of particular ages beyond those we have already described. *Children* are expected to behave differently from *adults,* and among adults a person in his twenties is expected to behave differently from someone in his fifties or sixties. *Elderly people* occupy still another role.

We will use the concept of role to help us create some orderliness out of the changes we see over age, particularly in the adult years. But the concept is also useful whenever we talk about *transitions* in the lives of children or adults. Whenever our roles change, especially if several roles have changed at the same time or if we have taken up several new roles, we can expect to find some role strain. This may be expressed in anxiety or disorganization or other signs of stress. This concept should be just as helpful in understanding the shift from preschooler to school child as it is in understanding the shift from nonparent to parent or from worker to retiree.

There is no single theorist whose use of the concept of roles precisely matches what we are saying here. However, we have nonetheless created a set of basic propositions (see Table 1.9) so that you can contrast them with the propositions of the other four approaches we have already described.

CONTRASTING THE THEORIES: THE ISSUES THAT DIVIDE

Each of the five theories we have sketched is particularly useful in explaining some facets of development. It would be difficult to talk about systematic changes in a child's motor skills without invoking the concept of maturation; it would be equally difficult to talk about the influence of parental disciplinary techniques on children without bringing in learning theory. In fact, we do not need to choose between them. All five are correct in some respects. But since they make very different assumptions about the nature and shape of development and since these differences affect the questions asked and the interpretations of evidence, it is useful to contrast the five views on a number of critical issues.

The Motivation for Development

Why does development occur at all? Why does a child learn to say "cookie" clearly when "coo" was successful for getting the desired food? Why do 6- and 7-year-old children develop individual friendships with peers while 2-year-olds do not? One of the differences among the several theories lies in whether they see the motive force for change as *intrin-*

TABLE 1.9
Some Basic Propositions of a Developmental Theory of Roles

Proposition 1:	Each individual—child or adult—occupies a set of roles, which may be defined as a set of integrated social norms. A person who occupies a role is expected to behave in particular ways and to have particular qualities.
Proposition 2:	The roles we occupy change systematically over the life span. There are changes associated simply with being a different age, changes in family roles, in worker/nonworker roles, and in sex roles.
Proposition 3:	Any change in roles is likely to be accompanied by strain or discomfort. Particular points in the age span at which there is an accumulation of role changes are thus likely to be associated with lower levels of happiness or satisfaction and with higher levels of problem behaviors or a sense of crisis.

sic or *extrinsic.* Learning theorists (both traditional and social learning theorists) generally look to extrinsic motivation as the source of behavioral change. Children and adults change because the reinforcement contingencies and models change. No inner force or motive is assumed. Similarly, a role-theory approach focuses on the impact of external events on the person's development. As the child or adult occupies a series of roles, the expectations and demands of those roles shape behavior to a considerable degree.

In contrast, the psychoanalytic, cognitive developmental, and biological theorists all see the primary motive force for developmental change as internal. Piaget sees the child and the adult as operating from a fundamental inner motivation to adapt to and understand the world. This leads to exploration, comparison, and examination. The particular experiences the child encounters will affect his understanding to some extent, so the environment does have an influence. The *motive* for development, however, comes from within.

Similarly, psychoanalytic theorists assume inborn instincts and drives, such as sexual and aggressive drives, that "push" the child and the adult. For maturational theorists such as Gesell, the force behind development is the unfolding set of signals contained in the genetic code.

Figure 1.4. Not so very many months ago this child was eating with her fingers. Why did she shift to eating with a spoon? Was it because her physical development had progressed so that she is now *able* to use spoons? Or did her parents shift the reinforcement patterns so that now she gets reinforced for spoon eating? Or is she delighted to discover that she can manage this new object? These possibilities illustrate the different views about the motive for development.

Major Influences on Development

A closely related set of arguments has to do with the factors that influence development. Are the changes we see over time the result of basic biological forces, or are they the result of environmental influences?

Virtually all developmental theorists, no matter what their basic orientation, agree that development is a result of *both* biological and environmental influences and of the interaction of the two. But the several theoretical groups obviously place emphasis on different elements in the equation. For biological theorists, both the unique genetic patterns and the physical changes that take place over the life span are critical ingredients—a framework within which all developmental patterns must be understood. For the learning theorists, the reinforcement contingencies and models in the environment appear to be the most critical ingredient. Role theorists, too, look primarily to environmental forces in accounting for developmental change.

Both psychoanalytic and cognitive developmental theories, on the other hand, place the emphasis differently. For theorists in both groups, the *motive* for development is internal, but the quality of the environment or the opportunity to interact with the environment is critical for development to occur. The child must have toys and objects to explore if assimilation and accommodation are to occur; the parents must respond predictably and supportively if the child is to develop a sense of trust. Thus in these theories it is the interaction of internal and external forces that shapes development.

The Nature of Developmental Change

A third issue that divides the five theories is the question of the nature of developmental change itself. When we say that a 2-year-old has no individual friends among his peers while a 6-year-old is likely to have several, we could think of this as a *quantitative* change from zero to some friends. Or we could think of it as a *qualitative* change from disinterest in peers to interest or from one type of friendship to another.

Both the psychoanalytic and the cognitive developmental theorists see development as a long series of qualitative changes. Piaget argues that the *way* a 5-year-old thinks is different from the way the 12-year-old thinks. The older child has had more experience, probably knows more words, is familiar with more things—all of which may be thought of as quantitative changes. But the types of analysis the older child brings to bear on problems is qualitatively different from what we see in the younger child.

The strongest position in favor of quantitative change is taken by traditional learning theorists, such as Baer, who sees development as the product of a long series of small quantitative steps. Within the social learning view, some element of qualitative change is introduced since an entirely new behavior can be added to the child's repertoire through modeling. But most of the changes we see over the life span would be analyzed by learning theorists into small changes in the frequencies of particular responses. The fact that a 6-year-old has more friends than a 3-year-old would be described by saying that the 6-year-old has more "friend-making" behaviors or shows "friend-seeking" behaviors more often.

Stages in Development

A highly related question is whether there are identifiable steps or stages in the course of development. Lawrence Kohlberg (1973) has argued that there are at least three kinds of stages we might see over the life span: (1) maturationally based stages; (2) age-linked stages, defined by particular social roles or developmental tasks (sequential theory); and (3) hierarchically organized stages, in which each stage is built on what has gone before. Of course, a fourth alternative is that there are no stages at all. Development may simply be a smooth and continuous process that is not broken up into distinct steps or stages.

All four of these positions are represented in the theories we have discussed. Maturational theorists argue for stages or steps based on biological programming. Freud's theory has a distinct maturational flavor as well, since he thought the psychosexual stages were based on shifts in the sensitivity of various parts of the body. Role theorists certainly emphasize sequential stages, as does Erikson to some extent. Successive roles need not be built on what has gone before. Instead, they are simply new sets of rules. Erikson's psychosexual stages, however, do have some flavor of genuinely hierarchical stages. He believes that the successful or unsuccessful resolution of the tasks of each stage affects the individual's ability to handle the subsequent tasks.

The most fully hierarchical stages have been proposed by Piaget and other cognitive developmental theorists. They see the child progressing through a specific sequence, with each step flowing logically from the steps that came before. You cannot change the order and you cannot move on to the next step or stage until you have mastered the prior one.

Social learning theorists, in contrast, see no need for any concept of stage at all. Donald Baer assumes that there may be *sequences* of learning experiences that will be required to yield any behavior change. But he does not think that an adolescent learns by different rules or that a fundamentally different sequence is required for a 4-year-old or a 12-year-old or a 25-year-old to learn the same thing.

Consistency of Behavior over Time

A final significant issue on which we can contrast the different theories is the question of consistency in individual behavior over the life span. Biological theorists who emphasize inherited behavioral tendencies argue that such tendencies continue to exist in much the same form over the entire life span. Basic temperamental differences that are visible in the infant should still be present in the adult 30 years later.

Psychoanalytic theorists, too, argue for a good deal of individual consistency over the life span. According to this view, many of our behavior patterns are formed in early childhood as we move through the first few stages in development. Those patterns *can* be changed later, but with relative difficulty. A child lacking basic trust (Erikson's first stage) will be affected by that lack throughout life unless psychoanalysis or other therapy or self-understanding intervenes.

Learning theorists argue that either consistency or inconsistency might be found, depending on whether the reinforcement contingencies encountered by an individual remain the same or change. A child or adult who shows gregarious behavior toward friends will continue to show that behavior as long as he continues to be rewarded for it.

One reason that reinforcement patterns might change, though, is that a person's roles change. We might expect that as roles shift with age or with the family life cycle, behavior will change as well. This is not incompatible with the learning view; it is in a sense an expansion of it.

The one theory that tells us little about consistent patterns over time for individuals is the cognitive developmental theory. Piaget and his followers have been primarily concerned with explanations of patterns of development that are shared by all of us. In this view we *all* change systematically with age. But these theorists have not asked whether there are individual consistencies or differences superimposed on the basic developmental pattern.

An Overview of Differences in Theories

We have summarized the differences among the five theories in Table 1.10. You should bear in mind that the contrasts we have made between these approaches are oversimplified. Each of these theories is more complex, more sophisticated than we have been able to suggest to you. But they do represent distinctly different ways of looking at development over the life span. We will use all five views throughout the book, contrasting them where that seems reasonable, combining them where that is fruitful.

TABLE 1.10
A Summary Comparison of the Five Theories on Several Basic Issues about Development

ISSUE	THEORIES				
	Biological	Learning	Psychoanalytic	Cognitive	Role
Motive for development: intrinsic versus extrinsic	Intrinsic	Extrinsic	Intrinsic	Intrinsic	Extrinsic
Influences on development: biological versus environmental	Primarily biological, though environment has some effect	Primarily environmental, though biology has some effect	Inborn instincts shape behavior, but environment has a major impact as well	Interaction of child with inborn skills with the environment	Primarily environmental influence through changes in role expectations
Nature of developmental change	Qualitative and quantitative	Primarily quantitative	Primarily qualitative	Primarily qualitative	Primarily qualitative
Are there stages or sequences?	Yes, maturationally based	No	Yes, sequential and partially hierarchical stages	Yes, hierarchical stages	Yes, sequential stages
Consistency over time?	Yes, such as temperamental characteristics	Yes or no, depending on reinforcements	Yes, because the early stages set the pattern	(Takes no position)	No, since role demands change

ANSWERING QUESTIONS

We have already asked a great many questions in this chapter and will ask hundreds more before we are through—questions about the patterns of development and about the reasons for developmental change. Before we go further, we need to say at least a few words about how psychologists answer questions like these: How do we go about *describing* behavior or development, and how do we *explain* the changes that we see? In the language we used earlier, how do we answer *what* and *why* questions about development?

Describing Behavior

The most basic need for any research on development is to be able to describe people's actual behavior accurately. What do children or adults do in particular situations? How does a 2-year-old react to the presence of a strange child? How does a 4-year-old react to the same stranger? How do teenagers behave in groups, and how does that compare to what we might see in a group of elderly adults in a nursing home? How happy or unhappy with their relationships are teenagers or 25-year-olds or 50-year-olds?

Observation.   One basic way to answer questions like this is simply to watch people, individually or in groups. Since observation is a common research technique within developmental psychology, especially in studies of children, we should say a word or two about some of the strategies.

There are almost as many ways to do an observation as there are observers, but we can give you some sense of the variety of techniques by suggesting four types of observation, which we've shown in Table 1.11. An observation can be highly *focused*. You may look for only certain specific behaviors—such as smiles between nursing home residents or number of shared toys among 4-year-old children in a preschool. On the other end of the continuum, an observation can be quite *unfocused*—you may try to record everything that happens in as much detail as possible. Unfocused observation is often done in the early stages of research when you are not sure just what elements of a situation may be important. For example, researchers (for example, Yarrow, Rubenstein, & Pedersen, 1975) have spent hours in homes recording details of encounters between parents and children, the toys available, the noise in the environment, the child's play with toys, sleep patterns, crying, and so forth.

A second dimension of differences among observations is the location or setting in which the observation takes place. One can se-

TABLE 1.11

PLACE OF OBSERVATION	AMOUNT OF FOCUS IN OBSERVATION	
	Unfocused: look at everything	Focused: watch only specific behaviors
Natural Setting	Examples: Watch children on a playground noting all individual and group behaviors, or observe behaviors of elderly adults in nursing homes and compare to behavior of elderly in their own homes.	Examples: Observe aggressive behaviors of children on a playground. Count nonverbal approval signals between spouses in a home setting. Observe and count the number of occasions a mother provides some kind of instruction to her child at home.
Special or contrived setting	Examples: Not often done but you could set up a special room for mothers with toddlers and observe all aspects of behavior, or note all facets of mother-infant interaction during a special feeding session in the hospital or equivalent.	Examples: Observe facial expressions of subjects watching selected films, or note degree of attachment shown by children for their mothers under slightly stressful contrived conditions.

lect a *natural setting,* as Leon Yarrow did in his studies of parent-child interaction, or one can create a special or *artificial situation,* as Mary Ainsworth has done in her studies of the development of children's attachment to their parents (Ainsworth, Blehar, Waters, & Wall, 1978).

Of these four types, focused observations in artificial situations are probably the most common because they simplify the task of the researcher. But there is presently a strong push to move back to observation in natural settings so that we can gain a better understanding of the complex dynamics of behavior (Bronfenbrenner, 1979).

Questionnaires and Interviews.   Because observation is a time-consuming procedure, researchers attempting to describe the behavior (or thoughts or feelings) of older children and adults frequently use a shortcut: They ask people about themselves using either interviews or questionnaires. In fact, a large portion of the description of adult development we will discuss in Chapters 11 to 14 is based on questionnaire or interview information. Since people do not always tell the full truth or do not *know* their own behavior accurately, this method has some pitfalls. But with care, it can yield useful descriptive information.

Describing Changes with Age

A special problem facing developmental psychologists is to figure out how to describe changes in people's behavior as they age. Developmental psychologists have devised two basic research designs to describe these age-related changes in behavior, each of which has certain advantages and disadvantages. On the one hand, we can study groups of people of different ages and compare them. This is called **cross-sectional** research. On the other hand, we can study the same individuals repeatedly over a period of time, which is called **longitudinal** research.

Cross-Sectional Research.   If we want to know whether 4-year-olds can learn the same kind of concept as 8-year-olds or whether 20-year-olds have more stereotyped sex roles than 50-year-olds or answer any one of hundreds of equivalent descriptive questions about development, the simplest and least time-consuming strategy is to study separate groups that differ in age—a cross-sectional study.

For example, Nancy Denney (Denney, 1972; Denney & Lennon, 1972) has studied the process of *classification* in both children and adults. The subjects were given sets of cardboard cutouts of various shapes and were asked to "put the things that are alike or the things that go together into groups." The 2-year-olds most often made designs out of the cutouts, while 4-year-olds and middle-aged adults created classes by putting things together into sets, such as square things or round things. Interestingly, a group of elderly adults (67 to 95 years old) responded very much like the 2-year-olds, making patterns or designs rather than classes.

On the face of it, these findings suggest that in the first few years of life, children do not yet understand completely that objects can be grouped into categories. Such an understanding seems to have been achieved by about age 4 and is maintained into middle age. In old age, though, there appears to be a kind of "regression" to the more primitive thinking characteristic of the 2-year-old.

But is this the only possible account of these results? Cross-sectional results like these can get you into big trouble if you are not careful, particularly when you compare groups of people of widely differing ages, such as middle-aged and elderly adults. Do the elderly in this case perform like 2-year-olds because they have *lost* some intellectual capacity they once had? Or do they perform this task differently because they come from a *different generation* from middle-aged persons? That is, can we be sure that the differences we observe are genuinely *developmental* differences or might they be explained by changes in society over the generations?

Widely spaced age groups are called **cohorts.** In our culture, different cohorts have had very different life experiences. Adults now in their seventies and eighties, for example, grew up in a time when young people frequently did not complete high school. They have also probably encountered fewer tests like the one that Denney gave them. So when we compare such adults with those now in their forties—who have had more education and more test experience—we are comparing groups that differ in age *and* in experience, and we cannot choose immediately between these two explanations.

Cross-sectional studies can be extremely useful in giving a first description of possible developmental patterns. When the groups being compared are fairly close together in age—such as 2-year-olds and 4-year-olds—we can be reasonably sure that the differences we see are age related and not the result of cohort differences. But when we are studying a wide age range, we must be cautious about interpreting the findings.

Longitudinal Research.   A second major strategy for describing developmental changes is to follow the same group of people over a period of time. There are several famous longitudinal studies in which children have been followed from infancy into adulthood (Kagan & Moss, 1962; Macfarlane, Allen, & Honzik, 1954) or from early adulthood to later adulthood (Vaillant, 1977). More commonly, a group of children or adults will be studied over a period of two to five years, which is a more manageable project.

Longitudinal studies have several virtues. They obviously solve the cohort problem that plagues cross-sectional studies. That is, any differences observed in a longitudinal study between 40-year-olds and 70-year-olds are much more likely to be the result of aging, not generational differences, because the 40- and 70-year-olds are the same people (and therefore belong to the same generation). So if we were to observe a decline in performance on intelligence tests over age in a group of people we had studied longitudinally, we would be safer in concluding that this decline is age related than if we had compared different groups of people across the same age range. Notice that even the longitudinal study does not tell us *why* there may be a decline or an increase in some ability with age; it simply describes such changes.

Longitudinal studies are also essential for studying consistency and inconsistency in behavior. If we want to know whether the outgoing 2-year-old is still highly social at 4 or 10 or 25 or whether your high school classmates will still have the same personality characteristics 25 years later, the *only* way to answer the question is to follow the same children or the same adults through a period of time. Detailed longitudinal analysis can also give us an irreplaceable sense of the actual journey of aging as it is experienced by individuals. An example of this is in Box 1.1.

Describing Relationships between Variables

Like other psychologists, developmental psychologists also need to describe *relationships* between variables: What types of behaviors go together? What are the features of the environment that are associated with rapid or slow development or with one pattern of development or another? The most common way to describe relationships of this kind is with a statistic called a **correlation.** Since we will refer to correlations throughout the book, you need to know a bit about how to interpret them.

A correlation is simply a number, which can range from −1.00 to +1.00, that describes the strength of a relationship between two variables. A correlation of .00 indicates that there is no relationship between the variables. For example, you might expect to find a zero or near-zero correlation between the length of big toes and IQ. People with toes of all sizes have high IQs, and those with toes of all sizes have low IQs, too. A correlation close to +1.00 means that two variables are closely related. For instance, the length of big toes is probably highly correlated with shoe size—the bigger the toe, the bigger the foot. Some other examples of high positive correlations are the relationship between height and weight (the taller you are, the more you are likely to weigh) or between hours of weekly exercise and aerobic capacity.

Negative correlations are a little harder to understand because they show that high scores (or large amounts) of something are related to low scores (or small amounts) of something else. There is a negative correlation, for example, between the number of calories you eat when you are on a diet and the number of pounds you lose. The more you eat, the less you lose. An example from developmental research would be the relationship between the number of years of education an elderly person has had and the amount of loss of intellectual skill. The more the education, the smaller the loss.

Perfect correlations (+1.00 and −1.00) are not found in the real world, but correlations of .80 or .90 sometimes occur, and they suggest very strong relationships between two variables. For example, the correlation between IQ scores of identical twins is in this range. Knowing one twin's IQ, you can predict the other's IQ with considerable accuracy. Correlations of .50 or .60, which are fairly common in psychological research, suggest moderate degrees of relationships, but with many variations or exceptions.

A correlation is an extremely useful statistic, but it is import-

BOX 1.1

One Life through Time

The study of individual lives over time, as in a longitudinal study, can yield fascinating insights and richness of data. Some of the most fascinating glimpses of development come from George Vaillant's (1977) descriptions of the lives of a group of Harvard men first studied in their late teens (as college freshmen) and then studied further on a regular basis into middle age (about 45 or 50). Here is part of one such life, that of a man Vaillant calls Richard Stover.

Dick Stover was a happy, healthy man. When I arrived for an interview, he was in his yard playing catch with his two sons. Putting away his glove, he motioned me into his house. We sat down together in his rustic, comfortable living room, he in a plaid lumber shirt, I in a stuffy business suit. He was a big man, with big hands and [a] reassuring naïveté and radiated an inner peace. His commonsensical, studied calm was reassuring rather than irritating, and it came not from the denial of a Pollyanna but from a man who derived peace of mind by living a simple life free of embellishments. . . .

Until he graduated from college, Dick Stover was the model of a boy scout, and a virtuoso of repression. He asserted that before he was sixteen he had never had sexual thoughts or feelings. He denied having been sexually curious in high school; and instead, he was shocked and disillusioned to think that his parents had ever had sexual relations. When the Study psychiatrist first asked him [in college] about masturbation, Stover said that he could not hear the question. When it was repeated, he replied that he was uncertain what masturbation meant (a unique response). Finally, he dismissed the question by saying that he had never engaged in masturbation except when he was half asleep and lacked the willpower to prevent it. . . .

In college, Stover's identification was thoroughly masculine; nothing was effeminate about Stover physiologically or in life-style. As the center on his college basketball team, he starred. Since he had never had a girl friend, his incredulous teammates all vied as to who would be the first to fix him up with a date; but throughout college, Stover ingeniously outmaneuvered them. Even during World War II, while stationed in Italy, he managed to meet no girls. . . .

Soon after returning from Italy, Stover married. He made an excellent and active sexual adjustment, and had no trouble fathering two sons and three daughters. At forty-nine, when I asked him about his early shyness with girls, he had lost all recollection of it. In a way, he resembled many girl-crazy sixteen-year-olds, who have no memory of hating girls in grammar school.

In real life, Stover saw crying as a sign of weakness, but in the movies, tears came easily. He knew that to others he seemed outwardly calm, but confessed, "People don't know what's going on inside." I asked him what did go on, and he said he did not know. At forty-six, Stover's philosophy over rough spots had become: "This too shall pass. Things work out OK as long as one works hard enough to make them come out that way" (Vaillant, 1977, pp. 129–131).

This brief description of 30 years of one man's life points up many of the issues we will deal with throughout the book: In what ways do people show consistency of temperament, attitude, or behavior over long periods of their lives? What role do close attachments (such as marriage or parent-child relationships) play in the lives of children and adults? How do adults handle stress, and how do they transform themselves? How do the experiences of childhood shape our adult selves?

ant for you to understand the limitations involved in interpreting such numbers. *Correlations describe; they do not explain.* They tell us the degree to which two variables, two measures, two things, go together, but they do *not* tell us *why* those things go together. An obvious example may make this clear. It is a fact that there is a correlation between the number of refrigerators sold each year since 1900 and the number of deaths each year from lung cancer. The more refrigerators sold, the more cancer deaths. But neither you nor we would ever draw the conclusion that the sale of refrigerators causes lung cancer. Rather, we would suspect that some third factor—sometimes called an *intervening variable*—is creating the correlation. Increased industrialization, for example, affected both the production of refrigerators and air pollution—which in turn may have influenced lung cancer.

The refrigerator example is an easy one because it is so clearly not a causal relationship. However, we need to watch out for other situations where we are strongly tempted to draw causal conclusions from purely correlational evidence. If the number of years of education is correlated with an older person's score on an IQ test, it is tempting to conclude that education causes greater retention of intellectual ability into old age. But there may well be other explanations (for example, smarter people may have gone to school longer and also retained more skill). The basic point is that a correlation describes a relationship. Explanation of that relationship requires other approaches or more careful analysis.

Explaining Development: Experiments and Quasi Experiments

When psychologists want to move beyond description to explanation, they normally move beyond observation of naturally occurring events and introduce some intentional variations or control the situation systematically. That is, they do **experiments.** Suppose, for example, that a psychologist wants to know whether students perform better or worse on examinations when they are anxious. He could try to answer this question by testing the level of anxiety of each student right before a test and then correlating students' anxiety scores with scores on the examination. If the two scores are negatively correlated (as they are likely to be), this tells us something; what it does not tell us is that high anxiety *causes* poor test performance.

A second way to answer this question would be to manipulate the level of anxiety intentionally. For example, before giving a test the experimenter could tell some of the students that this was an enormously important test and would affect all their grades in college (thus creating higher anxiety). He might tell a second group that the test didn't matter at all—it was just practice (low anxiety)—and tell still another group that the test was quite important but not a matter of life or death (medium anxiety). He would probably also have a group take the test without any information about how important it was. (This *nontreated* group is normally called the **control group.**) He can then compare the performance of these four groups on the test. As soon as the researcher introduces this type of systematic variation, we have an experiment, and we have an opportunity to answer causal questions.

Crucial Features of Experiments.   An experiment has several critical elements:

1. The experimenter has control over the critical or relevant aspects of the situation. Often we say that the experimenter has *manipulated* a variable. The aspect of the situation the experimenter controls is called the **independent variable,** while the aspect of behavior that is measured—which is changed as a result of the manipulation—is called the **dependent variable.** In the test-taking study, the level of anxiety is the independent variable, and the score on the test is the dependent variable.
2. Ordinarily only one variable is manipulated at a time, although it is possible to design complex experiments in which several different features are changed.
3. Subjects are assigned randomly to the different groups. This is an especially important ingredient in an experiment. If we assigned all the people who were typically or chronically highly anxious to the "high-anxiety" group in our experiment and they did poorly, we would not know whether they did poorly because they were made especially anxious for this test or whether all chronically anxious people have something else in common that leads them to do poorly. The only way we can be sure of the connection is to take average or random groups and subject them to the particular experiences we are interested in.

The Use of Experiments in the Study of Development.   As it happens, while tightly controlled experiments are usually seen as the ideal way to try to explain behavior, there are special reasons why these are difficult to conduct in studying the process of development.

Some questions of interest to developmental psychologists can be answered with experimental designs. For example, Nancy Denney wanted to know why older adults performed like 2-year-olds on her classification tasks. One of her ideas was that perhaps they didn't understand what was wanted. So she introduced an experimental variation by demonstrating more complex classification strategies to some elderly subjects and gave no modeling to another group (Denney, 1974). She found that the older people could easily perform complex classification after they had been shown what was wanted. The 2-year-olds, however, do not respond to modeling in this way, which tells us that there is a real difference between the behavior of the two age groups and moves us a step closer to an explanation. Experiments can thus be used to probe particular developmental patterns.

The central difficulty in using experiments to study development is that *we cannot assign subjects randomly to age groups.* Neither can we assign them randomly to sex or social class or education groups—and these are all vital aspects of any attempt to explain patterns of development. To put the problem another way, unlike psychologists studying other aspects of behavior, developmental psychologists *cannot* systematically manipulate the variables they are most interested in, such as age or broad environmental features.

Quasi Experiments.   To get around this problem, we use a series of research designs, sometimes called **quasi experiments,** in which we compare groups without random assignment. A few examples may make this point a bit clearer.

1. *Cross-sectional comparisons.* Comparing groups of people of different ages is a kind of quasi experiment. Thus all cross-sectional research has certain features of an experiment. We can increase the control if we design an actual experiment that is performed independently with *each* of a series of age groups, with subjects assigned randomly to groups *within* each age. An example would be providing models of complex classification for half the 2-year-olds and half the 70-year-olds, with the remainder of the subjects at each age left to approach the task without special conditions.
2. *Naturally occurring groups.* Other than different age groups, we may want to compare other types of people, such as men and women, children who experienced poor nutrition during pregnancy with those who had good nutrition, or children who established secure attachments with their parents with those who did not. Since again we cannot assign people randomly to these groups, such comparisons have built-in problems. However, such comparisons are often the first step in an attempt at explanation.
3. *Matching groups.* One way to strengthen any naturally occurring group comparison is to *match* the two groups on other features that we think might make a difference. If we want to compare 40-year-olds and 70-year-olds on cognitive skill, for example, we might match the two groups on years of education. Then if the two

equally educated age groups still differ in skill, at least we know it can't be because of the usual differences in level of education between these two cohorts. Or if we want to know if mothers who drink alcohol during their pregnancies are more likely to have premature infants, we would want to match the group of mothers who drink and the group of those who do not on such variables as age, education, smoking history, diet, and other factors that we know are likely to affect birth weight. Then if drinkers still have smaller babies, we have at least ruled out some of the more obvious alternative explanations.

All these strategies are common in developmental research. Explaining developmental sequences is a complex and difficult task, and researchers have become increasingly inventive in devising ways of sorting out the alternative possibilities.

SUMMARY

1. We must try to answer several basic questions about development: (1) How can we *describe* the patterns of development that we can see from conception to death? This breaks down into two subquestions: What are the shared patterns of development? And what are the unique individual elements of development? (2) How can we *explain* the patterns of development that we describe? Generally, what are the internal influences, what are the external influences, and how do the two interact? (3) How do we go about doing the research to answer either descriptive or explanatory questions?

2. Interactions between internal and external forces are of special concern since no behavior, no developmental pattern is the exclusive product of either. Most often, internal biological influences and environmental influences combine (interact) in special and often complex ways.

3. Five groups of theories have been proposed to explain development, each of which offers important insights into the causes of development.

4. Biological theorists focus on the role of genetic instructions in explaining both the ways in which we all develop similarly and the individual differences in rate and style.

5. Learning theorists invoke basic learning principles, such as classical and operant conditioning and observational learning, to account for the acquisition of new behaviors and the modification of old behaviors over the life span.

6. Psychoanalytic theorists emphasize the role of basic inborn instincts that shape the child's and the adult's behavior. These in-

stincts, in turn, interact with the environment to produce individually unique patterns of development.

7. Cognitive developmental theorists place greatest emphasis on the child's active role in discovering and exploring the world. Environment is needed for the child to proceed through the stages proposed. However, it is fundamentally the child's activity that is critical.

8. The concept of role, borrowed from sociology, can also be used as the basis for a developmental theory. Since roles change sequentially over the life span, each child's or adult's behavior is shaped into common developmental patterns to at least some degree because of shared roles at each stage.

9. While each theory offers important points, they differ from one another on a number of critical dimensions, including assumptions about the motives for and influences on development, the nature of developmental change, the existence of stages in development, and whether we should expect consistency in individual behavior over the life span.

10. Research techniques designed to yield valid descriptions of development include many forms of observation, such as detailed observations in natural settings or focused observations in artificial settings. Among older children, adolescents, and adults, questionnaires and interviews are also used to collect basic descriptive information.

11. Changes with age are normally studied with one of two research designs—cross-sectional or longitudinal. In the former type of design, separate groups of individuals, each group of a different age, are studied at one time. A longitudinal study, on the other hand, involves observation of the same group of people over a period of time. This type of design is particularly useful when we wish to study developmental changes that take place over large periods of time or consistencies or inconsistencies in individual development.

12. Descriptions of relationships between variables are often made with a statistic called a correlation, which ranges from $+1.00$ to -1.00.

13. Explanations of behavior are most often achieved through controlled experimentation, in which the experimenter manipulates at least one variable systematically and assigns subjects randomly to different treatment groups.

14. Experimental designs are used by developmental psychologists, but many of the explanations we search for do not permit complete control or random assignment. Quasi-experimental designs are more common, involving comparison of naturally occurring groups, with group matching on relevant variables.

Accommodation The process hypothesized by Piaget by which a person adapts existing structures—actions, ideas, or strategies—to fit new experiences.

Assimilation The process of taking a new experience or new information and adjusting it to fit existing structures. A cornerstone concept in Piaget's theory.

Chromosomes Tiny particles contained in the nucleus of every cell. Each human cell contains 23 pairs of chromosomes, which contain the basic genetic information for the development of that individual.

Classical conditioning One of three major types of learning. An automatic, unconditioned response such as an emotional feeling or a reflex comes to be triggered by a new cue, called the conditioned stimulus, after the conditioned stimulus has been paired several times with the original unconditioned stimulus.

Cohort A group of persons of approximately the same age who have shared similar major life experiences, such as cultural training, economic conditions, and type of education.

Conditioned stimulus In classical conditioning this is the cue that, after being paired a number of times with the unconditioned stimulus, comes to trigger the unconditioned response.

Control group A group of subjects in an experiment that is comparable in all ways to the experimental group except for the key manipulated variable.

Correlation A statistic *(r)* that can range from +1.00 to −1.00, describing the extent to which two variables are related to one another. The closer the correlation to +1.00, the stronger the relationship.

Cross-sectional study A study in which different groups of individuals of different ages are all studied at the same time.

Dependent variable The aspect of a subject's behavior that is expected to change because of the manipulation in an experiment.

Equilibration Another central concept in Piaget's theory; the process by which each individual attempts to keep assimilations and accommodations in balance so that one's theory of the world is as close as possible to one's experiences.

Erogenous zones Portions of the body that in Freudian theory are thought to be sequentially the seat of heightened sexual awareness, such as the mouth, the anus, and the genitals.

Experimental research designs Research intended to explain relationships or developmental patterns, involving control and manipulation of key variables and random assignment of subjects to treatment groups.

Genes Microscopic subdivisions of chromosomes. Each chromosome contains thousands of genes.

Independent variable The variable manipulated by the experimenter in a scientific experiment.

Instrumental conditioning Another term used for operant conditioning (see below).

Libido The term used by Freud to describe the pool of sexual energy in each individual.

Longitudinal study A study in which the same subjects are observed or assessed repeatedly over a period of months or years.

Maturation The sequential unfolding of physical or behavioral characteristics governed by instructions contained in the genes. Since all members of a species share thousands of genetic instructions, maturational sequences will be the same for all.

Modeling A term used by Bandura and others to describe observational learning.

Negative reinforcement Any event whose removal strengthens the probability of the behavior associated with its removal.

Observation One major way to obtain descriptions of behavior, involving primarily watching and recording of behavior in either standardized (often artificial) conditions or in natural settings.

Observational learning Another of the three main types of learning. The learning of motor skills, attitudes, or other behaviors through observing someone else perform them.

Operant conditioning A third major type of learning in which the principles of positive and negative reinforcement operate to shape behavior.

Partial reinforcement A pattern of reinforcement that occurs in most natural learning situations in which only some responses of a particular kind are reinforced.

Personality The collection of individual, relatively enduring, patterns of reacting to and interacting with others that distinguishes each child or adult.

Positive reinforcement Any event whose presence strengthens the probability of the behavior that occurred immediately before it.

Psychosexual stages The stages of personality development suggested by Freud, including the oral, anal, phallic, latency, and genital stages. The sequence is heavily influenced by maturation.

Psychosocial stages The stages of personality development proposed by Erikson, including trust, autonomy, initiative, industry, identity, intimacy, generativity, and ego integrity.

Punishment Unpleasant consequences administered after some undesired behavior. The purpose of punishment is usually to eliminate the undesired behavior, but in fact it seldom has that effect.

Quasi experiments Research designs that are like experiments in that groups are compared, but unlike traditional experiments in that naturally occurring groups are used rather than assigning people randomly. Comparisons of age groups or of gender or social class or experience groups are of this type. Such research is better if the groups are matched on critical variables.

Role A concept taken primarily from sociological theory. A role is the behavioral and attitudinal content of a social position, such as *employer* or *grandfather*.

Schemes Piaget's word for the basic actions, ideas, and strategies to which a new experience is assimilated and which are then modified (accommodated) as a result of the new experience.

Social learning theory   A subvariety of learning theory that places major emphasis on social reinforcements and on modeling or imitation as the source of new learning.

Temperament   Collections of typical responses to experiences that are visible in young infants and that show some stability over time. Sociability and activity level are two such dimensions.

Transaction   Term currently being used by developmental psychologists to describe interactions between two people (usually parent and child) in which each individual affects the other and in which the relationship systematically changes over time.

Unconditioned response   In classical conditioning this is the basic unlearned response that is triggered by the unconditioned stimulus.

Unconditioned stimulus   In classical conditioning this is the cue or signal that automatically (without learning) triggers the unconditioned response.

SUGGESTED READINGS

Achenbach, T. M. *Research in developmental psychology: Concepts, strategies, methods.* New York: Free Press, 1978.
This is an excellent source for more detailed information about developmental research.

Bandura, A. *Social learning theory.* Englewood Cliffs, N.J.: Prentice-Hall, 1977.
A very interesting, well-written description of the social learning approach, which includes a description of the cognitive elements new to this view. A bit tough for a beginning student, but it should be manageable.

Bijou, S. W., & Baer, D. M. *Child development* (Vol. 1). Englewood Cliffs, N.J.: Prentice-Hall, 1961.
A small pocketbook, easy to read and quite clear, that presents the operant conditioning view (the traditional view, as we have called it in this chapter) of child development. The authors do not address life-span questions, but presumably they would argue that the same principles apply at all ages.

Erikson, E. H. *Childhood and society.* New York: Norton, 1950.
The basic early presentation of Erikson's theory of development. Focus especially on Chapter 7.

Moore, S. G., & Cooper, C. R. Personal and scientific sources of knowledge about children. In S. G. Moore & C. R. Cooper (Eds.), *The young child. Reviews of research* (Vol. 3). Washington, D.C.: National Association for the Education of Young Children, 1982.
This is an excellent, brief discussion of the role of research in the study of children's development, touching more fully on many of the points we have made in this chapter.

Piaget, J. Development and learning. In R. Ripple & V. Rockcastle (Eds.), *Piaget rediscovered.* Ithaca, N.Y.: Cornell University Press, 1964, pp. 7–19. Also reprinted in C. S. Lavatelli & F. Stendler (Eds.), *Readings in child behavior and development* (3d Ed.). New York: Harcourt Brace Jovanovich, 1972.
Piaget's writing is ordinarily *very* difficult, but this fairly brief paper is not

as tough as usual. He discusses the roles of both maturation and learning in development, as well as other factors he thinks are important. Do not let the terminology throw you too much. It will get easier as you go along.

PROJECT 1.1
First Focused Observation

You will have opportunities to do focused observations in other projects later in the book, but you may want to start at this point by trying something fairly simple. The particular behavior we want you to observe in this case is *smiling.*

Step 1. Make arrangements with a local preschool or day care center to spend about an hour making observations. Ordinarily this will mean contacting the director of the school/center and inquiring about procedures for such observations. Assure the director that you will not be intervening in any way and will not interfere with the regular activities of the school. Make similar arrangements to spend about half an hour in the cafeteria at a local high school. Probably it is sufficient to call the principal, but you may need to call the school district office to obtain permission.

Step 2. Observe a group of preschool children one at a time for a total of at least a half hour. Observe an equal number of boys and girls, each for an equal amount of time. For example, you might observe 10 boys for 1½ minutes each and ten girls for 1½ minutes each. Alternate the boys and girls in your observations. If there are more children, then observe more of them for less time each, and so on. Keep track of the time with a stopwatch or other accurate method so that each child is observed for the same length of time. Note each time a child smiles while you are observing him or her, and be sure you can tell from your record whether it was a boy or a girl who smiled.

Step 3. Make a similar observation of teenagers in the high school cafeteria, making sure you observe as many boys and girls as you did in step 2. In this step and in step 4, do *not* select any person for observation who is eating alone.

Step 4. Do a similar observation in a college cafeteria or coffee shop, observing students or other adults.

Step 5. Compute the average number of smiles per minute for each sex at each age level and put your results into a table of some kind. Then try to figure out what your results might mean. There is some evidence from a study by Mackey (1976), as well as other research, that women smile more than men do, but there is some hint that this might be reversed in very young children. Do you find support for either or both of these expectations in your data?

Step 6. Prepare a written report of your project following guidelines specified by your instructor. You may want to consider the following issues:

- How did you decide what was a smile?
- Could you have agreed with another observer on what was a smile?
- How might the circumstances of the observations have affected the results? Were they very different from one age group to the next? Might those circumstances—rather than age—be producing any age differences you found?
- What can we conclude, if anything, about age changes in smiling?
- What did you learn about observations? About research design?

PROJECT 1.2
Experimentation: Smiling and Smiling Back

This time we want to introduce a small experimental manipulation, namely, whether you smile at each subject first or not.

Step 1. Find some location—in your dorm, near the student union or similar building on your campus, or even on a street corner—where you can stand for a period of time without looking too obvious or peculiar. (You might pretend that you are waiting to meet someone there.) As people come by you, greet them with some fairly typical comment, such as "Good morning" or "How are you?" either accompanied by a smile or *not* accompanied by a smile. Half the time, you smile when you say something; the other half of the time, you don't. Record whether you smile, whether the subject smiles back, and the sex of each subject. Continue this procedure, either in the same location or in several different locations, until you have at least 50 subjects of each sex, 25 of whom have been smiled at and 25 not smiled at. (If you cannot bear the idea of speaking to strangers, you can do this without the verbal greeting—merely meet the other person's gaze briefly and either smile or don't smile.)

Step 2. Compute the total number of smiles in each of the four categories (male/female, smiled at/not smiled at) and display them in a table.

Step 3. In a written report (if required by your instructor), discuss the design of this experiment. Which are the independent variables, and which are the dependent variables? Which things did you, as the experimenter, control? In addition, discuss any problems you discovered with this procedure. How might these flaws in the design be corrected? What about the results? Were there any differences? How might you explain them? Could you do the same experiment with young children and compare the results?

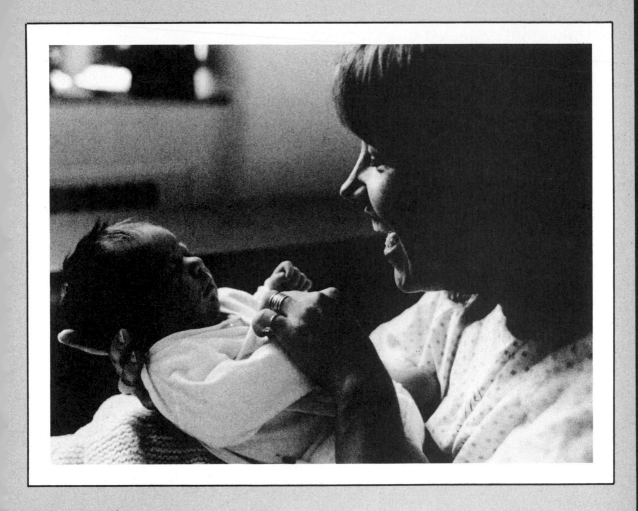

Chapter 2
The Beginnings:
Prenatal Development, Birth,
and Early Infancy

Suppose for just a moment that we asked you to picture in your mind's eye a human infant—a baby. What kind of picture would that be? Some of you would probably imagine a beautiful, clean infant wrapped in blankets and *sleeping* soundly—the kind of infant you usually find in a Nativity scene. Others would think of a baby who is *eating,* like those on the labels of baby food jars. And still others—perhaps the majority—would call to mind the picture of a *crying* baby, with her face wrinkled and red, making a lot of noise.

Let's start this chapter by comparing your mental pictures with the observations made by two kinds of experts in infant development—parents and pediatricians.

The charts shown in Figure 2.1 are records that were kept by parents of 1-month-old babies in a longitudinal study conducted by Kathryn Barnard and her colleagues (1979). The parents used symbols for eating, sleeping, crying, playing, and diapering to keep track of their infants' daily activities over the course of an entire week. As you

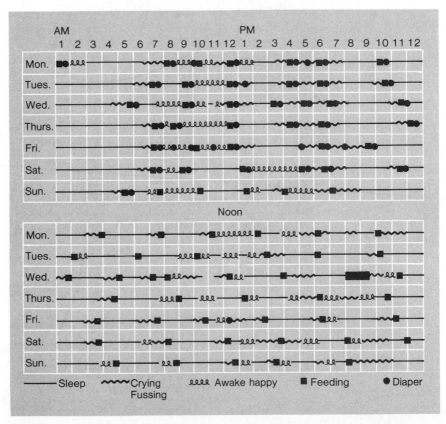

Figure 2.1. Sleep/activity records for two 1-month-old infants. The infant described in the upper chart has a very regular sleep-wake-cry-eat cycle, while the infant in the lower chart has a very irregular pattern and does not yet sleep through the night. (*Source:* Barnard, K. Unpublished data from the Nursing Child Assessment Project, University of Washington, 1976.)

can see, both of the babies shown in these charts did many of the things you thought of—eating, sleeping, and crying. But you should also notice that the two infants did them on quite different schedules. One baby had a regular, well-organized sequence of sleeping and wakefulness, while the other had a comparatively disorganized sequence of sleeping and activity. So our stereotypes of infant behavior have some basis in fact (that is, babies *do* a lot of eating, sleeping, and crying), but like all stereotypes, they do not do a very good job of describing individual infants.

The research done by T. Berry Brazelton and his colleagues (1973) has been aimed at describing and studying some of the subtle characteristics that account for how babies are different from one another. One of the first things they studied was what they call the baby's **state of consciousness.** This is very close to what parents and casual observers mean when they use labels like *awake, asleep,* and *crying.*

Brazelton (as well as other infant researchers such as Prechtl & Beintema, 1964) classifies infant state on a scale that has six divisions rather than the three that most casual observers use. Although the technical definitions of state include specific information about the infant's breathing rate and body movements, you can see that what this classification scheme actually does is break down each of the common-sense states into two parts: two kinds of sleeping, two kinds of wakefulness, and two kinds of crying (see Table 2.1). During some parts of sleep, babies have regular breathing and practically no body movements; during other parts of sleep, their breathing is irregular, and they make many small movements. These are called *quiet sleep* and *active sleep,* respectively. The two wakeful states are divided in a similar way:

TABLE 2.1
Basic States of Infant Sleep and Wakefulness

State	Characteristics
(1) Deep sleep	Eyes closed, regular breathing, no movement except occasional startles.
(2) Active sleep	Eyes closed, irregular breathing, small twitches, no gross body movement.
(3) Quiet awake	Eyes open, no major body movements, regular breathing.
(4) Active awake	Eyes open with movements of the head, limbs, and trunk; irregular breathing.
(5) Fussing	Eyes partly or entirely closed, intermittent fussy sounds, usually with irregular breathing.
(6) Crying	Eyes partly or entirely closed, vigorous diffuse movement with loud crying sounds.

Quiet-awake patterns are characterized by open eyes, regular breathing, and no major body movement; while *active-awake* patterns are those with more irregular breathing and more movement. Even crying has two divisions (though it doesn't always seem that way if you are baby-sitting for a crying baby). A *fussy* baby sounds as if he is complaining about something, with whimpers and on-and-off crying. But a *crying* baby is definitely crying—his whole body gets into the act, and he uses all of his lung capacity. You can see some examples of infants in the various states in Figure 2.2.

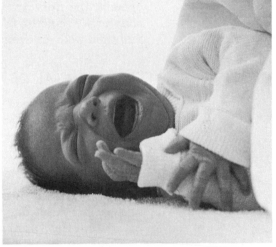

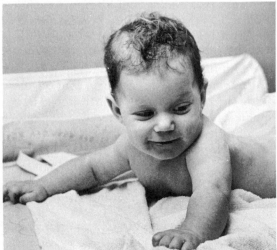

Figure 2.2. Infants in various states of consciousness. While it may be hard to distinguish some of the states in photographs, in-person observers can do so fairly easily.

Besides showing that infant state is more complex than most casual observers would notice, Brazelton has also demonstrated that very young infants have a wide range of behaviors that can be used to interact with adults. Newborn babies can turn toward the sound of a bell or a human voice, they can watch a bright object (even when that object is moving), and they can shut out repeated noises and sights. We will return to some of these social abilities at the end of this chapter, but the point to be made here is that although our view of the baby as an eater/sleeper/cryer is not incorrect, it *is* an underestimate of his abilities.

But where did these abilities come from, and how did they develop? Although most of us think of infancy as the beginning of human development, the story actually starts earlier than that. In the rest of this chapter we're going to look at what happens before and during birth and then take an even closer look at infants and their environments.

GETTING STARTED: PRENATAL DEVELOPMENT

The process of human development begins in a biological sense when an **ovum** (or egg) from a female is fertilized by a **sperm** from a male. The new cell formed by this union is called a **zygote.**

Conception

As we noted in Chapter 1, almost all the cells in the human body contain 46 **chromosomes.** These tiny parts of the cell, each of which is made up of thousands of still smaller parts called **genes,** carry the genetic information for the organism. Most of this information is *species specific;* that is, it concerns the characteristics that all humans share. We all have two arms, two legs, two eyes, and so forth, and all our basic body chemistry for things like eating, digesting, and reproducing is very much the same. Some of the information, however, concerns the characteristics that make every human a unique individual. So you can see, even when we are looking at something like biology, that developmental psychologists are asking the two questions we introduced in the first chapter: How do all humans change in the same way, and how do they change in different and unique ways?

There are, however, two important exceptions to the rule that all human cells have 46 chromosomes: The ovum and the sperm each have only 23 chromosomes; when they unite, the new cell they create (the zygote) has 46, exactly the right number for a new human organism to develop.

The 46 chromosomes are arranged in pairs in the cell, and one of these pairs is known to control the sex of the new zygote. In females this pair is made up of two chromosomes of about the same size (usually designated as XX), while in males this pair is made up of two chromosomes that differ in size (designated as XY). If the new organism has received X chromosomes from both the mother and the father, it will be a female; but if it receives an X from the mother and a Y from the father, it will be a male (Hsia, 1965). In general then, it is the genetic contribution from the father that determines whether a baby will be a boy or a girl, because only the father has both an X and a Y chromosome.

Both fertilization and the first steps in the growth of the zygote normally take place in the woman's **fallopian tubes,** which connect the ovaries (where eggs are produced) to the uterus (or womb). By the time the zygote reaches the uterus, its cells are not only growing and dividing, they have begun to separate into different kinds of tissue, a process known as **differentiation.** Some cells, in the center of the zygote, will develop into the infant itself. Others, now in a sphere surrounding the central mass, will develop into the structures that support the growth and development of the infant. These outer cells are the ones that develop microscopic tendrils that allow the zygote to attach itself to the side of the uterus to begin the period of prenatal growth in which it is known as the **embryo.**

The Embryonic Stage

The embryonic stage begins when the embryo attaches itself in the uterus and continues for about eight weeks. During this time both cell growth and differentiation take place very rapidly (Smith & Stenchever, 1978). The outer layers of cells develop into the membranes that surround and protect the developing embryo and into the special organ called the **placenta.** The placenta both separates the mother's bloodstream from that of the developing embryo and also connects the two so that oxygen and nutrients can pass from the mother's body to that of the developing child. You can see the ways in which these various structures develop in Figure 2.3.

Growth during the embryonic period is very swift, with rapid cell division and differentiation of function occurring among the developed cells. At the end of the stage, about eight weeks after conception, the embryo is about 12 centimeters (cm) long (½ inch) and has all of the following (Beischer & Mackay, 1976):

- Eyes
- Ears
- A mouth that opens and closes
- A nose
- A liver that secretes bile
- A heart that beats and a circulatory system
- Arms with elbows and legs with knees

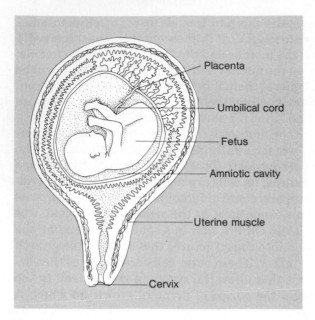

Figure 2.3. Schematic drawing of uterus, showing amniotic sac, placenta, and position of infant at about four months of gestation. Note that the only connection between the infant and the mother is through the placenta.

Placenta

Umbilical cord

Fetus

Amniotic cavity

Uterine muscle

Cervix

- Fingers and toes (although webbed, like duck's feet)
- A tail (it grows smaller after this stage; the tailbone at the end of your spine is the remnant of this tail)
- A spinal cord
- Bones

The Fetal Period

From the beginning of the third month of pregnancy to the end of the gestational period, the new organism is called a **fetus.** After reading the list of all the body systems that have begun their development during the embryonic period, you may be wondering what is left for the fetal period. Basically, what remains is the refinement and completion of all the systems that have been laid down.

It's a bit like the process of building a house. You first put up the floor and then the framework for the walls and roof. This skeleton of the house has the full shape of the final house; you can see where the windows and doors will go, what shape the rooms will be, how the roof will look. This stage is reached quickly, but after that there is a long process of filling around the skeleton already established. So it is with the embryo and the fetus. At the end of the embryonic period the main parts are all there, at least in some basic form; the next seven months are for the finishing process. The major exception to this developmental pattern is the nervous system, which is present in only rudimentary form at the age of 8 weeks. At that point only a small part of the brain and only the suggestion of a spinal cord have developed. The major development of the brain and the nervous system does not occur until the last 3 months of the pregnancy and the first 6 to 12 months after birth.

The major developmental changes during the fetal period are outlined in Table 2.2. You can see the changes in appearance in the sequence of pictures in Figure 2.4.

We mentioned earlier that the sex of the child is determined at the time of conception according to the X and Y chromosomes in the egg and sperm cells. However, the process of sex differentiation is not complete at that beginning point. Recent research with animals has led to the discovery that during the gestation period of a male organism there is a particular point when an infusion of **testosterone** (a male hormone) occurs (Grumbach & Van Wyk, 1974). The hormone apparently is produced in the child's own body and not by the mother. It is this infusion of testosterone that is critical for the later development of male genital organs, and it may also affect such later "boyish" behavior as rough-and-tumble play and aggression. If the hormone is *not* present at the appropriate time, the fetus develops as a female even if it is genetically XY. The reverse is also true. A genetically female fetus exposed to the male hormone at the critical time will develop some features of male genitals and will show more normally male patterns of behavior.

Obviously, most of the research about this process has been done with animals, mostly monkeys. But there is enough evidence from

TABLE 2.2
Major Milestones of Fetal Development

Gestational age	Average size of fetus	Major new developments
12 weeks	3 in.	Sex of child can be determined; muscles developed more extensively; eyelids and lips present; feet have toes, and hands have fingers.
16 weeks	4½–6 in. 3½–4 oz.	First fetal movements usually felt now; bones begin to develop; fairly complete ear is formed.
20 weeks	10 in. 10 oz.	Begins to grow hair; very human looking at this age; may show thumb sucking.
24 weeks	12–14 in. 1½ lb.	Eyes completely formed; fingernails, sweat glands, and taste buds all formed; some fat deposit beneath skin; capable of breathing if born prematurely, but low survival rate if born this early.
28 weeks	14 in. 2½ lb.	Nervous system, blood, and breathing systems all well enough developed to support life. Prematures born at this stage have poor sleep-wake cycles and irregular breathing.
29–40 weeks	18–20 in. 5½–10 lb.	Nervous system develops further; general "finishing" of the various body systems.

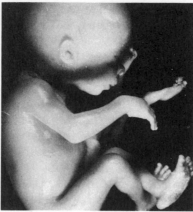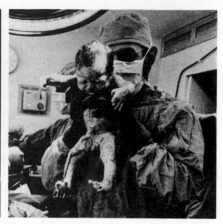

Figure 2.4. Changes in the developing fetus from 16 weeks to 27 weeks of gestation to the time of birth. Although you can see the framework of the infant in the earliest photo—including fingers, ears, and facial features—it doesn't really look like a baby until near the time of birth.

human cases to allow us to make several conclusions: (1) The basic form of the embryo appears to be female rather than male. That is, without the infusion of testosterone, both XX and XY fetuses will develop as females. (2) Male development depends on two processes—first, the genetically determined development of the testes (which produce testosterone), and second, the hormonally determined development of other sex characteristics. (3) Female development requires only one process—the one from the genetic material.

You are probably as interested as developmental psychologists are in understanding what, if any, differences there are between males and females and whether these differences are biologically or socially determined. It is clear that there are at least some biological differences during the period preceding birth—the genetic difference and the hormonal difference. We shall return to these facts later in this book as we look at the ways in which boys and girls are similar—and different—in the way they grow and develop.

INFLUENCES ON PRENATAL DEVELOPMENT

The developmental processes we have described so far are remarkable for their regularity and predictability. The changes that occur during prenatal development occur in what is apparently a fixed order in a fixed period of time. Although things can go wrong (for example, if there is a genetic error of some kind), for the vast majority of children, the developmental sequence runs its course without incident.

We do not have to look far to find an explanation. Whenever there is that much regularity in a fixed sequence, maturation seems the obvious answer. The fetus doesn't learn how to grow fingernails. It doesn't have to be stimulated from outside to grow them. Rather, the fingernails, along with all of the other parts of the complex system, apparently are controlled by the developmental code contained in the genes.

Genetic Influences

Occasionally the genetic information itself can be abnormal. When this happens, the process of development may be interrupted or changed. The most common genetic abnormalities are those that come about because of a failure of proper chromosome division at the time that an egg or a sperm cell is formed. In the normal process, the 46 chromosomes in a cell line up in 23 pairs, so that when the last cell division occurs, each reproductive cell will have exactly 23 chromosomes—one member of each of the 23 pairs. But what if the egg or sperm cell has the wrong number or the wrong kind of chromosomes?

Genetic Abnormalities. Most geneticists now believe that the majority of errors of this kind result in pregnancies that are self-terminating (Hsia, 1968), what most of us call **miscarriages.** (The medical term for this process is **spontaneous abortion,** which should not be confused with an **elective abortion,** in which a woman chooses to terminate a pregnancy.) There are some genetic abnormalities, however, in which pregnancy does continue, and some of these are listed in Table 2.3.

In **Down's syndrome** (which used to be called **mongolism**), the twenty-first chromosome pair does not separate during the cell division

TABLE 2.3
Genetic Anomalies Resulting from Incomplete or Incorrect Division of the Sex Chromosome

Pattern of sex chromosomes	Name for anomaly	Typical characteristics
XXY	Klinefelter's syndrome	These individuals are usually mentally retarded; and although they look like males, they have incomplete sexual development.
X	Turner's syndrome	These children look like girls but have incomplete sexual development. Not ordinarily mentally retarded, they frequently have major deficiency in spatial visualization.
XYY	(No special name)	These are physically males, often unusually tall, and ordinarily mentally retarded. They frequently have a history of high levels of aggression or delinquency.

process (Hsia, 1968). One of the resulting cells (which might be either an egg or a sperm) ends up with two number 21 chromosomes, while the other has none. The cell with too few chromosomes ordinarily does not survive, but the cell with an extra one may. A child born with this syndrome is usually (although not always) mentally retarded and ordinarily has characteristic physical anomalies (abnormalities), including a particular eye-fold pattern and a flattened face. Frequently they also have heart defects or other internal disorders. You can see some of the typical facial features in Figure 2.5.

There are several other genetic anomalies, listed in Table 2.3, which occur if there is an incomplete or incorrect division of the sex chromo-

Figure 2.5. Picture of a child with Down's syndrome. Note the characteristic facial features, especially the flattened cheeks and distinctive eyes.

some. Most of these are quite rare, but they have been of help to scientists in better understanding how the process of genetic programming takes place.

Prenatal Diagnosis.　　Some abnormalities, including Down's syndrome and those shown in Table 2.3, can now be diagnosed prenatally through a process called **amniocentesis.** A sample of the fluid surrounding the developing fetus (the **amniotic fluid**) is removed using a long needle inserted through the mother's abdomen. This fluid includes many cells sloughed off from the fetus, and these cells can be analyzed for their chromosomal makeup. If there is an abnormality present, the parents may choose to abort the fetus at this stage.

Amniocentesis is most often recommended for pregnant women over the age of 35, who have a higher than average probability of bearing a Down's syndrome child, and for women who have already given birth to a child with a genetic anomaly of some kind (Beischer & McKay, 1976). Unfortunately, most of the conditions that can be diagnosed prenatally cannot be treated, and the only choices available to parents are abortion (if that option is morally acceptable to them) and preparing to live with a handicapped child. Even though amniocentesis and other prenatal diagnostic procedures are becoming almost routine, the decisions that they occasion are difficult ones (see Box 2.1).

Environmental Influences

Physicians and scientists used to believe that embryos and fetuses were pretty well protected from environmental events that might be damaging. Beliefs that the developing infant might be affected by frightening events that happened to the mother or that pregnant women should follow specific dietary practices were generally dismissed as old wives' tales. To some extent this is true. The *bag of waters* (amniotic fluid) and the mother's body (especially the strong abdominal muscles) protect the baby from bumps and bounces. The placenta serves to keep some substances (particularly bacteria) out of the fetus's bloodstream. But in any system as complex and intricate as this one, there is some susceptibility to outside events.

As you read the next section, your first reaction will probably be alarm at the number of things that can go wrong. (I first saw a listing like this when I was about four months pregnant, and I was more than a little intimidated. [SM*]) So we would like to help you put these facts into perspective. Remember first that prenatal development is very robust. Moreover, most of the things that might adversely affect the

---

*Throughout the book, we use our initials to identify personal anecdotes.

BOX 2.1

Choices about Pregnancy

Most of you have your childbearing years ahead of you, so you may not realize that much of the information in this chapter about prenatal influences on development is relatively new—most of it was not known, for instance, at the time your mother was pregnant with you. Along with all this new knowledge come a number of decisions about childbearing, such as deciding when to become pregnant, what kind of diet and lifestyle to have during the pregnancy, and where to deliver the infant. Since couples are increasingly sharing the experiences of pregnancy and childbirth, these decisions are important for both men and women.

It seems to us that one set of decisions—mostly those about diet and lifestyle during pregnancy—should be fairly easy for most couples. As you will learn in this chapter, there is clear and convincing scientific evidence that poor diet, tobacco use, alcohol use, excessive radiation, and diseases like rubella can harm the developing embryo or fetus. These seem to be direct effects that are true for any pregnancy.

But there are two other kinds of decisions that can be very difficult. The first kind concerns topics where we just do not have as much scientific evidence as we would like. For example, some studies seem to have shown that caffeine intake during pregnancy is associated with birth defects, while other studies have failed to find this relationship. Similarly, there have been inconsistent results in studies of the effects of engaging in sexual relations during the last few weeks of pregnancy (Beischer & Mackay, 1976). Finally, there have been claims that certain practices during labor and delivery—especially those that are quiet, dark, and calming—result in more optimal later development. Once again, we just don't have enough data to be sure.

How can you make a decision when scientists disagree on the facts? Basically, you have to weigh your own values. Perhaps it is no great sacrifice to give up coffee and tea, and you would feel better if you knew you weren't taking any chances. And you might decide you prefer the less personal atmosphere of a hospital delivery room to the quiet, homelike setting where medical services and equipment might be less available in case of an unexpected emergency.

The second kind of hard decision is one that involves genetic conditions. It is fairly easy to diagnose some genetic conditions (such as Down's syndrome, described earlier in this chapter) early in pregnancy using amniocentesis. The hard decision comes when a diagnosis of such an abnormality is made. Should the pregnancy be ended (by abortion) or not? Many people have strong moral feelings about bringing handicapped individuals into the world, especially those who require long-term care; and of course many people have equally strong feelings about abortion. Couples in this unfortunate situation need sensitive personal counseling as well as accurate genetic counseling (Sorenson, Swazey, & Scotch, 1981). Decisions surrounding genetic conditions that cannot be diagnosed prenatally are even more difficult. For example, parents who have a child with cystic fibrosis, which is genetically determined, have a 25 percent chance of any subsequent children being similarly affected—and there is no way to diagnose this disease during pregnancy.

As we read in the newspapers about genetic engineering and test-tube babies (who are only conceived in test tubes, not grown there), the number of difficult personal decisions is likely to increase. Science can provide the information necessary for making these choices; but in the end, each individual couple must make their choice based on their own values and convictions.

course of that development are things that can be avoided by reasonable preventive or precautionary measures. Try to keep these hopeful points in mind as you read what follows.

Diseases of the Mother

Run-of-the-mill illnesses of a pregnant woman, like colds and flu, present almost no risk to the embryo or fetus. In fact, the number of diseases known to be dangerous is quite small. But since the effects of these diseases are quite profound and since these effects can almost entirely be prevented, they are important for prospective parents to know about.

Rubella.   The most common disease that is a problem is **rubella,** sometimes known as **German measles.** The mother herself may become only slightly ill from rubella, but if she is in the first three months (usually called the first **trimester**), the virus can pass from her body through the placenta to the developing embryo, where it may interfere with the organs and systems that are developing at that time. The most common abnormality among rubella babies is deafness, and they sometimes have cataracts on their eyes or heart defects. Sometimes these abnormalities are accompanied by a degree of mental retardation.

We should emphasize here, and in the discussions of other environmental effects, that the relationship between the specific environmental event—in this case, rubella—and the effect on the child is *not* invariable. *Most* infants whose mothers had rubella during the early months of the pregnancy do *not* show any abnormality. In one study (Sheridan, 1964), for instance, only 13 out of 200 children whose mothers had had rubella during the first 16 weeks of pregnancy had a significant hearing loss. Clearly there must be other factors operating, such as the severity of the infection, the timing of the illness, or the vulnerability of the fetus.

The other good news is that rubella can be prevented. A reliable rubella vaccine is now part of regular childhood immunization programs. Adult women can be given an inexpensive blood test to find out whether they have had the disease; and if not, they can easily be vaccinated. The only catch is that the vaccine itself can have the same unwanted effects as the disease—so vaccination must be done at least three months before a pregnancy begins (Beischer & Mackay, 1976). Many physicians now include this blood test in premarital examinations to be sure any necessary vaccination can be done in advance.

Sexually Transmitted Diseases.   Some sexually transmitted diseases also pose a threat to the developing embryo and fetus. About 25 percent of mothers who have **syphilis,** for example, pass the disease to their

offspring, while about 30 percent have spontaneous abortions (Beischer & Mackay, 1976). Often syphilitic fetuses are miscarried; if they are born, they have a high incidence of mental subnormality and physical deformities. These effects can be prevented, however, if the mother receives appropriate treatment early in her pregnancy. Many physicians routinely check pregnant women for the evidence of syphilis, and some patients are offended by this. However, it is clearly in the interests of good reproductive outcome to find out early if syphilis is present.

You have probably read in newspapers and magazines about the recent rise in the number of cases of **genital herpes** in this country. This disease, which is caused by a virus somewhat similar to the one responsible for cold sores and chicken pox, results in painful sores in the mother's reproductive tract, including the birth canal. A baby passing through the birth canal runs a serious risk of being infected; and among infants, such infections are frequently life threatening. Consequently, most physicians now choose to use surgical means (usually called a **Caesarean section**) to deliver babies whose mothers suffer from this disease. Although this does not cure the mothers, it does prevent the disease in the infant.

Other Diseases.   A few other diseases—most notably diphtheria, influenza, and typhoid—may be passed on to the fetus through the placenta. Generally, however, these diseases are infrequent and their effects on the infant are less severe than those seen in either rubella or syphilis.

Drugs Taken by the Mother

As we said earlier, it used to be believed that the placenta was effective in protecting the developing embryo and fetus from substances in the mother's bloodstream. In the early 1960s this belief was tragically contradicted when it was observed that many mothers who took a new tranquilizer called **thalidomide** were having babies with severe birth defects (usually without limbs or with limbs interrupted in very early stages of embryonic development and thus foreshortened). Fortunately, pregnant women are no longer being given drugs like thalidomide, especially during the early months of pregnancy. But many pregnant women *are* using other drugs, including alcohol and tobacco, which have now been shown to have some effects on the development of offspring.

Tobacco.   It now seems quite definite that women who smoke during their pregnancies are likely to have infants with lower than average birth weights. It also seems likely (though perhaps not as definite) that women who smoke are more likely to have infants with birth defects or to have stillborn infants. There are even now some studies indicating that children as old as 11 may show some effects of their mothers' smoking during pregnancy. One study (Nichols, 1977), involving over 28,000 children, showed that those youngsters whose mothers had smoked during pregnancy had more difficulties in school and were more likely to be hyperactive.

Ordinarily, we wouldn't draw such a strong conclusion from studies that are correlational in nature. The studies we have mentioned compared women who smoked with those who did not. Since these two groups probably differ in many other ways, too (perhaps in the amount of alcohol or coffee they drink or in the adequacy of their diets or in the amount of weight gained during pregnancy), you cannot say that any differences between the groups are necessarily due *just* to the use of tobacco.

In spite of these cautions, we feel confident in these conclusions for two reasons. First, investigators in several different countries have reported virtually the same results, and this **replication** (doing a similar study and getting the same results) is an indication of the validity of the findings. Second, some of the studies, such as the one we mentioned by Nichols involving thousands of children, have enough subjects that the investigators can choose special subgroups to compare, subgroups that really *do* vary on *just* the amount of smoking the mothers do. Taken altogether, the message from the evidence is clear: Pregnant women improve their chances of having a healthy baby if they avoid smoking.

Figure 2.6. This mother's smoking is a danger not only to her own health, but also to the health of her unborn child.

Alcohol.   There is also a growing body of literature showing the effects of alcohol on prenatal development. In the early 1970s, Kenneth Jones and his colleagues (Jones, Smith, Ulleland, & Streissguth, 1973) identified a pattern of mental retardation and physical abnormalities, which they named **fetal alcohol syndrome,** or **FAS,** common among children born to alcoholic mothers.

After the existence of FAS was established in the offspring of alcoholic mothers, investigators began to look for the more subtle effects of alcohol in the offspring of mothers who drank more moderately. In one such study, Henry Rosett (Rosett, Ouellette, & Weiner, 1976) compared heavy drinkers (those who had at least two drinks every day with occasional binges of more than six drinks) with those who rarely drank. The outcomes these researchers were interested in and the results they obtained are shown in Table 2.4. You can see that babies born to heavy drinkers were twice as likely to have physical abnormalities and more than three times as likely to have congenital problems than babies born to mothers who rarely drank.

Still other investigators have been looking at the long-term effects of drinking during pregnancy. In one of these studies—conducted by our colleague at the University of Washington, Ann Streissguth (Streissguth, Martin, Martin, & Barr, 1981)—drinking patterns during pregnancy were compared with infant development scores obtained when the children of these pregnancies were 8 months old. Babies whose mothers had been abstainers or very light drinkers showed normal or above normal development (on a mental development scale whose average score is 100, their scores were about 116). But babies whose mothers had been heavy drinkers showed slower development (their scores on that same mental development test averaged only 98). What is even more important, these results took into account other characteristics of the mothers, such as their ages and smoking habits. Just as in the case of smoking, the research evidence concerning alco-

TABLE 2.4
The Effect of Heavy and Low Levels of Alcohol Consumption on Characteristics of Newborn Infants

Characteristics of infants	PERCENT OF INFANTS SHOWING EACH CHARACTERISTIC	
	Heavy drinking mother	*Rarely drinking mother*
Any physical abnormality	71%	35%
Congenital anomalies	29%	8%
Growth abnormalities	53%	17%
Jitteriness	29%	10%

SOURCE: Rosett, H. L. From *U.S. Journal of Drug and Alcohol Dependence,* December 1977, Vol. 1, No. 11.

hol and pregnancy leads to one firm conclusion: It is safer for the developing fetus if the mother avoids alcohol.

Other Drugs.   There are other drugs that also seem to have detrimental effects on prenatal development. Addiction to barbiturate drugs (such as sleeping pills) during pregnancy may cause damage to the developing brain of the fetus, apparently as a result of loss of oxygen in the blood. Mothers addicted to heroin may actually pass their addiction on to their children. Such infants frequently show signs of withdrawal symptoms, including irritability, vomiting, and trembling, during their first few days of life.

One common treatment for heroin addiction is to substitute another drug called **methadone.** Although this may help the mother, a study by Milton Strauss and his colleagues (Strauss, Starr, Ostrea, Chavez, & Stryker, 1976) showed that it may not be helpful to the *baby.* Strauss found that infants of methadone-treated mothers showed withdrawal symptoms after birth and were smaller and slower in motor development when they were 1 year old.

The moral seems to be that several drugs have the potential of causing problems during prenatal development and that the safest course for a pregnant woman is to avoid any substances not specifically authorized by her own physician.

Radiation

Large doses of X rays, such as those used for the treatment of some kinds of cancer, may increase the risk of miscarriage in the mother and may also produce physical deformities in the child, depending on the timing. However, there is no evidence that single, brief doses of X rays (such as those used in dental exams) have any adverse effects.

Diet and Nutrition

For many years, pregnant women were advised to gain as little weight as possible during their pregnancies, certainly no more than 2 pounds a month or 18 pounds altogether. More recently, though, physicians and nutritionists have concluded that this practice may not be in the best interests of the health of the baby. The new recommendation is for a weight gain of about 24 pounds, with greater gains not causing any particular problem. As you might expect, this means that babies would be a bit heavier when born, and this additional weight seems to be a positive factor in the infant's health during the first few weeks after birth.

Why is the mother's diet so important? It is important because of the role of nutrition in promoting the development of the fetal nervous system. During the last trimester of pregnancy and the first two years of life, brain cells become increasingly interconnected. If the maternal diet (and later, the child's own diet) is not adequate, fewer of these interconnections are formed. Similarly, nerve cells in other parts of the body are becoming sheathed in a substance called **myelin,** which serves to insulate nerves from one another. Without adequate nutrition, these sheaths can be incomplete, which lets messages from one nerve "short circuit" onto another.

We cannot directly see effects like these on the cells of the nervous system, but we can look at children whose mothers have been malnourished for external effects of poor diet. One such study was done by Zena Stein and her colleagues (Stein, Susser, Saenger, & Marolla, 1975), who looked at the effects of a period of extreme famine in Holland toward the end of World War II when individuals were limited to 1000 calories per day or less. By looking at records of pregnancies, births, and deaths during and after this period, we can see the effects of such a restricted diet. Stein found that in general the effects of malnutrition were worst if it occurred during the final three months of the pregnancy. Babies from these pregnancies were lighter in weight at birth and had a greatly increased risk of dying in the first year (see Figure 2.7).

From data like this, we would expect the long-term outcomes for children like these to be poor, too. Stein and her colleagues, though, did *not* find any permanent damage for the children who survived the famine. Other researchers, such as Steven Richardson (1972), studying parts of the world where famine is a much more prevalent situation, *have* found long-term effects, as indicated by intelligence scores and school performance, especially if malnutrition continues during the child's early years.

Aside from avoiding malnutrition (which can come from misguided attempts at weight control as well as from famine), what should a pregnant woman eat? A well-balanced diet with about 1000 calories and 30 grams of protein per day more than the woman normally needs seems to provide for the developing fetus (National Research Council, 1974). Although our knowledge about specific nutrients during pregnancy is still quite sparse, we do know that iodine deficiency in the mother increases the risk of mental disability and physical impairments in the infant. Animal research suggests that zinc may also be particularly important during pregnancy, and iron deficiency (which is actually fairly common among American women) is likewise a cause for concern. For these reasons, physicians often prescribe vitamin and iron supplements for pregnant women, along with a good, high-protein diet.

Emotional Stress in the Mother

At the beginning of this section, we talked about some beliefs that are usually labeled old wives' tales. Several of these folk beliefs seem to

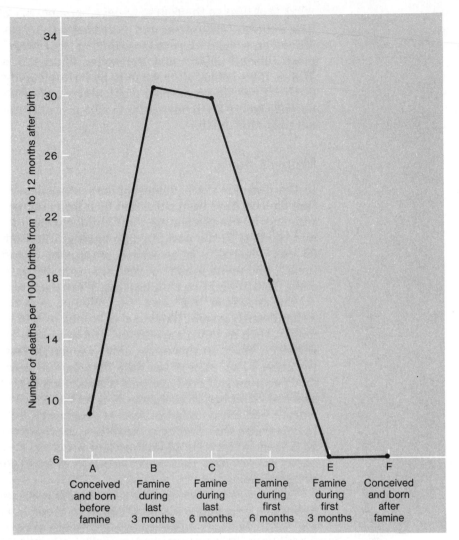

Figure 2.7. The results of Stein's study of the World War II famine in Holland. The infants most likely to die in the first year of life were those whose mother had been malnourished during the latter stages of pregnancy. (*Source:* Adapted from Stein et al., 1975, p. 161.)

center around the emotional state of the mother and its effect on the developing fetus. Is there any scientific evidence to support these views?

As it turns out, there is. During the times that a pregnant woman is under stress, the activity level of the fetus increases. Since part of the **stress response** in adults involves an increase in the hormone epinephrine (also known as adrenaline), it seems reasonable that the fetus may be responding to that substance. While we don't know exactly what that does to the course of development, it seems reasonable that long periods of such stress and increased activity might have an impact. Moreover, women who are tense during their pregnancies seem to have more difficult labors and deliveries (Sameroff & Chandler, 1975). Worse, their babies often seem to be irritable and cry more soon after birth. (It has always seemed particularly unfair that people who were nervous before birth have infants who probably make them even more nervous after birth.)

Mother's Age

In the past few years, demographers (statisticians who study population figures) have been surprised by a large increase in the number of women who are postponing their childbearing into their late twenties and thirties. In the past, anyone having a first child after the age of 35 was referred to as an *elderly primipara* (doesn't that sound ominous?), and many women of that age were discouraged by their physicians from attempting childbearing. Were those warnings appropriate?

The answer is "yes" *and* "no." Women over the age of 35 do have a significantly greater likelihood of having a child with a genetic abnormality, such as Down's syndrome, and are likely to have longer labors (Kessner, 1973). In this sense, older women do face a greater risk. On the other hand, some of the data that showed poor outcomes for older mothers were gathered in clinics where many of the patients were poor and had other health problems. It is probably not surprising that such women had many complications of pregnancy, but it would be wrong to generalize that finding to healthier, more affluent mothers getting good medical care. So while there are some risks associated with pregnancy at later ages, they can be partially offset by good health and good prenatal care.

Interestingly, there may be more health risks associated with pregnancies in very young mothers than with those in older mothers (Kessner, 1973). Mothers under the age of 15 seem to be in particular danger of stillbirth, miscarriage, and premature birth, presumably because they are still growing and have nutritional needs of their own to fulfill in addition to nurturing the unborn child. You can see the relative perils of young and old mothers in Figure 2.8.

GETTING GOING: BIRTH

Like prenatal development, the birth process itself seems to proceed without much influence from the environment around it. We will describe the birth process from the child's point of view here and from the mother's point of view in Chapter 8.

At the end of about 40 weeks gestational period, the mother's uterus

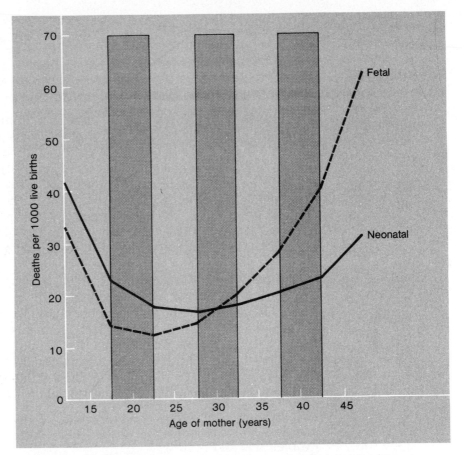

Figure 2.8. The relationship between mother's age and the risk that the fetus or neonate will die. This information came from a study of over 100,000 births in New York City during 1968. (*Source:* Kessner, 1973.)

begins to contract rhythmically, moving the infant down the birth canal. At the same time, the opening from the uterus to the vagina (or birth canal) gradually begins to open and becomes thinner and more elastic. Over the course of several hours (more in women having their first babies), these two processes work together to expel the baby into the world, where he draws his first breath and meets his parents.

In the United States, birth most often takes place in hospitals under the supervision of physicians or (increasingly) nurse-midwives. Increasing numbers of infants, though, are being born at home, at specialized *birthing centers,* or in less antiseptic *birthing rooms* in hospitals (see Box 2.2). Soon after birth, most medical attendants give the baby a quick examination and assign an **Apgar score** (named after Virginia Apgar, the prominent physician who developed the scoring system), which reflects the baby's health and vigor (Apgar, 1953). Happily, about 70 to 80 percent of infants score 9 or 10 on this 10-point scale, meaning they are getting off to a good start.

Use of Drugs during Birth

The process of childbirth can be anywhere from uncomfortable to downright painful for women, and it often seems either necessary or desirable to use drugs to lessen the pain and discomfort. These drugs (known as analgesics and anesthetics) are generally safe for the mothers, but what about the infants? You will not be surprised to learn that drugs administered during labor pass through the placenta as easily as those given earlier during pregnancy. Although they seem not to harm the infant in any specific way (that is, they don't impair breathing or other basic processes), they do have impact on the baby's behavior in the first days and perhaps the first months of life. In one study (Aleksandrowicz & Aleksandrowicz, 1974), babies whose mothers had had more drugs during labor were less likely to smile at examiners even a full month after birth. In another study (Murray, Dolby, Nation, & Thomas, 1981), babies were less alert after a birth that included having such drugs. No one would argue that painkilling drugs should be prohibited during difficult or especially painful deliveries, but evidence like this suggests that alternatives (such as childbirth preparation, including pain-management techniques) should be used whenever possible.

Problems at Birth

Although usually uneventful, there can be problems during the birth process. One of the most common of these is a temporary shortage of oxygen to the baby during the birth process. Sometimes this is caused by a delivery that is mechanically difficult (for instance, if the baby comes feet first instead of head first) and other times because of a delay in the infant's taking a first breath. Prolonged lack of oxygen (technically known as **anoxia**) can result in the set of motor problems known as **cerebral palsy.** The most common symptoms of cerebral palsy (which can also be caused by brain damage unrelated to the birth process) are tremors and uncontrolled muscular spasms. Some cerebral palsied children have difficulty in later years learning to walk and to speak clearly. Fortunately, it takes rather long periods of oxygen deprivation, longer than are likely in most medically attended deliveries, for such serious damage to occur. What evidence we have about shorter oxygen deprivations suggests that their effects are minimal by the time children reach school age.

BOX 2.2

The Good Birth: Who, Where, and How

For most parents, the birth of a child is a landmark in the family history. Increasingly, young parents are wanting to choose the location and type of delivery they experience. Part of this interest comes from the women's health movement, which emphasizes participation in all aspects of reproductive health, and part of it comes from research about the importance of the early acquaintanceship process for later parent-child relationships (which we will consider in some detail in Chapter 7).

The first issue that comes up is who should be present. Generally, a medical attendant (a physician or nurse-midwife) is there, and the father of the baby is usually included, too. Most women appreciate having their husband present; and if the couple have been involved in childbirth preparation classes, the husband is most likely serving as the coach, helping his partner remain controlled and relatively pain free during most of the labor and delivery process.

A new wrinkle in recent years has been encouraging the participation of other family members, including other children, in the birthing room. One of our colleagues enjoyed a home birth of this sort a few months ago, and all of the family found it a warm and growing experience. The practice is a bit more of a problem in deliveries performed in hospitals, but even there, it is fast becoming an option for parents who desire it.

In fact, the choice between hospital and home delivery is an increasingly controversial one. For several decades, most American babies have been delivered in hospitals, where equipment and personnel are available in case of some emergency. At the same time, many European infants have been safely delivered at home by trained nurse-midwives. Although home deliveries are sometimes attended by physicians and hospital deliveries by midwives, the contrast between a system that treats pregnancy and delivery as an illness (or at least a potential illness) and one that treats these conditions as normal can sometimes be dramatic. As a general rule, it appears as though home deliveries in uncomplicated pregnancies are completely safe; but when complications occur, hospitals may be safer.

Hospital deliveries can be very—well—hospitallike. Delivery rooms are generally brightly lit, heated for the comfort of fully clothed doctors and nurses, and loud or echoey. An influential French obstetrician, Frederick Leboyer (1975), has recently suggested that delivery rooms should be redesigned to better serve the purpose of welcoming a child *gently* into the world. That is, he supports the use of dimmer lights, a warmer room, less noise, and the like.

We suspect that this procedure is gentler for the parents as well as for the babies; however, as psychologists, we are particularly interested in whether or not birth practices such as those proposed by Leboyer make any difference in the child's later growth or development. One study (Rappoport, 1978) found that children who experienced gentle births were above average in walking and had few feeding or sleeping difficulties. Unfortunately, this study did not have an appropriate control group. In an experiment where some families were randomly assigned to some of the gentle birth conditions (Nelson, Enkin, Saigal, Bennett, Milner, & Sackett, 1980), no differences were found in the first few weeks after birth. Our interpretation is that such practices are clearly humane and pleasant, but when circumstances make them impossible (either because of recalcitrant hospital administrations or medical concerns), no damage is done to the infants or their families.

In summary, all of these choices seem to involve a decision by a couple about how *they* would like the conditions of their baby's birth to be. On the average, all of them represent safe alternatives that families can choose without concern that some poor outcome will result, except if it is known ahead of time that a medical risk is involved, in which case hospital delivery seems prudent.

Premature Birth

Another important problem arises when a birth is untimely, that is, too early. When most of you were born, any infant who weighed less than 5 or 5½ pounds was considered a **premature infant** (or *preemie,* for short). Today, physicians distinguish carefully between babies who are born earlier than expected (and are small because of their immaturity) and those who are born on schedule but are light in weight (Kopp & Parmalee, 1979). This latter group (not surprisingly labeled **small-for-date** infants) actually reflects some defect in the process of prenatal development, such as inadequate nutrition or a placenta that has functioned poorly.

Babies born too early need all types of special help just to survive. Their lungs, in particular, are not yet ready for the job they have to do. Preemies often have trouble regulating their own temperatures because their nervous systems are incomplete and they lack the layers of fat beneath the skin that act as insulation in babies who complete

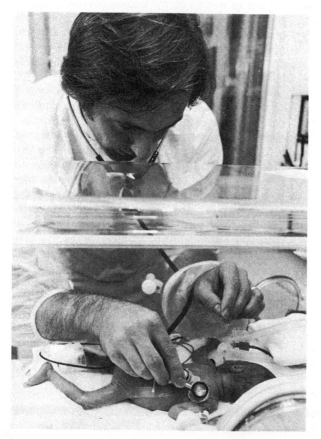

Figure 2.9.   A premature infant soon after birth. Babies this small need a lot of good medical care just to survive.

their gestational periods. Today there is a medical specialty, **neonatology,** concerned with the health of newborns and particularly that of premature newborns.

What about the long-term effects for premature babies? The answer depends on how early they were born and how much they weighed at birth. Larger preemies, those born after 34 weeks of gestation and weighing more than 1.5 kilograms (kg) (about 3.3 lbs.), who get good medical care seem to do about as well as full-term babies when they are raised in healthy, stimulating families. Smaller preemies, those born before 33 weeks of gestation and weighing less than 1.5 kg, do not fare as well. In one longitudinal study of these very low-birth-weight infants, Jane Hunt (1981) found that 46 percent of them had some identified disability by the time they started school (ages 4 to 6 years). By age 8, the situation was even worse—the children who had had problems continued to be in difficulty, and several who were developing normally in the preschool years showed new evidence of some disability. When Hunt compared the children with disabilities with the rest of the children, she found no differences in their birth weight or gestation age, nor in their mother's age or education. Even tests of infant development did not reveal the later disabilities. Apparently, whatever damage is done by premature birth does not appear until later in life. We have mentioned several environmental factors that are known to be related to premature birth (such as tobacco use and youthful motherhood), and we'd like to reemphasize the importance of preventing as many such births as possible by good prenatal care and health practices.

GETTING SETTLED: EARLY INFANCY

Unless you are a parent yourself, you probably have never seen a newborn infant (technically known as a **neonate**). Neonates look quite different from the stereotypes most of us have of older babies, as you can see in Figure 2.10. Much of their distinctive look has to do with the birth process itself. For example, the heads of neonates are often misshapen as a result of the trip through the narrow birth canal. The waxy substance (called **vernix**) that covered the skin prenatally is partially rubbed off, and the skin itself is usually somewhat red or mottled.

The neonate's state of consciousness seems to be affected by the birth process, too. Newborns (at least those whose mothers were not extensively medicated during labor and delivery) are more alert for the few hours following birth than they are for the several days that follow—they often smile, make gurgling noises, and establish eye contact with their parents or other caregivers. Our best guess is that the actual physical and tactile stimulation of birth plays some part in this alertness because infants born by Caesarean section (the surgical delivery

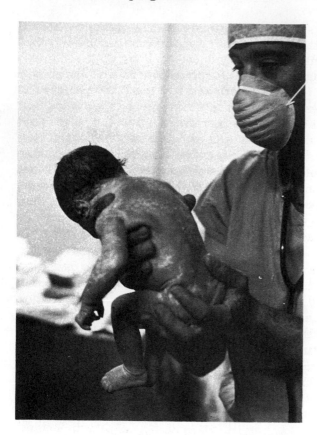

Figure 2.10. A full-term newborn baby. You can see some of the vernix on the skin. Compare the size of this infant with the premature infant in Figure 2.11.

procedure mentioned earlier) are less likely to show this behavior. As we shall see in Chapter 7, this early period of alertness seems to play an important part in establishing the relationship between the parents and the infant.

Well, what can these tiny babies do? We would like to answer that in two ways. First, we'll take a commonsense look at the daily life of infants—back to the sleeping, eating, and crying we started this chapter with—and second, we'll see how developmental psychologists have studied the special, but subtle, abilities of the very young.

The Daily Life of Infants

Sleeping.   The most obvious thing about the daily life of infants is that they spend a large part of their time sleeping. In fact, the newborn baby spends an average of 16 to 18 hours in the sleep states we described earlier, and a 1-month-old baby spends 14 to 16 hours sleeping (Berg & Berg, 1979). Although we cannot *ask* babies about their sleeping habits, we do know that sleeping isn't always *easy* for them. In fact, difficulty in sleeping, or in establishing regular cycles of sleeping and waking, is sometimes a sign of some neurological problem. Premature babies often have difficulty in sleeping, and their developing ability to sleep soundly is used as an indication that they are maturing in a healthy way.

It also seems likely that infants do about as much dreaming as adults. Again, we cannot ask them about this, but during dreaming most adults show a fluttering of the eyeballs under the closed lids (this is called **rapid eye movement sleep** or **REM** sleep). If anything, babies spend more of their sleeping time in REM sleep than adults do—perhaps as much as half of the total, compared to about one-fifth of the total in adults (Roffwarg, Muzio, & Dement, 1966). Even though babies sleep quite a bit, their brains are busy during these periods of REM sleep.

Eating.   If your stomach was only about as big as a pear and you were growing faster than you would at any other time in your life, how often would you have to eat to keep going? That's the situation for babies, and newborns have to eat as frequently as 10 times every 24 hours to get enough food into their systems for their rapid growth. Fortunately for the adults who feed them, most babies are down to five or six feedings a day by the time they are a month old (Barnard & Eyres, 1979).

What's the best way to feed a baby? From the point of view of nutrition, breast milk is probably the best food (Marano, 1979). Not only is it formulated precisely for the needs of a human baby (cow's milk, after all, fits the nutritional bill for cows, not people), it also seems to include some important protection for the baby against diseases. Some of the mother's antibodies (blood components that fight disease) are passed to the baby through the breast milk. Some nutritionists think that babies who are breast-fed are less likely to become obese or to develop allergies to foods. At the same time, it is also true that today's commercially prepared infant formulas are well suited to infants, and most infants can grow healthily using them.

What about the psychological effects of eating? Are breast-fed babies likely to be more loving or affectionate or more dependent or to interact with their mothers in any special way? Perhaps surprisingly, there is very little evidence to suggest that the parent-child interaction during feeding has much to do with whether the child is being breast-fed or bottle-fed. One study by Tiffany Field (1977), for example, showed that bottle-fed babies seem to engage in the same kinds of nonverbal "conversations" that breast-fed babies did. That is, their mothers talked to them, fondled them, burped them, and so forth about the same way regardless of the method of feeding. The answer to the question seems to be that breast feeding is somewhat more desirable for nutritional reasons, but that mothers who choose bottle feeding (because, for example, they need to be away from the baby for long periods during the day or because they want to share responsibility for feeding with their husbands) need not be concerned about the health or development of their babies.

Crying.   The other activity we associate with babies is crying. Prolonged crying (like the kind illustrated in the sleep/activity record at the beginning of this chapter) can be irritating and upsetting to parents, especially when it occurs during the night or at mealtime (dinner time seems to be a common time for crying bouts). However, shorter episodes of crying play an important part in the life of the infant because they represent one of the main ways of communicating with their adult caregivers (Wolff, 1971). The most common reason for crying is probably hunger, but babies also cry when they are sick or in pain. Many infants cry when they are overstimulated (such as when they are passed from lap to lap at a family reunion) or overtired (after a bath or a rough play session). Crying also serves to exercise the infant's lungs and circulatory system, much like jogging does for adults!

Most people would agree that it is sensible to feed a crying baby who is hungry. But what about other crying? Is it better to pick up a baby (and maybe "spoil" it) or to let him "cry it out"? Experts whose theories are primarily biological are inclined to dismiss this question, since they believe that the crying is simply part of the infant's behavior like sleeping and breathing. Learning theories have traditionally interpreted picking up a crying baby as reinforcing the crying and would predict that parents who did this would have babies who cried more as time went on. Psychoanalytic theories have usually interpreted picking up the baby as a way of establishing trust in her; so that when she needed help, the baby knew there was an adult who would give that help. Consequently, they would predict that babies who were picked up might be less likely to cry.

At least one study supports this latter position. Mary Ainsworth and her colleagues (Ainsworth, Bell, & Stayton, 1972) observed infants and their mothers over the course of the first year of life, visiting their homes every three weeks. When they compared the mothers' early responses to crying with the infants' later rates of crying, they found that the mothers who *waited* to respond to crying had babies who cried *more* often than did mothers who picked up babies right away. Other researchers (like Gewirtz & Boyd, 1977) have argued that these results are consistent with learning theory and that the mothers who respond later to their children are reinforcing long *bouts* of crying, which then increase in frequency.

However you interpret the findings, though, it seems very unlikely that picking up crying infants is detrimental to their healthy development. Still, new parents should expect to get considerable amount of contradictory advice on this point (see Figure 2.11).

Special Skills of Infants

Psychologists have had to be quite inventive and resourceful to study the skills of infants because infants have few ways of communicating their abilities to adults—they don't talk, and they usually refuse to fill out questionnaires! The best infant researchers are good observers of infants (though this does not mean that every study of infants is an *observational* study). What facts has their ingenuity revealed about infant behavior?

Reflexes.   Behaviors that are automatic and triggered by specific stimuli are known as reflexes (the kick you give when the doctor taps your knee with the little rubber hammer is one kind of reflex). Neurologists use 20 or more reflexes to test the normality of the nervous system of a newborn, but most psychologists are interested in only two clusters. One set of reflexes allows a newborn infant to eat. If you touch the cheek of a baby, he will turn toward the touch and search around for something to suck on; this is called the **rooting reflex.** If he gets something in his mouth, he will **suck** and **swallow** as well. This combination of rooting, sucking, and swallowing is obviously important to secure the survival of the young infant.

Figure 2.11.   One of the difficult things about being a new parent is getting conflicting advice. (*Source:* Johnston, 1977, p. 18.)

The other interesting reflexes are called the *primitive reflexes.* These seem to be controlled in the earliest-developing part of the brain called the midbrain. As the rest of the nervous system matures, the cerebral cortex takes over many functions and the primitive reflexes drop out. If the reflexes persist past the time they normally disappear, it can indicate that there is some problem with the nervous system.

One of these primitive reflexes, the **Moro reflex,** is the early response to loud noises or sudden lack of support (such as having the head fall backward unexpectedly)—the infant's arms fling outward and then back toward midline of the body. The hand grasp is another primitive reflex that you can test yourself on a young baby—the baby will tightly grasp any item that touches the palm of the hand. And the **Babinsky reflex** is a spreading then curling of the toes following a gentle stroke to the bottom of the foot.

Attention and Perception.   Nearly half of the pregnant women in a recent study thought that babies could not see or hear well until they were several months old (Snyder, Eyres, & Barnard, 1979). There is good evidence, though, that babies explore their worlds through seeing and hearing from the very first hours after birth. We will be looking at this evidence in some detail in Chapter 3, but we want to mention some basic findings here to give you more of an idea what a newborn baby *can* really do.

One classic study on vision was done by Philip Salapatek and William Kessen (1966), who used special photographic techniques to observe what parts of a shape young infants looked at most. When presented with the picture of a triangle, for instance, most babies spent their time looking at the edges, and particularly at the corners. Since these visual strategies appear very early in life, we can assume that they have some biological basis.

Infants also appear to have strategies for processing sounds. One item on a popular behavioral examination for newborns (Brazelton, 1973) has the examiner speak softly while just out of the baby's sight on one side. Amazingly, most babies can orient to the sound by quieting their ongoing activity and turning their heads toward the voice. Even more amazing, many crying babies stop their crying when they are talked to in a quiet voice. Clearly infants are attuned to some noises—human voices at least—from the time they are born.

Learning and Habituation.   If learning theories are to account for behavior changes during infancy, it is obviously necessary to demonstrate that learning (at least classical and operant conditioning) does take place in infants. But the question is not only theoretical; it is important for parents and other caregivers to know whether or not the infant will be learning new behaviors during the first weeks of life.

Several researchers have used the infant's ability to suck in studying operant conditioning in newborns. In one such study (Lipsitt, 1966), infants were reinforced (with sugar water) for sucking on a tube (they showed very short bursts of sucking on the tube when there was no reinforcement). After training, the length of time they sucked the tube increased, indicating that conditioning had occurred.

You may be surprised to learn that attempts to demonstrate classical conditioning in infants have not been entirely successful. Lewis Lipsitt and Herbert Kaye (1964) gave infants a nipple (an unconditioned stimulus that leads to the unconditioned response of sucking) at the same time they sounded a tone (the conditioned stimulus). If conditioning occurred, infants would show sucking when the tone came on, even without a nipple present. Lipsitt and Kaye found this effect in older infants (3 to 4 months old) but not in newborns. Rachel Clifton (1974) performed a similar study in which she also monitored the infant's heart rates during sucking. Normally, an infant's heart rate accelerates a bit when a nipple is put in its mouth. Even after many pairings of the nipple (the unconditioned stimulus) and a tone (the conditioned stimulus), there was no evidence of conditioning occurring. In fact, the first time the infants heard the tone without the nipple, they showed a heart rate *deceleration*.

Another important learning skill that infants seem to come equipped with is what psychologists call **habituation.** Habituation is the ability to tune out all sorts of sights and sounds and smells after they occur many times in succession. If you shake a rattle or ring a bell near a sleeping infant, he will respond with a startle or a facial grimace or perhaps just a change in activity level. If you keep on sounding the bell or rattle every 20 or 30 seconds, though, these responses become smaller until the infant does not respond at all. It is as if he has learned that this noise does not signal anything and has stopped paying attention to it. You can think of the stimulus "capturing" the infant's attention when it first occurs, but that capture wears off after several presentations. When that happens, the baby is more or less ready when another new stimulus occurs in the environment.

It may seem obvious to you that babies can respond to their environments by learning and habituating. However, many parents do not realize these things and consequently may provide too little stimulation and too few learning experiences for their babies. Knowledge of the newborn's abilities can lead infant caregivers to provide more appropriate nurturing during the early months of life.

Infancy and Later Development

It may seem to you that we have spent a rather long time discussing prenatal development, birth, and infancy, especially since this book is intended to cover development over the entire life span. We think the attention (and space) is warranted for several reasons. First, it shows that the theoretical issues we discussed in Chapter 1 apply to studies of early life just as much as they do to the studies of later childhood, adolescence, and adulthood. Second, it reflects a wonderful upsurge in knowledge—this chapter could not have been written 20 years ago or even 10 years ago because we lacked information on many aspects of prenatal development, birth, and infancy. Finally, it seems clear that there are aspects of very early development where thoughtful intervention can improve the quality of later life—intervention such as improved nutrition for pregnant women, moderate and appropriate sensory stimulation for infants, and changing the surroundings where birth actually occurs.

SUMMARY

1. The common stereotype of babies sleeping, eating, and crying is correct, but it fails to take into account individual patterns of these activities.
2. Human development begins when an ovum and sperm unite and begin dividing to form a zygote, later known as an embryo and then a fetus.
3. Most of the major systems of the body are formed during the embryonic period; only the nervous system takes shape during the later fetal period.
4. Genetic errors often end in miscarriages, but some result in abnormalities such as Down's syndrome. Prenatal diagnosis of some such conditions is now possible using techniques like amniocentesis.
5. Although most of prenatal development is a process of maturation, there are some environmental events that can influence the outcome, including the mother's illnesses, drug use, diet, mental state, and age.
6. Birth is a result of the rhythmic contractions of the uterus combined with the widening and softening of the birth canal.
7. Babies with low birth weights are more susceptible to a variety of difficulties, although this may vary according to whether the infant is premature or small-for-date.
8. The infants of mothers who were given drugs during labor and delivery often appear less alert and active for the first few days; there are no firm data that these changes persist longer or have any permanent effect.
9. Neonates are distinctive looking, partially because of the effects of going through the birth process; and (if their mothers did not have much medication during labor) they are often particularly alert during the first few hours following birth.

10. Infants sleep for large portions of every day and seem to spend a larger proportion of time in dream sleep than do adults.
11. Although breast-feeding is probably superior to bottle-feeding in terms of nutrition, there is no difference between the two methods in the nature of the parent-child interaction that occurs during feeding.
12. There is evidence to suggest that responding promptly to an infant's cries results in lower, rather than higher, rates of crying later in the first year of life.
13. Reflexes are the built-in, automatic associations between specific stimulation and motor responses. Infants have reflexes that aid in feeding and others that can serve as an index of central nervous system development.
14. It appears that both classical and operant conditioning can occur in babies and that babies are able to habituate. These facts are important for the learning theory approaches to development.
15. The study of infancy is especially important, even though it includes only a small portion of the life span, because it focuses on theoretical issues, it includes much recent research, and it offers opportunity for constructive intervention.

KEY TERMS

Abortion, elective Termination of a pregnancy by choice of the pregnant woman, whether for personal or medical reasons. Sometimes called an induced abortion.

Abortion, spontaneous Naturally occurring termination of a pregnancy, frequently referred to as a miscarriage.

Amniocentesis Method of prenatal diagnosis in which a small sample of amniotic fluid is drawn from the uterus and analyzed for chromosomal abnormalities.

Amniotic fluid The liquid surrounding the developing embryo and fetus in the uterus.

Anoxia Lack of oxygen during the birth process or immediately afterwards, frequently a cause of brain damage in infants.

Apgar score Scale used to judge the health of an infant in the few minutes immediately following birth. Apgar scores can range from 0 to 10.

Babinsky reflex When the bottom of the foot is stroked, an infant will spread his toes. This reflex generally disappears midway through the first year of life.

Caesarean section Delivery of an infant using surgical procedures. C-sections are done when delivery through the birth canal would be dangerous to the infant or mother.

Cerebral palsy Neurological disease characterized by tremors and uncontrolled muscular spasms. It is sometimes caused by perinatal anoxia.

Chromosomes Small threadlike structures in every living cell that determine its genetic character. Humans have 46 chromosomes arranged in 23 pairs.

Differentiation Development of cells in an embryo to become different body parts. Differentiation proceeds from the earliest stages of prenatal development.

Down's syndrome   A genetic condition caused by the presence of three (rather than the normal two) number 21 chromosomes. People with Down's syndrome, which used to be called mongolism, frequently have physical disabilities as well as mental retardation.

Embryo   The stage of prenatal growth beginning when the fertilized egg implants itself in the uterus and ending approximately eight weeks later.

Fallopian tubes   The tubes that connect a woman's ovaries to her womb. Most pregnancies are begun by the egg being fertilized in the fallopian tubes.

Fetal alcohol syndrome (FAS)   Pattern of birth defects associated with the mother's heavy use of alcohol during pregnancy.

Fetus   The developing child from the third month after conception until the time of birth.

Genes   Units of genetic transmission. Chromosomes are made up of many genes.

Genital herpes   A sexually transmitted disease for which there is currently no cure. Infants born to mothers with active infections face the chance of a severe infection themselves.

German measles   Common childhood disease that can cause severe birth defects when contracted by a pregnant woman, especially during the first trimester of her pregnancy.

Habituation   The way an organism learns to tune out repeated presentations of a stimulus.

Methadone   Addicting drug sometimes used in the treatment of heroin-addicted people. Both heroin and methadone seem to have adverse effects on the unborn child of pregnant addicts.

Miscarriage   Early self-termination of a pregnancy before the embryo or fetus is mature enough to live outside the womb. Technically known as a spontaneous abortion.

Mongolism   Down's syndrome.

Moro reflex   Infant's response to a loud noise and sudden loss of support, in which the arms are thrown open and the head is thrown back.

Myelin   Sheathlike covering of nerves. Made of fatty tissue.

Neonate   Newborn infant.

Neonatology   Medical specialty concerning the health of newborns.

Ovum   Egg cell from female (plural is *ova*).

Placenta   Specialized organ that connects the developing embryo/fetus to the mother's circulatory system without allowing actual mixing of the blood.

Premature infant   Infant born before the end of the appropriate gestation period (40 weeks). Usually infants born 37 weeks or earlier are called premature.

Rapid eye movement (REM) sleep   Stage of sleep characterized by rapid movement of the eyes behind closed eyelids. In adults, REM sleep is associated with the experience of dreaming.

Replication   Repeating a research study, sometimes with modifications, and obtaining the same results.

Rooting reflex   When the cheek of an infant is touched, the infant seeks the source of the stimulus with an open mouth. This reflex makes it possible for the infant to find the nipple when feeding.

Rubella   Same as German measles.

Small-for-date infant   An infant whose weight is not in proportion to its gestational age, that is, one who has had a growth problem in the uterus.

Sperm   Male cell needed to fertilize ovum.

State of consciousness   Condition of arousal exhibited by an infant as judged by sleep status, breathing, and activity.

Stress response   Body's reaction to stress, which includes production of the hormone epinephrine.

Sucking reflex   When an object is placed in an infant's mouth, she sucks on it. This is obviously important for early feeding of the infant.

Swallow reflex   Neurological organization that makes it possible for the infant to root, suck, and swallow in a coordinated way.

Syphilis   Sexually transmitted disease that can be given to unborn child.

Testosterone   Male sexual hormone produced in the testes.

Thalidomide   Tranquilizing drug given to pregnant women in the 1960s that caused serious birth defects.

Trimester   Three month period; the course of pregnancy is usually described as occurring in three trimesters.

Vernix   Waxy substance covering the skin of newborns.

Zygote   Fertilized egg ready for further development.

SUGGESTED READINGS

Nilsson, L. *A child is born.* New York: Dell (Delacorte Press), 1977.
This book is full of marvelous photographs of the embryo and fetus. It also has a good, basic text describing prenatal development and problems of pregnancy.

The Boston Women's Health Book Collective. *Our bodies, ourselves: A book by and for women* (2d Ed.). New York: Simon & Schuster, 1977.
Although this book is really focused on the adult female's body, it has an excellent discussion of health during pregnancy. You may not be entirely in sympathy with all the political views included, but there is no better compact source of information (including long bibliographies) on pregnancy.

Brazelton, T. B. *Infants and mothers: Differences in development.* New York: Dell, 1969.
This is a lovely book, written by a remarkably observant and sensitive physician. It describes the first year of life in some detail and also chronicles the progress of three infants who differ in basic temperament.

Macfarlane, A. *The psychology of childbirth.* Cambridge, Mass.: Harvard University Press, 1977.
Another lovely book, with both research information and opinions expressed in clear language.

McCall, R. *Infants: The new knowledge.* Cambridge, Mass: Harvard University Press, 1979.
This is an excellent book that reports recent research in an easy, readable style.

PROJECT 2.1
Observation in a Newborn Nursery

Although many hospitals now care for newborns in the same rooms with their mothers (a practice known as *rooming-in*), most still have newborn nurseries where people can look at the babies through a window. Since there are usually lots of friends and relatives admiring the babies, there shouldn't be much problem about your doing some brief observation. All the same, be sure to ask a nurse on duty before you begin your watching. Just explain that this is a class project, that you will only be watching through the window and taking notes. If more formal permission is needed, the nurse will let you know. If any of the other onlookers inquire, you can say the same thing—and say that you have permission to be there.

Once you have obtained permission, you can proceed with the following steps.

1. Set up a score sheet that looks something like this:

30-second intervals	Deep sleep	Active sleep	Quiet awake	Active awake	Crying fussing
1.					
2.					
3.					

Continue the score sheet for sixty 30-second intervals.

2. Reread the material in Table 2.1 until you know the main features of the five states (combining states 5 and 6) as well as possible. You will need to focus on the eyes (open versus closed; and rapid eye movement), the regularity of the baby's breathing, and the amount of body movement.

3. Select one infant in the nursery and observe that infant's state every 30 seconds for a half hour. For each 30-second interval, note on your score sheet the state that best describes the infant over the preceding 30 seconds. Do *not* select an infant to observe who is in deep sleep at the beginning. Pick an infant who seems to be in an in-between state (active sleep or quiet awake) so that you can see some variation over the half-hour observation.

4. If you can arrange it, you might do this observation with a partner, each of you scoring the infant's state independently. When the half hour is over, compare notes. How often did you agree on the infant's state? What might have been producing any disagreements?

5. When you discuss or write about the project, consider at least the following issues: Did the infant appear to have cycles of states? What were they? What effect, if any, do you think the nursery environment might have had on the baby's state? If you worked with a partner, how much agreement or disagreement did you have? Why?

Chapter 3
Physical and
Perceptual Development

(3)

A couple of years ago, my older daughter rather suddenly changed her eating habits. She picked at her food, even when I fixed her favorites—corn on the cob, steak, and caramel apples. At first we thought she might be sick, and then we wondered whether she was being negative for some reason. However, the answer turned out to be much simpler than that: She had lost her two front teeth, and it was hard to bite into things [SM].

Now this may seem like a trivial example (and you may be amused that it took us a few days to figure it out), but changes resulting from growth and physical development are easy to overlook when we are trying to understand the behavior of a particular child. Sometimes psychologists don't pay much attention to these physical processes, but it seems to us that there are several reasons why studying physical and perceptual development *is* necessary for understanding psychological development.

Growth as Limit Setting

First, physical capacities set limits on what children can do. A child whose maturation has not reached the point where he has control over the anal sphincter muscle cannot be toilet trained no matter how hard his parents try. (Sometimes mothers get quite skilled at noticing when a child needs to use the toilet and can put him on the pot; but that's a well-trained mother, not a toilet-trained child.) Similarly, a toddler can't pick up a raisin neatly until the development of thumb-forefinger opposition is complete, and a grade school student cannot ride a bike until balance and coordination develop. Obviously, it is important for parents, teachers, and others who work with children to have some idea what these limits are.

Growth as a Determinant of Experience

Second, these limitations affect the kinds of experiences a child can have; the nature of these experiences, in turn, influences the course of cognitive and social development. An infant who cannot crawl can only explore the environment that is within an arm's reach, but when she starts to move around on all fours, her horizons are widened considerably. Furthermore, her ability to get around changes her relationship with her caregivers—who must now deal with a moving explorer instead of a placid observer.

In fact, there is some evidence that children who are rapid in physical growth are also somewhat more rapid in mental growth (Tanner, 1970). Of course, we can't say for sure whether the more rapid growth of physical abilities *causes* the mental growth or whether both are the result of some third factor, such as good nutrition. Whatever the reason, though, the cognitive difference persists into adulthood long after the growth difference has disappeared.

Growth and Appearance

The third influence of physical development concerns the way others think of you. Children who are pretty or tall or well coordinated are frequently treated differently from those who are homely or petite or clumsy. A Little League baseball coach may be more supportive of a child with advanced large-muscle coordination (good for home runs), while a classroom teacher may be especially appreciative of children whose small-muscle coordination (used for writing and drawing) is superior.

In one study, Richard Walker (1962) had preschool teachers rate the social behaviors shown by boys with different body types. He classified the body types using a system originated by W. H. Sheldon (1940), which describes people as being predominantly **endomorphic** (rounded body contours), **ectomorphic** (tall and lean), or **mesomorphic** (well-muscled and square body contours). Walker found that endomorphic boys were rated by their nursery school teachers as being aggressive and assertive, the ectomorphs as being thoughtful and considerate, and the mesomorphs as being leaders and having high self-confidence. Of course, there were variations among the boys with each kind of body type, but the point to be made here is that teachers did view the boys differently depending on their physical characteristics.

Growth and Self-Image

Finally, physical development may affect the way a child feels about himself. Some of this is surely a reflection of the treatment he receives from others, but some of it is a realization of his own strengths and weaknesses. A child whose self-image matches the ideal held by his culture or by his family will have an easier time growing up than one whose self-image is a mismatch with those standards.

For all these reasons, we want to take a detailed look at physical growth and change before we consider other aspects of childhood development. We will start with the *outside,* at how children change in size and shape, and then move to the *inside* to see how bones, muscles, nerves, and hormones change. We'll see how both the outer and inner changes are reflected in motor development and look at some of the explanations for the ways in which that development proceeds. Finally, we'll switch to looking at development of perception and see how that links together our understanding of physical growth and the beginnings of cognitive development.

GROWTH ON THE OUTSIDE

Size

We have shown you the growth patterns for height in boys and girls in Figure 3.1, and you may be surprised to see that a baby starts out at about one third of his final adult height. But growth from birth to maturity is neither continuous nor smooth, and you can see from the graph that there are four different parts to the pattern.

First, from birth to about 3 years of age, growth (represented by the *slope* of the line) is rapid. In the second part of the pattern, the rate of growth slows but is steady from age 3 to about age 11. The third phase of growth begins with a dramatic adolescent *growth spurt.* This growth spurt comes earlier for girls than it does for boys; but since it is also shorter in duration for girls, they end up shorter in stature. The final part of the pattern is the leveling off at the beginning of adulthood, which marks the end of growth as we usually think of it (Tanner, 1970).

Shape

One of the reasons we are surprised to hear that a baby is one third the height of an adult is that infants are proportioned quite differently from adults. Compared to an adult, a baby's head is quite large: It accounts for about 25 percent of the baby's height at birth and about 20

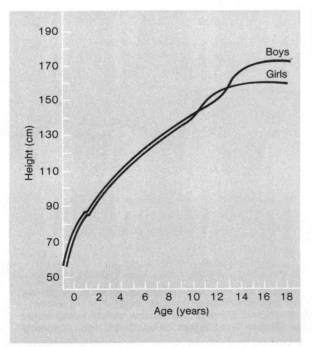

Figure 3.1. Changes in height during childhood. Note that girls are shorter than boys at every age except for a brief period during puberty, when girls have their growth spurt before boys do. (*Source:* Tanner, Whitehouse, & Takaishi, 1965, p. 467.)

percent at age 2, compared to approximately 10 percent in adulthood (Smith, 1978). You can see this comparison in Figure 3.2.

You can also see in this figure that there are other shape changes that have to do with how much baby fat a youngster has. Younger children have rounder contours than do older ones. Another thing not clearly visible from the drawing is that the shape of the face, as well as its size, changes with development. Particularly when the permanent teeth begin to come in, there are changes in the size and shape of the jaw (Smith, 1978). Sometimes it seems to adults that it takes a while for children to grow into their teeth, just as it takes time to grow into new clothes.

GROWTH ON THE INSIDE

Bones and Muscles

What we see on the outside of the body as changes in size and shape are really changes that have occurred inside, in the bones and muscles. What are some of these bone and muscle growth patterns?

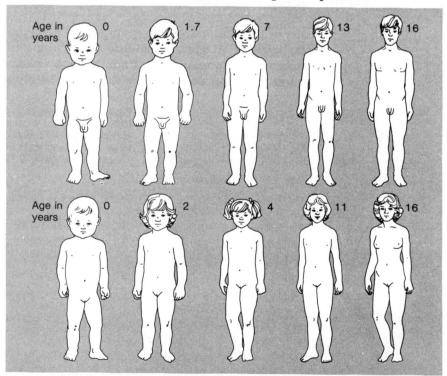

Figure 3.2. Changes in body proportions from birth through adolescence. As you can see, the head represents a very large proportion of the body length in young children, but a smaller proportion in older children. The legs also become proportionately longer and the trunk slimmer with age. (*Source:* The Diagram Group. *Child's body: A parent's manual,* p. D03.)

Bones   Earlier we described the skeleton as the framework for the body, but this framework is not entirely in place when a child is born. Bones continue to increase in number, in size, and in hardness.

At the time of birth, some parts of the skeleton are not yet complete. For instance, of the 28 separate bones in the adult wrist and hand, the 1-year-old infant has only three. The rest develop during childhood, with growth complete by adolescence (Teeple, 1978).

In one part of the body, though, the number of separate bones actually decreases. This is in the skull, where the infant has several bones, separated by spaces called **fontanels.** Fontanels allow the head to be compressed during the birth process without injury, and they also give the brain room to grow. Although many parents worry about these soft places on the baby's head, they may also protect the brain from injury by being more flexible than the later one-piece skull will be. In most children, the fontanels are filled in by bone by about age 2.

The skeletal change that is most obvious is the increase in length of the long bones of the body, especially those in the arms and legs. These continue to grow into the middle or late teens, when the ends of the bones (which are called **epiphyses**) become hard and no further growth is possible.

At the time of birth, some bones are actually made of cartilage (the same stuff that makes up the bridge of your nose), and all of them are softer and have a higher water content than will be true later. The process by which these soft tissues become bones is called **ossification.**

Although ossification occurs steadily from birth through puberty, the rate of progress varies for different parts of the body. The bones of the hand and the wrist harden quite early as do the bones of the head. By contrast, the long bones of the leg do not harden completely until the late teens.

Before you decide that bone hardening is a hopelessly boring topic, think of what having soft bones means to a young child: It means she can work herself into all sorts of flexible postures (such as putting her foot behind her head or in her mouth). However, it also means that she'll have a hard time sitting up. When we note that a baby is becoming less floppy, we are seeing the result of ossification as well as muscle development.

Muscles.   Unlike bones, babies are born with all the muscle fibers they will ever have (Tanner, 1970). The muscles do change, however, by becoming longer and thicker. This process takes place all during childhood; and like height and weight, it shows a spurt during adolescence.

Even before the adolescent growth spurt, though, there are significant sex differences between boys and girls on measures of strength. That is to say, the *average* boy is stronger than the *average* girl. However, there is a great range of strength in both boys and girls, and there is a sizable group of girls who are stronger than the average boy, as well as a few boys whose performance is much like that of the average girl (Faust, 1977).

Nervous System

We mentioned in Chapter 2 that the nervous system is not finished at the time a baby is born. Other body systems, such as the lungs and circulatory system, are fully operative (though not always completely mature) at birth; but the nervous system is still notably immature.

At the time of birth, the most fully developed portions of the brain are those included in the **midbrain.** This is the part of the brain in the lower part of the skull that regulates such basic things as attention and habituation, sleeping, waking, and elimination. These are the abilities that the newborn comes "wired for."

The least developed and most complex part of the brain, on the other hand, is called the **cortex.** This is the wrinkled gray part of the brain that is wrapped around the midbrain and is involved in perception, body movement, and all kinds of thinking and language. The cortex is present at birth, but the individual cells are not well connected with each other. During the first two years or so of life, additional brain cells develop and linkages between the cells increase. This process is about half complete at 6 months of age, and about three-fourths complete by age 2.

If you think back to Chapter 2, you will remember that some of the infant reflexes, like the Babinsky, drop out at about age 6 months. It appears that the cause of the dropout is the development of the cortex, which takes over the control of the baby's physical activities. Because of this natural sequence of appearance and disappearance of the reflexes, they are sometimes used by physicians in determining whether physical brain damage has occurred (Sells, 1978).

Like the rest of the body, the cortex develops unevenly—some parts grow more quickly than others. The parts that control seeing and hearing are relatively well developed at the time of birth, and the areas that control motor skills (such as head and trunk movements) develop fairly early, too. Later in this chapter when we look at the sequences in which these motor skills develop, we'll see that they parallel the development of the cortex.

A second important process in the development of the nervous system is the growth of coverings—like sheaths—around individual nerves. You can think of these myelin sheaths (whose role in prenatal development we discussed in Chapter 2) as being a kind of insulation material, keeping messages in one nerve fiber from being accidentally transmitted to another nerve fiber along the way. The process of myelin development is called **myelinization.**

At birth, for example, the spinal cord is not fully myelinized; and without this sheathing, the child has little ability to communicate with the lower half of her body. She can feel things down there, but because messages cannot be sent easily down the nerves, she has little muscle control. The process of myelinization occurs rapidly during the first months of life and is almost complete at age 2 for nerves leading to and from the brain. In the brain itself, though, myelinization continues as late as adolescence and perhaps into adulthood.

Hormones

The final set of changes inside the body concerns **hormones,** the substances that are produced by the **endocrine glands.** Hormones govern growth and physical changes in several ways, and we've summarized the most important of these in Table 3.1.

The most important of the endocrine glands for development is the **pituitary** gland, which is located in the middle of the head. Its special importance comes from the fact that it provides the trigger for the release of hormones from other glands. For example, the thyroid gland only secretes its hormone (called **thyroxine**) when it has received a signal to do so, in the form of a specific thyroid-stimulating hormone from the pituitary (Smith, 1978).

We mentioned in the last chapter that hormones play an important part in prenatal development. Although it is hard to study the exact role played by hormones (partly because it is difficult to separate hor-

TABLE 3.1
Major Hormones Involved in Physical Growth and Development

Gland	Hormone(s) secreted	Aspect(s) of growth influenced
Thyroid	Thyroxine	Affects normal brain development and overall rate of growth.
Adrenal	Adrenal androgen	Involved in some changes at puberty, particularly the development of secondary sex characteristics in boys.
Testes (in boys)	Testosterone	Crucial in the formation of male genitals prenatally; also triggers the sequence of changes during puberty in the male.
Ovaries (in girls)	Estrogen	Affects development of the menstrual cycle as well as the development of secondary sex characteristics in girls.
Pituitary	Growth hormone; activating hormones	Affects rate of physical maturation, signals other glands to secrete.

mones produced by the mother from those produced by the infant), it seems clear that thyroid hormone is present from about the fourth month, and it is involved in stimulating normal brain growth. Growth hormone (from the pituitary) is also present during the prenatal period, and scientists presume that it stimulates the rapid growth and development that occur then. And, as we mentioned earlier, testosterone, which influences the development of male genitals, is also produced in the testes of male fetuses. Clearly, hormones begin their work very early in development (Stechler & Halton, 1982).

Most of you are aware that hormonal changes signal the onset of puberty, and we will discuss that set of changes more thoroughly in Chapter 8. But what happens in the period between birth and adolescence? Well, the sex hormones are at very low levels, but the thyroid and pituitary hormones seem to be active in controlling the rate of physical growth and development. For example, thyroxine is produced in greater quantities during the first two years of life than it is later—which matches the pattern of height and weight increases in the child.

GROWTH ON THE MOVE

So far we have looked at basic changes in the child's body, inside and outside, and now we would like to turn to the ways that this growing body can be used. This is the topic usually called **motor development,** and it refers to all the ways that the organ systems of the body join forces for everyday activity. Most parents and teachers think of motor development when they think of physical development, but we should keep in mind that all those bone and muscle and nervous system changes contribute to the outward motor skills we can see.

General Trends

Two basic trends describe the child's motor development, especially during the early years of life. The first of these is the tendency for skills to develop from the head downward (**cephalocaudal**), and the second is the tendency for development to go from the center of the body outward (**proximodistal**). The terms may be awkward, but the principles are fairly simple: The baby can hold up his head before he can sit up —that's a cephalocaudal sequence; and he can lift his chest off the mattress before he can aim his arm and hand efficiently toward an object—that's a proximodistal sequence.

If you think back to our discussion of brain development, these sequences are entirely reasonable. The parts of the brain that govern the movement of the head and trunk develop before the parts that govern the movement of the hands and legs.

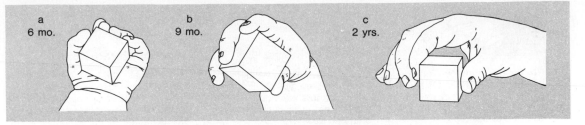

Figure 3.3. The development of grasping. The final stage of this sequence involves use of the thumb and forefinger in opposition and occurs at about age 2. (*Source:* The Diagram Group. *Child's body: A parent's manual*, p. D17.)

Some Basic Sequences

Since most motor behavior is easier to picture than to describe in words, we've given you several charts and diagrams to illustrate some of the important sequences in motor development. In Figure 3.3 you can see the development of grasping skill from the all-hand grasp of the 6-month-old to a full thumb-forefinger opposition in a 2-year-old. This sequence is important because it exerts so much influence over the kinds of interactions that young children can have with objects. A younger baby can pick up only those objects that *fit* his hand, for example, while an older child can pick up things that vary much more in size and shape.

Figure 3.4 shows the progression a child follows in learning how to crawl. Although our culture seems to recognize walking as the skill that separates infants from toddlers, we can't help feeling that crawling—the baby's ability to move around on his own—is really the more important event. Surely the start of locomotion changes the daily life of the child more than the switch from crawling to walking does.

Finally, we have shown you (in Figure 3.5) the difference in running style between an 18-month-old toddler and a 3-year-old youngster. How much of this difference is the result of maturation, and how much of it results from practice?

Practice

The answer to this question (and to other questions about motor skill practice in general) seems to depend on what kinds of skills are being studied and what kinds of practice are being used. Two older studies of the motor development of twins (Gesell & Thompson, 1929; McGraw, 1935) used basic motor skills like walking and climbing stairs and gave practice directed by an adult. These studies found little indication that this kind of practice was useful. As soon as the uninstructed twin was given the opportunity for brief practice, the two performed about equally. For these early motor tasks, a little bit of practice later was as good as a considerable amount of adult-directed practice early, presumably because maturation is the main determinant of when such abilities first appear.

Placed in a prone position, the newborn baby draws his knees up beneath his abdomen and lies with his pelvis high and his head directed to one side.

By six weeks old he tends to lie less tucked up. His pelvis is lower. Legs are more extended Sometimes he kicks out. Now and then he lifts his chin well up.

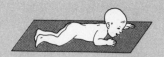

By 12 weeks the baby lies with legs fully extended and pelvis flat upon the bed or couch. He raises chin and shoulders and may hold his head almost upright.

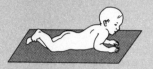

At 16 weeks he can press down with his forearms to lift his head and front part of the chest. He also stretches all his limbs, and "swims" on his abdomen.

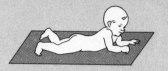

By 20 weeks the infant has had some weeks of practice and uses forearms in an even surer manner than before to help him lift up head and upper chest.

By 24 weeks he can lift his entire head, chest, and upper abdomen. Thrusting down with outstretched arms, he bears the weight of his upper body on his hands.

By 28 weeks he lies with the upper part of his body supported only on one hand. (By this time he is also able to roll over from abdomen to back and vice versa.)

The 36-week-old child learns that by thrusting down and forward on a surface he can move his body backward. He is well on the way to true crawling.

At 40 weeks he crawls forward on his belly, pulling himself along with his hands. At this stage his legs do no more than trail along unhelpfully behind.

By 44 weeks he has learned a more agile mode of crawling. Arms and legs all work together as he now creeps along on hands and knees, with belly held up off the ground.

At one year old he rests some weight upon his soles and ambles bear-like on his hands and feet. He has reached the final stage before unaided walking.

At 15 months he sometimes still feels safest on all fours, for instance when he starts tackling that formidable stepped cliff known to adults as a staircase.

Figure 3.4. The development of crawling in the first year of life. (*Source:* The Diagram Group. *Child's body: A parent's manual,* p. D11.)

On the other hand, there are other research results that strongly suggest that undirected practice—that is, the opportunity to practice the stages that *precede* a particular skill—may be quite important. For example, Wayne Dennis did a famous study of infants in an Iranian orphanage (Dennis, 1960). The babies in this overcrowded and under-

Figure 3.5. Running styles of 18- and 36-month-old youngsters. Changes in body proportion as well as changes in coordination help account for the difference in styles. (*Source:* Teeple, 1978, pp. 11 & 12.)

staffed institution were routinely kept on their backs in cribs. Instead of the normal sequence of crawling and walking, many of these infants would scoot around on their seats before learning to walk—and they did not walk until a year *later* than average. The reason for this seems to be that the babies were always placed on their backs (on soft mattresses that made it hard to turn over) and simply did not have a chance to practice the parts of the more common developmental sequence that includes creeping on the stomach.

Our conclusion from studies like these is that basic motor skills don't require specific, adult-directed practice and probably don't gain much from it. What they do require is general child-directed practice, that is, the opportunity to explore new forms of movement and to practice the preliminary skills needed to perform various motor skills.

What about nonbasic skills, things like ball throwing, tennis playing, and bike riding? In these cases the answer is easy: Practice (along with good coaching and perhaps general physical training) is needed just as it is for adults. It is interesting to note, in fact, that good coaches often try to break down complex skills into preliminary skills. This makes it possible for learners to go through preliminary sequences that may improve their final levels of performance.

Dangers

It is somewhat ironic that motor development, which opens the door to so many social and cognitive opportunities for youngsters, also represents the most serious threat to their lives. The leading cause of death (and the third leading cause of injury) in American children is accidents (Holm, 1978), and many of these accidents happen when a child is using a new motor skill.

A common (and usually minor) first accident is for an infant to roll over and fall off a bed or changing table while his parent turns away to pick up a diaper or clean clothes. The parent is invariably astonished that the baby is able to turn over so early. Stairways and open windows are hazards to crawlers, and nearly everything in a house that is sharp or poisonous is dangerous for a toddler. Preschool and school-aged children, while safe from many household hazards, are endangered by automobiles, by playground equipment, and by each other.

Many accidental injuries and deaths can be prevented, of course. Recent laws, such as the one requiring child-resistant tops on medicines and poisonous substances, can help; but the main responsibility for safety rests with parents and other caregivers. Child-proof environments (without dangerous objects and materials) and attentive supervision are both needed.

DETERMINANTS OF GROWTH

We've given you many facts so far about physical development, but we also need to think about the ways all of these changes might be explained.

Maturation

It seems clear that some set of internal signals controls the developmental sequences we have described. While *rates* of physical develop-

BOX 3.1

Motor Development and Toys

If you have ever tried to buy a toy for a child, you know how bewildering it can be to walk into a store and see aisles and aisles of bright attractive items. What makes a good toy, and what toys are good at what ages? The answer to these questions can come partly from what we know about a child's motor development.

BIRTH TO 6 MONTHS

Little babies use their hands and their eyes to play, so a good choice is something that is bright, safe to hold on to, and hooked to the crib so it won't fall. Mobiles and cradle gyms fit this description, and so do soft toys tied to the sides of the crib.

6 TO 12 MONTHS

Older babies are more mobile and are interested in toys that let them try out their new large muscle skills. Sling seats that hang from doorways and let babies jump are good and so are walkers, similar seats set on frames with wheels. Probably the best toy for a child this age is a child-proof house to explore, one in which hazards (such as sharp objects and poisons) have been removed. Playpens (now usually called *play yards)* are probably not as good, though they may sometimes be necessary for safety reasons.

Infants of this age also enjoy stacking and nesting toys. Measuring cups and pots and pans are often better for this than expensive baby toys.

SECOND YEAR

Give a toddler an expensive toy and chances are he will play with the box longer than with the toy. Since he can now pick things up with his thumb and forefinger, smaller objects (but not so small that they can be swallowed) are often favorites.

Toddlers like toys with wheels, but *push* toys are better than *pull* toys because the tots can see the object while it moves. Near the end of the year, towards the second birthday, the child can sometimes handle a big crayon or pencil and may enjoy drawing. For obvious reasons, washable colors are preferred.

THIRD YEAR

When in doubt, get something with wheels. Kid-die cars, tricycles, and other riding devices are favorites among large toys; and cars and trucks (for both sexes) are favorite small ones. Building toys start to be interesting, especially those with many possibilities, such as large wooden blocks (and again, homemade toys are just as satisfactory as expensive ones from a store).

Crayons and pencils are usually great favorites as are those messy classics, finger paints and play dough. As with younger children, "washable" is an important label to look for.

FOURTH TO SEVENTH YEAR

Small-muscle coordination develops rapidly during this period, and the child can manage toys like beads (to be strung on string) and more accurate cutting (although typical children's scissors are too dull for much accuracy; a sharp pair of scissors is a great gift for a child old enough to use them safely).

Large-muscle skills are improving too, and smaller balls (baseball or tennis size) can be used as well as larger ones. By the end of this period, the child can often manage a bicycle or at least start on one with training wheels.

ELEMENTARY SCHOOLS

These are the years during which coordination is really established. Most children can learn to ride a bike, throw a ball, and jump rope. Equipment for sports, though, needs to *fit* the child in both size and weight. For example, it is easier to start with bigger balls and lighter bats and rackets and then change to more traditional sizes after skills have developed somewhat.

Small muscles, perhaps because of practice in writing, are better developed, too. Children can begin building models, doing arts and crafts, and even sewing at this time.

A FINAL WORD

If you need to buy a gift and none of this information helps, our advice is to buy the *simplest* toy you can. A ball, a hula hoop, or a set of paints can be used in many ways by children of almost any age. If the gift is for a toddler, be sure it comes in a colorful box.

ment vary considerably from one child to another, the *sequence* of these changes is nearly invariant. In fact, we even see the same sequences in children who have marked physical or mental handicaps (Kopp, 1979). For example, Down's syndrome children are often slower in motor development than are normal children. Nonetheless, they move through the sequence of sitting and standing and walking in the same order (Carr, 1975; Dicks-Mireaux, 1972).

We don't know the entire explanation for these maturation changes. What we do know is that they seem to be part of the genetic code that applies to nearly all members of the human race.

Heredity

The other part of the genetic code controls those things that differ from one individual to the next—and this is what most people mean by heredity. We all know that physical features (such as eye color, hair color, or nose shape) are inherited, as are some patterns of physical development, such as height.

Height.   Tall parents tend to have tall children, and short parents tend to have short children. But, of course, we can't predict precisely how tall any child will be since environmental factors like diet and health will also influence final height. What seems to be inherited is some range of heights—and within that range, environmental forces can make a difference.

Growth Rate.   Rate of growth also seems to be an inherited trait. J. M. Tanner (1970), one of the foremost researchers in the field of growth, compared the similarity of girl twins, girl sisters, and unrelated girls in reaching various developmental milestones. (The method of using twins is a common one for studying heredity, as we shall see in Chapter 4.) The age of first menstruation is virtually the same for identical twins, somewhat similar in nontwin sisters, and not at all alike for unrelated pairs of girls. Studies of tooth development and bone ossification show this pattern, too, so it seems that the timing of growth is generally influenced by specific heredity.

Sex Differences.   There are few, if any, sex differences in the motor skills assessed by infant development tests. This may be because the kinds of general skills chosen for such tests are so basic that no sex differences would be expected. However, there are some differences in typical motor activities of babies, with 1-year-old boys spending more time in gross motor activities than girls, and the girls spending more time on fine motor activities (Malina, 1982).

Many more differences are apparent during the preschool and elementary school years. From ages 2 to 5, girls (on the average) excel in tasks requiring jumping, hopping, rhythmic locomotion, and balance; while boys perform better on strength and speed tasks. After age 5, boys do better in running, jumping, and throwing; while girls are better at hopping (Malina, 1982). There is, however, considerable overlap between boys' and girls' abilities, with the possible exception of ball throwing, where boys are substantially more able. (I regularly used to fail the fitness test for throwing, myself. [SM])

We need to interpret results like these carefully, though, because by elementary-school age (and perhaps during the preschool years as well), there are many factors influencing motor performance besides maturation and heredity. In particular, parent and teacher approval of different activities can be very influential in steering a child's interest toward sex-appropriate behaviors.

Other Influences

Birth Status   Several older studies (for example, Drillien, 1948) linked premature birth with delays in motor development. We need to view this evidence with caution, though, for three reasons. First, many premature infants have physical problems (such as anoxia) that may contribute to motor delays. Second, premature infants were sometimes compared to children of the same *living* age. Since premature infants were (by definition) born a month or more before the end of normal gestation, a better procedure is to correct the age of the prematures by comparing them with infants born at the time that the prematures *should* have been born, rather than when they actually *were* born. When such corrections are made, differences between premature and full-term infants decrease. Finally, we need to be careful about these results because the care of premature infants has improved dramatically in the past two decades. The appearance of neonatal intensive care units has meant a decrease in the number of children showing development delays.

Nonetheless, we want to remind you of the study by Jane Hunt that we reported in Chapter 2. Premature babies born *very* early and *very* small *do* run an increased risk of physical problems, including delays in motor development.

Nutrition.   The child's diet makes a major impact on the course of growth and development. Poorly nourished children grow more slowly and do not grow as large as well-nourished ones. More important, malnutrition in the early years seems to have a permanent effect on some parts of the brain and nervous system.

We've mentioned that brain development and myelinization continue during the first two years or so of life, so we'd expect malnutrition to have an effect during that time. The evidence we have (Lewin, 1975, for example) suggests that this effect is to reduce the amount of connective tissue between individual brain cells. The obvious result of this is that the cerebral cortex is not as heavy as it is in well-nourished children, but we do not have good evidence on the less obvious results. If a child is given a more adequate diet during these early years, it seems to be possible to make up the difference and have normal growth. If the inadequate diet continues throughout this period, though, the effects seem to be permanent.

The reason we are so tentative in describing the effects of nutrition is that most of the research in this area has been done with animals, since it is clear that *intentionally* giving children a poor diet is not ethical. When we compare groups of children who are already malnourished (those who have experienced a famine, for instance) with normal youngsters, we frequently find that the two groups differ in many ways besides diet—so we cannot make many firm conclusions.

There have been a few studies of specific dietary problems, though, and they support the importance of good nutrition. For example, Alice Honig and Frank Oski (1978) gave blood tests to a group of infants to find those with low levels of iron. Iron is important because it is part of the substance (called **hemoglobin**) that carries oxygen in the blood to all parts of the body, including the brain. These children were given a developmental test, and then half of them were given iron supplements. When they were tested a second time, about two weeks later, all the children showed increases (which we would expect, since they had had prior experience with the test). However, the group with the iron supplements showed much greater gains than did the group without them (see Figure 3.6). (By the way, the researchers gave the other half of the infants the iron supplement as soon as the second test was over, to be sure that all children in the study got the benefit of this procedure.) We don't have adequate studies on all aspects of diet, but we certainly have enough data to indicate strongly the importance of good nutrition in the early years of life.

Illness.   Another influence on growth is the occurrence of illness. Sick children generally grow more slowly, which may be a result of decreased activity, changed diet, or the disease itself. After recovery, though, growth tends to spurt ahead, usually showing a *catch-up* effect. As you can see in the example in Figure 3.7, the catch-up is not always complete, but children are almost always able to make up some of the growth lost during illness.

Overview.   The area of physical development is not the only place we shall see the contrast between *nature* and *nurture* in explaining devel-

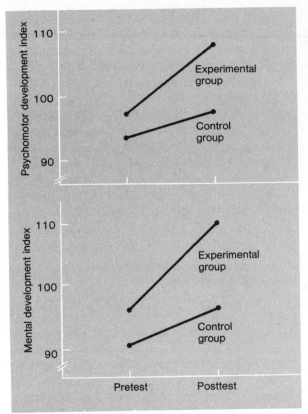

Figure 3.6. Effects of iron supplements on infant developmental test scores. All infants improved their scores on the Mental Development Index and the Psychomotor Development Index between the pretest and the posttest. The experimental group of babies, who were given an iron supplement, showed significantly greater improvement, though, than the control babies. (*Source:* Adapted from Honig & Oski, 1978.)

opment. But it is a place where we can clearly see that both nature (heredity and maturation) and nurture (experience and environment) can strongly affect the rate of development and the final outcome of that development.

GROWTH OF PERCEPTION

Another place where we can see this intricate connection between nature and nurture is in the development of the senses, usually called perceptual development. Among perceptual researchers and theorists, there has been a historical split between **nativism,** which stresses the importance of heredity and maturation, and **empiricism,** which stresses the importance of environment and experience. Before we can judge the strengths and weaknesses of these two theoretical positions, we need to look at what kinds of perceptual abilities infants have and how those abilities change and develop during childhood.

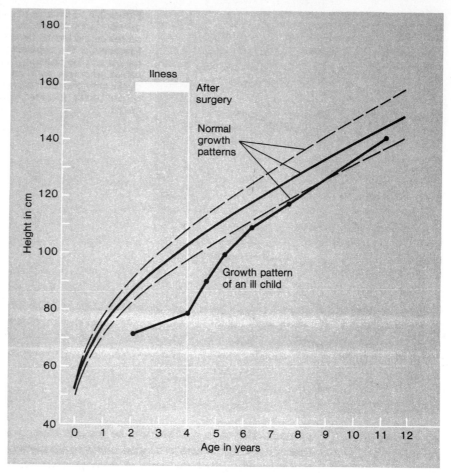

Figure 3.7. The catch-up phenomenon. Even though a child's rate of growth is slowed during illness, it speeds up afterward. This particular child had a tumor of the adrenal gland. After the tumor was surgically removed, she showed rapid growth. (*Source:* Prader, Tanner, & VonHarnack, 1963, p. 652.)

Studying Perceptual Abilities

Suppose you were a psychologist and you wanted to study infant vision. Since you can't ask a baby to read an eye chart or answer any questions, how would you go about your research? First, you would need to find some response that babies *could* make, such as gazing or sucking. Then you would have to devise some stimuli that would demonstrate whatever perceptual ability you were interested in—pictures or tape-recorded voices or smelly liquids. If the infant would gaze or suck in the presence of one stimulus and not in the presence of another, then you could conclude that he could perceive the difference.

This is exactly the kind of procedure that was pioneered by Robert

Fantz (1956) in his studies of infant vision. Fantz put babies in an infant seat with two drawings in front of them. Meanwhile a research assistant looked through a peephole (from behind the drawings) to see which of the pictures was reflected in the baby's eyes. If the baby looked longer at one picture than at the other (and they did), Fantz concluded that the baby could perceive the difference between the two.

Most of the studies of infant perception since that time have used some variation on this basic idea. Today, some researchers use sophisticated electronic equipment to measure brain waves and heart rate, as well as more direct responses like gazing. And some experiments use complex procedures involving learning or habituation. But the basic logic for all these studies is the same: If the baby can show some difference in responding to two stimuli, we know he can perceive the difference between them.

Vision

Acuity.   The word **acuity** refers to how well or how clearly you can perceive something. The eye test you took to get a driver's license, for example, was a test of visual acuity. The usual standard for visual acuity in adults is 20/20, and any number (called a *Snellen equivalent*) higher than that—like 20/50 or 20/200—represents poorer acuity.

Newborn babies have relatively poor acuity—about 20/800 (Dobson & Teller, 1978)—but it improves rapidly during early infancy so that most 4-month-olds have acuity ranging between 20/200 and 20/50. What does it mean to a baby to have limited acuity? Well, it means he will not be able to see things that are far away and even things fairly close will not be clear and crisp for the first few months. After that it shouldn't be much of a problem, especially since acuity continues to improve during childhood, reaching 20/20 at about age 10 or 11 (see Figure 3.8).

Scanning.   If you think of the human eye as a camera, then visual acuity is a measure of how well the camera can focus. But to be useful, the camera has to be aimed at the right things—it has to be used skillfully. Perceptual researchers have been especially interested in how babies develop this skillful use of their abilities. Several different theorists—including Gordon Bronson (1974), Philip Salapatek (1975), and Bernard Karmel and Eileen Maisel (1975)—have argued that visual attention during the first six to eight weeks of life is most concerned with *where* an object is. The baby is operating with what Bronson calls the **second visual system,** in which he can focus on objects near himself, move his eyes to track a moving object, and look at the edges of patterns and designs (recall the study of infants looking at the corners of triangles that we mentioned in Chapter 2). The general description is that the baby is somehow "captured" by movement and light/dark contrasts.

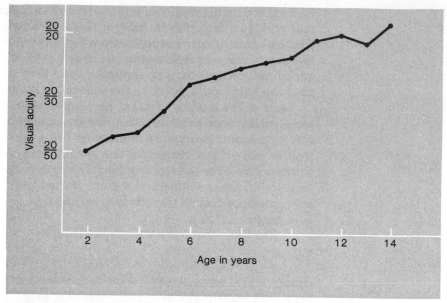

Figure 3.8. Development of visual acuity. Children's visual acuity improves steadily over the first 10 to 12 years. Acuity during infancy develops quickly from about 20/800 at birth to about 20/100 at 4 months. (*Source:* Weymouth, 1963, pp. 132 & 133.)

After about eight weeks of age, though, the emphasis changes to what Bronson calls the **primary visual system,** which is concerned with *what* something is. For example, Fantz and his colleagues Joseph Fagan and Simon Miranda (1975) studied infant preferences for designs that used curved lines versus similar designs with straight lines (see Figure 3.9). Younger infants (up to 6 or 8 weeks of age) showed no preference, but older babies (8 to 12 weeks) looked longer at the curved figures than at the straight ones.

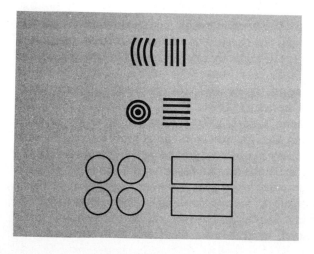

Figure 3.9. Patterns and designs used in studies of infant attention. This particular set was used to compare infants' preferences for straight versus curved lines. (*Source:* Fantz, Fagan, & Miranda, 1975, p. 277.)

This change from the secondary to the primary visual system is probably based on a maturational sequence that is going on at this time. It is also known, for instance, that the part of the cerebral cortex required for close detailed analysis of figures is not fully developed at birth but develops quickly during those first months of life.

Patterns.   The tendency for babies to prefer stimuli that are more complex (such as the curved designs in Fantz's study) continues during later infancy. For example, older babies prefer checkerboards with many squares, while younger ones prefer those with fewer squares. Older babies also show preference for designs with more contrast (that is, lines between light and dark spaces), with more brightness, and with more intensity (Acredola & Hake, 1982).

We can't tell from studies such as this one, though, whether the infants are really responding to the *pattern* as a whole or just to some characteristic like the contrast or brightness. Albert and Rose Caron (1981) have explored this issue by selecting stimuli that represent several different versions of the same pattern and using them in a habituation experiment. First the infant is shown several examples of a pattern (such as the "small shape above large shape" shown on the left side of Figure 3.10) until her gazing shows evidence of habituation (that is, she looks less). Then she is shown an entirely new stimulus that either matches or doesn't match the pattern (see the right side of Figure 3.10). If she is really habituated to the *pattern* (small above large), she will not be very interested in stimulus *A*, which is just another example of that pattern; however, she should show some interest (that is, look more) at stimulus *B*, which is a different pattern. Caron and Caron found that normal babies did show evidence of habituating to the pattern and not just to particular shapes.

Another kind of pattern that has been especially interesting to researchers is the human face. Some theorists, especially those with biologically oriented theories, have suggested that there is an innate

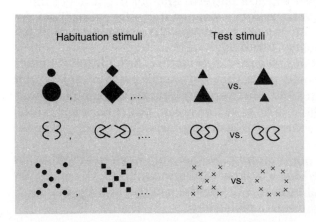

Habituation stimuli   Test stimuli

Figure 3.10.   Pattern stimuli used in experiments by Albert and Rose Caron. Infants were shown all of the stimuli on the left during the habituation phase. The stimuli on the right-hand side were used in the test phase. The 4-month-old infants showed renewed visual interest to stimulus B but not to stimulus A, which is an example of the sample pattern used during habituation. (*Source:* Caron & Caron, 1981.)

tendency for human babies to attend to human faces. Some early re-search, which showed that infants did choose faces over other stimuli (Fantz, 1963) seemed to support this position. However, when the other stimulus in such a study is made as complex as a human face, the pref-erence for the face is not found (Hershenson, 1964). In other words, it appears that infants have some built-in preference for a stimulus that is about the same complexity as the human face rather than for the human face itself.

Researchers have also found that infants look at faces in about the same way as they look at other objects. Younger infants (under 2 months of age) look mostly at the edges, while older ones look more at internal features, particularly the eyes (Cohen, DeLoache, & Strauss, 1979). At about 4 months, babies begin to show preference for real faces over schematic ones, and by 5 months they can discriminate between different faces. After that age it appears that they can tell men from women, one picture of an individual from another picture, and a color photo from a live face. As we shall see later in this book, these perceptual abilities play an important part in the infant's developing relationship with his parents—it's hard to have a relationship if you can't consistently recognize someone!

Visual Perception in Older Children.   Eleanor Gibson (1969) has stud-ied ways in which attention continues to develop during early child-hood. Her research indicates that there are four basic dimensions of that change:

1. *From capture to activity.* Even though young infants have system-atic visual scanning activity, much of their visual behavior is con-trolled by the nature of the stimuli—what Gibson calls *capture.* In-creasingly, though, the child looks at what she is interested in or, more simply, what she wants to.
2. *From unsystematic to systematic search.* Although young babies do look at more than just edges of patterns and objects, it is not until much later—perhaps 2 years or even as late as 6 years—that the child really begins to explore systematically, examining each fea-ture of a visual display carefully.
3. *From broad to selective pickup of information.* As children get older, they realize more and more that only some parts of objects and events are important and others are irrelevant. For example, it mat-ters whether a traffic light is red or green, but it does not matter what shape it is or whether it is on the corner or hanging over the street.
4. *Ignoring irrelevant information.* We not only have to attend to the right things, we also have to ignore the wrong things. Of course, the infant's ability to habituate is the first sign of this ability, and it con-tinues to improve through adolescence.

Perceptual Constancies.   Most of the research we have described so far used stimuli that were quite artificial. Researchers, though, have also been interested in how infants develop their ability accurately to perceive objects that exist in the real world. One of the most important skills for doing this is the ability to tell when two different visual images are actually the same object.

If we look at an object, such as a dinner plate, we see quite different visual images depending on the distance from which we see it (large if close up, small if far away), the angle at which we see it (a circle if seen straight on, an oval if seen from the side), and the lighting in which we see it (white in bright light, gray in the shadows). The knowledge that an object does not change size even though we see it from different distances is called **size constancy,** and the knowledge that it remains the same shape even though we see it from different angles is (not surprisingly) called **shape constancy.** The ability to recognize that colors are constant even in different amounts of light and shadow is, of course, **color constancy.** Taken together, the specific constancies add up to the larger concept of **object constancy,** which is the recognition that objects remain the same even when they appear to change in certain ways.

The aspect of size constancy that has been most studied concerns **depth perception.** When you watch someone walking away from you, the reason you know he isn't getting smaller is because you can judge how far away he is, which is what we mean by depth perception.

One of the earliest (and still one of the cleverest) studies of infant depth perception was the work of Eleanor Gibson and Richard Walk (1960), who built an apparatus called the **visual cliff.** You can see from the picture in Figure 3.11 that it consists of a large glass table with a runway in the middle. On one side of the runway there is a checkerboard pattern immediately below the glass; on the other side—the "cliff"—the checkerboard is several feet below the glass. If a baby had no depth perception, she should be equally willing to crawl on either side of the runway; but if she did have it, she should be reluctant to crawl out on the cliff side.

The original study by Gibson and Walk used babies 6 months old and older. By and large they would *not* crawl out on the cliff, even when their mothers stood on that side and urged them to do so. But what about younger babies, those not yet able to crawl? A more recent study by Joseph Campos and his colleagues (Campos, Langer, & Krowitz, 1970) used the same visual cliff with special equipment to record the heart rates of infants placed on one side or the other of the glass. In babies as young as 2 months, the heart rate went down a little when they were placed on the cliff side and did not change when they were placed on the other side. This indicates to us that they could tell the difference. Younger babies did not show this effect, probably because they lacked the visual acuity to see the checkerboard under the cliff.

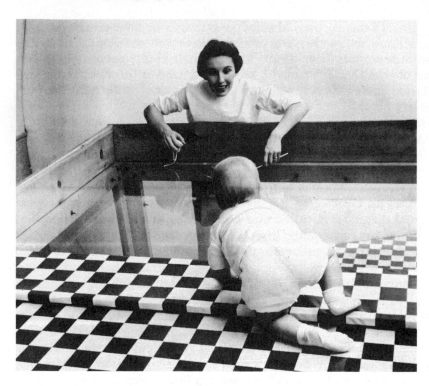

Figure 3.11. The visual cliff. This apparatus, designed by Eleanor Gibson and Richard Walk, has been used in many studies of infant depth perception. Infants of this age (6 months or older) will not go on the cliff side, even when urged to do so by their mothers. (*Source:* Gibson & Walk, 1960.)

Although we cannot be sure just when depth perception begins, studies like this one indicate that it is quite early in infancy.

Researchers interested in shape constancy have often used learning experiments in their studies. They teach babies to perform some behavior (usually head turning or sucking) when they see a particular shape. If the babies perform this behavior when they see a variation on the shape, we conclude that they think it is the same. Thomas Bower (1966) did a study like this using a rectangle as the stimulus, and he found that 2-month-old infants showed some shape constancy. That is, they responded to a slightly turned rectangle (whose visual image would be a trapezoid) as if it were still a rectangle. Studies like this one indicate that shape constancy is also present quite early in infancy.

Experiments about color constancy have used similar methods. For example, Marc Bornstein and his colleagues (Bornstein, Kessen, & Weiskopf, 1976) used different shades of colors in a habituation study (similar to that used in the pattern studies we described earlier). Bornstein showed a single color to an infant until she habituated; then he showed either a different color or a different shade of the same color. The 4-month-old infants gazed longer at the different colors, suggesting that they perceived the different shades as somehow the same as the original color.

Taken together, the evidence indicates that by 4 months of age (and perhaps sooner) infants have mastered the elements of object constancy. That is, they can use size constancy, shape constancy, and color constancy in their perceptions of objects in their environments.

Object Concept.   The next important perceptual development is the extension of this understanding to objects that may *not* be currently in their environments. This understanding is called the **object concept.** One aspect of the object concept is the understanding that objects continue to exist even when the infant cannot see them any longer. For example, even when mother goes out of the room, she still exists. That understanding is usually referred to as **object permanence.** The other aspect of the object concept is the understanding that individual objects retain a unique identity from one occasion to another; that is, mother is the same mother no matter when you see her. This is what we mean by **object identity.**

The first evidence that the baby is developing object permanence comes at about 2 months of age. Suppose you show a toy to a child of this age and then put a screen in front of the toy and remove the toy. When you then remove the screen, the child shows some indication of surprise, as if she knew that something should still be there (Piaget, 1954; Gratch, 1975). At the same time, though, infants of this age will not *search* for the toy that has been hidden.

Searching appears around the age of 6 months. At this age, when the baby drops a toy over the side of the crib, he will look down for it. He will even search for it if it is partly hidden by a cloth (or anything else) but not if it is entirely hidden. Search for completely hidden objects comes somewhere between 8 and 12 months (Piaget, 1954; Gratch, 1975).

One somewhat inconsistent piece of evidence about object permanence, though, comes from a study by Thomas Bower (1975). He found that while 5-month-olds would *not* search for an object that had just been covered with a screen, they *would* search for the same object if the lights were turned out. Why covering and darkness would have different effects on searching is still not clear, and this finding reminds us that the development of object permanence is probably a bit more complicated than our description indicates.

Object identity, too, is hard to study. One approach, used in another study by Bower (1975) is to present the infant with an impossible situation (that is, one in which object identity is violated) and see if the infant exhibits surprise. In Bower's study, he used mirrors to give the impression that several mothers were standing in front of the infant. Younger infants showed no surprise at this—in fact, they seemed to view the idea of multiple mothers with some pleasure. Infants 22 weeks of age or so were very upset by this state of affairs, though, suggesting that they realized there should be only one mother—evidence for object identity.

The reason we have discussed object constancy and the object concept in some detail is that they seem to form a bridge between perception and early cognitive development. As you shall see in Chapter 4, understanding these constancies is an important theme in cognitive development throughout the life span.

BOX 3.2

Reading and Perception

It is obvious that visual perception is an important skill for learning how to read. A child's perceptual learning during the preschool years, however, may sometimes make it more difficult, rather than easier, to learn to read.

In the first place, a child has already learned that objects are the same no matter how they are turned or rotated—a rectangle is a rectangle no matter what orientation it is in. Among letters, though, shapes that are turned are *not* the same shape anymore—*b* is different from *d,* and *p* is different from *q.* So a child has to *un*learn some aspects of shape constancy that she has been practicing before she can learn to read.

The second thing a child has to do is to transfer her knowledge of *spoken* language to a language that is *written.* Things like capitalization at the beginnings of sentences and periods at the ends of them don't exist in spoken language and have to be learned from scratch.

The steps that most children go through in learning how to read show that these factors do, in fact, sometimes cause problems. In the first step, when a child comes to a word he does not know, he substitutes one that fits the context of the sentence, even if it doesn't *look* (in its written form) at all like the word on the page. In the second step of this process, the child knows that what he reads has to correspond with what is on the page; so when he comes to a word he doesn't know, he just stops. He may stop altogether, or he may just skip it and read the rest of the words. Only in the third step of this

sequence does the child try to decode or sound out an unknown word.

It is important that adults helping children with reading understand these stages, or it is likely that they will make some incorrect interpretations of the children's behavior. A child who reads an entirely incorrect word or who leaves a word out is not necessarily a *bad* reader, just one who is not yet fully mature in his decoding skills.

Some children, though, do not go through this sequence smoothly. About 15 percent of school children in this country have a significant problem in learning how to read. A few are generally retarded or have some specific brain damage, but the majority are children who are basically normal. The term used to describe children like this is **dyslexia** or, more frequently, **specific learning disability.**

The fact that these children are given one label does not mean, though, that they all have the same problem. Some have general problems with language, and some have neurological deficits in sight or hearing. But for at least some of these children, perception seems to be the problem.

In particular, some children with reading difficulties have trouble decoding the visual information. For instance, the distinction between reversed letters seems to be hard for them to grasp. Other children seem to have difficulty in putting together the visual information (the letters printed on the page) and the auditory information (the sound of a word). This is often true in the early years of elementary school when much of reading is done aloud.

Hearing

Acuity.   Hearing is just as difficult as vision to assess in infants, but several different research methods seem to agree that infants can hear nearly as well as adults from the neonatal period onward (Morse & Cowan, 1982). In fact, even fetuses still in the womb respond to auditory stimulation (Murphy & Smith, 1962). The uterus is actually a fairly noisy place, with the heartbeat of the mother providing about as much noise as an average adult conversation (Morse & Cowan, 1982).

Speech Perception.   Although acuity is certainly important, in some ways it is more important to know how much *language* a child can understand. From quite early ages (approximately 1 to 2 months) infants can distinguish between individual speech sounds like *ba* and *ga.* Soon after, they can discriminate two-syllable words, like *bada* and *baga,* also. They can even respond to a syllable that is hidden inside a string of other syllables, like ti*ba*ti or ko*ba*ko (Morse & Cowan, 1982). This implies that babies can do a fairly good job of hearing what is said around them and to them.

Can they also tell who is talking? According to one study (DeCasper & Fifer, 1980), babies show a preference for their mothers' voices in the first few days after birth. Slightly older children (6 to 7 months old) can discriminate between male and female voices in the laboratory (Miller, Younger, & Morse, in press). In fact, if you put an infant of this age in a situation where he can see both his father and his mother and he can hear a tape-recorded voice of one of them, he will look toward the parent whose voice he hears (Spelke & Owsley, 1979).

In summary, then, very young infants seem to have the ability to hear speech sounds and to discriminate among speakers quite early in life. It seems likely, in fact, that babies may recognize their parents by *sound* slightly before they can recognize them by *sight.*

Smell and Taste

The senses of smell and taste have been much less studied than either vision or hearing, though we do have some basic knowledge. As with adults, the two senses are intricately related—that is, if you cannot smell for some reason (such as when you have a cold), you cannot taste, either. Taste is detected by the taste buds on the tongue, which can register only four basic tastes: sweet, sour, bitter, and salty. Smell is registered in the mucous membranes of the nose and has nearly unlimited variations.

A series of experiments by Jacob Steiner (1979) has shown that newborns can taste three of the basic flavors—sweet, sour, and bitter

—and, more important, they respond to those tastes in predictable ways. The experiments are simple. A newborn infant, who has never been fed, is photographed before and after flavored water is put into her mouth.

Some of Steiner's photos are shown in Figure 3.12, and you can see that there is remarkable similarity to the responses. The sweet liquid is responded to with a relaxed face and an expression of enjoyment resembling a smile. The response to the sour liquid is pursed lips, while the response to the bitter liquid is an arched mouth with sides turned down and an expression of disgust. Steiner has repeated this experiment with many other groups of subjects, including blind youngsters (to demonstrate they could not have learned the responses by watching others), handicapped children, and even seriously deformed children. He has also used sweet and bitter odors as stimuli. In all cases, he finds the same pattern of facial reactions—which is strong evidence in support of his position that they are innate and universal.

We know relatively little about the later development of taste or

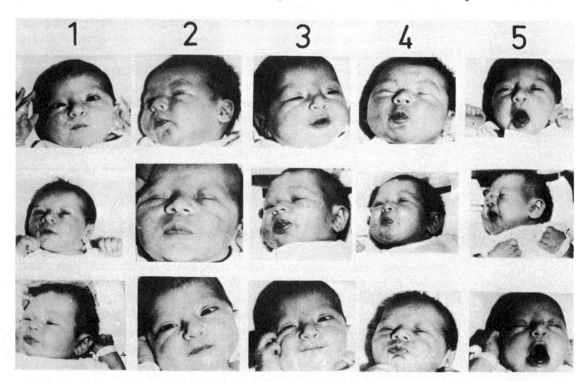

Figure 3.12.   Infants' response to sweet (left), sour (middle), and bitter (right) tasting liquids. Steiner believes these facial responses are innate and universal. (*Source:* Steiner, 1979.)

smell, except that the actual number of taste buds declines in adult-hood. This suggests that youngsters may have a reason for disliking spicy foods—they're just too strong for their taste.

PERCEPTUAL STYLES

So far we have talked as if all infants and children are quite alike in the ways they perceive things. But it is also true that there are some fascinating differences—styles—in the way people use perception. If you were to go to a museum, for example, and watch the visitors, you would see examples of these differences: Some people stand close to exhibits and look at them carefully for a long time, while others stand back and examine them more generally.

Reflection versus Impulsivity

One way of describing individual differences such as those mentioned above is to categorize them as **reflective**—slow and detailed observation—or **impulsive**—rapid and more cursory observation. Jerome Kagan (1971) refers to reflection and impulsivity as the two kinds of **conceptual tempo.**

Although reflection and impulsivity have been studied in infants, most of the research has been with older children. The task most often used is a picture matching game, and we have shown you an example of an item in Figure 3.13. The child's job is to find which of the six pictures at the bottom matches *exactly* the picture at the top (sometimes called the *standard*). A child characterized as reflective looks carefully at all the alternatives before making a choice and, not surprisingly, makes very few errors. A child who is impulsive, on the other hand, looks over the options quickly and chooses one—which is frequently incorrect.

Conceptual tempo seems to be fairly stable over the childhood years. In one longitudinal study, Kagan and his colleagues (Kagan, Lapidus, & Moore, 1978) compared measurements of tempo made when children were 8 months old with measures made at age 10 and found a signifi-cant correlation. That is, reflective infants were likely to become reflec-tive children, and impulsive infants were likely to become impulsive children.

It is easy to conclude that reflection is a more desirable conceptual tempo than impulsivity, especially when you consider that reflective children seem to have an easier time learning to read (Kagan, 1965). We need to remember, though, that only a few tasks in everyday life, such as learning to discriminate the letter *b* from the letter *d,* require

Figure 3.13. The picture test used to assess reflection versus impulsivity. The child taking the test must try to select the picture (from among the bottom six) that exactly matches the figure at the top. (*Source:* Kagan, Rosman, Day, Albert, & Phillips, 1964, p. 22.)

careful search and consideration. For other situations, like sorting apples and bananas, quick response is perfectly acceptable and often much more efficient than reflection.

Field Dependence versus Independence

Another way of studying perceptual style was originated in studies of adults by H. A. Witkin and his associates (Witkin, Dyk, Faterson, Goodenough, & Karp, 1962). Witkin was intrigued by the fact that some people's perceptions seemed to be influenced by the background environment, while other people's perceptions were not. This characteristic is often measured in children using the **Embedded Figures Test** (Coates, 1972). In this task (see Figure 3.14), the person is shown a simple figure, such as a square or a pie shape, and asked to find a figure like that in a complex drawing (you may have done puzzles like this in magazines when you were a child). People who can ignore the irrelevant background material are called **field independent,** while those who are captured by that background are called **field dependent.** Witkin's research suggests that children become increasingly field independent as they get older.

One of the reasons this way of classifying perceptual styles has been so popular among psychologists is that Witkin also suggested that these perceptual styles have personality correlates. The data are

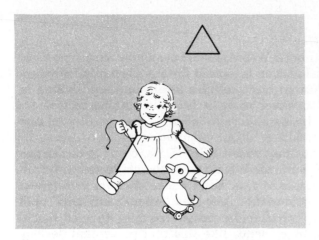

Figure 3.14. A sample item taken from the Coates Preschool Embedded Figures Test. The simple form in the upper right must be located in the complex figure below. How long does it take you to find it? (*Source:* Coates, 1972.)

somewhat less clear on this point, but the idea is an intriguing one that we shall return to in Chapter 4 when we consider *cognitive* styles.

NATIVISM AND EMPIRICISM

We began this section with the question of nativism versus empiricism: Are perceptual skills primarily the result of heredity and maturation or of environment and experience?

Many psychological questions are phrased in black-and-white alternatives—like this one—and most of the answers seem to turn out sort of gray. Nonetheless, let's have one last look at the evidence for the two positions so we can tell what shade of gray we have this time.

Nativism

We have seen that the neonate has a variety of perceptual skills: adequate acuity, some depth perception, and the beginnings of some of the perceptual constancies. Perhaps more important, she has a system for scanning and inspecting visual arrays. Although all of these seem to be present in some form from birth, there are also some changes (presumably maturational) that take place at about 2 months and others that continue through the fourth or fifth month of life.

In short, the newborn infant is quite a skilled perceiver—he knows what to look at and he is reasonably good at doing the looking. For these early abilities, the nativism position is clearly a strong one.

Empiricism

To explain the continued development of perceptual abilities, though, we need to take experience into account. At the biological level, several studies (for instance, Hubel & Weisel, 1963) have shown that some basic minimum of visual stimulation is needed for any perceptual development to occur. Beyond that basic cellular level, studies of infants in deprived environments, where there is literally nothing to look at, show that they have considerable retardation in both perceptual and motor skills (Dennis, 1960).

On the bright side, adding visual stimulation seems to encourage these skills. One study by Burton White (1967) was conducted with children in an orphanage such as this. Some of the children were given extra visual and tactile stimulation, and these infants were more rapid in their development of what White called "visually directed reaching"—a skill requiring good depth perception.

We are persuaded by evidence like this that perceptual development is dependent on nativism for a good start but needs continued varied stimulation for adequate progress to be made after the newborn period.

SUMMARY

1. Physical development can influence psychological development by setting limits on behavior, by determining experience, by determining appearance, and by influencing self-image.
2. Growth in height and weight is most rapid in the first year and during the adolescent growth spurt, which begins at about age 11 for girls and at age 13 for boys.
3. The number of bones in the body increases during childhood, and the bones also increase in size and become harder.
4. Since all the muscles are present at birth, further development consists of their changing size and shape.
5. During the first two years of life there is continued growth in the cortex of the brain and in myelinization of nerve fibers.
6. Hormones are important for growth, especially those from the pituitary gland, which sends out signals to stimulate other endocrine glands.
7. Motor development proceeds from the head downward (cephalocaudal) and from the trunk outward (proximodistal).
8. Studies of motor development seem to show that directed practice on basic skills is not necessary or helpful but that the undirected practice of general skills is important.
9. Most physical and motor development sequences seem to be heavily dependent on maturation.
10. Birth status, nutrition, and illness can, nonetheless, influence the rate (and end point) of physical growth.
11. Visual acuity is poor in newborns but improves rapidly during the first four months and continues to improve to about age 10.

12. Infants seem to have two kinds of visual scanning systems, one concerned with locating objects in the visual field and the other concerned with examining those objects.

13. As they develop, infants show increasing preference for looking at complex figures and increasing ability to discriminate among stimuli, such as patterns and human faces.

14. The development of attention continues through childhood as children are increasingly able to use active perceptual skills, systematic search, selective pickup of information, and ignoring of irrelevant information.

15. The concept of object constancy includes shape, size, and color constancy—all of which are concerned with recognizing things seen under varying conditions.

16. The object concept includes object permanence and object identity, both of which are concerned with things that are either not seen or are seen on different occasions.

17. Newborns can hear nearly as well as adults. By 2 months of age they can discriminate speech sounds, and by 7 months they can discriminate between voices.

18. Newborns can distinguish tastes and odors and show consistent facial responses to both.

19. One definition of perceptual style, conceptual tempo, compares reflective and impulsive ways of responding to tasks. Another definition contrasts field dependence and independence.

20. Both nativism and empiricism seem to describe some aspects of perceptual development: Many perceptual abilities and strategies are innate, but most require experience to develop fully.

KEY TERMS

Acuity   Clarity of perception; visual acuity is a measure of how well you can see and correctly identify small symbols at a set distance, usually 20 feet.

Cephalocaudal   Developmental sequence that proceeds from the head downward.

Color constancy   Recognition that objects are actually the same color even though they appear different in differing levels of brightness and shadow. Part of object constancy.

Conceptual tempo   General term for perceptual styles referred to as reflective and impulsive.

Cortex   Most advanced portion of the brain, consisting of the convoluted gray matter just under the skull. The cortex is involved in controlling perception, body movement, thinking, and language.

Depth perception   Ability to judge how far away an object is.

Dyslexia   Impairment in the ability to read or special difficulty in learning to read.

Ectomorphic   Body type defined by bone length; an ectomorphic man is tall and slender, usually with stooped shoulders.

Embedded Figures Test   Test for measuring field dependence/field independence in which a child is asked to find a simple geometric figure in a larger complex drawing.

Empiricism   Theory that perceptual development is mostly dependent upon experience.

Endocrine glands   Glands in the human body that produce hormones to regulate a large number of basic biological processes.

Endomorphic   Body type defined by amount of body fat; an endomorphic man is soft and round in shape.

Epiphyses   The ends of bones where growth occurs, until they become completely hard in late adolescence.

Field dependence   Tendency to have perceptual judgments influenced by the context or field.

Field independence   Tendency to have perceptual judgments that are minimally influenced by the context.

Fontanels   Spaces between the skull bones of a young infant. The fontanels disappear as the skull ossifies and grows together.

Hemoglobin   Substance in the blood responsible for transporting oxygen to all parts of the body.

Hormones   Substances produced within the body in endocrine glands that affect growth and development as well as other basic processes.

Impulsive style   Perceptual style characterized by rapid, but often incorrect, responding.

Mesomorphic   Body type characterized by amount of muscle mass; a mesomorphic man is square-chested, broad-shouldered, and muscular.

Midbrain   Part of brain in the lower part of the skull that regulates basic processes such as attention and habituation, sleeping, waking, and elimination.

Motor development   Growth and change in ability to do physical activities.

Myelinization   Process of myelin sheaths growing around nerve fibers.

Nativism   Theory that perceptual development is mainly dependent upon innate abilities and relatively independent of experience.

Object concept   Understanding that objects not in view continue to have enduring characteristics.

Object constancy   Recognition that though an object may look different under different circumstances, it is still the same object.

Object identity   Recognition that individual objects retain their unique identity even when they are not in sight or hearing.

Object permanence   Recognition that objects continue to exist even when they cannot be seen.

Ossification   Process by which soft tissues become bones.

Pituitary gland   Important endocrine gland that provides the trigger for many other glands to produce hormones.

Primary visual system   Perceptual activities concerned with identifying objects. It comes into play sometime after 6 to 8 weeks of age.

Proximodistal   Sequence of development proceeding from the center of the body outward.

Reflective style   Perceptual style characterized by slow, but correct, responding.

Secondary visual system   Early perceptual behavior concerned with locating objects or patterns in space. It includes focusing on objects, tracking moving objects, and looking at edges of patterns.

Shape constancy   Recognition that an object does not change shape even though we see it from different angles. Part of object constancy.

Size constancy   Recognition that an object does not change size even though we see it from different distances. Part of object constancy.

Specific learning disability   Special difficulty in learning some school subjects (usually reading) that is not caused by mental retardation or known brain damage.

Thyroxine   Hormone produced by the thyroid gland that affects normal brain development and overall rate of growth.

Visual cliff   Experimental apparatus for assessing depth perception in infancy. It consists of a glass-topped table with checkerboard patterns directly below the glass on one side and several feet below the glass on the other.

SUGGESTED READINGS

Bower, T. G. R. *The perceptual world of the child.* Cambridge, Mass.: Harvard University Press, 1977.
This brief book (only 85 pages long) covers most of the major aspects of perceptual development during the early years in a fairly readable fashion. If you are interested in this area, this book would be a good place to start.

The Diagram Group. *Child's body.* New York: Paddington Press, 1977.
This book is subtitled "An owner's manual"; and although we don't exactly *own* children, this is precisely that—everything you wanted to know about physical growth and health.

Malina, R. M. Motor development in the early years. In S. G. Moore & C. R. Cooper (Eds.), *The young child: Reviews of research* (Vol. 3). Washington, D.C.: National Association for the Education of Young Children, 1982.
This is an article written for preschool teachers and others who work with small children. It is clearly written and has an extensive bibliography if you are interested in reading more about any of the topics.

PROJECT 3.1
Plotting Your Own Growth

This project will work only if your parents are among those who routinely stood you up against a convenient door frame and measured you—and if you still live in the house with the marked-up door frame.

If you meet both of these conditions (or if your family kept some other record of your growth), you might find it interesting to go back and plot your rate of growth over the years of childhood.

When you look at your plot, see if you can identify the height spurt—that is, the time period when you grew the fastest. When did that happen to you? Was your rate of growth before that quite steady? Does your curve look like the one shown in Figure 3.1?

Finally, if your door frame has marks for other children in your family, plot their changes in height, too. Do the members of your family share a pattern of growth?

Chapter 4
Intelligence in Children: Power, Structure, and Style

Let's start this chapter by asking you to write down a list of behaviors that you think are characteristic of intelligence. Try to think of at least five different ones. Psychologist Robert Sternberg asked 476 people (including students, commuters, supermarket shoppers, and people who answered a classified advertisement) to do this, and you might like to see how your answers compare with those given in Sternberg's poll (Sternberg, Conway, Ketron, & Bernstein, 1981).

Most of the behaviors listed by the subjects in this study fell into three categories: practical problem solving, verbal ability, and social competence. Some examples of the behaviors actually listed are shown in Table 4.1, which also shows some of the kinds of behaviors listed by another group of people: 140 "experts" in the field of intelligence. You can see that the two lists have about the same categories but that some of the particular behaviors listed are different for the two groups.

Sternberg noted that there were two important differences between the lists (Sternberg, 1982). First, the experts considered motivation to be an important aspect of intelligence, especially academic intelligence. They included such behaviors as "displays dedication and motivation in chosen pursuits," "gets involved in what he or she is doing," "studies hard," and "is persistent." That is, they emphasized *intra*personal competence. Second, laymen seemed to place somewhat greater emphasis on the social-cultural aspects of intelligence than did the experts. They included behaviors such as "sensitivity to other people's needs and desires" and "is frank and honest with self and others,"

TABLE 4.1
Comparing Ideas about Intelligence

Laymen	Experts
Practical problem-solving ability	*Verbal intelligence*
Reasons logically and well	Displays a good vocabulary
Identifies connections among ideas	Reads with high comprehension
Sees all aspects of a problem	Displays curiosity
Keeps an open mind	Is intellectually curious
Verbal ability	*Problem-solving ability*
Speaks clearly and articulately	Is able to apply knowledge to problems at hand
Is verbally fluent	Makes good decisions
Converses well	Poses problems in an optimal way
Is knowledgeable about a particular field	Displays common sense
Social competence	*Practical intelligence*
Accepts others for what they are	Sizes up situations well
Admits mistakes	Determines how to achieve goals
Displays interest in the world at large	Displays awareness to world around him or her
Is on time for appointments	Displays interest in the world at large

which did not show up in the experts' category of practical intelligence. Here the emphasis was on the *inter*personal competence in a social context.

What seems striking to us, though, is not how much these two groups differ on their definition of intelligence but how much they are the same. All the respondents in Sternberg's study seem to view intelligence as a characteristic of people, the same as height or weight or blood count. The more of it you have, the smarter you are and the better you will be at doing all the individual behaviors listed in Table 4.1. The problems for theorists and researchers, in this view, are finding consistent and accurate ways to measure intelligence and finding the various other factors and characteristics that are related to it. This point of view is closely related to the physical sciences and conceptualizes intelligence as primarily a *quantitative* thing.

This perspective on human intelligence has a long history in American psychology. We like to think of it as a **cognitive power** definition of intelligence because it seems to emphasize how "strong" a person's mental abilities are: The stronger you are, the better you do on tests and other measurements of intelligence. The developmental questions in this view have to do with the origins of this mental power and the ways in which it can change with age and environmental events. You should notice, too, that the emphasis in this view is on *individual differences* in intellectual ability, since only by studying individual differences can we describe why some people have more of it than others do.

However, there is another, quite different way of looking at intelligence. Theorists and researchers in this second tradition view intelligence in much the same way biologists see processes like digestion. Instead of asking how much intelligence someone has (imagine asking how much digestion a person has), they ask about the *structure* and *functions* of intelligence. The answers to these questions are not quantitative; they are qualitative.

We'd like to refer to this perspective as **cognitive structure** because it seems to be focused on the organization of knowledge. More important, the developmental questions in this tradition have to do with the ways in which cognitive structures are formed and the reasons and ways in which they change as children grow older. You should notice that the emphasis here is on *universal similarities* rather than on individual differences. The name most associated with this approach is Jean Piaget, the late Swiss psychologist introduced to you in the opening chapter of this book.

There is also a third way of defining and studying intelligence; and although it is not nearly as popular as the study of cognitive power and cognitive structure, we think it deserves mention here. This is what Roger Webb (1978) calls **cognitive style.** You can think of cognitive style as the way in which people use their cognitive powers and processes in their real lives. It includes, therefore, factors like temperament and personality (which we will discuss in Chapter 6), perceptual styles (which we already discussed in Chapter 3), motivation, and creativity. Obviously, this is a much more complex notion of intelligence, but it is one that is probably quite close to what most of us mean when we describe a friend as intelligent.

We're going to describe these three views of intelligence separately in this chapter, but as you read it, we hope you will do some thinking about ways in which these perspectives might be combined and how those combinations might help us understand cognitive development in children.

THE MEASUREMENT OF INTELLECTUAL POWER IN CHILDREN

A Little Background

Although students usually find it boring to read about the history of ideas or concepts, we'd like to say a few words about the history of intelligence testing.

Early Tests of Intelligence.   The first modern intelligence test was published in 1905 by two Frenchmen, Alfred Binet and Theodore Simon (1905). It had been written at the request of the French government to identify children who would be likely to have trouble in school. From the very beginning, then, the practical purpose of intelligence testing was to predict school success, and the items included on the test were, well, schoollike: comprehension, reasoning, vocabulary, and so forth.

The system Binet and Simon worked out for measuring intelligence was later followed by Louis Terman and his associates at Stanford University (Terman & Merrill, 1937) when they translated and revised the test for use in the United States. Items were chosen to represent specific ages by choosing tasks that about half the children of that age could pass and that younger children could not usually pass. There were six items for each age level (4-year-olds, 5-year-olds, and so on), and each child taking the test was given these items in order from easiest to hardest until a level was reached at which he failed them all.

The score on the test was computed by comparing the child's chronological age (his real age in years and months) with his mental age (the level of questions he could answer correctly). This score, the **IQ**, was defined as

$$\frac{\text{Mental Age}}{\text{Chronological Age}} \times 100 = \text{IQ}$$

For example, a 7-year-old child who passes all the 7-year items plus three of the 8-year items would have a mental age of $7\frac{1}{2}$ and an IQ of

107 (7.5 ÷ 7 × 100). Children whose mental age is greater than their chronological age (who can do items typical of older children) have IQs of over 100; those whose mental age is less than their chronological age (can only do items appropriate for younger children) have IQs of less than 100. This old system of calculating IQs is not actually used anymore; instead, a child's score is directly compared with that of others his own age. But an IQ of 100 is still average, and higher and lower scores still mean above and below average performance.

Today's Tests of Intelligence.   The modern version of the original IQ test, now called the **Stanford-Binet** (Terman & Merrill, 1960), is still popular for assessing children's intelligence, as are two tests developed by David Wechsler, the **WPPSI** (Wechsler Preschool and Primary Scale of Intelligence, Wechsler, 1967) and the **WISC-R** (Wechsler Intelligence Scale for Children—Revised, Wechsler, 1964). These two tests are arranged by kind of question, rather than by age level, and are sometimes preferred when the examiner wants to know about the specific patterns of abilities that a child may show (see Table 4.2).

Since the WPPSI cannot be used before age 4 nor the Stanford-Binet before age 3, there has been considerable interest in tests for younger ages. The best known infant test used today is the **Bayley Scales of Infant Development** (Bayley, 1969), which includes items intended to measure both mental and motor development in babies from birth to about 30 months.

All of these tests must be given individually and take about an hour and a half. Obviously, such tests cannot be used on a large scale, so many paper-and-pencil tests of intelligence have been designed that can be given to groups of children. The scores from these assessments can be very useful to psychologists, teachers, and parents; but they cannot be interpreted in quite the same way as traditional IQ scores. The same can be said about tests of school achievement—the kinds of standardized tests you may have taken from time to time in elementary school or high school. Such tests *do* tell how a student is doing compared to other students in the same grade, but they are not intended as measures of intelligence and should not be interpreted that way.

TABLE 4.2
The Wechsler Intelligence Scale for Children

Verbal tests	Performance tests
Information	Picture Completion
Comprehension	Picture Arrangement
Arithmetic	Block Design
Similarities	Object Assembly
Vocabulary	Coding
Digit Span (optional)	Mazes (optional)

Some Basic Issues

Because intelligence tests are so widely used and IQ scores are discussed so often, we want to give you some basic information about these scores.

Competence and Performance.   When we give someone an intelligence test, we want to know what she can really do, her maximum potential, under the best of circumstances. This is what psychologists call **competence.** Unfortunately, it is not possible to measure competence—we cannot be sure that we are assessing any ability under the best of all possible circumstances. Instead, we inevitably measure what psychologists call **performance,** or the way someone acts under a particular set of real circumstances—which may be far from ideal.

The authors of the famous IQ tests believed that by standardizing the procedures for administering and scoring the tests they could come close to measuring competence (see Figure 4.1). While it is certainly

Figure 4.1.   A child taking a traditional standarized IQ test. The examiner must carefully follow the procedures so that every test is given in exactly the same way. Notice that even the room is chosen to limit the amount of distraction in the environment.

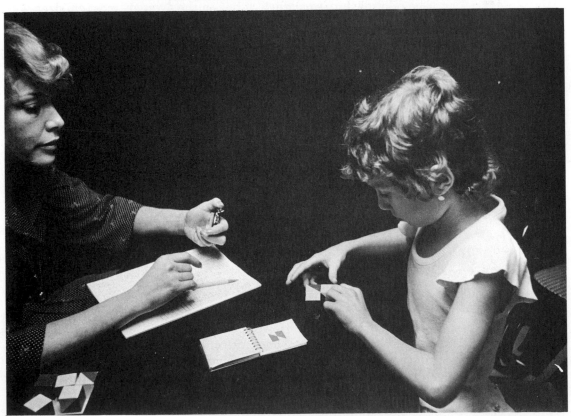

good practice to make the best possible test, no test really measures underlying competence—only *today's* performance.

Stability and Change in IQ.　If a child is given the same test more than once, will he get the same score? If he has an IQ of 115 when he is 10, is he likely to get that same score when he is 12 or 15?

That depends. If the tests are given within a short space of time, say a few weeks, the scores tend to be quite similar. But over longer periods of time, *most* children show wide fluctuations in their scores. Robert McCall and his colleagues (McCall, Appelbaum, & Hogarty, 1973), for example, looked at the test scores of a group of children who had been given IQ tests at regular intervals from the time they were $2\frac{1}{2}$ until they were 17. The majority of these children showed shifts of 20 to 30 points in their scores during childhood, and about 15 percent of them had shifted by 40 points or more. When infant tests are compared with childhood tests, the changes can be even more dramatic.

If there is one thing that *is* fairly stable during childhood, it is the extent to which IQ test scores are good at predicting performance in school. The correlation between a child's test scores and his grades in school or performance on other school tests is about .60 (Sattler, 1974). The relationship is not perfect; but on the average, most children with high scores on IQ tests also do well in school. Since the items on the major tests were chosen with exactly that goal in mind, this finding should not be at all surprising.

Environmental Influences on IQ Scores.　The fact that childhood IQ scores could be so variable led many researchers to study systematically what kinds of environmental events might affect scores on IQ tests. The results of a few of these studies are summarized in Table 4.3, and you can see that there is a wide variety of different kinds of environmental factors that can make some difference in the IQ score that a particular child gets on a particular test on a particular day.

This does *not* mean that IQ tests are useless nor that they fail to measure intellectual performance. It *does* mean that performance can be altered by environmental events. Most of all, it means we must remember that IQ tests are measures of performance, not of competence.

Heredity, Environment, and IQ

When Binet and Simon wrote the first IQ test, they did not assume that IQ was fixed or inborn. However, many of the American psychologists who revised and promoted the use of the tests *did* believe that intelligence was inherited and fixed at birth. The arguments about the **heritability** of IQ have been going on for more than 50 years, and there are still disagreements among researchers about the evidence related

TABLE 4.3
Environmental Influences on IQ Scores

Factors	Effect
Social class	Lower-class children, on the average, have lower IQ scores (Golden, Birns, Bridger, & Moss, 1971).
Home environment	Children with more responsive parents, on the average, have higher IQ scores (Bradley & Caldwell, 1975).
	Children whose parents are less punitive, on the average, have higher IQ scores (Ramey, Farren, & Campbell, 1977).
	Children whose parents are more involved in their development, on the average, have higher IQ scores (Hanson, 1975).
	Children whose parents provide appropriate play materials, on the average, have higher IQ scores (Tulkin & Covitz, 1975).
	Children whose parents use more descriptive language with them, on the average, have higher IQ scores (Clarke-Stewart, Vander Stoep, & Killian, 1979).
Birth order	First-born children, on the average, have higher IQs than do later-born children (Zajonc, 1975).
Preschool experience	Children who attended special preschool, on the average, had higher IQs immediately following (Gray & Klaus, 1965).
	Children who attended special preschool showed higher school achievement in the late elementary grades, on the average (not in earlier grades) (High Scope Foundation, 1977).
Testing situation	Children examined by an adult whom they know and like get higher scores, on the average, than those examined by a stranger (Sachs, 1952).
	Children who get the test in the traditional way (with items increasingly harder) get lower IQ scores, on the average, than do children who have hard and easy items mixed (Zigler & Butterfield, 1968).

to the so-called **nature–nurture** controversy and the correct interpretation of that evidence. How do scientists decide whether some characteristic is inherited or not, and what data are there about the inheritance of intelligence?

Before we can answer that question, we need to separate, as we will many times in this book, the question of *individual* differences in intelligence (in this case, whether children's IQs are largely determined by their parents' IQs) from the question of *group* differences in intelligence (whether racial or ethnic groups differ in average intelligence). Information about individual differences comes from studies compar-

BOX 4.1.

What to Ask about Your Child's Mental Test Scores

A friend of ours was recently called by her son's school and asked to come in for a conference about the results of "some tests." The friend called us to find out what she ought to do to prepare for this conference. Since many of you will be teachers or parents, we would like to share with you the pointers we gave our friend for talking to school personnel about the results of mental tests.

1. *Find out why the test was given in the first place.* Some schools give tests (especially achievement tests) as part of their regular schedule, usually to give some feedback to the teachers and administration about the success of their program. Other schools only test youngsters when there is some concern about their academic performance (either higher or lower than expected for their age and grade). Many schools notify parents when tests are going to be given, but if you weren't notified or if you did not understand the reason for the test, be sure to ask.

2. *Find out what kind of test was given.* One thing to ask is whether the test was administered individually or to a group of children. More important, you need to ask exactly *what* the test is intended to measure. Was it a test of intelligence, or of school achievement, or did it try to measure a personality factor such as motivation? Even good tests are only useful for the purpose they were intended—we wouldn't want to put a child into a class of gifted youngsters on the basis of a personality test alone, for example.

3. *Find out the results of the test.* Some schools may prefer not to give you the child's exact score but will give you a general description of his performance, like "above average" or "in the bottom 10 percent of the children his age." Some results are given in terms of *grade equivalents,* and others may use special scores like *percentiles;* so be sure you understand exactly what the test results mean before you try to make any decisions based on them.

4. *Find out if the test results match other information about the child.* In particular, see if you agree with what the test shows and ask whether the child's teacher agrees. Sometimes very low scores on a test are due to illness or a child's forgetting his glasses, and a parent's or teacher's observations can help explain it. In the state of Washington, where we live, decisions about a child's eligibility for special services *must* be based on at least two pieces of information. If the pieces of information do not match, you'll need to gather further information before you make any decision.

5. *Find out if any other information is needed.* A sudden change in a child's school habits can be related to undetected health problems or to some emotional upset. If you think this might be the case, a physical or psychological examination would be a wise idea. And don't overlook the possibility that hearing or vision problems may be present.

6. *Find out what the options are for your child.* Chances are that the school psychologist or teacher will have some recommendation. It might be for a special class (for gifted children or those with learning disabilities, for example) or for some special extra help, like speech correction or tutoring. If their recommendations do not seem appropriate to you, you'll probably want to explore some other options on your own.

Even after you have asked all of these questions, you may find that the decision rests on your own personal values and preferences. For example, suppose the question is whether your $4\frac{1}{2}$-year-old child should be the youngest child in this year's kindergarten class or the oldest one in next year's class. Although mental tests might provide some information, you will also need to take into account factors like the child's social maturity, your feelings about the kindergarten teacher, or your own work schedule.

The point to be made is that there is nothing *magical* about mental test scores. When they are used appropriately, they are a helpful source of information for decision making. However, the decision itself should be made on the basis of the whole picture, not just a single test score.

ing IQ test scores obtained by family members with their known genetic similarities. Some of the studies use family members whose genetic makeup is known to be similar (usually identical twins), while others use family members whose genetic makeup is known to be dissimilar (adopted children and their families). Information about group differences, though, must come from studies comparing groups known to differ in some particular genetic or environmental manner.

Twin Studies.   The most straightforward way of studying the link between heredity and IQ is to look at pairs of individuals who have exactly the same genetic makeup—identical twins. The technical name for identical twins is **monozygotic** twins, because they both develop from the same zygote (see Figure 4.2). Generally, IQ similarity between identical twins is compared with IQ similarity between fraternal twins

Figure 4.2.   Identical and fraternal twins. The identical twins share exactly the same genetic makeup, so they are often used as a natural experiment for studying the effects of environment. Fraternal twins, although they are born at the same time, are no more genetically alike than any other sibling pair.

(technically known as **dizygotic,** because they develop from two separate zygotes). In fact, several studies have found that IQ scores of identical twins are more alike than scores of fraternal twins (Loehlin & Nichols, 1976; Newman, Freeman, & Holzinger, 1937; Wilson, 1977, 1978). This evidence clearly supports the hereditarian argument.

But wait a minute. Could there be any other kind of difference between identical and fraternal twins that might account for the pattern of results? One possibility is that identical twins may be treated more alike by their parents and by others than are fraternal twins. Hugh Lytton (1977) made observations showing that parents did treat identical twins more alike. Thus part of the similarity in the IQ scores of identical twins may be due to the fact that their rearing is similar, even more similar than it is for fraternal twins.

The logical way to test this possibility is to look at the IQ scores of identical twins who were not reared together, perhaps because they were separated by adoption at an early age. Over the years there have been several attempts to locate such people, and the evidence from these studies has always seemed to support the hereditarian view—that is, the IQs of the twins were still very similar. Recently, though, Susan Farber (1981) undertook a reanalysis of all the known data about identical twins reared apart—physical and personality characteristics as well as IQ. She found (as had earlier authors such as Kamin, 1974) that few of the twin pairs had actually been raised completely apart. Generally, they lived in the same geographic area—sometimes in the same town or village—and many were aware of the fact that they had a twin somewhere. Twins whose backgrounds were the *least* similar had IQ scores that were less similar, too. And when Farber limited her analysis only to healthy twins for whom accurate and reliable IQ data were available, the apparent influence of heredity decreased even further.

Adoption Studies.   If intelligence were inherited, we would expect a stronger relationship between IQ scores of children and their *biological* parents than between the children and their *adoptive* parents. Sandra Scarr and Richard Weinberg (1977) looked at these relationships in a group of black children who had been adopted into white families. Just as the hereditarian position would suggest, the children's IQs seem to be more closely related to the IQ (or education, which is often the only information known) of the biological mother than to the IQ of the adoptive mother (the correlations were .32 and .23, respectively). But other data from this same study also suggest a strong environmental position: The IQs of unrelated children adopted into the same family are nearly as similar as those of natural siblings (brothers and sisters with the same biological parents).

It is not easy to put together research results like these, but our feeling is that both heredity and environment have been shown to be potent influences on the development of intellectual power.

Racial Differences in IQ. Few topics in developmental psychology have caused as much controversy as the question of whether racial differences in IQ are caused by hereditary factors. The basic finding is actually *not* disputed: On the average, black Americans score about 15 points lower on IQ tests than whites do. The way you interpret this fact can have enormous implications for social attitudes, educational practices, and government policy. Let's start with some of the evidence about this difference and then see the various ways in which this evidence might be interpreted.

1. The average IQ difference between blacks and whites is found in numerous studies, those conducted in the North as well as those conducted in the South (Loehlin, Lindzey, & Spuhler, 1975).
2. The difference is *not* found among infants. There are essentially no differences among racial and social-class groups during infancy, except that black children exhibit somewhat faster motor development than do white children (Bayley, 1965). The difference between blacks and whites on IQ tests is first seen when the children are between 2 and 4 years old (Golden, Birns, Bridger, & Moss, 1971).
3. Within both the black and white groups, there are social-class differences: Middle-class blacks, on the average, achieve higher scores than do poor blacks, as is the case among whites (Loehlin, Lindzey, & Spuhler, 1975).
4. School performance is about equally well predicted by the IQ test scores in each group: Black children who have high IQ scores are more likely to do well in school than are black children with low scores, again just as is the case among whites (Kennedy, Van de Reit, & White, 1963).

There are really only two ways of looking at this set of information: One is to assume that we are seeing a genetically determined difference—that blacks are simply less able on the average than whites are; the other is to assume that there are so many cultural and environmental differences between blacks and whites in America that these differences probably account for the results.

The genetic position is, of course, the more controversial. Since evidence shows that there is an important genetic contribution to the measured IQ score, it may seem logical for the racial difference to be explained the same way. It may *seem* logical, but it is *not*. It is entirely possible that individual IQ scores are influenced by heredity but that group differences are entirely or largely the result of environmental differences. (Incidentally, that is one of the reasons we emphasize the difference between questions about individual differences and questions about group differences.) An example on a less controversial issue may help you to see this point more clearly.

Suppose you go to a very poor village in an underdeveloped country and study the relationship between parents' and children's heights. You will undoubtedly find that height is highly heritable: Tall parents tend to have tall children. Now go to a city and do the same thing. Again you will find a strong genetic effect. But now compare the average height of the children in the village with the average height of children in the city, and you will probably find that the village children are considerably shorter (you'll remember from Chapter 3 that this is probably because of differences in diet). There is a major influence of genetics within each group, but there is also a difference between the groups that is a result of an environmental variable.

The same logic can be applied to studies of IQ scores of blacks and whites. If you look at Table 4.3, you will probably have some idea of the kinds of environmental factors that some researchers believe account for racial differences in IQ scores. In particular, many psychologists have focused on aspects of the black child's home environment that may influence his IQ test performance. For instance, black children are more likely to be poor, to grow up in a family headed by a woman, and to experience prejudice and rejection from others.

It is also possible that the tests themselves and the ways they are given contribute to some of the observed racial differences. For example, some of the questions on IQ tests—such as "Why is it better to pay bills by check than with cash?"—make sense only to children with certain backgrounds. Moreover, the tests tend to be highly verbal; and as we shall see in Chapter 5, many black children speak a dialect different from standard English. These arguments all have some truth to them; but when researchers like Gerald Lesser and his co-workers (Lesser, Fifer, & Clark, 1965) made special efforts to design and administer tests in the best and fairest ways that could be devised, there were still some differences between racial groups.

Overall, although we cannot entirely reject the possibility of a genetic difference, it seems to us that there is ample reason to suppose that racial differences in IQ scores are largely the result of environmental differences and that, to a lesser extent, characteristics of the tests themselves may add to these effects.

Is Intelligence Just Cognitive Power?

On an intuitive basis, defining intelligence as cognitive power makes considerable sense. But as we finish looking at some of the evidence gathered using this definition, it seems to us that there is much left to learn about the ways children think. In the first place, we hope you have noticed that one of the main aspects of the layman's notion of intelligence has been almost completely ignored—the *social* part. Although children's IQ tests include items related to social situations (like "What is the thing to do if you lose a ball that belongs to one of your friends?"), the scoring reflects general knowledge rather than real social skill. For example, "Tell him you're sorry" is *not* scored as a correct answer to this question! The kind of cognitive power we have discussed in this chapter has more to do with the power of thinking about abstract ideas than it does with thinking about social relationships or interpersonal interactions.

A slightly different question is how cognitive power relates to actual social behavior. Our colleague Wendy Roedell studied this question as part of a research project on the development of children with very high IQs who attended a special preschool at the University of Washington (Roedell, 1978; cited in Roedell, Jackson, & Robinson, 1980). In this study, the children's social skills were measured in three ways. First, their teachers in the preschool rated their social behaviors with other children. Second, research assistants observed their behavior during free activity periods in the preschool. Finally, the children were given something called the "Preschool Interpersonal Problem-Solving Test," in which they had to think of ways in which social problems might be solved. Their scores on the PIPS test (as it is nicknamed) reflected how many solutions they thought up and told the examiner. Other researchers (Spivack & Shure, 1974) had found that the PIPS test was related to general classroom adjustment among disadvantaged preschool children. In this group of very bright children, however, there was no relationship between PIPS scores and either teacher ratings or observed behaviors. The PIPS scores were, however, related to the children's IQ scores—children with higher IQs could think up more solutions than could children with lower (but in this case, still high) IQs. Even more interesting is the fact that *neither* teacher ratings *nor* observed behaviors were related to IQ. In other words, the most intellectually advanced children were *not* the most socially advanced. Thus cognitive power may help in *understanding* social situations but not in actually *behaving* in those situations.

However, there is a second, more serious problem with definitions of intelligence that center on cognitive power. These definitions, and the research based on them, simply leave us with too much still to learn about the ways in which children think. The power definitions may tell us about *how much* intelligence children have, but they haven't told us very much about *what kind* of intelligence they have. More important, they tell us practically nothing about the ways that thinking changes during childhood.

It was this very dissatisfaction with traditional mental testing that led Jean Piaget to begin work on an entirely different kind of theory of intelligence, a *structural* theory, which we will now examine.

COGNITIVE STRUCTURE IN CHILDREN

When he was a young man, Jean Piaget (Figure 4.3) worked briefly as an examiner administering one of the early IQ tests. His job, like that of all examiners, was to mark down all the children's correct answers so that he could compute IQ scores for them. He soon found, though, that he was much more interested in the children's *wrong* answers than in their correct ones. It seemed to him that there were some important patterns in the kinds of errors children made, with children of similar ages often making similar mistakes.

Because Piaget's work was published in French and because it seemed unscientific to American psychologists (who, as we said earlier, were thinking like physicists while Piaget was thinking like a biologist), his work had very little impact in this country during the 1920s and 1930s when it first appeared. In the early 1960s, though, psychologists studying learning in children were finding that traditional learning theories—which assume that children think like unskillful adults—were not describing the behavior of children well at all. Piaget's theory—which proposes that children at different ages think and learn in different ways—became and has remained a dominant force in the study of children's thinking.

Figure 4.3. Jean Piaget, the Swiss developmental psychologist. Piaget often referred to himself as a "genetic epistemologist"; *genetic* indicating growth and *epistemology* meaning the understanding of knowledge.

Introduction to Piaget's Theory

The Central Assumptions.   We introduced you to this theory in Chapter 1, but let's take a closer look at its basic assumptions and important terms now.

1. For Piaget, cognitive development is the result of *active, voluntary exploration* by the child. For infants this may mean watching, listening, and putting things in their mouths; for preschoolers it may mean making mud pies and playing with blocks; for older children, asking questions and doing science experiments. Piaget believed that it is the child, and not the parent or the environment, that provides the drive for development.
2. Piaget believed that cognitive development begins with certain *inborn strategies* for interacting with and exploring the environment. The earliest of these strategies are primarily perceptual (such as visual scanning, which we discussed in Chapter 3), but other more complex strategies develop later.
3. In Piaget's theory, these strategies for exploring change in *predictable sequences*. Piaget viewed these sequences as being based on mental adaptation to the environment.
4. This is a *stage* theory, stating that a child's behavior at a particular age reflects his general place in the sequence of cognitive development. Piaget believed there were important *qualitative* changes between stages rather than just *quantitative* differences between ages.
5. Finally, Piaget firmly deemphasized the role of the environment in shaping or explaining cognitive development. Although he admitted that very "rich" or very "impoverished" environments might speed up or slow down a child's development, basically he found the question of individual differences to be of no particular interest.

Some Piagetian Terminology.   Because of his background in biology, formal logic, and philosophy, Piaget uses terms in his theory that are unfamiliar to most psychology students. We introduced three of these to you in the opening chapter of this book: assimilation, accommodation, and equilibration. Piaget uses these words to describe the process of **adaptation,** which he believes to be the most general process of life, both biological and psychological. Assimilation and accommodation are the reciprocal processes by which information is taken in and the mental structures are changed in the course of development (Piaget, 1970).

The other term important in understanding Piaget's theory is **scheme.** Schemes are organized patterns of behaviors, approximately what we mean when we talk about mental strategies. Some schemes, especially those used by newborn infants, are visible: looking, grasping, sucking. Other schemes (sometimes called **operations**) are more complex and invisible: comparing, classifying things into categories, adding, or subtracting.

Piaget's Clinical Method.   Perhaps because of his experience in giving IQ tests, Piaget was not at all interested in recording the correctness of children's answers to preset questions. Instead, he developed a technique known as the *méthode clinique* (**clinical method**).To start such an interview, Piaget would set up some physical materials—blocks, clay, beakers of water, or the like—and let the child examine them. Then he would introduce some change in the materials and ask the child a question about the result. This was not, however, a question with a right answer. Rather, it was a question to help the interviewer understand the way the child was thinking. The initial question might be followed by other questions or with other activities using the materials, until the interviewer was sure he understood the child's reasoning about the situation. You can see why American psychologists, used to the carefully standardized conditions of IQ testing, thought that Piaget was unscientific.

You can see from both Piaget's assumptions and his terminology that this theory of cognitive development describes an active, changing organism adapting to an environment. This is a far different picture from the one we got from looking at scores on IQ tests.

Themes in Cognitive Development

In the writings of Piaget and his followers, development is always described in terms of stages. However, you have realized by now that we think it is easier to understand development if we look at topics rather than at ages and stages. So we are going to take the rather unconventional step of breaking down Piaget's theory into a set of six *themes*, which we think describe the changes that occur from birth through middle childhood. We have summarized these themes (and Piaget's stages) in Table 4.4. We're going to discuss the themes first and then look at the stages.

Theme One: Constancies.   One basic cognitive task is recognizing that objects have a continued existence in spite of many kinds of apparent changes they may undergo.

You will recall from the last chapter that during infancy (which Piaget calls the **sensorimotor period**), babies learn two general rules about physical objects. The first is object constancy—the understanding that although something may *look* slightly different (because of lighting or angle of sight), it is still the same object. The second idea is the object concept, which extends these constancies to objects that may be out of sight. An infant who has achieved the object concept, for example, will

TABLE 4.4
Themes in Piaget's Theory of Cognitive Development

THEMES	PIAGETIAN STAGE		
	Sensorimotor	*Preoperational*	*Concrete operational*
Constancies	Object constancy	Constancy of some properties of objects	Constancy of some properties when others are changed —conservation
Perspective taking	Self separate from others	Egocentrism	Decentering
Symbol use	Internal representation	Language	Rules
Logic	Means-ends relationship	Transductive reasoning	Inductive reasoning
Reversibility	No	Forward only	Reversible
Classification	Sensorimotor schemes	Common features	Logical features

look for a toy that has been hidden under a cloth, while a baby who has not yet achieved the concept will not (Gratch, 1975).

During the preschool years (Piaget calls it the **preoperational period**), this understanding is applied to certain properties of objects, as well as to the objects themselves. A child of this age, for example, knows that you stay the same sex for your entire life (Slaby & Frey, 1975). But this understanding is fairly fragile: The same child may say that if her brother wore a dress, he would be a girl.

It is only during middle childhood (Piaget's period of **concrete operations**) that the child begins to understand that changing some characteristics of an object (such as a person's clothes) does not necessarily change other characteristics (like his gender). Some of the most famous studies of Piagetian theory have explored this understanding, which is known as **conservation.**

One classic experiment about conservation (Inhelder & Piaget, 1958) uses two equal-sized lumps of clay. The experimenter takes one lump and squashes it like a pancake. The question for the child is, "Is there the same amount here (pointing to the pancake) as there is here (pointing to the ball)? Or is there more here, or more here?" A preschooler nearly always thinks the amount of clay is different (most think the pancake has more), but older children realize that the pancake and the ball are still the same. In Piagetian terms, the child has conserved the *quantity* of clay because he knew it was the same, even when the shape changed.

Another classic experiment involves the conservation of *number* (Piaget, 1952). In this case, the child is shown two identical rows of objects, usually buttons or coins. The experimenter then moves the objects in one row so that they are farther apart (see Figure 4.4). The question for the child is, "Are the two rows of things the same now, or does this one have more (pointing to the spread-out row), or does this one have more (pointing to the unchanged row)?" The child using preoperational thought thinks the spread-out row has more, while the concrete operational child realizes that moving the objects did not change their number.

As the child grows, then, her understanding of constancy grows from the recognition of a single object from different visual perspectives to the recognition that things can be smashed, moved, or otherwise manipulated without losing their identity. We think of this as a long-term process of learning which aspects of objects are invariant and which can be changed.

Theme Two: Perspective Taking.   Another important cognitive task is the ability to see things from more than one point of view. For the in-

Figure 4.4. Conservation of number. Regardless of the kind of objects that are used in this experiment, younger children usually think that the spread-out row has more than the cluster. Children must reach the stage of concrete operations before they can understand that the arrangement of objects does not affect their number.

fant, this means coming to understand that she is separate from other objects and from other people. This may sound basic, but children younger than 4 months or so do not seem to have this knowledge (Lewis & Brooks-Gunn, 1979).

Preschoolers know they are separate persons all right (ask the mother of any 3-year-old), but they can see things only from one point of view, their own. Piaget refers to this as **egocentrism** (Piaget, 1954), but he doesn't mean that in a selfish way. Rather, the child thinks everyone sees things the way he does.

We have a picture (Figure 4.5) of a classic experiment illustrating this kind of egocentrism. The child is shown a three-dimensional scene with mountains of different sizes and colors. From a set of drawings, he picks out the one that shows the scene the way he sees it. Since the mountains are quite different from one another, most preschoolers can

Figure 4.5. A demonstration of egocentrism. This is a task designed to determine whether or not the child can understand that different people would see different views of this scene. The child is asked to indicate which picture is the one that the doll is seeing. Preoperational children are not able to take the perspective of another person.

make this choice without much difficulty. Then the examiner asks the child to pick out the drawing that shows how the *examiner* sees the scene, and preoperational children cannot do it. Most often they pick the same drawing they did in the first part of the study; but even if they don't do that, they cannot mentally put themselves into someone else's place.

The process of **decentering** takes place during the middle childhood years (Piaget, 1970). One aspect of the process is perceptual—the ability to solve problems, such as the drawings of the mountains. The other aspect is social—the understanding of other peoples' feelings and beliefs. We shall see in Chapter 7 that this social process begins early in childhood, but it is not clearly seen until the concrete operational period.

Theme Three: Use of Symbols. We are so used to using symbols—words, mental pictures, ideas—that it is hard for us to imagine thinking without them. But that is exactly what infants must do: One of the *last* accomplishments of the sensorimotor period is the use of **internal representations.** Not surprisingly, this occurs close to the time that the child learns his first word.

During the preschool years, one of the outstanding developments is the mastery of language, which we will describe fully to you in the next chapter. At the end of the preoperational stage, the language system and the cognitive system seem to become synchronized, and they start to work together more effectively.

This linkage of language and thought continues through the elementary-school years, giving the child enormous power to learn. More important, language begins to be used for rules that describe general conditions and sometimes can be used for the self-regulation of behavior. The rules at this stage are quite concrete (they become more abstract in adolescence, which we will discuss in Chapter 9), but they represent an important step forward.

Theme Four: Logic. One of the major milestones in infancy is the understanding that certain events lead to certain other events. This **means-ends** relationship is, of course, basic for learning of many kinds.

In preschoolers, logic can often appear illogical. For example, a young friend of ours, upon missing her nap one day, insisted that she couldn't have dinner because it was not afternoon yet. She correctly associated naps and afternoons, but she incorrectly assumed the relationship was directly causal. Illogical (to us) logic like this is sometimes called **transductive** logic.

Elementary-school-age children rarely make that kind of error, and (as we saw in the case of conservation) they can sometimes use reasoning about several qualities of objects at the same time (weight and shape, for instance). Children of this age often use **inductive reasoning,** a type of summarizing of information by making a general rule.

Theme Five: Reversibility.   This concept is a bit harder to grasp than the others, and perhaps we should have called it *directionality* rather than reversibility. The issue is whether or not the child can understand that certain processes work both ways. Things that are added can be subtracted; things that are squashed can be made back into lumps. Infants, of course, do not have this ability because they can deal only with their immediate experience (remember that internal representations do not occur until the end of infancy).

Preschoolers seem to operate only in the forward direction. When faced with the conservation problem, they almost never mention that the action taken on the clay could be reversed. As another example, consider the following conversation I had with one of our children:

Me: Do you have a sister?
Child: Yes.
Me: What's her name?
Child: Colleen.
Me: Does Colleen have a sister?
Child: Nope (followed by much giggling). (SM)

As far as she was concerned, the sister relationship went only one way—from herself to Colleen. It wasn't until she reached the stage of concrete operational thought that she could see that the relationship was reciprocal.

In fact, there are several kinds of reversibility that are important for thought in middle childhood. One is reciprocity, like knowing that sisterhood works both ways. Another is realization that things can be undone—knots can be untied, steps can be retraced, wrong homework answers can be erased. In school, children of this age are introduced to the idea that certain **operations** have corresponding reverse operations: adding and subtracting, multiplying and dividing. This ability to see relationships, events, and operations in two directions adds greatly to the flexibility and richness of the child's reasoning.

Theme Six: Classification.   The last of our cognitive tasks is that of putting things into groups. Sometimes classification is straightforward, like sorting socks after doing the laundry. But it can also be complex, like matching a patient's symptoms to a medical diagnosis.

As far as we know, the only way that infants can make classifications is according to which sensorimotor schemes they are using. All of the things that you look at, for instance, would be in one group, and all of the things that you chew on (or gum on, before teeth) would be in another.

Young children's classification strategies have been the subject of considerable research, and a study by Nancy Denney (1972) can give you a good idea of the general findings. She gave a batch of paper cut-outs of various sizes, shapes, and colors to preschoolers and asked them to "put the things together that go together." Denny found great differences among the children in the ways they did this, and you can see some of their responses in Figure 4.6. The most common response from the children seemed to be to focus on some *common features* of the cut-outs—usually the shape—and use that to put them into groups.

Older children can do this same kind of classification in a more complex way by using two or more features at the same time. A 10-year-old might first sort all the pieces by color and then divide each color group into different shapes. They can also group in other ways, such as putting things in order of size or brightness (called **seriation**).

A Word of Caution.   We do not want you to think that everything in Piaget's theory of cognitive development can be reduced to just these six themes. We do think, however, that looking at changes in the themes can help you understand Piaget's notions about *stages* in mental development.

Stages in Cognitive Development

If you were to go back and read the first paragraph of each of our themes, you would have a good description of the sensorimotor period. Second paragraphs would take care of the preoperational period; and third paragraphs, the period of concrete operations. Piagetian theory, however, assumes that stages are more than just collections of individual behaviors or cognitive skills, so let's just say a few words about the stages in general.

Sensorimotor Stage.   Although this period is the shortest chronologically, the number and range of changes that occur in the infant's behavior are very large. In fact, Piaget describes in detail *six* substages in the development of thought: The first one involves innate, reflexive behavior, and the sixth one involves internal representation of objects and events (Table 4.5). This intricate set of observations (originally made on his own three children) and their interpretation as evidence of enormous cognitive growth are major contributions Piaget has made to developmental psychology.

You should notice one important way in which this period differs from those that follow: The child is not really thinking in the sense

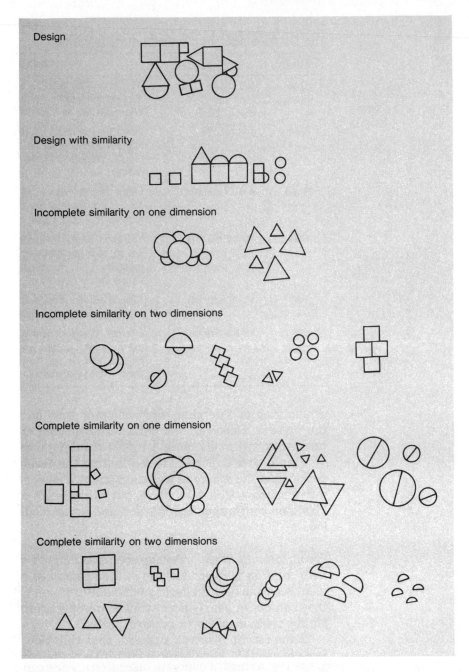

Design

Design with similarity

Incomplete similarity on one dimension

Incomplete similarity on two dimensions

Complete similarity on one dimension

Complete similarity on two dimensions

Figure 4.6. How young children classify objects. In her study, Nancy Denney found that the youngest children tended to use the classifications shown at the top, while the older ones made the groupings at the middle and bottom of the diagram. (*Source:* Denney, 1972, p. 1165.)

TABLE 4.5
The Six Substages of the Sensorimotor Period

Substage	Age	Characteristics
One	0–1 month	Almost entirely practice of built-in reflexes, such as sucking and looking. These reflexes are modified (accommodated) as a result of experience.
Two	1–4 months	Infant tries to make interesting things with her body happen again, such as getting her thumb in her mouth. Visual and tactile explorations are more systematic.
Three	4–10 months	Infant tries to make interesting external things happen again, such as controlling the movement of a mobile. The object concept is also developed.
Four	10–12 months	The infant begins to combine actions to get things he wants, such as knocking a pillow away in order to reach for a toy. He uses familiar strategies in combination and in new situations.
Five	12–18 months	Experimentation begins; the infant tries out new ways of playing with or manipulating objects.
Six	18–24 months	Internal representation readily apparent; the child uses images, perhaps words or actions, to stand for objects, and he can do primitive internal manipulations of those representations.

of planning or intending. Sensorimotor intelligence is very much in the present. However, the child *is* developing the underlying structures that will make more complex thinking possible at later ages.

Finally, it is important to realize that the development through this period (and the others as well) is gradual. Piaget emphasizes the qualitative changes that take place, but many small quantitative changes (based on continuing assimilation and accommodation) are occurring, too.

Preoperational Stage.   Perhaps because Piaget's own first experiences with children involved looking at their mistakes, this stage in development seems to be described by what children *can't* do rather than what they *can* do. In nearly every theme, preoperational children are notable for their inability to perform tasks.

Some recent research suggests that this view is unduly negative. Preschoolers *do* have notable cognitive skills, some of which seem to be the beginnings of concrete operations. For example, we made much of the fact that preschool children are egocentric, but Marilyn Shatz and Rochel Gelman (1973) have shown at least one way that youngsters of this age can take someone else's point of view. They compared the kind of language that 4-year-old children used when they talked to adults and when they talked to a younger child (2 years old). Adults make adjustments in their language according to the person they are talking to. So did the 4-year-olds in this study, who used shorter and simpler sentences with the younger children. One interpretation of this result is that the preschoolers had some notion that different people have different abilities.

There is even some indication that the perceptual abilities of preoperational children may have been underestimated in studies, such as the one using the three mountains. In one study, Helen Broke (1975) found that 3- and 4-year-olds could tell that someone standing on the opposite side of a scene would see a different view.

What these studies, and others like them, tell us is not that Piaget was wrong about preoperational thought, but that the tasks he used may have been too hard to display what children in this stage *can* do. Thus the task that required the child to pick out a drawing of what the mountain scene looked like to the examiner is failed by the preoperational child, but an easier question ("Does he see the same thing you see?") is passed successfully.

In summary, we see the preoperational period, with emphasis on the *pre,* as a time when the earlier kinds of operational logic are growing and where children can show us these abilities if we carefully structure our inquiries to find them.

Concrete Operations.   For Piaget, the onset of concrete operational thought is marked by an entire set of new and powerful cognitive skills. The child has important new operations—such as arithmetic and seriation—available to use as tools in his encounters with the world, and nearly every one of these tools is reversible, making them even more powerful. With these operations, the child is able to undertake inductive reasoning, which we mentioned earlier.

To some extent, though, the concrete operational child is still characterized by things he *cannot* do. He cannot, generally, use **deductive** reasoning, that is, go from some general rule to some anticipated experience. Nor is he successful in imagining things he has never experienced or in classifying things that exist only in his own mind (instead of concretely or in language symbols). Most of these deficits are things that develop fully in the final stage of mental development, that of **formal operational** thought, which we will discuss in Chapter 9.

Continuity of the Stages.   One way of seeing the continuity that runs through all three of these stages is to consider the degree of abstractness that the child can use in thought. The infant basically thinks with *objects* in a physical way, by handling and watching them. At the end of infancy (or at least at the end of the sensorimotor period), he develops the capacity to use *internal representations,* which makes it possible for him to think with *symbols* (many of which are probably words). This is a big step forward in efficiency, especially since it lets him think about things that are not currently in front of him.

That ability to think with symbols continues during the preschool years (during the preoperational stage), until at the end of this time the child develops the ability to think more effectively with *language*. That is, the language system has become tied in with the cognitive system, which makes both of them more useful to the child.

The key event at the end of the concrete operational stage, the one that opens the door to formal operational thought, is the ability to think about *thoughts*. Once a child can do that, there is no end to the complexity and flexibility of his thought.

In summary, Piaget's stages reflect a progression in cognitive ability: thinking with objects, thinking with symbols, thinking with language (and symbol systems like mathematics, too), and thinking about thoughts.

Is Intelligence Just Cognitive Structure?

Theories of cognitive structure do seem to answer many questions that were left unanswered by theories of cognitive power. But although these theories have looked at children's thinking about a variety of topics, the general kind of thinking has always been the same—problem solving. Researchers studying cognitive power looked at children's skill in solving problems, and those studying cognitive structure looked at children's process of solving problems. However, there is much of our everyday thinking that is not at all related to problems. That kind of thinking has been studied by theorists and researchers interested in cognitive *style*.

COGNITIVE STYLES IN CHILDREN

Of the three ways of looking at intelligence in children, the notion of cognitive styles is both the easiest to understand and the hardest to define and study. Maybe an example will help. If the two of us were sitting in a seminar discussing a research article we had read, one of us (SM) would be thinking about the methodological problems in the study, the other (HB) would be thinking about applications of the results, while some of our colleagues might be thinking about the theoretical or public-policy implications. Some people at the seminar will spout off a lot of thoughts of variable quality, and others will have just one or two good ideas. Some will jump into the discussion, and others will wait until later. Some comments will be specifically about the topic, and others will be somewhat off-base. The point is that none of these styles requires any more cognitive *power* than any of the others, and none requires any unusual cognitive *structure* (although I hope we will all be using formal operational thought!). But they certainly represent different *styles* of thinking.

There is no single theory of styles in childhood thinking, but there are several lines of research relating to some of the variables that we think can be interpreted as cognitive styles.

Perceptual Definitions of Cognitive Style

The perceptual styles we described in Chapter 3 (conceptual tempo and field independence versus dependence) might also be considered cognitive styles, since they are measured by tests that require thinking as well as perceiving.

Conceptual tempo, you will recall, is the speed with which a child makes a first response to some problem or task. According to Jerome Kagan and his colleagues (Kagan, Rosman, Day, Albert, & Phillips, 1964), children who respond rapidly (impulsive) often make more errors than those who respond more slowly (reflective). These impulsive children also tend to have lower scores on IQ tests, especially when the tests are based on recognizing pictures. Although there are few sex differences in conceptual tempo among school-aged children, preschool girls seem to develop reflective styles somewhat earlier than boys do (Kogan, 1976).

Girls also seem to develop field independence somewhat earlier than boys do (Kogan, 1976). This cognitive style (Witkin, Dyk, Faterson, Goodenough, & Karp, 1962) is defined by how much a child is influenced by background conditions when making perceptual judgments.

Children who can disregard the background (field independent) usually also get high scores on perceptually related parts of IQ tests, such as the Block Design subtest of the WISC-R. Preschool children whose perceptions are captured by the background (field dependent), on the other hand, are more likely to be rated by their teachers as requiring "structure and direction" or as "giving up in the face of frustration" (Kogan, 1976).

Since older children are more likely to be reflective and field independent than younger ones, these are usually considered the more mature and more desirable styles. However, both Kagan (Kagan & Kogan, 1970) and Witkin (1973) have recently emphasized that each style has its own virtues. Reflective responding is helpful in tasks like reading, which require attention to detail; while impulsive responding works well for tasks not requiring such detail, such as choosing the correct tool from a drawer. Similarly, field dependent perception may make it easier to attend to the social environment around yourself, while field independent perception makes it easier to concentrate on a task. The point is that no single cognitive style is superior on all occasions.

Categorization Definitions of Cognitive Style

Another way psychologists have studied cognitive styles is by looking at the ways in which children put objects into categories. In one typical study (Sigel & Olmsted, 1970), children were shown 12 everyday objects: a pencil, a spoon, a cup, a can opener, and so forth (see Figure 4.7). The experimenter chose one item (say, the spoon) and asked the child which of the other items were similar to or belonged with it. This procedure is repeated for several objects, and the child's score is the number of items she can put into each category. Interestingly, preschool children who put many items into the categories are seen *less* positively by their teachers than those who use fewer items (Kogan, 1976). Among school-aged children, though, youngsters who put more items in each category also tended to be more creative (Wallach & Kogan, 1965).

We know less about categorization styles than we do about other kinds of cognitive styles, but they seem to show some promising relationships with both personality traits and cognitive skills in children.

Temperamental Definitions of Cognitive Style

Some researchers and theorists whose main interest is personality have studied factors that are closely related to cognitive style. We will see in Chapter 6 that theorists who focus on temperament (like Thomas, Chess, & Birch, 1970)—the basic behavioral styles shown by a person in many situations—include traits that seem quite close to what we mean by style, such as *rhythmicity* and *approach-avoidance*. The general idea is that basic themes of behavior may influence cognitive functioning just as much as they do social and emotional development.

Divergent Thinking as a Cognitive Style

In a classic theoretical paper about intelligence, J. P. Guilford (1956) made a distinction between traditional problem solving, which he called **convergent thinking,** and another cognitive process called **divergent thinking.** Guilford chose the name convergent thinking to represent the process of mental abilities coming together (converging) on a single correct answer to a question.

People engage in divergent thinking, on the other hand, when they need to generate more than one new or original idea. In fact, what Guilford means by divergent thinking is quite close to what most of us mean

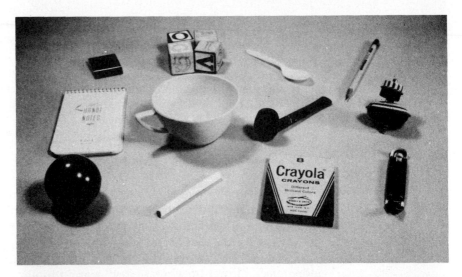

Figure 4.7. The objects used in the Sigel Object Categorization Task. The examiner chooses one item and asks the child to say which other items go with it and why. Researchers are interested in how many objects the child puts into each category and the rules she uses for doing it. (*Source:* Sigel & Olmsted, 1970.)

by **creativity,** namely, the ability to come up with novel ideas, those that diverge from what has been thought of before. Both convergent and divergent thinking are used to solve problems but in different ways. The person who invents the proverbial better mousetrap will probably be using divergent thinking, but the person who uses the mice in a psychological experiment will be using convergent thought.

An older study by Michael Wallach and Nathan Kogan (1965) will illustrate how divergent thinking is often measured. Children were asked to think of as many specific examples of a general class of objects as they could. For example, the experimenter would say the following:

> In this game I am going to tell you something and it will be your job to name as many things as you can that are like what I tell you. For example, I might say "things that hurt." Now you name all the things you can think of that hurt. (The child practices, and then the interviewer continues.) Name all the round things you can think of (Wallach & Kogan, 1965, page 29).

For this particular question, you'll be interested to know that Lifesavers, mouse holes, and drops of water were unique answers (that is, given by only one of the children in the study); while plates, buttons, and doorknobs were given by several youngsters.

Another task required the child to think of possible uses for a common object. "Rip it up when angry" was a unique use for a newspaper, while "make paper hats" was not unique. Similarly, "a hatch on a toy submarine" was a unique use for a button, while "puppet's eyes" was not.

Children can be given creativity scores based on their responses to tasks like these. Although most of the tasks require verbal answers, rather than drawing or producing music, for example, they do seem to generally identify children who can do divergent thinking skillfully.

Overview of Cognitive Styles

Although these four views of cognitive style differ in many ways, we can make some general statements about them (Kogan, 1976).

First, although the perceptual origins of the styles can sometimes be measured in infants and toddlers, most of the styles themselves cannot be seen clearly until the preschool years. Even then, children show many changes in their use of the styles, with girls usually developing somewhat ahead of boys in their efficient use.

Second, the styles seem to be linked with both cognitive variables and with some personality traits and social behaviors. However, the nature of these linkages changes rapidly during the preschool and elementary school years.

Finally, cognitive styles do not seem to be applied to all tasks and to all materials in the same way, especially among younger children. By middle childhood, youngsters are used to problem solving and probably meet new tasks with the style that is most developed (and perhaps also most comfortable) (Figure 4.8). Preschoolers, though, are new to problem solving and seem to be more variable in their use of styles.

Figure 4.8. This child is trying to memorize the objects on the table. Judging by his age, what kinds of mental strategies is he probably using?

LINKING POWER, STRUCTURE, AND STYLE

Until now, we have discussed power, structure, and style as if they were completely separate and independent. It is true that the psychological studies of children's thinking have generally been oriented to only one of these viewpoints at a time. Before we leave the subject, though, we want to mention some lines of research that are starting to cross over from one perspective to another.

Style and Power

We can understand this linkage more easily if we think of cognitive style measures falling into two groups (Kogan, 1973, 1976). The first group includes tests that measure specific *skills* and abilities, such as the Matching Familiar Figures test (for reflection/impulsivity) and the Embedded Figures Test (for field independence/dependence). Scores on these tests tend to be moderately correlated with scores on traditional IQ tests. The reason for this is probably that reflective and field independent thinking are helpful in developing the skills measured by IQ tests. In a real sense, then, these definitions of style bridge the gap between our study of perception and our study of cognitive power.

The second group of cognitive style measures consists of tests that measure *preferences,* such as classification schemes and divergent thinking tasks. Scores on these tests (especially if they are presented as *games* rather than as tests) tend to be much less strongly related to IQ scores. At the same time, the results from these tests have been shown to be related to a variety of personality and social-emotional factors (Wallach & Kogan, 1965). So perhaps it is appropriate to think of these definitions of style as providing the link between personality and cognitive development.

Style and Structure

Although it seems logical to us for these topics to be considered together, we don't know of any research that does this. We do know, however, that a child must develop some divergent thinking skills before he can leave the period of concrete operations and enter the period of formal operations (which we will describe in Chapter 9). This final stage in the Piagetian theory of intelligence requires that a person think of many possible alternatives before deciding upon a solution to a problem. In a sense, then, divergent thinking provides a link between concrete and formal operation thinking, as well as between theories of cognitive style and those of cognitive structure.

Power and Structure

One way to link together notions of cognitive power and cognitive structure is to try and apply measurement techniques (like those used for IQ tests) to the assessment of cognitive structures. In other words, you can try to make a Piagetian intelligence test. Several researchers have done just this; and in general, scores on these new tests closely resemble the scores that the same children get on traditional IQ tests (DeVries, 1974; Jensen, 1980). What this probably means is that both tests are measuring the child's place in a general developmental sequence, with the Piagetian test simply making it easier to interpret that place in light of a specific theory of cognitive development.

Is That All There Is?

Even when the power, structure, and style aspects of intelligence are linked together, they do not tell us very much about the specific mental processes that are involved in cognitive development. We might be able

BOX 4.2

The Influence of School on Cognitive Development

Back in the 1960s, many educators and policy makers were concerned about the high rate of school failure occurring for children from poverty backgrounds. The solution that they suggested, and that was implemented on a national scale, was to place such children in special preschool programs to help stimulate their cognitive development and help them do better in elementary school. Project Head Start was the best known and largest of these programs, but smaller local and experimental programs were started at about the same time for about the same reasons. Our question is whether or not this effort was successful: Does preschool "inoculate" a child against school failure?

The first evidence collected to answer this question consisted of IQ tests given to children before and after they participated in one of these programs. Generally speaking, the IQ test scores increased by about 10 points during the preschool year, but this gain seemed to fade once the children entered regular school (Gray & Klaus, 1965; Klaus & Gray, 1968; Bissell, 1973; Weikart, 1972). Needless to say, these results were very discouraging for those who had hoped special preschools would help to solve the problem of school failures.

Fortunately, researchers have continued to follow the progress of children who participated in the programs, and recent reports have been more encouraging than the early ones were. By the late elementary-school years (sixth through eighth grade) there seems to be a growing difference between those who attended preschool and those who did not. A delayed effect like this is sometimes known as a **sleeper effect.** One example of this is cited in the study by David Weikart, who found that children with preschool showed higher scores on the California Achievement Test starting in sixth grade and that this difference got *bigger* as the children got older (Bulletin of the High/Scope Foundation,

1977). Children who had attended Weikart's preschool were also less likely to require special education classes or other remedial services than children who had not attended.

What about elementary school? When the first Head Start results were reported, many educators assumed that the problem was not the failure of preschool but the failure of elementary school to maintain the gains made by children. Robert Rosenthal's (1968) famous study of teacher expectations suggests that this factor may be very important in children's education. Rosenthal told teachers, supposedly on the basis of special tests, that some children were about to make substantial cognitive gains. In fact, he had chosen these children's names at random. Nonetheless, the children "identified" by Rosenthal showed greater cognitive gains during the year than those not chosen.

Eigel Pederson and his co-workers (Pederson, Faucher, & Eaton, 1978) have also described an educational situation that seemed to have a big effect—an exceptionally good first-grade teacher. Students of Miss A showed better performance in school and in later life than children who had had other first-grade teachers in the same school.

Interestingly, not all educators think school makes all that much difference. Christopher Jencks and his colleagues (Jencks, Smith, Acland, Bane, Cohen, Gintis, Heyns, & Michelson, 1972) have argued that most features of schooling matter relatively little in the long run.

This is obviously a situation where it is very hard to do good research—the outcomes we are interested in happen much later than the school settings we are investigating. Findings like the ones mentioned here, though, suggest that really *good* programs and teachers may have long-term effects on the students.

to say that knowing $8 \times 9 = 72$ will predict later school performance, and that this fact is more likely to be known by a child in the concrete operational period, and even that it is more likely to be known by a reflective than an impulsive child. But that still does not tell us much about how the number 72 is retrieved from memory when the problem 8×9 is presented. Researchers and theorists interested in how thinking actually occurs have developed another way of looking at intelligence, usually referred to as the **information-processing** approach.

A NEW VIEWPOINT: INFORMATION PROCESSING

The information-processing approach sees people as manipulators of symbols (Siegler & Richards, 1982). Thus researchers have focused their work (logically enough) on the symbols and the manipulations. The research on symbols has particularly centered on how things are remembered and how memory strategies change as children get older. The work on manipulation, on the other hand, has centered on how problems are solved and how the solutions change with age.

Memory

If we gave a memory task, like learning the names of all the state capitals, to children of varying ages, we would expect that the older ones would do better than the younger ones would. One possible explanation for this fact is that older children have a greater *capacity* for remembering. In fact, if we recite a list of digits to a child and ask him to repeat them back in reverse order, we find that 5- or 6-year-olds can repeat only two digits, while adolescents can repeat about six digits. This is not a large change, and researchers using other tasks have noted even smaller age differences in pure memory (for example, Hoving, Spencer, Robb, & Schulte, 1978). Since the change in ability for things such as state capitals is fairly large, another kind of explanation must be found.

This other explanation concerns the kinds of *strategies* that youngsters use to help them remember things. These strategies are much like a computer program in that they consist of a set of directions for doing something. A strategy for rehearsing the list of state capitals, for example, might be, "Repeat the name of each capital and state until you can do it without looking at the list, then add one more capital and state; continue the process until you can repeat the whole list." Rehearsal is not the only memory strategy, of course, but it is one that has been extensively studied.

Rehearsal. Preschool children seem not to use rehearsal (or other strategies, for that matter). In one study (Keeney, Canizzo, & Flavell, 1967), children were shown seven pictures to remember, and then delayed for 15 seconds before they were allowed to recite. The 10-year-olds spent the 15 seconds rehearsing the items (either aloud or by just moving their lips), while 5-year-olds did not. Children of all ages who rehearsed did better than those who did not; and when nonrehearsers were taught the strategy, their recall improved, too. Nonetheless, when the children who had been taught rehearsal were later given another memory task, they did not rehearse. This pattern indicates what John Flavell (1970) has called a **production deficiency**—the ability to *use* strategies like rehearsal when suggested by others but the inability to spontaneously *produce* them.

Even when they begin to spontaneously rehearse, though, younger children do not rehearse in the same way that older ones do. When learning a list of words, for instance, 8-year-olds practiced the words one at a time ("cat, cat, cat"), while 13-year-olds practiced them in groups ("desk, lawn, sky, shirt, cat") (Ornstein, Naus, & Liberty, 1975). Efficient and silent rehearsal does not become common until children are 9 or 10 years of age.

Organization and Elaboration. Other strategies that help improve memory involve putting the items to be learned into some meaningful organization. For example, if we give a list of words to be learned that includes four types of furniture, four animals, and four foods (though in scrambled order), children are likely to group the categories together when they recall the words. Even 2-year-olds show evidence of this (Goldberg, Perlmutter, & Myers, 1974); but as we would expect, younger children are generally less efficient than older ones. For instance, they tended to use a greater number of small categories rather than fewer large ones (Worden, 1975).

Another way to put items into context is to imagine some visual link between them. If a child needed to remember to take his math homework and his football jersey to school, he might visualize the paper and the jersey flying from the school flagpole. This strategy, known as **elaboration,** is used more often—and more effectively—by older children than by younger ones. Part of the increased effectiveness results from the fact that older children's elaborations are more active ("the LADY whacked the gopher with the BROOM" rather than "the LADY held the BROOM"), and this added distinctiveness seems to further improve memory (Siegler & Richards, 1982).

Differential Study Time. Another basic strategy for learning is dividing your time to spend on each thing to be remembered. John Flavell and his colleagues (Flavell, Friedrichs, & Hoyt, 1970) studied this process in children by giving them 10 items to learn, with each item hidden behind a window in the experimental apparatus (see Figure 4.9). To study each picture, the child had to push a button that would reveal it. Overall, older children (up to age 10) spent more time looking at the objects and used more strategies (like rehearsal and elaboration) for remembering what they had seen. After a test on the items, older children (and adults) were more likely to spend their time looking at items they had missed than at those they had recalled correctly.

We can say, then, that all of these strategies—rehearsal, organization, elaboration, and differential study time—substantially increase a child's ability to learn. Most of the strategies can be applied by 5- and 6-year-olds, but they are not spontaneously used until later than that, with good mastery demonstrated by age 10 or so. It is striking that this is the very age range that Piaget describes as the period of concrete operations, since these memory strategies bear quite a resemblance to the concrete operations themselves.

Prior Knowledge.   Another kind of memory aid is not a strategy at all but rather the fund of prior knowledge that a child has accumulated.

Figure 4.9. An apparatus for observing how children divide their study time among items to be remembered. The child must push a button to see each item, so the experimenter has an object measurement of attention to each item. Older children use more complex strategies than younger children do for memorizing items like this.

One especially dramatic example was demonstrated in a study by M. T. Chi (1978). Chi compared the memory of 10-year-olds and adults on two problems: recalling digits that were presented orally and recalling the placement of chess pieces on a chessboard. The clever thing about this study is that the 10-year-olds were all expert chess players, while the adults were novices at the game. You can see the outcome in Figure 4.10: Adults were better (as we would expect) at remembering digits, but the youngsters were better at the chess problems. In this case, the influence of previous knowledge is clearly more important than age or any strategy.

Problem Solving

Information-processing research about problem solving has generally centered on the relationship between the capacities of the problem solver and the characteristics of the problem. The capacities of the problem solver are thought of as similar to computer capabilities: input, memory, retrieval, comparison, output, and the like. The re-

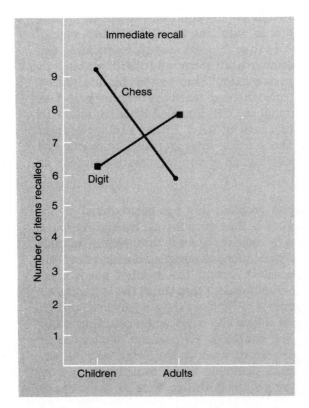

Figure 4.10. Different kinds of memory skills. Adults have better memories for some kinds of material (like recalling digits), but people with special knowledge—even if they are children—can do better on tasks that use that knowledge. (*Source:* Chi, 1978.)

searcher's job is to design a problem that will use only those parts of the system that she is interested in. The task of repeating digits backward, for instance, is thought to use only memory; while repeating digits forward is believed to involve strategies like rehearsal also.

Transitivity Problems.   One task that has been studied in this way is that of recognizing **transitive** relationships. For instance, if Abigail is taller than Bernice and Bernice is taller than Catherine, then logically Abigail is also taller than Catherine. Sometimes this relationship is represented as

$$\text{If } A > B$$
$$\text{and } B > C$$
$$\text{then } A > C$$

Children younger than 7 years can rarely solve these transitivity problems. Piaget (1970) has suggested that the reason for their failure is that they do not yet understand the logical relationship of transitivity.

Thomas Trabasso and his co-workers (Trabasso & Bryant, 1971) have studied these problems from an information-processing framework. They analyze the solution as requiring three steps: first, memorizing the pair-wise relationships (like $A > B$); second, integrating the pair-wise relationships into some overall form; and third, making an inference from the overall representation. They tested this analysis by giving specific training to help preschoolers learn the original pair-wise relationships. With such training, the children had little trouble with the transitivity problem. In this case, at least, Piaget's interpretation seems less compelling than the simpler interpretation that younger children have trouble remembering all of the information needed to solve the problem.

Counting.   A somewhat simpler problem that has been studied by information processing researchers is that of counting. Straightforward as it may seem, counting actually requires at least three skills (Gelman & Gallistel, 1978). First, each object must be assigned one and only one number (one-to-one correspondence); second, the number words must be recited in the correct order (stable order); and third, the last number used in the sequence is the number of items in the set (cardinal principle). Even very young children follow the rules when counting small arrays. Among 3-year-olds, for example, 70 percent demonstrated one-to-one correspondence, 80 percent used stable order, and 50 percent showed use of the cardinal principle when counting things in groups of five or less. For larger groups of things, though, their use of all of these skills dropped dramatically. The 5-year-olds, on the other hand, were nearly as skilled with large arrays as they were with small groups of things.

It appears that even counting is a fairly complex skill when seen from an information-processing point of view. A strong point of this view, it seems to us, is that it specifies quite clearly *what* it is that changes with age. In this example, children gain only slightly from ages 3 to 5 in their ability to count small arrays, but they gain substantially in the ability to count large ones. If, for some reason, we wanted to train children to count large groups of things, we would be better off to try and extend the abilities they already have than to teach them new ones.

Information Processing and Intellectual Power

Not surprisingly, researchers have been interested in how these information-processing variables relate to traditional tests of mental abilities. A study by Daniel Keating and Bruce Bobbitt (1978), although it is fairly complex, will give you the flavor of this line of inquiry. Keating and Bobbitt used a perceptual/cognitive task in which children were given small cards that had two letters printed on them. On some cards the two letters were identical, like *AA* or *bb*; on other cards, the letters were the same but uppercase and lowercase, like *Aa* or *bB*. Still others had letters that did not match at all, like *Ab*. The first part of the children's task was to sort out all the letters that were physically identical (like *AA* or *bb*), and the experimenter noted how long this sorting took. The second part was to sort out all the cards that had letters with the same name (*aA* or *Bb*). This is a little harder, since you have to think of the name of the letter rather than just match its physical appearance.

In Figure 4.11 we have shown you the amount of time it took children of different ages and intellectual-ability levels to do these tasks. Older children are faster than younger ones, and those with high ability (on IQ tests) do better than those with average ability. This is evidence that the basic processing abilities have some relationship with the scores that children get on traditional IQ tests.

There have also been recent reports from longitudinal studies of development linking infant information-processing skill with later intellectual ability. Michael Lewis and Jean Brooks-Grunn (1981) found a significant relationship between scores on a visual-attention task given at 3 months and scores on the Bayley Scales (the infant-development test we mentioned earlier) at 2 years of age. Similarly, Joseph Fagan and Susan McGrath (1981) reported data comparing infant recognition-memory performance and scores on vocabulary tests given at 4

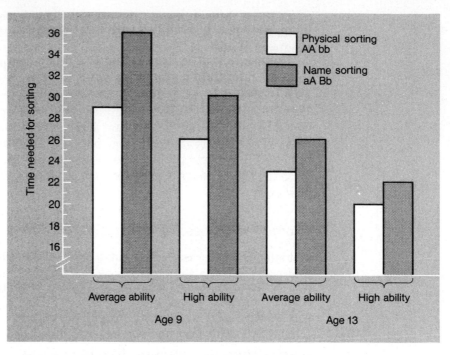

Figure 4.11. Results of the information-processing study by Keating and Bobbitt. This experiment compared how long it took children to sort cards that had letters that matched physically (like AA or bb) with how long it took them to sort cards that had letters that matched in name but not in appearance (like Aa or bB). Both age and mental ability were related to the length of time the sorting took. (*Source:* Adapted from Keating & Bobbitt, 1978.)

and 7 years of age. They, too, found a significant correlation between the two sets of data.

Although the relationships reported in these two studies were not very large, the results do suggest that certain basic information-processing abilities may underlie what we have called cognitive power. That does not mean that IQ is entirely the result of perceptual skill, but it probably does mean that having good perceptual skills in infancy makes it easier to develop good cognitive skills during childhood.

Is Intelligence Just Information Processing?

It is tempting to avoid all of the complexities of traditional IQ testing and Piagetian theory by embracing information processing as the only way to study intelligence. But we need to avoid the temptation. We do not, for example, have any tests of information-processing ability yet that could replace the careful use of IQ tests in schools and clinics. Nor do we have any stage theories of information processing that explain all of the differences we see between infants, preschoolers, and older children in various Piagetian stages. Information processing does not even explain the general kinds of cognitive styles we have discussed. In short, information processing is an important addition to our understanding of cognitive development, but it does not explain away all of the other approaches.

A FINAL WORD

At this point, you may be discouraged by the lack of a single theory for describing cognitive development. Studies of cognitive power tell us a good deal about how children differ from one another; studies of cognitive structure tell us about the basic thought process of children at different ages; studies of cognitive style give us an idea of the variety of ways in which cognitive skills can be deployed; and studies of information processing help us understand the individual mental processes that go into them all. But cheer up. Developmental psychologists (and future developmental psychologists like you) are busy looking for ways to blend these threads into a single fabric.

SUMMARY

1. Psychologists and laymen agree that intelligence is defined by problem-solving ability and verbal fluency. Laymen also emphasize social skills, which are often not included by psychologists.
2. In the United States, intelligence has usually been considered from the viewpoint of *power,* that is, as something that individuals have in some measurable amount. Alternative views of intelligence include *structural* definitions that emphasize function and process, and *style* definitions that emphasize everyday usefulness.
3. IQ tests were originally designed to predict school success. Most of the famous tests are individually administered and have items that cover a variety of topics and formats.
4. Although scores on IQ tests are fairly stable in the short run, over the course of childhood they may vary considerably. Hence, no single test is a dependable measure of a child's ability.
5. Many environmental events can influence IQ scores, including things in the child's home and upbringing, as well as in the testing situation itself.
6. Individual differences in IQ are partly determined by heredity, but group differences (such as racial or social-class groups) cannot be attributed to heredity without more evidence.
7. Piaget's theory of cognitive development is a structural theory based on biological concepts such as adaptation. Piaget believed that development begins with inborn strategies and advances in

predictable sequences by means of the child's voluntary exploration, with little influence from the environment.

8. Although it is intended to be a stage theory of development, Piaget's theory can also be thought of as describing the child's progress in six areas (themes): constancies, perspective taking, symbol using, logic, reversibility, and classification.

9. The sensorimotor period is characterized by thinking in the here and now, while practicing skills to be used in a later period.

10. The preoperational period is a period of transition during which thinking becomes less egocentric, and the ability to classify concepts and objects gradually becomes more complete.

11. The period of concrete operations is characterized by the ability to use operations on sets of objects and experiences.

12. There are a variety of definitions of cognitive style, centering on perceptual skills, categorization preferences, temperament patterns, and divergent thinking.

13. Most cognitive styles seem to develop somewhat earlier in girls than in boys and appear to be linked with both cognitive variables and personality traits.

14. Although cognitive power, structure, and style are usually considered separately, there are some links between them.

15. Information-processing researchers have found that memory strategies, rather than just memory capacity, increase during childhood.

16. Studies of problem solving have shown that even simple problems may involve several mental processes.

17. Scores on traditional IQ tests are related to some information-processing skills, including those demonstrated during infancy.

18. Although information processing is an interesting and useful theory about cognition, it does not replace theories of cognitive power, structure, or style.

KEY TERMS

Adaptation In Piaget's theory, the basic biological and psychological process. Consists of assimilation and accommodation.

Bayley Scales of Infant Development Standardized developmental test for infants that yields two scores, a Mental Developmental Index (MDI) and a Psychomotor Development Index (PDI).

Clinical method A research method in which the interviewer asks unique questions of each subject to make sure the subject's reasoning is understood correctly.

Cognitive power Theories of cognition that see mental abilities as primarily quantitative and focus on individual differences.

Cognitive structure   Theories of cognition that see mental abilities as primarily qualitative and focus on universal processes.

Cognitive style   Theories of cognition that center on the ways that mental abilities are used by individuals.

Competence   The behavior of a person as it would be under ideal circumstances. It is not possible to measure competence directly.

Concrete operational period   The stage of development proposed by Piaget for the ages 6 through 12, in which mental operations such as subtraction, reversibility, and multiple classification are acquired.

Conservation   In Piaget's theory, the understanding that some aspects of objects are unchanged even while their appearance is changed. Researchers have studied conservation of number, mass, volume, and other concepts.

Convergent thinking   Thinking with the goal of solving a problem by bringing together information and reasoning.

Creativity   Similar to divergent thinking; the ability to generate new possibilities or ideas.

Decentering   The process of learning to take another person's perspective; growing out of egocentrism.

Deductive reasoning   Reasoning from a general rule to a specific instance.

Divergent thinking   Thinking with the goal of generating new ideas; similar to creativity.

Dizygotic twins   Also known as fraternal twins, these are children who develop from separate zygotes and therefore share only about as much genetic similarity as other brothers and sisters do.

Egocentrism   In Piaget's theory, the notion that children can see events only from their own points of view; the inability to take the perspective of another person.

Elaboration   Strategy for improving memory by imagining a dramatic and active link between two or more elements to be recalled.

Formal operational thought   In Piaget's theory, thought that is complex, logical, and involves the generation of hypotheses and use of deductive logic.

Heritability   The extent to which a trait is passed on from one generation to the next. Since it cannot be measured directly, heritability is usually estimated on the basis of the similarity between family members.

Inductive reasoning   Reasoning from specific instances to general rules.

Information processing   Way of looking at cognition that emphasizes people as mental manipulators of symbols.

Intelligence Quotient (IQ)   As scored on the original intelligence test, this was the ratio of mental age to chronological age. In today's tests, it is an indication of how well a child does compared to others of the same age. An IQ of 100 is average, with scores below and above that number indicating below and above average mental performance.

Internal representation   In Piaget's theory, the infant's first thoughts, which consist of symbols representing outside events or objects.

Means-ends relationship   Understanding of basic cause and effect for infant's own behavior.

Monozygotic twins   Also known as identical twins, these are children who both develop from a single fertilized egg. Because they have exactly the same genetic makeup, they are often subjects in studies to determine the heritability of various characteristics.

Nature-nurture controversy   The argument as to whether certain traits or characteristics are caused by genetic factors (nature) or by environmental ones (nurture).

Operation   In Piaget's theory, a complex, internalized set of behaviors for interacting with the environment.

Performance   The behavior shown by a person under actual circumstances. Even when we are interested in competence, performance is what we measure.

Preoperational period   Piaget's term for the second major stage of cognitive development from age 2 to 6 years.

Production deficiency   Characteristic of child's memory skills when she can use helpful strategies suggested by other people but cannot produce the strategies spontaneously herself.

Scheme   In Piaget's theory, an organized pattern of behaviors for interacting with the environment.

Sensorimotor period   Piaget's term for the first major stage of cognitive development, covering approximately the first two years of life.

Seriation   The ability to put objects together in order of size, brightness, or other characteristic.

Sleeper effect   The delayed result of a developmental intervention. Sometimes the size of the effect increases as time goes by.

Stanford-Binet Intelligence Scale   Most famous American intelligence test, based on early French test by Binet and Simon.

Transductive logic   In Piaget's theory, immature reasoning in which cause and effect are confused.

Transitive relationship   A logical relationship such that if A > B and B > C, then A > C.

Wechsler Intelligence Scale for Children—Revised (WISC)   American intelligence test with items organized according to topics rather than according to ages.

Wechsler Preschool and Primary Scales of Intelligence (WPPSI)   American intelligence test for young children based on the WISC-R.

SUGGESTED READINGS

Beck, J. *How to raise a brighter child.* New York: Pocket Books, 1975.
This is one in a long line of books about how to raise your child's IQ. It includes some good suggestions for games and activities to do with children, but it also illustrates nicely the American preoccupation with going faster.

Flavell, J. H. *Cognitive development.* Englewood Cliffs, N.J.: Prentice-Hall, 1977.
This is a first-rate basic text in the field, written by one of the major figures in current cognitive developmental theory. The writing style is easy to read, but it does get technical at points. A very good next reference if you are interested in knowing more about this topic.

Siegler, R. S., & Richards, D. D. The development of intelligence. In R. J. Stern-

berg (Ed.), *Handbook of human intelligence.* New York: Cambridge University Press, 1982.
A short encyclopedia of what we know about the development of intelligence. The writing is clear and straightforward but not always easy. If you want more information about a specific aspect of intellectual development, this article will have a description and some good recent references.

PROJECT 4.1

Conservation of Number, Mass, and Weight

Subjects and
Materials

For this project you will need
- A child between 5 and 10 years old
- 2 balls of clay or play dough
- 14 pennies or identical buttons

General Instructions

As we said in the chapter, the concept of conservation involves the understanding that some features of objects remain invariant despite changes in other features. The weight of an object remains the same regardless of how its shape is changed; and the number of objects in a row remains the same regardless of how widely spaced the objects are.

In this project you will be testing your subject for three kinds of conservation: number, mass, and weight. Typically, number and mass conservation occur at about age 5 or 6, and conservation of weight occurs later, at about age 8 or 9. If your subject is between 5 and 8, you may find that he or she can manage the first two conservations but not the last.

The Task

Part One. Begin with the two balls of clay. Handle each of them yourself and then hand them to the child asking, "Is there the same amount of clay in each of these balls? Are they the same?"

If the child agrees that they are the same, proceed. If not, say to the child, "Make them the same." The child may want to squash them a little or may actually shift some clay from one ball to the other. That's quite all right. When he is done, ask him again, "Is there the same amount of clay in each of these balls? Are they the same?"

Once he has agreed that they are the same, proceed with the actual test. Say to the child, "Now I'm going to squash this one into a pancake" and proceed to do so. Then place the two objects—the ball of clay and the pancake in front of the child. Read these questions (and the ones in parts two and three) exactly as written and record exactly what the child says.

1. "Is there the same amount of clay in this one (pointing to the pancake) as there is in this one (pointing to the ball), or is there more here (pointing to the pancake), or is there more here (pointing to the ball)?"
2. "Why is there more here?" or "Why are they the same?"

Part Two. Mold the pancake back into a ball and set the two balls of clay aside for the moment. Bring out your pennies or buttons and place them between yourself and the child, spaced equally in two rows of five, as follows:

X X X X X

X X X X X

Ask the child, "Are there the same number of pennies (buttons) in this row as there are in this row (pointing), or are there more here (pointing to the child's row) or more here (pointing to your own row)?" The child may move the objects around, which is fine, before he agrees.

Procedure

Now spread the objects in your row so that it is now noticeably longer than the child's row but still contains the same number of objects:

X X X X X
X X X X X

Now ask these questions and record the child's exact answers:

3. "Are there the same number of pennies in this row as there are in this row, or are there more here, or more here?"
4. "Why are they the same?" or "Why are there more here?"

Now spread out the child's row and add two objects to each row, so that your row and the child's row are again exactly matched, with seven items equally spaced in each. Ask as before,

5. "Are there the same number of pennies in this row as there are in this row, or are there more here, or more here?"
6. "Why are they the same?" or "Why are there more here?"

Now move the objects in your own row closer together so that the child's row is now longer. Ask again,

7. "Are there the same number of pennies in this row as there are in this row, or are there more here, or more here?"
8. "Why are they the same?" or "Why are there more here?"

Part Three.   Now remove the buttons and bring the balls of clay out again saying, "Now we are going to play with the clay again." Again show the balls to the child asking, "Do these two balls weigh the same? Do they have the same amount of weight?" If the child agrees, proceed. If he does not, say, "Make them the same," and give him the balls to manipulate as he sees fit. Do not proceed until he agrees that they weigh the same.

Then say, "Now I am going to make this one into a hot dog," and roll one of the balls into a hot-dog shape. When you have completed the transformation, put the two pieces of clay in front of the child and ask,

9. "Does this one (pointing to the hot dog) weigh the same as this one (the ball), or does this one weigh more, or does this one weigh more?"
10. "Why do they weigh the same?" or "Why does this one weigh more?"
    When you have finished, thank the child for his help and offer to give him the clay or the pennies.

Scoring

For each of the crucial questions, decide whether or not the child conserved. Not only must he give the right answer, he must also give a correct reason, such as

- "You haven't added any or taken any away"
- "One is longer, but it is still the same"
- "If I made it back into a ball it would be the same"

Analysis

1. Did the child show conservation on any of the tasks? Which one or ones? Is this consistent with the pattern of acquisition we have described?
2. If several students do this project, put your data together, looking at which con-

servations are done correctly by children of different ages. Do these data fit the pattern we have described?

3. As a result of your interview with the child, how would you change the procedure if you wanted to repeat this study?

Chapter 5
The Development of Language in Children

(5)

Several years ago I listened with fascination as my 3-year-old and my 6-year-old daughters argued about the relative dangers of forgetting to feed the goldfish versus overfeeding them:

6-year-old: It's worse to forget to feed them.
3-year-old: No, it's badder to feed them too much.
6-year-old: You don't say badder, you say worser.
3-year-old: But it's baddest to give them too much food.
6-year-old: No, it's not. It's worsest to forget to feed them. [SM]

If you listen to children, especially when they are between about 2 and 6 years old, you will be enchanted by the wonderfully inventive constructions: "Bees eat bruises because people don't want them," or "The moon has melted! Did the wind blow it away?" What is perhaps most astonishing is the speed with which the changes occur. An 8-month-old is making sounds like *kikiki* or *dadada*. By 18 months the child will probably be using 30 or 40 separate words; and by 3 years children construct long and complex sentences, such as those created by the 3-year-old in the example above.

From the beginning, children's language is *complex, abstract, creative, and rule governed.* It is abstract in the sense that most of the individual words describe classes of things or categories rather than individual instances; it is creative in the sense that the child combines words into patterns he has never heard; it is rule governed in the sense that even the first two-word sentences follow certain rules. The daughters in the example were trying to apply the rules for creating superlatives and just happened to hit on an irregular version of that rule. But the fact that they were creating words that followed a logical pattern (even though the words were grammatically incorrect by adult standards) shows that they were operating with a rule.

For psychologists, the puzzle is to explain how this complex, abstract process can occur in a 2- or 3-year-old whose thinking is otherwise characterized by very limited abstractness, as we saw in the last chapter. We also need to understand how the process comes to happen so similarly in widely varying environments.

In attempting to solve these mysteries, we want to divide the question in the same way we did in Chapter 4, by looking at structure, power, and style. The vast majority of research on language development in the past two decades has focused on structural changes in both grammar (which the linguists call **syntax**) and word meaning (called **semantics**). Lately there have also been some attempts to explain differences in the *rate* of language development from one child to another, which takes us into the realm of power differences. There are also some intriguing hints of style differences among children as well.

WHAT IS LANGUAGE ANYWAY?

Let us begin by being more specific about what we mean by *language*. Roger Brown defined it as an arbitrary system of symbols

> which taken together make it possible for a creature with limited powers of discrimination and a limited memory to transmit and understand an infinite variety of messages and to do this in spite of noise and distraction (Brown, 1965, p. 246).

The critical element in this definition is the phrase "infinite variety of messages." Language is not just a collection of sounds. Even very young babies make several different sounds, but we do not say they are using language. Chimpanzees and other primates have vocabularies of sounds, each used in a particular situation. Apparently, though, they do not *combine* the individual sounds into different orders to create new and different meanings.

There is presently a fairly hot debate among linguists about whether primates can be *taught* to use words or symbols in this creative way (Gardner & Gardner, 1980; Savage-Rumbaugh & Rumbaugh, 1980; Stahlke, 1980; Terrace, Petitto, Sanders, & Bever, 1980). Most observers think they can and that there may be other mammals (such as perhaps dolphins or whales) who use language in this sense. Whatever the outcome of this argument, we do know that *humans* use language creatively. Virtually all children, without special training other than exposure to language, develop complex and skillful language use within the first three years of life. Even deaf children can learn a *language* in Brown's sense of the word, since gestural languages, such as American Sign Language, involve arbitrary symbols combined in creative, rule-governed ways.

THE DEVELOPMENT OF GRAMMAR IN CHILDREN

Before the First Word

The sounds a child makes before 10 months or 1 year of age, when he speaks his first words, are really not language at all. Linguists (for example, Dale, 1976) usually call this the **prelinguistic phase.** Within this period, however, there are several recognizable stages or steps that appear to occur in the same order in all children (Kaplan & Kaplan, 1971). The rate of progression through these steps varies from one baby to another, but the sequence seems to be consistent.

Crying.   From birth to about 1 month of age, just about the only sound an infant makes is a cry. Crying may be irritating to the parents, but it is helpful to the child in several ways. It helps to improve lung capacity and cardiovascular development (like aerobic exercise in an adult), and it signals to the caregivers that the infant is in need. Infants seem to have several different cries to signal different kinds of discomfort or problems. Many parents become quite skilled in "reading" these cries to diagnose the baby's particular need at that moment. Physicians can also use the sound of a cry as a hint of possible disorder in the infant.

For example, Philip Zeskind and Barry Lester (1978) found that babies born after high-risk pregnancies or deliveries had higher pitched and more piercing and grating cries than did babies from low-risk pregnancies, even though both groups appeared healthy on a normal physical examination (see Figure 5.1). Adult listeners can also tell the difference between the cries of babies with different temperaments. Babies rated by their mothers as having "difficult" temperaments (a concept

Figure 5.1.   College students and young parents listened to tape recordings of the cries of some babies whose mothers had had high-risk pregnancies and deliveries and of some babies with no history of risk. When they rated the cries of these babies (without knowing ahead of time which was which), the differences shown in the figure emerged. High-risk babies' cries were much more unpleasant to listen to. (*Source:* Zeskind & Lester, 1978, Table 3, p. 584.)

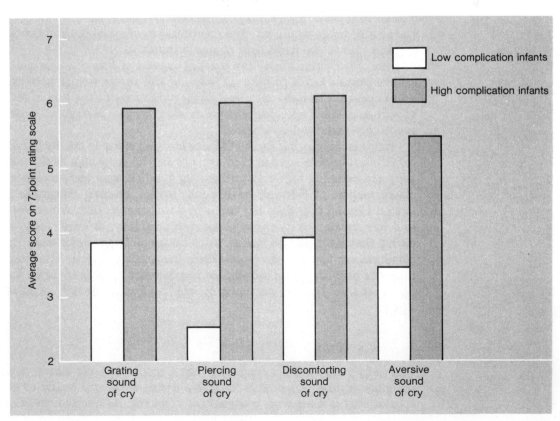

we'll describe more fully in Chapter 6) sounded to other listeners as if their cries showed more anger or irritation or "spoiledness" than did babies rated by their mothers as having "easy" temperaments (Lounsbury & Bates, 1982). Research like this suggests that an unpleasant crying sound in an infant may turn out to be a fairly accurate signal of potential problems for the baby.

Cooing.   Starting at about 1 month of age, the baby begins to add some noncrying sounds to his repertoire, of which vowel sounds like *uuuu-uuu* are typical. For obvious reasons, this is called **cooing.** Such sounds seem to be associated with pleasurable times for the baby.

Babbling.   By about 6 months of age the infant begins to use a much wider range of sounds, including a lot of what we would call consonants, such as *k* and *g.* Frequently, the baby combines a consonant sound with a vowel sound to produce a kind of syllable, such as *ba* or *gi* or *da* (a sound much loved by fathers). Toward the end of the babbling period—late in the first year of life—the baby frequently can be heard repeating such syllables over and over, such as *dadadadada* or *gigigigi.* This apparently endless repetitive game is called **echolalia:** The child repeats (apparently for his own pleasure) his own sounds and the sounds made by others. The combination of syllables and echolalia is what makes the **babbling** period distinctive.

One of the particularly fascinating aspects of this phase is that the child's sounds begin to take on some of the *intonational* patterns of adult speech. The baby may use rising inflections at the end of strings of sounds or use a speechlike rhythm, even though she is still babbling seemingly meaningless sounds.

Another intriguing facet of the babbling period is the fact that infants often babble sounds that are not in the language of the adults they are listening to. Children hearing English may use vowel sounds characteristic of German or French; babies hearing Japanese may use an *l* sound that does not occur in Japanese. In fact, Janet Werker and her colleagues (Werker, Gilbert, Humphrey, & Tees, 1981) have found that 7-month-old babies were better able to make discriminations among two sounds from Hindi than adults were. The point is that the infant's sound repertoire has not yet narrowed down to the set of sounds he will be using in the language he will eventually speak.

The First Words

The baby's first word is an event that parents eagerly await, though it's easy to miss. A *word,* as linguists define it, is any sound or set of sounds that is used with a consistent referent. As Scollon (1976) puts it, it requires "a systematic matching of meaning and form" (p. 42). But it can be *any* sound. It does not have to be a sound that matches words the adults are using. The little girl Scollon listened to, whose name was Brenda, used the sound *nene* as one of her first words. It seemed to mean primarily liquid food, since she used it for milk, juice, and bottle; but she also used it to refer to mother and sleep. Another of Brenda's words was *aw u,* which seemed to mean "I don't want" or perhaps "away"; while still another early word was *da,* which meant only "doll."

Brenda's first words illustrate the two ways in which young children seem to use their first words. Some of the time they use words merely to label objects, such as cookie or doll. But a lot of the time they use a single word to convey an entire sentence of meaning, something linguists call **holophrases.** The combination of the word, gestures, intonation, and context tells the listener what the child means. Parents usually become skillful at decoding these meanings.

Adding New Words.   Once the milestone of the first word is reached, toddlers go through a period of slow vocabulary growth. Katherine Nelson (1973) found that it typically took three to four months for a child to add the next 10 words. But past the 10-word point, there was a rapid increase in vocabulary, with a new word added every few days. Eighteen-month-old children typically have vocabularies of 40 to 50 words, and by 24 months the average is nearly 300 words. The change in Brenda's vocabulary from 14 to 19 months, which we have listed in Table 5.1, illustrates the first stages of this vocabulary spurt.

TABLE 5.1
Brenda's Vocabulary at 14 and 19 Months

14 months	*19 months*[a]		
aw u (I want, I don't want)	baby	nice	boat
nau (no)	bear	orange	bone
d di (daddy, baby)	bed	pencil	checkers
d yu (down, doll)	big	write	corder
nene, (liquid food)	blu (pu)	paper	cut
e (yes)	Brenda	pen	I do
maem (solid food)	cookie (kuki)	see	met
ada (another, other)	daddy	shoe	Pogo
	eat	sick	Ralph
	at	swim	you too
	(hor)sie	tape	climb
	mama	walk	jump
	mommy	wowow	

SOURCE: R. Scollon, *Conversations with a one year old.* Honolulu: The University Press of Hawaii, 1976, pp. 47, 57–58.
[a]Brenda did not actually pronounce all these words the way an adult would; we have given the adult version since that is easier to read.

Kinds of New Words.   The early words in children's vocabularies are most likely to be what Katherine Nelson (1973) calls *general nominals*—names for classes of objects or people, such as *ball, car, milk, doggie, he,* or *that.* Over half of the first 50 words of the children she studied were of this type—what we normally call nouns—while only 13 percent were action words, as you can see in Table 5.2.

Nelson was also struck by the fact that many of the early words labeled things the child could do something with or play with or objects that made interesting noises or moved in interesting ways. Names of static objects, or objects the child couldn't play with, were much less likely to appear in the list of early words. This observation is consistent with what Piaget has said about this *sensorimotor* stage: The child is still focused on action and perception.

The First Sentences

Much more interesting than the mere addition of words to the child's vocabulary is his growing ability to string those words into sentences. The first two-word sentences usually appear at about 18 months. (In fact, you can see two examples in the list of Brenda's 19-month vocabulary.) For some months after this, the child continues to use single words as well as two-word sentences. Eventually, the one-word utter-

TABLE 5.2
Six Main Categories of Words Used by Young Children among Their First 50 Words

Type of word	Percentage of all words in that category
General nominals: words for classes of objects or people, such as *ball, car, milk, he, that.*	51
Specific nominals: words used to name unique objects (for example, people and animals), such as *Spot* or *daddy.*	14
Action words: used to describe or accompany actions or to express or demand attention, such as *go, byebye, up, look, hi.*	13
Modifiers: words that refer to properties or qualities of things, such as *big, red, pretty, all gone, there.*	9
Personal-social words: words that say something about the child's feelings or social relationships, such as *ouch, please, no, yes,* or *want.*	8
Function words: words that have only a grammatical function, such as *what, where, is, to,* or *for.*	4

SOURCE: Nelson, 1973, p. 18.

ances drop out almost completely, and the child begins to use three- and four-word sentences and to create more complex combinations of words. Linguists now commonly divide the developmental progression into two stages.

Stage-1 Grammar.　There are several distinguishing features of the Stage-1 sentences. First, they are *short*—usually only two or three words. Second, they are *simple*. Nouns, verbs, and adjectives are usually included, but virtually all the purely grammatical markers (which linguists call **inflections**) are absent. Children in Stage 1 of grammatical development do not use the *s* for plurals or put the *ed* ending on verbs to make the past tense. They don't use possessive markers or auxiliary verbs.

Because only the really critical words are present, Roger Brown (Brown & Bellugi, 1964; Brown, 1973) describes the sentences of the child at this stage as **telegraphic speech.** The child's language is rather like what we use when we send a telegram. We keep in all the essential words—usually nouns, verbs, and modifiers—and leave out all the prepositions, auxiliary verbs, and the like.

We see the same pattern not only in children's spontaneous speech but also in their imitations of other people's sentences. If you ask a child of 20 to 24 months to say "I am playing with the dogs," the child is likely to say "Play dog," or "I play dog," thus omitting the auxiliary verb *(am),* the verb ending *(ing),* the preposition *(with),* the article *(the),* and the plural ending *(s).*

Despite these limitations, it is important to understand that this earliest language is nonetheless *creative.* Just as you can create totally new sentences following the rules of adult grammar, the very young child seems to construct totally new sentences following another set of rules.

Martin Braine (1963) was one of the first linguists to try to write down the rules that seemed to govern children's early sentences. Table 5.3 lists the first 50 sentences Braine heard from Gregory, one of the three boys he studied. Gregory didn't speak these sentences in the order listed in the table. The sentences were spread over several days or weeks. When Braine looked at the 50 sentences, though, there seemed to be considerable order. There were some words Gregory used in many different sentences, usually as the first word. Braine called these *pivot words.* Then there were words that went with pivot words. There were more of these, and they each occurred in fewer combinations. Braine called these *X words.* The basic grammatical rule seemed to be to "pick a pivot word and then select any *X* word to go with it." For obvious reasons, this way of describing children's language came to be called **pivot grammar.**

One of the intriguing things about this way of looking at children's

TABLE 5.3
Gregory's First Sentences

14 combinations with *see,* such as:	nightnight boat
see boy	hi plane
see hot	hi mommy
see sock	big boss
31 combinations with *byebye,* such as:	big boat
byebye plane	big bus
byebye man	more taxi
byebye hot	more melon
pretty boat	allgone shoe
pretty fan	allgone vitamins
my mommy	allgone egg
my daddy	allgone lettuce
my milk	allgone watch
do it	
push it	Plus 20 unclassified
close it	sentences, such as:
buzz it	mommy sleep
move it	milk cup
nightnight office	ohmy see

SOURCE: Braine, 1963, p. 5.

sentences is that it helps us make sense out of some of the peculiar combinations that children come up with. "Byebye hot" is a combination an adult would not make, but it is perfectly legal in Gregory's pivot grammar.

As it turns out, pivot grammar doesn't adequately describe the complexities that exist in even these very simple first sentences. Most important, the pivot grammar concept seems to gloss over some interesting **semantic** (meaning) distinctions that occur in the child's first sentences. For example, young children frequently use a sentence made up of two nouns, such as "Mommy sock" or "Sweater chair" (to use some examples from Lois Bloom's 1973 analysis). In a simple pivot grammar, the word *mommy* would probably be considered a pivot word. But such a classification misses what the child was saying in some instances. The child in Bloom's study who said "Mommy sock" said it on two different occasions. The first time was when she picked up her mother's sock, and the second time was when the mother put the child's own sock on the child's foot. In the first case, "Mommy sock" seems to mean mommy's sock—a possessive relationship. In the second instance, though, the child seems to convey "Mommy putting on my sock," which is an *agent* (mommy)–*object* (sock) relationship.

So hidden within the apparent simplicity of Stage 1 grammar are important complexities. From the earliest two-word sentences, the child appears to be able to express a series of different relationships.

She can express location (as in "Sweater chair"), possession (as in "Mommy coat"), recurrence (as in "More milk"), and so on. In adult language each of these different relationships is expressed with different grammatical forms. Since the young child often uses the same kinds of word combinations to express these different relationships, it is easy to miss the complexity. But if you listen to the child's language in context, you can see that the child is indeed expressing a rich array of meanings from the very earliest sentences.

Stage 1 continues for about a year or less, depending on the overall rate of the child's linguistic development. During this time, the child's sentences get longer, but they do not get significantly more complex. In the terminology of linguistics, the **mean length of utterance** (MLU) increases, but the child has not yet added the grammatical inflections, such as plurals, past tenses, or auxiliary verbs.

Stage-2 Grammar.   The beginning of Stage 2 is defined by the first use of any of those grammatical inflections and continues for several years. Children differ markedly in the age at which they arrive at this stage and in the rate at which they move through it, as you can see in Figure 5.2. The three children represented in the figure were studied by Roger Brown over a period of years; and as you can see, they differed widely in rate of language development. The horizontal line at 2.5 meaningful units per sentence represents the approximate point at which most children shift from Stage-1 to Stage-2 grammar. Eve made this transition at about 21 months, while Adam and Sarah passed over this point at about 34 to 35 months.

Within Stage 2 there are further regularities or sequences. The various grammatical inflections seem to appear in children's sentences in a fairly predictable order. Among English-speaking children, Brown (1973) finds that prepositions are added fairly early, as are plurals. Irregular verb endings also appear early (as in *went* or *saw*), while possessive forms, such as *its,* come later in the sequence. Kuczaj (1979) has also recently found that suffixes are learned before prefixes.

Another intriguing phenomenon of Stage-2 grammar is **overregularization** or overgeneralization. This is what the two daughters in our early example were doing when they created new regularized forms of superlatives (badder, baddest, worser, and worsest). We see the same thing in the use of past tenses as well. Children say *wented* or *goed* or *ated.* Stan Kuczaj (1977, 1978) has found that young children initially learn a small number of irregular past tenses and use them correctly for a short time. Then, rather suddenly, the child seems to discover the rule of adding *ed* and overgeneralizes this rule to all verbs. This type of "error" is particularly common among children between ages 3 and 5. Note, though, that this only occurs be-

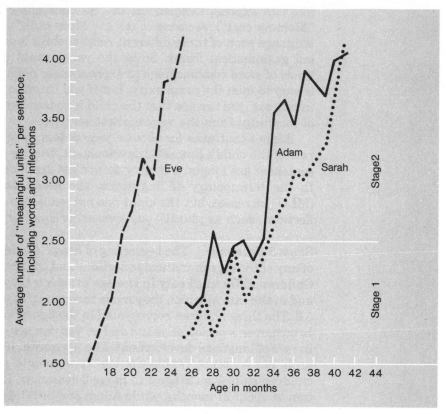

Figure 5.2. This figure shows the rapidly increasing sentence length for three children studied intensively by Roger Brown and his colleagues. The break between Stage 1 and Stage 2 grammars occurs at about 2½ words per sentence. As you can see, the pattern of change is very similar from one child to the next, but the ages at which the steps occurred differed markedly among the three children. (*Source:* Adapted from Brown, 1973, p. 55.)

cause the child is operating with a set of rules. If English were perfectly regular, we would not be able to see this principle in operation.

During Stage 2, the child learns to ask questions and to create negative sentences and even passive ones (such as "The wagon is pulled by the boy"). In each case, the child seems to move through a predictable sequence. Along the way, the child goes through periods when he creates types of sentences that he has not heard adults use but that are consistent with the particular set of rules he seems to be using. For example, in the development of questions, there is a point at which the child gets a *wh* word *(who, what, when, where, why)* at the front end of a sentence but does not yet have the auxiliary verb put in the right place, such as, "Why it is resting now?" Similarly, in the development of negatives, there is a stage in which the *not* or *n't* or *no* is put in, but the auxiliary verb is omitted, as in "I not crying" or "There no squirrels."

This series of changes is delightful to listen to. The changes are important for theorists as well, who are impressed with the fact that the child creates sentences he could not have heard but which make excellent sense within the rules of his own grammar.

Later Language Development

By age 5 or 6, a child's language is remarkably like that of an adult. He can construct most kinds of complex sentences, and he can understand most of them. Despite this excellent skill, however, there are some specific kinds of errors that still occur and some systematic changes that take place over the elementary-school period. For example, children 5 and 6 years of age have difficulty with passive sentences ("The food is eaten by the cat"). They don't spontaneously produce many passive sentences at this age and have more difficulty understanding this construction than they do the active version of the same meaning ("The cat is eating the food"). They also make more mistakes with pronouns (as in "Him and me went to the movies") than do teenagers, although this error is still fairly common among adults.

Obviously language development does not end in first grade. Vocabulary continues to increase, and more complex sentence forms are learned later. However, the really giant strides occur between 1 and 5 years of age, as the child goes from single words to complex questions, negatives, and commands.

Overview of Grammatical Development

Let us pause for a brief summary of the key points before we look at the various attempts to explain grammatical development.

1. Even children's earliest sentences show regularities and rules. The rule system is not the same as it is for adult language but is unique to children.
2. The same rules seem to develop, in roughly the same order, in children learning all types of different languages. We find something similar to a Stage-1 grammar in children learning Russian, French, and so forth.
3. The child's grammar changes gradually in a sequence that seems roughly the same for all children who have been studied. The *rate* of development varies, but the sequence seems to stay about the same, especially the early steps in the sequence.
4. Children's language is creative from the very beginning. The child is not simply copying sentences she has heard; she is creating new ones according to the rules of her own grammar.

EXPLAINING GRAMMATICAL DEVELOPMENT

The problem for the theorist is obviously to develop a theory that takes these basic facts into account. Theories of language development are immensely complex—no doubt because the process itself is complex—so we cannot delve into them fully. But we can sketch the alternatives and tell you about some of the current thinking of researchers in this field.

Imitation

Probably your first idea about how a child learns language is that it is a process of imitation. Imitation obviously has to play *some* part, since the child does learn the language he is hearing and doesn't invent his own. Furthermore, children acquire the accent of the people they grow up with. However, if you look at the summary points about grammatical development that we just listed, you'll see that imitation won't help us account for much of what actually happens. Most important, children create types of sentences and forms of words that they have never heard. When a child regularizes the past tense and invents words such as *goed* or *beated,* she is following her own grammatical rules, not imitating what she hears. Furthermore, when children do imitate adult sentences directly, they reduce them to a form that is like their own sentences.

The conclusion of linguists like Roger Brown (1973) or David McNeil (1970), among many others, is that imitation plays some role in language development, but that it is not the central process, no matter how much common sense says otherwise.

Reinforcement

A second apparently logical possibility is that children are *taught* language directly by their parents or by others around them. B. F. Skinner, one of the major exponents of reinforcement theory, has attempted to apply a learning model to language (1957). He argues that adults around the child *shape* the child's first sounds into words, and then the words into sentences, by selectively reinforcing those that are understandable or correct.

It is difficult to see how such a reinforcement view can account for the facts we have already listed—particularly for the creative and rule-governed aspects of children's early language. Furthermore, when Roger Brown and his colleagues Courtney Cazden and Ursula Bellugi (1969) recorded actual exchanges between parents and children, they found that parents responded to their children's language based on the "truth value" of the sentence and not the grammatical correctness

(Brown, Cazden, & Bellugi, 1969). As a general rule, parents seem to be remarkably accepting of children's language efforts. They try to interpret incomplete or primitive sentences and very rarely correct the child's grammar or withhold treats or other reinforcements until the child says it better. The entire process just does not sound like shaping. In fact, the evidence for a reinforcement theory of language is so weak that this view has been widely discarded.

Before we cast the reinforcement explanations of language completely into outer darkness, however, we should note that shaping *is* used in programs designed to teach language to children whose language has been delayed for some reason, such as retarded children or those with a disorder known as *autism.* Such children may be taught both specific words and basic sentences through complex shaping programs (Lovaas, 1976) or may be positively reinforced for speaking as part of a program to encourage greater language use (Reynolds & Risley, 1968). Such applications of reinforcement principles show that language, like other behaviors, can be affected by basic processes of learning. However, the vast majority of children do not require this kind of careful programming to learn language. Shaping or other kinds of reinforcement programs may thus be useful backup systems when the normal acquisition process fails, but they appear to play relatively small roles in the normal process.

Innateness Theories

At the other end of the theoretical spectrum is a collection of proposals by Noam Chomsky (1965), David McNeill (1970), and others to the effect that both the capacity to develop language and the general form of language are built into the brain. According to this view, language is not learned; it unfolds or emerges as part of the maturational process we talked about in Chapter 1 and Chapter 3. Just as the maturation of physical skills like walking requires a basic, supportive environment, so the maturation of language skill requires that the child hears language being spoken around him. The built-in mechanism, which McNeill calls the **language acquisition device,** is not programmed especially for English or Urdu or Swahili. It is programmed for language in some more general sense. The particular language the child is hearing is then passed through this system, and the child emerges with the appropriate set of rules for the language he hears and speaks.

Transformational Grammar.   Now what exactly could it be about language that is built into the language acquisition device? Chomsky argues that what is built in is **deep structure.** He proposes, in essence, that every sentence exists at two levels. The *meaning* of the sentence is contained in the deep structure. That meaning is then transformed into **surface structure,** which is the sentence that we actually see or hear. The rules for turning basic meaning into sentences Chomsky calls transformational rules, and the entire system has come to be called **transformational grammar.**

For example, if the basic deep structure meaning were something like "I like cookies," this could be transformed into a variety of surface structures (actual sentences), such as "Do I like cookies?" or "What do I like?" or "I do not like cookies." In each case, we have applied a transformational rule to the basic meaning to create a question or a negative form. If we applied rules for creating passive sentences, we could say "Cookies are liked by me."

If you think about the basic sequences of grammatical development we have already described, it begins to look like the child's earliest sentences are straight out of deep structure. The child uses a few words to convey whole meanings, and the adult listener fills in around the edges. As the child's language improves, what she seems to do is learn the transformational rules—the rules for turning those basic meanings into various kinds of complex sentences in the language she is hearing.

This approach helps to explain why children's language is rule governed from the beginning and why we hear children create forms of sentences they have never heard—they are simply applying an incomplete set of transformational rules. When we hear a child say "Why it can't turn off?" she is getting the *wh* word in the right place and has the negation rule in place but has not applied the rule that determines the location of the auxiliary verb. If we assume that children initially apply rules one at a time and then learn how to apply two or more at once, then much of what we hear children doing begins to make better sense.

Despite the attractiveness of innateness models, however, many linguists (for example, Derwing, 1977) are dissatisfied with this view. It seems too mechanistic and does not seem to take the child's creativity into account. There is also a great deal of vagueness in the "strong innateness theories" about just what the language acquisition device consists of.

A Combined View

Most current theorists have arrived at a compromise view that assumes some innate "bias" to the system but also assumes that the child plays a large part in the process as well. As Stan Kuczaj (1982) puts it, "The child *creates* language within the limits set by his or her processing and organizing predispositions and the input" (p. 53).

From this perspective, language development is influenced by three things. First, there are innate "organizing predispositions." We talked about innate scanning strategies when we described perceptual development in Chapter 3. Newborn infants seem to be programmed to look at the edges of things and at movement. The sensorimotor schemes Piaget described can also be thought of as organizing predispositions. It seems equally logical to assume that there are built-in *listening* strategies or "rules to listen by," such as attending more to the ends of strings of sounds (which would lead to attention to suffixes before prefixes, for example) or attending to the sequence of sounds.

A second critical influence is the *input,* the set of language experiences actually encountered by the child. A child who hears *no* language or only limited language—like Genie, whom we have described in Box 5.1—will not develop in the same way as does a child who encounters a rich array of sounds and sentences.

The third crucial element, though, is what the child *does* with the input. The child begins with strategies (rules), receives input (hears people talking), processes that input according to the initial strategies, and then changes the strategies or rules to fit the new information. The result is a series of rules for understanding and creating language. These rules change over time as the child notices more and more subtleties in the language he hears and then applies that information to the sentences he constructs. The strong similarities we see among children in their early language constructions come about because all children share the same initial processing rules, and because most children are exposed to very similar input from the people around them.

If you think about this combined view, it sounds very much like Piaget's description of cognitive development. Piaget assumes that the child begins with a set of primitive schemes, which she applies to experiences. The schemes, however, change (are accommodated) as a result of those experiences. Both the initial schemes and the experiences are crucial in understanding cognitive development, but from Piaget's perspective the key element is the processing of the experience that the child engages in.

We find Kuczaj's approach appealing partly because it is so much like Piaget's; it is certainly parsimonious to think that language and thought may develop in parallel ways, even though the initial built-in strategies may be quite different in the two cases. We also like the fact that this approach retains some of the elements of innateness theory and some role for the environment. But just how does the language environment affect the child? We have already said that pure imitation or reinforcement theories don't do a very good job of describing language development. How else can we conceptualize the language environment?

BOX 5.1

Genie: The Child No One Talked To

Linguists have long been interested in children who grew up without language. Studies of deaf children have helped to uncover some of the secrets of language development; and an early study of a "wild boy" in France, who had apparently grown to age 12 without human contact, was also of great interest. In particular, linguists have wanted to discover whether there is a **critical period** in the development of language. Do children have to learn language during the first 2 to 4 years of age, when the innate programming is "ready" for language? Or can a first language be learned at any time? Both Erik Lenneberg (1967) and Noam Chomsky have taken the first position, while social learning theorists have taken the second view.

In 1970, another "wild child" was found, this time in California (Curtiss, 1977; Pines, 1981). Genie was 13 when she came to the attention of authorities. She had apparently spent nearly all of the first 13 years of her life tied to a potty chair in a back room of her parents' house. She was naked except for a harness she wore, and no one had spoken to her for most of her life. Her father—clearly a very disturbed man—used grunts and animal noises when he was with her; her older brother, who fed her, was instructed not to talk to her at all. When her father died, her mother (who was blind) tried to obtain public assistance, and in the process Genie was found. She weighed only 59 pounds, was incontinent, unable to walk, malnourished, and totally without language. Genie is now 25, and over the intervening years many linguists and therapists have tried to teach Genie all the skills she would need to survive in the world, including language. Susan Curtiss (1977) was the most diligent and has provided us with the most detailed descriptions of Genie's language.

After being released from her captivity, Genie rather quickly developed a small vocabulary of individual words—rather like the first level of vocabulary development in a child of 12 to 18 months. She said "Sorry" and "Stopit" and "Nomore" and "Pillow." She also showed that she understood much of what was said around her. Six months after she was hospitalized, for example, a "teacher asked [another child] who had two balloons how many he had. He said 'Three.' Genie looked startled and gave him another balloon" (Curtiss, 1977, p. 15).

About a year after her treatment began, she started using simple two-word sentences (Stage 1

The Role of Environmental Input

Many early language theorists were so determined to reject narrow reinforcement views of language acquisition that they went too far in casting out nearly all environmental influence (for example, Chomsky, 1965; McNeill, 1970). Recent research and thinking have moved the pendulum back at least part way. It is now clear that some elements of the language the child hears help to foster the child's early language development.

Talking to the Child.   It may seem a little silly to begin at this simple level, but it *does* matter how much adults around a child talk to her: Children who hear a lot of language develop vocabulary a little faster in the early years than those who are talked to less (Engel, Nechlin, & Arkin, 1975; Elardo, Bradley, & Caldwell, 1977; Clarke-Stewart, Vander

grammar), such as "Big teeth" and "Little marble" and "Two hand." In the beginning there were no verbs in these two-word sentences, but within another few months she had included verbs, too, like "Want milk."

Despite these early advances, however, Genie's language has never developed much beyond primitive Stage-2 grammar. She never used questions and continues to speak in "telegraphic language" even as an adult. She does not appear to understand the difference between various pronouns and does not grasp the difference between passive and active verbs at all.

Intellectually, Genie showed some progress. When her IQ was first tested (using a test designed for deaf children), she achieved a score of 38 (in the range of severe mental retardation). By 1977, after seven years of treatment, she scored 74 on the same test, and there were some kinds of tasks at which she was remarkably good. She could recognize faces better than most adults could, for example. Her ability to understand sounds, though, seemed to be especially poor.

Curiously, Curtiss has found that Genie's language—such as it is—seems to be processed with the *right* half of her brain. In nearly all adults (as we'll see more fully in Chapter 9), the language cen-

ter is in the left half of the brain; but Genie doesn't seem to use the left part of her brain for much of anything. Any task that can be accomplished with the right brain—including spatial abilities and face recognition—Genie is good at; but for anything that usually demands the left side of the brain, she does very poorly. This pattern is intriguing to linguists and to physiologists because it suggests that the process of acquiring a language in the early years of life may be necessary to program the left side of the brain properly. At the moment, this is still speculation, but it is fascinating speculation nonetheless.

Genie's case has yielded many clues to the process of language development. While Genie did learn *some* language, which shows that such learning is possible past the age of 4 or 5, she didn't learn full adult language skills despite valiant efforts. At the same time, it is extremely interesting that the early steps in her language development were so much like the first steps we see (hear) in children learning language in the normal manner. All of this makes it appear that these first steps, at least, may be "built in" in some way. Development beyond those first steps, however, seems to require both early and extensive exposure to language in the child's world. If the child does not have that exposure, it can't be made up later.

Stoep, & Killian, 1979). Allison Clarke-Stewart (1973), for example, observed and listened to a group of 36 infants and their mothers. You can see in Figure 5.3 that those mothers who talked to their children more in the early months of life had children who knew and used more words at 17 months. At the very least, we know that there is some *minimally sufficient* amount of exposure to language that is necessary for children to develop language at all. Beyond that minimal level, the effect is less clear; but it appears that children who are exposed to more words, more different grammatical forms, may develop somewhat faster.

Simpler Language to the Child.   Other than simply talking to the child, one of the most critical things that adults do that seems to aid the process of language development is to speak in very simple sentences to the child. Since this distinctively simpler language is often heard when mothers talk to their infants or toddlers, it has acquired the name of **motherese.**

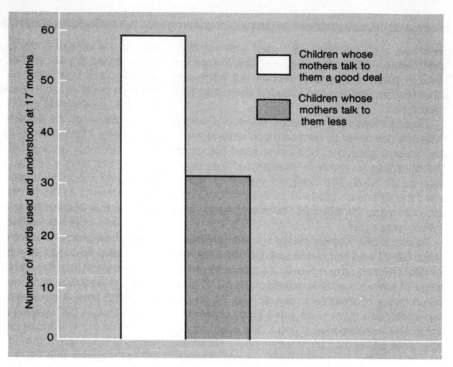

Figure 5.3. The figure shows the relationship between the rate of the child's vocabulary development during the second year of life and the amount the mother talked to the child during the *first* year of life. Children whose mothers talked to them more, later knew and used more words than did those whose mothers talked to them less. The fact that the effect can be traced over a year later suggests that the child is not triggering this causal chain. In other words, early talking children do not stimulate more conversation from their parents; rather, the more talkative parents seem to produce (cause) faster vocabulary development in the child. (*Source:* Clarke-Stewart, K. A., 1973, p. 82. With permission by the Society for Research in Child Development, Inc.)

Motherese has several key features (Gelman & Shatz, 1977; Snow & Ferguson, 1977):

1. The sentences are nearly always grammatical.
2. The sentences are short.
3. The grammatical forms used are quite simple. There are many questions but few past tenses, for example.
4. It is highly repetitive. The adult tends to use the same sentences, or minor variations of the same sentences, over and over when talking to a young child. ("Where's the ball? Can you see the ball? Where is the ball? There is the ball!")
5. Most of the conversation deals with the immediate present and not the past or the future.
6. The vocabulary is fairly concrete, and only a small selection of words

is used. The adult intentionally chooses words that she thinks the child will understand.

7. When parents imitate their child's sentences, they often *expand* or *recast* the sentences into slightly longer, more grammatical forms. (If the child said "Mommy coat," the mother might say "Yes, that's mommy's coat.")
8. The words are spoken in a higher-pitched voice, at a slower pace, and with a wider range of pitch and speed than we use when we speak to adults.

What is really fascinating about this adult-child interchange is that most adults are so attuned to the child's developing language skills that they steadily *adapt* the level of complexity of their language as the child becomes more capable. Juliet Phillips (1973), for example, has found that mothers gradually increase the length of sentences they use with their children as the children's own sentences get longer. The mother's sentences are always longer than the child's, but she moves ahead slowly, just a notch ahead of the child's language.

Obviously, mothers and fathers don't do all this in order to teach the child grammar. They do it in order to communicate with the child. However, it's hard to imagine a more useful set of circumstances for the child trying to learn the language. He hears simpler forms and hears them repeated and varied. He also hears his own simple sentences turned into more complex ones when the parent expands his sentences. This is just the sort of "food" the child needs to develop basic rules and then to enlarge on those rules as the input becomes more and more complex. Thus what the parents say, as well as how much they say, seems to be an important element in the language acquisition process (Nelson, 1977; Brown, 1977).

Still, it is important to reemphasize the fact (at least we think it is a fact) that the really crucial element in the process is not the input but what the child *does* with that input—whether he notices what the adult has said and how he interprets it or categorizes it or organizes it. The input is a necessary but not sufficient condition for grammar to develop.

THE DEVELOPMENT OF WORD MEANING

Although linguists obviously still disagree on the explanations of grammatical development, there is at least some agreement on the description of the developmental steps. Systematic study of the development of word meaning (semantics), however, is much newer, and there is still dispute about both the descriptions of the meanings the child attaches to words and about the appropriate explanations of the process.

Obviously, we are touching here on a set of questions that overlaps with what we have already said about cognitive development. Nearly all words represent *classes* of things; so when we ask about children's word meanings, we are asking something about the kinds of classes they create.

If a child calls the family cocker spaniel a dog, what other types of creatures or objects is the child likely to put into the same class with the same word applied? Are the early word categories very narrow, or are they extremely broad? Does the child generalize (extend the class) on the basis of the perceptual properties of the objects, such as calling all furry things or all four-legged things *dogs?* Or does he generalize on the basis of what he can do with the object, such as "dogs are things you pet"? Answers to all these questions are still coming in, but let's take a look at some of the current ideas.

Which Comes First, the Meaning or the Word?

The most fundamental question is whether the child learns a word to describe a category or class he has *already* created through his manipulations of the world around him (Nelson, 1973; Nelson, Rescorla, Gruendel, & Benedict, 1977) or whether he creates new cognitive categories to handle those things that are named with the same word (Clark, 1973). This may seem like a highly abstract argument, but it touches on the fundamental issue of the relationship between language and thought that we talked about in the last chapter. Does the child learn to represent objects to himself *because* he now has language, or does language simply come along at about this point and make the representation easier?

The answer seems to be both (Greenberg & Kuczaj, 1982). In the early stages of language development, children seem to apply words (or even to create words) to describe categories or classes they have already created mentally. Probably Brenda's word *nene* (liquid food and the pleasure that goes with it) is an example of this. But it seems equally clear that the child's classification system is affected by the labels attached to objects, too. A child who has never seen a horse may be taken to the county fair and hear the word *horse* used to describe several different animals. This naming of instances obviously helps to create a category, a class, for the child.

Extending the Class

Let us go back to the family cocker spaniel. The 2-year-old correctly uses the word *dog* when referring to this animal. That is helpful for communication, but it doesn't tell us much about the word meaning the child has developed. What does the word *dog* mean to the child? Does he think it is a name only for *that particular* creature? Or does he think it applies to all furry creatures, in which case cats and maybe sheep would be in the same class, but Great Danes might be excluded. Does he think it is for all animals of about that same *size?* If so, then again large cats might be included in the same class, but probably sheep would not, and many other dogs would be excluded as well.

Our current information tells us that children *overextend* their early words more often than they *underextend* them, so we are more likely to hear the word *dog* applied to sheep and even to cows than we are to have it used for just one animal or for a very small set of animals or objects. Some examples of the kind of overextensions that children create, collected by Eve Clark (1975), are given in Table 5.4.

All children seem to show overextensions like these. But the particular classes the child creates are unique to that particular child. There doesn't seem to be any tendency for all children to use the word *dog* to apply to all four-footed animals or to all furry creatures or whatever. Each child overextends his words using his own distinct rules, and those rules change as the child's vocabulary grows.

Another way to look at the naming process is to realize that part of the child's problem is that he simply doesn't know many words. If he wants to talk about something, point out something, or ask for something, he has to use whatever words he has that are fairly close. Overextensions may thus arise from the child's desire to communicate and may not tell us that the child fails to make the discriminations in-

TABLE 5.4
Some Examples of Overextensions in the Language of Young Children

Word	Object or event for which the word was originally used	Other objects or events to which the word was later applied
mooi	moon	cakes, round marks on windows, writing on windows and in books, round shapes in books, tooling in leather book covers, round postmarks, letter *O*
buti	ball	toy, radish, stone spheres at park entrance
baw	ball	(by another child) apples, grapes, eggs, squash, bell clapper, anything round
sch	sound of train	all moving machines
em	worm	flies, ants, all small insects, heads of timothy grass
fafer	sound of trains	steaming coffeepot, anything that hissed or made a noise
va	white plush dog	muffler, cat, father's fur coat

SOURCE: Reprinted with permission from Eve V. Clark, "Knowledge, context, and strategy in the acquisition of meaning." In: Georgetown University Round Table on Language and Linguistics 1975, *Developmental psycholinguistics: theory and applications,* edited by Daniel P. Dato. Copyright © by Georgetown University, Washington, D.C., pp. 83–84.

volved. The example Clark (1977) uses is of a child who wants to call attention to a horse. She may recognize that the horse is different from a dog, but she doesn't know the word. So she says "Doggie." As the child learns the separate labels that are applied to the different subtypes of fuzzy four-legged creatures, the overextension disappears.

This possibility came back to me when I was recently in France, struggling with my highly primitive and unused French. I spent most of one day trying to buy my mother a sweater. The problem was that I couldn't remember the word for *sweater,* so I used the next-closest word that I did know, which was the word for *blouse.* Since I did remember the word for *wool,* I started out asking for a *wool blouse,* which amused the salespeople no end. I was reduced to pointing in short order, until I managed to pick up the word for *sweater* from the replies of the salespeople. It struck me that young children in the early stages of language acquisition must often find themselves in a similar position—knowing that the word they are using is incorrect, but simply not knowing the right word. [HB]

Parents may actually contribute to a child's overextensions. Carolyn and Cynthia Mervis (1982) found that mothers were likely to use simple words to describe quite broad classes when speaking to their toddlers, such as calling leopards and lions *kitty cats* or labeling toy fire engines as *cars.*

Form versus Function: What Does the Child Attend To?

A third dispute among researchers studying the development of word meaning is whether the child initially creates categories based on what objects *look like* (form) or whether he bases his early classifications mostly on what you can *do with* the object (function).

Eve Clark (1973) originally took the first view; and if you go back and look at the overextensions in Table 5.4, this position makes a lot of sense. Children do seem to be basing their overextensions on the shape of objects or their sounds or textures—all perceptual qualities.

The second view has been proposed by Katherine Nelson (1973), who was very much struck by the fact that the child's first words nearly always referred to objects that had particular functions or objects that the child could play with or move. The young child is more likely to learn the word *ball,* for example, than the word *sofa* even though both are part of her world on a daily basis. Similarly, words that describe changes in state, like *dry* or *dirty,* are understood and spoken earlier by most children than are words that describe constant qualities, like *rough* or *square.*

Nelson concluded that children's concepts are thus organized around a "functional core"—a set of things that the object does or is.

A ball *is* something round that rolls, bounces, and can be thrown. Extensions of this concept may be based on perceptual qualities, as Clark suggests. New round things may be labeled as *balls,* for example. However, if the child discovers that the new round thing does not bounce, it would no longer belong in the same category.

As we have found so often when we compare two contrasting theories, the evidence tells us that both theories are at least partly correct. Children's early word meanings seem to be based on both function and form. There is some indication, in fact, that what children do is to develop a sort of mental *prototype* of each category (Anglin, 1977; Greenberg & Kuczaj, 1982) and generalize to other examples based on how close the new instance is to the prototype. Adults do this, too. Think of a *vase.* Vases can come in a large variety of shapes and sizes, but probably when you first thought of the word *vase* a picture of a *particular* vase came to your mind. This is your prototype of a vase—the central example that defines the category for you. When you encounter some object that *might* be a vase, you compare it mentally to the prototype to see if it fits.

Children seem to do the same thing. Their early prototypes may be based on either form or function, and the prototype changes as the child has more experience with instances and as the child learns new words for related categories. When the child learns the word *horse,* she stops calling horses *dogs* and develops a horse prototype as well as a dog prototype.

The whole process of developing word meanings is clearly complicated and seems to vary more from child to child than does the process of grammatical development. Obviously what linguists are searching for are the rules that govern this process so that we can understand why children use words the way they do. So far, a few general principles have emerged, but the study of semantics is still very much in the toddler stage.

INDIVIDUAL DIFFERENCES IN LANGUAGE DEVELOPMENT: POWER AND STYLE

The distinctions between questions about structure and those about power or style are the same when we look at language development as they were when we looked at cognitive development. Psychologists interested in structural change are struck by the fact that all children seem to go through similar steps or stages in development. Other psychologists are struck by the fact that there are such marked differences in the *rate* of development. Still others have noticed that there are some subtle differences in the quality of children's early language—differences that may be analogous to the variations in style we have talked about earlier. Both the similarities in pattern and the differences in rate (or style) are real and important; but they have led to quite different sets of research, as we have seen in the last chapter.

Differences in Rate of Language Development

Anyone who has been around children knows that there are marked differences in the timing of children's language development. Eve, Adam, and Sarah—whose progress we showed in Figure 5.2—are a good illustration of the variation. Systematic attempts to explain this variation, though, are comparatively new.

Genetic Explanations.   One fairly obvious possibility is that language development may be partially controlled by the genetic code. Certainly if we assume that part of language is built into the brain, it makes sense to think that some children may inherit a more efficient built-in system than others.

As with studies of the genetic contribution to IQ, there are two basic research designs available: twin studies and adoption studies. In one twin study, Harry Munsinger and Arthur Douglass (1976) tested groups of identical and fraternal twins, plus a group of nontwin siblings, using a standardized test of language skill. The subjects ranged in age from 3 to 17, so we are dealing here more with the final level of language skill than with the rate of initial development. Still, the results suggest that there is some genetic component involved. As was true in studies of IQ, Munsinger found that the correlation between the language scores of identical twins was considerably higher (.83) than the correlation between the language scores of fraternal twins (.44).

Studies of adopted children also point to some genetic influence. In the first year of life, children's language comprehension and production can be predicted better by knowing the *natural parent's* cognitive ability than by knowing the *adoptive parent's* skill (Hardy-Brown, Plomin, & DeFries, 1981).

Unlike the studies of heritability of IQ, however, in this case there are no studies of language skills of identical twins reared apart to help us sort out the effects of similar environments. These first studies of the genetics of language development make it clear, though, that we must continue to consider the possibility of an inherited element influencing both the rate of language development and the skill level finally achieved.

Environmental Influences.   The other side of the coin is environmental influence. We have already pointed out that when parents talk to their children a lot, their youngsters have more rapid language development in the early years. This *could* be a disguised genetic effect: Parents who have more language facility both talk to their children more and are more likely to pass on "good language" genes to them as well. But at least one study of adopted children indicates that the impact of the language environment is important by itself. In the study by Karen Hardy-Brown (Hardy-Brown, Plomin, & DeFries, 1981), the amount that the *adoptive* mother imitated the infant's vocalizations and the amount of her "contingent vocal responses" to the child were both related to the infant's language development at 1 year of age. Since Hardy-Brown was studying the adoptive mother and not the natural mother, we can be sure that this is an effect of the environment and not a combination of heredity and environment.

As we found with IQ, it seems obvious that both the particular genes the child inherits and the environment provided for the child contribute to the rate of language development the child shows. We should emphasize once again, too, that although children do differ widely in the timing of their language development, virtually all children progress adequately through the sequence of steps of grammatical and semantic development we have described. Nearly all children learn to communicate at least adequately; most do so with great skill, regardless of their early rate of progress.

Sex Differences in Language Development. One additional aspect of individual differences in language we should touch on, if only because it is so much a part of our stereotypes, is sex differences. Our cultural stereotype is that women are more talkative, more verbal, than men. But is this true? Can we see differences as early as the first year of life? Yes and no. Table 5.5 summarizes the findings on sex differences in verbal ability, and you can see that in the early years there are some differences in favor of girls (Schachter, Shore, Hodapp, Chalfin, & Bundy, 1978). Note, though, that there seem to be no differences in the rate of *structural* development. The differences, when they are found at all, occur in vocabulary, talkativeness, and clarity of speech. Girls do not seem to arrive at Stage-2 grammar any sooner.

In adolescence, girls seem to score higher than boys on most measures of language, but once again we should emphasize that most of these are measures of language power and tell us little about language structure.

Still, when differences are found, girls seem to show greater language facility than boys. The difference is small, but it has been found by several different researchers. How can we explain it? One possibility is that early language is partly determined by physiological maturation. Since girls are on a slightly faster developmental timetable (as

TABLE 5.5
Summary of Sex Differences in Language Development and Skill

SKILL	DIRECTION OF DIFFERENCE
	Infancy and early childhood
Vocabulary	Girls *may* be a bit ahead up to about age 3, but many studies show no difference.
Amount of talking	Girls may talk a bit more in the early years, although this finding, too, is not consistently reported.
Grammatical skill	There seems to be no difference.
Articulation (speaking clearly)	Girls are better, and remain better through school; more boys need the help of speech therapists in elementary school.
	Adolescence and adulthood
Spelling	Girls and women are better on average.
Punctuation	Girls and women are better on average.
Comprehension of complex written material	Girls and women are better on average.
Verbal reasoning	Girls and women are better on average.

we pointed out in Chapter 3), they may simply be biologically ready for language a bit earlier than boys are. Another possibility is that parents expect girls to be more verbal and thus talk to them more. There is some evidence to support this possibility. Michael Lewis (1972) has consistently found that mothers talk to their daughters more than to their sons. Other observers, though, have not noticed the same differences in parental treatment of the two sexes (Maccoby & Jacklin, 1974; Schachter, 1979). Still, there is at least a suggestion here that some parents may provide a more encouraging climate for language development for girls than for boys.

Differences in Style of Language Development

Aside from differences in rate, children also may differ in the way they use language and in the kind of vocabulary they develop in the early stages. We have described one such difference in style—black English—in Box 5.2. A broader look at style differences comes from Katherine Nelson (1981). She thinks there are two general types of early language: **expressive** and **referential.** We have summarized the differences in Table 5.6, but a few examples would probably help as well.

Children who use language referentially develop early vocabularies

TABLE 5.6

Some Differences between Expressive and Referential Language Users in Their Early Vocabulary and Sentence Structure

	Expressive	*Referential*
Types of words learned and used initially	Vocabulary is diverse, with many personal-social words as well as nominals. High rate of pronoun use compared to referential children.	Many more general nominals (names for things) than expressive children and fewer pronouns.
Types of early sentences	Many social routines used in their entirety, such as "I want it" or "Stop it."	Few social routines.
	Many formulas or rote strings of words inserted into sentences in their entirety, such as "What do you want?" or "I don't know where it is."	Very few rote strings. As a result, the referential child's early sentences may be shorter than those of expressive children.

SOURCE: Based on Nelson, 1981.

that consist mostly of names of individual objects—mostly *specific nominals,* to use the terminology we introduced earlier. Their sentences tend to be short—at least at first—and they don't seem to use language very much for social interactions with adults. In contrast, children who use language expressively seem to be focused much more on the communicative aspect of language. They also seem to learn more from imitation. Their early sentences often include entire chunks of adult sentences spoken without any pauses or inflections, as if the word strings were single words. One child of 18 months that Nelson describes used the phrase "I don't know where it is" in this way. If we look only at the complexity of the sentence, we might conclude that this child was in Stage-2 grammar; but Nelson thinks not. Rather, the child has learned this "formula" as if it were a single word.

Most children use a mixture of these two styles. However, Nelson's observations suggest that some children seem to use primarily one mode or the other in their early language. In Nelson's studies, predominantly referential children were likely to come from families in which the mother does a lot of naming and uses a lot of nouns in relation to pronouns. So perhaps the child's style is basically imitative of the parent's style. Alternatively, it could reflect a more fundamental individual difference in children's orientation toward objects or toward relationships. It would be extremely interesting to see whether expressive children interact differently with other children than do referential children, or whether their play with toys is qualitatively different from one another. Until such research is done, these style differences in language remain merely suggestions or hints.

BOX 5.2

Black English

Many black children in the United States speak differently from whites. Until fairly recently, teachers and others who dealt with black children assumed that this difference was really a deficit, that the children just had not learned properly. But a number of linguists, perhaps most notably William Labov (1972), have argued that what black children learn is a perfectly legitimate dialect of English. In our terms, the difference is one of style rather than one of either power or structure.

Anastasiow and Hanes give a lovely example of the difference:

A petite five-year-old black girl sits across from an experimenter. He asks her to repeat a sentence spoken in typical school English and played on a tape recorder. The tape recorder plays the sentence: "I asked him if he did it and he said he didn't do it." She smiles, presses down the folds of her thin dress and says, "I asks him if he did it and he says he didn't did it but I knows he did" (Anastasiow & Hanes, 1976, p. 3).

The message is the same, but this child has made some specific changes in the sentence she heard; she has *transformed* the sentence into black English dialect.

When linguists have analyzed black English, they have found that there are very specific differences, particularly in the use of verbs. In the Green Road Housing Project in Ann Arbor, Michigan (a largely black neighborhood), the children say "He be gone" when they mean "He is gone a good deal

Standard English	Black English Version
He is going home	He going home
John runs	John run
I have lived here	I have live here, or I lived here
Didn't anybody see it?	Didn't nobody see it?
She came home	She come home
He doesn't have any toys	He ain't got no toys, or He don't have no toys

SOURCE: Examples from Dale, 1976; Baratz, 1969.

SUMMARY

1. From the earliest use of two-word sentences, children's language is complex, abstract, productive, and rule governed. We can study it as we did cognition by looking at structure, power, and style.
2. *Language* can be defined as an arbitrary system of symbols that permits us to say and to understand an infinite variety of messages.
3. Prior to about 1 year of age, linguists talk about the prelinguistic phase, which is broken up into steps: crying, cooing, and babbling.
4. At about 1 year of age the earliest words appear. The child begins to use sounds with consistent referents. These early words are normally used to convey entire sentences of meaning.
5. By age 2, most children have a vocabulary of 50 words, and the first two-word sentences normally appear between 18 and 24 months.

of the time." They say "He been gone" when they mean "He's been gone for a long while." Some other examples of standard and black English translations are given in the accompanying table.

The black English versions are predictable enough so that it is quite possible for someone to learn the dialect. But is the black English dialect less complex? (Does it require less linguistic "power" or involve qualitatively different structures?) Philip Dale (1976), among others, argues that it is just as complicated as standard English. When the black child says "She come home" rather than "She came home," it doesn't mean that there is no past tense in black English; rather, it means that both the present and the past tense are formed with the word *come.*

Virtually everyone—educators and linguists alike—now agrees on the basic point that black English is a legitimate dialect of equivalent complexity. The argument now is over whether the black child should be allowed or encouraged to use this dialect in school or whether he should be required to use standard English. Parents in the Green Road Housing Project went to court to force the Detroit school system to provide better training for their teachers so that the children could use their dialect in school. They won the suit (*Time,* August 20, 1979).

There is a parallel between this issue and the question of whether children who come to school speaking an entirely different language (Spanish or Vietnamese or whatever) should be taught in their own language or required to learn standard English. Most school districts now begin instruction in the child's native language and teach English as a second language. Perhaps black English should be treated in precisely the same way—the child could be taught originally in the dialect and taught standard English as a second language later, after reading and writing had already been mastered.

The other side of the argument is taken by many black leaders who emphasize the fact that like it or not, standard English is the basic language of the culture, and black children need to become skillful in its use. They think that children should use the standard language from the beginning.

At the moment, we simply lack the evidence that would permit us to choose. We do not know whether black children taught originally in their own dialect would have less difficulty with schooling than many of them now have. Furthermore, we don't know whether such instruction would foster or inhibit the development of facile use of standard English at a later point. No doubt the question will be with us for a long time to come.

6. Grammatical development can be divided into two stages. In Stage 1 the child may construct two- or three-word sentences (or longer) but omits all the grammatical inflections. Stage 2, which normally begins about a year later, is defined by the beginning use of such inflections.

7. During Stage 2, the child progressively adds questions, negatives, superlatives, past tenses, and other grammatical forms.

8. Several theories have been offered to explain grammatical development. Imitation clearly plays some part, but linguists agree that it is not an adequate explanation. Similarly, while reinforcement may have some impact, it cannot explain the creative aspects of language.

9. Innateness theorists emphasize the inborn capacity to learn language and the built-in form of language. The child merely learns the transformational rules that change basic meaning into acceptable sentences.

10. A combined theory emphasizes the role of inborn "rules to listen by," the importance of the language input to which the child is exposed, and the child's own construction of language.

11. The aspects of language input that appear to be important are the amount of language spoken around the child and the use of simplified motherese in speaking to the child.

12. The development of word meanings (semantic development) follows a less predictable course. Most children overextend their early word meanings—applying a word to a very broad category of objects that does not match the adult usage. These overextensions appear to be based on both the form and the function of the originally named object.

13. Children also differ in the rate of development of both grammar and vocabulary. Genetic explanations of such differences receive some support from the results of comparisons of language skill in identical and fraternal twins and from studies of adopted children.

14. Environmental explanations of individual differences receive support from studies showing that the amount parents talk to their children affects the rate of development.

15. Girls develop language slightly faster in the early years and are again ahead of boys in language skill in adolescence. The differences are very small and not found by every researcher. Explanations of this difference emphasize differences in maturational rate and differences in parental treatment.

16. Some differences in language style have also been noted in young children. Some children's language can be described as referential, with heavy use of nouns. Other children's language is more expressive, with more pronouns and more rote strings.

17. Despite these variations in early patterns, most children learn to speak skillfully by about age 5 or 6.

KEY TERMS

Babbling   The repetitive sounds, usually involving at least one consonant and one vowel, shown by the baby from about 6 to 12 months.

Black English   The dialect of standard English spoken by many black children and adults in the United States.

Cooing   An early stage during the prelinguistic period in which vowel sounds are repeated, particularly the *uuu* sound.

Critical period   A specific period in an organism's development during which that organism is especially responsive to a particular stimulus or group of stimuli; the same stimulation at other points in development have little or no effect. Example: Rubella produces defects in the fetus only if the mother contracts it during a particular range of weeks of gestation.

Deep structure   The underlying meaning of a sentence—a concept first proposed by Noam Chomsky.

Echolalia   A characteristic of the babbling period. The child repeats (echoes) the same sounds over and over.

Expressive language style   One of two language styles described by Nelson, including high use of social routines, pronouns, and rote strings.

Holophrases   The expression of an entire idea in a single word. Characteristic of the child's language from about 12 to 18 months.

Inflections   The grammatical markers, such as plurals, possessives, past tenses, and equivalent.

Language acquisition device   A hypothesized brain structure that may be programmed to make language learning possible.

Mean length of utterance   Usually abbreviated MLU; the average number of meaningful units in a sentence. Each basic word is one meaningful unit, as is each inflection, such as the *s* for plural or the *ed* for a past tense.

Motherese   The word linguists often use to describe the particular pattern of speech by adults to young children. The sentences are shorter, simpler, repetitive, and higher pitched.

Overregularization   The tendency on the part of children to make the language regular, such as using past tenses like *beated* or *goed*.

Pivot grammar   The description of the first two-word sentences first offered by Braine. The child's sentences appeared to have two kinds of words: pivot words and *X* words.

Prelinguistic phase   The period before the child speaks his first words.

Referential language style   The second style of language proposed by Nelson, including high use of object labels (nouns) and low use of pronouns and "rote strings."

Semantics   The study of word meaning.

Surface structure   The phrase used by Chomsky to describe the actual grammatical construction of a sentence. Surface structures are created from deep structure by use of transformational rules.

Syntax   Grammar or sentence structure.

Telegraphic speech   A characteristic of early child sentences in which everything, but the crucial words, is omitted, as if for a telegram.

Transformational grammar   The phrase used broadly to describe Chomsky's theory of language and language development. It describes the rules by which deep structure is transformed into surface structures.

SUGGESTED READINGS

Brown, R. Development of the first language in the human species. *American Psychologist,* 1973, *28,* 97–106.

A wonderful, brief description of some of the major findings in language development written in Roger Brown's usual clear style. Bear in mind when you read this article, however, that a great deal of research has been done since 1973 that changes some of his conclusions.

Pines, M. The civilizing of Genie. *Psychology Today,* 1981 (Sept.), *15,* 28–34.

A highly readable and fascinating description of the most recent information on Genie's progress. Many of the key issues in language development are mentioned.

Terrace, H. S. How Nim Chimpsky changed my mind. *Psychology Today,* 1979, *13* (No. 6), 65–76.

This is the paper that has sparked a renewed controversy about whether chimps really create complex sentences or not. A very interesting paper.

PROJECT 5.1

In Table 5.3 we have given you the sentences used by Gregory when he was at Stage 1 of grammatical development. In this project we want you to collect a similar sample of sentences from a child.

You will need to find a child as close to 20 to 24 months as you can. He or she should be speaking at least some two-word sentences. Arrange to spend enough time with the child (at his or her home or in a day care center or in any convenient setting) so that you can collect a list of 50 different utterances, including one-word utterances and two-or-more-word sentences. Write them down in the order they occur and stop when you have 50. It may take several sessions with the child before you get this many, and you may find it helpful to have the child's mother or some other adult play with the child while you listen and write things down. Whenever you can, make notes about the context in which each sentence occurred.

When you have your list of 50 utterances, consider the following questions in a written paper or in a report in a form desired by your instructor:

1. Are there pivot words? Which words are they?
2. What are the *X* words in your child's grammar?
3. Is your child still at Stage 1 or has he moved into Stage 2? How can you tell?
4. How many different *meanings* can you detect, such as subject-object relationships or attribution (for example, *big boat*)?
5. What is the mean length of utterance (MLU)? If you want to figure this out fairly precisely, follow the rules suggested by Brown (1973, p. 54) or by Dale (1976, p. 19).

Chapter 6
The Self and Personality in Childhood

THE CONCEPT OF SELF: DEVELOPMENTAL PATTERNS
The First Step: The Existential Self
The Next Step: The Categorical Self
The Categorical Self during the School Years
Self-Esteem

INDIVIDUAL DIFFERENCES IN THE SELF:
TEMPERAMENT AND PERSONALITY
Temperament Theory of Personality
Psychoanalytic Theory
Social Learning Theories
Cognitive Developmental Theories
A Tentative Synthesis

SUMMARY
KEY TERMS
SUGGESTED READINGS
PROJECT

Try an experiment: Before you read any further, write down 20 separate answers to the question, "Who am I?"

Now look over your list. Have you included descriptions of your appearance (for example, "I am skinny"), your beliefs ("I am a Protestant"), your skills and problems ("I am a good cook" or "I have trouble getting along with bosses"), or your roles ("I am a parent" or "I am a psychologist")? Did you include some statement about your gender in the list somewhere ("I am a male" or "I am a female")?

Each of us carries around a detailed, pervasive set of ideas about ourself, collectively called the **self-concept.** These ideas affect our relationships with others, our choice of activities or occupation, and our confidence (or lack of it) in many situations. The self-concept is also a highly significant part of what is usually called the **personality,** which we may define as *that unique, individualized pattern of thinking and reacting to the world around us that is characteristic of each of us.*

In this chapter we want to search for the roots of that individuality. How does each person develop a unique personality? How does each of us end up with a different self-concept?

Paradoxically, we need to start this search for the source of individual patterns by understanding the shared patterns in the development of the concept of the self. How do infants and young children discover that they are unique individuals? What aspects of their own behavior, or their qualities, do they pay attention to in the early years? Once we have laid this basic developmental groundwork, we can look at the ways in which children's self-concepts, and their broader personalities, differ from one another.

Examining the developmental patterns in the concept of the self also helps link cognitive development (which we discussed in Chapter 4) and the development of the unique self. The key point to bear in mind is that the self-concept is first of all a *cognitive* accomplishment, an accomplishment that should be related to the development of other basic concepts about the world. We have already seen that the child's ideas about objects, about friendships, and about other people's understanding change systematically with age. We should expect that the child's concept of herself should also show changes in both content and complexity over the first years of life.

THE CONCEPT OF SELF: DEVELOPMENTAL PATTERNS

The First Step: The Existential Self

Both Piaget and Freud have emphasized that in the first months of life the infant does not distinguish between himself and other people. Freud talks about the *symbiotic* relationship between the mother and the infant in which the two are joined together as if they are one. For the infant, the first step in developing a self-concept thus must be to understand that he is a separate and distinct entity. Michael Lewis and

Figure 6.1. This little boy seems to be having a grand time playing by himself. Does he usually play in this solitary way—that is, is it part of his personality? Or is there something about this situation—the play materials or the behavior of the teacher—that has encouraged him to play alone? Psychologists have always been interested in how much personality accounts for behavior and how much environment is responsible.

Jeanne Brooks-Gunn call this first step the development of the **existential self** (Lewis & Brooks, 1978; Lewis & Brooks-Gunn, 1979; Lewis, 1981).

Lewis and Brooks-Gunn argue that the basic underpinnings of this sense of separateness are the contingent interactions the baby has with the people around him. When he cries, someone picks him up; when he drops his rattle, someone returns it to him; when his mother smiles, he smiles back. By this process the baby slowly begins to grasp the basic difference between self and other. We have already pointed out the importance of contingent responsiveness for the development of both language and cognitive skills in the infant and young child. Now we see that this pattern of interaction between parent and child may also be vital for the development of the concept of self as well.

This first primitive step in the development of the self-concept appears to take place during the first six months of life, at about the same time as the child is developing the concept of the permanence of objects (which we described in Chapter 3). While the child is figuring out that the bottle he handles continues to exist from day to day even when it is out of sight, he is also figuring out that he exists separately and continuously too. You can see these parallel developments in the results of a study by Bertenthal and Fischer in Figure 6.2.

One of the techniques used to explore early self-awareness involves the use of a mirror. First the baby is placed in front of a mirror, just to see how she behaves. Most infants of about 9 to 12 months will look at their own images, make faces, or try to interact with the baby in the mirror in some way. After allowing this free exploration for a time, the experimenter, while pretending to wipe the baby's face with

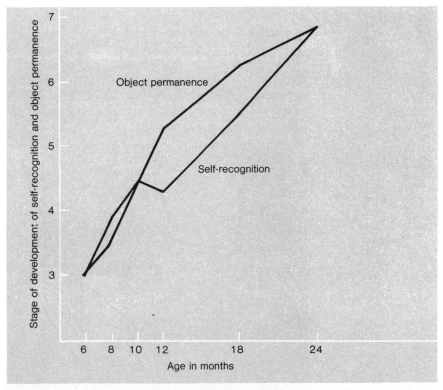

Figure 6.2. In this study, Bertenthal and Fischer tested children's object permanence and their self-recognition separately. As you can see, they found that these two types of understanding develop at about the same rate in the early months of life. (*Source:* Bertenthal & Fischer, 1978, Figure 1, p. 49.)

a cloth, puts a spot of rouge on the baby's nose and then again lets the baby look in the mirror. The crucial test of self-recognition, and thus of awareness of the self, is whether the baby reaches for the spot on her *own* nose (not the nose on the face in the mirror).

Figure 6.3 shows the results from one of Lewis's studies using this procedure. As you can see, none of the 9- to 12-month-old children in this study touched their noses; but by 21 months, three quarters of the children showed this level of self-recognition. The figure also shows the rate at which children refer to themselves by name when they are shown a picture of themselves. You can see that this development occurs at almost exactly the same time as self-recognition in a mirror. The results of this research make it clear that most toddlers of 21 to 24 months have developed a clear notion of their own separation from others and have some sense of their own appearance. When you think about it, that is quite an accomplishment in only two years.

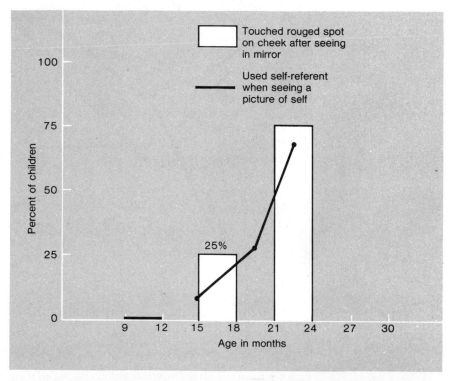

Figure 6.3. Both the growth of children's use of self-referents in their language and their recognition of themselves in the mirror show that the basic sense of a separate self is well established in most children by age 2. (*Source:* Lewis & Brooks, 1978.)

The Next Step: The Categorical Self

Once the infant has clearly understood that he is separate and distinct from others, the process of defining the self begins—a process that continues over the entire life span. Lewis and Brooks refer to this as the **categorical self** because the definition takes the form of placing yourself in a wide range of categories. Like the beginning sense of separation of self from others, the development of a categorical self requires that the child compare himself with other people along a range of dimensions. If you think of yourself as *young,* you are comparing yourself with other people who are *old;* if you are *clumsy,* you are contrasting your behavior with the *coordinated* or skillful behavior of others.

One of the earliest dimensions young children appear to focus on is age/size. Edwards and Lewis (1979) have found that children from 2 to 5 years of age are already categorizing themselves and other people as old or young, big or little. When 3 to 5-year-old children were asked to sort photographs of infants, toddlers, children, and adults, they made separate groupings for *big children* and *little children,* and *parents* and *grandparents.* The category of *little children* seemed to include everyone up to about age 5, while *big children* included those up to about age 13 or so. Everyone older than that was a grown-up from the perspective of the preschool-age child.

The Gender Concept.   Another dimension on which children define themselves during these same early years is gender. "Am I a boy or a girl? Are mommies boys or girls? Are the other children I play with boys or girls?" Just as the young child notices size, she also notices gender in others and thus defines her own gender as well. This aspect of the self-concept is especially important because it forms the foundation for a more general concept of how boys and girls are *supposed* to behave. That is, once children discover which gender category they belong to and that the gender is permanent, they begin to pay serious attention to the *roles* of boy and girl—to use the sociological terminology we introduced in Chapter 1. What do boys *do?* How do grown-up women behave? What are "girlish" or "boyish" toys, attitudes, or skills? These are all part of what is usually called a **sex role.** We will use the phrase **gender concept** to refer to the basic understanding that people (and other creatures, too, of course) can be divided into two gender categories, and that membership in such categories is a permanent quality. We will use the phrase *sex role* or *sex-role concept* to refer to the broader set of ideas the child develops about the expectations and properties of "boyness" and "girlness."

The child's basic concept of gender appears to develop in four steps, which we've summarized in Table 6.1. The first visible indication that

TABLE 6.1
Stages in the Development of the Gender Concept

Awareness	Child begins to notice gender differences; the dimension of gender becomes relevant for the categorical self (ages 12 to 24 months).
Labeling	The child correctly labels his own gender and the gender of others (ages 2 to 3).
Stability	The child understands that gender remains stable over time—that if he is a boy now, he will be a boy when he grows up (ages 3 to 5).
Constancy	The child understands that gender does not change when a person's outward appearance has been changed.

gender is an important part of a toddler's categorical self is simply **awareness** of other children's gender. Michael Lewis noticed that in groups of 12- to 18-month-old children, the boys looked more at other boys, and the girls looked more at other girls. It is not clear just what cues the children are using to detect boyness or girlness at this early age. But they do seem to be paying attention to something. Whether this means they have any kind of concept of gender, however, is debatable.

The second step in this sequence, **gender labeling,** is evident at about 24 months, when we hear children labeling themselves and others correctly as boys or girls, men or women (Eaton & Von Bargen, 1981). Spencer Thompson (1975) found that about half of the 2-year-olds in his study were labeling themselves correctly, and this had risen to nearly 100 percent in a group of 3-year-olds.

The third step is **gender stability,** which involves the understanding that you (and other people) stay the same gender throughout life. To check whether children have achieved this understanding of gender, psychologists ask them questions like "When you were a baby, were you a little boy or a little girl?" or "When you grow up, will you be a mommy or a daddy?" Or the child may be shown a photograph of a boy or a girl and asked something like "Will Johnny be a mommy or a daddy when he grows up?" This aspect of the gender concept seems to develop by about age $4\frac{1}{2}$ (Slaby & Frey, 1975; Eaton & Von Bargen, 1981), although the timing varies quite a bit from one child to another.

The final step is the development of true **gender constancy,** which develops for most children at about age 5 or 6 (Slaby & Frey, 1975; Marcus & Overton, 1978). It involves a recognition that one's gender remains the same even though there may be changes in activity, dress, or appearance. For example, boys don't change into girls by wearing different clothes or by having different hair lengths. It may seem odd that a child who understands that he will stay the same gender throughout life (gender stability) can nonetheless be confused about the effect of changes in dress or appearance on gender. This sequence of development, though, has been found in both cross-sectional and longitudinal studies and seems to hold.

The underlying logic of this sequence becomes a bit clearer if we draw a parallel between gender constancy and the concept of conservation we described in Chapter 4. Conservation of mass or number or weight involves recognition that an object remains the same in some fundamental way even though it changes externally in some fashion. Since gender constancy involves recognition that gender remains the same despite external changes in a person's appearance, we can think of it as a kind of "conservation of gender." As such, it is a more abstract understanding of gender than what we see in gender stability.

In one interesting study, Dale Marcus and Willis Overton (1978) have looked specifically at the links between gender constancy and other forms of conservation. They found that gender constancy usually develops just after the child has mastered the conservation of quantity, as you can see in Table 6.2.

Once children have achieved a complete concept of gender, including gender constancy, they seem to pay more attention to the way other people of the same sex behave. It is as if the child now realizes that he really will be a boy for the rest of his life, so he'd better learn what boys do (learn the role). Children who are still at earlier stages of the development of the gender concept do show some sex-differentiated behavior, such as preference for certain types of toys (for example, dolls for girls, trucks for boys), but it isn't until after the child achieves full gender constancy that we see more consistent imitation of same-sex than of opposite-sex models.

A recent study by Diane Ruble (Ruble, Balaban, & Cooper, 1981) shows this pattern very nicely. She showed children a cartoon with a "commercial" in the middle. The commercial showed either two girls playing with a toy or two boys playing with the same toy. After the cartoon was over, the viewing children were encouraged to play with any of the toys in the room, which included the toy they had seen during the commercial. As you can see in Figure 6.4, children who had al-

TABLE 6.2
Relationship between Gender Constancy and Conservation of Quantity

Pattern of constancy and conservation	CHILD'S GRADE IN SCHOOL		
	Kindergarten	1st	2d
Child has neither	17	4	1
Child has conservation but not gender constancy	3	4	4
Child has both	4	14	18

SOURCE: Marcus and Overton, 1978, p. 440. © The Society for Research in Child Development, Inc.

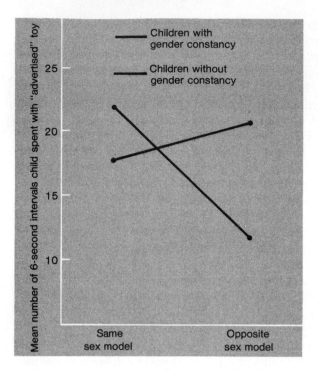

Figure 6.4. Results from Ruble's study show that children who had already achieved gender constancy were much more likely to imitate the same-sex model than the opposite-sex model, which suggests that once children figure out that gender is permanent, they spend considerable time trying to figure out just what they are supposed to do in order to be a boy or a girl. (*Source:* Ruble, Balaban, & Cooper, 1981, adapted from Figure 1, p. 670.)

ready achieved full gender constancy were much more influenced by the gender of the models in the commercial than were children who were at earlier levels of development of the gender concept.

Sex-Role Concepts and Sex-Role Stereotypes. As a result of observing and imitating the behavior of males and females, children begin to develop their ideas about how men and women are "supposed" to behave. That is, they gradually learn the *role* that is associated with their own gender and the role for the opposite gender as well. When these "generalized expectations" for other people's behavior become strong and rigid, we call them **stereotypes.** You will see the phrases *sex-roles concept* and *sex-role stereotypes* used almost interchangeably in many places, presumably because the evidence suggests that both adults and children have very powerful (and usually quite rigid) ideas about male and female roles and about appropriate male and female qualities.

We see the first signs of sex-role concepts and stereotyping in children as young as 3 (Kuhn, Nash, & Brucken, 1978); and by school age, children's ideas about appropriate or expected behavior for men and women match adult sex-role stereotypes quite closely. Studies of children in the United States, England, and Ireland by Deborah Best, John Williams, and their colleagues (Best, Williams, Cloud, Davis, Robertson, Edwards, Giles, & Fowles, 1977; Williams, Bennett, & Best, 1975) have found that by fourth or fifth grade, children see women as weak, emotional, softhearted, sentimental, sophisticated, and affectionate. They see men as strong, robust, aggressive/assertive, cruel, coarse, ambitious, and dominant. These lists of traits are remarkably similar to equivalent lists given by adults (Rosenkrantz, Vogel, Bee, Broverman, & Broverman, 1968).

There are two intriguing sidelights to the research on sex-role stereotypes in children and adults. First of all, stereotyping appears to be *strongest* at about ages 5 to 10, after which it declines somewhat (Ullian, 1981). Once the child figures out her gender, there seems to be a period of intense interest in all gender-related issues. Children of this age show almost total same-sex play groups, for example, and they are highly curious about "appropriate" behavior for males and females. During this period children are highly stereotyped in their views about acceptable behavior. You may recall from Chapter 4 that at the same age, we also see children insisting that the rules of games are absolute and unchangeable; this fixedness of approach to sex roles may thus be part of a larger cognitive strategy of searching for clear, fixed rules.

Once the child reaches preadolescence or early adolescence, however, *some* (but by no means all) of this absolutism disappears, and the child becomes more able to accept variations and alternatives.

A second interesting sidelight is that the male stereotype is consistently more clearly defined and more widely held than is the female stereotype. This greater clarity of the male role is evident in very young children and seems to continue into adulthood. In these days of the women's movement, you may be accustomed to thinking of the traditional female role as being the one that is narrowly defined and confining. However, the evidence we know of points to a greater rigidity in the male role. Male qualities are more highly *valued* by both men and women (Broverman, Broverman, Clarkson, Rosenkrantz, & Vogel, 1970), but the role is much more narrowly defined, beginning as early as age 5 or 6.

The Categorical Self during the School Years

By about age 5, a child can give you quite a full description of himself on a whole range of dimensions, including size, age, and gender. We have to remember, though, that the self-concept continues to undergo the same types of cognitive changes as do other concepts. Given what we know about cognitive development from ages 5 to 12 (Piaget's period of concrete operations), we would expect the content of the child's self-concept to get more complex, more elaborated, less and less focused on the external characteristics and more and more focused on internal qualities. This is precisely the shift that Montemeyer and Eisen (1977) have found in a study of the self-concept during the elementary-school years.

Using the "Who am I" procedure we had you try at the beginning of this chapter, these researchers found that the younger children in this study used mostly surface qualities to describe themselves, such as their age, their address, their appearance, and their favorite activities. By 11 to 12 years, the children had shifted toward descriptions of more internal qualities, such as likes and dislikes or personal skills or personality characteristics. The two quotes following can give you the flavor of the difference. A 9-year-old in the fourth grade:

> My name is Bruce C. I have brown eyes. I have brown hair. I have brown eyebrows. I am nine years old. I LOVE! Sports. I have seven people in my family. I have great! eye site. I have lots! of friends. I live on 1923 Pinecrest Dr. I'm going on 10 in September. I'm a boy. I have a uncle that is almost 7 feet tall. My school is Pinecrest. My teacher is Mrs. V. I play Hockey! I'm almost the smartest boy in the class. I LOVE! food. I love fresh air. I LOVE school.

An 11-year-old girl in the sixth grade:

> My name is A. I'm a human being. I'm a girl. I'm a truthful person. I'm not pretty. I do so-so in my studies. I'm a very good cellist. I'm a very good pianist. I'm a little bit tall for my age. I like several boys. I like several girls. I'm old-fashioned. I play tennis. I am a *very* good swimmer. I try to be helpful. I'm always ready to be friends with anybody. Mostly I'm good, but I lose my temper. I'm not well-liked by some girls and boys. I don't know if I'm liked by boys or not.

Both of these children have a concept of themselves; but as they have moved through the concrete operations period, the categories on which they are comparing themselves with others have become more complex and less external. As you'll see in Chapter 10, this process continues during adolescence, when the self-concept becomes still more abstract.

Self-Esteem

So far, we have talked about the self-concept as if there were no values attached to the categories by which we define ourselves. But that's clearly not the case. Look again at the 11-year-old's description of herself. Quite a few of her definitions are negative, while young Bruce C's description of himself is almost entirely positive. This positive-negative dimension of the self-concept is usually referred to as **self-esteem.** Children or adults with high self-esteem are those whose definitions of themselves are primarily positive, while those who define themselves in mostly negative terms are said to have low self-esteem.

Self-esteem is usually measured by having the child or adult answer a series of questions about himself, such as those we have listed in Table 6.3, taken from Stanley Coopersmith's instrument (1967). Using measures like these, several researchers have found that self-esteem is quite stable over time. The 6- or 7-year-olds who describe themselves in positive terms are likely to be doing so three or four years later as well. More important, children who differ in self-esteem also differ in other significant ways:

1. Children with high self-esteem usually do better in school than do children with less positive self-images, although this is not found in every study. Figuring out the causal connections in this case is extremely difficult. Do children who think well of themselves do well in school because they have high self-esteem, or do they have high self-esteem because they do well? No doubt both are partly true. Children who think well of themselves approach school tasks with a different attitude and different motivation than do those who see themselves as unsuccessful. But then achieving success in school reinforces the child's original view of herself, so the link between the two gets stronger. In younger children, too, successful mastery of new tasks raises the self-esteem, which encourages the child to try new, perhaps more difficult tasks.
2. They are usually found to have an internal rather than an external "locus of control." That is, they see themselves as responsible for their own success or failure, rather than seeing their behavior as controlled by such external events as luck or the whims of others.
3. They see themselves as having better relationships with their parents. Again there is a chicken-egg problem here. No doubt a good parent-child relationship contributes to high self-esteem—a possi-

TABLE 6.3
Some Sample Items from a Measure of Self-Esteem

I often wish I were someone else.

I am often sorry for the things I do.

I'm pretty sure of myself.

I can make up my mind and stick to it.

I wish I were younger.

I don't like to be with other people.

I'm pretty happy.

There are many times when I'd like to leave home.

My parents usually consider my feelings.

I'm a lot of fun to be with.

I'm doing the best work that I can.

I often get discouraged in school.

SOURCE: Coopersmith, 1967, pp. 265–266.

bility we explore in Box 6.1. However, it is probably also true that the child with high self-esteem enters into the parent-child encounter with a different attitude from the child who thinks ill of himself.

4. They have more friends than do children with lower self-esteem.

If we add up these characteristics, we can see that the child or young person with high self-esteem not only thinks well of himself but is generally successful—in school, in friendships, in relationships with parents. The sense of self-worth is an inner one, but it affects a wide range of outward behavior.

INDIVIDUAL DIFFERENCES IN THE SELF: TEMPERAMENT AND PERSONALITY

We have taken a brief look at differences in self-esteem, which is one of the major dimensions of individual differences in the self. Now let us cast our net a bit wider. Children not only differ in self-esteem, they also differ in the actual *content* of their self-concepts. One child behaves

BOX 6.1

Rearing a Child with High Self-Esteem

Where does high self-esteem come from? Is it something you just have, like blue eyes or black hair? Or are there specific experiences that foster it? This question has considerable personal relevance for at least two reasons. You may want to understand better where your own level of self-esteem came from, and you may want to rear your own children so that they have the benefit of high self-esteem.

All the evidence tells us that the child's self-esteem is heavily rooted in his family experiences. Stanley Coopersmith (1967), who has been one of the major researchers in this area, found that school-aged children with high self-esteem had parents with high self-esteem, too (which may suggest that some work on your own self-esteem would be a good first step if you are concerned about your children). More important, in families in which the children liked themselves, the children were treated as responsible individuals. Mothers in these families were more accepting and positive toward their children, more affectionate, and more

likely to praise the children for their accomplishments. They were interested in their children and showed it. They expected the children to have opinions and wanted them to share those opinions with others.

The parents of the children with high self-esteem also set fairly strict and clear limits for their children's behavior and applied those limits consistently. Such parents provide consistent guidance and discipline and are loving at the same time. You can see the differences between families of low and high self-esteem children on some of these dimensions in the table that follows.

This combination of firm but reasoned control, positive encouragement of independence, and a warm and loving atmosphere shows up again in a particularly interesting study of preschool children by Diana Baumrind (1972). She selected children who were content with themselves—self-reliant, self-controlled, and explorative—and compared them with children who had poor self-esteem, little curiosity and exploratory behavior, and little

in an outgoing and cheerful way with others. His self-concept may include the element of *friendliness*. Another child is quiet and studious. Her self-concept may include the element of *smartness*. Both children may have high self-esteem, but their behavior, as well as their self-concepts, differ markedly. Where do such differences come from?

We can think of several possible sources of such differences, all of which we want to examine more fully. First and most obviously, children may see themselves differently because they *are* different. Parents and researchers have noticed that beginning in the first days of life, infants differ in their reactions to the world around them. Some are easily soothed; others are cranky. Some react strongly to any new sensation; others are more placid. These differences seem to be inborn.

Additional differences in behavior are shaped by the environment in which the child grows. Some parents reward assertive or aggressive behavior in their children; others do not. Some children are rewarded by success when they attempt to throw a ball or hammer a nail; others are less successful and may begin to avoid physical activities that demand such coordination. These actual experiences are assimilated into

Some of the Characteristics of Parents of Children Who Are High, Medium, or Low in Self-Esteem

STATEMENTS THE PARENTS WERE GIVEN	PERCENT OF PARENTS WHO AGREED WITH THE STATEMENT WHOSE CHILD HAD		
	Low self-esteem	Medium self-esteem	High self-esteem
"The child should not question the thinking of the parents." *Authertaurian*	50%	25%	19%
"A child has a right to his own point of view and ought to be allowed to express it" *Permissive*	68%	100%	90%
"Children should have a say in the making of family plans." *Democratic*	41%	68%	77%

SOURCE: Coopersmith, 1967, pp. 209, 210, and 212.

self-reliance. The children with the highest self-esteem, self-reliance, and explorative tendencies had parents with the same combination of traits that Coopersmith found in parents of children with high self-esteem. Baumrind calls this combination **authoritative** parental behavior, in contrast to either **authoritarian** behavior (detached, controlling, and less warm) or **permissive** behavior (noncontrolling and undemanding, but quite warm and affectionate). In her study, the least self-reliant and effective children were likely to have permissive parents; the most positive and competent children were likely to have authoritative parents; and the children of authoritarian parents fell in between.

If you want your own children to emerge from early childhood with a strongly positive view of themselves, the moral is that you will need to love and respect the child, respond to his or her individual needs and skills, and set clear limits for the child's behavior. As parents, we both know that this formula is easier to state than to do, but it is clearly worth the effort.

the child's self-concept, and the concept accommodates to the new information.

Children also assimilate the comments other people make about them. "What a clumsy girl you are!" "John is so smart; he always does so well in school." "I don't think you've ever hit the ball straight." "My, how pretty you look today!" Such comments are part of what social psychologists describe as *attributions*. Each of us seeks to understand and explain our own behavior as well as the behavior of those around us. In particular, we try to figure out whether a particular behavior (our own or someone else's) is caused by some *internal* factor, such as a personal skill or trait, or by some *external* factor, such as luck or chance or special circumstances. When parents, teachers, or other children provide such explanations of a child's behavior, that information is absorbed by the child and may become part of his own *self-attributions*. So, for example, the next time the child hits a foul ball in the baseball game, he attributes this to some lack of skill on his part (an internal attribution) rather than to some other circumstance, like being especially tired that day. A personal example may help underline the power of this process:

I recall very vividly in my own early years that when something was broken in our house, no one asked, "Who broke the dish?" The question seemed (to me) to be instead, "Helen, when did you break the dish?" I have no way of knowing whether in fact I broke more things than other children did, but I came to *believe* that I did. My self-image then, and still, includes a sense of physical clumsiness. Nowadays when I break something, I automatically attribute it to clumsiness rather than to some external circumstance, like a slippery dish or someone bumping into me. [HB]

The roles we occupy also affect our concept of ourselves. We have already talked about the sex role, but there are many others that shape early behavior. The role of *child* has a certain content. As long as a youngster occupies that role, her concept of herself will conform, in part, to the role content. When her roles change, her self-concept will change as well.

Of these four sources of information for the self-concept—inborn differences, environmentally shaped differences, attributions by others, and role demands—psychologists have focused by far the most attention on the first two. Inborn differences in patterns of reactivity are described by the term **temperament.** The more inclusive term **personality** describes those unique individual patterns of behavior that are the product of both temperament and environmental influences. Since the self-concept is *part* of the personality, we can restate our original question: How do children come to have different personalities?

As you might guess, this is not a simple question to answer. Different theorists have offered distinctly different views of the origins of personality differences, each theory leading to somewhat separate sets of research. We can make the greatest sense out of this mixture by looking at the alternative theories and the evidence supporting each view. Then we can offer a beginning attempt at a synthesis of the several theories.

We have talked about each of these theories in earlier chapters, so this is not new territory. Now we need to see how the alternative theoretical approaches are applied to the specific question of personality development.

Temperament Theory of Personality

Many researchers and theorists have argued that infants, children, and adults are characterized by fundamental, inborn differences in *style* of responding—a concept that will be familiar from Chapters 4 and 5 (Thomas & Chess, 1977; Buss and Plomin, 1975; Rothbart & Derryberry, 1981). The most influential of these theorists have been Thomas and Chess, who describe nine dimensions of temperamental differences, which we've listed in Table 6.4. These nine dimensions, in turn, can be clustered into several basic types:

1. The "easy child" approaches new events positively, is regular in biological functioning (has a good sleep cycle, eats at regular intervals, and so on), is usually happy, adapts to change easily, and is moderately responsive to stimulation.

TABLE 6.4
Thomas and Chess's Nine Temperament Dimensions

Activity level	The amount of typical movement by the infant, and the amount of active time each day.
Rhythmicity	The predictability or unpredictability of the child's daily patterns.
Approach/withdrawal	The child's initial response to a new stimulus.
Adaptability	How easily the child's initial response to a new stimulus can be changed.
Threshold of responsiveness	The intensity of some stimulus required to trigger a response.
Intensity of reaction	The level of energy of the child's response, regardless of whether it is positive or negative.
Quality of mood	Pleasant, joyful, or friendly behavior in contrast to unpleasant or unfriendly behavior.
Distractability	Degree to which child's behavior can be interfered with or altered by an outside event.
Attention span and persistence	How long the child pursues any one activity, even in the face of obstacles.

SOURCE: Thomas & Chess, 1977, pp. 21–22.

2. The "difficult child," in contrast, is less regular in body functioning and is slow to develop regular sleeping and eating cycles. She shows negative reactions to new things and to change, cries, is often irritable, and is highly responsive to stimuli. This child reacts vigorously, often negatively. Once the difficult child has adapted to something, she is often quite happy about it; but the adaptation process itself is difficult.

3. The "slow-to-warm-up" child is not as negative in responding to new things or to new people as is a "difficult" child, but he shows a kind of passive resistance. Instead of spitting out new food violently and crying, as a difficult child might do, the slow-to-warm-up child may let the food drool out and may resist mildly any attempt to feed him more of the same. These children show few intense reactions, either positive or negative. Once they have adapted to a new person or to a new experience, however, their adaptation is generally positive.

Buss and Plomin (1975) have offered a somewhat simpler list of temperamental dimensions, which we have listed in Table 6.5. Obviously, there is not yet agreement on just what aspects of behavior we should label with the term *temperament*. There is agreement among temperament theorists, however, on two basic propositions: (1) temperament is inherited, and (2) it persists over time.

Since these are clear hypotheses, it ought to be possible to test them empirically. In recent years, a number of researchers have tried to do just that.

The Inheritance of Temperament. Studies of the genetic element in temperament have primarily used the twin study strategy we described in Chapters 4 and 5. If temperament is at least partly inherited, we should find the identical twins more like each other in temperament than are fraternal twin pairs.

TABLE 6.5
Buss and Plomin's Four Dimensions of Temperament

Temperament	Extremes of the dimension	Aspect of behavior
Activity	Active-lethargic	How much behavior does the person show?
Emotionality	Emotional-impassive	How intense is the behavior?
Sociability	Gregarious-detached	How close to others does the person seek to be?
Impulsivity	Impulsive-deliberate	How quickly does the person react, or how inhibited is the person's behavior?

SOURCE: Buss & Plomin, 1975, Table 1.1, p. 8.

Several studies provide support for this expectation. Buss and Plomin (1975) had mothers rate the temperaments of their twins on the four dimensions we listed in Table 6.5 and found that the correlations between the scores of identical twins were *much* higher than for fraternal twins, as you can see in Table 6.6. (You will recall that the closer a correlation is to 1.00, the stronger the relationship it describes.) What the numbers in Table 6.6 tell us is that mothers describe their identical twins very similarly, while their descriptions of fraternal twins vary a lot.

One of the problems with this study, though, is that the ratings are made by the mothers, who know that their twins are identical or fraternal. Perhaps they simply *expect* identical twins to behave more like each other and therefore rate them more similarly. One way to get around this problem would be to have independent observers provide ratings of temperament in identical and fraternal twins. As it happens, several groups of researchers have done just this. Goldsmith and Gottesman (1981) studied over 500 pairs of twins who had been tested as part of a large longitudinal study. When the children were given standardized IQ tests at 8 months, 4 years, and 7 years, the examiner rated each child on a series of behaviors such as shyness, irritability, and persistence. Usually the twins were tested by different examiners; thus if the identical twins were rated as having more similar behavior than were the fraternal twins, it would be good evidence for an inherited pattern. In fact, Goldsmith and Gottesman did find that there were several behaviors on which identical twins were seen as more alike than fraternals, such as activity level at 8 months, irritability at 4 years, and fearfulness at 7 years.

Since a number of other researchers have obtained similar results (Matheny, 1980; Torgerson & Kringlen, 1978; Plomin & Rowe, 1979), it looks very much as if there may be at least some genetic element in temperament. In particular, activity level and persistence seem to be especially influenced by heredity.

TABLE 6.6
Similarity of Identical and Fraternal Twins on Buss and Plomin's Temperament Dimensions

| TEMPERAMENT | CORRELATIONS BETWEEN SCORES OF PAIRS OF TWINS | | | |
| | FRATERNAL TWINS | | IDENTICAL TWINS | |
DIMENSION	*Boys*	*Girls*	*Boys*	*Girls*
Emotionality	.00	.05	.68	.60
Activity	.18	.00	.73	.50
Sociability	.20	.06	.65	.58
Impulsivity	.05	.59	.84	.71

SOURCE: Buss & Plomin, 1975, p. 19.

Consistency of Temperament over Time.   Consistency of temperament is also found, to at least some degree, in a number of recent studies. Adam Matheny and his colleagues (Matheny, Wilson, Dolan, & Kranz, 1981) have found that both negative responding (such as frequency of temper tantrums or irritability) and positive sociability (such as smiling or cuddliness) were somewhat stable over the first 6 years of life. Others, such as McDevitt and Carey (1981) and Rothbart (1981), have found that mothers' ratings of children's temperament are stable over the early years of life, especially in activity level and such aspects of sociability as smiling and laughter.

It may sound from this list of studies that we know quite a bit about the heritability and consistency of temperament. But that is misleading. There is still an enormous amount that we do not know. Researchers have used many different measures of temperament, so they have not all studied the same behaviors. Some have had parents describe their children; others have observed the children themselves for brief periods. Most have studied only young infants. We know far less than we would like about the consistency of temperament past about age 3 or 4. Nonetheless, despite the gaps in our knowledge, it does appear that each child begins life with *some* measurable and reasonably stable behavioral tendencies. Clearly not all behavior we see in a child is based on inherited temperamental differences. Temperamental patterns may, however, be the starting point from which personality develops.

Psychoanalytic Theory

We see a considerable change in theoretical emphasis when we turn to psychoanalytic theories of personality. For Freud and Erikson, personality arises not from largely inborn temperamental patterns but from the interactions of the child's needs and drives with the qualities of the environment. In particular, they see the response of the child's parents as especially critical in shaping the child's personality.

Among the several psychosexual and psychosocial stages proposed by Freud and Erikson, two seem to be particularly important for the development of the personality. The first stage, which Freud called the **oral stage** and Erikson calls the period of **trust versus mistrust,** is the time when the child develops the first, basic attachment to the caregiver (usually the mother). In order for the child to emerge from this period with a firm, secure sense of trust, Erikson believes the parents must be loving and must respond predictably and reliably to the child. Those infants whose early care is erratic or harsh may develop mistrust instead. Furthermore, the resolution of this first stage should affect the quality of the child's relationships with other people at future stages. For example, a child who achieves a basic, secure attachment should get along better with other children, with teachers, and eventually have more successful intimate relationships with others as an adult.

Figure 6.5. These two pictures show consistency in temperament very graphically. Both are of the same pair of identical twins, in the same order. The child on the right in both pictures was consistently of a more "difficult" temperament, while her sister on the left was consistently "easy." The photos also illustrate the fact that while temperament may be inherited, other factors must be at work too, since even identical twins can have different temperaments. (*Source:* Photos by Suzanne Szasz.)

Some Findings on Early Trust.   We will have a great deal more to say about the process of attachment in the next chapter. For now, we want only to point out that this particular feature of psychoanalytic theory has received a good deal of support from recent studies, particularly from the work of Alan Sroufe (such as Sroufe, 1978; Waters, Wippman, & Sroufe, 1979; Arend, Gove, & Sroufe, 1979). Children rated as being "securely attached" to their mothers at 12 or 18 months of age, compared to children with "insecure" attachments, have been found to be more friendly and outgoing with other children at ages 2 and 3 and to be more persistent and curious in their play and in school. Some typical results from a more recent study in this same area by Donald Pastor are in Figure 6.6.

Pastor had rated a group of 18-month-old children on the security of their attachment. Three to six months later, when the toddlers were 20 to 23 months old, he observed each child again in a standard situation, playing with another child who was a stranger to the subject. Observers rated the behavior of the children in a number of ways. For our purposes, the critical scores were a rating of "sociability," which included friendliness and cooperativeness to both the mother and the other child, and "orientation to peer," which included the degree of interest and attention the child showed toward the strange playmate. As you can see in Figure 6.4, toddlers who had been rated as securely attached when they were 18 months old were more sociable and more strongly oriented toward the other child than were toddlers who had been rated as insecurely attached.

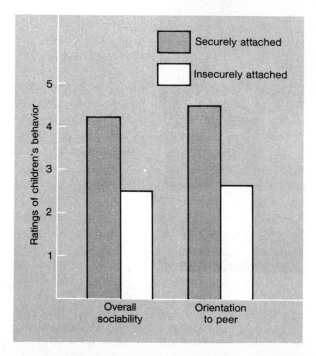

Figure 6.6.   A number of recent studies, like this one, have shown that children who are securely attached in the first 12 to 18 months of life are more sociable and skillful in their interactions with peers than are less securely attached children. (*Source:* Pastor, 1981, from Table 1, p. 331.)

Neither Pastor nor the other researchers in this area have followed their subjects much past early elementary school, so we don't know how lasting these differences may be. However, the research so far suggests that the resolution of the first stage of psychosocial development may have a major impact on the child's subsequent relationships. In extreme cases, where the parents are completely "psychologically unavailable" to the child (to use a phrase suggested by Sroufe), the effect appears to be particularly pervasive. Sroufe's research shows that children growing up with such parents are nearly always insecurely attached and show angry, noncompliant, and aggressive behavior with other children (Sroufe & Egeland, 1981).

The Oedipal Conflict and Its Consequences.   A second critical stage for the development of personality is the period around age 4 or 5, which Freud described as the **phallic stage** and which Erikson called the period of **initiative versus guilt.** It is during this period that Freud believed the **Oedipal conflict** occurred. He described this conflict more fully (and more credibly) for boys than for girls, so let us trace the proposed male pattern for you.

The theory suggests that at about age 4, maturational changes in the body lead to increased sensitivity in the genitals. At about the same time, the boy somehow becomes "intuitively aware of the mother as a sex object" (Rappoport, 1972, p. 74). Precisely how this occurs is not completely spelled out, but the important point is that at about age 4 the boy begins to have a type of sexual attachment to his mother and to regard his father as a sexual rival. His father sleeps with his mother, holds her, and kisses her, and generally has access to her body in a way that the boy does not. The boy's view of his father becomes complex and conflicting: The father is simultaneously seen as loving and protective and as powerful and threatening (with the ultimate power to castrate). The boy is caught between desire for his mother, his desire to keep his father's love and protection, and anxiety about his father's power. This conflict is resolved, Freud thought, by the boy's repression of his feelings for his mother and his **identification** with his father.

Identification is a process of taking in, of incorporating all that the father is—his behaviors, mannerisms, ideas, attitudes, morals, and sex role. In other words, it results in the child's adoption of that very set of behaviors and attitudes that we call personality. The boy thus becomes like his father, not because he inherited similar patterns but because he has intentionally created the similarity. He thinks that the more like his father he becomes, the more his father will love and shelter him and the less his father will aggress against him. In addition, by being like his father, he may also earn more of his mother's love.

The equivalent process (sometimes called the *Electra complex*) in girls is described less clearly in both Freud's work and in that of his followers. Supposedly, the girl sees her mother as a rival for her father's attentions, but her fear of her mother is less (perhaps because she assumes that she has already been castrated), and there may therefore be less full identification. For the girl the situation is different in still another way. Like the boy, her original love attachment is to her mother; but where the boy shifts to an identification with his father and continues to love his mother, the girl must shift her love to her father while maintaining an identification with her mother.

Despite the difficulties in the psychoanalytic interpretation of the phallic stage for girls, it is clear that in this theory identification is the central process in the development of personality in both sexes. Successful completion of the Oedipal crisis and full identification with the parent of the same sex are crucial for development of appropriate sex-role behavior, as well as for successful resolution of stages still to come.

There are several interesting implications of this view. First of all, if Freud is right, it is obviously important for children to have both parents present during the Oedipal period for the whole process to be successfully resolved. If one parent is absent because of divorce or other separation, then we ought to see significant disruption and incomplete identification. Furthermore, if it is the father who is absent—the most common pattern in our society—the effect ought to be greater for the boy than for the girl, since the boy would lack a male figure with whom to identify.

Research on children in divorced families supports the second of these hypotheses from Freudian theory but not the first. Judith Wallerstein and Joan Kelly (1980), in their extensive study of 136 children in 60 divorcing families, found that the child's age at the time of the divorce was not related to the likelihood of long-term problems. Children who were younger than 5 years of age when the divorce occurred showed more immediate difficulty; but five years after the divorce they were no more likely than were older children to be having problems.

On the other hand, it does appear to be the case that boys are more severely affected by divorce than girls are. Wallerstein & Kelly found this in their study, particularly if the boy did not have a continuing, loving relationship with his father after the separation. Hetherington, Cox, and Cox (1978, 1979) have found the same thing in a separate group of 72 divorcing families whom they followed for several years. Overall, it appears that the availability of a loving parent of the same sex is an important ingredient in the healthy growth of the child. It does not appear, though, that the Oedipal period is an especially crucial one for the formation of the relationship with that parent.

Social Learning Theories

Learning theory explanations of the results from studies of divorcing families would be quite different. Boys may show greater effects not because of any Oedipal conflict or failure to identify with the father, but simply because the reinforcement contingencies may change more for boys than for girls. In fact, that appears to be the case. Hetherington and her colleagues, in their study of divorcing families, found that mothers' behavior toward their sons was more critical and less positive than was their behavior toward their daughters (possibly because they saw their sons as more like the divorced/rejected husband). What should be clear from this example is that social learning approaches to the explanation of personality are logical extensions of learning explanations of other behavior. The fundamental proposition is that those characteristic behaviors that we call *personality* are the product of basic rules of learning, just as any other behaviors are. Since the likelihood of any behavior is increased if it is reinforced, then whatever patterns of behavior the parents (or others) reward ought to increase. Parents who reward aggression ought to have more aggressive children; parents who reward gregarious behavior, or kindness toward others, should have children who have more friends.

Partial Schedules of Reinforcement.   If you look back at our discussion of learning in Chapter 1, you'll discover another principle that has direct relevance for the development of personality in the child. Behaviors that the parents reward on a partial schedule—only rewarding the behavior occasionally instead of every time—ought to become particularly persistent and difficult to extinguish. Since most parents are inconsistent in their responses to their children's behavior, in the real world children experience many partial schedules of reinforcement.

There is considerable support for this aspect of the theory, both from experimental studies and from observations of actual family interactions. For example, in an older study, Sears, Maccoby, and Levin (1957) interviewed a large group of mothers of 5-year-olds. Based on the interviews, they rated each mother's *permissiveness* toward aggression (whether she allowed it to go on in the home) and her *punitiveness* toward aggression (whether she spanked the child, sent him to his room, or used some other form of punishment when the child did behave aggressively). Each child's level of aggression was also rated.

The pattern of permissiveness and punitiveness toward the child's aggressiveness that is most like a partial schedule of reinforcement would be a combination of high permissiveness and high punishment. Parents who show this combination are normally allowing the aggression to go on; but when they do react to it, they come down hard with punishment. Since the child may frequently get what he wants from the permitted aggression (taking another child's toy, for example), he is getting reinforced at least part of the time and punished part of the time. Given the fact that such parents are also providing the child with a *model* of aggressive behavior, this pattern of child rearing ought to be associated with high rates of aggression in the child. The pattern that ought to be associated with the *least* aggression in the child would be nonpermissiveness and nonpunishment, since children who encounter this combination of treatment are rarely reinforced for the behavior and are not seeing the parents demonstrate aggression either.

The results from the Sears, Maccoby, and Levin study show just this pattern, as you can see in Table 6.7. The parents who were both permissive and punitive toward aggression in their children had the most aggressive youngsters, and this was true for both sons and daughters. No doubt many parents who show this pattern believe that since they are disciplining their children when they behave aggressively, the children ought to be less violent. In fact, however, the parents have put the children on a partial schedule of reinforcement.

Gerald Patterson (1975) in his splendid book *Families* has described the ways in which these principles can be used by families with disobedient, aggressive, or uncontrollable children. In virtually every instance, the parents have unwittingly rewarded the child for the very behaviors they detest. Patterson helps families change the system by having them keep detailed records of the child's behavior and of their own responses. In this way the parents become aware of the reinforcement patterns they are actually using. Step by step, Patterson then has the parents introduce small changes into the system, altering the rewards. In this way, families that had despaired of ever being able to manage their children find that apparently intractable problems can be changed.

This illustrates an important point about social learning views of personality. If our behavior is a product of the reinforcement patterns we have experienced, then our behavior can change. In this view, children are not shy because they have an inborn temperamental disposition toward shyness or because they had an insecure first attachment to their mothers, but because they have been rewarded for shy behavior. If they can now be reinforced for more gregarious behavior —smiling, eye contact, intent listening, and the like—they should

TABLE 6.7

The Effect of Parents' Permissiveness and Punitiveness on Their Children's Aggressiveness

Pattern of discipline	PERCENT OF HIGHLY AGGRESSIVE CHILDREN	
	Boys	Girls
Low permissiveness, low punishment	3.7%	13.3%
Low permissiveness, high punishment	20.4%	19.1%
High permissiveness, low punishment	25.3%	20.6%
High permissiveness, high punishment	41.7%	38.1%

SOURCE: Sears, Maccoby, & Levin, 1957, p. 260.

become more friendly. A number of researchers, in fact, have been able to change shyness in elementary-school children by enrolling the youngsters in special social skills training groups (Ladd, 1981).

Observational Learning.   Another highly significant element in the social learning explanation of personality development is observational learning. Children learn a full range of behaviors from watching others perform them—everything from generosity to critical language. They learn from their parents, their peers, from television, books, and from all other sources. Some of these models, such as television, are the same for most children, which should tend to create similar patterns of behavior in all children who share those models. (We have discussed some of the effects of television models on children's behavior in Box 6.2.) Parental models, though, also differ from one family to the next, so the child's learning will be individual as well as collective.

There is an apparent parallel here between the concept of modeling and Freud's concept of identification. In both theories, many of the child's individual patterns of behavior are thought to arise out of imitation of the parents. However, the social learning theorists do not feel the need to introduce a complex internal process like identification to explain the child's imitation. They assume that learning by imitation is a normal process in human behavior and that the child is directly reinforced for imitating the parent. Thus while the two theories have some surface similarity, the assumptions underlying the process are quite different in the two cases.

Cognitive Developmental Theories

The three theories we have already discussed represent the major, currently influential views of the origins of personality in early childhood. Neither Piaget nor any of his many proponents has offered a cognitive theory of personality development. Given the general silence of cognitive theorists on this subject, it seems a bit presumptuous of us to suggest a fourth theory—but we will do it anyway. It seems to us that the self-concept can be used as the centerpiece of a cognitive theory of personality and can help to integrate much of what we have said in Chapter 4 and in our discussion so far in this chapter.

The key notion is that the self-concept can be thought of as a *scheme* in Piaget's sense. The child assimilates experiences and information to this scheme, and the scheme changes (accommodates) over the early years of life. As we have already indicated, the developmental patterns for this process seem to be very similar from one child to the next, but the actual content of the self-concept differs among children. By the age of 4 or 5, each child has a self-concept scheme with unique content.

BOX 6.2

Television as a Source of Models for Children

Children obviously learn from observing their parents and other live models such as peers and teachers. In our modern culture, though, past the age of about 2 or 3, many children spend as many or more hours each day watching models on television than they do watching live models. The average preschooler watches about three to four hours a day, and the average 9- to 10-year-old watches four to six hours a day (Liebert & Schwartzberg, 1977).

What are children learning from all those hours in front of the television? Obviously, many things. Television characters demonstrate a wide range of behaviors, any of which a child might learn through viewing. Two kinds of possible effects of television viewing, however, have received the bulk of the research attention: the effects on aggression and the effects on children's sex-role stereotypes. Let us take a brief look at each of these.

EFFECTS OF TELEVISION VIOLENCE

The definition of violence used in most studies is "the overt expression of physical force against others or self, or the compelling of action against one's will on pain of being hurt or killed" (Gerbner, 1972, p. 31). By this definition, the average television drama has 6 acts of violence each hour, while children's cartoons have about 17 episodes of violence per hour (Gerbner, Gross, Morgan, & Signorielli, 1980). Even more disturbing is the fact that vio-

lence is concentrated in programs during the times of day when children are watching (Slaby, Quarfoth, & McConnachie, 1976). The highest levels of aggression were noted during the early morning, after school, and on Saturday mornings. On the whole, the violent episodes children see are performed by the "good guys" as well as the "bad guys" and are rewarded about as often as they are punished.

What is the effect of this extensive exposure to violent models? If social learning theory is correct, it ought to increase children's aggressive behavior because they will learn new kinds of violent actions and because they are "vicariously reinforced" by seeing the violent actor get rewarded for his aggression.

There has been a vast amount of research exploring exactly this question, and the conclusion now seems quite clear: The more violent television a child watches, the more aggressive he is likely to be. This is somewhat more true of young children, but it is found in studies of older children and adolescents as well (Comstock, 1980). The effect has been demonstrated in laboratory experiments in which children have been exposed to controlled doses of violent television fare and in studies of real-life situations. For example, one isolated Canadian town did not receive any television signals at all until fairly recently. Researchers were able to observe the children in the town before television was introduced and then again afterward. They found

Once this has occurred, both the child's thinking and her behavior are affected by the content of this scheme.

Remember that one of the characteristics of the process of assimilation is that a new experience or piece of information is modified as it is taken into existing categories. So once the child has developed his self-concept scheme, new information is *interpreted* in light of the existing scheme. Once a child believes he is uncoordinated, then the occasional times when he catches a ball well, or gets a hit in the baseball game, are chalked up to luck rather than to skill; and the underlying scheme isn't modified (accommodated) very much.

Thus the self-concept, once well formed, serves as a central mediating process for each of us, leading to stable differences in behavior. It affects the activities the child will choose and his interpretations (attri-

that the level of aggression among the children increased after television viewing became common (Roberts & Bachen, 1981).

In addition to affecting behavior, viewing violence on television affects children's *attitudes* about aggression and makes them more fearful. Joseph Dominick and Bradley Greenberg (1972) found that elementary-school-aged children who watched many violent programs were more likely to think that aggression was a good way to solve problems and were more willing to use violence to solve their own problems.

The Dominick and Greenberg study also showed that the effect of television was smaller when the parents disapproved of aggression and controlled it in the home. Parents who provide children with nonaggressive models in their own behavior may also reduce the impact. However, the overall effect seems clear from the research.

EFFECTS OF SEX-ROLE STEREOTYPING
ON TELEVISION

The portrayal of men and women in television programs is highly stereotyped. Gerbner (1972) and Sternglanz and Serbin (1974) have found that women are shown as more conforming, less effective, more dependent, and less physically active than men. Far more men occupy the central roles in television programs; and their characters have higher status, are more dominant and aggressive, and solve problems. The women characters mostly serve as handmaidens who stand around and hand the man his coat, type his reports, or listen to his troubles. Gerbner also found that female characters were more often shown as being powerless, rather than powerful. Once again we must ask: What is the effect of repeated exposure to such models?

The research evidence is not nearly as substantial as for television aggression, but the limited research suggests that children are indeed affected by the sex roles they see on television. Terry Freuh and Paul McGhee (1975) found that children who watched more than 25 hours of television a week had more traditional sex-role concepts than did children who watched less than 10 hours a week. Even more persuasive is an experiment by Emily Davidson (Davidson, Yasuna, & Tower, 1979), who found that children who were shown highly sex-stereotyped cartoons gave more stereotyped answers to questions about the qualities of men and women than did children who had seen cartoons depicting men and women in more equal roles.

It seems very clear that in our present culture, children are acquiring many of their ideas about society, about adult roles, about men and women, and about the appropriate use of violence from watching television. Television is not a harmless entertainment: It is an educational medium from which children and adults learn both behaviors and attitudes. For parents, the moral seems straightforward: If you want to control or influence your children's sex-role ideas and aggressive behavior, one of the things you will have to do is control or restrict the television they watch.

butions) of the events that take place. It *can* be modified (accommodated) if the child accumulates enough experience or evidence that does not fit with the existing scheme. If the child began to get a hit half the times he batted, he could not assimilate this information to his existing self-concept forever before there would be some change in the concept. However, since the child will tend to choose activities that fit his self-concept (such as avoiding baseball completely if he thinks of himself as uncoordinated), he will be partially protected from such nonconfirming experiences.

This view of the self-concept bears a good deal of resemblance to the theory of **self-efficacy** recently proposed by Albert Bandura (1977, 1982), whose social learning theory we described in Chapter 1. In discussing self-efficacy, Bandura has moved beyond the original limits of social learning theory to a consideration of internal influences on behavior. He argues, basically, that each person's beliefs about what he can and cannot do affect his thought patterns, his actions, and his emotional reactions. Adults choose activities at which they believe they can do well and expend more effort trying to succeed at such activities. They avoid those they feel incapable of managing. Both children and adults perform better on difficult tasks if they believe ahead of time that they can succeed. Interestingly, a person's perception of his skill (his interpretation of it, if you will) is more important than his actual performance in determining later skill.

All of Bandura's research on self-efficacy in adults lends considerable support to our proposal of a self-concept theory of personality. Thus far there is little information on the *origins* of feelings of self-efficacy in children. No doubt the factors that influence high self-esteem (see Box 6.1, page 222) are part of the picture, along with actual experiences of success. It does seem abundantly clear, though, that what a child believes about himself (his self-concept) shapes his behavior, his attitudes, his feelings, and his thoughts in pervasive ways.

A Tentative Synthesis

We have presented four different views of the origins of those unique, individual patterns of behavior we call personality. Each view can be at least partially supported with research evidence, so it seems impossible to choose one of the four as the "correct" view. We would argue instead that they are all partially correct. Can we add all of these partially correct ideas into a complete theory? If we merely add all the elements together, we might get a theoretical model that looked something like the one in Figure 6.7.

What we have suggested in this first attempt at synthesis is that personality is somehow the sum of the child's temperament, his experiences after birth (specific reinforcement patterns and general family environment), and his self-concept. Surely, though, this is much too simple. The outcome we see is *not* just the sum of three independent forces. The several factors interact in complex ways. The actual process probably looks much more like Figure 6.8.

In this second synthesis, we still see inborn temperament as the beginning point—the base on which everything must be built (arrow number 1). The treatment the child receives from the parents is still influential as well (arrow 2). However, these two elements are not independent of one another. The way a child is treated is influenced by her temperament (arrow 3). Cranky, difficult children elicit different responses from their parents than do more placid, easygoing, sociable children (Campbell, 1979). Difficult children are punished more (Rutter, 1978), for example, which may only increase the likelihood that they will behave in less pleasant ways.

Both the basic temperament and the environmental events, in turn,

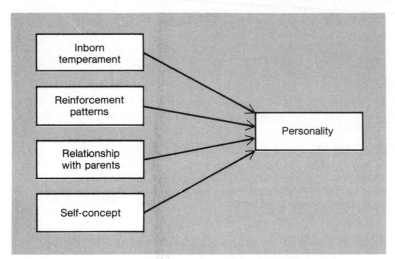

Figure 6.7. A simple additive model for the way personality might be formed from separate influences of temperament, reinforcement, general environment, and self-concept. While all these elements appear to be important, this view of the way they might operate is far too simple.

affect the child's self-concept (arrows 4 and 5). And the self-concept, in turn, affects the behavior we see.

A recent study by Susan Crockenberg (1981) nicely illustrates one way in which this interactive system can work. Crockenberg studied a group of 46 mothers and infants over the first year of the child's life. The child's irritability (an aspect of temperament) was measured when the baby was 5 to 10 days old, and the security of the child's attachment to the mother was measured when the child was 12 months old. We might expect that irritable babies would be more likely to be insecurely attached, merely because they are more difficult to care for. In fact Crockenberg did find that. But the picture is even more complicated than that. Crockenberg also measured the level of the mother's social support—the degree to which she had family and friends who were sufficiently helpful to assist her in dealing with the strains of a new child and any other lifestyle changes she might be experiencing. The results of the study, which are summarized in Table 6.8, show that when the mother had *both* an irritable baby *and* low levels of support, the infant was likely to be insecurely attached. However, either factor by itself

TABLE 6.8
Influence of Child's Temperament and Mother's Social Support on Children's Secure or Insecure Attachment
An Example of an Interaction of Influences on the Development of Personality

Child's irritability	Mother's support	Children with secure attachment	Children with insecure attachment
High	Low	2	9
High	High	12	1
Low	Low	7	2
Low	High	13	2

SOURCE: Crockenberg, 1981, p. 862, Table 5.

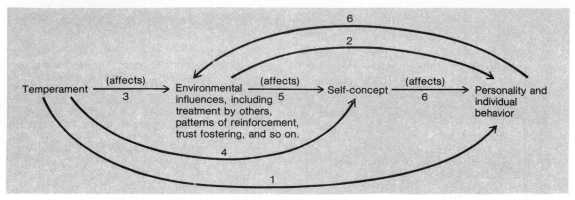

Figure 6.8. A more complex, interactive model for the formation of personality. Rather than merely adding, the environmental effects and the child's temperament both influence each other, and both affect the child's self-concept. What we think of as personality is a complex product of all three.

had little effect on the security of the child's attachment to the mother. Mothers with adequate social support were able to care for their irritable babies in ways that fostered secure attachment; those with inadequate support whose babies were not irritable were also able to support the baby's attachment. Only when the two difficult conditions occurred together did a poor outcome result for the child.

Finally, arrow 6 again points to the *transactional* aspects of this system. Once the child's unique pattern of behaviors and attitudes (personality) is formed, this affects the environment he will encounter, the experiences he will choose, the responses of the people around him.

What we call personality is thus a blend of innate temperament with the patterns of stimulation and care the child receives from the parents and others. The parents are, in turn, influenced by the child's temperament and emerging personality, and their ability to respond supportively to the child is affected by a wide range of things in their own lives. All of these elements affect the child's self-concept, which, once formed, serves as a mediator for the system, directing the child's behavior and making change more difficult.

Obviously, this is only a very primitive synthesis. There is much we do not yet know. Still, searching for the ways in which the several causal forces interact with one another seems to us to be a large step forward from a position of competing theories. The theories can be, and are being, fruitfully combined.

SUMMARY

1. The self-concept is a detailed, pervasive set of ideas about the self that develops early in childhood and persists throughout life. It is a cognitive accomplishment but has its roots in social interactions.
2. The earliest stage in the development of the self-concept is the development of the "existential self," which occurs in the first months

of life as the child figures out that she is separate from others. Such an awareness of self is clearly present by 18 months.

3. Beginning at 18 to 24 months, the child begins the development of the "categorical self" by comparing himself to others on a range of dimensions. Among the early relevant dimensions are size, age, and gender.

4. The gender concept appears to develop in stages between 12 months and about 6 years. The earliest step is simply awareness of the dimension of gender in the self and in others.

5. The remaining steps are gender labeling, observed at about age 2, followed by gender stability and gender constancy. By about age 5, most children understand that their gender will remain the same throughout their lifetimes and cannot be altered by changes in appearance.

6. During these early years children also develop ideas about the appropriate behaviors for each sex role. Sex-role concepts are maximally stereotypic during the early elementary-school years, and the male role is more fully defined than the female role.

7. Over the elementary-school years the categorical self becomes increasingly complex as the child defines herself using more and more abstract categories.

8. The positive/negative dimension of the self-concept is self-esteem. Children with high self-esteem ordinarily do better in school, see themselves as in control of their own destiny, have more friends, and get along better with their families.

9. Children from families in which their independent achievements are valued and praised, in which there are warm, affectionate relationships between parents and children, and in which clear limits are set are more likely to have high self-esteem.

10. Individual differences in the content of the self-concept arise from actual differences such as temperament, from differences in treatment by parents and others, and from actual experiences. Collectively, the individual, unique pattern of behavior and self-concept is called the personality.

11. Four different theories about the origins of personality offer insights into the source of individual differences.

12. Temperament theorists argue that basic behavioral tendencies are inherited and persist over the life span. Research evidence provides at least preliminary support to both ideas.

13. Psychoanalytic theorists (Freud and Erikson) emphasize the role of the interaction between the child's needs and drives and the responses of the people around the child. In particular, the first relationship with the major caregiver is critical, as is the period around ages 4 to 5 when the Oedipal crisis is thought to occur.

14. Considerable evidence supports the expectation that the first attachment is important. Children insecurely attached in the first

year of life have greater difficulty relating to peers later. Evidence supporting the importance of the Oedipal period is far weaker.

15. Social learning theorists explain personality differences by relying on basic principles of learning. The concept of a partial schedule of reinforcement is particularly helpful in accounting for the effects of parental discipline on children's behavior.

16. Observational learning (modeling) is also a major source of children's behavior. For example, children learn both aggressive behavior and sex-role stereotypes from watching television models.

17. A cognitive developmental theory of personality is also possible. The self-concept can be thought of as a scheme to which information is assimilated. Once well formed, the self-concept serves as a mediator, affecting the child's choice of activities, behaviors, and feelings.

18. All four views are partially correct and can be combined into an interactionist view of personality development. Temperament serves as the base from which personality grows. It affects behavior directly and also influences the way others respond to the child. Both in turn affect the child's self-concept, which then helps to create stability in the child's unique pattern of behavior.

KEY TERMS

Authoritarian parental style   Pattern of parental behavior described by Baumrind that includes high levels of directiveness and low levels of affection and warmth.

Authoritative parental style   Pattern described by Baumrind that includes high levels of control and high levels of warmth.

Categorical self   The major content of the self-concept. Descriptions of the self in terms of categories such as size, age, color, gender, beliefs, and personality traits.

Existential self   The most basic part of the self concept: the sense of being separate and distinct from others.

Gender awareness   The first step in the development of the gender concept. The child becomes aware of the dimension of gender.

Gender concept   The broad concept of his own gender and the gender of others, developed by each child during the first 5 to 6 years.

Gender constancy   The final step in development of a gender concept. The child understands that gender does not change even though there are external changes like clothing or hair length.

Gender labeling   The second step in gender concept development. The child labels herself and others correctly according to gender.

Gender stability   The third step in gender concept development. The child understands that a person's gender continues throughout the lifetime.

Identification   The process of taking into oneself the qualities and ideas of another person, which Freud thought was the result of the Oedipal conflict, at ages 3 to 5.

Initiative versus guilt   The third psychosocial stage proposed by Erikson, corresponding in time to Freud's phallic stage and the period of the Oedipal crisis.

Oedipal conflict The pattern of events Freud believed occurred between ages 3 and 5 when the child, in part because of fear of possible reprisal from the parent of the same sex and sexual desire for the parent of the opposite sex, identifies with the parent of the same sex.

Oral stage The first psychosexual stage proposed by Freud.

Permissive parental style A third style described by Baumrind, including high warmth and low levels of control.

Personality The unique, individualized pattern of thinking and reacting to the world around us that is characteristic of each child and adult.

Phallic stage The third psychosexual stage proposed by Freud. Heightened sensitivity in the genitals during this period is one factor triggering the Oedipal conflict.

Self-concept The broad idea of the self including the existential self, the categorical self, and the self-esteem.

Self-efficacy Term suggested by Bandura to describe the degree to which a person feels capable of performing some action.

Self-esteem The positive or negative quality of the self-concept.

Sex role The "job description" for male and female behavior in a given culture, including behaviors that are expected and those that are discouraged or forbidden, as well as the attitudes and skills that go with the role.

Stereotypes A fixed set of ideas or expectations about a group of people—such as males, females, blacks, or other groups—that are applied to each new member of the group automatically, without adjustment for individual characteristics.

Symbiotic Freud's word to describe the mutually interdependent relationship between the mother and infant during the earliest months of life.

Temperament An inborn, persisting set of behavioral tendencies on such dimensions as activity level, persistence, and sociability.

Trust versus mistrust First psychosocial stage proposed by Erikson. If no trust relationship is formed in the first year of life, mistrust may result.

SUGGESTED READINGS

Baumrind, D. Socialization and instrumental competence in young children. In W. W. Hartup (Ed.), *The young child: Reviews of research* (Vol. 2). Washington, D. C.: National Association for the Education of Young Children, 1972.

An excellent and not very difficult paper describing Baumrind's research on the development of competence in young children.

Comstock, G. New emphases in research on the effects of television and film violence. In E. L. Palmer & A. Dorr (Eds.), *Children and the faces of television.* New York: Academic Press, 1980.

A reasonably up-to-date and well-written review of the research in this important area.

Rivers, C., Barnett, R., & Baruch, G. *Beyond sugar and spice. How women grow, learn, and thrive.* New York: Putnam, 1979.

An excellent, very readable new book on sex-role development in girls. The book was designed for a nonprofessional audience, so you will find it less technical than some other books we have suggested.

PROJECT 6.1
Sex Roles on Television

As a follow-up of Box 6.2, we thought you would find it both instructive and enjoyable to watch a little television and see what sort of sex-role stereotypes are portrayed. This time we would like you to design your own project, using one of the following general formats or introducing elements of your own.

Option 1. Watch at least eight hours of television, spread over several time periods, and record the number of male and female characters and whether they are the central character or a minor character.

Option 2. Watch four to six hours of television, selecting among several different types of programs, and note the activities of each male and female character in the following categories: aggression, nurturance, problem solving, conformity, constructive/productive behavior, and physically exertive behavior.

Option 3. Watch four to six hours of television, selecting among several different types of programs, and focus on the consequences of various actions by male and female characters: positive outcome resulting from own action, positive outcome resulting from the situation or from someone else's action, neutral outcome, negative outcome resulting from own action, negative outcome resulting from the situation or the action of others.

Option 4. Watch and analyze the commercials on at least 10 programs, making sure that the programs cover the full range of types, from sports to soap operas. You might count the number of male and female participants in the commercials and the nature of their activity in each case, using some of the same categories listed in Option 2.

Whichever one of these projects you choose, you must define your terms carefully and record your data in a manner that makes it understandable. In writing up your report, include the following: an *introductory* section, in which some of the background literature is described and your hypotheses are given; a *procedure* section, which must include details of the programs you observed, how you selected them, what specific behaviors you recorded, how you defined your behavioral categories, and any other details a reader would need to understand what you actually did; a *results* section, in which the findings are reported, using graphs or tables as needed; and a *discussion* section, in which your results are compared to those of other researchers (as cited in the book or elsewhere) and any puzzling or unexpected findings are discussed and explained if possible. Additional research projects may also be suggested.

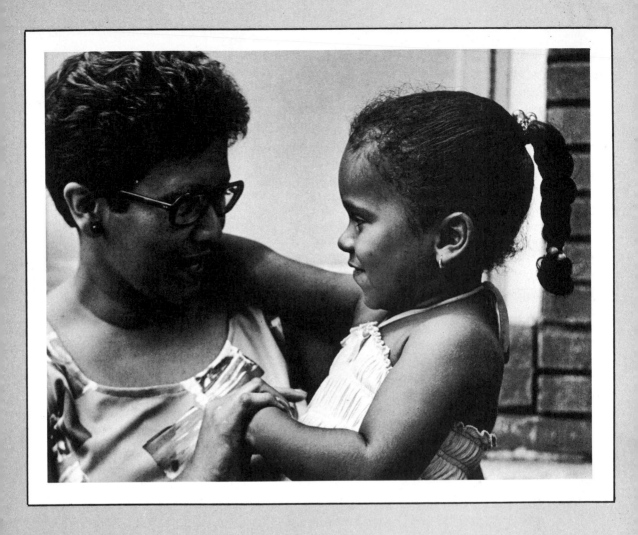

Chapter 7
Social Relationships in Children

(7)

Six months ago I watched my sister-in-law, Donna, with her 2-month-old son Lars. She was sitting with her knees bent and raised with the baby lying on her lap, his head on her knees. By raising her legs or bending her upper body she could vary the distance between them, and she could look directly into his face all the time. Anyone who has watched such an interchange will know the feeling that I experienced—I smiled from ear to ear as I saw the two of them launch into an intricate, joyful, "dance" with one another. Donna leaned over so that her face was close to the baby's, raised her eyebrows, smiled widely, and spoke in a lilting voice. "Lars (pause). Lars (pause). Are you going to look at me?" Lars locked his eyes on hers, and her smile grew even wider. *That's* a good boy (pause). Can you smile at your momma? Can you? Is that a smile I see?" She waited a moment and then reached her hand to his face, touching him lightly. A small smile crept into his expression, which gradually widened. For about 5 seconds the two of them sat there beaming at one another before Lars broke off the contact by looking away.

Lars is now 8 months old, and he is much more skillful at this "dance." He smiles more, coos, babbles a little, kicks his feet, reaches out for his mom. She talks to him in more complex sentences, tickles him more, and uses many more playful actions with him. But there is another change, too. When he was 2 months old, Lars would let me "dance" with him, too. I could entice a small smile and feel him relax in my arms. Now he clearly prefers his mother and father to anyone else. His best smiles, his warmest greetings, are reserved for them. [HB]

This brief description of Donna and Lars focuses our attention on an aspect of development we have largely neglected so far, namely, the child's relationships with others. We pointed out in the last chapter that the self-concept develops out of interactions with and comparisons with others. But just what is the nature of those interactions?

The central concept we will use in most of our discussions of social relationships is that of **attachment.** We can see examples of attachment in the interactions of Donna and Lars. She was clearly attached to him when he was 2 months old (in fact, from the time of his birth), and he shows attachment to her at 8 months.

The use of the attachment concept to describe the interactions of the infant with his parents has become familiar in developmental psychology. However, we agree with John Bowlby (1969, 1973, 1980) that most of the close, intimate relationships between individuals throughout the life span can be thought of in terms of attachments. Furthermore, we can understand many of the major transitions in life—such as children leaving home, the death of a parent or a spouse, a divorce or the breakup of a love affair, even the loss of a job—in terms of *de*-tachment. Throughout our lives we become attached to other individuals. Those attachments may strengthen and endure, or they may weaken and disappear. In every case, though, our relationships with others are colored by the pattern of attachments in our lives.

If this is a reasonable way to think about social interactions over the life span—and we think it is—then it is important for us to begin here by exploring the first attachment between child and parent and between parent and child. We can then move outward to look at the child's relationships with other children.

ATTACHMENT AND ATTACHMENT BEHAVIOR: DEFINITIONS

As Bowlby has described it, an attachment is an important emotional link, an "affectional bond" between two people. The child or adult who is attached to another person uses her (or him) as a "safe base" from which to explore the world, for comfort when stressed or distressed, and for encouragement. A parallel concept in theories about adult relationships is that of the **social network,** which we might think of as a set of attachments serving important equivalent functions, such as providing intimacy, nurturing, reassurance, and assistance (Weiss, 1969). When we talk about attachment in this way, we are talking about an invisible internal structure (perhaps even a scheme in Piaget's language).

This definition of attachment raises a problem. If an attachment is invisible, then how do we know when it exists? We *infer* it from the presence of **attachment behaviors,** just as we infer a child's intelligence or cognitive competence by looking at the way she solves problems. Attachment behaviors are all those behaviors that allow a child or adult to achieve and retain proximity to someone else to whom he is attached. This could include smiling, making eye contact, calling out to the other person across a room, touching, clinging, crying. It is important to make clear that there is no one-to-one correspondence between the strength of the underlying attachment and the number of attachment behaviors a child (or adult) may show on any particular occasion. A child with a strong, secure attachment to a parent may play happily in the same room with the parent, showing only occasional glances or other contacts. On another occasion, the same child may show high levels of attachment behaviors. The task of inferring the quality of the attachment from the observed behaviors is thus a complex one.

Still, this distinction between attachment and attachment behavior is an essential one, particularly when we talk about the infant's attachments and attachment behaviors toward the parent. Furthermore, it is relevant when we look at the parent's involvement with the child as well. Let us begin by looking at the way in which parents form their attachment to the baby and then turn to a look at the development of the child's attachment to the parents.

THE ATTACHMENT PROCESS: PARENT TO CHILD

Current research points to a two-step process in the development of the parent's attachment to the child. There appears to be an early bond (attachment) formed at birth or shortly after. This bond is then strengthened by the opportunity to engage in mutual attachment behaviors with the baby.

The First Step: The Initial Bond

Several years ago, two pediatricians, Marshall Klaus and John Kennell, suggested that there was a critical period immediately following the birth of a baby for the formation of the mother's attachment to her child (Klaus & Kennell, 1976). They argued that mothers who have the opportunity to fondle and hold their infants in the first few hours after delivery should have much stronger bonds to their babies than should mothers who were separated from the infant for a period after delivery.

Klaus and Kennell's early research on parent-infant bonding was flawed in a number of respects, and they may well have generalized beyond their data. However, the issue they raised had considerable practical as well as theoretical relevance. The common practice in hospitals in the United States in the 1970s (and still in many hospitals today) was to separate mother and infant immediately after birth, with no extended contact until 12 to 24 hours later. If Klaus and Kennell were correct, this practice might well be detrimental to the mother and child. Because of the importance of the question, their proposals spurred improved research by a number of investigators whose results are now available.

The basic design has been to give one group of mothers either early contact with their infants or extended contact with the infant over the first few days of life, or both. Another group is given normal hospital treatment involving delayed or less extensive contact with the baby. These several groups are then observed with their infants in the hospital, or later at home, to see whether there are any differences in the attachment behaviors the mothers show toward their children.

Short-term Effects.   The results of all this research suggest that *early* contact does have some effect on mothers, at least in the first few days or weeks of the child's life (Campbell, Taylor, & Taylor, 1980; Carlson et al., 1979; de Chateau, 1980).

Some findings from a well-designed, recent study done in Germany by Karin Grossmann and her colleagues (Grossmann, Thane, & Grossmann, 1981), which we have shown in Figure 7.1, make the point clearly. In this study mothers were assigned randomly to one of four groups: (1) an early contact group, in which the mothers had a minimum of half an hour to handle the infant immediately after birth, (2) an early and extended contact group in which the mother had the first half-hour contact plus a rooming-in arrangement, which allowed an additional

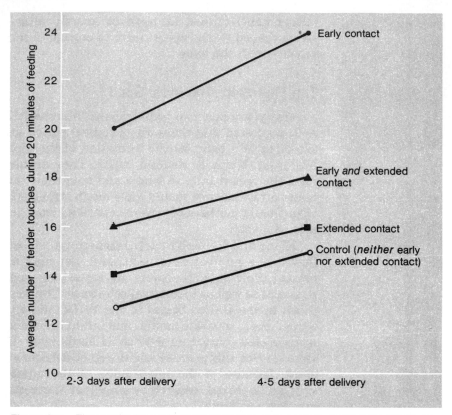

Figure 7.1. The results from this study show that early contact, and not the length or frequency of contact, is the important ingredient in affecting the earliest bond between mother and infant. (*Source:* Grossmann, Thane, & Grossmann, 1981, Figure 2, p. 164.)

5 hours per day of contact with the baby while in the hospital, (3) an extended-contact group *without* the first hour of early contact, and (4) a normal hospital group that had neither early nor extended contact. The mothers in all of these groups were observed periodically while feeding their infants. What we have shown in Figure 7.1 is the amount of tender touching the mothers showed toward their babies during these observations. As you can see, both groups with early contact showed more tender touching than did the extended contact or normal groups, which suggests that it is the timing and not the amount of early contact that really makes a difference. (Unexpectedly, the early contact only group showed the highest level—a finding that neither we nor Grossmann can easily explain.)

There are some qualifications to this conclusion. For example, de Chateau (1980) found that the positive effect of early contact was especially marked for mothers with their first babies, and a few researchers (for example, Svejda, Campos, & Emde, 1980) have found no effect at all of early contact. The weight of the evidence, though, points to at least a small initial effect. Mothers with early contact appear to be more strongly "bonded" to their infants.

We do not yet know enough about the nature of the "glue" that is involved in forming this strong, early bond between mother and child. Why is the glue stickier if there is early contact? Klaus and Kennell argue that there is some physiological readiness of the mother to form an attachment in the hours immediately after birth. If that time goes by without an opportunity for contact, the special moment of readiness is lost. Another ingredient in the mixture may be the particular alertness the baby displays in the first hours after delivery, which may enhance the mother's responses. Whatever the explanation, the phenomenon itself is quite well documented. The next critical question is whether the effect of this early bond persists past the first days of the child's life.

Long-term Effects of the Early Bond.   When we turn to look at research on the longer-term effects of early contact, the conclusions become far more tentative. Klaus and Kennell (Kennell, Jerauld, Wolfe, Chesler, Kreger, McAlpine, Steffa, & Klaus, 1974; Ringler, Trause, & Klaus, 1976) found some effects of early contact lasting as late as age 2. One year after delivery the early contact mothers in this study showed more soothing behavior toward the baby when he cried and were more involved and attentive when a physician examined the baby. At age 2, the early contact mothers used more complex language in talking to their infants than did mothers in the control group. Similarly, de Chateau (1980) found that the early contact group in his study breast-fed their infants longer and returned to work later than did the mothers who lacked early contact.

Other researchers have *not* found lasting effects. In the study by Grossmann that we showed in Figure 7.1, the higher level of tender touching in the early contact group did not persist. The control group mothers showed an increase in tender touching, and all the other groups declined, so that nine days after delivery there were no group differences. Furthermore, in a study done in Sweden, Carlsson (1979) found that the effect of early contact on specific maternal caregiving behaviors washed out after six weeks.

Our conclusion is that early contact has only a small and not very lasting effect on the amounts of such *specific* behaviors as smiling or touching. However, it does appear to have some small lasting effect for at least some mothers if we look at broader measures of the mother's attachment, such as whether she chooses to stay home with her child longer or whether she cares for the child adequately.

The most persuasive evidence we know of on this point comes from a study by Susan O'Connor and her colleagues (O'Connor, Vietze, Sandler, Sherrod, & Altemeier, 1980). They have followed a large group of poverty-level mothers who were given early and extended contact through a rooming-in arrangement in a Nashville, Tennessee, hospital. Other similar mothers in the same hospital were randomly assigned to a more traditional care arrangement, and these two groups have now been followed through the first 18 months of the children's lives. O'Connor's interest has been in a global measure of the mother's behavior, which she calls "adequacy of parenting." Inadequate parenting was indicated if the child was physically abused or neglected, if the child was repeatedly hospitalized, or if the parents relinquished custody of the child.

Table 7.1 shows the number of rooming-in and normal-hospital-routine mothers who were rated as showing inadequate parenting. As you can see, the actual number of inadequate parents is quite small. Only about 7 percent of the control group (normal-hospital-routine) mothers showed inadequate parenting. Obviously, the lack of early contact did not have a major negative effect in most cases. But the rate of inadequate parenting was *less* in the early contact group. Thus among mothers who may be especially high risk for abuse or for other failures of parenting, early contact may help *prevent* such abuse by aiding the formation of a stronger initial bond. For the majority of mothers, however, early or extended contact does not seem to be an essential ingredient in the long-term bonding process.

The Second Step: The Meshing of Attachment Behaviors

Not all parents are able to form a strong initial attachment at birth. There may be delayed contact, the infant may require special medical treatment that prevents early or regular contact (as is true of low birth weight infants, for example), or the child may be adopted. For any of these reasons, the child and parents may begin their home life together without a strong bond. The fact that most of these parent-child pairs

TABLE 7.1
Frequency of Parenting Inadequacy and Abuse in Families in Which the Mother Had Extended (Rooming-In) Contact or Regular Hospital Contact with Her Newborn

	Rooming-in group (143 cases)	Regular hospital group (158 cases)
Number with any kind of parenting inadequacy	2	10
Number referred to Children's Protective Service for suspicion of abuse	1	5
Number of children hospitalized for illness or failure to thrive	1	8

SOURCE: O'Connor, Vietze, Sandler, Sherrod, & Altemeier, 1980, pp. 356–357.

nonetheless manage to form such a bond over the first few months tells us that there must be a powerful backup system.

Over the early weeks and months, there develops between parent and child a mutual, interlocking pattern of attachment behaviors. The baby signals her needs by crying or smiling; she responds to being held by soothing or snuggling; she looks at the parents when they look at her. The parents, in turn, enter into this two-person "dance" by coming near the baby when she cries or gurgles, by picking her up, by waiting for and responding to her signals of hunger or other needs, by smiling at the baby when she smiles, by gazing into her eyes. It was exactly this mutual system that was visible between Donna and Lars.

One of the most intriguing things about this process is that we all seem to know how to do this particular dance. In the presence of a young infant most adults will automatically shift into a baby play act, which includes smiling, raised eyebrows, very wide open eyes, and a quiet, high-pitched voice. The baby runs through his half of the dance quite automatically, too. But while we can perform all these attachment *behaviors* with many infants, we do not become *attached to* every baby we coo at in the grocery store.

For the adult, the critical ingredient for the formation of a genuine attachment seems to be the opportunity to develop real mutuality—to practice the dance until the partners follow one another's lead smoothly and pleasurably. This takes time and many rehearsals. The parents of a newborn, especially if it is a first child, may feel clumsy or awkward with their infant. They don't read the baby's cues easily, and the interaction may be out of synchrony. As they care for the infant, play with him, and talk to him, the synchrony improves. The mother and father learn how to extract a smile from the baby and how to get the baby to look at them. They learn how to soothe and feed the baby. The smoother and more predictable the process becomes, the more satisfying it seems to be to the parents, and the stronger their attachment to the infant becomes.

Attachments by Fathers

Although we have used the word *parents* in the paragraphs you have just read, most of the research we have talked about so far has involved studies of mothers. Are all the same things true of fathers as well? Are fathers affected by an opportunity for early contact? Do they form attachments to their infants? The preliminary answer appears to be "yes" to both questions.

Fathers who are present at delivery, or who have some other opportunity to hold and fondle the child shortly after birth, report stronger feelings of attachment to the baby (Greenberg & Morris, 1974; Peter-

BOX 7.1

When Mutuality Fails: *Child Abuse and Other Consequences* *of Failure of Attachment*

The two-part system for fostering strong attachment by the parent for the infant is normally robust and effective. Most parents *do* become attached to their babies. However, attachment is a process requiring two partners, both of whom have the necessary signals and skills and the energy to enter into the "dance." When either partner lacks the skills, the result can be a failure of attachment or a weaker attachment by the parent to the child. Child abuse or neglect is one possible consequence of such a failure.

WHEN THE INFANT LACKS SKILLS

For the system to work, the baby has to possess a full repertoire of attachment behaviors. If there are some missing, real problems can ensue. For example, Selma Fraiberg (1974, 1975) has studied a group of blind babies, who smile less and do not show mutual gaze. Most parents of blind infants, after several months of this, begin to think that their infant is rejecting them, or they conclude that the baby is depressed. These parents feel less attached to their blind infants than to their sighted infants.

Similar problems can arise with parents of premature infants, who are usually separated from their parents for the first weeks or months (which may interfere with the first bond) and then are unresponsive for the first weeks after they are home from the hospital. Most mothers of premature infants work especially hard in those first months to stimulate their infants. In fact, these mothers show *higher* rates of involvement with and stimulation of their babies in the early months than do mothers of full-term babies (Field, 1977; Barnard & Bee, 1982). But eventually the mothers withdraw somewhat from the interaction since the babies so seldom respond with real mutuality.

Obviously, not all blind infants or premature infants or others who are different in some way end up being physically abused. Many parents manage to surmount these problems. But the rate of abuse is higher among prematures than term infants. Klein & Stern (1971) found, for example, that about a quarter of the abused children in their study had been born prematurely, even though prematures represent only about 8 percent of the total population. This doesn't mean, by the way, that a quarter

son, Mehl, & Leiderman, 1979). Whether this effect lasts we do not know, since no one we know of has followed a group of early contact fathers past the first days of the child's life. Still, it is an intriguing question, well worth exploring.

We do have information, though, about fathers' actual attachment behaviors toward their infants. The evidence suggests that the fathers' *initial* reactions to the newborn are virtually identical to the mothers' reactions, but that over the first months of life fathers develop a distinctive role that is different from that of mothers.

Ross Parke, in several studies (Parke, O'Leary, & West, 1972; Parke & O'Leary, 1976; Parke & Sawin, 1975; Parke, Grossman, & Tinsley, 1981), has observed fathers and mothers with their newborns and finds that when fathers are actually holding their infants, they touch, talk

of all prematures are abused. It does mean that they are overrepresented in the group of abused children.

WHEN THE PARENT LACKS SKILLS

The other partner in the dance is obviously the parent, and failure of attachment can just as well come from the parent's end of the system. A parent might lack attachment skill because she herself did not form a secure attachment with her own parents and did not learn the needed behaviors in later relationships. In fact, the majority of abusing parents were *themselves* abused as children, which makes this argument seem plausible.

Another factor that can affect a parent's ability to enter fully into the attachment process is the amount of other stress in his life. Parents with many children, with small living spaces, with uncertain incomes, and who lack friends or other sources of emotional support are much more likely to abuse their children than are parents with lower levels of stress (Light, 1973; Justice & Justice, 1976; Garbarino & Sherman, 1980).

When these two elements are combined—a child who is less able to respond fully for some reason and a parent who is less skillful in forming attachments or who is experiencing heightened stress—the likelihood that there will be a failure of attachment, and possibly neglect or abuse of the child, is greatly increased.

WHAT CAN BE DONE?

Fortunately, it is possible to intervene to help the unattached parent become more attached. Fraiberg (1974) found she could help the parents of blind babies to "read" the child's hand and body movements instead of waiting for smiles or eye contact. After such training, the parents of the blind babies found that their attachment to the baby was strengthened. Rose Bromwich (1976) has used a similar procedure with parents of children with other physical handicaps. She begins by finding some activity that the child and parent can do together that brings pleasure to both. When the level of basic mutual pleasure has been achieved, she then tries to help the parent become more attentive to the child's individual signals. Through this process, the parents' attachment to the child can be enhanced.

When actual abuse has already occurred, more extensive intervention may be needed. Henry Kempe and his colleagues in Denver (Kempe & Kempe, 1978), for example, report that they have had an 80 percent success rate with abusing families using a combination of a crisis hot line (to deal with their life stresses, among other things) and personal counseling to help the parents deal with their own early relationships and develop the skills needed to relate to their child. This is not a simple or quick process, but it can and does succeed.

to, and cuddle their babies as much as and in the same ways that mothers do. Mothers typically spend more time holding the baby; so the actual quantity of affectionate behavior shown to the infant by the father may be less, but the quality is the same (Parke & Tinsley, 1981). These findings suggest that the father's attachment to the infant is as strong as is the mother's.

Past the early weeks of life, however, we see differences in the behavior of fathers and mothers with their infants or toddlers. The *mother role* seems to involve not only routine caregiving, it also includes more talking and more quiet interactions. The *father role* involves more playfulness. Fathers do more physical roughhousing with their children and are more likely to play a game of some kind with the child. This distinction between the two roles has been found re-

Figure 7.2. Until the past few years, fathers have been the forgotten group in studies of infant development. However, recent research shows that fathers typically become strongly attached to their babies, as this father seems to be.

peatedly in studies in a number of countries (Parke & Tinsley, 1981).

Why does this difference occur? One possibility is that the person who is doing the major physical caregiving quite logically ends up doing less playing. Since mothers do most of the caregiving—and they do, even in families in which both parents work—perhaps these *mother* and *father* roles are really *caregiver* and *noncaregiver* roles. If that's true, then in those few cases in which the father is the major caregiver we ought to see a reversal of the typical care/play roles.

Michael Lamb and his colleagues (Lamb, Frodi, Hwang, Frodi, & Steinberg, 1972) have recently studied just such a group of caregiving fathers in Sweden, where the custom of paternal leave from work at the birth of a child is quite well established. Lamb located a group of families with 8-month-old children in which the father had spent at least one of the previous three months as the major caregiver. He compared the behavior of fathers and mothers in these families with the behavior of parents in more traditional families during a home observation when both parents were present with the child.

Surprisingly, the father's involvement in caregiving had little effect on the patterns of interactions Lamb observed. As you can see in Figure 7.3, mothers talked to and held the infants more and showed more affection and more physical care, regardless of whether they were the major caregiver or not. Fathers who were involved in the child's care did show less play than did fathers who were less involved, but they did not show more physical caregiving. Lamb concludes that "somewhat unexpectedly, the results of this study indicate that gender has a more important influence on parental behavior than does the individual's involvement in caretaking" (Lamb et al., 1981, p. 219).

This research still does not tell us whether the father and mother roles are somehow instinctive. They could still be products of broader cultural forces and imitation of other males. But the findings are intriguing. We hope other researchers will focus attention on this question in the future. For now, we can say that both parents seem to be equally attached to their infants, but that past the first few days of life they display that attachment somewhat differently.

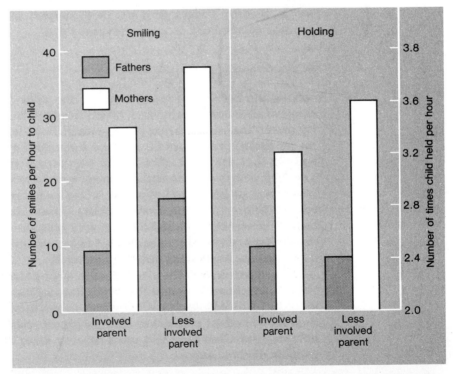

Figure 7.3. The involved parents in this study had all been the major caregiver for their 8-month-old infants for at least one month out of the previous three months. This major caregiving responsibility for the involved fathers, however, did not seem to have affected their patterns of interactions with their infants when mother, father, and infant were all together. Could this mean that mothers are naturally more likely to smile at and hold babies? Or could this difference still be culturally determined? (*Source:* Lamb, Frodi, Hwang, Frodi, & Steinberg, 1982, p. 218.)

THE ATTACHMENT PROCESS: CHILD TO PARENT

The process of attachment formation for parents seems to begin with the development of an initial bond and then extends to more skillful attachment behaviors. In contrast, the infant seems to begin with the attachment behaviors and develops the attachment itself somewhat later.

John Bowlby, in his extensive writings on the process of attachment (1969, 1973, 1980), has argued that a basic repertoire of attachment behaviors is instinctive in the infant and present at birth. As we pointed out in Chapter 2, newborn babies can cry, make eye contact, cling, cuddle, and respond to caregiving efforts by being soothed. These are all highly effective attachment behaviors since they keep people close by, providing care to the child. If an older infant or child directed such behaviors at someone, we would take it as evidence that the child was attached to that person. But the newborn shows no *preference* for any particular caregiver. There is thus no sign of an actual attachment. Based on their research, Mary Ainsworth and her colleagues (Ainsworth, Blehar, Waters, & Wall, 1978) suggest that the emergence of genuine attachment occurs in several steps.

Phase 1: Initial Preattachment

During the first 3 to 4 months of life, the baby displays a wonderful range of attachment behaviors, which Ainsworth describes as "proximity promoting"—they bring people closer. But because the child shows no consistent preference for any one individual over another, we cannot say that she is attached to any one person yet. (At 2 months, for example, nearly anyone could "dance" with Lars.) This preattachment phase *may* be linked to the young infant's relative lack of skill in discriminating one person from another. While discrimination on the basis of smell or sound may occur in very young infants, discrimination on the basis of visual cues seems not to be well established until about 3 months (as we pointed out in Chapter 3).

The importance of the visual cues in aiding the infant's discrimination is underlined by Selma Fraiberg's fascinating observations of blind infants (1975). Although such children do eventually establish clear attachments to their mothers or other caregivers, the process is considerably delayed since the child must develop other methods for making reliable discriminations.

Phase 2: Attachment in the Making

At about 3 months (when the baby can tell the difference between familiar and unfamiliar folks), she begins to dispense her attachment behaviors more discriminatingly. She smiles more at the people who regularly take care of her and may not smile readily at a stranger. Still, this is not yet a full-blown attachment to a *single* figure; there are still a number of people who are favored with the child's "proximity promoting" behaviors.

Phase 3: Clear-cut Attachment

Two important changes take place at about 6 to 7 months of age. First and most important, the child typically now has *one* person toward whom attachment behaviors are primarily directed. We can say for the first time that the child is genuinely *attached* to someone. Second, the dominant mode of his attachment behavior changes: He shifts from using mostly "come here" signals (proximity promoting) to what Ainsworth calls "proximity seeking." Because the 6- to 7-month-old begins to be able to move about the world more freely by creeping and crawling, he can move *toward* the caregiver as well as entice the caregiver to come to him. We also see a child of this age using the "most important person" as a safe base from which to explore the world around him.

Separation Protest and Fear of Strangers. In many children (but not all) one of the striking signs of this strong single attachment is that the child may show both protest at separation from the preferred person and fear of strangers. Separation protest—if it occurs at all—is usually seen sometime around 6 to 8 months, after which it fades (Ainsworth, Blehar, Waters, & Wall, 1978). Fear of strangers begins to emerge at about 8 months and continues until about 12 months, after which it too gradually fades (Emde, Baensbauer, & Harmon, 1976).

We want to reemphasize that not all infants show fear of strangers. Some children show only brief wariness; others show more striking withdrawal such as crying, clinging to the parent, or other signs of fear (Sroufe, 1977; Batter & Davidson, 1979). The likelihood of a fear reaction is increased if the stranger comes up right next to the child or if the child is in a new or stressful situation. Nearly all attachment behaviors, in fact, are heightened in stressful or fearful situations, so it is not surprising that wariness of strangers should show such a pattern as well.

Phase 4: Multiple Attachments

During the second and third years we see several changes in the child's attachments and attachment behaviors. Most children show a spread of attachment to more than one significant person—to father, grandparents, siblings, day care workers. These attachments have the same qualities as the attachments to the principal caregiver: The child can use any one of her preferred adults as a safe base for exploration and may turn to any of them for comfort in distress. She also shows the positive forms of attachment, including smiling and seeking proximity, more to these adults than to others, although she still chooses her central person if that person is available.

At the same time, the overall level of proximity seeking declines. A 12-month-old child stays pretty close to the safe base most of the time, remaining within sight of the mother or other caregiver. But by 2 or 3 years of age, children seem to be comfortable being on their own more. Remember that the $2\frac{1}{2}$-year-old can now talk well enough to call out to his mom or dad from some distance away and stay in contact with them. Alison Clarke-Stewart (Clarke-Stewart & Hevey, 1981) tracked this change in a group of 63 children she observed in their homes from ages 12 to 30 months. One of the items she noted was the percentage of time the child spent in the same room with the mother. As you can see in Figure 7.4, this percentage declined steadily over the second and third years of life. To be sure, the $2\frac{1}{2}$-year-olds in this study were still in the same room with their mothers nearly three-quarters of the time. That is still a significant drop from the 85 percent Clarke-Stewart observed at 12 months.

This reduction in proximity seeking does not mean that the child is less *attached to* the caregiver. Rather, it says that the attachment behaviors change and become less visible. We can still see clear attachment behaviors in 2-, 3-, or 4-year-old children who are frightened, tired, or under stress. In normal circumstances, however, they move more freely from the safe base of their preferred person(s).

Later Steps

We assume that the child's attachment to his parents remains strong throughout the period of elementary school, although the attachment behaviors toward the parents become less visible. The character of the relationship to the parents changes as well. As the child comes to understand something of the parent's perspective, the relationship takes on more properties of what Bowlby (1969) calls a "goal-corrected partnership." At the same time, the child's social horizons are widened considerably by the establishment of individual friendships with other children.

Attachments to Fathers and Mothers

We have pointed out that both fathers and mothers appear to become attached to their infants, although their behavior with infants varies somewhat. But what about the child's half of this attachment? Are in-

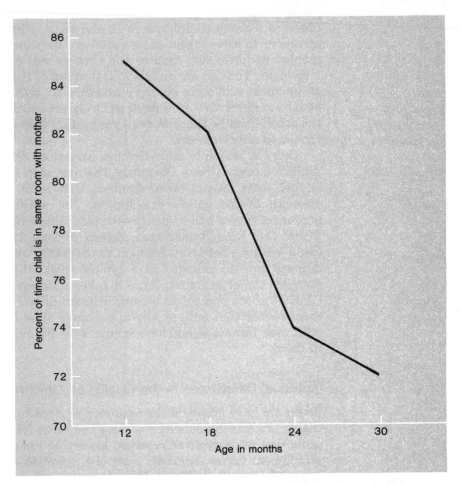

Figure 7.4. One of the attachment behaviors we see in children during the first years of life is simply staying near the preferred person. As you can see from these results from Clarke-Stewart's longitudinal study, though, this form of behavior declines slowly between 12 and 30 months as the child becomes able to maintain contact in other ways. (*Source:* Clarke-Stewart & Hevey, 1981, Figure 1, p. 134.)

fants and young children equally attached to their fathers and their mothers?

Michael Lamb (1977) argues that they are. He points out that from the age of 7 to 8 months, when strong attachments are first seen, infants prefer *either* the father or the mother to a stranger. Furthermore, when both the father and the mother are available, an infant will smile at or approach both, *except* when he is frightened or under stress. When that happens, most children turn to the mother rather than to the father (Clarke-Stewart, 1978; Lamb, 1976).

Mary Main and Donna Weston (1981) have recently documented this roughly equal status of fathers and mothers in another way. They observed a group of children at 12 and 18 months and rated their attachment to each parent as "secure" or "insecure"—a distinction we mentioned in the last chapter and that we will explore more fully in a moment. You can see in Table 7.2 that out of this sample there were 15 children who were securely attached to *both* parents and about equal numbers who were more securely attached to one parent over the other. Finally, there were 10 youngsters who were not securely attached to either parent.

There is certainly no indication here that mothers are generally preferred over fathers. Obviously, the next step is to find out what it is that some fathers do or don't do that leads to variation in the strength of the child's attachment. Not surprisingly, the simple amount of time a father spends with his child seems to be an important factor. Gail Ross (Ross, Kagan, Zelazo, & Kotelchuk, 1975) found she could predict a baby's attachment to the father by knowing how many diapers the dad changed in a typical week; the more diapers, the stronger the attachment! Since it takes time for the partners in the "dance" of attachment to become attuned to one another's signals, it makes sense that fathers who invest more time in their relationship with their infants should have infants who are more strongly attached to them.

Individual Differences in the Quality of Attachments

So far we have sketched the sequence of steps in the development of the child's attachments as if it were the same for all children. At the same time we have given repeated hints that the *quality* of the child's attachment varies markedly from one infant to another. Mary Ainsworth (Ainsworth & Wittig, 1969; Ainsworth et al., 1978) suggests that the best way to think about such differences in quality is in terms of the **security of attachment.**

Ainsworth developed a technique for observing attachment behaviors in children that has come to be called the **strange situation.** It consists of a series of episodes in a laboratory setting in which the child is with the mother, with the mother and a stranger, alone with the stranger, completely alone for a few minutes, and then reunited with

TABLE 7.2
The Security or Insecurity of Children's Attachments to Their Fathers and Mothers at 12 to 18 Months of Age

CHILD'S ATTACHMENT TO MOTHER	CHILD'S ATTACHMENT TO FATHER	
	Secure	*Insecure*
Secure	15	13
Insecure	11	10

SOURCE: Main & Weston, 1981, from Table 1, p. 836.

the stranger and then with the mother. Based on the child's reaction to this set of experiences, the child is classed as being **securely attached** or as one of two types of **insecurely attached.** We have shown one child's reaction to this setting in Figure 7.5, and we've listed some of the characteristics of securely and insecurely attached children in Table 7.3.

There is an obvious parallel between Ainsworth's secure/insecure attachment distinction and Erikson's trust/mistrust distinction. Erikson sees the first attachment as the model for later relationships, a view

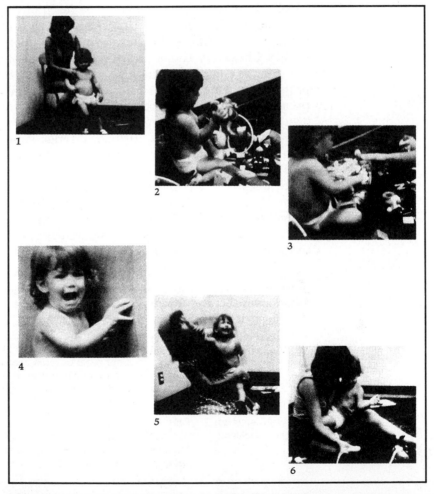

Figure 7.5. In an unfamiliar playroom this securely attached baby leaves her mother (1) and plays happily (2). The approach of a stranger does not bother her (3). Left alone in the room, however, the baby becomes distressed (4), and the return of the stranger (5) fails to pacify her. Only the mother's return (6) brings comfort, and the baby seeks contact as soon as the mother enters the room. This child is considered securely attached despite her tears because she used the mother as a safe base initially and was consoled by the mother's return. (*Source:* Sroufe, 1978, pp. 52–53.)

shared by current theorists studying attachment (Ainsworth et al., 1978; Sroufe, 1979). Because the present work on the security of attachments has so many theoretical and practical ramifications,we need to take some time to explore some of the issues and implications.

Security of Attachment versus Temperament.   The assumption that underlies all the current work on security of attachment (and Erikson's theory as well) is that a secure or insecure attachment is largely the product of the child's interaction with the parents. But is that the whole explanation? If you look again at the description of the insecurely attached child—especially the resistant/ambivalent type—you may find that it sounds a lot like Thomas & Chess's descriptions of temperamentally "difficult" children that we talked about in Chapter 6. In fact, Chess and Thomas have recently suggested that "the items of the infant's behavior in the Ainsworth Strange Situation could be appropriately rated under the temperamental categories of approach/withdrawal, adaptability, quality of mood, and intensity" (Chess & Thomas, 1982, p 220). Maybe there is really no separate process of secure attachment. Instead, we may simply be seeing another manifestation of underlying, inherited differences in temperament.

   This possibility deserves more attention than it has received, but there are several bits of evidence that lead us to conclude that temperamentally difficult children may be more *likely* to be insecurely attached but that there are two separable processes involved. Everett Waters and his co-workers (Waters, Vaughn, & Egeland, 1980) found that infants who were rated as resistant/ambivalent in their attach-

TABLE 7.3
Behavior of Securely Attached and Insecurely Attached Infants in Ainsworth's Strange Situation at 12 Months of Age

Group	Behavior
Securely attached	Child shows low to moderate levels of proximity seeking to mother, does not avoid or resist contact if the mother initiates it. When reunited with the mother after absence, child greets the mother positively and can be soothed if upset. Clearly prefers mother to stranger.
Insecurely attached: detached/avoidant	Child avoids contact with mother, especially at reunion after an absence. Does not resist the mother's efforts to make contact, but does not seek much contact. Treats stranger and mother about the same throughout.
Insecurely attached: resistant/ambivalent	Greatly upset when separated from mother, but the mother cannot successfully comfort the child when she comes back. Child both seeks and avoids contact at different times. May show anger toward mother at reunion and resists both comfort and contact with stranger.

SOURCE: Based on descriptions of Sroufe & Waters, 1977; Ainsworth, Blehar, Waters, & Wall, 1978.

ment at 12 months, compared to securely attached 1-year-olds, had been rated as more irritable, less motorically mature, and less responsive to stimulation when they were 7 days old. One possible way to account for this finding is to argue that parents respond differently, perhaps less optimally, to more irritable or "difficult" infants, which increases the likelihood of an insecure attachment.

This possibility is further strengthened by the results of Susan Crockenberg's study (1981), described in Chapter 6 (see Table 6.8). You may recall that she found that infants rated as irritable were more likely to be later rated as insecurely attached *only* if the mothers also lacked the level of social support they required to handle the complexities of their lives. Since not all irritable babies ended up as insecurely attached, it seems clear that an insecure attachment is not just another way of describing a "difficult" temperament. However, the possibility clearly remains that a part of what has been described as the quality or security of a child's attachment may be understood as a reflection of temperamental variation.

Is the Security of Attachment Stable over Time?   Assuming that we are in fact talking about something more than just temperament, it is still legitimate to ask whether a securely attached child seen at 12 months is still likely to be securely attached a year later. Once established, does the quality of a child's attachment remain stable forever, or can it change?

The answer seems to be that when the child's family environment or life circumstances are reasonably consistent, the security or insecurity of attachment does remain stable. For example, Everett Waters (1978) found that only 2 out of the 50 infants he studied changed in their category of attachment from 12 to 18 months. But equivalent stability is *not* found in studies of poverty-level families or families in which abuse or neglect has occurred. Egeland and Sroufe (1981), for example, found that in a group of abused children, the percentage rated as securely attached rose from 38 percent at 12 months to 56 percent at 18 months. In a larger sample of low-income families, Vaughn (Vaughn, Egeland, Sroufe, & Waters, 1979) found that 31 out of 100 children had shifted from secure to insecure, or vice versa, between 12 and 18 months. When such shifts occurred, they were usually accompanied by a change in the stress level in the family or in the availability of alternative caregivers. In abusing families, for example, the child's attachment might shift from insecure to secure if the grandmother came to live with the family or if the level of family stress went down.

These findings tell us that the security of a child's central attachments at 12 months of age is not necessarily a permanent characteristic of that child's relationships with the adults around her. The specific family circumstances affect the stability of the child's early relationships, too. The quality of the baby's temperament or of the first attachment, however, may *predispose* the child toward later secure or inse-cure relationships with others.

How do children become securely attached?   We have implied all along that the quality of the infant's attachment is a product of the relation-ship between the infant and the caregivers, most often the mother. But just what is it that some mothers do or don't do that makes a differ-ence?

Mothers of securely attached infants are more supportive of their infants' independent play, more sensitive to their child's needs, and more emotionally expressive toward their babies (Blehar, Lieberman, & Ainsworth, 1977; Main, Tomasini, & Tolan, 1979; Londerville & Main, 1981). Our favorite from this collection of studies is the work of Mary Blehar, Alicia Lieberman, and Mary Ainsworth (1977). They use the wonderfully descriptive phrase "contingent pacing" to characterize the behavior of the mother of the securely attached child. A mother who is using this type of interaction paces her actions "slowly and gent-ly, modifying them in keeping with infant cues, pausing if needed to allow him time to mobilize a response" (p. 185). Moreover, these moth-ers encourage further interaction by allowing the baby enough time to respond during their play and are playful themselves. The mothers of securely attached babies are also rarely routine in manner with their babies and rarely silent or unsmiling. In our terms, the mothers of se-curely attached infants are "dancing" well with their babies.

Attachment and Separation: Day Care.   If good dancing is required to foster secure attachment, then it might seem logical that a mother who works full time, and whose child is in some form of alternative care, might be a less skillful dancer and thus have a less securely attached child. Since at least 40 percent of the mothers with children under age 3 are working part time or full time, this is a question with enormous practical importance. It also has theoretical importance, since Erikson, Freud, Bowlby, and other theorists have placed such strong emphasis on the importance of the first mother-infant relationship.

Our conclusion is that Erikson and Bowlby are probably right about the importance of that early relationship but that they are wrong to assume that secure attachment requires a *constant* contact between mother and child. The sort of predictable, repeated separation that oc-curs when the mother works need not weaken or reduce the quality of the child's attachment to the mother (Rutter, 1982), just as the lesser availability of the father in most families does not prevent a child from becoming attached to him.

This conclusion is supported by the findings from dozens of studies, virtually all of which show that children in day care settings still prefer their parents over day care workers, will turn to the parents rather than to the day care worker for comfort even when both are available, and show the same proportions of secure and insecure attachment as do children reared entirely at home (for example, Caldwell, Wright, Honig, & Tannenbaum, 1970; Farran & Ramey, 1977; Kagan, Kearsley, & Zelazo, 1978).

We are reasonably confident about these generalizations, but a few cautions are in order. Children who are moved frequently from one care setting to another do show some signs of disturbance, and the quality of the day care experience makes a difference as well. Our summary of the research should not lead you to conclude that *all* day care experiences have no detrimental effect, nor that all children in day care are securely attached to their parents. What we can conclude is that a well-chosen alternative care arrangement need not *interfere* with the formation of a strong and secure attachment of child to the parent if the parent-child interaction is of the type that will normally foster such security. Neither will day care—no matter how good—create a secure child-parent attachment bond where one did not exist before. The great lack at the moment is research on the impact of such separation on the *parent's* attachment to the child.

Long-term Effects of Secure or Insecure Attachment.   As we pointed out in Chapter 6, there is now an accumulating body of information showing long-term effects of the security or insecurity of the child's first attachments. Those children rated as securely attached to their mothers have also been found to be more sociable, more positive in their behavior toward others, and more emotionally mature in their approach to school and other nonhome settings. If, as we have suggested here, these differences are not just a restatement of temperamental differences and are reasonably stable over time, then this entire body of research offers striking support for Erikson's or Freud's general view of the importance of early relationships.

BEYOND THE FIRST ATTACHMENT: CHILDREN'S RELATIONSHIPS WITH OTHER CHILDREN

Thus far in our discussions of the development of social interactions we have looked almost exclusively at the child's relationship with his mother and father, with occasional references to such other adults as day care workers or grandparents. Beginning in the preschool years, however, other children play an increasingly central role in a child's social world.

Most of the work on children's social interactions with one another has focused on the two ends of the positive-negative continuum. On the positive end, researchers have looked at children's friendships, at popularity, at helpfulness or generosity among peers. On the negative end, psychologists have looked at aggression among peers and at dominance in play groups. For both convenience and clarity we will divide our own discussion in a similar way, beginning with a look at the friendly and helpful side of children's relationships with each other. But we should emphasize at the outset that positive versus negative is an overly simplistic way of describing the complex social interactions we see among children (or among adults). We can see signs of a shift in the descriptions of social interactions in some of the recent research, which emphasizes such dimensions as the cohesiveness of a group or the synchrony or reciprocity of actions. We will use such concepts wherever we can to give a richer description of the quality of children's relationships with one another.

Positive Social Interactions among Children: Developmental Patterns

Following our usual pattern, let us begin our exploration of positive social interactions among children by describing some of the developmental changes that take place from infancy through the early school years. We can then turn to the question of individual differences in popularity or social skill.

In Infancy and Early Childhood.   Children first begin to show some positive interest in other infants at 10 to 12 months of age, when they will touch each other, imitate each other's actions, and smile at one another (Eckerman & Whatley, 1977). Children at this early age apparently still prefer to play with objects but will play with other little bodies if no toys are available. By a year and a half, however, we begin to see two or more children playing with each other and with toys at the same time. Some results from a short-term longitudinal study by Joseph Jacobson (1981), which we have shown in Figure 7.6, illustrate this. Jacobson observed the same children from 10 to 14 months in a series of 20-minute episodes. As you can see in the figure, play interactions centered around a common toy increased sharply over the four-month period, while interactions involving no toy leveled off.

Besides the steady increase in social exchanges, two facets of this developmental change deserve some emphasis. First, the quality of children's play interactions changes, shifting from what Piaget calls **parallel play** to **cooperative play.** In parallel play, two children may be using the same materials or the same toys, but each is playing independently, such as two children each painting a picture. In cooperative play, the children join in a common project. (We've shown both types of play in Figure 7.7.) Cooperative play becomes more common in children 3 and 4 years of age, although you can see it occasionally in younger children.

A second interesting aspect of children's early social exchanges is

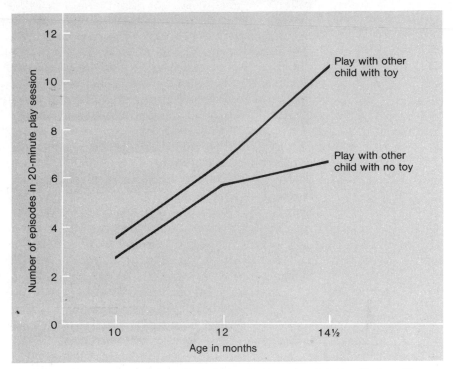

Figure 7.6. Recent research has shown that even very young infants will play with one another if left alone; but in the second year of life (14 ½ months in this study), their play is increased if there is a toy (which they both enjoy) involved in the interaction. (*Source:* Jacobson, 1981, p. 623.)

that to some extent, young children seem to have to learn how to play with one another. In one study, Edward Mueller and Jeffrey Brenner (1977) observed two different preschool groups, one of which began when the children were about 12 months old and the second when the children were 17 months old. Mueller and Brenner observed the interactions of each group for a six-month period, looking particularly at the rate of social exchanges between the youngsters. In both groups the rate of social behavior increased as the children spent time with one another. However, the older children, who did not start interacting with one another until they were 17 months old, started out with a level of social interaction that had been typical of the younger group at age 14 months. Apparently there are some aspects of the child's interest in and skill with other children that are related to broader developmental patterns, such as the changes in social cognition we talked about in Chapter 4. But specific experience with other children is also important—a good argument for play groups or preschool experience for children of this age.

While 1- and 2-year-old chilren show real social interactions, they do not appear to have *attachments* to other children. The first signs of "best friends" are seen at about age 3 to age 5 (Hartup, 1975). We

Figure 7.7. These two photos illustrate parallel play (on the bottom) and cooperative play (on the top). During the preschool years there is a shift from a dominance of parallel play to a predominance of cooperative play.

know far less about the quality of these early friendships than we would like. Do children of this age use their friends as a safe base or go to them for comfort? In other words, are these friendships genuine attachments? We don't know. We do know that 4- and 5-year-old children exhibit more positive and less negative behavior toward their friends than toward nonfriends (Masters & Furman, 1981), and that they make a major effort to be responsive to their friends' needs and to be understood by their friends (Gottman & Parkhurst, 1980). We also know that many of the early friendships are reciprocal (Strayer, 1980). At the same time, the early friendships seem to be less stable and more based on proximity and shared play interests than are friendships in older children (Berndt, 1981).

Very young children—as young as age 2—also show another type of positive social behavior, **altruism.** They will offer to help another child who is hurt, offer a toy, or try to comfort another child (Zahn-Waxler, Radke-Yarrow, & King, 1979). The fact that such young children behave in this thoughtful and helpful way toward one another is especially interesting because of what we know about the typical levels of egocentrism of 2- or 3-year-olds. While it appears to be the case that children of this age have trouble understanding that others feel differently from themselves, they obviously understand enough about the emotions of others to respond in supportive and sympathetic ways when they see other children hurt or sad. It turns out, though, that children vary markedly in the amount of such altruistic behavior they show at this early age. For those of you interested in knowing more about how helpful children come to be that way, we have summarized some of the research in Box 7.2.

Positive Social Interactions at School Age.　　Individual friendships play a still larger role in the social patterns of elementary-school-aged children. In one study, John Riesman and Susan Shorr (1978) found that second graders named about four friends each; by seventh grade this had increased to about seven friends each.

There are some curious inconsistencies in the information we have about the quality of these relationships. On the one hand they seem to be more stable than are the friendships of younger children (Berndt, 1981a). On the other hand, elementary-school-aged children treat friends and strangers more alike than do younger children (Berndt, 1981b; Gottman & Parkhurst, 1980).

At the moment the most reasonable resolution of this apparent contradiction seems to be that older children are simply more polite to strangers. They show many of the same positive, sharing, considerate behaviors toward strangers that they show toward friends. School-aged children *do* make clear distinctions, though, between friends and nonfriends among those children they know well. So it is not that 5- to

BOX 7.2

Rearing Helpful and Altruistic Children

We have said that children as young as 2 or 3 years of age will show helpful and kind behavior toward one another at least occasionally. This is quite true, though some children show much more altruism and kindness than others do. Since most of us would *like* our children to behave in this way toward us, toward their brothers and sisters, and toward other children, it's worthwhile to take a look at what we know about the kind of family environments that seem to foster this type of positive social interaction.

At least four things that parents can do seem to make a difference.

EXPLAINING WHY AND GIVING RULES

Probably the most significant element in the equation is to explain to children what the consequences are of their own actions and to give them clear, elaborated rules.

Carolyn Zahn-Waxler and her colleagues (Zahn-Waxler, Radke-Yarrow, & King, 1979) have given us the best evidence about this. They asked a group of 16 mothers of young children to keep daily diaries of every incident in which someone

around the child showed distress, fear, pain, sorrow, or fatigue. For example, John's mother described an incident in which her 2-year-old son was visited by a friend, Jerry:

> Today Jerry was kind of cranky; he just started completely bawling and he wouldn't stop. John kept coming over and handing Jerry toys, trying to cheer him up, so to speak. He'd say things like "Here, Jerry," and I said to John: "Jerry's sad; he doesn't feel good; he had a shot today." John would look at me with his eyebrows kind of wrinkled together like he really understood that Jerry was crying because he was unhappy, not that he was just being a crybaby. He went over and rubbed Jerry's arm and said "Nice Jerry" and continued to give him toys (pp. 321–322).

What Zahn-Waxler found was that mothers who *both* explained the consequences of the child's actions (for example, "If you hit Susan it will hurt her") *and* who stated the rules clearly, explicitly, and with

12-year-old children treat all other youngsters alike. They don't. They have stable, positive friendships that play important roles in their lives. But they have also learned the proper or polite way to act toward others more thoroughly than have 2- to 5-year-olds, and we see this polite behavior with strangers in first encounters.

Aside from the growth of individual friendships, the most striking thing about peer relationships during the years from about 5 to 12 is that the groups children form then are almost exclusively sex segregated. Obviously, in many schools children interact with peers of both sexes, but in their own chosen play groups girls play with girls and boys with boys. Perhaps in recognition of this preference, most organized children's activities at these ages, such as Boy Scouts and Girl Scouts, are also sex segregated. Interestingly, this is not an isolated Western culture phenomenon. Such sex segregation of groups has been observed in widely varying cultures (Rubin, 1980).

emotion ("You mustn't hit people") had children who were much more likely to react to others with helpfulness or sympathy. John's mother did the first of these by explaining why Jerry was crying.

BEING HELPFUL

Children also learn to be helpful by being helpful. This sounds simpleminded, but we often forget the simple things. Children can be encouraged to do helpful things in several ways. You can have them playact the role of the person needing help and of the person doing the helping. If you also talk about what is happening and get the children to talk about how they are feeling, this strengthens the effect (Staub, 1975, 1979; Friedrich-Cofer, Huston-Stein, Kipnis, Susman, & Clewett, 1979).

Another way to encourage responsible or helpful behavior is to give children genuinely responsible tasks. Ervin Staub found, for example (1970), that a child put in charge of the care of a younger child is much more likely to respond to the sound of a child crying in a nearby room than is a child who has no responsibility. Furthermore, in studies of other cultures, John and Beatrice Whiting (1973, 1975) have shown that in cultures where children are given responsibility for the care of younger siblings,

the youngsters are likely to show heightened levels of helpfulness in other situations as well. In this study, American children showed the *lowest* levels of altruism, which suggests that many of the conditions that promote such helpful behavior are less common in our modern society.

TUTORING

Children also learn altruistic or helpful behavior by teaching younger children to behave this way. Staub (1975) has found that the role of *tutor* is beneficial for both the learner and the tutor. If you ask an older child to show a younger one how to share, *both* children may show more sharing later.

MODELING

The final and obvious way to encourage altruism and helpfulness in your children is to behave that way yourself. We have pointed out repeatedly that children learn things through modeling, and altruistic behavior is no exception. Sharing your own things with your children, taking the casserole to the recently widowed neighbor, and responding to a friend's tears with affection will all demonstrate to the child the very behaviors you would like him to show toward others.

It is worth noting in passing that this maximum sex segregation of children's groups occurs during the period Freud described as *latency,* when sexual energies were thought to be relatively quiescent. It is also the period after children have fully grasped the permanence of gender, when they seem to be focused on learning their sex roles.

Links between Friendship Patterns and Cognition. We are getting a little ahead of ourselves, but we wanted at least to mention some intriguing connections between friendship patterns and children's *ideas* about social relationships—links we will describe more completely in Chapter 9. Prior to about age 5, children define friends as people who are available, who will be there to play with you. After age 5, children begin to see friendship as a system of exchange. This shift in the understanding of friendship is partially reflected in the changes we see in actual behavior toward friends. Friendships seem to become more enduring, more reciprocal, among children in elementary school, both of which are changes we would expect based on children's changed understanding of the *role* of friend.

Individual Differences in Positive Interactions

Superimposed on these developmental shifts are significant differences in children's competence in social interactions and in their popularity with others. We have already described the findings from several studies that seem to show that children who are securely attached to their parents are also more skillful in playing with and relating to their peers in the preschool. To give you a more concrete notion of just what those differences are, we've selected some comparisons from a study by Sroufe (1978) to show in Figure 7.8. Securely attached children were

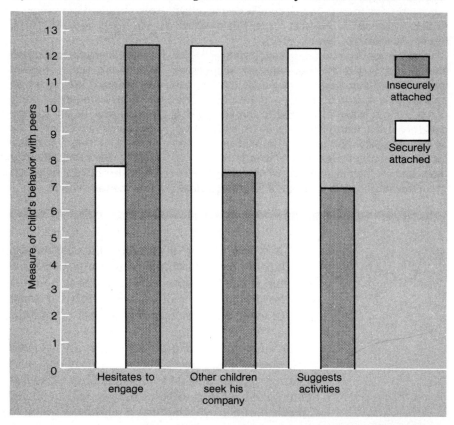

Figure 7.8.   Some of the results of Sroufe's study of peer interactions among children who were rated as "securely" or "insecurely" attached at 15 months and who were then observed playing with peers at 3 ½. Securely attached children were generally more competent in their relationships with peers. (*Source:* Adapted from "Attachment and the roots of competence" by L. Alan Sroufe, in *Human Nature,* October 1978. Copyright 1978 by Human Nature, Inc. Used by permission of the publishers.)

more often sought out by other children, were more likely to suggest activities to others, and were more willing to engage in play or other activities with other children in the play group.

We do not know whether this link between security of attachment and skill with peers persists into elementary school, but it is reasonable to expect that it would. Among other things, children who have early success in their interactions with others continue to be reinforced for their social overtures, so that their skill ought to be both maintained and increased.

Popularity.   Another way to explore individual differences in social skill is to ask which children are *popular*. In Table 7.4 we have listed some of the characteristics of children who are chosen as playmates or who are leaders of groups. Some of the items in this list are things that a child can't control, such as his physical size or attractiveness. These characteristics do make some difference, but the crucial element in popularity is not what you look like but how you *behave*. Popular children are liked because they behave in positive, supporting, non-punitive ways toward most other children. In a sense, what we term *popularity* is simply the sum of the positive qualities of a child's inter-actions with his peers. To put it rather baldly and simplistically, the more people you are nice to, the more popular you will be.

What kinds of families do popular children come from? We have already mentioned two elements: Families that foster secure attach-ment probably have more popular children (although this link has not been directly studied), and families that foster high self-esteem have

TABLE 7.4
Some of the Characteristics of Popular Children in Elementary School

Friendliness	Popular children are friendlier toward others, less punitive, more reinforcing.
Outgoingness	Gregarious children are more popular than withdrawn children.
Success in school	Children who get better grades or have better academic skill are more popular.
Family position	Youngest children in a family are usually more popular than first-born children.
Physical attractiveness	The more attractive the child, the more he is liked by peers. (This does not seem to be a factor in the friendships of preschoolers.)
Physical size	Tall or physically mature children are more popular.
Specific task ability	Children who are very good at sports or at any task valued by the group they are in are more popular.

SOURCE: Based on information in Asher, Oden, & Gottman, 1977; Masters & Furman, 1981.

more popular children. Other literature suggests three other aspects of families of popular children (Hartup, 1970): (1) they discourage aggression and antisocial behavior in their children, (2) they try not to frustrate the child and use little punishment, and (3) they like their children and tell them so. For a boy to be popular with his peers, a strong father figure, one who is warm and positive toward the son, also seems to be important. If you think back to what we said in Box 6.1 (page 222) this combination of parental treatment sounds a great deal like the pattern Baumrind calls "authoritative" child rearing. Thus the origins of high self-esteem and the origins of popularity seem to be very similar.

Negative Social Interactions among Children

If you have watched young children together you know that all is not sweetness and light in the land of the young. Children do show affection and helpful behaviors toward one another, but they also tease each other, fight, yell, and argue over objects and territory. (Of course, adults do most of these things, too; we just disguise it better or call it by different names—we *discuss* instead of argue, and we *assert* ourselves rather than behaving aggressively.)

Researchers who have studied this negative side of children's interactions have looked mostly at aggressive behavior, which we can define as behavior with the apparent intent to injure some other person or object (Feshbach, 1970).

The Development of Aggressive Behaviors.   Aggression is seen to at least some degree in every child. The basic built-in signal for aggression in most instances seems to be frustration. Some early theorists (Dollard, Doob, Miller, Mowrer, & Sears, 1939) argued that aggression always followed a frustration, and that all aggressions were preceded by frustration. That extreme version of the "frustration-aggression hypothesis" turns out to be invalid, but it does seem to be the case that the human child is born with a fairly strong natural connection between frustration and aggression, just as she naturally exhibits attachment behaviors when she is hungry, frightened, or in need.

Over the early years of life, the frequency and form of aggression change, as we've summarized in Table 7.5. When 2- or 3-year-old children are upset or frustrated, they are more likely to use physical aggression. As their verbal skills improve, however, there is a shift toward greater use of verbal aggression, such as taunting or name calling.

Individual Differences in Aggression: Sex Differences.   Superimposed on these basic developmental changes there are (as usual) individual

TABLE 7.5
A Summary of Developmental Changes in the Form and Frequency of Aggression in Children

	2- to 4-year-olds	*4- to 8-year-olds*
Frequency:		
Physical aggression	At its peak from 2 to 4.	Declines over the period from 4 to 8.
Verbal aggression	Relatively rare at 2; increases as the child's verbal skill improves.	A larger percentage of aggression in this period is verbal rather than physical.
Form of aggression	Instrumental aggression (aimed at obtaining or damaging an object) is the major form at this age.	Hostile aggression (aimed at hurting another person or their feelings) is the major form at this age.
Occasion for aggression	More often occurs after conflicts with parents.	More often occurs after conflicts with peers.

SOURCE: Based on data from Goodenough (1931) and Hartup (1974).

differences in the frequency of aggressive behavior. The most noticeable difference is that boys consistently show higher rates of aggression than girls do (Maccoby & Jacklin, 1974; Barnett, 1979). It is extremely important for you to understand that these are *average* differences we are talking about; the range of aggressiveness in boys and the range in girls overlap a great deal. Many boys are less aggressive than the average girl, and many girls are more aggressive than the average boy. Still there *is* an average difference, and we need to try to explain it.

Where might such a sex difference in aggressiveness come from? Eleanor Maccoby and Carol Jacklin (1974, 1980), after reviewing all the evidence, have concluded that there is an important biological basis for the aggression differences:

> Let us outline the reasons why biological sex differences appear to be involved in aggression: (1) Males are more aggressive than females in all human societies for which evidence is available. (2) The sex differences are found early in life, at a time when there is no evidence that differential socialization pressures have been brought to bear by adults to "shape" aggression differently in the two sexes. (3) Similar sex differences are found in man and subhuman primates. (4) Aggression is related to levels of sex hormones, and can be changed by experimental administration of these hormones (Maccoby & Jacklin, 1974, pp. 242–243).

Other psychologists have emphasized that there are important social influences, at least in our culture, which also foster higher levels of aggression in boys as well (Brooks-Gunn & Matthews, 1979; Tieger, 1980).

It seems clear to us that both biological and environmental influences play a role. There may well be hormonal or other biological factors creating higher rates of aggressiveness in boys to begin with. However, as we pointed out in Chapter 6, there is also pressure from parents, particularly fathers, for 4- or 5-year-old boys to adopt more boyish behaviors and attitudes, which include playing physical games and being assertive with others. We also pointed out in the last chapter that the ways parents respond to children's aggressive outbursts—whether they are permissive or punitive—affect the rates of the child's aggressive behavior. Thus aggressiveness is obviously not purely determined by biology; it is also heavily influenced by the reinforcement systems existing in the child's environment.

Competition and Dominance.   A related but separable aspect of negative encounters between children is **competition** and **dominance.** Whenever there are too few toys for the number of children, not enough time with the teacher to go around, or some other scarcity of desired objects, there will be competition. Sometimes competition results in outright aggression. More often, though, competition results in the development of a clear **dominance hierarchy,** more popularly known as a *pecking order.* Some children seem to be more successful than others at asserting their rights to desired objects, either by threats, by simply taking the object away, by glaring at the other child, or the equivalent.

Clear dominance hierarchies are seen in play groups of children as young as 2 to 5 years of age (Strayer & Strayer, 1976; Strayer, 1980; Vaughn & Waters, 1981). That is, among 10 or 15 children who play together regularly, it is possible to predict who will win in any given competition over some desired object or space. Children high in the dominance hierarchy win out over nearly all other children; children at the bottom of the pecking order lose to everyone. Similar dominance hierarchies have been observed in groups of primates, as well as in other animals, so this is not at all unique to human children or adults.

Recent work on dominance in children has revealed some extremely interesting patterns. Among young children (2 to 5 year olds), a child's place in the group dominance system is *not* related to the amount of friendly, affiliative behaviors from the child or to the child (Strayer, 1980; Vaughn & Waters, 1981). Put another way, a child can be at the bottom of the pecking order and still be popular with others or be the most dominant and not be particularly well liked by others. The two systems seem to be largely independent among the younger children.

But among children of kindergarten or elementary-school age, the dominance system and the friendship system seem to be more connected. When Strayer (1980) observed 5- and 6-year-old play groups, he found that the dominant children *were* the ones who were also chosen as playmates. This finding suggests that among the older youngsters popularity is a much more unitary process, involving both dominance and positive, helpful activities.

Overall, the picture that emerges is that past the age of 4 or 5, *socially competent* children are those who are at the middle to higher end of the dominance hierarchy, who are positive, helpful and supportive of others, and who refrain from overt acts of physical aggression. Popularity or social effectiveness thus seems to result from a combination of positive and negative actions by the child.

SUMMARY

1. Relationships with adults and peers are of central significance in the development of all children. Of particular importance is the formation of basic attachments to others in infancy and later childhood.
2. An important distinction is made between *attachment behavior* and underlying *attachment*. The latter is the basic bond between two people; the former is the manner in which that bond is expressed in actual behavior.
3. The parents' attachment to the infant develops in two phases: (1) an initial strong bond may be formed in the first hours of the child's life; (2) a growing attachment results from the repetition of mutually reinforcing and interlocking attachment behaviors.
4. The strength of the first bond appears to be somewhat increased if the parents have immediate contact with the newborn, but the long-term effect of this early contact is relatively small.
5. Fathers as well as mothers form strong attachments to their infants. Some differentiation of interactive pattern occurs past the early weeks of life, however, as fathers show a more playful interactive pattern with their children than do mothers.
6. The development of the infant's attachment to the parents follows a somewhat different course, beginning with a period in which the baby shows attachment behaviors toward nearly everyone but shows no preferential attachment.
7. By 5 to 6 months, most infants have formed at least one strong attachment, usually to the major caregiver.
8. In older children, the basic attachment remains but the form of attachment behaviors changes, becoming less clinging except when the child is under stress, in which case the earlier forms reappear.
9. Children differ in the security of their first attachments. The secure infant uses the parent as a safe base for exploration and can be readily consoled by the parent.
10. Secure attachment appears to be fostered by attentive, loving,

"contingently paced" interactions between parent and child. Securely attached children appear to be more skillful in later years with peers and more curious and persistent in approaching new tasks.

11. Children's relationships with other youngsters become more and more central to their social development from age 1 or 2. Toddlers are aware of other children and will play with them; by 2 or 3 children show specific social approaches to others.

12. By age 4 or 5 children have formed individual friendships and show preferential positive behavior toward friends. Friendship becomes more common, and more stable, in the elementary-school years.

13. Among preschool and elementary-school-aged children, some are consistently more popular than others—receive more positive bids from other children. Such popular children show more positive approaches to others and are more likely to be supportive and sharing.

14. Young children also show such negative social patterns as aggressiveness and dominance. Physical aggression peaks at 3 or 4 and is gradually replaced by verbal aggression among older children.

15. Boys are found to be consistently more aggressive than girls, probably because of a combination of biological and environmental forces.

16. Among children's groups, clear dominance patterns are also visible. In preschool-aged children, dominance and popularity are unrelated, but the two are positively related among school-aged children.

KEY TERMS

Aggression   Usually defined as intentional physical or verbal behaviors directed toward a person or an object with the intent to inflict damage on that person or object.

Altruism   Giving or sharing objects, time, or goods with others, with no obvious self-gain.

Attachment   The positive affective bond between one person and another, such as the child for the parent or the parent for the child.

Attachment behavior   The collection of (probably) automatic behaviors of one person toward another that brings about or maintains proximity and caregiving, such as the smile of the young infant.

Competition   Interaction between two or more persons aimed at gaining control over some scarce resource, such as toys, attention from a preferred person, or success.

Cooperative play   Play between two children in which both are joined in a common enterprise, such as building a block tower together.

Dominance   The ability of one person consistently to win competitive encounters with other individuals.

Dominance hierarchy   A set of dominance relationships in a group describing the rank order of winners and losers in competitive encounters.

Insecure attachment   Includes both ambivalent and avoidant patterns of attachment in children; the child does not use the parent as a safe base and is not readily consoled by the parent if upset.

Parallel play   A pattern of play in which two or more children play next to each other but each at his own game or task, with no mutual activities.

Secure attachment   Demonstrated by the child's ability to use the parent as a safe base and to be consoled after separation, when fearful, or when otherwise stressed.

Social network   A set of individuals to whom one is attached, and from whom one receives nurturance, reassurance, assistance, and intimacy.

Strange situation   A series of episodes used by Mary Ainsworth and others in studies of attachment. The child is observed with the mother, with a stranger, left alone, and reunited with stranger and with mother.

SUGGESTED READINGS

Brooks-Gunn, J., & Matthews, W. S. *He and she. How children develop their sex-role identity.* Englewood Cliffs, N.J.: Prentice-Hall, 1979.

If you are interested in sex differences—particularly in aggression, attachment, and other areas we've discussed in this chapter—this is an excellent, readable summary.

Oden, S. Peer relationship development in childhood. In L. G. Katz (Ed.), *Current topics in early childhood education* (Vol. 4). Norwood, N.J.: Ablex, 1982.

A very clear, up-to-date discussion of this important topic.

Rubin, Z. *Children's friendships.* Cambridge, Mass.: Harvard University Press, 1980.

Zick Rubin writes wonderfully; this book is both delightful and informative.

Stern, D. *The first relationship: Infant and mother.* Cambridge, Mass.: Harvard University Press, 1977.

Another lovely book, full of good examples and clear descriptions of research.

PROJECT 7.1
Television Aggression

In the last chapter we had you watching sex-role portrayals on television. This time we would like you to observe types and frequencies of aggressive episodes. Using the definition of violence offered by George Gerbner (see Box 6.2, page 236)—that is, "the overt expression of physical force against others or self, or the compelling of action against one's will on pain of being hurt or killed"—select a minimum of four half-hour television programs normally watched by children and count the number of aggressive or violent episodes in each. Count also episodes of verbal aggression, in which the apparent intent is to hurt the other's feelings, as well as episodes of physical aggression. You may select any four (or more) programs, but we would strongly recommend that you distribute them in the following way:

1. At least one educational television program, such as "Sesame Street" or "Mister Rogers" or "The Electric Company."
2. At least one Saturday morning cartoon. "The Road Runner" is a particularly grisly example, but there are many others. If you have time, it would be worthwhile to watch an entire Saturday morning of cartoons, so that you can get some feeling for the fare being offered to young children.
3. At least one early evening adult program that young children can watch: a family comedy, a western, a crime film, or one of each.

For each program that you watch, record the number of violent episodes, separating the verbal and physical violence in your record. In thinking or writing about the results of your observations, consider the following questions:

1. What kind of variation in the number of violent episodes was there among the programs that you watched?
2. Are some programs more verbally aggressive, others more physically aggressive?
3. Do the numbers of violent episodes per program correspond to the figures Gerbner reported (Box 6.2)?
4. What about the consequences of aggression in the television films? Are those who act violently rewarded or punished? How often do reward and punishment occur?
5. What behaviors other than aggression might a child have learned from watching the programs you viewed? This question is particularly relevant for "Sesame Street," "Mr. Rogers," and other educational programs but applies to entertainment programs as well.

Part I Summary
The Developing Child

After reading seven chapters about children's development, you know that we have quite intentionally chosen to present information by topic rather than by "ages and stages." We are convinced that you can get a better feeling for the patterns of development by concentrating on one series of changes at a time. The risk with this strategy is that you may come away with a very fragmented view of the developing person. In this brief chapter, and in similar brief discussions at the end of the adolescence and adulthood chapters, we want to try to put the person back together for you by looking more carefully at the things that are happening at the same time.

We also want to address some of the persisting issues and unanswered questions about development, some of which we raised in the first chapter: What is the impact of major environmental variations, such as poverty or family interaction patterns, on the child's development? Are there important individual variations in the rate or shape of development? Are there sex differences? Is early experience more important or more formative than later experience? Let us begin with a look at the simultaneous developments during several broad periods in childhood.

STAGES OF DEVELOPMENT IN CHILDHOOD

Transitions and Consolidations

Our own reading of the process of development is that it is made up of alternating periods of rapid growth (accompanied by disruption or disequilibrium) and periods of relative calm or consolidation. Change is obviously going on all the time, from conception throughout childhood (and adulthood, too). However, we are persuaded that there are particular times when the changes pile up or when one central change affects the entire system. This might be a major physiological development, or a change from one status to another (baby to toddler, for example), or from one role to another (such as at-home child to going-to-school child). Frequently, these role or status changes are accompanied by the development of major cognitive or language skills, too. These pile-ups of change often seem to result in the child's coming unglued for a while. The old patterns of relationships, of thinking, and of talking don't work very well any more, and it takes a while to work out new patterns.

Erikson frequently uses the word **dilemma** to label these periods. Klaus Riegel (1975) once suggested the phrase **developmental leaps,** which conveys nicely the sense of excitement and blooming opportunity that often accompanies these pivotal periods. We will use the term **transition** to describe the times of change and upheaval and the term **consolidation** to describe the in-between times, when change is more gradual.

From Birth to 18 Months

We have summarized the many changes of infancy in Table I.1. As you can see in the table, we think there are really three subperiods here, with one transition point at about 2 months and another at 8 months.

The overriding impression one gets of the newborn infant—for all her remarkable skills and capacities—is that she is very much on automatic pilot. There seem to be built-in rules or schemes that govern the way the infant looks, listens, explores the world, and relates to others.

One of the really remarkable things about these rules is how well designed they are to lead both the child and the caregivers into the dance of interaction and attachment. Think of an infant being breast-fed. The baby has the needed rooting, sucking, and swallowing reflexes to take in the milk; in this position, the mother's face is at just about the optimum distance from the baby's eyes for the infant's best focusing; the mother's facial features—eyes and mouth, particularly—are just the sort of visual stimuli that capture the baby's attention; the baby is most sensitive to sounds that are at the upper end of human voice frequencies, so the higher-pitched, lilting voice most mothers use is easily heard by the infant; and during breast feeding, the release of a hormone called *cortisol* in the mother has the effect of relaxing her and making her more alert to the baby's signals. Both the adult and the infant are thus primed to interact with one another. (Obviously, the infant's half of this readiness applies during bottle

TABLE I.1
Summary of Development from Birth to 18 Months

Age	Physical and perceptual development	Cognitive development	Language development	Social development
0–2 months	Major neurological change at about 6 to 8 weeks. Activity mostly controlled by primitive portion of brain before that point. Built-in schemes control	Child's built-in schemes, primarily reflexive actions, dominate his interactions with the environment.	Crying and a few pleasure noises are the prelinguistic vocalizations.	Child comes equipped with good proximity eliciting attachment behaviors and can discriminate between others to some degree on the basis of smell and feel. No clear-cut attachment to a single individual, however.
2–8 months	Major neurological change leads to more voluntary control by child: can sit up and reach for things; examines objects for *what* they are, not just *where* they are. Vision improves; can see parent at a distance.	Infant explores and examines objects and people more systematically, repeats interesting actions; develops early steps of the object concept.	Cooing and babbling sounds dominate; child seems to play with sounds; discriminates among many sounds, including those not in the language being heard.	The first central attachment is formed. Child now shows preference for one or more adults over others. Still little interest in other infants.
8–18 months	Child learns to crawl, then walk during this period. Neurological development largely complete by 18 months.	Child completes sensorimotor period; can represent things to himself internally; experiments more systematically with objects; uses chains of actions to gain desired outcome.	First words and beginning two-word sentences for most children. Many overextensions of early words.	First attachment spreads to other caregivers, plus major increase in interest in other children. Attachment behaviors now include moving toward as well as eliciting caregiving. Attachment behaviors less often displayed, however. Child more independent.

Sometime around 6 to 8 weeks of age, however, there are several changes in the system. Perhaps because of the child's early explorations and perhaps because of simple physical maturation, the child's actions and perceptual examinations of the world seem to switch into a different gear, one controlled much more by the cortex and less by the primitive portions of the brain. The child now looks at objects differently, begins to discriminate one face from another, smiles more, sleeps through the night, and generally becomes a more responsive creature.

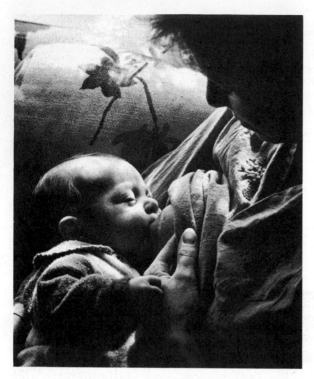

Figure I.1. Newborn infants come into the world remarkably well equipped to enter into the "dance" of interaction: They can suck and swallow, can focus their eyes on the mother's face at this distance, can hear the mother's voice clearly, and can take turns in even these early interactions.

Because of these changes in the baby, and also because it takes most mothers six to eight weeks to recover physically from the delivery, there are big changes in mother-infant interaction patterns as well. The need for routine caretaking continues, of course (ah, the joys of diapers), but as the child stays awake for longer periods, smiles and makes eye contact more, there are more playful and smoother-paced exchanges between parent and child.

During the period of consolidation from 2 to 8 months, change continues steadily. There are gradual neurological changes, with the motor and perceptual areas of the cortex continuing to develop. The child is also exploring the world around him in an active way, which seems to be essential for the development of the object concept and other changes in cognitive skill. The child is busy assimilating new experiences and accommodating old strategies to handle the new information.

Somewhere around 6 to 8 months, two changes bring about a brief disequilibrium (transition point): (1) the child forms a strong central attachment and may start to show distress or fear with strangers, and (2) the child learns how to crawl. The combination of these two changes—one motor and one social/cognitive—requires a new adaptation both by the child and by the parents.

The period from 8 to 18 months is a time of intense activity and change. Social relationships are dominated by the central attachments, language begins, the child learns to walk and move about more confidently. Cognitively there are rapid changes toward the eventual milestone of internal representation. Descriptively we can see all these things happening at the same time. What we still don't understand is how these several lines of development are linked together.

There are some suggestions (discussed in Chapters 4 and 5) that the early cognitive developments are a necessary underpinning for beginning word use: The child may develop the concept and then learn the word to attach to that concept. There is also a growing body of evidence (Bates, Bretherton, Beeghly-Smith, & McNew, 1982) linking the security of the child's first attachment with cognitive development. Securely attached children seem to explore more freely, to persist longer in their play, to develop the object concept more rapidly, and the like.

Such a link might exist because the securely attached child is simply more comfortable exploring the world around him and thus has a richer and more varied set of experiences to stimulate more rapid cog-

Figure I.2. A child in the period from 2 to 18 months, a time of rapidly increasing perceptual-motor skills and significantly changing personal relationships.

nitive development. A second possible explanation is that the type of parent-child interaction that fosters a secure attachment may *also* be optimal for fostering language and cognitive skill. In particular, one of the magic ingredients seems to be *contingent responsiveness*. We have seen that parents who use contingent pacing have more securely attached children; we have seen that parents who respond contingently to their infant's vocalizations have infants who talk sooner; we have seen that responsive toys and responsive parents foster more complex play and more rapid development. Presumably most parents provide similar levels of contingent responsiveness in many domains, so that the rate of children's development on all three fronts will be similar.

From 18 Months to 6 Years

The transition at 18 to 24 months is marked by the achievement of internal representation and by the development of more complex language. Children passing through this transition frequently show disruption of sleeping or eating habits as symptoms of the disequilibrium being experienced.

We have summarized the changes from 2 to 6 years of age in Table I.2. We see this as a single period, without significant subperiods or transitions.

One way to think of this stretch of four years is as a long consolidation. The major breakthroughs in language and cognition at 18 to 24 months usher in entire collections of new skills and opportunities, and

TABLE I.2
Summary of Development from 2 to 6 Years

Physical and perceptual development	Cognitive development	Language development	Social development
With major brain growth complete, there are no new major motor skills but considerable refinement of existing skills occurs. Coordination improves, particularly small muscle coordination; child begins to play games and use large game equipment, such as bats and balls.	Preoperational stage of development according to Piaget. The child's logic is still fairly primitive, but he can use words or images to stand for things in his play, begins to be able to take other people's perspectives, becomes able to classify fairly skillfully, and develops a full gender concept.	Child moves from Stage-1 to Stage-2 language, constructing more complex sentences. By age 6, language is used skillfully by most children. The meaning of words has come to match the meaning in the adult language fairly well.	Primary attachments to parents are still present and visible, especially when the child is under stress. Child explores farther and farther from this safe base, however, and develops more relationships with peers. Primitive forms of early friendships are formed, and sharing and generosity as well as aggression can be seen. Play choice begins to be with the same sex and with sex-stereotyped toys and games.

it takes the child three to four years to master the new skills completely.

Another way to look at the preschooler is in terms of his striving
for independence. He can get around in the world much better than
he could before, and he pushes for the freedom and opportunity to go
his own way. It is this element of the period that Erikson emphasizes
in his stages of autonomy versus shame and doubt and initiative versus
guilt.

It seems to us that the advances in language and cognition and the
push for independence are not separate from one another. Each makes
the other possible to some degree. They also combine to influence the
form of the child's attachment behavior. When language is rudimentary and the child's locomotion is poor, then clinging, touching and
holding, or crying are just about the only stress-related attachment behaviors available to the child. However, as language becomes more
skillful, she becomes able to stay in touch with adults and peers in new
ways; she can call to her mother, "Mommy, are you still there?" or ask
for attention, "Daddy, look at my picture!" The attachment may be no
less strong, but it can be maintained at greater physical distances.

These new skills also clearly affect the child's developing
self-concept and sex-role identity. The child understands that there is
a continuing self and begins to define the dimensions of that self—size,

Figure I.3. Independence at last! The child from 2 to 6 demands independence, learns
to play with peers, makes significant cognitive strides, and develops skillful use of
language.

age, gender, and the like. He also now comprehends the things that other people say about him, and that information is also factored into the self-concept.

For most children, the next major transition occurs somewhere between ages 5 and 7. Again the cognitive shift is probably the critical experience, although the fact that most children start school at this time is clearly of importance as well. (It's not accidental that these two things occur together. Schooling is begun at about ages 5 to 7 in virtually every culture, presumably because of some recognition that children of that age are now cognitively and socially ready for the demands of formal schooling.)

Like the earlier transitions, this one is often marked by increases in problem behavior, difficulties adjusting to school, loss of appetite, or other symptoms. But it is also frequently a time of excitement, even joy, for children. Whole new vistas open up. The child is more independent, more focused on the peer group and less on the parents, and is learning immensely powerful new cognitive and academic skills.

From 6 to 12 Years

We have summarized the changes that take place from ages 6 to 12 in Table I.3. Freud called this the *latency period,* as if it were a period of waiting, with nothing very important happening. In one sense he was right; it appears to be a relatively calm period. Nonetheless, there

TABLE I.3
Summary of Development from 6 to 12 Years

Physical and perceptual development	Cognitive development	Language development	Social development
Physical growth continues at a steady pace without any major spurts until puberty. Among girls, puberty may begin during this time. Gross-motor skills continue to improve; the child can ride a bike, play ball, and perform other complex motor tasks. Adult levels of visual acuity are reached.	This is the period Piaget called *concrete operations.* The child's thinking becomes reversible; and she can use the operations, such as addition, subtraction, and serial ordering. She is less tied to the physical features of objects, more able to perform actions in her head. She also grasps conservation. Inductive logic is now seen.	Although the basic language skill has been acquired, the child normally learns to read and write in this period and becomes more skillful with advanced forms of sentence construction, such as passive sentences.	Freud called this the *latency period* because sexual interests seem to be largely submerged. Peers become very important, but nearly all peer groups are same-sex groups. Children are exploring and learning their sex roles partly through imitation of same-sex models. Attachments to parents are less visible but still present. Individual friendships become important, especially for girls.

is a great deal of change. Unlike the earlier periods we have talked about, though, in which there are significant changes in many areas—language, cognition, social and physical development—the changes from 6 to 12 seem to center mostly in one area, cognition.

During the elementary-school years, the child's understanding of the world, and of people and relationships, shifts fundamentally from an egocentric to a more reciprocal view. We can see this in the quality of children's friendships, which move toward sharing and exchange; we see this in children's judgments of other people's actions, which shift to an emphasis on intentions rather than on consequences; we see this certainly in children's understanding of the lawful relationships among objects. The school-aged child is no longer tied down by what things look like on the outside; she can understand that there are constancies—qualities of people, of friendships, of objects—that remain the same even when they appear to be different.

Figure I.4. Individual friendships become important in the social lives of children of elementary-school age; their understanding of what friendship means also changes during this period, becoming more reciprocal.

We do not want to leave the impression that social relationships are unimportant at this age. They are vitally important. Whether a child has friends at this age, for example, is one of the few things about childhood that predicts emotionally stable or unstable adulthood (Kohlberg, LaCrosse, & Ricks, 1972). But the most striking characteristic of this period is the development of more complex mental abilities, which in turn affect a wide range of behaviors and relationships.

THE ROLE OF THE ENVIRONMENT

Some of the patterns of developmental change we have described are obviously strongly influenced by maturation: motor development, early language, possibly cognitive development as well. But no development is purely maturational. At the very least, expression of any physiologically programmed development requires a minimally supportive environment. Infants need to spend time on their stomachs if they are to learn to crawl at the normal time; toddlers need to be exposed to language if they are to develop language themselves. There are many other examples.

For some kinds of development, and possibly for some periods of development, the range of acceptable environments may be quite broad. For example, several respected theorists, including Sandra Scarr (Scarr-Salapatek, 1976) and Robert McCall (1981), have recently suggested that cognitive development in the first 12 to 18 months of life is highly *canalized* (a term first suggested by Waddington, 1957). That is, the path or sequence of early development is very powerful (a narrow canal), and nearly all basic child-rearing environments provide enough support for it to proceed normally. Furthermore, infants seem to have excellent "self-righting" tendencies: If the child is deflected from the underlying pathway because of some inadequacy of the environment or some accidental occurrence, the power of the underlying developmental system is such that the child can often recover later. A child who is ill in the early years, for example, may show slower development during the illness but then later largely catches up to her healthier peers. Beyond infancy, however, canalization seems to be much weaker. Optimum development seems to demand much more specific input, so that a narrower range of environments provides sufficient support.

Despite such apparent built-in directionality, however, and despite differences in specific heredity, the environment in which a child is reared clearly has a *major* impact on the rate of development and possibly on the final level the child achieves. We've mentioned such environmental effects as we have gone along, but let us summarize:

1. Physical development is affected perhaps least by the environment,

though diet has a significant effect on the rate of growth, on final height, and on the development of brain cells. Children who have been deprived of adequate diets prenatally and in the early years frequently also show intellectual deficits, and these deficits may remain even if the diet later improves (Zeskind & Ramey, 1978, 1981).

2. Both the rate of development of cognitive structures, and the level of cognitive power (as measured by IQ tests, primarily) are affected by the richness and variety of the objects available to the child, by the regularity and predictability of experiences, by the amount of encouragement for exploration, and by the amount of parental support and involvement (Bee, Barnard, Eyres, Gray, Hammond, Spietz, Snyder, & Clark, 1982; Bradley & Caldwell, 1978; Ramey & Haskins, 1981; Wachs, 1979). Comparisons of children from middle-class and poverty-level families (who differ on many of these dimensions) show that by age 3, children from middle-class families have IQs that are 15 to 20 points higher, on the average, than children from working-class families (Golden, Birns, Bridger, & Moss, 1971). Some of that difference *may* be genetic. Current research suggests, though, that much of the effect is environmental.

3. Language development appears to move along with only basic environmental support—mainly exposure to language from adults. But as we've already pointed out, parents who talk more to their children, and who respond contingently to their child's language efforts, have children who develop language more rapidly. Such children also show higher IQ scores (Clarke-Stewart, VanderStoep, & Killian, 1979).

4. The influence of the environment seems to be especially strong in the area of social and emotional development. Attachment behaviors in the early months may well be instinctive, as Bowlby suggests, but the security of the attachment seems to be largely a function of the child's experience with the major caregivers (Ainsworth, Bell, & Stayton, 1972; Blehar, Lieberman, & Ainsworth, 1977). In older children, behavior disorders and problems with relationships with others seem to be a function of both the security of the early attachment and the level of stress or support in the family environment (Rutter, 1978, 1979).

We can illustrate the degree of the potential impact of the environment quite clearly by looking at the results from a fascinating intervention study by Rick Heber and his colleagues (Heber, 1978). Heber selected a group of 20 infants born into poverty circumstances to mothers with IQs below 75. Without intervention, such children are also likely to end up with very low IQ scores. Heber wanted to find out if that probable retardation could be prevented if the infants were given a massive dose of a well-designed, stimulating environment—one that embodied all the optimal features we have just listed. The intervention began in the first weeks of life and continued to school age. It included five-day-a-week, all-day day care for the infants and vocational and educational rehabilitation for the mothers.

Figure I.5 shows the IQ scores of these 20 children compared to another group of 20 from the same kinds of families who did not receive the special care. As you can see, this rich environment did, in fact, prevent intellectual retardation for this group of children. The fact that the children were still above average even three years after the intervention stopped suggests that the effect may be permanent.

We should emphasize that Heber's study does not prove that all mental retardation could be "cured" with appropriate environmental interventions. Heber did not include in his group any children with known brain damage or other physical abnormality—either of which might cause lasting retardation. What his study does show is that for

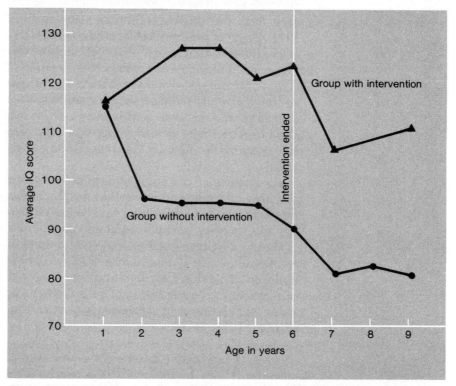

Figure I.5.   In Heber's study, 20 children received massive intervention, including enriched day care for the infant and educational training for the mother. Twenty children from equivalently impoverished families received no such intervention. The figure shows the IQ scores of these two groups of children over time. The treated group's IQ does drop when the intervention stops but continues to be more than 20 points above the IQ of the nontreated group. (*Source:* Heber, 1978, p. 59, combination of Figures 4 and 5.)

those children who have the environmental deck stacked against them, changing the environment greatly alters the outcome. Since briefer or less massive interventions attempted by other researchers have resulted in somewhat smaller intellectual gains (Ramey & Haskins, 1981; Madden, Levenstein, & Levenstein, 1976), the case for the importance of the environment is further strengthened.

INDIVIDUAL DIFFERENCES IN DEVELOPMENT

We have been talking right along about differences in rate of development and about some of the explanations of those differences. But there is one aspect of individual differences that we have sidestepped a bit, namely, sex differences. Do boys and girls develop in the same way, at the same rate?

Sex Differences

Table I.4 summarizes the major sex differences in development during childhood that have been reasonably well established. Two points are worth making about these differences.

First, even where the difference is very clear, such as with aggressiveness, *the actual magnitude of the difference is small* (Plomin & Foch, 1981), and the two distributions (male and female) overlap almost completely. That is, *within* each sex there is almost a full range of performance or skill on each of the dimensions listed in the table. (Many boys have fast maturation, or low tolerance for pain, or low levels of aggression, or poor math skill; many girls are competitive, or noncompliant, or field independent, or good at spatial visualization tasks.) It is only when we look at the average scores for the two sexes that we see a difference. It is worthwhile to try to explain such differences, but it is important to keep in mind that the actual impact of gender on behavior is really very small.

Second, both biological and environmental causes seem to be at work in producing the differences we do see. The difference in aggressiveness seems to have biological roots, such as varying hormone patterns (Maccoby & Jacklin, 1980) (as we pointed out in Chapter 7), but parental treatment may well magnify the biological effect. Similarly, differences in early language skill may be partly biological (varying maturational rates) and partly caused by differing amounts of exposure to language. We realize that it is not popular (at least not within the women's movement) to look for *any* biological causes of sex differences. However, the evidence we have at the moment compels us to accept the plausibility of some biological effects interacting with environmental shaping.

TABLE I.4

Summary of Sex Differences in Development in Childhood

Physical development:

Rate of maturation	Girls seem to be on a bit faster developmental timetable, with slightly more advanced development at birth and with earlier puberty.
Quality of maturation	Girls' physical growth is more regular and predictable with fewer uneven spurts.
Strength and speed	Little difference in the early years.
Fat tissue	Girls have a thicker layer of fat tissue, just below the skin, from birth onward.

Perceptual development:

Sensitivity to pain	Boys appear to have a greater tolerance for pain, but the sex difference is small.
Responsiveness to taste	Girls appear to be somewhat more responsive to taste stimuli.
Perceptual style	Girls are more likely to be field dependent; boys are more likely to be field independent.

Cognitive development:

Cognitive structure	No sex differences on any measure of structure during childhood is found consistently.
Cognitive power: IQ	No sex differences on total IQ scores is found.
Verbal skill	Girls slightly better at some verbal skills, particularly in the early months of life and again in late elementary school.
Math skill	No difference in this age period, except that girls are sometimes better at computation.
Spatial skills	No difference in spatial visualization skill at this age.

Social development:

Aggression	Boys are more aggressive on nearly all measures, beginning in toddlerhood.
Competitiveness	Boys show more competitiveness than girls, although this difference does not appear as early as the aggression difference.
Dominance	Boys again show more dominance in play with other children.
Nurturance	No clear sex difference found in this age period.
Sociability	Girls typically have fewer but closer friendships; boys have more, but less intimate, friendships.
Compliance	Girls appear to be somewhat more compliant to adult requests, especially in early childhood.

SOME LINGERING UNANSWERED QUESTIONS

We cannot leave this summary without talking at least briefly about some of the questions and issues about development in childhood that are currently being discussed. The field of developmental psychology is presently in a state of considerable theoretical ferment. Old assumptions are being questioned right and left, and new theoretical paradigms have not yet emerged. Two questions, in particular, are the focus of present debates.

Are There Really Stages?

We raised this question in Chapter 1, when we contrasted the several major theories. But the question is being asked now in a somewhat different form: Is there any *synchrony* in development, any pattern of connectedness or overall organization that characterizes each of a series of ages? We often talk as if there is, such as in the discussion of the period from ages 6 to 12 that you read a few pages back. However, many psychologists are now asking whether development is really a set of largely unrelated sequences or whether there are overriding characteristics at particular ages that affect all the child's behavior. There is evidence on both sides, and the argument will no doubt continue.

Is Early Experience Really More Important than Later Experience?

The assumption that experience in the first years is more important, more formative, than later experience has been around a long time (Lomax, Kagan, & Rosenkrantz, 1978). Obviously, Freud believed it, as do Erikson and many others. One way to get a handle on this issue is to use an analogy suggested by A.D.B. Clarke (1968; Clarke & Clarke, 1976): When we construct a house, does the shape of the foundation determine the final structure completely, or does it partially influence the final structure, or can many final structures be built on the original foundation? Perhaps even more important, if there are flaws or weaknesses in the original foundation, are the weaknesses permanent, or can they be corrected later, after the house is completed?

Put more precisely, we are asking whether the early years of life (infancy, or even childhood as a whole) are a **critical period** in development—a period during which a particular experience or set of experiences has a lasting effect that cannot be undone later (Colombo, 1982). Current theorists also talk about the *resiliency* of children. Are they resilient enough to recover from deprivation or abuse if they are later placed in better circumstances?

Again, there are data on both sides. Some prenatal influences are permanent, such as the effect of rubella in the early months of pregnancy. Some effects of poor diet in the early years also do not seem to be outgrown, and some effects of early cognitive impoverishment may also be very long lasting, as may the effect of abuse or neglect or insecure attachment.

At the same time, there is evidence that children can and do recover from many such early experiences. Many preterm infants, and others who suffered from prenatal trauma, seem to turn out quite normally if they are later reared in supportive environments (Sameroff & Chandler, 1975); longitudinal researchers who have hunted for permanent effects of early experiences frequently have not found them (Kagan, 1979); and as we will see in the chapters on adult development, those who experienced poor early childhoods may sometimes be "healed" by particular relationships or experiences in adult life.

Our own conclusion at the moment is that children (and adults) are probably considerably more resilient than many of us had thought a decade ago. But we think there is a danger that the theoretical pendulum is now swinging too far toward the *resilience* side of the argument. Alan Sroufe has stated the middle ground well:

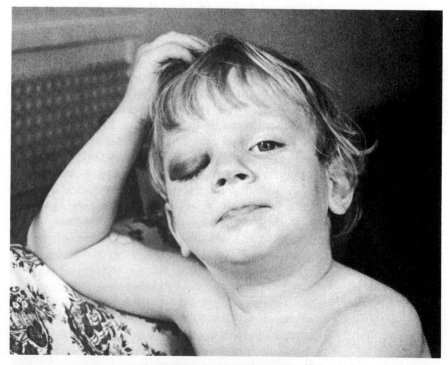

Figure I.6. Will the abuse this child has experienced in the first few years of life mark her for life? Or can she recover if she is given a better environment later?

There is reason to doubt that children are infinitely resilient, even given the flexibility of our species. . . . What children experience, early and later, makes a difference. We cannot assume that early experiences will somehow be canceled out by later experience. Lasting consequences of early inadequate experience may be subtle and complex, taking the form of increased vulnerability to certain kinds of stress, for example, or becoming manifest only when the individual attempts to establish intimate adult relationships or engage in parenting. But there will be consequences (Sroufe, 1979, p. 840).

When we talk about continuity and discontinuity in development or individual consistency or inconsistency over time, we are really raising variations on these same two fundamental themes. We will meet these questions again as we explore development in adolescence and adulthood.

KEY TERMS

Consolidation   The term used in this book to refer to those periods in development between transitions when the child is expanding and consolidating major gains or changes made at transition points.

Developmental leaps   Term used by Klaus Riegel to describe points of transition in development, when the child appears to shift into a different gear.

Dilemma   Term used by Erikson and others to describe the central task on which the child (or adult) is focused in each of several periods or stages of development.

Transition   The term used in this book to refer to those periods in development when major changes in cognitive skill, social interaction pattern, or physical development appear to disturb the equilibrium of the previous consolidation period and require a new equilibration process.

PART II
The Developing Adolescent and Youth

Chapter 8
Physical Development in Adolescence and Youth

Because my family lives more than 2000 miles away, I usually only see them once or twice a year. So I have watched my younger cousins grow up as though I were seeing their pictures in a family album—one glimpse every 6 or 12 months. The last time I went home was a particular shocker. The youngest boy in the family, who had been collecting baseball cards and wearing dirty T-shirts when I saw him last, had traded his cards for rock records and his T-shirts for button-down collars and a blow dryer. His little-boy skinniness had been replaced by wider shoulders and muscular hips and legs, and I didn't recognize his new, lower voice on the telephone. The change in his older brother was no less noticeable: A tall, gangling, and somewhat awkward teenager had returned from his first term at college looking a lot less skinny (from dormitory food, no doubt) and a lot more coordinated. [SM].

These changes are probably more recently familiar to many of you than to us, since we are some distance away from them. Adolescence is a time of rapid physical growth and development, more so than any other period except early infancy. Babies, though, are not aware (as far as we know) of the changes in their bodies, while adolescents most certainly are.

In this chapter, we want to look at how growth proceeds in the period from about age 12 to about age 22, both in the ways that show (like height and weight) and in the ways that don't show (like changes in bones, muscles, and hormones). We also want to look carefully at the set of physical changes that accompanies **puberty,** the physical onset of sexual maturing, and the set that goes along with growing a new life in pregnancy. Finally, we'll take a look at some issues of health and illness during these years, just as we did in our discussion of physical development in childhood.

Before we move into the material on physical changes, though, we need to say a word about terminology and about the ages we will cover in the chapters in this section of the book. We want to talk here about a span of years that extends somewhat beyond what is normally considered *adolescence* and to include a part of the early twenties.

This is not a totally arbitrary choice. We can think of the period from 12 to 22 as a time of physical transition (puberty) and also as a time of psychological transition to full adulthood, culminating in the achievement of independence from one's parents. For most of us, this is not completed until the early twenties. But we do not want to apply the word *adolescent* to a young person of 19 or 20 or 22; instead, we will use both the phrase *young adult* and the word *youth* (a word Kenneth Keniston, 1970, suggested) to describe the period from about 18 to 22. We will thus talk about the years from 12 to 22 as the period of *adolescence and youth.* For some purposes, such as the discussion of health and accidents, we can combine our discussions of these two subperiods. However, many aspects of physical development are different in adolescence and in youth, so we will divide our description into two parts.

Figure 8.1. We can distinguish between two subperiods in the years from 12 to 22, one which we have called adolescence (12 to 18) and one which we have called youth (18 to 22). Most of the major physical changes we will be charting take place during the first of these, but as you can see there are changes in appearance and behavior as well.

PHYSICAL DEVELOPMENT IN ADOLESCENCE

Growth on the Outside: Size and Shape Changes

Height. If you look back at Figure 3.1, page 91, you can see that there is a growth spurt in the early adolescent years, when both height and weight increase rapidly. We would like to show you those data in a slightly different way (Figure 8.2) that highlights how sizable that spurt really is. In this graph, we have plotted how much *growth* occurs in each year, rather than total height. Although growth during adolescence is not as rapid as during infancy, it is certainly much more rapid than during the rest of childhood. As we have mentioned before, the spurt both begins and ends earlier for girls and never reaches quite the same high rate as it does for boys (Tanner, 1978).

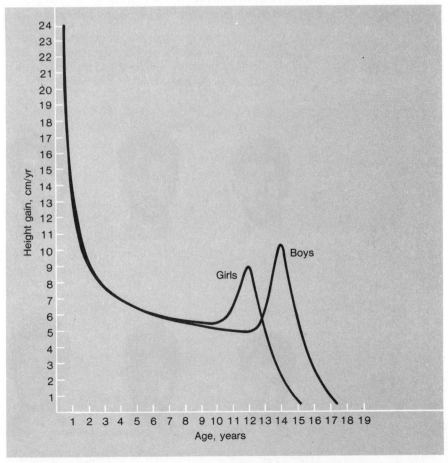

Figure 8.2. The velocity of growth. The rate of growth during adolescence is greater than at any other time except during early infancy. (*Source:* Tanner, 1978, p. 14.)

Shape.   During adolescence, the proportions of the body (that is, the relative sizes of the head, trunk, and legs) change. The legs increase in length first, some six to nine months before the trunk does. (This is the reverse of the proximodistal rule that described development in infancy, since the limbs seem to grow before the center of the body.) The stereotype that young teenagers are all arms and legs is based on this fact. So is the observation that teenagers start outgrowing their pants before they start outgrowing their jackets.

Although the head does not change a great deal in size, it does change in other ways. The forehead becomes more prominent and both jaws grow forward, the lower more than the upper (see Figure 8.3). These changes are often quite striking, especially in boys, who are also beginning to grow facial hair. In the intermediate stages, before all the changes have coalesced into the pattern that will be the adult features, the difference between the childhood face and the adolescent face may be startling, even disconcerting, to parents.

My son went through this stage during a time when unkempt below-shoulder-length hair was the style for teenage boys. The combination of the hair and his suddenly larger jaw and forehead makes photos of him at this age almost unrecognizable as the same child he had been or the adult he has become.[HB]

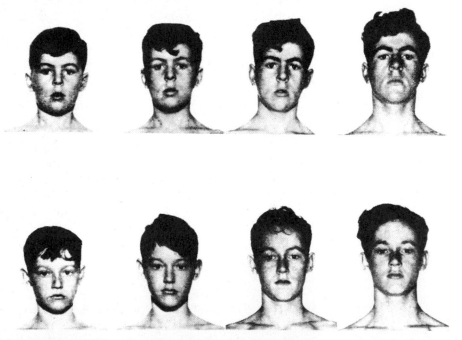

Figure 8.3. Changes in the shape of the head during adolescence. Although the head does not increase much in size, the shape of the face and the features change substantially during puberty. (*Source:* Tanner, 1978, p. 68.)

Another important change in shape at puberty concerns the width of the shoulders and the hips. Both boys and girls show a spurt in growth of the pelvis (the large, flat bones that determine the shape of the lower trunk), but boys also show a similar spurt in shoulder width, which is not seen in females. Incidentally, this is why physical anthropologists can usually determine the sex of a skeleton, even one that is millions of years old—the ratio of shoulder size to hip size is always greater among males.

Population Differences in Size and Shape.   If living conditions are optimal, blacks are taller and heavier than whites during adolescence, and Asiatics are smaller and lighter than whites and blacks (Chumlea, 1982). These are the same differences that are found among adults, in fact (Eveleth & Tanner, 1976).

The reason we emphasize that these differences occur under optimal living conditions is that living conditions can themselves have a big impact on growth measures. For example, Harbine Young and Lucy Rau Ferguson (1981) studied three groups of adolescent boys whose grandparents had come from southern Italy. Some were still living in southern Italy (in the city of Palermo), some had emigrated with their families to Rome, and still others had moved to Boston, Massachusetts. Since the genetic backgrounds of the three groups were similar, any differences between them must be due to environmental influence. Young and Ferguson found that the boys now living in Boston were both taller and heavier than those remaining in Italy; and among those, the ones in Rome tended to be larger and heavier than those in Palermo.

We want you to notice that there are two kinds of population differences seen in these growth measures. One kind is a difference *between* racial groups, no matter where they live, and the other is a difference *within* a racial group, depending upon where they live. This is important because when we compare two or more groups of people, they often differ in *both* racial composition and standard of living. We encountered this problem when we tried to sort out the influences of race and environment on IQ scores (Chapter 4), and it is just as much a problem here. Since both factors can affect growth, we need to be sure that we control one of these variables before we conclude that the other is the cause of growth differences.

Cohort Effects.   Changes in standards of living may also help us understand the fact that boys and girls today are taller and heavier than their parents or grandparents.

It is worth taking a look at these changes because they give such a dramatic example of what we called *cohort* effects in Chapter 1. If you will recall, a cohort is a group of persons of about the same age who share similar major life experiences, such as growing up in a particular historical era. When we compare groups of people of widely differing ages, we have to be cautious about assuming that the differences we see are due to age, since they might also be due to the differences in general experiences encountered by the several cohorts. Studies of adolescent growth changes in different historical periods illustrate just how large such cohort effects can be.

Boys and girls living today in the United States, western Europe, and Japan are taller, heavier, and more mature than were their parents, grandparents, and particularly their great-grandparents during adolescence (Chumlea, 1982). These differences are referred to as **secular trends,** and as you can see in Figure 8.4, they are fairly substantial. Does this mean that American youngsters will all be 6 feet 5 inches tall by the end of the century? Probably not. It seems likely that these improvements are related to improvements in the standard of living—mostly diet—and that they have reached about the peak they are likely to achieve.

Individual Differences in Size and Shape. One thing you should remember as we discuss both the outer and inner changes that occur in

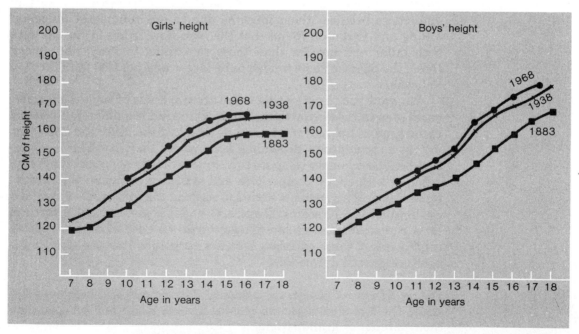

Figure 8.4. Secular trends in height. These data are from Sweden, where excellent medical and growth records have been kept for many years. It appears that the rate of increase in height from one generation to the next is slowing down. (*Source:* Ljung, Bergsten-Brucefors, & Lundgren, 1974.)

teenagers is that there is a wide range of normal times for them to occur. Children of the same age may—in fact, usually do—differ widely in their physical maturation. As you can see in Figure 8.5, some 14-year-old males look like little boys, while others are definitely young men. The same thing is true, of course, of girls, and it is noticeable at an earlier age. All of this variation is perfectly normal; but there are some effects of being very early, or very late, in physical change that we will discuss later in this chapter.

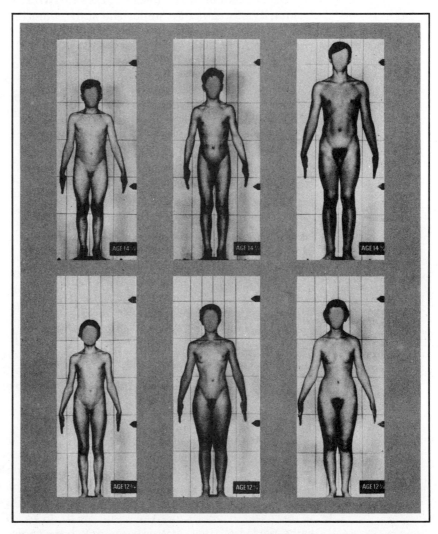

Figure 8.5. The variability of growth during adolescence All of the boys are the same age, but one looks like a little boy and another looks like a young man. The same thing is true of girls, although it is obvious at an earlier age. (*Source:* Tanner, 1975, p. 28.)

Growth on the Inside: Muscles, Fat, and Hormones

Although we cannot see growth in bones, muscles, and nerves as easily as we can see changes in height and weight, these body parts also show important changes during adolescence.

Lean Body Mass: Bones and Muscles.   It is sometimes helpful to think of bodies as being made up of two kinds of tissues, **lean body mass** (LBM) and **total body fat** (TBF). Lean body mass includes all of the bones, internal organs, muscles, and skin; while total body fat includes primarily storage of fat under the skin (sometimes called **subcutaneous fat**).

Several of the outside changes we described in the last section are actually a result of changes in lean body mass, particularly bone maturation. The long bones in the body, particularly those in the arms and legs, grow as the cartilage near the ends of the bones becomes ossified. During adolescence this process increases, gradually tapering off at about age 18 for girls and age 20 for boys.

Because of the regularity and predictability of the sequences of bone changes, it is actually possible for physiologists to estimate a child's or adolescent's overall level of maturational progress by assessing **skeletal age**—that is, by determining the maturity of the bones. Most estimates of skeletal age are based on careful classification of X-ray pictures of a joint, usually the hand or knee (Tanner, Whitehouse, Marshall, Healy, & Goldstein, 1975). Measures of skeletal age tend to be more closely related to other physical development events—like the beginning of sex-organ development—than chronological age is.

Both boys and girls increase their LBM up to age 15 or so; girls then show no further changes until considerably later in life. Boys, on the other hand, continue to increase in LBM through the end of the teen years and perhaps into the early twenties (Chumlea, 1982). Not surprisingly, these differences in lean body mass are reflected in the relative strengths of teenaged boys and girls (see Figure 8.6). Boys are consistently stronger, and their advantage continues to grow throughout adolescence.

Total Body Fat.   Girls have slightly more total body fat than do boys at the beginning of puberty; and this difference becomes greater during adolescence, as females show increases and males show decreases. Among boys, TBF declines from 17 to 20 percent at the beginning of puberty to 10 to 12 percent of body weight at full growth; among girls, it increases from 19 to 23 percent up to 25 to 28 percent during the same period of time. Not only do girls have more subcutaneous fat, it is located in different places: There are noticeable deposits on the breasts, buttocks, thighs, and across the back of the arms (Sinclair, 1978).

BOX 8.1

Scoliosis

Scoliosis is a sideways bending of the spinal column that often begins in early adolescence. It affects about 1 percent of the teenagers in this country, four-fifths of whom are girls. No one knows exactly why some children develop this problem; but if it is not treated, the body compensates with a second sideways curve. This double bend can lead to considerable discomfort or even permanent disability.

Traditional treatment for scoliosis has been the use of a cumbersome garment called a *Milwaukee brace*. This brace, which looks like some medieval instrument of torture, consists of a strap around the neck under the chin with a back like a high collar. A wide belt of cloth or leather goes around the hips, and another under one arm, and both of these are attached to the collar by three upright metal bars.

Needless to say, most teenage girls are unhappy about wearing such an unsightly and uncomfortable appliance, especially since it must be worn virtually all the time (usually 23 hours per day is the prescription). At the same time, parents and doctors are not very happy about having scoliosis go untreated.

Recently, Barry Dworkin (1982) has invented an alternative to the Milwaukee brace. Dworkin, who is a health psychologist, had noted that the brace was most successful when the patients tried actively to hold the prescribed position. That is, they seemed to use the brace as a reminder of the correct posture rather than passively letting the brace hold them. So he invented a relatively unobtrusive device that could do the job of reminding the child to stand or sit correctly.

This device is much lighter and less obtrusive than the brace. It consists of narrow nylon cords going over the shoulders and between the legs. Another cord around the chest keeps everything from slipping and holds a small electronic device. This electronic device detects when the shoulder and lower cords are not lined up and sounds a quiet beep to remind the child to resume the correct posture. If the child does not straighten up, a louder tone (audible to others) sounds.

The real question, of course, is whether the behavioral device is as effective as the Milwaukee Brace in preventing permanent damage. Although carefully controlled studies are just now being done, a preliminary study found that 10 out of 12 children who used the device were considered cured by their own doctors.

One of the reasons we chose to include scoliosis in this chapter is that a psychologist seems to be a good guy in this story (as opposed to the typically brainless way they are usually portrayed in movies and on television). Scoliosis, though, is no joke, and because the traditional treatment is so unsightly and uncomfortable, many patients (especially girls) are reluctant to carry through with it. The lesson is that good medical treatment for adolescents has to take psychological factors into account—or even the best prescriptions will not be followed.

Of course, as with all averages, these descriptions do not fit everyone. In particular, girls who are involved in serious athletic competition (or, for that matter, ballet training) often show substantially lower percentages of TBF than indicated here. Such a lowering of body fat *may* be implicated in the observed fact that most female athletes tend to begin menstruation later than nonathletes do (Malina, 1981). We know from studies of adults experiencing serious loss of body fat under conditions of famine that women typically cease menstruating (Stein, Susser, Saenger, & Morella, 1975). There are also reports from adult

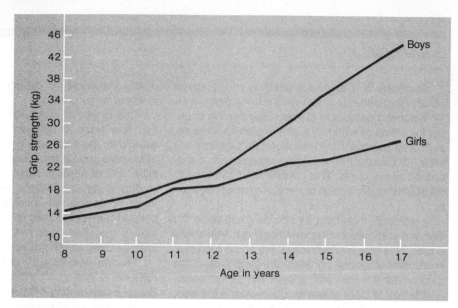

Figure 8.6.   Grip strength in boys and girls. Boys show greater strength over the entire age range studied, but the difference begins to increase at about age 13. By the end of adolescence boys are substantially stronger. (*Source:* Chumlea, 1982, p. 477.)

women athletes that they cease menstruating when their body fat falls below some critical level—perhaps 8 to 10 percent. By extension, it may be that delayed first menstruation in teenage girl athletes is also related to lowered body fat.

Changes in the Glandular System and Hormones.   Although the basic growth processes of the nervous system (cell division and myelinization) are complete before adolescence, the brain continues to play an important part in physical development. We noted in Chapter 3 that the pituitary gland controls the output of other hormones in the body. During puberty, the pituitary gland is itself under the control of the part of the brain called the **hypothalamus.** Cells in the hypothalamus, called **neuroreceptors,** serve to keep the concentration of hormones in the body at a preset level. If the concentration rises, a neuroreceptor causes the hypothalamus to reduce the amount of stimulating hormone it sends out, therefore lowering the level. Similarly, if the concentration becomes low, another neuroreceptor causes the hypothalamus to increase the amount of stimulating hormone it sends out, causing the level to rise.

The hormone levels to which the neuroreceptors respond are under the control of maturation (and to a lesser extent, environmental) influences. The *set points* for the neuroreceptors are quite low in children but get higher at the onset of puberty. Although it is undoubtedly true that hormones affect the brain, the first change that occurs seems to be that the brain affects the hormones. The hormones, then, proceed to direct the maturation of sexual characteristics in both males and females.

Growth and Sexuality

The most striking changes of adolescence are not those of height and weight, nor even of body composition, but those that concern the development of sexual characteristics. We usually divide these characteristics into two groups: The **primary sex characteristics** are those that are necessary for reproduction. They include the testes and penis in the male, and the ovaries, uterus, and vagina in the female. The **secondary sex characteristics** are those that are not necessary for reproduction, and these include breast development, pubic hair growth, lowered voice pitch, and hair growth on the face and underarms. (For those of you who do further reading in this area, we should note that there is some confusion about whether the development of testes and penis should be considered a primary or a secondary sex characteristic. Both labels are sometimes used. However, since the changes in male genitalia are essential for reproduction, we have included them as part of primary sex characteristics.)

In some cultures, the maturing of the primary sex characteristics (marked by a girl's first menstruation or a boy's first nocturnal emission) is an important developmental milestone. In our own culture, we (at least we psychologists) tend to place more emphasis on the secondary sex characteristics. There are probably two reasons for this. First, our culture defines both menstruation and nocturnal emissions as private events, not discussed in public and not evident to a bystander. At the same time, the visible changes in bodies are public events, easily seen by all. Second, we assume that an adolescent's appearance influences the behavior of people who interact with him. Since the secondary sex characteristics are those that affect appearance, we would expect them to show a closer relationship to psychological development.

Primary Sex Characteristics: Girls.   For girls, as well as for boys, changes in the reproductive organs are gradual; but there is a clearly marked single event that is often taken as a measure of sexual maturity, namely, the first menstruation, called **menarche** (pronounced me-narkee).

Most of us assume that the first menstruation signals that the girl is fertile and biologically ready to have children. This is not quite the case. In most girls, the first several menstrual periods are not accompanied by the production of an ovum. For a while only some cycles are fertile, until finally full fertility is achieved.

For most girls in the United States and western Europe, menarche occurs between the ages of 10 and 16. It usually follows soon after the peak of the growth spurt has been reached and thus is fairly late in the sequence of pubertal changes in girls, as we have outlined in Table 8.1.

The age of menarche has been steadily declining in the industrialized nations over the last two centuries or so (Roche, 1979). Since girls growing up in less developed countries show later menarche, we assume that this secular trend (like the one for height and weight) is related to diet. The observation mentioned earlier—that young women athletes often begin menstruating relatively late—suggests that total body fat, rather than diet itself, may be the controlling variable.

Primary Sex Characteristics: Boys.   In boys, there are major changes in reproductive organs beginning at about ages 11 to 12. The first signs of change are an enlargement of the testes and scrotum; the penis begins to enlarge a little later. The entire process of change normally takes three or four years to complete and is commonly divided into steps or stages (Tanner, 1962), as we've outlined in Table 8.2.

Pinpointing the achievement of male reproductive maturity within this sequence has proved to be difficult. Not only is the first nocturnal emission a private event (sometimes even regarded as shameful), it is also hard to tell when the seminal fluid begins to include viable sperm. What data we do have suggest that reproductive fertility begins sometime between ages 12 and 16 for most boys in industrialized nations.

Table 8.3 summarizes the several changes in boys during puberty. Typically, a boy begins to show development of testes and penis before he shows rapid growth in height. The point of reproductive fertility is not shown in this table, but it would appear to occur sometime near the end of the height spurt.

Although the onset of menstruation and emission mark, in a general way, the biological ability to conceive offspring, we should not conclude that they mark the beginning of optimal childbearing. The body

TABLE 8.1
Summary of Pubertal Development in Girls

Characteristic	Average age of onset	Normal range of onset ages	Average age at completion
Height spurt	10 ½	9 ½–14 ½	14
Menarche (first menstruation)	12 ½	10–15 ½	—
Breast development, beginning with first breast buds	10 ¾	8–13	14 ¾

SOURCE: Adapted from J. M. Tanner, "Growth and Endocrinology of the Adolescent," in Gardner, L. J. (Ed.): *Endocrine and Genetic Diseases of Childhood and Adolescence*, 2d ed. © 1975 by the W. B. Saunders Co., Philadelphia, PA.

TABLE 8.2
Five Pubertal Stages in the Genital Development of Boys

Stage	Description
1	Penis, testes, and scrotum are all about the same size and shape as in early childhood; this is, then, a *pre*pubertal stage.
2	Scrotum and testes enlarge slightly. The skin of the scrotum reddens and changes in texture. However, there is little or no enlargement of the penis at this stage.
3	The first change in the penis is a slight increase in length, accompanied by a further enlargement of testes and scrotum.
4	Further enlargement of the penis occurs, with growth both in breadth and development of glans. Still further enlargement of testes and scrotum also occurs at Stage 4, and the skin of the scrotum becomes still darker.
5	Genitalia are adult in size and shape.

SOURCE: Adapted from Tanner, 1962; Peterson & Taylor, 1980.

of an adolescent may not be adequate for good development of a fetus, even if one is conceived. Furthermore, we shall see in Chapter 10 that the adolescent is usually unprepared psychologically for bearing and rearing children.

Secondary Sex Characteristics. The most important (or at least the most studied) changes in secondary sex characteristics are in breasts (for girls) and pubic hair (for both boys and girls). Table 8.4 shows the five stages of development suggested by Tanner (1962) for both sets of changes.

Development within each of these categories, as well as in primary sex characteristics, seems to be controlled largely by maturation. That is, nearly all youngsters go through the sequences listed in Tables 8.2 and 8.4 in the order described. However, there is frequently inconsistency in rate of development *across* sequences. For example, a boy may be in Stage 2 of genital development but already in Stage 5 of pubic hair development (Petersen & Taylor, 1980).

TABLE 8.3
Summary of Pubertal Development in Boys

Characteristic	Average age of onset	Normal range of onset ages	Average age at completion	Range of ages at completion
Height spurt	12 ½	10 ½–16	16	13–17 ½
Accelerated growth of penis	12 ½	10 ½–14 ½	14 ½	11 ½–16 ½
Accelerated growth of testes	11 ½	9 ½–13 ½	15	13 ½–17

SOURCE: Adapted from J. M. Tanner, "Growth and Endocrinology of the Adolescent," in Gardner, L. J. (Ed.): *Endocrine and Genetic Diseases of Childhood and Adolescence,* 2nd ed. © 1975 by the W. B. Saunders Co., Philadelphia, PA.

By now it should be no surprise that girls begin development of the secondary sex characteristics before boys do. You can see both the usual timing and sex differences in breast, pubic hair, and male genital development in Figure 8.7, where the dots indicate the average age for each stage. We also want you to look, though, at the vertical lines in this figure, because they show the amount of variability in attaining each stage. Once again we are reminded how early—and how late—puberty can begin and yet be perfectly normal.

Hormones and Pubertal Development. We psychologists sometimes assume that research in the physical and biological sciences is somehow tidier than in our own area. The study of hormones in adolescence quickly shows us how wrong we are. It is difficult and expensive to do the chemical tests that identify hormones, some of which are detected more easily in the blood and others in the urine. Many hormones show cycles in their levels, that is, they are higher at certain times of the day or (especially for females) at certain times of the month. Furthermore, many other factors, such as diet and exercise patterns, can sometimes change the levels of hormones. So a good study of hormone development in adolescents is a costly and a time-consuming endeavor.

Despite these limitations, however, we do now have a fairly good

TABLE 8.4
Five Pubertal Stages in the Development of Pubic Hair and Breasts

Stage	Pubic hair development	Breast development
1	There is no pubic hair at this first stage. Thus, again, this is a prepubertal stage.	Only the papilla are elevated.
2	First sign of pubic hair, chiefly at the base of the penis and along the labia. The hair is sparse, long, slightly pigmented, tawny, straight or slightly curled.	Breast bud stage. The breast and the papilla are elevated as a small mound. The diameter of the areola is increased over Stage 1.
3	Hair darkens and becomes coarser and more curled and is spread sparsely over the pubic area.	Both the breast and areola are enlarged and elevated more than in Stage 2, but there is still no separation of their contours.
4	The hair is now adult in type, but it covers a smaller area than it will in adulthood. There is no spread to the thigh surface, for example.	The areola and papilla form a secondary mound, which projects from the contour of the breast.
5	The hair is now distributed in quantity and area as in an adult.	Mature stage: The papilla only projects with the areola recessed to the general contour of the breast.

SOURCE: Tanner, 1962; Peterson & Taylor, 1980.

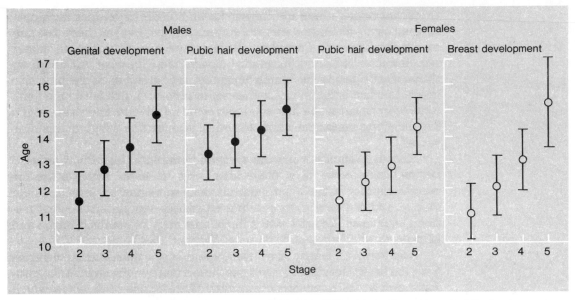

Figure 8.7. The ages at which the various stages of sex characteristic development occur. Once again we see that girls begin to mature earlier than boys. Also notice the wide range of ages included for each stage. (*Source:* Petersen & Taylor, 1980, p. 128.)

picture of how hormones influence the growth patterns in puberty. The beginnings of this process are found way back during the prenatal period, when the neuroreceptors we described earlier seem to be set to maintain low levels of sex hormones in the bloodstream. This probably happens around 21 or 22 weeks of gestational age.

The low set point continues to control the levels of hormones until late in childhood (the exact age, of course, varies with different children). Gradually, the set point changes, and the levels of these hormones in the blood increase. We don't know precisely what begins this process, but it seems likely that the adrenal gland is involved (Sizonenko & Paunier, 1975).

Now things begin to get complicated. The pituitary gland begins secreting **gonadotropic** hormones (two in males, three in females), which are hormones that stimulate the sex organs to develop. At the same time, the pituitary also secretes three hormones related to growth but not to sexual development: one that regulates the adrenal gland, one that regulates the thyroid gland, and one that regulates general growth, especially of the bones.

What all of this means is that there are at least five hormones (six in the female) that influence growth and development during puberty. Together they regulate the form and function of the endocrine system, basal metabolism, skeletal growth, and both primary and secondary sex characteristics (Dreyer, 1982).

As if that biochemical system weren't complex enough, the gonadotropic hormones stimulate the ovaries and testes to produce hormones of their own—**estrogen** and **androgen.** It appears that these two hormones are the most important for the development of the secondary sex characteristics and for genital development in boys. Although we think of estrogen as the female hormone and androgen as the male hormone, the fact is that everyone has some of both. A girl develops a feminine body because she has more estrogen relative to androgen, and a boy develops masculine characteristics because this relationship is reversed.

Although scientists now have a good understanding of how puberty begins, they have very little idea why it ends. Apparently the neuroreceptors in the hypothalamus reach some mature level and hold steady, and the secondary sex characteristics complete their maturational sequence. Exactly which hormones may be involved in the end of puberty still remains to be seen (Dreyer, 1982).

To summarize briefly, the development of sex characteristics begins with the brain (specifically the hypothalamus), which controls the pituitary gland, which controls the growth of the ovaries and testes, which control the amounts of androgen and estrogen in the body. There is probably no other time during the life span, except perhaps for pregnancy, when the body undergoes so many complex hormonal changes. Perhaps it is not surprising that adolescence is thought of as a time of wide mood swings and bodily concerns—so much development is going on.

Timing of Sexual Development: Psychological Effects

The changes in size, shape, and biological functioning that we have just described obviously affect the appearance of adolescents. Equally obviously, they affect the way the young person is treated by others and the way she feels about herself. Psychologists have explored the links between the physical changes and the psychological ones primarily by looking at the effects of *timing* of puberty. What are the consequences for a young person of going through pubertal changes extremely early (say, at age 10 for girls, or 11 or 12 for boys) or extremely late?

We have two somewhat conflicting sets of information about the effects of pubertal timing on psychological development. On one side we have results from the Berkeley and Oakland Longitudinal studies, begun in the 1920s. Results from these studies have been analyzed by several investigators, including Mary Cover Jones (1957, 1965) and Harvey Peskin (1967, 1973). On the other side we have a growing collection of recent research—most of it cross-sectional studies—including work by Gail Jaquish and Ritch Savin-Williams (1981), Diane Ruble and Jeanne Brooks-Gunn (1982), and Alan Apter and his colleagues (Apter, Galatzer, Beth-Halachmi, & Laron, 1981).

The early findings suggested that for boys, early puberty carried a clear advantage, at least during the adolescent years. Ratings made by parents, peers, and the teens themselves all suggested that early maturing boys were more poised, relaxed, good natured, and unaffected. They were more popular with peers and more likely to be school leaders. Furthermore, they were described as being less impulsive and more concerned with self-control and with making a good impression on others.

The picture of the late-maturing boy was much less complimentary. He was described as being more tense, restless, talkative, attention-seeking, and as less popular with peers. In these early studies, late maturing boys had more negative self-concepts and expressed more feelings of inadequacy and rejection. They were unlikely to be dominant or to take leadership positions and more inclined to seek encouragement from others.

When these boys were followed into adulthood, much of the advantage for the early maturing group seemed to disappear (Jones, 1957, 1965). Still, some differences remained. The early maturers were more successful in their careers and more concerned about making a good impression. At the same time they were more cautious, rigid, and even anxious (Peskin, 1967, 1973). Later maturers, on the other hand, were more tense but were also seen as more tolerant and flexible.

Among girls, the early studies of timing of puberty showed fewer clear-cut differences, but in general it appeared that early maturing was not such a plus for girls as it was for boys. For example, early maturing girls were rated as being lower on traits like sociability, poise, and expressiveness and were less likely to take an active role in school activities. Peskin (1973) found them to be more introverted and shy and generally experiencing greater stress during adolescence than later-maturing girls. Interestingly, however, Peskin concluded that in adulthood it was the early maturing girls—those who appeared to struggle the most in adolescence—who made a better adult adjustment.

Findings from the more recent studies make this picture more complex. Jaquish and Savin-Williams's study (1981) is perhaps the most intriguing. They gave seventh-grade students "beepers" (small, portable signaling devices) and asked them to fill out a brief mood questionnaire each time they were beeped (which was eight times per day). If the youngsters indicated a positive mood, it was taken as a sign of a positive self-esteem, while negative moods were interpreted as negative self-esteem. They also took physical measurements of the children, including height, weight, and development of secondary sex characteristics.

The results seem exactly the opposite of what we would expect, given the earlier studies: Boys who were taller and heavier (presumably earlier developers) tended to have *lower* self-esteem than smaller and lighter boys, while girls with more advanced breast development had *higher* self-esteem than their less-developed peers.

Similarly, Apter (Apter et al., 1981), in an Israeli study, found that among both boys and girls, height and not stage of pubertal development was the best predictor of self-image: Taller adolescents thought better of themselves than did very short ones.

How can we reconcile these apparently contradictory findings for boys and girls and from early and recent research? We think that the most helpful way to look at this question is in terms of the typical or normal development for each sex. If you look at the growth curves for boys and girls on the same graph, as we have done for you in Figure 8.8, you will see a large area of overlap that we might call the time of *normative* development. The youngsters whose growth spurt and sexual development occur before this normative period (that is, the early maturing girls) or after it (the late-maturing boys) have more difficulty than those whose growth falls in the middle period. In addition, within each sex, those whose pattern of development falls well outside the norm are likely to experience greater difficulty.

We can even make sense of Jaquish and Savin-Williams's data when we look at it this way. Boys who are very tall or large in the seventh grade are really very early developers (outside the male norm) and may well be earlier in development than the early developers in the classic studies. Consequently, their self-esteem suffers somewhat. Seventh-grade girls who are developing breasts, on the other hand, are *not* unusual. Among current generations, such development at seventh grade is considered early normal and is thus associated with greater self-esteem.

Given the steadily lowering age of puberty, truly early developing girls begin menstruating in the fifth or sixth grade (age 10 or 11), and

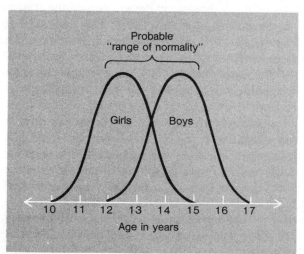

Figure 8.8. The overlap of developmental schedules for boys and girls. Youngsters who begin puberty before the middle or normative period seem to do better during adolescence than those who begin early (the early maturing girls) or late (the late-developing boys).

recent data (for example, Ruble and Brooks-Gunn, 1982) show that (as we would expect) such girls have a more difficult time with menarche and report more symptoms and distress than do girls whose development is in the seventh or eighth grade.

In general, then, we are suggesting that very early or very late development is a somewhat negative experience for both boys and girls, while on-time development is most optimal for self-esteem. For boys, there may also be an additional wrinkle: Early developing boys are more likely to be of the *mesomorphic* body type (which we described in Chapter 3)—a body type that is close to the all-American-boy image of broad shoulders and narrow hips. Given the emphasis on athletic skill within the male high school culture, boys with such body types are likely to have greater popularity and visibility in the peer group. Thus the somewhat early developing boy has a double advantage: He is at the leading edge of the range of normality, and he fits the masculine physical stereotype more completely than does the late-developing boy, who tends to be more *ectomorphic* (tall and skinny) in build.

Doubtless there are also some cohort differences hidden in these results as well. The meaning of early and late development within the adolescent peer group may well have changed over the past decades. The current research, which shows a smaller effect of pubertal timing than did the older studies, is probably a more accurate representation of the present-day situation.

Sexual Activity in Adolescence

If research about hormonal development is complex, it is still less troublesome than research about sexual activity in adolescents and young adults. Whenever researchers ask questions about personal matters like sexual experiences, they run into two problems. First, people who agree to answer questions about personal matters may be different in important ways from those who decline to answer these questions. We might expect to find differences in age, in personal characteristics like religious beliefs, and perhaps in the kinds of sexual experiences they have had. When the research involves teenagers, it is necessary to have the parents' permission as well as the subject's agreement, so that family characteristics (like the willingness to talk about sexual matters) are also probably different for those who participate and those who do not.

A second problem is that there is no way to tell whether subjects in such studies are telling the truth or not. While this is true of any study, it seems especially troublesome in research about very personal matters. Some individuals might feel the need to brag about their sexual exploits, while others might be too shy to mention them, even in an anonymous questionnaire or interview.

With these difficulties in mind, are there any conclusions we can reach about sexual activity in young people? In one of the best studies on this topic, A. Vener and C. Stewart (1974) collected data by questionnaire from a large sample of high school students in Michigan. In Table 8.5, we've shown you some of the results of this study. Adolescents appear to begin sexual behaviors with simple hand holding and progress through activities including sexual intercourse (technically known as coitus). It is noteworthy that boys are (or profess to be) generally more experienced than girls at every age, in spite of the fact that their physical development is less advanced.

Not surprisingly, there are significant secular trends in adolescent sexual activity, with more younger teens engaging in premarital relationships than ever before (Zelnik, Kanterner, & Ford, 1981). At the same time, the rate of teenage pregnancy has not changed much recently: About 30 percent of sexually active young women became pregnant in 1971 compared to 28 percent in 1976 (Zelnik & Kanter, 1978a). What *has* changed is the actual *number* of these pregnancies—even though the rate of pregnancy is the same, there are *more* teenagers now and *more* of them are sexually active. That is why the newspapers and magazines have been full of articles about the "problem of teenage pregnancy."

There has also been a secular trend in attitudes toward the expression of sexual feelings. In one study, Reiss (1967) asked both students and parents if they approved of petting and full sexual relationships between partners who were engaged, those who were in love, those with strong affection, and those with no affection. Students and parents agreed that both kinds of sexual activity were more appropriate for couples who were engaged or in love than for others, but the students

TABLE 8.5
Levels of Adolescent Heterosexual Activity

	PERCENTAGE OF HIGH SCHOOL YOUNGSTERS WHO HAVE PARTICIPATED AT LEAST ONCE					
	13 years and younger		*15 years*		*17 years and older*	
LEVELS OF SEXUAL ACTIVITY	Boys	Girls	Boys	Girls	Boys	Girls
I. Held hands	80	84	93	89	92	97
II. Held arm around (or been held)	67	72	87	87	90	96
III. Kissed (or been kissed)	65	68	84	82	87	96
IV. Necked (prolonged hugging and kissing)	48	43	70	65	78	84
V. Light petting (above the waist)	40	31	66	55	71	71
VI. Heavy petting (below the waist)	34	17	56	40	62	59
VII. Going all the way (coitus)	28	10	38	24	34	35
VIII. Coitus with two or more partners	17	4	21	10	23	14

SOURCE: Vener & Stewart, 1974.

were much more approving overall of these activities, regardless of the relationship between the two people.

We have introduced the topic of sexual activity here because it is closely linked to the development of the primary and secondary sex characteristics. But although physical maturity is necessary for full sexual activity, being physically mature is certainly not the only thing that enters into the decision to be sexually active. A variety of personal values and psychological characteristics is involved, and we will look at some of them in Chapter 10 when we look at how couples get together.

PHYSICAL DEVELOPMENT IN YOUNG ADULTS

Most of the major changes associated with puberty are completed by age 18 (although there are small increments in height still to be achieved for some late-developing teenagers, particularly boys). So we could probably omit a section called *physical development in young adults*. However, we think it is important to take at least a few pages to describe the nature of sexual functioning after the changes of puberty have been completed.

We have also included in this chapter a description of the body changes associated with pregnancy and delivery. Obviously, childbearing is an important part of the adult-life period for most women, and we might logically have included such a discussion later in Chapter 11 when we examine physical development in adults. It makes sense to include it here, however, both because it is part of mature sexual functioning and because at least half of all women who bear children have their first child before the age of 22 (U.S. Bureau of the Census, 1980). Thus for the majority of women, childbearing does in fact begin during the period of youth or young adulthood.

Mature Sexual Functioning

Females.   The outstanding feature of adult female sexual functioning is the menstrual cycle. This cycle, which takes 28 to 30 days in most women, can be divided into four parts. During the first phase (sometimes called the **follicular** phase), the pituitary gland secretes a hormone that stimulates the ovaries to produce an egg, a process called **ovulation.** As the egg enters the fallopian tubes to travel toward the uterus, a small remnant of the ovum begins producing the hormone progesterone, which characterizes the second phase (the **luteal** phase) of the cycle. If the egg is not fertilized, the second phase is ended by a drop in progesterone, which brings on the third or **premenstrual** stage. Rounding out the cycle is a **menstrual** phase of three to seven days duration.

Are there any psychological changes that accompany these physiological changes? A study by Alice and Peter Rossi (1980) suggests that mood changes may follow the cycle. They gave a group of young women a diary to fill out every day for 40 days, including information about their menstrual cycle and their moods—both positive and negative. You can see in Figure 8.9 that positive moods predominated near the time of ovulation, and negative moods predominated during the end of the luteal and beginning of the premenstrual phases.

We should point out, though, that these effects were fairly subtle. Furthermore, there was also evidence that mood was affected by the day of the week as well. Women felt most positive on Friday and least positive on Tuesday. Moods, like other traits and behaviors, are usually caused by a combination of variables; and no single factor—even a potent biological one like hormonal patterns—can explain them completely.

Males.   Male sexual functioning, in contrast, is primarily episodic, rather than cyclical. Rising and falling hormone levels are the result of specific stimuli, rather than of some underlying ebb and flow.

Nonetheless, there is some evidence of cyclical behavior in males. In the study we just described, Rossi and Rossi (1980) also had a number of young men keep diaries of their moods and activities. Like the

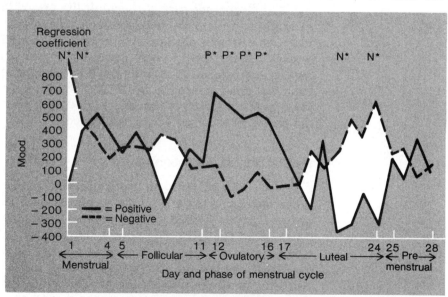

Figure 8.9.   Day-to-day changes in mood during young women's menstrual cycles. Positive moods outweigh negative ones in the middle of the cycle, around the time of ovulation, while negative ones prevail immediately before and immediately after that time. (*Source:* Rossi & Rossi, 1980, p. 284.)

women, they showed a strong weekly cycle in positive and negative mood, with a peak on Saturdays and a low point on Mondays. It may or may not be a coincidence that most social (and probably sexual) activity occurs on the weekends, and this time is marked by a positive mood peak. The point to be made, though, is that there are many cyclical mood changes in humans, only some of which are directly caused by sex hormones.

Reproduction: Pregnancy

In Chapter 2 we described the prenatal period for you from the point of view of the infant. Now we'd like to look at some of the same set of events from the point of view of the mother.

The General Course of Pregnancy.   During the first trimester, a large number of physiological and biochemical changes take place soon after conception occurs. Many women feel nauseous (sometimes called **morning sickness**) or bloated. Most experience extreme tiredness and such troublesome symptoms as frequent urination and vaginal discharge.

During the second trimester, these bodily adjustments have been made, and most women report a feeling of well-being. During this time the mother can first feel the baby moving (this is called **quickening**) and often begins to refer to the child as a separate person, perhaps with a nickname. [Our first baby was nicknamed Bronco when I was pregnant, because she kicked so much. (SM)]

The fetus grows quite rapidly during the third trimester, and most women experience discomfort due to crowding in their bodies. Simply put, the baby takes up so much room that everything else—lungs, stomach, bladder—gets pushed out of the way. At the end of this period, these discomforts are ended by labor and the delivery of the baby.

A woman's experience of pregnancy does not end with delivery, though. There is a period (sometimes called the fourth trimester of pregnancy) of recovery during which her reproductive organs return to their prepregnant state. At the same time, she is also recuperating from the hard work of labor and perhaps from any damage done to her body during the delivery.

Physical Changes during Pregnancy.   Although the experience of pregnancy can be complicated, most of the changes we have just described can be explained in terms of a few underlying physical changes that occur during gestation.

Some of the most important of these changes take place in the bloodstream. The volume of blood increases dramatically, presumably because it must carry enough nutrients and oxygen for the developing fetus, as well as for the woman herself. A common part of medical prenatal care is the use of iron supplements to ensure that this increased blood volume is well supplied with hemoglobin, the substance that transports oxygen. In fact, a fair proportion of the weight a woman gains during pregnancy is due to this increased blood volume, over and above the weight of the infant's body. To move all of this blood efficiently, the heart rate also increases slightly.

A second important set of changes is in the muscular system. The uterus, like many of the internal organs, is made up of fibers called **smooth muscle.** During pregnancy, the smooth muscles of the uterus must soften and stretch enormously (to contain the growing fetus), and when they do, so do the other smooth muscles in the body. Several of the normal symptoms of pregnancy can be traced to this fact. Indigestion, heartburn, and constipation, for example, are all related to the sluggish operation of the gastrointestinal system.

The skeletal muscles and ligaments also soften and stretch during pregnancy (to make room for the fetus to travel down the birth canal during delivery). At the same time, the weight of the baby means that the distribution of weight in the woman's body changes markedly. Taken together, these facts mean that a pregnant woman generally changes her posture and may be more susceptible than usual to backaches and similar complaints.

Of course, the most dramatic changes during pregnancy are those directly concerned with the growth and development of the fetus. The uterus, which is usually about 7 cm long and weighs about 60 g, grows to 35 cm in length and 1100 g in weight, while its volume increases 500 to 1000 times (Stenchever, 1978).

The breasts also get bigger as the blood vessels enlarge and the milk ducts develop. The area around the nipple frequently becomes larger and darker in color, and there may be stretch marks present.

The final set of changes during pregnancy concerns the skin. The skin on the abdomen, of course, must stretch a great deal. In this process it becomes tender and tight and may develop stretch marks. Some women notice blotchy areas on the face, which are a reaction to hormonal changes.

The Pregnant Father.   For men, pregnancy is an interpersonal event, not a physical one. However, many men—no one knows exactly how many—experience symptoms like morning sickness when their wives are pregnant. This phenomenon is called the **couvade.** In some primitive cultures, men are expected to experience such symptoms, and some even take to their beds during labor and delivery. In our own culture, less dramatic symptoms may reflect either empathy with the mother or anxiety about new parental responsibilities.

Reproduction: Labor and Delivery

Physicians and midwives divide the period of labor into three unequal parts.

First Stage of Labor.   The first and longest stage of labor consists of uterine contractions that begin widely spaced and become more frequent and rhythmical as labor proceeds. While it is obvious that one purpose of these contractions is to move the infant down the birth canal, two other important processes are also involved. The **cervix,** the opening at the bottom of the uterus, is normally thick and tightly closed. During the first stage of labor, the cervix must begin to open like the lens of a camera (called **dilation**) and also flatten out (called **effacement**). The cervix must be entirely effaced and dilated (about 10 cm in most women) before the baby can be born. Normally, by the end of the first stage of labor the cervix is dilated about 7 to 8 cm.

We have a stereotype of women going into labor and being rushed to a hospital, but most of the time there is no rush. The first stage of labor, particularly in first pregnancies, lasts for many hours and need not take place in a hospital. The usual advice is not to head for the hospital until the labor contractions (sometimes inaccurately called labor pains) are about five minutes apart.

Many women control their discomfort during this stage of labor using special concentration and breathing techniques learned in prenatal classes. The father of the baby is often the "coach" for these techniques, giving him an active part in the labor (and possibly increasing the strength of his attachment to the infant, too, as we pointed out in Chapter 7), rather than relegating him to a passive role in the waiting room.

Transition Stage.   At the end of the first stage there is a (usually brief) period in which the final 2 to 3 cm of dilation are achieved. This period is very uncomfortable for many women, since the uterine contractions come quite close together and are very strong. Following this comes the urge to help the infant out by pushing. When the birth attendant is sure the cervix is fully dilated, she or he will encourage this pushing, and the second stage of labor begins.

Second Stage of Labor.   The second stage of labor includes what we would think of as *delivery,* that is, the expulsion of the infant through the birth canal.

Most infants are delivered head first, facing the floor (if the mother is lying on her back). The birth attendant supports the head, then may gently twist the baby to help the shoulders emerge one at a time, followed by the rest of the body. If the opening in the birth canal is not large enough for the birth to proceed easily, a small incision (called an **episiotomy**) is made to enlarge the opening. A few babies are born feet first or bottom first. In these deliveries the birth attendant must often take a more active role, perhaps using medical instruments to aid the baby's descent.

Third Stage.   Technically, the third stage of labor consists of the delivery of the placenta and other material from the uterus. No one but the attendant is much interested in this process, since the mother (and often the father, too) is usually busy looking at and holding the baby.

Age and Reproduction

The adolescent and young adult years include both good and poor times for women to bear children. As we mentioned back in Chapter 2, very young mothers (those under 15 or so) are more likely to have complications of pregnancy, especially premature birth. Apparently the nutritional and physiological demands of pregnancy, added to normal adolescent development, are just too great. While not every infant born to a mother in prime childbearing age (about 18 to 35 years) will be healthy, the odds are better for them than for infants born to very young mothers.

GROWTH AND HEALTH IN ADOLESCENCE AND YOUTH

Most of us think of adolescence and youth as healthy periods of life, and by and large this is true. There are, however, a few basic health problems during these years that can have an impact on psychological functioning and development.

Accidents

The major causes of death and injury to adolescents and young adults involve accidents and acts of violence (see Figure 8.10). In fact, the single greatest risk to teenagers comes from *automobiles,* either alone or in combination with the use of alcohol.

You can see that suicide and homicide are also leading causes of death in young people. Adolescent girls are more likely to make suicidal gestures than are adolescent boys, but the boys are more likely to be successful in their attempts (Hammar, 1980). We think of homicide primarily in the case of violent crime, but sanctioned homicide—war—is responsible for a large part of the death toll among young people. We were horrified to learn that between 1940 and 1974, 27 percent of male deaths in the 20 to 34 age group were war related (Henley & Altman, 1978).

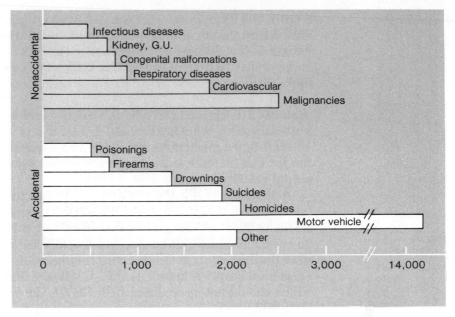

Figure 8.10. Causes of death among adolescents and young adults. The greatest risk comes from the automobile, and the next greatest from acts of violence. (*Source:* Smith, Bierman, & Robinson, 1978, p. 178.)

Less serious accidents are also an important problem for this group. In a study of why patients visit their family doctors (Marsland, Wood, & Mayo, 1976), nearly 7 percent of all visits by young adults were for musculoskeletal disorder and trauma—in other words, injuries. This percentage was exceeded only by the common cold (respiratory infections, 15.6 percent).

An important cause of accidents in young people seems to be a tendency toward risk-taking, especially among young men. While this is obvious in people who take up hobbies like skydiving and motorcycle riding, it is equally present, but less obvious, in those who abuse drugs (especially alcohol), fail to use seat belts or observe speed limits, or misuse their bodies in other ways.

Illnesses

In this day of antibiotics, we sometimes assume that contagious diseases no longer threaten us. Recent experience, however, indicates that several such diseases occur with considerable frequency among young people.

Infectious Mononucleosis. *Mono* used to be called the "kissing disease," but it is actually not often spread in that way. It is caused by a virus, and its main symptoms are chronic fatigue or listlessness along with a sore throat, swollen glands, and an enlarged spleen. The main danger of this disease, which normally runs its course in 4 to 14 days, is that hepatitis (liver infection) is a fairly common complication (Hammar, 1980).

Sexually Transmitted Disease.   Of the two best known sexually transmitted diseases, there has been a decrease in one (syphilis) over the past 15 years and a precipitous rise in the other (gonorrhea). The exact reason for this increase is not known, although generally higher rates of sexual activity certainly play a part.

A newer sexually transmitted disease, genital herpes (which we mentioned in connection with prenatal development in Chapter 2) also seems to be on the rise. Since it is caused by a virus, antibiotics offer no cure; and in fact, there are very few medications that will even relieve the discomfort associated with this disorder. The virus responsible for genital herpes is known as HSV-II (Herpes Simplex Virus, Type II), which should not be confused with HSV-I, the virus that causes common cold sores.

Hepatitis.   Viral hepatitis is an acute infection of the liver. Hepatitis A (which used to be called infectious hepatitis) is spread by poor sanitation practices, and its incidence has been declining steadily in the last decade. Hepatitis B (formerly called serum hepatitis, because it was known to be spread by blood transfusions) has not been declining at the same rate, partly because about 10 percent of the people who get it become carriers—that is, they can transmit the disease even though they suffer no symptoms themselves.

Both kinds of hepatitis occur most commonly between the ages of 15 and 30, and more often in males than in females. Hepatitis B, in particular, seems to be seen more frequently among white male homosexuals, but the reason for this is still under study.

Lifestyle

As we look at young adults, and more so when we look at middle-aged and older people in Chapter 11, our concern with health will lead us to concerns about several aspects of lifestyle, such as substance use and abuse (see Box 8.2), diet, and nutrition.

Diet and Nutrition.   One major health problem for adolescents is **obesity.** Current estimates are that 16 to 20 percent of the teenagers are significantly overweight (Hammar, 1980). Generally, obesity does not begin in adolescence but follows a childhood weight problem (Zack, Harlan, Leaverton, & Cornoni-Huntley, 1979).

There seem to be three factors that can cause obesity in youngsters. First, a tendency to overweight can be inherited. Jean Mayer (1975) found in one study that only 7 percent of the children of normal-weight parents were obese but that 80 percent of those with two obese parents were themselves seriously overweight. (Since these same relationships are found between child weight and natural-parent weight in cases of *adopted* children, we can be reasonably sure that this is really a genetic influence and not caused by the fact that overweight parents feed their children more.)

The child's diet during the early years does have an effect, however. Fat cells are added to the body during the first two years of life and then again at adolescence. The more fat cells a person has, the harder it is to lose weight. Children who are overfed in infancy may develop extra fat cells that cause a problem later.

A third contributor to weight problems is lack of exercise. Jean Mayer, in his study of overweight and average-weight youngsters (1975), found that overweight children don't move around very much. For example, normal-weight girls were in motion about 90 percent of the time while playing tennis; obese girls moved only 50 percent of the time. While this may reflect some underlying temperamental difference, Mayer found that the overweight girls could be helped to lose weight by introducing a regular exercise program, without any changes in diet.

The other major nutritional problem that frequently affects teenagers is a disease called **anorexia nervosa.** Most of the sufferers are teenage girls, among whom as many as one girl in 250 may show this disorder (Vigersky, 1977). The main symptom is the refusal (or perhaps more accurately, the inability) to eat normally. Often the girls have gone on a diet to lose weight (though their original size usually was not obese) and then continued to limit their food intake drastically. Some of them also suffer from a disorder known as **bulimia,** in which they periodically gorge themselves with food, then either vomit or take huge doses of laxatives to purge themselves. Anorexia and bulimia are serious psychiatric disorders as well as nutritional problems and require both medical and psychological treatment.

Health and Development.   Until recently, young people had a choice of obtaining health care from a pediatrician (a children's physician) or a family doctor or internist (often primarily an adult's physician). But you can see from our description of their health problems that none of these specialties is entirely appropriate. The new specialty of adolescent medicine is growing but still small and limited to cities with major medical centers. Until these specialists are more available, family physicians, parents, and teachers will carry most of the responsibility for monitoring the health and safety of adolescents and youth.

BOX 8.2

Alcohol and Drugs in Adolescence and Youth

Widespread use of alcohol and other drugs is one of the major health problems among adolescents and youth. The accompanying table shows the percentage of teenagers and young adults who indicated that they had ever used, or had recently or regularly used, alcohol, marijuana, and harder drugs such as heroin or cocaine. These figures come from a recent national survey that included over 2000 teenagers and over 2000 young adults, carried out by the National Institute on Drug Abuse (1979). There are the usual problems about accuracy with numbers like these, especially since they involve reports of illegal drug use. However, the respondents' answers were anonymous; and if anything the sensitivity of the questions would lead to underestimates rather than overestimates of the amount of marijuana and hard-drug usage actually occurring.

Obviously, the use of alcohol and other drugs increases with age. But it begins early for many young people. Over 7 percent of 12- and 13-year-olds said they had had at least one drink in the past month, and about 3 percent of the 12- to 13-year-olds had smoked marijuana in the same period. Usage of all types of drugs is generally higher among males than females, but this difference is beginning to disappear in the younger age groups (Hartford, 1975). For example, in the 1979 National Survey represented

Alcohol, Marijuana, and Hard Drug Usage Reported in a National Survey

	PERCENTAGE WHO REPORTED USING		
	Alcohol	Marijuana and hashish	Cocaine and heroin
Teenagers (12- to 17-year-olds)			
Who *ever* used	70.0%	30.9%	5.9%
Who used in past month	37.2%	16.7%	1.4%
Regular users (five or more times in past month)	8.9%	8.4%	0.5%
Young adults (18- to 25-year-olds)			
Who *ever* used	95.0%	68.2%	31.0%
Who used in past month	75.9%	35.4%	9.3%
Regular users (five or more times in past month)	37.2%	22.5%	0.5%

SOURCE: National Institute on Drug Abuse, 1979.

SUMMARY

1. There is a growth spurt for both height and weight during adolescence. This spurt starts and ends earlier for girls.
2. Body proportions change during adolescence as the legs increase in length, the shape of the head changes, and the shoulders (in boys) and hips (in both sexes) become wider.
3. Among different ethnic groups, blacks are usually taller and heavier than whites, while Asiatics are smaller and lighter than either of the other groups. Moreover, children in more developed countries are usually larger than those in less developed countries.

in the table, 39 percent of the boys and 36 percent of the girls aged 12 to 17 had had at least one drink in the past month.

Use of all drugs has been increasing over the past decades as well. In 1972, only 24 percent of adolescents had had a drink in the past month, compared to 37 percent in 1979. Marijuana use among adolescents has doubled in the same period (from 14 percent to 31 percent), and cocaine use has tripled (from 1.5 percent to 5.4 percent).

Young people begin using alcohol or other drugs for a variety of reasons, including a desire for the "high" sensation, peer pressure, and low self-esteem. However, those young people whose parents and friends use drugs are more likely to do so as well, illustrating the effect of both access and modeling (Huba & Bentler, 1980, 1982).

A number of researchers have found a distinct progression of drug use, beginning with alcohol and moving toward marijuana use (Kandel & Faust, 1975; Huba & Bentler, 1982): (1) beer or wine, (2) hard liquor or cigarettes, (3) marijuana, and (4) other illicit drugs. It's perfectly clear from the data in the table that not all teenagers or young adults move past Stage 1 or 2, since there are many more young people who drink than there are those who use either marijuana or cocaine or heroin. But virtually all youth who arrive at Stage 4 have been through the previous steps. This does not mean that smoking marijuana *causes* the use of harder drugs; all we know is that for a subsample of young people, they follow one another.

The consequences of drug use are myriad. In the 1979 National Survey, about 40 percent of the young people said that marijuana use was associated with poorer performance (slowed reflexes, apathy, dulled senses, reduced driving ability, and the like), and 30 percent thought that there were negative mental reactions, such as memory loss or hallucinations. Alcohol use has similar associated hazards; in fact, alcohol has been reported to be involved in half of the highway deaths in this country and in half of the homicides committed (Henley & Altman, 1978).

All drugs have some side effects. By definition, a drug is any substance (excluding food) that when ingested alters one or more body function (Katchadourian, 1977). The three groups of drugs we have talked about here—alcohol, marijuana, and hard drugs such as cocaine—clearly alter the body's functioning in various ways. Regardless of one's attitude about the morality or legality of their use, we should all be concerned about the massive increases in drug use among teenagers and young adults. Not only does such widespread use increase the risk of accidents, it also increases the likelihood of drug dependence or abuse in later life and alters the social interactions of young people with one another.

4. Humans have been growing taller and heavier over the past few centuries, and these cohort effects are known as secular trends.
5. There are large individual differences in growth quite apart from population differences and secular trends.
6. The long bones grow markedly during puberty and finish their ossification at about age 18 for girls and 20 for boys.
7. During adolescence, boys increase their lean body weight and decrease their total body fat; at the same time, girls show no change in lean body weight and an increase in total body fat.
8. The changes associated with puberty are triggered by the activity of the part of the brain called the hypothalamus.

9. Pubertal changes are divided into two groups: primary sex characteristics, which are directly involved in reproduction, and secondary sex characteristics, which are not.

10. Primary sex characteristics include the menarche in girls, genital development and the onset of nocturnal emissions in boys. Female development is ahead of male development in this area, too.

11. Secondary sex characteristics include pubic hair development in both sexes and breast development in girls. Girls begin developing earlier and finish sooner, but there is a wide range of variability within each sex as to when the changes begin and end.

12. Development of sex characteristics is initiated by the hypothalamus and involves the pituitary gland and the ovaries and testes as well, in a complicated hormonal system.

13. Mature sexual functioning in the female is described by the menstrual cycle, while in the male it tends to be episodic rather than cyclical.

14. Sexual activity develops gradually during adolescence, with boys generally being more experienced than girls. There has been a secular trend toward more sexual activity among teenagers.

15. The experience of the three trimesters of pregnancy can be largely explained by physical changes in the circulatory system, the muscles, the skin, and the uterus and breasts.

16. Labor and delivery are accomplished by strong contractions of the uterine muscles, which expel the fetus through the birth canal.

17. Although adolescents and young adults are usually healthy, accidents and some infectious diseases are still a problem. Lifestyles that involve alcohol and drug use or inadequate nutrition also threaten the health of young people.

18. Early maturing boys and late-maturing girls seem to be most popular and successful when they are teenagers. Later in life, the differences are fewer and tend to represent differences in style rather than in quality of life.

KEY TERMS

Alcoholism Chronic dependency upon alcohol.

Androgen Male sex hormone.

Anorexia nervosa Illness in which a patient, usually a young woman, is unable to eat and suffers considerable weight loss.

Bulimia Illness in which a person grossly overindulges in food and then vomits or purges herself with laxatives.

Cervix Opening from the uterus to the birth canal.

Couvade The mimicking by a father of the symptoms of his wife's pregnancy, including morning sickness in the early months and, possibly, pain during delivery.

Dilation Opening of the cervix, usually to a size of about 10 cm, to allow birth of a baby.

Effacement   Flattening of the cervix to allow birth of a baby.

Episiotomy   Small surgical incision made during delivery to ensure easy passage of the baby.

Estrogen   Female sex hormone.

Follicular phase   First stage of female menstrual cycle.

Gonadotropic hormone   Hormone produced in the pituitary gland, which stimulates the sex organs to develop.

Hypothalamus   Part of the brain that controls the pituitary gland and therefore indirectly controls the development of primary and secondary sex characteristics during puberty.

Lean body mass (LBM)   Proportion of body weight accounted for by muscles, bones, nervous system, and other organs; excludes the amount of body fat.

Luteal phase   Second stage of the female menstrual cycle.

Menarche   Onset of menstruation in girls.

Menstrual phase   Final stage in the female menstrual cycle.

Morning sickness   Nausea, which is a symptom of early pregnancy.

Neuroreceptors   Cells in the hypothalamus that help to regulate the levels of hormones in the body.

Obesity   Overweight.

Ovulation   Ripening of an egg in the ovaries of a woman and expulsion of the egg into the fallopian tubes.

Premenstrual phase   Third phase of the female menstrual cycle.

Primary sex characteristics   Sexual characteristics related directly to reproduction, including development of the uterus and testes.

Puberty   The collection of physical and hormonal changes at adolescence that bring about full sexual maturity and full adult size.

Quickening   First movements of the fetus that can be felt by a pregnant woman.

Scoliosis   A sideways bending of the spinal column, often beginning in early adolescence.

Secondary sex characteristics   Sexual characteristics not directly involved in reproduction, including breast and body hair development and changes in body size and proportions.

Secular trends   Cohort differences in patterns of growth and development.

Skeletal age   Estimate of the extent of bone development in an individual. Sometimes used instead of chronological age to predict other developmental milestones.

Smooth muscle   Fibers that make up the internal organs of the body, including the uterus and the digestive tract.

Subcutaneous fat   Fat stored underneath the skin, sometimes called storage fat.

Total body fat (TBF)   Proportion of body weight attributable to fat.

SUGGESTED
READINGS

O'Neill, Cherry. *Starving for attention.* New York: Continuum, 1982.
  Those of you interested in anorexia nervosa may find this firsthand account particularly fascinating.

Smith, D. W., Bierman, E. L., & Robinson, N. M. (Eds.). *The biologic ages of man: From conception through old age.* Philadelphia: Saunders, 1978.

Like Tanner's book (below), this volume contains a wealth of useful information about physical growth and change over the life span.

Tanner, J. M. *Fetus into man. Physical growth from conception to maturity.* Cambridge, Mass.: Harvard University Press, 1978.

A detailed but very thorough small book that will probably tell you more than you want to know about physical development.

PROJECT 8.1
Plotting Your Own Growth

This project is only feasible if you happen to be one of those rare people whose parents routinely stood you up against a convenient doorjamb and measured you—and if you (or your parents) still live in the house with the marked-up doorjamb. It will also work if you have a friend who happens to have access to such a measuring system. But if you are one of that select group, you will find it of interest to plot your rate of growth (or that of a sibling or a friend) over the years of childhood and adolescence. The maximum point of height spurt is considered to be the period in which you grew the most inches in a fixed period of time. When did that happen for you? During elementary school, did you grow about the same number of inches per year, as Figure 8.2 suggests? Did your growth spurt take place at about the average time (again in comparison to Figure 8.2)? How old were you when you stopped growing altogether?

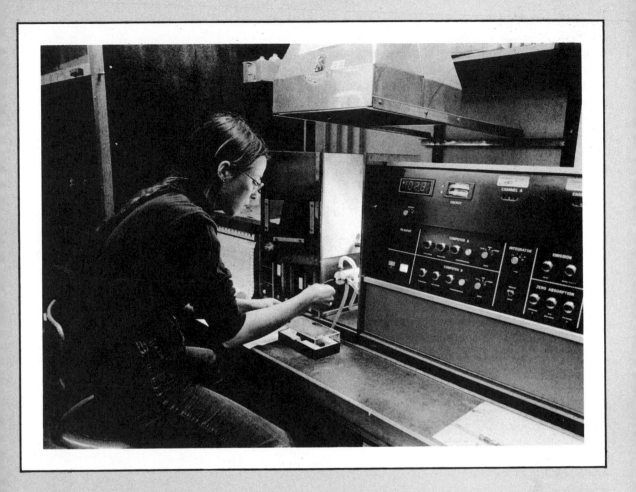

Chapter 9
Intelligence in
Adolescence and Youth:
Power, Structure, and Style

One of my all-time favorite comic strips is the story of a wizard mixing up a magic potion. In the first line of the strip, he feeds some of this potion to a nearby hen who promptly turns into a baby chick. "Eureka," shouts the wizard, "I have found the secret of eternal youth!" In the next picture the wizard gives some of the stuff to the king, who promptly turns into—a baby chick. [SM]

The reason we can laugh at this story is that we can see what the wizard *didn't* see—that there are several possible explanations for the effects of his magic potion on the chick. The wizard leaped to the first conclusion that came to his mind (that the potion caused youth), but the king suffered quite different consequences.

One of the hallmarks of adolescent and adult thought is the ability to avoid the wizard's error. We can think of several different possible explanations for things that happen, and then we can systematically test those possible explanations until we find the one that is correct (without, we hope, doing irreparable damage to the king). These are important cognitive abilities, and in this chapter we are going to see how these abilities develop and change during the adolescent and young adult years.

Just as we did in Chapter 4, we're going to separate our discussion of adolescent cognition into sections—power, structure, and style. The measures of intellectual *power* that most affect many adolescents and youths are the standardized tests that are used for college entrance, and we are going to look at some of these examinations and the way they are used. There are several theories of cognitive *structure* that are important during these years: Piaget's theory of formal operational thought deals with ways of thinking and reasoning about academic topics; theories of interpersonal understanding and moral reasoning are extensions and elaborations of this structural theory to more socially oriented content. Finally, the study of cognitive *styles* extends to adolescence and youth as well. As we did in Chapter 4, we will also look at the role of information processing as a link between power, structure, and style.

COGNITIVE POWER IN ADOLESCENCE AND YOUTH

When we discussed the nature of intelligence in children, we began by considering quantitative or power definitions. We'll begin this chapter in the same way, looking at the ways cognitive power is measured in adolescents and young adults.

Measuring Cognitive Power

The tests that are used to assess intelligence in adolescents and young adults are either the same or very similar to those used with children. The Stanford-Binet, for example, includes age categories up to the adult level, and the WISC-R is intended for use up to age 16 or so. Beyond that age, there is another test known as the **WAIS** (Wechsler Adult Intelligence Scale, Wechsler, 1958). The important thing to notice is that adolescent and adult intelligence is not considered to be any different from children's intelligence. Although the questions on the WAIS are harder than those on the WISC-R, they are still divided into subtests presumed to measure verbal and performance IQ.

Chances are that most of you have never taken an intelligence test of this kind, at least not as an adolescent or young adult. But there is another kind of mental test that nearly all of you *have* taken—a college entrance exam.

In some ways, these exams are very much like IQ tests. They include many items intended to cover different kinds of thinking and reasoning. A person's score, although not usually expressed as an IQ, *does* represent how well he has performed compared to other people with similar educational backgrounds. People with high scores are presumed to be smarter or to have higher achievement potential than people with low scores.

However, there is an important difference in the way tests like this are used. Most IQ tests given to children are for *diagnostic* or *predictive* purposes. Theoretically, at least, the intention is to use the information from the test to help the child, for example by suitable placement in a special class. College entrance exams, on the other hand, are used for *selection* purposes. The intention is to use the information to help someone (usually a school or college) decide who will be accepted and who will be rejected. Although in the long run it is expected that this will help most students, in the short run, most high school and college students see exams of this kind as barriers to their progress rather than as aids for diagnosis or prediction.

Influences on College Entrance Exam Scores

The best-known college entrance tests are those conducted by the American College Testing Program (usually called the ACTs) and by the College Entrance Examination Board (the Scholastic Aptitude Test or SAT). Obviously, both of these organizations (which are private, nonprofit institutions) are interested in the factors that might influence test scores.

Environment and Experience.   The results of research on the SAT are summarized for you in Table 9.1. Generally, it appears that factors under the influence of the test taker (such as coaching, practice, anxiety) make little difference on test scores, while factors not under her influence (like sex or race) are related to scores. Of course, these differences are just averages, and individuals may score quite differently than the averages predict. [Back when I took the tests, I scored higher

TABLE 9.1
Factors That May Influence College Entrance Exam Scores

Factor	Effect
Coaching	Small gain, if any.
Practice	Small gains when test is retaken.
Fatigue	Students who take several tests in one day score as well as those who take only one test.
Anxiety	Scores obtained under nonanxious conditions not different from scores under usual conditions; some tendency for women to score higher on verbal tests and lower on math tests when anxious.
Sex	Few differences on verbal tests, but a substantial difference favoring men on math tests.
Race	Whites generally score higher than blacks.
High school grades	Modest positive correlation.

SOURCE: Summarized from Fremer & Chandler, 1971.

on the math than on the verbal section, which was and is unusual for women. SM]

Historical Influences. Environment and experience may influence the scores of individuals or of specific groups, but recently there has been considerable publicity about factors that may influence the general levels of cognitive power—at least as shown in tests like the ACT and the SAT—for all young adults. The data that are the basis for these questions show that average scores on the major college entrance examinations have been going down for the past several years. From 1964 to 1975, the average score on the ACT (which has a possible range of 1 to 36) has declined about 1.2 points (Munday, 1976). The greatest decline was found on the social studies subtest, next greatest on mathematics and English, and no decline on natural sciences. In three of the four areas, declines were greater for women than for men. Similar data have been reported for the SAT (see Figure 9.1): Scores on this test can range from 200 to 800, and the drop from 1963 to 1977 was about 49 points on the verbal subtest and 32 points on the math subtest (College Entrance Examination Board, 1977).

How would you interpret these findings? Well, first remember that not *all* students take college entrance examinations—only those planning to go to college usually go to the trouble. Historically, then, only the smartest students took the tests. If this situation were to change so that more students, including those in the range of moderate ability, took the test, scores would go down. This seems to be what happened

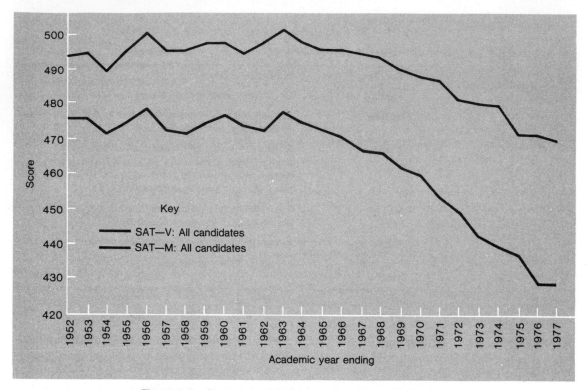

Figure 9.1.   Changes in scores on the Scholastic Aptitude Test from 1952 to 1977. You can see that scores on both the verbal and the math portions of the test have declined steadily since the mid-1960s. (*Source:* College Entrance Examination Board, 1977.)

during the middle and late 1960s: An increasing number of students from lower socioeconomic and minority groups began to take the test. Since on the average they got lower scores, the average for the total group went down.

This change in the test population was largely completed by 1970, so the decline in test scores since that time must be the result of some other factor. Our best guess is that changes in high school curricula account for the changes since 1970. For a variety of reasons too complex to list here, many schools had less rigorous programs during the 1970s than they had had previously, and the continued decline in test scores during this period is probably related to that fact (College Entrance Examination Board, 1977).

Prediction of College Success

Since the purpose of most college entrance exams is to select students who will do well in college, it is important to know how good a job these test scores do in predicting college success.

Most studies of this relationship have compared scores on the tests with the grades earned in the first year of college. As many of you have probably learned from experience, this is not a perfect measure of college success. Many students have trouble during their first year because of personal adjustments or ill-chosen courses, but they later go on to do well.

In general, correlations between test scores and college grades range from .30 to .45 (Schrader, 1971). (You will recall from Chapter 1 that correlations range from 0 to 1.0; the higher the correlation, the stronger the relationship between the two variables.) Interestingly, if you divide students into three groups (those with low, moderate, and high examination scores), the *least* accurate predictions are made for the students with the highest scores. The best interpretation of this peculiar fact seems to be that some basic level of intelligence is needed to succeed in college, but above that level, more intelligence doesn't always help. Instead, success in freshman courses may have more to do with motivation, course selection, or even luck.

Perspective on Cognitive Power and Selection

When you were in high school and applying to colleges, you were probably greatly concerned with your scores on exams like these. You might have felt better if you had seen the results of a survey of 1463 college and university admissions officers (Undergraduate Admissions, 1980). Only 48 percent of the schools actually *required* test scores for admissions, and only 2 percent of them felt the test scores were the "single most important factor" in deciding who was admitted. High school graduation rank and high school grade averages were considered more important than tests by most schools, and the pattern of courses taken in high school was close behind.

It should be clear that measures of cognitive power in adolescence and young adulthood, no matter how used, have the same shortcomings as they did among children: They fail to tell us much about how young people think or how their thinking changes as they mature; and they are always measures of performance, not competence. As we did in Chapter 4, we must turn to theories of structure and style to answer these questions.

COGNITIVE STRUCTURE IN ADOLESCENT THOUGHT

We have already described how the child learns to think about *objects* in many different and flexible ways during the period of concrete operations. Even without objects being physically present, she can categorize them, put them in logical sequences (such as ordering them by size or weight), and can demonstrate conservation of quantity, number, and weight. So what is left to learn? According to Piaget's theory of cognitive development, what is left to learn is how to think about *ideas* in different and flexible ways. This is the task of the stage of **formal operations.**

The Stage of Formal Operations

Most of the research about cognitive structure has focused on young adolescents—ages 11 to 15—because this is the period when formal thought shows clear developmental changes. The themes of cognitive development that we introduced in Chapter 4 are one way of tracing these changes; but before we look at them again, we would like to give you a quick overview of the special cognitive achievements that mark this period.

Thinking about Possibilities.   One of the basic steps in starting to think about thoughts is for the child to extend his reasoning abilities to objects and situations that he has not seen or experienced firsthand, or that may not exist at all. This shift can be seen in a study by Frederic Mosher and Joan Hornsby (1966), which involved two versions of the game "Twenty Questions."

In the first version of the game, the child was shown a set of 42 pictures of animals, people, toys, machines, and the like. Each child was told that the experimenter was thinking of one of the pictures, and that he was to figure out which one by asking questions that could be answered "yes" or "no."

One way to play this game is to go from picture to picture asking, "Is it this one?" until you get to the correct answer. The 6-year-olds in Mosher and Hornsby's study used this strategy most of the time. Another way is to classify the pictures hierarchically into groups. So you might start by asking, "Is it a toy?" If the answer were "yes," the next question might be, "Is it a red toy?" and so on until you got the answer. This strategy was preferred by both 8- and 11-year-olds, though they did not use it for every question.

The second version of the game given these children used a story instead of pictures. The child was told, "A man is driving down the road in his car. The car goes off the road and hits a tree. Find out what happened." The big difference between this game and the one with the pictures is that the child must imagine all of the possible answers before he can arrange them hierarchically to use in guesses. Both the 6- and 8-year-olds approached this problem by asking questions about one reason at a time, such as "Was the man stung on the eye by a bee?" Obviously, they could *imagine* reasons for the accident (just as children this age have shown other evidence of divergent thinking). What they couldn't do was to *organize* those imaginary reasons into categories and ask questions about entire categories of reasons. In this study, only the

11-year-olds, who are presumably beginning to think formally, were able to ask questions like "Did the weather cause the accident?" or "Did the driver make some kind of mistake?"

Systematic Problem Solving.   Thinking up solutions and organizing them are not all that is needed. To solve a problem, the adolescent must learn to test each of the possible solutions mentally until he finds one that works. So another important feature of the stage of formal operations is that the youngster is able to systematically and methodically evaluate the possible answers to a problem.

This aspect of formal operations was extensively studied by Piaget and his colleague, Barbel Inhelder (Inhelder & Piaget, 1958). They used problems taken from the physical sciences to observe the complexity and organization of children's problem solving. In one of these tasks, the youngsters were given a long piece of string and a set of objects of various weights, which could be tied to the string to make a swinging pendulum (see Figure 9.2). They were shown how to start the pendulum by pushing the weight with differing amounts of force and by holding the weight at different heights. The subject had to figure out which one or combination of these four factors (length of string, weight of object, force of push, or height of push) determined the *period* (amount of time for one swing) of the pendulum. (One interesting thing about this problem is that only one factor—the length of the string—actually matters, and all the rest are quite irrelevant.)

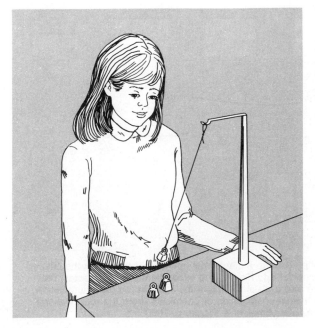

Figure 9.2.   One of the best-known tasks for measuring formal operational thought is the pendulum problem used by Barbel Inhelder and Jean Piaget. This young teenager has just tried a light weight on a long string. What do you think she will try next?

If you give this problem to a concrete operational thinker, she will try out many different combinations of length and weight and force and height, but she will try them in inefficient ways. For instance, she might try a heavy weight on a long string and then a light weight on a short string. Since both string length and weight have changed, there is no way to make a conclusion about either factor.

An adolescent is likely to try a more organized approach. An 11- to 15-year-old might start with a long string and try all three different weights and then repeat the procedure using a short string. Of course, not all adolescents (or even all adults) are quite *this* methodical, but nearly all of them make some attempt to solve the problem in an organized fashion.

Multiple Causation. The adolescent, unlike the younger child, is able to imagine solutions that involve several factors acting together, rather than just those involving single factors. In another of Piaget and Inhelder's tasks, the experimenter demonstrated that when a drop of something labeled *g* was put into a glass of colorless liquid, the liquid became yellow. The child was then given four beakers of clear chemicals and asked to recreate the demonstration (see Figure 9.3). The correct answer required that two of the clear chemicals be mixed in the

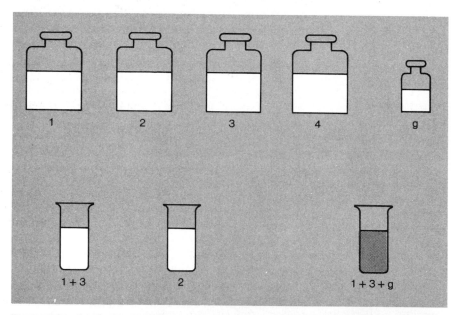

Figure 9.3. Another task often used to study formal operational thought is the colored liquids problem devised by Inhelder and Piaget. The experimenter demonstrates that putting a drop of substance *g* into a glass will make the liquid in the glass turn yellow. The youngster must figure out what combination of chemicals (from the four beakers) needs to go into the glass. (*Source:* Inhelder & Piaget, p. 108.)

glass. Almost no concrete operational children solved this problem, because they lacked what Piaget called the **combinatorial** property of formal operational thinking (Inhelder & Piaget, 1958).

Themes in Formal Operational Thought

The themes of cognitive development that we introduced in Chapter 4 (constancies, perspective taking, symbol use, logic, reversibility, and classification) continue to be important during the growth of formal operational thought. However, since the adolescent's thinking is becoming increasingly more integrated and organized, the themes show much more overlap and are less distinctly different from one another than they were during childhood. Thus rather than discussing the themes one at a time, as we did before, we'd like to give you some examples of how the individual concrete skills come together and how they are coordinated in the process of deductive reasoning (see Figure 9.4).

Constancies and Classification.   The two themes that involve comparisons—constancies and classification—become more alike during the formal operational period, and both seem to be especially influenced by the ability to reason about possibilities. When an adolescent is able to imagine changes in objects or groups of objects, then the distinction between conservation (continued identity of *one* thing in spite of visible changes) and classification (identity of *two or more* things in spite of visible differences) decreases.

The ability to reason systematically also influences these two themes, since it means that comparisons between objects and events can be made more methodically. A young person who understands multiple causation can make more complex and sophisticated comparisons and distinctions among objects and events

Perspective Taking and Reversibility.   The concrete operational child can take the perspective of another person and can understand that operations can be reversed. The formal operational youngster, who can think about possibilities, joins these two themes by the ability to think about things that are contrary to fact. Not only can she imagine what it would be like "if I were Marjory," she can also imagine what it would be like "if I came from Mars."

Systematic reasoning and the understanding of multiple causation also play a part in this more organized way of looking at hypothetical situations. For instance, an adolescent can take a mental list of possible solutions to a problem (like which people to assign to a committee) and methodically try out different combinations mentally until a suitable one is found.

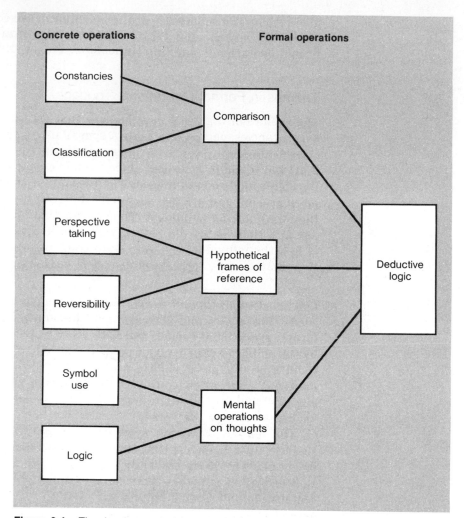

Figure 9.4. The development of formal operations in adolescence.

Symbol Use and Logic.   These themes, too, are profoundly influenced by the ability to think about possibilities. Deductive logic (which we will describe in more detail in a minute) and the use of formal systems like those in mathematics and computer programming both depend upon the ability to adopt a frame of reference that may not have much relation to reality. For example, the study of trigonometry requires the student to deal with the relationships among many imaginary triangles.

Both logic and symbol use are made more powerful by the child's systematic problem solving, and both make use of the youngster's understanding of multiple causation. Doing a chemistry experiment, for example, requires both a methodical approach and an appreciation that some outcomes may have several contributing causes.

Deductive Logic.   We hope that these examples do not give you the idea that only these pairs of themes are linked. In fact, all of the themes become interrelated during this period of development, so that mature formal thought uses them together in organized and coherent ways. Perhaps the best example of this kind of organized thought is **deductive logic.**

We noted earlier that the concrete operational child can use inductive logic, that is, he can arrive at a conclusion based upon individual experiences. In other words, he can reason from the particular to the general. During the period of formal operations, the child develops the ability to use the more difficult kind of reasoning that involves going from the general to the particular.

This is seen most obviously in the formal operational child's ability to understand if-then relationships. *If* "all people are equal," *then* "you and I must be equal." This deductive reasoning may not seem very important, but remember that a great deal of the logic of science is of this type. We begin with a theory and propose, "If this theory is correct, then I should observe such and such."

You can see that deductive logic requires the child to use all of the basic formal operational abilities we have mentioned—thinking about the possible (the "if" part of the logic), systematically evaluating alternatives, and recognizing the possibility of multiple causation. You should also notice that deductive logic requires skills in making comparisons (shown at earlier ages as constancies and classification), in using a hypothetical frame of reference (seen earlier as perspective taking and reversibility), and in using mental operations on concepts and ideas (symbol use and logic).

Piaget's theory of formal operational thought is a theory about competence (not performance), and the particular competence that is central to this period is the ability to organize and coordinate mental operations (Neimark, 1982). You can think of the concrete operational period as being a time of perfecting individual mental skills (operations), and the formal operational period as being a time of extending these skills and organizing them into efficient mental strategies.

The Development of Formal Operations

We know that children do not just wake up one morning in a new stage of cognitive ability. When *do* children start using formal thought, and how does that use change and mature?

In Piaget's original work, he set the beginning of the period of formal operations at about 11 or 12 years of age (Ginsburg & Opper, 1969). A large cross-sectional study by Suzanne Martorano (1977), however, suggests that American children master these skills at somewhat later ages. In her study, Martorano tested children from 11 to 17 years old on a number of the problems devised by Inhelder and Piaget. Some of the results of that study are shown in Figure 9.5. You can see that older children generally do better than younger children (that's no surprise, after all), but the problems seem to be quite different in their level of difficulty. Why might this be?

The easiest problem, called *colored tokens,* asks the child how many different pairs of colors can be made using tokens of six different colors. This requires only thinking up and organizing possible solutions. The next easiest problem, *chemicals* (colored liquids), requires this skill plus an understanding of multiple causation. The pendulum was the

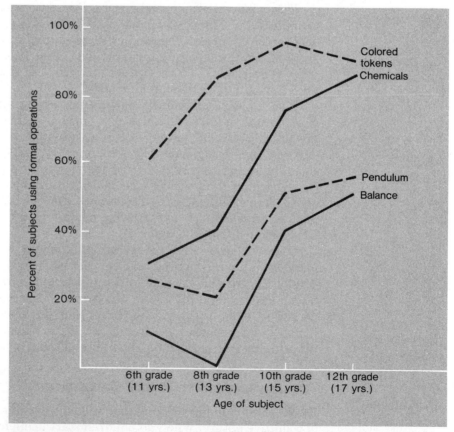

Figure 9.5 These American youngsters seem to develop formal thought at a later age than Piaget originally reported for European students. You can also see that teenagers seem to use formal thought for some problems much earlier than they do for others. (*Source:* Martarano, 1977.)

third hardest problem, since it added the requirement of considering several possible factors simultaneously. The most difficult problem for all of the children was the *balance* problem, which tests the youngster's ability to predict whether or not two weights on either side of a scale will balance (a laboratory version of the seesaw). This may *sound* easy, but the weights can be hung at different distances from the center point of the scale, which means that the child must consider both weight and distance at the same time.

There are three important things to notice about Martorano's results. One is that the biggest leap in the ability to use formal operations seems to occur between eighth and tenth grade or between 13 and 15 years of age. (Remember, this was a cross-sectional study, though, so we don't know whether all individuals advance most quickly at these ages.) The second thing is that not everyone—not *nearly* everyone—achieves formal operational thought. Martorano reports that only 2 of her 80 subjects used formal operations on all 10 of the problems. The stage of formal operations seems not to be universal in the same way that the earlier stages of cognitive development were. Finally, at almost every age, youngsters are solving some of the problems and failing to solve others. Formal operational thought is not an all-or-none process; different aspects of thinking formally seem to develop at different rates and to be used for different kinds of problems.

Should we conclude that American children lag behind Swiss children in logical thinking? Perhaps not. A study by Fred Danner and Mary Carol Day (1977) suggests that the way the problems are presented may make a difference in how children answer them. In this study, they gave the pendulum and two similar problems to groups of 10-, 13-, and 17-year-olds, using Inhelder and Piaget's rather vague instructions. After the child finished each of the first two problems, the experimenter noted how many of the possible factors (like string length or weight used) the child had systematically varied and then asked a set of leading questions to help the child solve the problem successfully. As you can see in Figure 9.6, this instruction was apparently helpful, since the children scored much higher on the third problem than they did on the first or even the second. The point to be made is that performance on formal operations tasks does not depend *only* on the child's level of reasoning, it also depends on the way in which the problems are presented. When the children in this study understood the demands of the problems, some evidence of formal thought was found in the youngest children, just as Piaget had predicted.

The parts of Piaget's theory we have discussed so far have been very influential in the study of adolescent thought. Both Piaget and other cognitive developmental theorists, though, have also been concerned with more social subject matter, and we now turn to these topics.

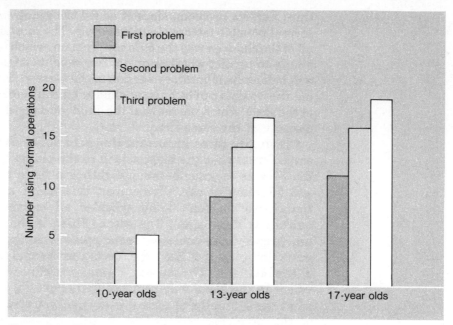

Figure 9.6. The use of formal operations is increased when the problem is made more explicit. When children were directly asked about various factors, their problem solving became more mature. (*Source:* Danner & Day, 1977.)

COGNITIVE STRUCTURE OF INTERPERSONAL UNDERSTANDING

Over the past several years we have seen research articles in psychological journals with titles like "The development of the child's understanding of refrigerators." That's not a real title, of course, but researchers have applied structural theories of cognitive development to the understanding of many topics, some of which (like the refrigerator) seem to be a bit trivial.

However, there have also been studies where these same theories have been applied to topics of particular relevance for young people, and we think the studies of the growth of interpersonal understanding fit this latter category. Why do we think interpersonal understanding is more important than refrigerators? Two reasons. First, as we will see in Chapter 10, the adolescent and young-adult years are times when issues like personal identity, religion, career choice, love, truth, and justice are important for the development of the personality. Second, there is a final characteristic of the formal operational period that we have not yet mentioned: The ability to think about abstract thoughts allows the forces of the emotions to be combined with the forces of the intellect. While we would be hard pressed to describe that linkage in very precise terms, most of you have probably had the experience of solving problems (perhaps personal or moral dilemmas) in which both cognitive and emotional factors were involved.

The researcher and theorist who has studied the growth of interpersonal understanding most thoroughly is probably Robert Selman (1980). Selman has been interested, as we are, in both stages of development (including childhood as well as adolescence and youth) and in themes that traverse those stages.

Selman's methods are, not surprisingly, quite a bit like Piaget's. He uses a clinical interview in which the interviewer is more interested in *assessing* the reasons for a child's answer than in *scoring* the answer itself. Just as studies of formal operational thinking use physical materials, Selman's studies of interpersonal thinking use social materials—stories in which the main character is faced with a particular social problem. You will find an example of one of Selman's stories in Table 9.2. After reading the story, the youngster is asked what he thinks the person in the story should do. Follow-up questions center on how each person in the story feels and how those feelings reflect relationships between the characters. One distinctive feature of Selman's work, however, is that he and his colleagues explicitly consider a set of concepts, similar to what we have called themes, which they trace through the various stages of the development of interpersonal understanding.

TABLE 9.2
Sample Story Used in Robert Selman's Research on Interpersonal Understanding

Charlene and Joanne had been good friends since they were five. Now they were in high school and Joanne was trying out for the school play. As usual she was nervous about how she had done, but Charlene was there to tell her she was very good and give her moral support.

Still, Joanne was worried that a newcomer in school would get the part. The new girl, Tina, came over to congratulate Joanne on her performance and then asked if she could join the girls for a snack.

Right away Charlene and Tina seemed to hit it off very well. They talked about where Tina was from and the kinds of things she could do in her new school. Joanne, on the other hand, didn't seem to like Tina very well. She thought Tina was a little pushy, and maybe she was a bit jealous over all the attention Charlene was giving Tina.

When Tina left the other two alone, Joanne and Charlene arranged to get together on Saturday, because Joanne had a problem that she would like to talk over with Charlene. But later that day, Tina called Charlene and asked her to go to Washington to see a play on Saturday.

Charlene had a dilemma. She would have jumped at the chance to go with Tina, but she had already promised to see Joanne. Joanne might have understood and been happy that Charlene had the chance to go, or she might feel like she was losing her best friend when she really needed her (Selman, 1980, p. 322).

Themes in Interpersonal Understanding

During their clinical interviews, Selman and his colleagues have focused on four domains of interpersonal understanding: individuals, friendships, peer groups, and parent-child relationships. We would like to look at these domains much as we looked at themes in our earlier discussion of cognitive development—focusing on the developmental changes that occur within each topic. We summarized both the themes and the stages proposed by Selman in Table 9.3, which you will probably want to look at as we discuss each one. Although age ranges are included for each of the stages, you undoubtedly realize by now that such ranges are always only approximate.

Theme 1: Individuals. This theme is very similar to the cognitive theme of *perspective taking* and refers to the youngster's understanding of how others think and feel. At first (Stage 0), the child does not separate thinking and acting, even for himself. That is, he believes that a person's thoughts must always be the same as his behavior. Soon, though (Stage 1), he realizes that thinking and acting are separate. Along with this comes the realization that different people may react differently to some events and that people may have several reactions to any one event. Only in Stage 2 does the child come to understand, though, that people can hide or disguise their true feelings. He can then appreciate the little white lie designed to save hurt feelings, for instance.

In Stages 3 and 4, the child develops an understanding of others as complex but organized personalities. In Stage 3, others are seen in terms of strong general traits, what we might call stereotypes. At Stage 4 comes the more complex understanding that people's selves are made of both conscious and unconscious thoughts and emotions.

TABLE 9.3
Summary of Selman's Stages of Interpersonal Understanding

	Stage 0 *(3–6 yrs)*	*Stage 1* *(5–9 yrs)*	*Stage 2* *(7–12 yrs)*	*Stage 3* *(10–15 yrs)*	*Stage 4* *(12–adult)*
Individuals	Physical entities	Intentional subjects	Introspective selves	Stable personalities	Complex self-systems
Friendships	Momentary physical interactions	One way assistance	Fair-weather cooperation	Intimate and mutual sharing	Autonomous interdependence
Peer groups	Physical connections	Unilateral relations	Bilateral partnerships	Homogeneous community	Pluralistic organization
Parent-child relationships	Boss-servant	Caretaker-helper	Counselor, need satisfier	Tolerance and respect	Unknown

Theme 2: Friendships. The earliest understanding of friendships (Stage 0) is based mainly on physical characteristics. If you ask a young child how people make friends, the answer is usually that they "play together," that is, spend time physically near one another.

At Stage 1, children begin to notice that friendship involves two people, but they can see only one person's point of view at a time. The notion of real reciprocity, that it takes two people to have a relationship, doesn't appear until Stage 2 in the process. To some extent, this is just another example of perspective taking; however, this level of social understanding means that a child can understand that friendship has advantages for both friends.

In Stage 3 of this sequence, reciprocity extends to the point of mutual sharing and genuine intimacy. This is closely related to the notion we introduced earlier, that emotions become part of the social understanding system sometime early in adolescence. Along with intimacy comes the feeling of exclusion, or even jealousy, if a friend chooses other companions. Only at Stage 4 are young people able to understand that friendships must include both independence and shared intimacy. Again, the ability to fully take the perspective of the other is necessary for this level.

Theme 3: Peer Groups. In the early stages, children's understanding of groups is very much like their understanding of friends. In fact, groups are often seen as bunches of friends who happen to be in the same place at the same time (Stage 0). At Stage 1, children see groups as ways to provide enough people for desired activities. Selman refers to this as the unilateral function of groups.

By middle childhood (Stage 2), children have begun to understand the reciprocal nature of groups and use words like *teamwork* to describe the way they can work together for mutual goals. But they still think of a group as a bunch of overlapping dyads rather than as a complex structure.

Real *groupness* is not understood until Stage 3, when the peer group is seen as a homogeneous community. The group now appears to have some wholeness of its own, held together by common interests and beliefs. If you think about your own teenage years, this was probably the time you were most interested in what your friends thought (and least interested in what your parents did). In Stage 4, this is modified so that there is more latitude for individual differences, while there is still a strong need for group feelings or mutual concerns. The group is seen, then, as a pluralistic organization, and there is often felt the need for agreements and contracts to formalize that organization.

Theme 4: Parent-Child Relationships. Although both friendships and parent-child relationships involve the child with a single other, there are important differences in the way children think about the two. At Stage 0, the young child sees her relationship with her parents as a boss-servant one with the parent as the boss. A Stage-0 child may know that bad behavior and punishment from a parent occur together, but she does *not* know which is the cause and which is the effect (sounds like transductive reasoning, doesn't it?). The situation is only slightly modified in Stage 1, which Selman refers to as the caretaker-helper relationship. The child understands that the parent is not just bossy, but she does not yet see the parent-child relationship as reciprocal.

As with other themes, the reciprocity of the relationship is first understood during Stage 2. Youngsters at this stage understand that parents get some satisfaction from their roles and have some ideas about the fact that "good" parents give up other pleasures for the sake of their children.

Stage 3 is concerned with a more intimate relationship, in this case one of tolerance and respect. While love and closeness are now important (as is intimacy in friendships), there are also some natural conflicts that occur because of the unequal relationship between parents and children. Stage 4 in this process has not been well documented, but Selman proposes that it would involve both autonomy and interdependence, fluctuating through the rest of the life cycle.

Research on Selman's Stages

Selman and his colleagues (Selman, 1980) have studied several groups of children, and in Figure 9.7 we have shown you one example of this research. Using the answers given in the clinical interviews, each child was assigned a score corresponding to a stage (or in some cases, to a point intermediate between stages). Then these scores were averaged for children of different ages. You can see that growth in understanding is fairly steady over the middle years of childhood and early adolescence, and that understanding is about equal for the three domains pictured (individuals, friends, and peer groups).

Interpersonal Understanding and Behavior

Our last remaining question about the course of development of interpersonal understanding is whether or not the stages reported in interviews can be seen in actual behavior. A study by Daniel Jaquette (1980) helps to answer this question.

Jaquette observed eight children during weekly class meetings (in a special clinic school) over the course of the year. Some of these meetings were used to discuss hypothetical problems, while others concerned real issues from the classroom. The children also participated

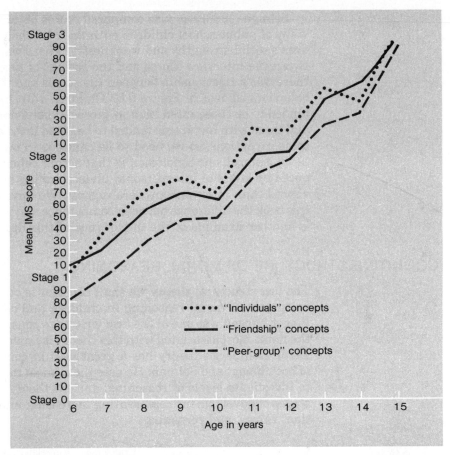

Figure 9.7. The development of the understanding of interpersonal relationships. Understanding of individuals, friendships, and peer groups all seem to grow steadily during the elementary-school years and early adolescence. (*Source:* Selman, 1980.)

in clinical interviews, and these also included both hypothetical and real-life problems. Each child's statements were coded in all four situations using the stages we have described and then compared from situation to situation. Overall, the children showed lower levels of functioning in real-life situations than they did in interviews. Jaquette believes that this is because many factors entered into the real-life situations—the actions of others, occasional intervention by teachers, and the limitations on time that occur in the classroom. Furthermore, among the real-life measures of social understanding, those concerned with hypothetical problems showed higher scores than those concerned with real problems. Again, it can be argued that many factors enter into behavior about real problems, while only the cognitive factors influence hypothetical ones.

Selman (1980) has also compared scores obtained in clinical interviews of public-school children with their teachers' ratings of the children's social strengths and weaknesses. There was no relationship between the interview scores and the ratings of *negative* behaviors, but there was a relationship between the scores and the ratings of *positive* behaviors (shown in Figure 9.8). Children with high interview scores tended to be those rated high in prosocial behaviors by their teachers, and those with low scores tended to be rated low. Of course, there were some exceptions, so we need to be cautious in our interpretations.

In general, our conclusion is that actual behavior is strongly influenced by levels of interpersonal understanding but is usually less advanced than interview answers suggest. We have discussed earlier in this book the difference between competence and performance, and this is another example of the importance of this distinction.

COGNITIVE STRUCTURE OF MORAL REASONING

The last structural theory we shall consider is concerned with the development of moral reasoning in children and adolescents. Although Piaget himself was one of the first writers to consider moral reasoning, the name most associated with this theory is Lawrence Kohlberg (1964, 1978). Kohlberg's theory has a great deal in common with the ideas of both Piaget and Selman: He uses the clinical method; he uses stories to investigate levels of reasoning; and his theory is strongly based on stages of development representing increasing integration of information, values, and reasoning.

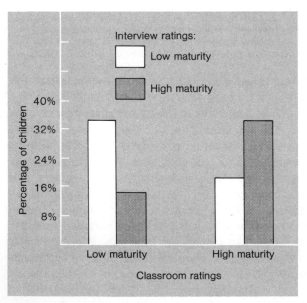

Figure 9.8. The relationship between interview measures of interpersonal understanding and actual behavior in the classroom. These public-school children were rated by their own teachers and also given Selman's interview. Those with mature behavior at school also showed mature understanding in the interview. (*Source:* Adapted from Selman, 1980.)

Before we look at the theory, though, we must ask exactly what moral reasoning is. For Kohlberg, moral reasoning is thinking about and embracing moral principles, those universal standards of conduct that we believe should be shared by all people (Kohlberg, 1970). Therefore, he is less interested in specific laws and rules, or even in specific behavior, than he is in the kind of reasoning that goes into making laws and rules or determining behavior.

Stages in Moral Reasoning

In contrast to the other structural theories we have looked at, this theory is not easily broken down into themes or domains. Instead, Kohlberg implies that there is a single theme in the development of moral reasoning, which we would describe as the focus of authority. That is, Kohlberg is describing the ways in which the child comes to shift his understanding of the source of moral authority from the concrete and immediate to the abstract and infinite. Let us start, then, by describing this sequence of development in more detail.

Level 1: Preconventional Morality.   In these earliest stages of moral reasoning, the child's judgments are based on sources of authority who are close by and physically superior to himself—primarily the parents. The standards he uses are external, based on what others will do as a result of his behavior, rather than internal, or based on some belief system of his own.

The first stage of this level, which Kohlberg calls the *punishment and obedience* orientation, is characterized by the child's reliance on the physical consequences of his action. If he is punished, the behavior was wrong; if not, it was right. His obedience to adults is based on their obvious size and power, not on moral authority or position.

In the second stage, the child has an *instrumental-relativist* orientation. Instead of only avoiding punishment, he can begin to do those things that are rewarded and avoid those that are punished. There is some beginning, during this phase, of concern for other people, but only if that concern can be expressed as something that benefits the child himself, as well. So he can enter into agreements like "if you help me, I'll help you," but even this is based on the idea of rewards and punishments.

Level 2: Conventional Morality.   Two changes mark this level of moral reasoning. First, and most obvious, groups replace parents as the source of authority. The reference group may be the family, the nation, or just the gang at school, but what the group defines as right *is* right in the eyes of the child. Second, this authority is no longer expressed only outwardly in rewards and punishments. Instead, the child carries around in his head (what we usually refer to as a **conscience**) the idea of what the group thinks is right and wrong.

The first stage of this level (which is Stage 3 overall) is called the *good boy/nice girl* orientation by Kohlberg. Children at this stage believe that good behavior is whatever pleases other people. Another mark of this stage is that the child begins to make judgments based upon intentions as well as on outward behavior. If someone "means well" or "didn't mean to do it," their wrongdoing is less serious than if they did it "on purpose." This can be thought of as yet another way that moral reasoning is going on 'inside' the head and not just in overt behavior.

The latter stage at this level (Stage 4) shows the child turning to larger social groups for his norms. Kohlberg has labeled this the *law and order* orientation, because children focus on doing their duty, respecting authority, and following rules and laws. The emphasis is less on what is pleasing to particular people (as in Stage 3) and more on adhering to a complex set of regulations. However, the regulations themselves are not questioned.

Level 3: Principled Morality.   The final stage of moral reasoning is also characterized by two shifts. First, the source of authority is no longer the group as an outside entity, but rather a group in which the youngster (who is probably now a young adult) is a full member. The group becomes *we* rather than *they*. The second shift is from accepting and following rules to formulating, challenging, and (if necessary) changing them. Rules, laws, and regulations are seen as important ways of ensuring fairness, but people operating at this level also see times when the rules, laws, and regulations need to be ignored or changed. Our American system of government is based on moral reasoning of this kind, which Kohlberg has labeled the *social contract* or *legalistic* orientation.

In his original writing about moral development, Kohlberg also included a sixth stage, *universal ethical principle* orientation. People who reason in this way assume personal responsibility for their own actions based upon fundamental and universal principles, such as the sacredness of human life. More recently, though, Kohlberg (1978) has come to the conclusion that there may not be a separate sixth stage at all. As he put it,

> . . . my sixth stage was mainly a theoretical construction suggested by the writings of "elite" figures like Martin Luther King, and not an empirically confirmed developmental concept (Kohlberg, 1978, p. 86).

It seems likely that universal ethical principles guide the moral reasoning of only a few very unusual persons, probably those who devote their lives to humanitarian causes.

Sequence and Universality of Moral Reasoning

Although the stages of moral reasoning play a central part, we should also consider two other facets of Kohlberg's theory: (1) that the stages progress in an invariant sequence, and (2) that the stages occur in all cultures.

Sequence.   The evidence seems fairly strong that the stages described by Kohlberg do occur in the order he states. The best data come from a longitudinal study of 30 men who were interviewed every three years from their teens until about age 30 (Kohlberg & Elfenbein, 1975). From one interview to the next, the men all remained in the same stage or moved up one stage, rather than going backward.

Universality.   Although psychologists have not given moral dilemmas to children from every culture in the world, there have been enough studies (including Taiwan, Turkey, Mexico, Kenya, India, and the Bahamas) to be fairly persuasive. In every case, the older children studied had higher levels of moral judgment than the younger children and used forms of judgment that were parallel to those found in American children. There are some suggestions, however, that the rate of moral development may vary from culture to culture. Kohlberg (1969), for example, found that Stage 4 was the highest reached by 16-year-olds in Mexico and Turkey, in contrast to the 10 percent or so of American 16-year-olds who show Stage-5 reasoning. It seems likely, then, that the sequence described by Kohlberg may be experienced at different rates depending upon specific cultural experiences.

Another issue of universality has recently been raised by Carol Gilligan (1982). She criticizes the fact that Kohlberg's theory categorizes some types of answers—mainly those that emphasize relationships rather than logic—as either not scorable or as a low level of reasoning. She suggests that a different categorization system may be appropriate for these responses, which are quite frequently made by girls and women.

Moral Reasoning and Moral Behavior

We saw earlier that interpersonal understanding, assessed in hypothetical terms, seemed to overestimate somewhat the kinds of behaviors that children would perform in real-life situations. How about moral reasoning?

In one study, Kohlberg (1975) found that 85 percent of the students showing at least some use of the principled level of reasoning resisted cheating when given the opportunity, compared to 45 percent of those using primarily conventional morality and 30 percent of those using primarily preconventional reasoning. A study of much younger children by Nancy Eisenberg-Berg and Michael Hand (1979) showed a similar result: Children who were hedonistic in their moral reasoning (what feels good is right; what feels bad is wrong) were less likely to share toys than children who showed more mature moral reasoning.

However, we should be aware again that the correspondence between the reasoning and behavior is not perfect. After all, in Kohlberg's study, 15 percent of the principled moral reasoners *did* cheat, and some preschoolers who talked about sharing failed to share. It seems likely that real-life situations involving moral reasoning, just like those situations involving interpersonal understanding, sometimes make it hard for children's best and most mature thinking to be expressed.

COGNITIVE STRUCTURE: A BEGINNING SYNTHESIS

We hope you have noticed that theories of cognitive structure during adolescence and early adulthood seem to have many similarities. We'd like to try and compare the nature of formal thought, interpersonal understanding, and moral reasoning before we move on to consider cognitive styles.

In Table 9.4, we have tried to pull these different threads together. In order to make a table that would fit on one page, we've taken one theme from cognitive development (perspective taking), one from interpersonal understanding (peer groups), and one from moral reasoning.

TABLE 9.4
Structural Theories of Adolescent and Young Adult Thinking

	APPROXIMATE AGES				
	3–6 yrs	*5–9 yrs*	*7–12 yrs*	*10–15 yrs*	*12 yrs–adult*
Cognitive development (perspective taking)	Preoperational egocentrism	Concrete operational	Decentering	Formal operational	Hypothetical frames of reference
Interpersonal understanding (peer groups)	Stage 0 physical connections	Stage 1 unilateral relations	Stage 2 bilateral partnerships	Stage 3 homogeneous community	Stage 4 pluralistic organization
Moral development (authority source)	Stage 1 punishment and obedience	Stage 2 instrumentalist relativist	Stage 3 good boy/ nice girl	Stage 4 law and order	Stage 5 social contract legalistic

As always in comparisons like this, the ages listed at the top are only approximate.

The fit between the growth of interpersonal understanding and moral reasoning is very close. (Selman was, in fact, much influenced by Kohlberg's work.) General cognitive development is somewhat less closely linked.

Although we drew up Table 9.4 on a theoretical basis, we would like to mention two studies that support the relationship among these various themes. Carol Tomlinson-Keasey and Charles Keasey (1974) presented moral dilemmas to two groups: 12-year-old girls and college women. On the basis of their responses, each subject was classified as preconventional, conventional, or principled in moral reasoning. A few months later, all subjects were given three cognitive tasks; and their performance was rated as being at the concrete operational level, at the formal operational level, or at the transition between the two levels.

Figure 9.9 shows some of the results. Among the 12-year-olds, concrete operational thought was associated with preconventional morality, formal operational thought was associated with conventional morality, and transitional thought was split between the two kinds of moral reasoning. Conventional moral reasoning was the most common level for all of the college women, regardless of cognitive level. Interestingly, though, only women with transitional or formal thought showed principled levels of reasoning.

Lawrence Walker and Boyd Richards (1979) have looked at this question in a slightly different way. They assessed the ease with which adolescents could be trained to use Stage 4 moral reasoning and found that youngsters who were already using formal operational thought learned most easily.

It seems reasonable to us, then, to conclude that all of these theories of cognitive structure are reflecting some basic changes in the organization of thought during the adolescent and early adult years. We are especially struck by the fact that all of these theories seem to *end* at about the same age, as though there is some definite end to cognitive change in the structural sense. We'll be returning to answer that question in Chapter 12.

COGNITIVE STYLES IN ADOLESCENCE AND YOUTH

Field Dependence and Independence

You will recall that in Chapter 4 we described the difference between field dependent persons, whose perception is greatly influenced by the background and environment, and field independent people, whose per-

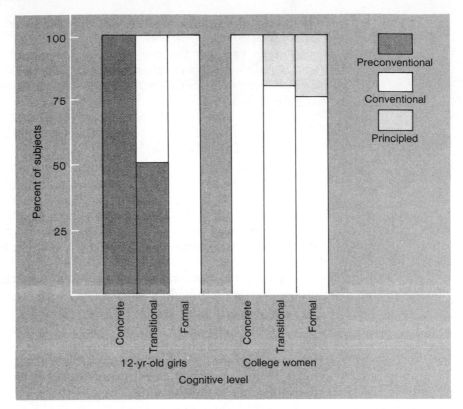

Figure 9.9.   The relationship between cognitive and moral reasoning levels of girls and college women. There is clearly a relationship between the general level of cognitive development and the general level of moral reasoning. Still, many adults who use formal thought do not display principled moral thinking. (*Source:* Tomlinson-Keasey & Keasey, 1974.)

ception is largely free of these influences. At least some of these differences seem to continue their influence into the adolescent and young adult years.

For example, people who are relatively field dependent seem to pay more attention to other persons (including looking more at their faces) than do those who are relatively field independent (Konstadt & Forman, 1965). This interest in people was also shown in a study of student nurses (Quinlan & Blatt, 1972): Those who excelled in psychiatric nursing were more likely to be field dependent, while those who excelled in surgical nursing were more likely to be field independent. There is also evidence that students who are relatively field independent are more likely to succeed in college majors such as math, science, engineering, or architecture (Witkin, 1977).

At the same time, it appears that measures of this perceptual style are *not* related to general success in college (as measured by grades).

BOX 9.1

The Development of Extraordinary Musical Ability

All of the theories we have talked about in this chapter have limited their concerns to the kinds of thinking that are related either to academic or everyday activities. Now let us take a minute to look at another kind of mental ability—the ability to play musical instruments and compose music.

Jeanne Bamberger (1982) has studied the development of musical skill in musically naive children and adults, novice musicians (those with a few years of training), and expert musicians. In one task, the subjects were asked to play a familiar tune (like "Twinkle Twinkle Little Star") using a set of bells that all look the same and can be moved around freely.

Bamberger found that subjects used two quite different methods for playing the tune. Musically naive subjects usually found (by trial and error) the bells necessary to play the song and placed these bells in a line so that the song could be played just by going down the row. She calls this a **figural** solution to the task. The figural arrangement for "Twinkle Twinkle" would be

C G A G F E D C

The other strategy, used by the novice musicians, was to find (also by trial and error) the bells that make up a musical scale and put them in order from highest to lowest:

C D E F G A B C

The song is played by ringing the bells in a specified order. Bamberger refers to this as a **formal** solution to the problem.

You can see that the advantage of the formal solution is that once the bells are put into a musical scale, any melody can be played (as long as you know or can figure out the correct pattern). So you might think that expert musicians would use this method. What Bamberger found, though, was that expert musicians use *both* figural and formal strategies when remembering melodies and for other musical activities like playing instruments.

These studies (and others about rhythm) suggest that most musicians begin their training by learning formal strategies for making music and later add figural strategies. Bamberger, though, suggests that one group of musicians probably follows a different course. This group includes children who are musical prodigies—those whose extraordinary abilities are recognized very early in life and who often begin performing by the age of 5 or 6.

Among these prodigies, it appears that figural strategies for music are highly developed from a very early age. These strategies tend to be specific and also to be highly organized and extremely well practiced. When such a child begins music lessons, she is introduced to formal strategies, which seem quite foreign and perhaps even incompatible with the way she has played music before. Consequently, many prodigies face a crisis during their teen years when they must try and reconcile these two different approaches to music. Some youngsters never make this switch, while others do it successfully.

This switch is undoubtedly related to the onset of formal operational reasoning—thinking about thought. It seems to us, in fact, that the clash of early, specific concepts with later more abstract concepts is a description of cognitive development as well as of musical development.

Perceptual styles, at least those defined in this way, seem to be related to school and career preferences rather than just to mental ability.

Spatial Visualization as Style

In most tests of mental abilities (like the WAIS, WISC, or college entrance exams), spatial reasoning is considered to be just one facet of general intellectual functioning. Another view of spatial reasoning is that it is a mode of thinking, separate from—and sometimes competing with—verbal reasoning.

The origin of this notion comes from biology and medicine more than from psychology. As you may know, the part of the brain known as the **cerebral cortex,** which seems to be responsible for all kinds of thinking, is divided into right and left halves (sometimes called **cerebral hemispheres**). The right half controls the left side of the body, and the left half controls the right side of the body. In addition, the left side seems to control language functions, while the right side seems to control spatial functions (at least among right-handed people).

There has been much interest in this **cerebral specialization** in both the scientific literature and in the popular press, chiefly because many theorists and researchers have characterized left-brain and right-brain thought in more general terms: left-brain being logical and analytical thought, and right-brain being intuitive or artistic thought (Edwards, 1979). This distinction, although it is certainly an oversimplification of complex brain functioning (Gardner, 1978; Kinsborne, 1982), is a powerful one and reminiscent of the distinction between convergent and divergent thought. Moreover, the well-documented sex difference in spatial reasoning (favoring men on the average) has made this a controversial topic.

We cannot untangle the web of evidence about sex differences and cerebral specialization for you here, but we'd like to describe a couple of studies representative of the issues involved. One example comes from Deborah Waber (1977), who assessed verbal and spatial reasoning in adolescents. Both boys and girls who physically matured early had better verbal than spatial skills, while those who matured relatively late had better spatial than verbal skills. Since on the average girls mature earlier than boys, we would expect more of them to show verbal superiority, which is exactly what the results of many other studies have shown.

A second example of research in this area comes from a study by Sarah Burnett, David Lane, and Lewis Dratt (1982), which specifically addressed the link between cerebral specialization and spatial reasoning. They found that intermediate levels of cerebral specialization were associated with the best performance on the spatial task. In other words, the best way to solve visual problems is to use *both* sides of the brain, rather than having one side (even the right side) clearly dominant.

It seems likely to us that spatial and verbal skills are better seen as complementary than as competing. Future research needs to ask *when* and *how* these skills are used, rather than which one is stronger.

Divergent Thinking as Style

One of the best-known studies of divergent thinking was done by Jacob Getzels and Phil Jackson (1962), who compared youngsters who were high on IQ tests but low on creativity with those who were high on creativity but slightly lower on IQ.

Getzels and Jackson selected their subjects from a private school in Chicago where the average IQ was quite high, as you can see in Table 9.5. Although the groups differed (by definition) on IQ, their school achievement scores did not differ, nor did their scores on a personality test that measured their motivation to achieve. Nonetheless, their teachers found the high IQ students to be more desirable class members than the high creative students. As you can see in Table 9.6, stories written by students in the two groups differed in many ways.

Getzels and Jackson also found that the homes of the high IQ students seemed to be especially intellectually stimulating (for instance, containing many books and magazines), while the homes of the high creative students were more accepting (for example, the mothers reported fewer unfavorable characteristics of their children) and independence fostering.

TABLE 9.5
Characteristics of High IQ Children and High Creative Children

Characteristic	High IQ	High creative	Other children
IQ	150.0[a]	127.0	132.0
School achievement	55.0[a]	56.3[a]	49.9
Personality: need for achievement	49.0	50.0	49.8
Teacher rating: desirability as a student	11.2[a]	10.5	10.2
Drawings: presence of humor	18%	54%	
Drawings: presence of violence	4%	35%	
Home life: seven or more magazine subscriptions	68%	33%	
Mother reports: child has more than one unfavorable characteristic	43%	10%	

SOURCE: Abstracted from Getzels & Jackson, 1962.
[a]Significant difference from other groups.

TABLE 9.6
Examples of Stories Written by High IQ and High Creative Adolescents

Stimulus Picture: Man sitting at a desk, most often seen as someone working late at the office.

A High IQ Child:

There's ambitious Bob, down at the office at 6:30 in the morning. Every morning it's the same. He's trying to show his boss how energetic he is. Now, thinks Bob, maybe the boss will give me a raise for all my extra work. The trouble is that Bob has been doing this for the last three years, and the boss still hasn't given him a raise. He'll come in at 9:00, not even noticing that Bob has been there so long, and poor Bob won't get his raise.

A High Creative Child:

This man has just broken into this office of a new cereal company. He is a private eye employed by a competitor firm to find the formula that makes the cereal bend, sag, and sway. After a thorough search of the office he comes upon what he thinks is the cereal formula. He is now copying it. It turns out that it is the wrong formula and the competitor's factory blows up. Poetic justice.

SOURCE: Getzels & Jackson, 1962, p. 40.

Although this study has many limitations (such as the high level of mental ability in both groups), it does make the point that creativity is partly separate from general intelligence and may help to determine how that intelligence is displayed.

LINKING POWER, STRUCTURE, AND STYLE

Information Processing

The work of information-processing researchers has extended from childhood to adolescence and youth. Although their intent is not to show links with formal operational thought, evidence of this kind of organized approach to thinking, learning, and remembering can be seen in their experimental results.

One group of experiments has studied *studying* by high school and college students. These older students are able to use their study time better than younger children because they can pick out important facts from less important details (Brown & Smiley, 1977). Furthermore, they show more complex strategies for taking notes (Brown & Day, in press). That is, college students are more likely to make notes that use general terms to describe specific items or events and are more likely to use (or write, if necessary) topic sentences for each paragraph. Notice that all of these more mature strategies require the student to take an active role and use classification, categorization, and evaluation rules.

The same trends can be seen in studies of writing. Beginning writers (and that includes students up through high school age) tend to use a writer-based method—they describe everything they know about a topic, even if it doesn't match the question or assignment. Although many college students do this too (especially on essay exams, as we have noticed), more mature writers use a reader-based method where they marshall their facts to fit the assignment or the reader (Brown, Bransford, Ferrara, & Campione, 1983). This, of course, requires fairly advanced skills in perspective taking, such as those found in the formal operational period.

It is worthy of note that information-processing researchers have found the same tendency for uneven development of mental skills that Piagetian researchers have. As Ann Brown and her colleagues (Brown, et al., 1983) have phrased it, the early state of a skill is fragile, and the skill can be used only with limited kinds of subject matter. Later, the skill becomes more "robust," and is applied much more generally.

A FINAL WORD

At the end of Chapter 4, we were able to list for you the several ways in which psychologists were trying to link together definitions of intelligence based on power, structure, and style. Unfortunately, we cannot write a conclusion to this chapter that so neatly combines the three. Although there have certainly been many studies that have used intelligence tests along with measures of formal operations or interpersonal understanding or moral reasoning or creativity, the goal of these studies has been comparison rather than synthesis.

We suspect that this lack of synthesis is related to the fact that power, structure, and style begin to play quite different roles in the lives of adolescents and young adults than they did in childhood. As one example, consider education. During the early years, school curricula are pretty standard (reading, arithmetic, social studies), and a child's success in mastering school work is strongly related to measures of cognitive power. Similarly, cognitive styles are usually considered in relationship to school performance. Cognitive structures seem to develop according to a maturational timetable; and although teachers use their knowledge of those structures to design good programs, measures of cognitive stage are not particularly related to school achievement. In late adolescence, however, the situation changes. The school curriculum no longer consists of only core material; instead, there is a variety of different subjects that can be studied. All of them require about the same levels of cognitive power and structure, and choices between them become increasingly made on

BOX 9.2

Education for Gifted Adolescents

We have discussed some personality and family characteristics of adolescents with strong convergent thinking abilities and strong divergent thinking abilities (the high IQ and high creative youngsters from Getzels and Jackson's study). Do these young people need special educational programs, or are they well enough served by regular classroom experiences?

There have been two important influences on thinking about this problem over the last 30 years (Tannenbaum, 1979). The first was the launching of the first earth satellite by the Soviet Union in 1957. Although that seems quite minor to us now, at the time it seemed to be evidence that the American educational system was not producing enough talented scientists and engineers to meet the challenges of developing space programs. One way to meet these challenges was to improve school curricula generally, and much effort was put into new ways of teaching math and science, which we now take pretty much for granted. Another way to produce more scientists is to do a better job of identifying able students early in their school years and offering them special opportunities. This latter strategy became very popular during the late 1950s and early 1960s, with many high schools offering special accelerated classes for bright students.

The other influence was an awakened concern about equality of opportunity. After the United States Supreme Court ruled in 1954 that separate educational facilities for black children were inherently unequal, and therefore unconstitutional, educators became very sensitized to the fact that programs for gifted children usually included very few minority group children. Since participation in such programs was often determined by scores on standardized tests, this should not have been surprising. Still it became (and remains) a difficult policy question: how to serve the needs of intellectually ad-

vanced children while maintaining equal educational opportunity?

Several strategies have been tried to deal with this dilemma (Fox, 1979). Among those most aimed at identifying and encouraging the intellectually advanced students are those that involve special schools, or at least special classes, for them. Among those most aimed at ensuring educational equality are those that offer enriched curricula while keeping the able students in classrooms with children their own age.

The issue of *what* is to be taught in these special programs is closely related to our notions of cognitive power, structure, and style (Hogan, 1980). If you focus on intellectual *power,* then you tend to emphasize speeding up the rate of learning. Julian Stanley and his associates (1974), for instance, have taught four and a half years of college mathematics to gifted youngsters in as few as 120 hours. Robinson and Robinson (1982) have encouraged very able students to enter college as early as age 11. If you focus on intellectual *structure,* however, then you tend to emphasize increasing the amount of hands-on learning to ensure the best development of the cognitive structures. Finally, if you focus on intellectual *style,* you may intentionally try to influence the rates of creative or divergent thinking. Robert Hogan and his associates (1977) found that such a course improved scores on a divergent thinking test for a group of high school students taking a college-level introduction to the social sciences.

Although we are not educators, we suspect that the recent emphasis (and legal mandate) on education for all—which was originally intended to improve education for disabled youngsters—will encourage programs for gifted children that are integrated into regular classrooms. Whether communities and school districts will be willing and/or able to fund such programs remains to be seen.

the basis of personal preferences, which may be strongly influenced by cognitive styles. College achievement is somewhat less related to measures of cognitive power than high school achievement is, and more related to variables like motivation and personal maturity. In short, cognitive development becomes more interwoven with personality during this period, a linkage that continues through adult life.

SUMMARY

1. Measures of intelligence in adolescents and young adults are basically similar to those used in childhood. But while intellectual tests are usually used for guidance and placement with younger children, they are often used for selection of adolescents and young adults.

2. College entrance examinations share many characteristics of traditional IQ tests, including their susceptibility to certain environmental influences. There has also been a decline in scores on these tests over the last 15 to 20 years.

3. College entrance examinations are moderately good at predicting college grades, although this relationship is not strong among the most able students.

4. Formal operational thought is characterized by the youngster's ability to think about imaginary and hypothetical situations as well as real ones, to engage in systematic problem solving, and to understand multiple causation.

5. Formal operational thought can be described in terms of the same themes used to describe earlier mental development, but these themes show more overlap and are less distinctive than they were previously.

6. Although older children can perform formal operational tasks more often than younger children can, some of the tasks are easier than others (suggesting that this stage is not an all-or-none situation), and many young people seem to use formal operational thought infrequently or not at all (suggesting that this stage is not universal).

7. The understanding of interpersonal relationships seems to develop in a way that is parallel to the understanding of physical and logical relationships. Selman's theory provides a set of stages and themes that describe this developmental sequence.

8. Actual behavior in social situations is related to levels of interpersonal understanding but is often slightly less advanced than interview responses would suggest.

9. Reasoning about moral dilemmas also follows a developmental course related to cognitive development. Kohlberg's theory de-

scribes this developmental course using a single theme that is related to the source of authority or power.

10. Although there is considerable evidence to suggest that the sequence of stages described by Kohlberg occurs among members of many cultures, there may be some cultural (and perhaps gender-specific) differences not expressed in the theory.

11. Since Kohlberg's theory focuses on reasoning and since several kinds of reasoning can lead to the same moral decision and behavior, it is difficult to study the relationship between moral reasoning and moral behavior. The data we do have suggest an imperfect correspondence between the two.

12. The three theories of cognitive structure we have described seem to have a great deal in common, especially concerning the progression through a series of stages.

13. The cognitive styles of field dependence and field independence are related to school and career choices among young people but not to their level of academic achievement.

14. Some researchers think that people who are skilled in spatial visualization have dominant right cerebral hemispheres, while those who are skilled in verbal abilities have dominant left cerebral hemispheres.

15. Studies of divergent thinking in adolescents and young adults suggest that this skill is partially distinct from IQ.

16. Studies about studying and writing suggest that these skills require formal operational thought, and that they develop in much the same way that formal thought does.

17. There are few theories that link together cognitive power, structure, and style in this age group, but there is reason to think that structure and style may be more important for daily life and personality development than power.

KEY TERMS

Cerebral cortex   The part of the brain responsible for conscious thought and reasoning. It is the outer layer of the brain, characterized by a convoluted surface.

Cerebral hemisphere   One half of the cerebral cortex. The right cerebral hemisphere controls the left side of the body, and the left cerebral hemisphere controls the right side of the body. In most people, the left hemisphere also controls language and speech.

Cerebral specialization   The extent to which the cerebral hemispheres have different functions, as opposed to their working together. Many authors have characterized the left cerebral hemisphere as the logical and analytical side and the right hemisphere as the intuitive and artistic side, but this is an oversimplification.

Combinatorial property   The aspect of formal operations concerned with multiple causation. That is, the understanding that certain results are the combined results of several causes.

Conscience Set of ideas about what is morally right and wrong.

Conventional morality The second level of moral judgment proposed by Kohlberg, in which the person's judgments are dominated by considerations of group values and laws.

Deductive logic Reasoning from general rules to specific instances. Sometimes referred to as *if > then* logic.

Figural musical reasoning Way of thinking about melodies as being fixed patterns of notes, with each melody having a unique pattern.

Formal musical reasoning Way of thinking about melodies as being variable patterns of notes, with many such patterns sharing the same basic set of notes (usually a musical scale).

Formal operational thought Piaget's name for the fourth and final major stage of cognitive development, occurring during adolescence when the child becomes able to manipulate and organize ideas as well as objects.

Preconventional morality The first level of moral development proposed by Kohlberg, in which moral judgments are dominated by consideration of what will be punished and what feels good.

Principled morality The third level of morality proposed by Kohlberg, in which considerations of justice, individual rights, and contracts dominate moral judgment.

WAIS Wechsler Adult Intelligence Scale. An adult IQ test with items arranged in subtests that measure verbal and performance IQ.

SUGGESTED READINGS

Hargadon, F. Tests and college admissions. *American Psychologist,* 1981, *36,* 1112–1119.

This is a nontechnical article about college entrance testing that appeared in a special issue of this journal dedicated to psychological testing.

Lickona, T. (Ed.). *Moral development and behavior: Theory, research, and social issues.* New York: Holt, Rinehart and Winston, 1976.

This is a very good collection of articles about moral development and also includes several other approaches to morality that we have not discussed here.

Niemark, E. D. Adolescent thought: Transition to formal operations. In B. B. Wolman (Ed.), *Handbook of developmental psychology.* Englewood Cliffs, N.J.: Prentice-Hall, 1982.

This is the most up-to-date summary about formal operations that we have found. Parts of it are technical, but it is well written and has plenty of suggestions for further reading.

Selman, R. L. *The growth of interpersonal understanding: Developmental and clinical analyses.* New York: Academic Press, 1980.

This is the main source for reading about Selman's theory, and fortunately it is quite clearly organized and written. It also includes a considerable amount of clinical material about children in a special school that you will find fascinating.

Witkin, H.A., Moore, C.A., Goodenough, D. R., & Cox, P. W. Field-dependent and field-independent cognitive styles and their educational implications. *Review of Educational Research,* 1977, *47,* 1–64.
This is one of the most readable accounts of research on this cognitive style dimension. Witkin pulls together a great many threads in this article and discusses the applications as well as the basic research.

PROJECT 9.1
The Pendulum

This project is a simplified version of Inhelder and Piaget's pendulum problem. It is suitable for use with youngsters starting at about age 8, and can also be used with teenagers, adults, and the elderly. If your class is working on this project together, your instructor may assign each of you to find a person of a different age, so that you can do a real cross-sectional study.

Equipment

Since the physical objects are so important in this problem, collect your equipment carefully and test it before you start. You will need three pieces of string (about 25 cm, 37 cm, and 50 cm long) and three weights. The string needs to be strong enough not to break but flexible enough to swing. It is best if the pieces of string can be tied to something overhead, like a door frame or a shower-curtain rod. If you can't manage that, then *you* hold the top end of the string while your subject works on the problem. The weights can be anything that is heavy and can be tied to the bottom end of the string—fishing sinkers and keys work well. They need to be light, medium, and heavy weights.

Procedure

First, show your subject how the weights attach to the string and how to give the weight a push to start the pendulum swinging. Then say,

"I am doing a class project about how different people go about solving a problem. The problem I would like you to solve is to find out what makes this pendulum swing faster or slower. You can use any of these three strings and these three weights to help you figure this out. I'll be taking notes about what you do and say while you are working on the problem."

Report

Look over your notes for your subject and try to answer these questions:

1. Did he solve the problem? That is, did he figure out that it was the length of the string and not the weight that determined the speed of the pendulum?
2. How many trials did it take for him to reach his conclusions (right or not)? Each combination of a string and a weight is one trial.
3. Did he systematically plan combinations of length and weight to help answer the question? Did he talk out loud about this strategy?
4. Did he mention having had a course where he studied this problem (like general science or physics)?

If your class is working on a cross-sectional experiment for this project, pool your results and try to answer these questions:

5. Are people of different ages more or less likely to solve the problem? You might compare preteens with teenagers or adults with elderly people to answer this question.
6. Do people of different ages take more trials to reach their conclusions?
7. Are children and the elderly less likely to try different combinations of length and weight systematically? Why might this be so?

PROJECT 9.2
Moral Reasoning

Locate two subjects who are at least 13 years old. If possible, try to get people of different ages or different sexes or different ethnic backgrounds. If your entire class is doing this project, your instructor may assign students to find particular types of subjects.

Procedure

Present the following dilemma to each subject:

In Europe a woman was near death from a very bad form of cancer. There was one drug that the doctors thought might save her. It was a type of radium for which a druggist was charging 10 times what the drug cost him to make. He paid $200 for the radium and charged $2000 for a small dose of the drug.

The sick woman's husband, Heinz, went to everyone he knew to borrow the money, but he could only get together about $1000, which is half of what it would cost. He told the druggist that his wife was dying and asked him to sell it cheaper or to let him pay later. But the druggist said, "No, I discovered the drug, and I'm going to make money from it." So Heinz became desperate and broke into the man's store to steal the drug for his wife. Should the husband have done that? Why?

Report

Analyze the answer given by each subject in terms of Kohlberg's six stages of moral development. Then, either by yourself or with your class, try to answer these questions:

1. Did you have difficulty classifying the subjects' answers, or was each answer clearly in one particular stage? If you had trouble, what does that tell you about the research on moral reasoning?
2. Was there a relationship between the subjects' level of moral reasoning and their ages?
3. Could you detect any differences between the answers given by people in different groups, like men and women, white and minority? Were these differences in the stage of moral development or in some other aspect of the answer?
4. Do you think your results are consistent with those obtained by Kohlberg and his colleagues? If they are not, how do you account for the differences?

Chapter 10

The Self and Relationships with Others in Adolescence and Youth

(10)

Henry is a somewhat shy, sensitive and studious young man. He is taking a college preparatory course [in high school], likes physics and math, and is clearly excited about school and what he is learning. . . . Outside of school, Henry works 20–30 hours as a clerk and is saving his money for college. His dream is to be accepted by a good university so he can study engineering. . . . Henry's father is a mechanic—and an alcoholic. Henry feels little relationship with his father and portrays him as a man who, when he is home, "cusses and yells" and makes everyone's life difficult. With some sympathy for his father, however, Henry reports that his father "had a hard life," having to quit school and go out to work when his father died. . . . Henry has little time for involvement with peers, but he has several close friends with whom he shares his sports activities. He feels that, above all, a friend should be "a helping hand—when someone's in trouble, help them out the best you can" (Josselson, Greenberger, & McConochie, 1977a, pp. 38–39).

Henry, who was in the eleventh grade at the time he was interviewed, was part of a study on psychosocial maturity in adolescence by Ruthellen Josselson and her colleagues. Henry's ideas about himself, his parents, and his friends illustrate a number of points we have already made about adolescent development and suggest some of the directions we will go in this chapter as well.

Henry's acceptance of his father's failings reflects Selman's final stage of social perspective taking. You will remember from Chapter 9 that at this level, found in young people in their late teens or early twenties, other people are seen as partly a product of their own history,

Figure 10.1. Adolescents like these face two major tasks or dilemmas, according to Erikson's theory: establishing a clear personal identity and forming intimate relationships.

so that they can't always help doing what they do or being what they are. Henry shows similarly advanced levels of social cognition in his ideas about friendship as well.

At the same time Henry is also showing signs of struggling with the two tasks that Erikson says are vital in the period of adolescence and young adulthood: **identity versus role confusion** and **intimacy versus isolation.** Henry is trying to figure out who he is and what he will be when he grows up. He is also moving toward the development of relationships of real intimacy. In the language we used in Chapters 6 and 7 when we talked about the social development of young children, the teenager must develop a mature sense of self and must establish new central attachments.

Erikson's theory provides a very useful framework for our discussion of these two facets of adolescent development, so let us describe his proposals in somewhat more detail.

ERIKSON'S THEORY OF DEVELOPMENT IN ADOLESCENCE AND YOUTH

You will recall from Chapter 1 and Chapter 6 that Erikson's basic idea is that development over the life span is made up of a series of stages, each of which involves a central task or dilemma. The nature of each task is determined partly by biological changes, such as puberty, and partly by changing social demands placed on the individual. Erikson places two such tasks in the period of adolescence and early adulthood.

Identity versus Role Confusion

All eight of Erikson's stages/tasks involve some aspect of the formation of a personal identity. Erikson believes that a person's identity undergoes change throughout the life span, becoming increasingly complex, increasingly integrated. In Erikson's view, though, it is in adolescence that the question "Who am I?" becomes absolutely central for the developing person. Thus the first of the two tasks of adolescence, in Erikson's theory, is to resolve the dilemma between identity and role confusion.

Obviously, the teenager has already developed a sense of self, as we described in Chapter 6. But the old definitions are called into question because of the sexual changes of puberty and because of the teenager's new intellectual and physical capabilities. In addition, there are new expectations from parents, from schools, from society in general. The 14- or 15-year-old is expected to be more independent, more responsible for herself. These physical, mental, and social changes, in Erikson's view, throw the adolescent into an *identity crisis.*

To resolve this crisis, the adolescent must develop three aspects of a new identity: (1) a *sexual identity* (not to be confused with the gender concept, which was developed much earlier) that includes a mature sex-role concept as well as some understanding of her own sexuality; (2) an *occupational identity,* an idea of what she will *do* as an adult; and (3) an *ideological identity,* which touches on the adolescent's beliefs, her attitudes, and ideals. In a sense, what the adolescent must figure out is what her *role* will be as an adult.

If the adolescent does not find an appropriate role and does not develop the accompanying ideology, she will remain in a state that Erikson described as *role confusion* or *identity diffusion.*

Intimacy versus Isolation

Once an identity has been formed, the young adult now faces new pressure to form a family, eventually to have children. Erikson argues that this pressure triggers a new dilemma. The young person has already established a number of important attachments, particularly the attachments to the parents in the early years of life and later with peers. Now there is a new level of intimacy required if stable, lasting relationships are to be created. To Erikson, the key to true intimacy is total openness, a willingness to give up, at least partially, the sense of separateness and create a new union that is *we* rather than *I.* Clearly such an intimate relationship is a form of attachment, but it is an attachment created after each person has established an independent identity. Such relationships normally involve sexual intimacy, but they include emotional and mental intimacy as well.

A young person who has not successfully completed the stage of identity formation may be unable to form an intimate relationship, since he does not have the ability to give completely. If there is no complete sense of *I,* then there is no self to give up in the merging of the intimate pair. Lacking a successful intimate relationship, the young person may experience a sense of *isolation* from others.

Let us keep this theoretical formulation in mind as we look at the development of the sense of self and at changes in the relationships between teenagers and their parents and peers.

THE SELF IN ADOLESCENCE AND YOUTH

If Erikson is correct, we ought to see at least two kinds of changes in the self-concept of teenagers and young adults. We should see a shift in the categories or dimensions on which young people define themselves—an aspect we talked about as the categorical self in Chapter 6. We should also see a reduction in signs of identity crisis or role confusion.

Developmental Changes in the Categorical Self

In Chapter 6 we quoted from two children's answers to the question "Who am I?" from a study by Montemayor and Eisen (1977). Let us give you a third example from the same study to illustrate the further changes that take place at adolescence. These answers were given by a 17-year-old girl in the twelfth grade:

> I am a human being. I am a girl. I am an individual. I don't know who I am. I am a Pisces. I am a moody person. I am an indecisive person. I am an ambitious person. I am a very curious person. I am not an individual. I am a loner. I am an American (God help me). I am a Democrat. I am a liberal person. I am a radical. I am a conservative. I am a pseudoliberal. I am an atheist. I am not a classifiable person (i.e. I don't want to be) (p. 318).

Notice how abstract the self-definition of this high school girl is, especially compared to those we quoted in Chapter 6. She is far less tied to her physical characteristics or even to her abilities than the younger children were in this same study. This increasing abstractness reflects the basic *cognitive* shifts we described in Chapter 9, the shift from concrete to formal logic.

At the same time, notice how preoccupied this girl seems to be with *ideology,* with what she believes or does not believe. Such a focus on ideas is part of what Erikson thought occurred during this period as the teenager struggles to figure out who she is and what she believes.

You can see these same changes graphically in Figure 10.2, based on the answers of all 262 subjects in the Montemayor and Eisen study. Each of the subjects' answers to the "Who am I" question was placed in one or more specific categories, such as mention of gender, social status, sense of competence, or political affiliation. You can see from the figure that references to the physical self drop sharply over the teen years, while references to beliefs and ideology increase, just as Erikson (and Piaget) would expect.

Sex Roles in Adolescence.   As we pointed out in Chapter 6, one of the crucial dimensions on which young children define themselves is gender. Since that is a physical characteristic, we might expect that references to this part of the self would decline with age. However, as you can see in Figure 10.2, gender references did *not* show any systematic decline with age in the Montemayor and Eisen study. Such self-definitions were very high among 12-year-olds (at the beginning of puberty) and then very high again at the end of high school. Clearly gender continues to be a highly relevant aspect of a young person's self-definition.

There are, nonetheless, changes in the form and content of adoles-

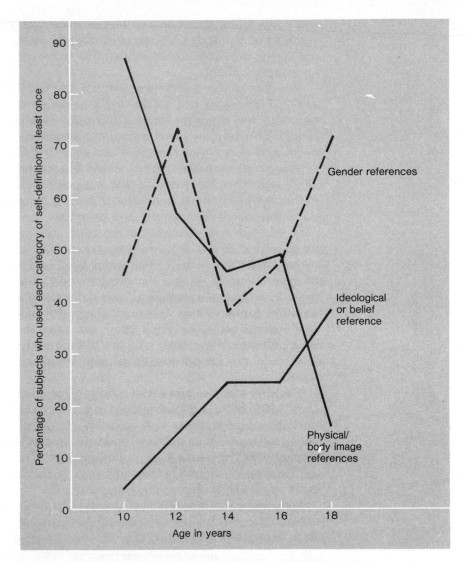

Figure 10.2. Adolescents' self-concepts change in expected ways: References to the physical self decline with age, while references to ideology or belief increase. Self-definitions by gender, however, remain high at every age. (*Source:* Montemayor & Eisen, 1977, p. 316.)

cents' gender definitions. First of all, adolescents seem to have somewhat more flexible ideas about sex roles than do younger children, particularly about acceptable behaviors for their *own* gender (Urberg & Labouvie-Vief, 1976; Huston-Stein & Higgins-Trenk, 1978; Emmerich & Shepard, 1982). As we pointed out in Chapter 6, children in the concrete operations period, especially when they first discover the constancy of gender, seem to treat gender roles as if they were absolutely fixed rules. But with the advent of the early stages of formal operations, adolescents' thinking becomes more flexible, more open to exceptions and new possibilities. Greater flexibility in sex-role conceptions is just one example of this.

One sign of this greater flexibility is the fact that a significant minority of teenagers and youths begin to define themselves with *both* masculine and feminine traits. Until quite recently psychologists had thought of masculinity and femininity as opposite ends of a single dimension. A person could be one or the other but couldn't be both. Lately, though, Sandra Bem (1974), Janet Spence and Robert Helmreich (1978), and others have argued that it is possible for a person to express both masculine and feminine sides of herself, to be both compassionate and independent, both gentle and assertive.

In this new way of looking at sex roles, masculinity and femininity are conceived as two separate dimensions. Any person can be high or low on either one or both. The terms used to describe the four possible types created by this two-dimensional conception are shown in Table 10.1. The two traditional sex roles are the masculine and the feminine combinations. However, there are two new types that become evident when we think about sex roles in this way: **Androgynous** individuals are those who are high in both masculine and feminine traits, and **undifferentiated** individuals are those who are low in both.

Table 10.2 shows one set of results from Spence and Helmreich's study (1978) of the self-descriptions of nearly a thousand junior and senior high school students. You can see that androgyny is fairly common among teenagers. You may also notice in the table that more girls were androgynous than were boys, a finding that runs throughout Spence and Helmreich's data. This sex difference in the rate of androgyny was found in all social-class groups they studied.

Spence and Helmreich's finding is simply one part of a more general pattern: It is much more common for girls to prefer boys' activities, to adopt masculine characteristics, or even to prefer to be boys than it is for boys to adopt girls' activities or behaviors (Huston-Stein & Higgins-Trenk, 1978). This is true among younger children as well, as we pointed out in Chapter 6. This greater preference for the male

TABLE 10.1
Score on Masculinity and Femininity Scale

SCORE ON FEMININITY SCALE	SCORE ON MASCULINITY SCALE	
	High	*Low*
High	Androgynous	Feminine
Low	Masculine	Undifferentiated

TABLE 10.2
The Percentage of High School Students
Showing Each of Four Types of Sex-Role Concepts

	Males	*Females*
Masculine	44%	14%
Feminine	8%	32%
Androgynous	25%	35%
Undifferentiated	23%	18%

SOURCE: Spence & Helmreich, 1978, from Table 5-5, p. 54.

role by both boys and girls becomes even more clear in adolescence.

There are several possible explanations for this intriguing pattern. We have already pointed out that the male role is much more rigidly and clearly defined, and that boys are more strongly socialized to adopt the male role. Girls are allowed a wider latitude in behavior, including more tomboyishness. Perhaps we simply see the outcome of this latitude in adolescence. Another possibility is that the male role is more greatly *valued*. The set of traits that are part of the male stereotype includes more elements that both men and women think are better to have (Broverman, Vogel, Broverman, Clarkson, & Rosenkrantz, 1972). Perhaps, then, both boys and girls come to choose the male role, or the traditional male qualities, in an effort to adopt the higher status role.

Figure 10.3. Not only do young girls show more cross-sex play and less strict attention to same-sex models, among adolescent girls we can also see more signs of cross-sex behavior than among boys. Tomboyishness like this girl shows is much more common than is girlish behavior in a 14-year-old boy.

Whatever the explanation, there are some interesting implications of the pattern of sex-role preferences among teenagers, some of which we have explored in Box 10.1.

Developmental Changes in Identity or Identity Crisis

Most researchers studying changes in adolescents' self-concepts have not asked about changes in the categories by which young people define themselves or even the content of those categories. Instead, they have asked whether there really is an identity crisis and whether such a crisis actually gets resolved over time. The simple answer to both of these questions seems to be "yes," although as usual there are a few qualifications needed.

Marcia's Identity Statuses.   Nearly all the current research on the identity crisis in adolescence has been based on James Marcia's description of **identity statuses** (Marcia, 1966, 1980). Following Erikson's basic formulation, Marcia argues that there are two key parts to any adolescent identity formation: a *crisis* and a *commitment*. By a crisis Marcia means a period of decision making when old values, old choices are reexamined. This may occur as a sort of upheaval—the classic notion of a crisis—or it may occur gradually. The outcome of the reevaluation is a commitment to some specific role, some particular ideology.

If we put these two elements together, as we have in Table 10.3, you can see that four different *identity statuses* are possible.

Identity achievement occurs when a decision-making period has been experienced and the individual has resolved the conflict and reached a commitment.

Moratorium is a combination of decision making and *no* commitment. The individual in this status is in the midst of the crisis, is struggling with the issues, but has not yet resolved it. (As an example, the twelfth grader whose self-description we gave earlier appears to be in moratorium.)

Foreclosure is in some sense the opposite of a moratorium status: Someone in this status has made a commitment without ever going through a period of decision making. No reassessment of old positions, old choices, or old roles has occurred. Instead, the young person has simply accepted a parentally defined commitment.

Identity diffusion is a status in which no commitment has been made. Often these young people have simply not been through a period of self-examination; other teenagers and young adults in this status have been through an identity crisis and have still not emerged from it with commitments made. Diffusion may thus represent either an

BOX 10.1

Is It Better to Be Androgynous?

One of Sandra Bem's original proposals about masculinity, femininity, and androgyny is that it is psychologically *healthier* to be androgynous. Since androgynous people can express both their masculine and feminine qualities, they can be more flexible in their approach to a new situation. She also expected that androgynous young people or adults would have higher self-esteem and lower levels of anxiety.

Bem turns out to be right, at least judging by the information we have at the moment. Spence and Helmreich (1978), in their studies of masculinity and femininity, have found that among both high school and college students, androgynous people have higher self-esteem than any other group. The second highest self-esteem scores—among both males and females—are usually found among those who describe themselves as masculine. Christopher Massad (1981) has found a similar pattern in his recent study of high school students, as you can see in the table.

**Self-Esteem Scores
for Androgynous, Masculine, Feminine,
and Undifferentiated Adolescents**

	SELF-ESTEEM SCORE	
	Males	*Females*
Androgynous	65.5	68.4
Masculine	63.4	61.6
Feminine	55.7	61.8
Undifferentiated	56.8	56.7

SOURCE: Massad, 1981, p. 1295.

Not only are androgynous people higher in self-esteem, they are also more empathetic, have stronger achievement orientations, are better adjusted, and are better liked by their peers (Massad, 1981; Spence & Helmreich, 1978; Wells, 1980). In Massad's study, androgynous girls were best liked, while among boys, being either masculine or androgynous was associated with greater peer acceptance.

What are the implications of these results? For boys, the situation seems fairly easy. A boy can achieve high self-esteem, mastery and maturity by seeing himself as traditionally masculine, or by seeing himself as having both masculine and feminine qualities. The androgynous pattern is slightly "better" but for a boy the masculine choice is also adaptive.

For girls the picture is much more complex. In our culture, at least, a positive self-image, empathy, maturity, even success in a later career seem to be associated with some expression of traditionally *masculine* qualities. As Caryl Rivers, Rosalind Barnett, and Grace Baruch (1979, p. 58) put it:

> For a woman to be a healthy, self-confident individual, she must identify with virtues that have been associated with the male role in our society. While there is plenty of evidence that this will be healthy for her, there is no evidence that it will be harmful.

In our culture, then, adolescent girls and young women hear two somewhat conflicting messages: Be independent and capable (part of the masculine stereotype) and be nurturing, caring, and dependent (part of the feminine stereotype). The solution to this dilemma would seem to be the expression of both, which is precisely what the concept of androgyny describes. The fact that more teenage girls than boys do describe themselves as androgynous on Bem's Sex-Role Inventory suggests that, in fact, many girls have resolved the dilemma in precisely this way. And since androgyny seems to be the most mature, healthiest alternative, the confusing cultural pressures may actually accelerate the psychosocial development of girls more than boys. (We hasten to add that this is a speculative interpretation of the situation for girls—but it is intriguing speculation, especially for two women who have been through the process themselves.)

TABLE 10.3
Level of Reexamination and Commitment

LEVEL OF COMMITMENT TO NEW VALUES AND ROLE	LEVELS OF REEXAMINATION OF VALUES	
	High	*Low*
High	Identity achievement status	Foreclosure status
Low	Moratorium status	Identity diffusion status

early stage in the process or a failure of identity achievement at a later stage.

Using Marcia's classification system, we can ask several questions about the development of a clear identity during adolescence and early adulthood.

Is There Really a Crisis? We don't know if *every* teenager goes through a period of moratorium, but we do know that when you test a group of young people using Marcia's interview system, you find that some are indeed in each of the four statuses he describes. Some sample findings in Table 10.4 from a study by Caroline Waterman and Jeffrey Nevid (1977) of a group of college-level introductory psychology students illustrate this basic fact.

The table also shows that an identity is not a unitary thing. Many of the young people in this study obviously had worked their way through periods of questioning about their religious and sexual beliefs before they had fully resolved the question of their occupational identity.

When Does the Crisis Occur? Erikson places the identity dilemma during the period of puberty and adolescence, perhaps from ages 12 to 16 or 17. But virtually all the evidence we have points to a later transition than this, at 18 to 22 or even later (Meilman, 1979). Take another look at Table 10.4. If the identity crisis were confronted and completed dur-

TABLE 10.4
Percentage of College Students Who Are in Each of Four Identity Statuses, in Each of Four Different Areas

Identity statuses	SUBJECT AREAS			
	Occupational identity	*Religious identity*	*Political identity*	*Sexual identity*
Identity achievement	17%	23%	14%	30%
Moratorium	24%	15%	10%	11%
Foreclosure	21%	28%	11%	51%
Diffusion	39%	34%	64%	8%

SOURCE: Waterman & Nevid, 1977, adapted from Table 1, p. 339.

ing high school, we should find that nearly all of the college students are in either the identity achievement or foreclosure status, which is clearly not the case. The *issue* of identity definition becomes highly relevant for many young people in their early and middle teens, but for most of us the resolution of this dilemma comes later than Erikson thought.

This conclusion about the timing of the identity dilemma, however, requires one qualification: Probably this dilemma is resolved earlier among young people who go to work immediately after high school than among those who go to college. Attending college is, in some sense, a postponement of full adult status. The years in college are a period in which students are actively encouraged to question, doubt, and try out alternatives. Those who go directly into the working world do not have that luxury. Gordon Munro and Gerald Adams (1977) found that among a group of 18- to 21-year-olds, 45 percent of those who were already working could be described as in the identity achievement status, while only 7 percent of the college students in the same study had achieved a stable identity.

Does Identity Develop?   The really key question in this series is not whether some people have crises or when they have them, but whether the identity statuses Marcia has described are really part of a developmental sequence that is common to all or most teenagers and young adults. Does each of us move from diffusion or foreclosure, to moratorium, to an achieved identity, as Erikson's theory suggests? Or do Marcia's statuses simply represent temporary states, with fluctuation back and forth depending on circumstance?

The answer to this question is the least clear of the three, since no one has followed the same group of young people through their adolescence to see if they shift statuses in the expected ways. The closest we can come is a set of studies by Caroline and Alan Waterman (1971; Waterman, Geary, & Waterman, 1974; Waterman & Goldman, 1976) in which a group of college men were retested at regular intervals throughout college. Most of the men did move through the identity statuses from diffusion or foreclosure through moratorium to identity. However, there were some who showed reversals as well, going from an achieved identity in freshman year to diffusion or moratorium. Marcia (1976) also found that some of a small group of men he studied over a seven-year period through their twenties "regressed" to moratorium or even to foreclosure.

Our own sense of the process of identity formation is that there are repeated episodes of crisis and commitment throughout adulthood. Adolescence and early adulthood may be the time in which the first such major reformulation takes place, but it is not the last. Thus identity achievement at 18 or 20 or 22 is not a permanent state. Reaching the point of identity achievement does seem to require a period of moratorium (or *disequilibrium,* to use Piaget's term); that portion of the hypothesized developmental sequence seems to be valid. But adults' identities do not stay achieved forever.

Such a statement does not refute Erikson's model. As we have pointed out earlier, Erikson believes that all of the dilemmas he describes involve some change in the person's identity, so major reappraisals in later adulthood are both expected and essential if the final integration of the identity in old age is to be achieved.

Summary of Developmental Changes in the Self

Let us summarize all of this for you. During adolescence and young adulthood, the concept of the self undergoes two kinds of systematic changes. The content of the self-concept becomes more abstract, more complex. At the same time the entire self-concept appears to undergo a kind of reorganization, with a new future-oriented sexual, occupational, and ideological identity created. The first of these two changes takes place gradually over the period of formal operations, but the second process seems to be particularly visible in the late teens and early twenties.

Some Individual Differences in Identity Achievement

It is certainly clear from what we have said so far about the process of identity formation that not all adolescents go through this process at the same speed nor with the same degree of success. In Marcia's terms, some remain in (or return to) a state of *identity diffusion,* while others achieve a clear identity.

As you might expect, the speed and completeness of the identity process is related to a cluster of other personal characteristics as well. Teenagers and young adults who are in the identity achievement or moratorium statuses, compared to those in diffusion or foreclosure, are more independent and autonomous, get better grades in college, and are higher in self-esteem (Marcia, 1980). LaVoie's results (1976) from a study of ego identity in high school students, which we have given in Figure 10.4, are typical. LaVoie also included a measure of the degree of trust versus mistrust (Erikson's first stage, as you'll recall) and found that those teenagers with a clearer identity also described themselves as having more "basic trust." Such a link between the successful resolution of the earlier and later dilemmas is certainly consistent with Erikson's theory, although LaVoie's study does not tell us whether this is a *causal* connection or not.

An even more vivid picture of the characteristics of identity achievers versus nonachievers comes from a series of case studies of

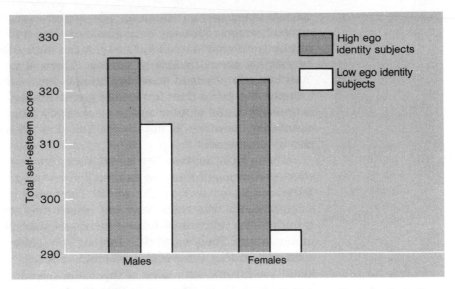

Figure 10.4. Achieving a clear identity is associated with higher self-esteem for both males and females. These data are from LaVoie, but others have found the same effect. (*Source:* LaVoie, 1976.)

psychosocially mature and immature eleventh-grade boys and girls by Ruthellen Josselson and her colleagues (Josselson, Greenberger, & McConochie, 1977a, 1977b). Josselson has not used Marcia's categories, but it is clear that the mature young people in her studies are those who are either struggling toward or have reached a completed identity.

Among the boys, those with low maturity were heavily focused on the here and now. They made few plans for the future, and their behavior was guided by what other people thought of them or did for them. Someone else decided whether they should go to college or get a job after high school; their self-esteem was dependent on being liked by their friends. Many of these boys were popular, and many were actively involved in sports. Nearly all the boys in the immature group also had a steady girl friend.

By contrast, high-maturity boys in this study were very future oriented (like Henry, whom we described at the beginning of the chapter). They thought about what they would do with their lives. For them, self-esteem arose from what they did more than from what other people thought. They were often quite introspective and tried to understand other people's motivations.

One of the very interesting findings in this study was that among the boys, those who were *low* in maturity were the most popular, the most likely to be seen as leaders in their group. The low-maturity boys were very friend oriented and cared a great deal about being accepted by and being part of the gang. The higher-maturity boys were often active in school, but they were also more self-sufficient. Josselson's results suggest that success for a boy in the high school culture may not be a sign of overall health or growth. (There is an interesting parallel here to early *physical* maturing among boys, which we described in Chapter 8. During the high school years, the boy who develops early is typically more popular and is more likely to be a leader. This early popularity, however, is not always linked to greater emotional maturity in adulthood.)

Among girls, on the other hand, it was the *high*-maturity girls who were seen as popular and as leaders. These were girls "who [took] themselves seriously" as Josselson put it. They were introspective and had thought about who they were and where they were going. But their thinking was much less focused on an occupation than on their own inner nature. They wanted to find out *who* they were, not what they would do. So they differed from the high-maturity boys in their attitude about the future. Still, most of them had specific career plans and expected to work in addition to marriage.

Outwardly, the low-maturity girls were very similar to the high-maturity girls. Both groups were involved in school activities, both had friends, and both dated. Inwardly, though, there were differences in values. "The world of the low-maturity girls is dominated by two concerns: having fun and having things" (p. 152). As a group these girls were outgoing, often cheerful, sometimes successful with their peers. But they were *diffuse,* in Marcia's terms.

Where do these differences come from? A logical place to look would be the teenager's family. We have already pointed out that among younger children, mature, competent behavior is associated with a combination of firm and loving behavior by parents—a combination Baumrind calls *authoritative.* Baumrind (1975) argues that a continuation of this type of parental control into adolescence helps to foster the development of a sense of social responsibility in teenagers, and that high expectations by parents help to foster greater achievement and independence.

Both of those hypotheses may be true, but we have remarkably little evidence one way or the other. There have been hundreds of studies of parental behavior with young children but only a handful of such studies of adolescents. The little evidence we have (for example, LaVoie, 1976; Enright, Lapsley, Drivas, & Fehr, 1980) suggests that identity achievement is more likely in families that Baumrind would describe as authoritative. The young person is encouraged to try things on his own, to have his own opinions; but the parents have not given up firm control. At the same time, the parents are positive and supportive of their children.

Young people showing foreclosure status report similar parental patterns—firm and positive—except that they are apparently given less freedom, less encouragement to try things out on their own. Those in diffusion status, in contrast, often report that their relationships with their parents are detached and somewhat negative.

These findings are generally consistent with Baumrind's hypotheses and with what we would expect from Erikson's general formulation. But at the moment we have only the barest sketch of the complex relationships between family patterns and the development of identity in adolescence.

THE YOUNG PERSON'S RELATIONSHIPS TO OTHERS: PARENTS, PEERS, AND PARTNERS

Besides the development of a clear identity, the second major task of adolescence is to complete a complex shift of central attachments from parents to a partner. In fact, most adolescents accomplish this transition as a two-step process: parents to peers and peers to partner. The intense involvement with a peer culture that we see so vividly among many teenagers is thus partly a way of creating an intermediate level of emancipation from the parents without the full commitment to an intimate relationship with a partner that we see in the early twenties.

Relationships with Parents

A 10- or 11-year-old's life is still very much centered around his family. He may have many friends and playmates and he goes to school each day, but the rules for his life are still laid down by mom and dad. At this stage he has little quarrel with that (except for the expected arguments about cleaning his room or helping with the dishes, of course). His level of moral reasoning is perhaps at Kohlberg's Stage 3, the good boy/nice girl orientation, so he is still trying hard to please his parents (and his friends) and accepts their definitions of good and bad.

When the physical changes of puberty arrive, however, the family pattern as well as the physical patterns are significantly altered. The young person begins to look more and more like an adult, begins to think of himself in more adult terms, and is seen by the parents as more mature, more potentially independent. In the first stages of this emancipation process, the level of conflict between parents and children increases. Teenagers begin to interrupt their parents more, to question their parents' decisions and rules. Parents, in response, heighten their attempts to control the adolescent. Needless to say, this produces conflict. In most families, though, the tension does not last forever. The parents accept some new level of independence for the teenager, and a new family equilibrium is achieved.

You can see both parts of this process in Laurence Steinberg's (1981) study. He observed mother-father-son triads during decision-making discussions at intervals during a one-year period. The sons were between 11 and 14, at various stages of puberty. Steinberg found that the maximum amount of conflict, particularly between the boy and his mother, occurred at the very beginning of the pubertal cycle, regardless of the boy's actual age. But as the boy moved through the pubertal changes, the conflict declined. These older boys explained themselves less to their parents, but their parents also asked for fewer explanations; thus the confrontation level was reduced. The emancipation process is a gradual one. The young person does not wake up one morning at age 14 or 15 and sever all emotional ties to the parents. Strong attachment bonds to the parents remain throughout adolescence. But there is a gradual shift toward greater and greater involvement with the peer group, and less and less participation in the family.

Some years ago, Bowerman and Kinch (1959) suggested that we ought to look at three different aspects of the parent-to-peer transition: (1) Who does the adolescent *identify* with, parents or peers? For example, does she think that when she grows up she would rather be like her parents or like her friends? (2) Who determines the *norms* for the adolescent's behavior? Does the teenager think her ideas and preferences are more like her peers' or like her parents'? (3) Who does she spend the most time with?

Results from Bowerman and Kinch's study, as well as more recent evidence (such as Wright & Keple, 1981), suggest that teenagers spend more time with their peers, and that their norms for behavior are increasingly determined by the peer group, but that identification with the parents remains quite strong throughout high school. You can see some typical findings from Bowerman and Kinch's study in Figure 10.5. They show that by tenth grade less than a third of the students reported that their likes and dislikes (norms) were more influenced by parents than by peers, but half of the same students said that their strongest identification was still with their parents.

Making the Break: Moving Away from Home.   The culmination of this gradual emancipation, at least for most young adults, is an actual departure from home—to college, to marriage and an independent household, or to some other form of separate existence. As Goleman (1980) puts it,

> The real significance of leaving home . . . is an inner one, not an outer one. . . . Leaving home is an apt metaphor for finishing the developmental tasks of adolescence; this act, more than any other, symbolizes childhood's end (p. 61).

Paradoxically, relationships with parents often actually *improve* after

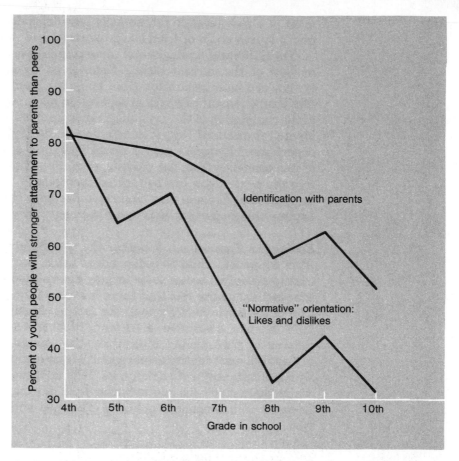

Figure 10.5. The involvement of adolescents with their families declines with age, but these findings from Bowerman and Kinch's study show that identification with parents remains strong for many young people throughout high school. The peer group does increasingly define the norms for teenagers' behavior, however. (*Source:* Bowerman & Kinch, 1959.)

the young person has left home. This effect is very clear in a recent study by Kenneth and Anna Sullivan (1980) of over 200 young men beginning college. About half the men continued to live at home and commuted to college, while the others lived in a dormitory or an apartment away from home. Both the parents and the young men were questioned about their relationships with one another at the end of the senior year of high school, when all the men were still living at home, and then again in the first months of the freshman year in college.

   The really intriguing finding in this study is that the young men who physically left home showed an increase in affection toward their parents, improved communication with them, and a greater sense of independence. Far from weakening the emotional tie to the parents, the greater independence seemed to allow or encourage the development of a new level of autonomous interdependence, rather like Selman's fourth stage of friendships we described in Chapter 9.

The Sullivans' findings raise some provocative questions, especially in view of the current trend—fostered partly by economic necessity—toward later separation from home for many young adults. Does this postponement of physical separation also result in postponement of the completion of the psychological tasks of childhood? Does it delay identity formation? Does it interfere with the development of adult independence? Erikson's theory would lead us to expect that some level of independence from the parents, some *de*tachment, is necessary before the next stages can be tackled successfully. The Sullivans' study suggests that Erikson may be correct. We hope that other researchers explore this important issue over the next few years.

Easing the Transition.   Whether the transition from parent to peer, from dependent child to independent adult, occurs smoothly or with extended conflict seems to be largely determined by whether the parents can accept the fact that there is a need for a change in the definition of the adolescent's role in the family (Ausubel, 1977; Alexander, 1973; Morton, Alexander, & Altman, 1976). Not surprisingly, the same pattern of parent-child interaction that seems to foster both high self-esteem and identity achievement is also associated with lower family conflict throughout adolescence. That apparently optimum pattern, which Baumrind calls *authoritative* child rearing, includes the encouragement of independent opinions combined with firmness and affection.

Relationships with Peers

Despite the continuing influence of parents, there is no denying the fact that peers assume a far more central role in the lives of teenagers and young adults than they have earlier or than they will at any later time. In some sense the heavy involvement with peers that we see at 13 and 14 and 15 is a *mechanism* for assisting the young person in making the transition from dependent child to independent adult.

The Influence of Peers.   The impact of the peer group on ideas, customs, and behaviors seems to be at its peak between ages 12 and 14—at least in the United States. Look back at Figure 10.5 and you'll see that the sharpest decline in parental definitions of behaviors and ideas was at about seventh or eighth grade, which is approximately age 12 or 13. It is also clear from several studies that teenagers' conformity to peer influence is at its height at the same time (Costanzo & Shaw, 1966).

Thomas Berndt's study (1979) shows the conformity effect quite clearly. He asked children and teenagers a series of questions about hypothetical situations in which they disagreed with their peers about what they'd enjoy doing or what they ought to do. For example, one of the antisocial situations was

> You are with a couple of your best friends on Halloween. They're going to soap windows, but you're not sure you should or not. Your friends all say you should because there's no way you could get caught. What would you *really* do? (Berndt, 1979, p. 610)

Berndt found that the influence of peers in neutral or prosocial conflicts (such as helping other children) remained at about the same level from third to eleventh grade, as you can see in Figure 10.6. For antisocial conflicts, however, the group that said they'd be most likely to go along with the gang were ninth graders—about age 14.

The Structure of Peer Groups.   The period of maximum influence of the peer group seems to occur when the teenager has begun to shift away from small groups of same-sex friends to associations with larger groups, which Dunphy (1963) calls **crowds.**

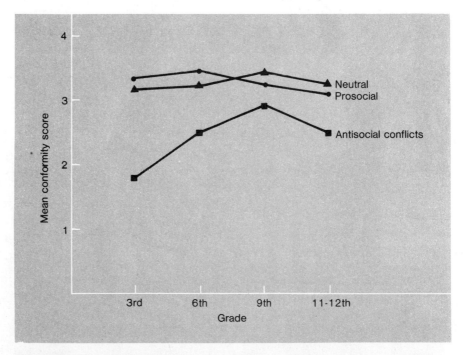

Figure 10.6.   Berndt asked young people what they would do in situations in which their peers wanted to do something different from what they wanted or from what they knew was right. The figure shows that teenagers in ninth grade were most likely to report that they would go along with the gang on some antisocial activity. (*Source:* Berndt, 1979.)

Dunphy's study of the several steps or stages in the shape and function of the peer group during adolescence is particularly fascinating. He observed the formation, dissolution, and interaction of teenage groups in a high school in Sydney, Australia, between 1958 and 1960. Two types of groups were visible. The first type Dunphy called **cliques.** They were made up of four to six young people who appeared to be strongly attached to one another. Cliques had strong cohesiveness and high levels of intimate sharing. In the early years of adolescence, these cliques are almost entirely same-sex groups—left over from the preadolescent pattern. Gradually, however, the cliques combine into larger sets made up of several cliques, which Dunphy called *crowds.* Finally, the crowd breaks down again into heterosexual cliques, and eventually into loose associations of couples.

Figure 10.7. A crowd of teenagers, made up of several cliques of close friends. Dunphy's observations of teenagers in Australia led him to conclude that crowds came later than cliques and that crowds eventually broke up into individual couples.

Stage 1 (isolated unisex cliques) occurs in preadolescence or very early adolescence. The period of the fully developed crowd can be seen from about 13 to 15 or so, at the same time that we see maximum peer pressure toward conformity and maximum compliance with that peer pressure.

According to Dunphy, the crowd performs the highly important function of serving as a vehicle for the shift from unisexual to heterosexual social relationships. The 13- or 14-year-old can begin to try out her new heterosexual skills in the somewhat protected environment of the crowd; only after some confidence is developed do we see the beginnings of committed pair relationships.

Pairs: Friendships and Partners

We need to look at two kinds of pair relationships. Individual friendships, which can be seen in young children, continue to be of major importance in adolescence. However, a new kind of intimate pairing occurs in late adolescence as well. It is this later kind of pairing that Erikson refers to in talking about *intimacy,* but the capacity for intimacy is not restricted to sexually intimate heterosexual (or homosexual) pairs. We also see an increase in intimacy in same-sex friendships and in cross-sex friendships as well. As Selman (1980) has found, young people in late adolescence see friendship as involving autonomous interdependence. Friends are people you share with and who share with you. These increasingly intimate friendships no doubt help to set the stage for the development of loving, intimate partnerships or marriage in the late teens and early twenties.

Friendships in Adolescence.   Most junior high school age students (ages 12 and 13 or so) say that they have about seven or eight friends—more than a clique but less than a crowd (Riesman & Shorr, 1978). While the number of good friends remains about the same during high school and into young adulthood, the *quality* of the friendship seems to undergo specific changes, involving more giving and sharing, more exclusiveness, stronger attachment, more frankness and spontaneity (Sharabany, Gershoni, & Hofman, 1981). All of these elements of friendships increase over the high school years. At the same time, some dimensions of friendships remain stable, including trust, wanting to spend time with the friend, and feeling free to receive things from the friend. These qualities of friendship exist in elementary-school children, and they continue to be a part of friendship on into adolescence.

Beyond these developmental changes, the most striking thing about friendships among adolescents is the fact that friendships seem to be more central in the lives of girls than of boys. Girls' friendships with each other are more intimate in almost every way than are those be-tween boys. Girls report being more strongly attached to their girl friends, with higher levels of giving, sharing, trust, and loyalty between them. Boys' relationships with one another are more centered around activities such as sports, and they apparently spend less time sharing secrets or discussing feelings.

We can see both of these effects—the developmental changes and the sex differences—in the results from a study by Judith Fischer (1981). Fischer asked high school and college students to describe their closest friend on a number of dimensions. Based on their answers, she was able to categorize the friendship patterns into four types: (1) uninvolved friendships that are neither intimate nor especially friendly, (2) friendly friendships that center mostly around activities but involve little intimacy, (3) intimate friendships that include sharing and close-ness but not much mutual activity, and (4) integrated friendships that involve both intimacy and friendliness.

Fischer found that the dominant form of friendship for high school students in her study was the uninvolved type (34 percent), while the most common form of friendships described by the college students was the integrated type (37 percent). The sex difference Fischer found was of the same kind: Males more often reported uninvolved friendships while females reported integrated ones. Among college women, 72 per-cent of the friendships were described as either intimate or integrated compared to only 43 percent for college males. We will be returning again to this sex difference in friendship style when we talk about at-tachments in adulthood. In our culture, at least, intimate friendships between men are the exception rather than the rule. We first see this difference in elementary-school-age children and continue to observe it over the entire life span.

The Development of Intimate Partnerships

The young person in his late teens and early twenties, having coped to at least some degree with the task of identity formation and having practiced intimacy in friendships and in other peer relationships, turns to a new central task: the creation of a lasting, fully intimate partner-ship. This is not an instantaneous process. Finding a long-term partner is complex and often takes many trial relationships before a permanent relationship is formed.

Finding a Partner.   A number of theorists have suggested that the search for a partner can be thought of as a process involving a series of *filters* or steps (Adams, 1979; Udry, 1971; Lewis, 1975).

The first filter is simply *propinquity*. You can only choose from among the people you meet, the people you see on some regular basis. But among those we meet, we do not choose partners randomly. A second crucial filter in the mating system is *perceived familiarity*. This is a basic principle of attraction not only among prospective mates but between friends as well (Heider, 1958; Newcomb, 1956; Byrne & Nelson, 1965). Lewis (1975) calls this the **principle of homogamy,** which translates as the "tendency of similar persons to marry."

Homogamy is an enormously powerful force in shaping mate selection. Most of us choose to marry people who are from the same race, the same religious background, the same social class, with similar levels of education and similar interests. Obviously, there are exceptions to this rule, but it is nonetheless a significant element for most adults.

A third filter (which may sometimes operate temporally before similarity can be determined) is our *physical attraction* to the other person. Similarity once again plays a role. We tend to be drawn to people we see as similar to ourselves in interests or abilities and to people whom we see as roughly the same level of physical attractiveness as ourselves (Walster & Walster, 1978). So some aspects of attraction are predictable and somewhat understandable. The rest of the equation, though, is often mysterious and unexpected. We may find our hearts beating wildly at the sight of someone quite unlike ourselves or find no chemistry with someone who shares many interests.

Once the first filters have been passed and dating or courtship has begun, the couple must try to discover if more fundamental compatibilities exist. Are they able to be open with one another, sharing flaws as well as triumphs? Are their interactions more rewarding than punitive, more positive than negative? Are their identities or sex-role concepts compatible with one another (Winch, 1974; Lewis, 1975)? If any of these tests is not passed, the pair will tend to dissolve, and each member of the pair will seek another partner, beginning the filtering process all over again. But if the tests are successfully passed, the couple begins to think of marriage or of living together on some permanent basis.

The Timing of Marriage.   Consistent with Erikson's theory, which places the task of intimacy in early adulthood, the majority of people do in fact marry in their late teens and early twenties. Figure 10.8 shows the median age at first marriage—the age by which half of all people had married at least once. As you can see, women (on the average) marry somewhat younger than men do, but for both men and women the age of first marriage has been rising in recent decades. The median age is now almost two years later for both males and females than it was two decades ago.

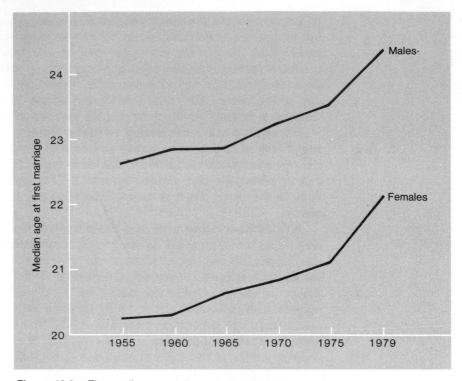

Figure 10.8. The median age at first marriage for males and females in the United States over a 25-year period. Clearly people are marrying later now than they did several years ago. (*Source:* Marital status and living arrangements: March 1979. Current population reports, Series P-20, # 349. U.S. Department of Commerce, Bureau of the Census. Washington, D.C.: U.S. Government Printing Office, 1980.)

Still, the early twenties is by far the most common time for first marriages. As one example, according to data from the U.S. Bureau of the Census, about 45 percent of the women marrying for the first time in 1979 were between 20 and 25 years old, and another 19 percent were 18 or 19.

Making It Last.　Getting married is obviously not the end of the story. *Staying* married and being satisfied with the quality of your marriage are other tests of the successful resolution of the intimacy task.

Studies of the stability or quality of marriage have mostly been done by sociologists. The findings from this extensive body of research, summarized by Robert Lewis and Graham Spanier (1979; Spanier & Lewis, 1980), suggest a number of influential factors, which we have listed in Table 10.5.

The second item on the list, "availability of premarital resources," is particularly interesting since it fits nicely with Erikson's model. This

TABLE 10.5
Some of the Factors That Influence Marital Quality and Stability

Homogamy	Those who marry others who are different from themselves in education, religion, race, age, or social class are more likely to divorce than are those who follow the principle of homogamy.
Availability of premarital resources	Those who are better educated, older, more skilled in social relationships before they marry have more lasting and satisfying marriages.
Positive parental models	Those whose parents had lasting and satisfying marriages are more likely to have similar marriages themselves.
Approval from others	If your parents and friends support your marriage, it is more likely to succeed than if you marry against the wishes or judgments of others.
Absence of premarital pregnancy	Regardless of the age of the couple, those who marry when the bride is already pregnant are less likely to have lasting or satisfying marriages.
Greater socioeconomic adequacy	When the husband has a higher-status job with reasonable income and stability of income, the marriage is more likely to last than if the husband is in a lower-status or lower-paying job. If the wife works, marital quality is associated with both her own and her husband's satisfaction with her work status.
Perceived similarity	Beyond basic similarity of background, continued similarity of interests and personal qualities is associated with permanence and satisfaction in marriage.
Positive interactions	Good marriages have a higher ratio of positive to negative interactions than do poor marriages—more approval, more affection, more support, more laughter.
More effective communication	Greater self-disclosure, greater communication accuracy, and greater frequency of communication are all associated with greater stability and satisfaction in marriage.
Role fit	The more each partner fulfills the role expectations of the other, the more stable and higher quality the marriage.

SOURCE: Based on information in Lewis & Spanier, 1979.

is a bit like saying that people who are more ready for marriage are more likely to have satisfying and lasting marriages. But what does "readiness" for marriage mean? In Erikson's theory, people who have successfully achieved an occupational and ideological identity and who have developed the capacity for intimacy ought to be better marriage prospects. Since resolving these dilemmas takes time, one simple measure of readiness should be simply age: Those who marry later ought to have a greater chance for a lasting marriage than those who marry early. We have explored this important question more fully in Box 10.2.

Age, though, is not the only relevant aspect of readiness. Lewis and Spanier (1979) also list higher levels of education, higher levels of interpersonal skill, better physical health, and greater self-esteem and emotional health as significant elements as well. A longer acquaintance with the prospective spouse is also predictive of more lasting and satisfying marriage.

IDENTITY AND INTIMACY: THE LINKS BETWEEN THE TWO

We have talked separately about the two major tasks of adolescence, identity and intimacy. But Erikson's theory would lead us to expect important links between the two. Specifically, we ought to find that those teenagers or young adults who have successfully mastered the task of identity should be more skillful in creating genuine intimacy. Do we have any evidence that this is true?

Yes and no. For young men, the relationship seems to hold strongly: Those who have achieved an identity, especially an occupational identity, are much more likely to describe their relationships with others as being deep and committed (intimate) rather than brief or superficial (Hodgson & Fischer, 1979; Kacerguis & Adams, 1980; Orlofsky, Marcia, & Lesser, 1973). For women, the picture is less clear. Kacerguis and Adams (1980) found that for both college-age men and women, achievement of occupational identity was a good predictor of intimacy status. But Hodgson and Fischer (1979) have found that among women, intimacy was much less strongly related to identity. In this study, 19 out of 21 college women who were rated as identity achievers were also rated as showing intimacy in their relationships. However, 15 out of 29 women who had *not* reached identity-achievement status were also rated as showing intimacy. Among the men in this same study, only 3 showed intimacy without identity.

It is risky to place too much emphasis on this one finding. After all, Kacerguis and Adams, in a very similar study, did not find the same pattern. But some speculation is in order anyway, if only because Hogdson and Fischer's results point to the possibility that identity may be defined differently for women or that Erikson's stages may be accomplished in a different sequence for women than for men—a possibility suggested by several other authors as well (Gilligan, 1982; Gould, 1978, 1980; Sanguiliano, 1978). Hodgson and Fischer propose the following tentative hypothesis:

The evidence suggests . . . that the woman's task in response to "Who am I?" revolves around who she can be in relation to others. . . . Her

BOX 10.2

Early versus Delayed Marriage. Does It Matter?

We have suggested in the discussion of marital stability and quality that later marriages ought to be more stable or more satisfying. This may be true because teenagers, or those in their early twenties, are more likely to lack the various educational and emotional skills that are required for creating a stable marriage.

This question has some theoretical importance for Erikson's theory. The ability to enter fully into intimate relationships is clearly a requirement for a decent marriage, and intimacy seems to develop in the early twenties, if not later. But the question of timing of marriage is also a highly relevant practical issue for many of you. Just what does the evidence tell us?

The simplest statement is a clear one: The later you marry the more stable and satisfying your marriage is likely to be.

Very early marriages are especially risky. Men who marry in their teens are more than twice as likely to divorce as those who marry in their early twenties and three times as likely to divorce as those men who wait until their late twenties. Among women, those who marry between 14 and 17 are four times as likely to divorce as those who marry in their late twenties (National Center for Health Statistics, 1978).

Some of you may well be thinking back to the discussion of teenage pregnancy in Chapter 8. Could it be that when we are describing very early marriages we are really talking mainly about couples who have married because the wife was pregnant? Such couples are more likely to divorce later, no matter how old they were when they married. However, that is not the full explanation of the relationship between early marriage and marital stability. Even among those pairs in which pregnancy is not an issue, very early marriages are more likely to fail. Such early marriages are also likely to lead to dropping out of school (Chilman, 1980), which makes things still riskier (see Table 10.5).

Even among those who wait until their twenties there are still differences between early and later marriages. In one study, Rachel Cox (1970) followed a group of college students for the first 10 years after their graduation. Their marital happiness, measured when they were in their early thirties, was clearly related to the age at which they had married: Those who married after age 23 were far more likely to be moderately or very happy than those who married before that age. More generally, sociologists and psychologists have found that earliness of marriage is associated with higher risk of divorce, even when education, income, and length of courtship have been controlled (Lee, 1977; Otto, 1979).

These results seem very clear, but two qualifying points are worth making. First, these are all *probability* statements. Early marriages have a higher probability of failure, but there are still many couples who marry in their teens or early twenties who achieve satisfying relationships, and many who marry in their late twenties who do not.

Second, we should note that most of these studies are making comparisons within a fairly narrow range of ages, from the late teens to the mid-twenties. We know much less about people who marry for the first time in their thirties or forties. It's not even clear whether we should expect the later is better rule to hold over the entire adult life span. On the one hand, we might predict that late marriages would always have a better chance of success since the partners would have achieved their own identities and be prepared for intimacy. On the other hand, we might predict that very late first marriages would be generally less than successful, since the partners would be involved in other developmental tasks, such as the struggle between generativity and stagnation, which Erikson describes as central to middle adulthood. As the number of people marrying (and remarrying) later in life increases, we can hope to see psychological studies of marriage at all points in the life span.

identity issues therefore seem to be based on *relating,* as if her sense of self rests on the success with which she can resolve issues of getting along with others in ways that satisfy both herself and those important to her (p. 47).

We will be returning to this question in Chapter 13 as we explore the roles and pathways in men's and women's adult lives. For now, it appears that Erikson's theory has considerable validity for men. The question remains open for women.

SUMMARY

1. The two central social and emotional tasks of adolescence and young adulthood appear to be to form a clear identity and to establish one or more truly intimate relationships outside the family circle.
2. In Erikson's theory, the task of identity versus role confusion is faced during early and middle adolescence and requires the development of sexual, occupational, and ideological identities.
3. The task of intimacy versus isolation is encountered in the early twenties when lasting marriages or other partnerships are formed.
4. The self-concept of the adolescent becomes more abstract and complex compared to the concepts of younger children.
5. One element of the self-concept, the gender concept, also undergoes changes at adolescence, becoming somewhat more flexible, particularly for girls. Some adolescents are able to define themselves in terms of both masculine and feminine traits—a combination called androgyny.
6. Androgynous adolescents and young adults, compared to those with more traditional masculine or feminine sex-role concepts or those with undifferentiated sex roles, have higher self-esteem and are better liked by their peers.
7. The adolescent's self-concept also appears to go through structural changes—usually called the identity crisis.
8. An adolescent's sense of self can be described as being one of four identity statuses: identity achievement, moratorium, foreclosure, or identity diffusion.
9. The identity crisis—a reevaluation of old values and goals and the commitment to new values and goals—appears to occur during the late teens and early twenties.
10. Those young people who have successfully completed this restructuring of the self-concept have higher self-esteem, are more independent and autonomous, and are more successful in school. They appear to come from families that encourage the students' indepen-

dence but that also provide clear rules and strong emotional support.

11. Relationships with others, during the same period, shift from dominance of family relationships, to dominance of peers, to a focus on intimate paired relationships.

12. The beginning separation from family-centered orientation can be seen at the onset of puberty, when family conflicts increase. The influence of the family on the young person's value system, the identification of the teenager with the parents, continues to be strong throughout these years, however.

13. The physical transition away from home, usually accomplished in the late teens or early twenties, may have the effect of improving the relationship with the parents, rather than weakening it.

14. The influence of the peer group appears to be at its maximum (at least in the United States) in early adolescence, at 12 to 14.

15. The structure of the peer group undergoes systematic change at the same time, moving from unconnected same-sex cliques, to connected same-sex cliques, to crowds that include both sexes, to heterosexual cliques made up of loosely related couples.

16. Individual friendships between teenagers, especially between same-sex pairs, remain an important element in the social relationships of adolescents, particularly for girls. Among girls, friendships are more intimate, more personal than among boys.

17. In both sexes, however, friendships become more intimate over age, so that such relationships in college youth involve more exclusiveness, stronger attachment, and more frankness than in high school students.

18. Intimate partnerships can be seen among students in high school, but the major development of the skills of intimacy appears to occur in the early twenties. Most marriages occur during this period.

19. Finding a partner is a complex process involving propinquity, perceived familiarity, physical attraction, and finally the development of mutuality and shared role concepts.

20. The stability of and satisfaction from such partnerships (including marriages) are influenced by a number of factors, including the emotional, educational, and financial readiness of the couple; the support of friends and family; the effectiveness and positiveness of the communications between the partners; and the degree of role fit.

21. As a general rule, later marriages are more lasting and more satisfying than early marriages.

22. The tasks of identity and intimacy are linked in much the way Erikson proposed: Those young adults who have developed a clear

identity are more likely to enter into successful intimate relationships as well. The relationship is clearer for males than for females, however.

Androgyny   A self-concept including, and behavior expressing, high levels of both masculine and feminine qualities.

Clique   A group of six to eight friends with strong attachment bonds and high levels of group solidarity and loyalty.

Crowd   A larger and looser group of friends, with perhaps 20 members normally made up of several cliques.

Foreclosure   One of four identity statuses proposed by Marcia, involving an ideological or occupational commitment without having gone through a reevaluation.

Identity achievement   One of four identity statuses proposed by Marcia, involving the successful resolution of an identity crisis, resulting in a new commitment.

Identity diffusion   One of four identity statuses proposed by Marcia, involving neither a current reevaluation nor a commitment.

Identity statuses   The four types or stages of identity formation proposed by Marcia.

Identity versus role confusion   The first of two crises or dilemmas Erikson suggests occur during the adolescent years. The young person must successfully reexamine old values and goals and make a new commitment, or suffer from role confusion.

Intimacy versus isolation   The second of the two crises or dilemmas Erikson suggests occur during adolescence. The young person must establish a fully open, deep, committed relationship, or face a sense of isolation.

Moratorium   One of four identity statuses proposed by Marcia, involving an ongoing reexamination but without a new commitment as yet.

Principle of homogamy   The basic rule of partnerships or marriages that like chooses like.

Undifferentiated   A self-concept and behavior including low levels of both masculine and feminine qualities.

Gilligan, C. Why should a woman be more like a man? *Psychology Today,* 1982, *16* (June), 68–77.

Carol Gilligan has recently been proposing a new and highly interesting theory about the different pathways of development for girls and women during adolescence and young adulthood. This is an easily readable version of her views.

Goleman, D. Leaving home: Is there a right time to go? *Psychology Today,* 1980, *14* (August), 52–61.

For those of you now in your late teens or early twenties, this should be an especially interesting discussion of an important element of the emancipation process.

Sangiuliano, I. *In her time.* New York: Morrow, 1978.

A lovely book (written for a lay audience rather than for fellow psychologists) about the development of girls and women. (If we seem to have a bias toward books on women's development, perhaps that is understandable! It is also a refreshing change from the usual dominance of studies of male development.)

PROJECT 10.1

Attachment between Young Adults and Their Parents, Peers, and Partners

Since young adulthood is the time in which intimacy is a central task and since most of you are young adults, you can collect data on yourselves this time. The table shows a somewhat modified version of a questionnaire called the Family Attachment Scales, designed by Lillian Troll and Jean Smith (1976). The questions were designed to tap as many different aspects of attachment as possible, as you will see when you fill it out yourself.

Family Attachment Scales

Gender of respondent: _____ Age of respondent: _____
Relationship described: Mother _____ Friend _____ Partner _____

Score

1. Know personally (now or at the time of death) _____
   1. don't know at all
   2. know slightly
   3. know casually
   4. know well
   5. know intimately

2. Amount of influence this person has on you (as of now) _____
   1. no influence—know very little about
   2. some influence
   3. moderate influence
   4. strong influence
   5. mirror image

3. Contact frequency (now or at the time of death) _____
   1. have never been in contact with
   2. in contact with a few times in life
   3. in contact with several times a year
   4. in contact about once a month
   5. in contact frequently—once a week or more
   6. live with or see daily

4. Residential contiguity (as of now) _____
   0. not alive
   1. lives in a different country
   2. lives in a different state
   3. lives in a different city, but in the same state
   4. lives in a different neighborhood
   5. lives in the same neighborhood
   6. lives on the same street
   7. lives in the same house

5. Strength of relationship (as of now) _____
   1. neutral, indifferent toward the person

  2. mild interest
  3. moderate interest
  4. moderately strong feelings toward (+ or −)
  5. very strong feelings for (+ or −)

6. Quality of relationship (rate each item on a 7-point scale and enter score on the right)

3	2	1	0	−1	−2	−3		
love						hate	————
like						dislike	————
approve						disapprove	————
accept						reject	————
admire						despise	————
want to be like					want to be different from		————
would seek out						would avoid	————
would expect support and get approval from					would expect disapproval from		————

7. You owe something to   ————
   0. not at all
   1.
   2.
   3. very much

8. You feel responsible for   ————
   0. not at all
   1.
   2.
   3. very much

9. You feel obligated to keep in touch with. If dead, feel obligated to remember in ritual.   ————
   0. not at all
   1.
   2.
   3. very much

   Total score: (Add up the points for each item)   ————

SOURCE: Troll and Smith, 1976, pp. 166–167.

We would like you to complete this questionnaire *three times:* (1) describing your relationship to your mother, (2) describing your relationship to your best friend at this moment, and (3) describing your relationship to your current partner (spouse, lover, or closest dating partner). You will need to make copies of the table for this purpose, and be sure to fill out each copy with your age, gender, and the relationship you are describing in that version.

The sets of three questionnaires for each student in the class can then be combined and analyzed as a class project. Any or all of the following comparisons would be of interest:

1. For the class as a whole, are the total scores on the scale different for mothers, friends, and partners?
2. Are there sex differences in the level of scores? (This will require computing

mean scores for mothers, friends, and partners separately for male class members and for female class members.)

3. Looking specifically at the responses under "quality of relationship," are the average scores on these individual items different for mothers, friends, and partners?

4. Is there any relationship between the age of the respondent and the level of attachment described? Specifically, is there some age range, such as very early twenties, when attachment scores are higher than at other ages? (You will need to compute separate mean scores for each age or each age range, such as 17 to 19, 20 to 22, and so forth. If you want to get really elegant, you could determine whether there were separate age patterns for attachments to parent, friend, and partner.

How do your results compare with the findings and theory described in this chapter? What other information would you like to have in order to interpret the findings better?

Part II Summary
The Developing Adolescent and Youth

Our task here, as it was in the summary of childhood, is to try to pull together the several developmental progressions and create a more integrated look at the span of years from 12 to 22. How do physical, mental, and social development in adolescence and youth connect and affect one another? Is there a genuine stage, or are there merely a set of themes, each changing in a predictable sequence but without cross connections? As we did before, we also want to look at some individual differences, especially sex differences.

STAGES OF DEVELOPMENT FROM 12 TO 22

Throughout the chapters in this section, we have been working on the assumption that there are two periods or stages within the years from 12 to 22. The first of these, which we have called adolescence, runs from the beginning of puberty to about age 18—until the young person leaves home for college or a job or independent living. The period of youth begins at about 18 and lasts until 22 or so, when college is completed or when a transition to more complete independence has been made. Obviously, for those young people who marry during or immediately after high school and move directly into a full-time job, the period of youth is foreshortened. From our point of view, though, it still makes sense to divide this stretch of years into two stages or phases. We have summarized them in Table II.1.

417

TABLE II.1
Summary of Development during Adolescence and Youth

Age	Physical development	Cognitive development	Social development
Adolescence: 12–18	Puberty is completed during this period with *widely* varying rates for both onset and duration of pubertal changes. Full sexual maturity is achieved, as is adult height and most of adult proportions. For boys, this is accompanied by increases in muscle tissue and growth of greater lung and heart capacity, producing a surge of strength and speed.	Early stages of formal operations are visible for many, but not all, adolescents during this period. These early stages (age 14 or so) are accompanied by conventional moral reasoning (Stage 4) and by Selman's third stage of social cognition. By age 17 or 18, some adolescents have achieved a more consolidated formal operations, accompanied by principled moral reasoning (Kohlberg's Stage 5).	A period of social disequilibrium with increased problems in parent-child relationships, maximum influence of peer pressure, and peak of behavior problems and depression. Teenager begins to question old values, old roles, old ideas of identity. Individual friendships are important throughout this period, although heterosexual relationships begin as well.
Youth: 18–22	No real physical changes, although the final bits of height and some other pubertal changes may still be continuing for those young people who experienced very late puberty. A peak of sexual capacity is reached (especially for males) during this period, and this stage may contain peak performance for some physical efforts involving speed.	Consolidated formal operations continue to be developed in some young people, with accompanying development of Stage 4 social cognition. Relationships are seen as fundamentally reciprocal, and other individuals are seen as complex products of their own histories. Not all young people reach these levels of reasoning.	The identity crisis is resolved for many young people by developing a new concept of the self—occupational, religious, sexual identities are all worked out in this period. Intimate relationships—both with prospective partners and with friends—are also developed in these years, presumably as an outgrowth of the mature identity and of the new levels of understanding concerning the nature of relationships.

Adolescence

The period of adolescence is marked by major changes in all three domains. Physically, the teenager experiences all the many body changes of puberty. Not only does the young person become physically capable of reproduction, she also quickly reaches close-to-adult stature. These changes not only alter her relationships with peers, they also affect her relationships with her parents. At about the same time, most teenagers begin to take the first steps toward formal operational thinking and the first steps toward constructing an occupational and sexual identity.

In some ways the first few years of this period remind us a bit of the early years of toddlerhood. Toddlers (2-year-olds) are famous for their negativism, for their constant push for more independence, and for their struggles to learn a vast new array of skills—walking well, talking, playing with new toys, understanding objects. Many of these same qualities, at more abstract levels to be sure, are characteristic of the early years of adolescence. There is usually an increase in conflict with parents, as we pointed out in Chapter 10, which often appears as a kind of negativism. There is certainly a demand for greater independence, for a chance to try out some of the pieces of the adult role. In addition, there is a new level of complexity of intellectual tasks to be faced in school. In our culture, junior high school is normally begun at about age 12, and senior high school at 14. Each of these changes in school calls for new social and cognitive skills.

Descriptively, then, there seems to be a major *disequilibrium* on virtually all fronts, particularly in the first few years of adolescence. Old patterns are pushed aside, and new patterns must be found—sexually, intellectually, and socially. In the terms we introduced in the summary of childhood, early adolescence is a time of major *transition*.

Youth

If adolescence is, in some sense, a long transition, then the period of youth may be thought of as a period of consolidation. For most young people, the beginning of the period of youth is marked by the physical transition of leaving home. Of course there are new issues and tasks that emerge during the period of youth as well, most notably the task of establishing intimate relationships. But to a large extent the years from 18 to 22 are marked by resolutions or completions of the tasks of adolescence. In other words, a new equilibrium is created: The questioning and doubting of adolescence shift toward achievement of an identity; moral development normally reaches (and then stays at) the conventional or principled level of reasoning (Stages 4 or 5 in Kohlberg's system); social cognition normally reaches Selman's fourth stage of autonomous interdependence. The 19- or 20-year-old understands that other people are complex products of their own histories. Friendships are seen as mutually sharing, and friends are treated with greater tolerance and respect. Such an understanding not only forms the root of forgiveness, it is also one of the underpinnings of intimacy. Many young people establish enduring individual friendships and lasting intimate partnerships during this period.

Norma Haan (1981) suggests that one way to contrast the periods of adolescence and youth is to think of adolescence as a period focused on *assimilation* and youth as a time focused on *accommodation*. Any time a child or adult is faced with new environments, new tasks, or changes in his body, there is likely to be a heightened level of assimilation. The young person absorbs (takes in) large amounts of new information, new data. However, until this information has been digested, a state of disequilibrium has been created. The resolution of the disequilibrium is to accommodate, to change your ways of thinking, create a new identity, alter the patterns of your relationships. This is what we see in the period of youth—a new equilibrium created after the upheaval of early adolescence.

Links among the Domains of Development

It is fairly simple to describe all the simultaneous changes and easy to apply a label like *disequilibrium.* It is far harder to figure out how the changes are related. Does the teenager develop formal operations *because* of the physiological changes of puberty? Does the young person develop a new identity *because* he is now capable of formal operations? Oddly enough, the sort of study we would need to answer these questions has never been done. No one has followed a group of children from preadolescence through the teenage years and assessed *all* the domains at repeated intervals along the way. A number of investigators, though, have looked at pieces of the puzzle, and a few conclusions are emerging.

The most consistent finding seems to be that the ability to use at least the beginning levels of formal operations seems to be a *necessary but not sufficient* condition for the development of a full identity, for principled moral reasoning, or for the most mature forms of social understanding. Formal operations involves propositional (if . . . then) logic as well as the ability to think of unexperienced alternatives and to examine all possible explanations or causes systematically. These are the very elements of thinking that are necessary if the young person is to develop an adult identity or the more mature forms of moral reasoning. If you are trying to work out what the future will be like, what kinds of jobs you might have, what kind of person you will be, you must be able to think about things you have not yet experienced and mentally consider the consequences of each of several alternative courses of action. Being *able* to think in this way does not guarantee that you *will* think this way, but it makes complex and flexible decision making possible.

Some examples should help make these connections clearer. Bonnie Leadbeater and Jean-Paul Dionne (1981) studied a group of high school seniors using Marcia's measure of identity status. They also administered a pencil-and-paper measure of formal operational thinking, which tested the teenager's ability to draw inferences, to use deductive logic, to interpret and evaluate arguments. Figure II.1 shows the average formal operations score for each of the identity status groups. As you can see, those high school students who were either in the middle of or had just gone through a period of questioning (moratorium and identity achievers) had higher scores on formal operations than those in the diffusion or foreclosure groups. This finding is certainly consistent with the view we are proposing but doesn't reveal the causal connections as much as we would like.

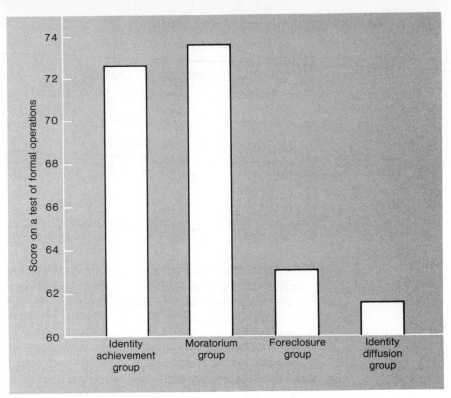

Figure II.1. Those adolescents who have achieved a mature identity, or who are in the midst of working toward such a mature identity (moratorium status), have higher scores on a test of formal operations, which is consistent with the position that formal operations is a necessary but not sufficient condition for achieving a full identity. (*Source:* Leadbeater and Dionne, 1981, p. 116.)

A study by Ian Rowe and James Marcia (1980) helps us a bit more. With a small sample of youth (18 to 26 years old), they measured formal operations using the beam balance and colorless liquids tests developed by Inhelder and Piaget (described in Chapter 9). They also tested the level of moral reasoning using Kohlberg's interview and identity status using Marcia's technique. The number of people showing each combination of identity status and cognitive level is shown in Table II.2. The particular pattern in the table does in fact point to a "necessary but not sufficient" relationship between formal thinking and identity achievement. None of the concrete operational or early formal operational thinkers had achieved a full identity, while three of the formal operational thinkers had. At the same time, many of those who could use formal operations logic had not managed to work out a clear identity. Formal operations thinking thus seems to *enable* the young person to rethink many aspects of his life but does not guarantee that he will do so.

Incidentally, all three of the youth in this study who showed both formal operations and identity achievement *also* showed postconventional moral reasoning. In a separate study, Marvin Podd (1972) has

TABLE II.2
The Relationship between Identity Status
and Formal Operational Thinking in a Small Sample

| | STAGE OF LOGICAL THINKING | | |
Identity status	Concrete operations	Early formal operations	Full formal operations
Diffusion	0	6	4
Foreclosure	1	4	4
Moratorium	0	3	1
Identity achievement	0	0	3

SOURCE: Adapted from Rowe & Marcia, 1980, Table II, p. 93.

also found that the majority of identity achievers were using postconventional or late-conventional moral reasoning.

Before we become too enchanted with the consistencies across domains we should raise a note of caution. There is actually very little research that touches on the questions we are asking; and in most of those few studies, only male subjects have been used. For example, all of Leadbeater and Dionne's and Podd's subjects are males, as are all but four of Rose and Marcia's. Any conclusions about the orderliness of development during adolescence and youth should thus be very tentative.

We know even less about the connections between the physical changes at puberty and the cognitive and social changes of adolescence. There are at least two ways that puberty could cause a chain reaction of cognitive and social changes. One possibility is that the hormonal changes themselves affect the brain as well as the reproductive system and trigger the development of new levels of cognitive ability.

J. M. Tanner (1970), one of the leading experts on physical development at adolescence, makes such a point when he says

> There is clearly no reason to suppose that the link between maturation of [brain] structure and appearance of [cognitive] function suddenly ceases at age 6 or 10 or 13. On the contrary, there is every reason to believe that the higher intellectual abilities also appear only when maturation of certain structures is complete (Tanner, 1970, p. 123).

Some of the research we described in Chapter 9 that shows a link between the timing of puberty and the development of such cognitive skills as spatial visualization provides some support for a biological explanation of the changes in adolescence (Waber, 1977; Burnett, Lane, & Dratt, 1982). But there is far too little research available at this point to go beyond a statement that it is *possible* for hormonal and other maturational changes at puberty to cause changes in cognitive skill and social behavior.

An indirect effect of physical change is also plausible. When the child's body grows and becomes more like that of an adult, the parents begin to treat the child differently, and the child begins to see himself as a soon-to-be adult. Both of these changes may trigger some of the searching self-examinations that are part of this period of life. The change in status is also acknowledged socially by a change in schools and by new cognitive demands. Thus *looking* like an adult, as well as feeling the sexual impulses of an adult, may be the single element that unbalances the system and forces the new accommodations.

If this were true, then the timing of puberty ought to be a much better predictor of adolescent behavior and self-concept than actual age. As we saw in Chapter 9, there is some evidence to support this. Teenagers who experience early puberty do have quite different adolescent experiences than do those who go through puberty later (Livson & Peskin, 1980). In addition, as we mentioned in Chapter 10, Steinberg (1981) found that the level of stress between adolescents and their parents was related to the young person's degree of pubertal change much more than to actual age. Again, though, the quantity of evidence is very small. To answer any of these questions more fully, we are going to need many more studies of adolescents in which *pubertal age,* rather than chronological age, is examined systematically.

Storm and Stress in Adolescence and Youth

We cannot leave this discussion of the stage of adolescence without a word about "storm and stress." This phrase (or its German equivalent *sturm und drang*) has been used almost universally in texts and in the popular press to describe the period of adolescence. But is adolescence really stormy and stressful? And if it is, is that a bad or a good thing?

Yes and no. Yes there is a disequilibrium—a broad questioning of old values, old patterns, and a search for new values and behaviors to replace them. And yes, in the very *early* years of adolescence, between about 12 and 14 or 15, this disequilibrium is often accompanied by short-term emotional instability (Anthony, 1970; Siegel, 1982) or a loss of self-esteem (McCarthy & Hoge, 1982). Such unhappiness or emotional unsteadiness seems to be more characteristic of girls in this period, but it is more likely in both boys and girls at the beginning of adolescence than in late high school or in the period of youth. Thus while storm and stress may describe a brief period in the early teens for some young people, it is not a good description of the entire period of adolescence or youth.

The really intriguing thing about that early upheaval, though, is that there are hints that it is *beneficial* in the long run for many adolescents. One of these hints comes from Norman Livson and Harvey Peskin (1980), who have followed the lives of a group of children in the Berkeley Guidance study through adolescence and young adulthood.

Figure II.2. Parents are usually warned about the storm and stress of adolescence, and it is true that conflicts with parents do increase during the early years of puberty. For most adolescents, though, the years from 12 to 18 are less stressful than the stereotype would lead us to believe.

They found that those teenagers (especially girls) who experienced an upheaval or distress in early adolescence were psychologically *healthier* as 30-year-olds. This pattern was even more clear among those young people who had good intellectual development before adolescence. As they put it:

> The availability of cognitive capacities increases the likelihood that adolescent stress is nutriment for self-constructive processes of ego control and mastery (Livson & Peskin, 1980, p. 78).

Just as in psychotherapy, when the client frequently gets worse before he gets better, so the storm and stress of early adolescence may serve an important purpose. This does not mean that all depressed or delinquent adolescents are really healthy and moving toward greater self-understanding through misbehavior. Just as there are adults who show serious emotional disorders, so for some adolescents the unhappiness of the early teen years becomes pathological. For most young people, however, the upheaval is more accurately described, in Erikson's term, as a **normative crisis**—a *necessary* transition if more complex forms of identity and thinking are to be achieved.

INDIVIDUAL DIFFERENCES IN DEVELOPMENT DURING ADOLESCENCE AND YOUTH

In talking about individual differences in development during childhood, we focused primarily on differences in the *rate* of development. Nearly all children seem to pass through the same *structural* sequences, although they do so at varying speeds. The vast majority of children achieve at least concrete operational thinking, acquire a full gender concept, develop the ability to take other people's perspectives to some degree, and so on. In adolescence, however, we see differences not only in rate but in the final level of development achieved.

Differences in rate are obvious when we look at pubertal development. Anyone who has observed a group of junior high school students can readily see differences in the timing of puberty (and most of us can still remember the agonies of early adolescence when we wondered if all those changes were *ever* going to happen to us). Still, virtually all children eventually pass through the predictable changes of puberty.

In contrast, in the cognitive and social domains the outcome is not nearly as predictable. As we pointed out in Chapter 9, many teenagers and youth do not seem to achieve full formal operational thinking. Even among adults, formal thinking is not the norm at all. Most of us muddle along using concrete operational thinking most of the time (Tomlinson-Keasey, 1972). Achievement of formal operations is partially predictable from IQ scores: Those teenagers and adults with higher IQs are more likely to show formal operations reasoning (Keating, 1975; Keating & Schaefer, 1975). Those young people with more education, and those from middle-class families, are also more likely to show formal thinking (Neimark, 1975; Keating, 1980).

If at least beginning-level formal thinking is a necessary condition for some of the other changes of adolescence, then the fact that not everyone achieves formal reasoning raises some interesting questions. Is the achievement of a clear adult identity the prerogative of only a privileged few, such as middle-class, college-educated adults? Is principled moral reasoning, Stage 4 of Selman's social understanding, found only in a minority of adults? There are several answers to these questions.

First, descriptively it does seem to be the case that some young people do *not* achieve a complete or stable identity, and many adults do not show the higher levels of Kohlberg's or Selman's stages. If intimacy is really built on these more decentered forms of thinking, then some adults may well be at a disadvantage in forming intimate relationships. As one example of the type of question that flows from this logic, we know that formal operations thinking is less common among the poor and the working class and that divorce is also higher in this group. We do not know if this is a causal relationship. We would very much like to see some research focused directly on this question, since it seems to us to have both theoretical interest and great practical relevance.

A second important point is that for day-to-day purposes formal thinking doesn't seem to be that essential. We will be addressing this more fully in Chapter 12, when we talk about thinking in adults.

Sex Differences in Development

We have summarized the existing information on sex differences among adolescents in Table II.3. As you can see, some of the differences that were evident in childhood, such as speed of maturation and aggressiveness, are still visible in adolescence and youth. However, there are several new areas of difference, too. In particular, several persistent differences emerge in the cognitive domain.

The most striking cognitive sex difference is that boys are better at tasks involving spatial visualization. As was true of all the differences we described in childhood, there is a great deal of overlap in the distributions of spatial skill for males and females. Many girls are very good at spatial tasks, and many boys are not. But there is a significant difference between the sexes when groups are compared. A number of recent studies suggest that at least part of this difference is biological in origin. Deborah Waber's study (1977), which we mentioned in Chapter 9, shows that late-developing adolescents of either gender are more likely to be good at spatial tasks, and Anne Peterson (1976) found that physically androgynous teenagers (girls who were least physically feminine and boys who were least physically masculine) were most likely to score well on tests of spatial ability. The best current hypothesis seems to be that spatial visualization requires balanced involvement of both cerebral hemispheres. Late puberty seems to promote such balance, as does physical androgyny. Because of prenatal hormones or because of rate of development during puberty, boys are simply more likely to end up with such a balance.

Still, cultural pressures may also play some role. Certainly such pressures are part of the cause of the sex difference we see in mathematical and verbal abilities. Judith Meece and her colleagues (Meece, Parsons, Kaczala, Goff, & Futterman, 1982) have concluded that there are strong environmental forces pushing girls away from mathematics achievement. Teachers interact more with boys in math and science classes; adolescent girls are much more likely to believe that they cannot perform well in math; girls take fewer advanced mathematics classes than boys do. Furthermore, math ability is part of the masculine stereotype in our culture. For a girl to choose mathematics classes requires bucking the stereotype.

This set of conditions produces a spiraling effect: Girls begin to receive many messages in late elementary school suggesting that math is not their domain; as a result, they choose fewer math courses and believe they will not do well in the ones they take. The predictable result is that girls end up by tenth grade and later with lower scores on math tests.

It is conceivable that the observed sex difference in formal-operations logic has similar origins. To the extent that formal thinking is fostered by science and mathematics instruction that demands deductive and propositional thinking, girls exposed to fewer such courses may simply not develop formal operations as completely. Whatever the reason, the fact that fewer girls seem to develop full formal thinking may be linked to the sex difference in identity formation, as well. Note, though, that females show *more* intimate relationships in the period

TABLE II.3
Summary of Sex Differences in Development during Adolescence and Youth

Physical development

Rate of maturation	Girls are still on a faster timetable, arriving at puberty 1 to 2 years sooner than boys.
Strength and speed	Beginning at puberty, boys are both stronger and faster; they develop a larger percentage of muscle and a smaller percentage of fat than girls do.
Heart and circulation	At adolescence boys develop a larger heart and lungs and a greater capacity for carrying oxygen in the blood than girls do.

Cognitive development

Spatial visualization	Boys begin to be better at tasks involving spatial visualization sometime in adolescence, with consistent differences beginning at about age 14 or 15. (Spatial visualization involves the ability to manipulate abstract shapes, to visualize three-dimensional space from two-dimensional drawings, and equivalent skills.)
Mathematics	Boys are normally better on tasks involving mathematical reasoning, beginning in high school. On Scholastic Aptitude Tests, for example, boys are usually higher on the math test than on the verbal. No difference is found, or girls are slightly better, however, on measures of mathematical computation.
Verbal skills	Girls are normally better on tasks involving verbal reasoning. They are also a bit more talkative and use longer sentences.
Cognitive structure	There is some indication that boys are more likely than girls to achieve the level of formal operational thinking.

Social development

Aggression/dominance	Boys continue to show more aggressiveness during adolescence and youth.
Identity	Not much evidence, but there are a few hints that boys may be more likely to achieve a mature identity during the period of youth.
Intimacy	Not much evidence, but there are some hints that girls may be more likely to achieve fully intimate relationships (in Erikson's sense of the word). Friendships between teenage girls or young women are more intimate than are the friendships of boys and young men.

of youth than do males, which certainly argues that formal operations is not a necessary condition for the establishment of intimacy.

Let us reemphasize the fact that few of the differences listed in Table II.3 are very large. The development of males and females during adolescence and youth is much more similar than different. Still, there are signs here that there may be somewhat different developmental pathways for males and females and that those pathways begin to diverge during adolescence. Such divergence results partly from differences in cultural definitions of sex roles, but it may also reflect differing emphases on relationships rather than on achievement or identity. These different pathways will become still more evident when we look at development in adulthood.

KEY TERM **Normative crisis** Phrase used by Erikson to describe the central dilemma of any one stage. The word *normative* implies that this is a normal, predictable dilemma.

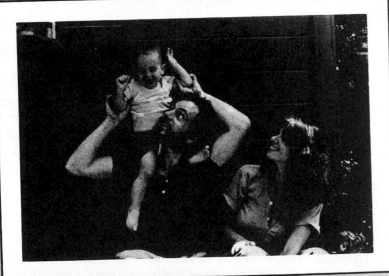

PART III
The Developing Adult

Chapter 11
Growth and Health in Adults

(11)

Last weekend I went to a dinner party where I had the chance to see and talk with some old friends. One couple in their late forties, tan and lean, had just returned from running the Honolulu Marathon. Although they insisted they were just "weekend runners," we real weekend runners knew what an accomplishment this was. At the other end of the table, our host—also in his forties—was wearing a cast on his foot instead of his Adidas. "I don't know how you did it," he mused. "Look at what I did to my foot just jogging to the grocery store." Another guest reported that he had switched from running to swimming because of a stubborn back injury. Not all the talk was about exercise, though. One woman was caring for an elderly relative recovering from surgery, and still another was showing off a 25-pound weight loss. Our bodies were very much on our minds! [SM]

AGING AND DEVELOPMENT

Most of us realize sometime during our thirties and forties that our bodies no longer look, feel, or perform as they used to. These changes in the way we look, feel, and act play a big part in changing the kinds of social, intellectual, and personal activities we enjoy. They may set limits on the kinds of jobs and hobbies we can pursue, where we decide to live, how we eat, and many more details of our daily lives. In other words, you cannot hope to understand the course of adult development without also understanding the physical changes that occur during these years.

When we left the human body at the end of Chapter 8, it had just survived the enormous spurt of growth that characterizes the teen years and early twenties. Because growth of that kind comes to a halt, we are inclined to think that bodily change and development have halted, too. Nothing could be further from the truth. All of the organ systems in the human body show normal, predictable changes in form and function during the adult years.

Before we discuss those changes, we should say a word about the differences between Chapters 3 and 8—which dealt with children, adolescents, and youth—and this chapter. In the first place, this chapter has fewer facts to report. The plain truth is that we know considerably less about the nature and sequence of the changes that occur during adulthood than we do about those that occur earlier.

Second, we cannot specify ages at which most developmental changes can be expected to occur. The physical changes that we see in adults are less tied to chronological age and maturation, and more tied to social and interpersonal factors, than were the changes in children and youth. We can say, for example, that normal babies start walking at the end of the first year of life or that the adolescent growth spurt in girls starts at about age 12. But we cannot state a normal age for adults to start getting gray hair or arthritis.

Finally, our perspective is different in this chapter. In young people, we usually think of physical development as the force that influences social and cognitive development. In adults, though, we usually turn this around and ask how social and cognitive factors may influence physical changes and well-being.

These physical changes begin in middle (or even early) adulthood, and they can be divided into two groups: those that are bad news and those that are good news. Like corny vaudeville comedians, we will start with the bad news.

THE BAD NEWS

Most of the bodily changes associated with aging can be summarized in five words: *smaller, slower, weaker, lesser,* and *fewer*. We have illustrated some of these changes for you in Figures 11.1 and 11.2 (these are also summarized in a slightly different way in Tierney, 1982).

Smaller

In the first place, human bodies get shorter as they get older. A man who is 5 feet 10 inches tall at age 30 will be (on the average) only 5 feet $9\frac{5}{8}$ inches at age 50 and 5 feet $8\frac{7}{8}$ inches at age 70. Although the long bones of the body (those in the legs and arms) do not actually get

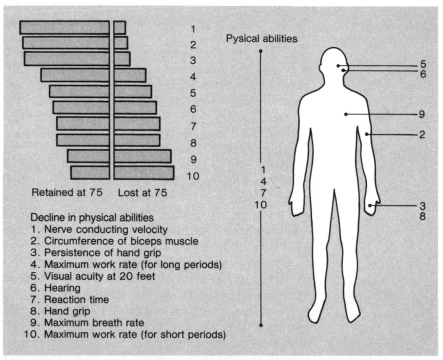

Figure 11.1. Some physical abilities decline with age, although as you can see, others are retained at a higher level to age 75. (*Source:* The Diagram Group, *Man's body: An owner's manual,* p. L07.)

any shorter, the connective tissues that hold them together (that is, tendons, ligaments, and muscles) become compressed and flattened. This is particularly true of the material that separates and cushions the individual bones in the spine (Tonna, 1977).

Weight also goes down, but only during the second half of adulthood. A person who weighs 184 pounds at age 50 will weigh only about 178 pounds at age 70. What may be the extra bad news is that this person probably only weighed 165 at age 20.

Some of the internal organs actually shrink. A woman's uterus and vagina may shrink to a size smaller than those of a preadolescent girl, for example, though no corresponding changes are seen in the male testes (Talbert, 1977). The urinary bladder often shows a decrease in size, which may contribute to incontinency in the elderly.

Slower

As we get older, our bodies generally slow down. All of us have noticed that older relatives and friends seem to walk, talk, eat, and live more slowly than we do. Part of this slowdown is due to a basic biochemical

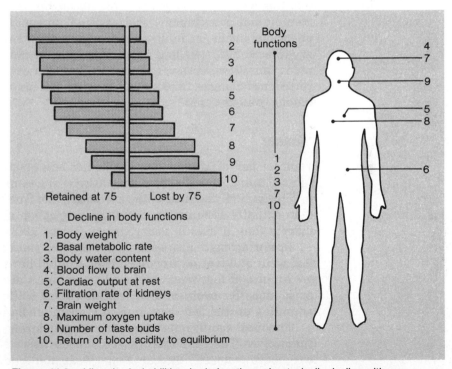

Decline in body functions

1. Body weight
2. Basal metabolic rate
3. Body water content
4. Blood flow to brain
5. Cardiac output at rest
6. Filtration rate of kidneys
7. Brain weight
8. Maximum oxygen uptake
9. Number of taste buds
10. Return of blood acidity to equilibrium

Figure 11.2. Like physical abilities, body functions also typically decline with age, although again there are substantial variations among body functions in the amount of loss typically experienced. (*Source:* The Diagram Group, *Man's body: An owner's manual,* p. L01.)

change that occurs with aging: Because of loss of neurons, as well as degeneration of the nerve pathways, nerve impulses travel more slowly to the brain and back as people get older (LaRue & Jarvik, 1982). Because of this, reaction times are slower, which makes it seem that older people often pause frequently and respond more slowly than younger people.

Other internal processes slow down, too. The kidneys take longer to filter the blood, and the bladder reflex is slower (Goldman, 1977). Even the growth of the fingernails and hair slows down.

The most important slowing in the body, though, concerns its ability to regulate its own internal state, sometimes referred to as **homeostasis.** In order to stay alive we must maintain a fairly uniform internal environment: a steady body temperature, moderate levels of blood sugar, correct acid levels in the blood, appropriate levels of different hormones, and so forth. If any part of this environment is altered, the body must respond and make adjustments or it will die. If we get too hot, we need to sweat; too cold, we need to shiver. If we exercise hard, our hearts must beat faster and our lungs breathe more quickly and deeply.

Under normal conditions, older people can maintain homeostasis about as well as younger ones. In the face of stress, though (like extremely hot or extremely cold weather, unusually vigorous exercise, emotional strain, or injury), older people show much less rapid recovery (Shock, 1977). As long as an older person can control the environment, this slower recovery is not an issue. However, unexpected environmental changes take a much greater toll among older people than among younger ones.

Weaker

Another fact of aging is that our bodies become progressively weaker. For one thing, bones become more brittle and seem to break more easily. This is partly because of the loss of calcium from the bones. The skeleton actually accounts for a smaller proportion of total weight in the elderly than it does in young people (Bortz, 1982).

Loss of strength also seems to result from the accumulated mechanical wear and tear of carrying a body around for many years. You can get an idea of that wear and tear if you think that a person takes 1600 or so steps for every mile of walking. Over a lifetime that's a lot of pounding on the feet, legs, hips, and even on the backbone.

The most significant change in strength, however, is in the muscles themselves. There is a loss of actual muscle tissue (Novak, 1972), which is replaced primarily by scar tissue (wear and tear strikes again). The remaining muscle tissue, however, appears to get weaker as well, so that older people may have more trouble with gardening, working, and household chores than they had earlier.

It is not only the muscles of the arms and legs that are affected—so are the muscles of the chest and diaphragm, which are used in breathing. Less efficient breathing can contribute to chronic lung ailments. Muscles in the face (used for chewing and facial expressions) and those in the urinary bladder (used for control) may also show decreased strength.

Vision and Hearing.   Both vision and hearing become weaker with old age. The most common visual change is a tendency to farsightedness, and many middle-aged people are chagrined to have to start wearing glasses so late in life. At the same time, visual acuity is declining, such that fewer than 30 percent of 70-year-olds still have 20/20 vision.

To get some sense of the combined effect of these changes, take a look at Figure 11.3, which comes from the work of Leon Pastalan (Pastalan, Mautz, & Merrill, 1973). Pastalan's photographs (of which this is only one pair), which simulate the visual changes of aging, have been used effectively to sensitize health professionals and others who work with elderly people to the consequences of visual loss.

Hearing loss is also a common experience with advancing age. Figure 11.4 shows the incidence of deafness among people of various ages, so you can see very vividly that there is a sharp increase after about age 65. Among those over 75, over 15 percent are listed as deaf. An even larger number of older adults experience partial loss of hearing, particularly for very high and very low frequency sounds (Corso, 1977). Fortunately, most adults (those who are not actually deaf) retain their best hearing ability in the frequency range of the human voice. Nonetheless, the ability to discriminate speech (to tell what is being said at a given level of loudness) declines markedly with age. Older adults may require that conversations be both some-

Figure 11.3. The photograph on the left shows a typical urban street scene as it might look through the eyes of a young adult. The photo on the right shows the same view as it might look through the eyes of someone 80 years old. (*Source:* Adapted from slides prepared by Leon Pastalan.)

what louder and somewhat slower paced for their understanding.

Such normal losses of hearing with aging appear to be largely the result of degeneration of elements of the auditory system (wear and tear, again). Such degeneration is worse in adults who have been consistently exposed to high levels of noise in their work or leisure (Corso, 1977). (Loud-rock-music fans take note; habitual exposure to very loud music greatly increases the chances of degenerative hearing loss.)

These declines in vision and hearing may be small or large, but many of them can be overcome by the use of proper eyeglasses and hearing aids. If not corrected, they can pose a real threat to the individual's safety. Normal activities like crossing the street or taking prescription medicine can be hazardous to someone with impaired sight or hearing, and social activities can become frustrating rather than enjoyable.

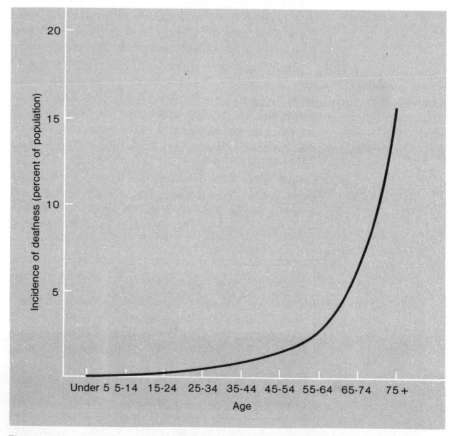

Figure 11.4.   The percentage of children and adults classified as deaf increases with age. Among those over 65, approximately 10 percent are listed as deaf, and many more experience lesser degrees of hearing loss. (*Source:* Corso, 1977, p. 536.)

Lesser

Many of the glands and organs in our body have a lesser output as we get older. The salivary glands in our mouths, for instance, become less active, and we may experience the sensation of a dry, "woolly" mouth. The digestive acids and enzymes of the stomach are secreted in lesser amounts, too. These two changes mean that food may be less adequately chewed and digested by older people, and this may have an important impact on the amount and kinds of food they choose to eat.

We don't get any less skin, but the oil producing glands in the skin slow down or stop altogether. As a result, older skin is usually dryer and more susceptible to breaking, cracking, and peeling than younger skin. Sweat glands may also decrease their production. While this may decrease body odors, it can be a serious problem for people in hot climates: Perspiration serves an important purpose in maintaining body temperature. Without an adequate cooling system, old people are especially susceptible to heat exhaustion and heat stroke.

The amount of subcutaneous fat is also decreased in old age, which accounts for the loose, baggy appearance of older faces. This loss is more than just a matter of appearance, as these fat layers are part of the body's protection against cold. Without them, the elderly are more susceptible to drafts and chills. Body fat also serves as padding to cushion the body during periods of sitting or standing. Without this padding, the elderly are more prone to develop bedsores and other skin disorders.

Fewer

Finally, our bodies actually have fewer and fewer parts as we get older. The amount of hair on the body decreases, for example. The number of taste buds on each little bump on the tongue also declines, from 245 in a young adult to only 88 or so in an elderly person.

Many adults lose all or some of their teeth during adulthood, though this is usually because of dental or gum disease, rather than a normal aging process.

How Bad Is the News?

Though these changes sound awful when listed all together, their real impact is not always great. A fraction of an inch of height or a few pounds of weight do not change a person's life very much, nor does a gradual slowdown in response speed. Weakness in sight and hearing can frequently be corrected, and modern dentistry can minimize the impact of lost teeth. Tools can often make up for lack of strength (consider power steering or the wheelbarrow), and so can social skills (asking for help with heavy jobs).

Sometimes the news really is bad, though. For one thing, the various declines or losses tend to be additive—being weaker *and* slower is worse than being weaker *or* slower. And for another, nobody likes them very much. Our culture tends to value speed and strength more than it values wisdom and age, so we label these changes as unpleasant when they might otherwise be nothing more than inconvenient. If nothing else, they also serve as unremitting reminders of getting old.

THE GOOD NEWS

Growth

Although they have slowed down their rate of growth, both hair and fingernails continue to grow during adulthood and old age. More obviously, the bones and cartilage of the head continue to grow. The ears, for example, may add a half centimeter or more between the ages of 30 and 70 (Smith, 1978). Furthermore, the nose may grow in both width and length. (Think about witches in fairy tales—they are always old and have enormous noses.)

Female Sexuality

Sexual Functioning.   The normal menstrual cycle, which we described in Chapter 8, begins to change in the late thirties or early forties. Menstrual periods become less regular, and ova are not produced during every cycle. Around age 50, menstrual periods cease altogether (the **menopause**). Changes in the reproductive organs (mostly shrinking) continue for some years after that in a process that is known generally as the **climacteric.** There is some variability in the age at which the menopause occurs. Relatively late menopause is more likely among women who have borne children, had early puberty, had a mother with a late menopause, are thin, financially well off, and are of white, northern European extraction. Early menopause is more common among blacks, women of southern European extraction, and among those who have not borne children, are overweight, or had late puberty (The Diagram Group, 1977a).

The main symptom of menopause (or more generally, the climacteric) is the loss of fertility. However, along with this, many women experience other symptoms that cause them discomfort and inconvenience. The most common of these are hot flashes, nighttime sweating, and accelerated loss of calcium from the bones (called **osteoporosis**). We really do not know exactly how frequent these discomforts are—studies have reported hot flashes in anywhere from 30 to 80 percent of middle-aged women.

Traditionally, it has been assumed that a variety of other symptoms also accompanied the menopause, things like weight gain, depression, crying spells, and feelings of inadequacy. Careful review of the evidence, though (for instance, Nathanson & Lorenz, 1982), shows that these are no more frequent among menopausal women than among women of the same age and general health who are not going through menopause.

The source of the real symptoms is well known: the reduced levels of the female hormone estrogen produced by the ovaries. Serious symptoms (particularly osteoporosis) have, in fact, been treated with prescription drugs containing the hormone. Whether this is a wise or even necessary medical intervention, however, has become very much a subject of debate among physicians and women's groups—a debate we have explored in Box 11.1.

Male Sexuality

Sexual Functioning.   There is no single event to mark the male climacteric in the way that cessation of menstruation marks the female experience. Production of the male hormone testosterone does decline with age, but the changes are gradual, and it is well known that men can sire offspring even fairly late in life.

Some researchers have suggested that there may be male counterparts to the symptoms of the menopause, especially things like depression, insomnia, and weight gain. Again, however, there is no valid evidence that these ailments are connected with hormonal changes, nor that they occur in unexpected numbers among men in this age group.

Despite the changes in hormone patterns in both men and women, sexual activity need not be impaired in either group. Sexual activity does typically *decline* over the years of adulthood, but it may remain a markedly pleasurable part of life for many adults well into their seventies or eighties, as we have described in Box 11.2.

Exercise and Fitness

Until fairly recently, most people accepted drastic decreases in physical fitness and in feelings of well-being as part of the process of aging. However, as you all know, sports and exercise have lately become enormously popular in this country. Many of us have realized that although it may be *typical* to be overweight and out of shape, it is neither normal nor healthy. In fact, there is now enough accumulated evidence to conclude that at least part of the body changes we have just described to

BOX 11.1

Hormone Treatment for the Symptoms of the Menopause

One of the themes running through this chapter is that some physical conditions that used to be thought of as part of the normal aging process—like elevated blood pressure or poor physical fitness—are today seen as signs of illness or disease. We now know ways in which these disorders can be prevented and ways in which they can be treated if they do occur. Something of the same logic has been applied in recent years by many physicians, and many women, to the symptoms of the menopause, which are treated as disorders rather than normal aging processes. In this case, however, we think the logic is incorrect or at least risky.

The normal menstrual cycle, as we described in Chapter 8, requires a specific sequence of hormone secretions to be maintained. At the time of the menopause, this sequence begins to break down. Although the pituitary gland continues to function and to secrete its hormones, the ovaries no longer respond to the stimulation. Fewer ripe eggs are produced, until fertility is lost altogether. Menstruation becomes irregular and then stops. Along with these events, the ovaries greatly reduce their production of estrogen and progesterone. It is this decline in

estrogen that seems to be the causal factor for most of the symptoms of the menopause: hot flashes, night sweating, and a loss of calcium in the bones (called **osteoporosis**) that can lead to higher rates of broken bones, particularly spine and hip fractures.

Since the loss of estrogen is the cause of the symptoms, it seems entirely logical to treat these symptoms by providing replacement estrogen. In fact, the symptoms *can* be largely eliminated by such treatment—a finding that led to widespread use of estrogen treatment. During the mid-1970s, one group of researchers (Stadel and Weiss, 1975) estimated that 50 percent of menopausal and postmenopausal women had replacement estrogen for at least three months, with the median usage being *10 years.* Many physicians, in fact, recommended continued use of estrogen throughout the remaining years of women's lives in order to prevent or reduce such effects of aging as osteoporosis, vaginal atrophy, or bagging of the skin.

Recent medical research, however, calls this practice into question. Serious side effects have been found (Hulka, 1980), of which the most serious

you (smaller, slower, and so forth) are the result of *disuse* and not of aging per se.

Walter Bortz (1982) has provided an especially fascinating review of the information on the effect of exercise and disuse on body functioning. Bortz, who is a physician, notes that many of the body changes we think of as aging are also consequences of bed rest. Most intriguingly, many of the same changes are seen among astronauts who experience periods of weightlessness. For example, both bed rest and weightlessness are accompanied by loss of lean body mass, loss of calcium in the bones, reduction of maximum oxygen-carrying capacity of the blood (which affects virtually every body system), a rise in blood pressure, and lowered androgen levels in men. Look over that list, and you will recognize many of the changes we think of as aging.

What is more, such changes from bed rest or weightlessness or even

is a greatly increased risk of cancer of the lining of the uterus (endometrial cancer). In women using estrogen replacement, the risk of such cancer is estimated as 3 to 12 times higher than among women of the same age not using such therapy (Nathanson & Lorenz, 1982). The longer a woman uses estrogen, and the larger the dosage, the greater the risk. Furthermore, the use of estrogen does *not* appear to reduce the risk of heart attack, as early evidence suggested, nor does it seem to affect the rate of arthritis or other diseases of aging. The other side of the argument is that estrogen replacement *does* reduce hot flashes and does significantly reduce the risk or severity of osteoporosis.

Given the arguments on both sides, how is an individual woman (or her physician) to weigh the risks and benefits? Most physicians have responded to the latest findings by substantially decreasing their rate of estrogen prescriptions (and the rate of endometrial cancer has dropped off as a result). However, the treatment is still prescribed for short periods in cases of severe menopausal symptoms. When estrogen is prescribed, it is now typically given in much lower doses than had been true in the early days of this treatment—a strategy associated with much lower risk of cancer. Exercise is also now being prescribed more often, even in cases in which the osteoporosis is advanced.

The more general question raised by these findings is how we are to decide which normal aging process can or should be "corrected" by intervention and which should be left alone. Many normal aging changes, such as loss of visual or auditory acuity or the reduction in cardiac efficiency, can be corrected or modified with intervention (glasses, hearing aids, improved physical fitness), with few apparent negative side effects. But some—including the changes of menopause—are probably best left alone. At the moment, most of the decisions about which aging changes are to be prevented or treated and which are not are made by health professionals. Their judgments, in turn, are shaped by their own values, by their education, by the culture we all live in. It is partially the general cultural perception of menopause as unpleasant or associated with a loss of femininity that led to attempts to intervene medically. If that perception changes, then the assumptions about the need for treatment will also change.

Ultimately, decisions about health practices, fitness (or lack of it), and medications designed to prevent or modify the symptoms of physical aging are up to each of us. The better informed you are about the risks and benefits of each treatment, the better the decision you can make.

mere passage of sedentary years can be reversed (partially or fully) by regular exercise. The several hundred studies Bortz reviews show that androgen levels rise, oxygen-carrying capacity of the blood increases, calcium levels in the bones increase, and blood pressure decreases in adults who have begun exercise programs compared to those who remain sedentary.

The gains can be striking. In one study, Fred Kasch (1976) studied two groups of men both before and after they were enrolled in an exercise program. The first group had all been college athletes and had remained fit by regular exercise. The second group was made up of men who had not exercised since their youth (and not all of them had done much then, either). The men in both groups began a vigorous program of physical training: running or swimming for at least an hour a day, at least three times a week, continued for 8 to 10 *years*.

BOX 11.2

Sexual Activity in the Adult Years

The potential for sexual functioning is well established by the early twenties and remains available well into old age. But do adults across these years change in their sexual activity in predictable ways? The cultural stereotype is that adults are most sexually active in their twenties, and that sexual activity drops to nearly zero by the sixties or seventies. That is *partially* true, but misleading.

A word of caution before we describe the research findings: Almost everything we know about developmental changes in adult sexual activity concerns *married,* heterosexual adults. Obviously, this represents the majority, but it ignores significant minority groups. Interestingly, an exception to this rule have been studies of sexual activity among the elderly, which often include both married and unmarried adults. Since women typically outlive men, more elderly women are unmarried and (as a result) frequently lack a readily accessible partner. When groups of such women are compared with groups of married elderly men, we should not be surprised that women appear to be less sexually active. However, we should not leap to the conclusion that older

women are, therefore, less *interested* in sexual activity. With this in mind, let's examine the data.

The first figure shows the average number of times per month that married couples had sexual intercourse, as a function of the age of the couples. We have combined data here from two national surveys, one by Kinsey, completed between 1938 and 1949 (Kinsey, Pomeroy, & Martin, 1948; Kinsey, Pomeroy, Martin, & Gebhard, 1953), and one by Hunt, completed in 1972 (Hunt, 1974). We have also combined the data for males and females in each case, to simplify the chart.

Two things are evident from the figure. First, it appears to be true that sexual activity (at least intercourse) declines over age. Second, there are important secular trends: Frequency is higher at every age in 1972 than it had been 30 years earlier. Since these are *cross-sectional* comparisons (different groups at each age), rather than longitudinal ones, we cannot tell whether declining sexual frequency is characteristic of the life pattern of each adult (undoubtedly it is not). However, it certainly appears to be the normative pattern.

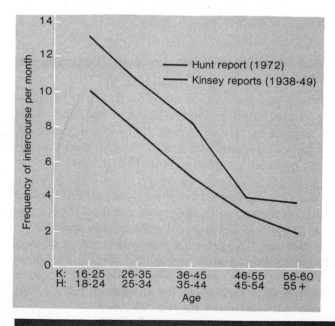

Box 11.2A. The monthly frequency of sexual intercourse for married couples (male and female estimates combined), as a function of age. Two separate surveys, one completed in the 1940s and one in the 1970s, are shown. Both surveys show a decline in sexual activity with age, but the more recent survey shows higher levels at every age. (*Source:* From Mussen, Conger, Kagan, and Geiwitz. *Psychological development: A life-span approach.* New York: Harper & Row, Inc. 1979. Copyright 1979 by Harper & Row, Publishers, Inc. Reprinted by permission.)

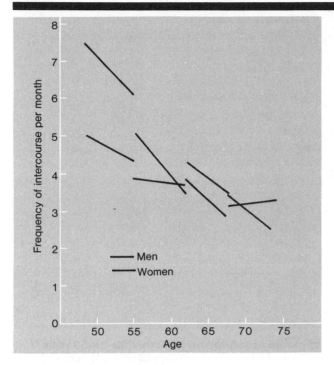

Box 11.2B. The frequency of intercourse declines in later years, but among married adults, as these subjects all are, the average frequency remains at about two to three occasions per month well into old age. Each line on this graph represents one group of people followed for a period of eight years. We have shown the level of sexual activity they reported when the study began and the level they reported eight years later. (*Source:* Palmore, 1981, p. 88.)

We find the same thing when we look at frequency of intercourse as a function of length of marriage, rather than the age of the adults. Sexual activity is typically very high in the first months of marriage and then drops rather markedly—from perhaps an average of 14 or 15 times per month in the first year to approximately 8 times per month in the second year. Thereafter, it drops much more slowly (but steadily) to a level of perhaps 3 or 4 times per month among couples married 30 years (Broderick, 1982).

The best longitudinal data available, and by far the best information about sexual activity in old age, come from the Duke longitudinal studies (Palmore, 1981). They have studied several groups of middle-aged and elderly adults, following each group for periods of eight years. The second figure shows the frequency of reported intercourse among the married adults in each age group. Each line in the figure represents one age group (cohort) and shows the change in sexual activity for that group over the eight-year period of the study. Thus the men who were first studied in their late forties reported that

they had intercourse an average of 7 or 8 times per month. Eight years later, these same men reported between 6 and 7 instances of sexual intercourse. Women in the same age group declined from 5 per month to about $4\frac{1}{2}$ eight years later.

Overall, this figure shows that among older adults who have access to a regular partner, sexual intercourse declines with age but certainly does not disappear. Among those in their seventies, a frequency of about 3 times a month was still the average—hardly support for the usual image of asexuality among the elderly that most of us carry around. Obviously, there is variability. Some older adults *do* cease all sexual activity; others actually show an increase (particularly women in their forties and fifties).

Palmore and his colleagues have found that the best single predictor of continued sexual activity over the eight-year period of the study was reported sexual activity when young. That is, those adults who have an active (and presumably pleasurable) sexual life in their twenties, thirties, and forties are most likely to continue to be sexually active in their fifties, sixties, seventies, and beyond.

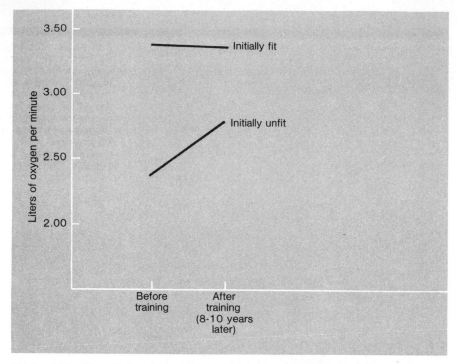

Figure 11.5. The effects of exercise upon breathing efficiency. After 1 to 10 years of vigorous exercising, the breathing capacity of former college athletes shows no decline. Even men who were initially out of shape improved their lung capacity as a result of the exercise program. (*Source:* Kasch, 1976, p. 66.)

The measure of physical fitness Kasch used was the efficiency of the lungs at using oxygen, usually described as *maximum oxygen uptake.* (This is an indirect measure of the oxygen-carrying capacity of the blood.) In Figure 11.5 you can see the average efficiency of these two groups (measured in liters of oxygen per minute) before and after the exercise program. The men who had remained fit throughout their adult lives showed superior oxygen efficiency throughout the study. The initially unfit men, though, obviously showed a great improvement in their performance. Since we know that maximum oxygen uptake ordinarily *decreases* over the adult years among men who are not physically active, the effect of exercise in this case was to reverse the typical aging trend.

Our conclusion based on the existing research is that it is far better to stay fit throughout adulthood than to go through a (sadly common) period of sloth and flabbiness. People who exercise regularly have fewer health complaints in general and appear to age more slowly (Cureton, 1969; Bortz, 1982). The good news here is that it is never too late to improve. Even elderly women who suffer from serious osteoporosis can show improvements in calcium levels in the bones after a program of regular, gentle exercise. So start now!

How Good Is the News?

It seems to us that there are at least three kinds of good news here. First, the body continues to repair itself and to provide replacements for its disposable parts, like hair and fingernails. Second, in spite of hormonal and physical changes, the majority of sexually active people can continue these activities late into life. And third, taking good care of yourself can actually reverse or delay the "normal" trends of aging.

This is not to say, however, that there are no real body changes associated with aging. Clearly there are. As Bortz puts it:

> It is wrong to suggest that exercise might halt the fall of the grains of sand in the hourglass. It is proposed, however, that the dimension of the aperture may be responsive to the toning influence of physical activity, and consequently the sand may drain more slowly. A physically active life may allow us to approach our true biogenetic potential for longevity (1982, p. 1206).

THEORIES OF AGING

What *is* it, exactly, that causes the body to become smaller, slower, weaker, lesser, and fewer? In Bortz's language, why does the sand fall through the hourglass at all? Of course, there is no single, simple answer to this question. Aging, like earlier growth, is the outcome of many different factors acting together. We know that genetic factors play a role—you are much more likely to have a long life if your parents and grandparents did. We also know that environment plays a part; for instance, Americans who reside in rural areas live longer than those who live in cities.

When we ask about theories of aging, though, we are usually looking for something more specific than family history and place of residence. Several quite different kinds of theories have been devised to explain the many biological and physiological changes that occur as people grow older (Shock, 1977). Some of these theories are focused on the smallest units of life—individual cells. The idea is to explain aging as a result of the minute changes that occur within single cells as they get older. Another family of theories is focused upon particular organs and systems in the body—the heart and circulatory system are the most common—and the changes they undergo with age. Finally, the most global kinds of theories look at the human body as a whole, as a complex system whose internal operations change in systematic ways with advancing age.

Cellular Theories of Aging

Theories that are focused on individual cells are concerned with the fact that with advancing age, body cells die and are not replaced. Many laboratory experiments have shown that if you take a human cell and grow it in a test tube, it will divide (that is, reproduce itself) only a set number of times. The exact number depends upon what kind of cell it is. For instance, one type of cell (called fibroblasts) from human embryos has been shown to make about 50 divisions before it stops altogether. Studies with animal cells have also shown that cells from older animals will divide fewer times than cells taken from younger ones (Shock, 1977).

One possible explanation for findings like these is that there is some kind of genetic programming for longevity. That is, a particular cell is programmed to live only a certain length of time. Another possible explanation is that the cells somehow become damaged after a certain period of time, and this accumulated damage causes them to cease reproducing. Damage might be caused by radiation, improper synthesis of cellular proteins, or inadequate nutrition by an aging circulatory system.

Theories like these may seem far away from the physical changes we have described (and the psychological changes we will describe in future chapters). Still, research on cellular processes plays an important part in advancing our general understanding of aging.

Organ System Theories of Aging

Most of us are not, after all, terribly concerned about why our *cells* get old; we want to know why our *bodies* grow old. To answer that question, we can turn to those theories that look at individual organs and organ systems.

One such theory focuses upon the importance of the circulatory system. The blood vessels carry blood, with its oxygen and nutrients, to every part of the body. With advancing age, there are certain predictable changes in these blood vessels—that is, they become brittle, less flexible, and are smaller inside because of deposits of fatty acids (like cholesterol). The changes in the blood vessels mean that not as much blood is delivered to all of the other body parts and organs, which may mean, in turn, that their functioning will be decreased or altered.

Other similar theories can be advanced, which concentrate on the importance of other bodily systems. One of them focuses on the sex hormones in the blood; another focuses upon the functioning of the thyroid gland. What they all share is the emphasis upon the importance of changes in function of one organ system upon the aging of the body as a whole.

Systems Theories of Aging

The most complex theories of aging are those that emphasize the entire human body as a complicated system. There are systems theories in other disciplines, too (like engineering, management, and computer science), because they provide a general way of describing complex inter-related sets of events. In the field of aging, such theories try to explain aging in terms of the relationships between different organs and systems in, for example, their response to infection.

As you probably know, the human body makes a complex set of chemical responses when it is invaded by some external agent (like a cold or flu virus). These are called the **immunological responses,** and they depend upon changes in the blood chemistry, body temperature, and many other factors. There is growing evidence that as aging progresses, the efficiency of these immunologic responses decreases somewhat (Shock, 1977). This means that older people may be less able to fight off illness and may therefore become sick in circumstances where a younger person would remain well.

Another important aspect of this immune systems theory concerns the body's ability to destroy its own cells when they are imperfect. When the immune response declines in efficiency, some of these imperfect cells—including cancer cells—may survive to cause disease.

We mentioned earlier that older people respond more slowly than younger ones to environmental events that may upset their internal homeostasis. Other systems theories of aging are concerned with the maintenance of blood components, hormone levels, and internal temperature.

Too Many Theories?

As we have seen for many topics in developmental psychology, there is no single theory of aging that explains all of the changes that are observed. Cellular, organ, and systems theories are all promising, but all require much more research before they can be either accepted or rejected. At the moment, they serve to remind us just how complex the process of aging really is.

AGING AND HEALTH

Many of the changes associated with aging are virtually inevitable—nearly everyone gets shorter and loses taste buds and slows down in reaction time. However, there are other important bodily changes that occur during adulthood that are not so inevitable, namely, those that have to do with illness and disease. Just like aging, wellness and illness can affect our jobs, homes, and personal lives.

Life Expectancy

In one basic way, we can be sure that people are much healthier today than they were in the past: They live longer. We have illustrated this dramatic secular trend for you in Figures 11.6 and 11.7. You can see that the most dramatic changes in life expectancy are during the childhood years. Of all the infants born in the year 1840, 25 percent were dead by the age of 3. Babies born in 1910 had a much better chance for survival; they reached the age of 55 before 25 percent of their number were dead. And you who were born since 1960 are luckier still—three quarters of you will still be alive at the age of 75.

The reasons for these dramatic changes in life expectancy are quite simple: the conquest of infectious diseases by inoculations and antibiotic drugs, as well as better sanitation. Except for the very young and the very old, infectious diseases cause relatively few deaths in our country today.

It's also interesting to note that the total human life span—the width of the graph—has *not* changed very much over the years. A few people born in 1810 lived to be 90 years old, and a few people born in 1960 will live to be 90 or 100. What *has* changed is the proportion of people who survive to enjoy most of that life span.

These changes in life expectancy have implications for public poli-

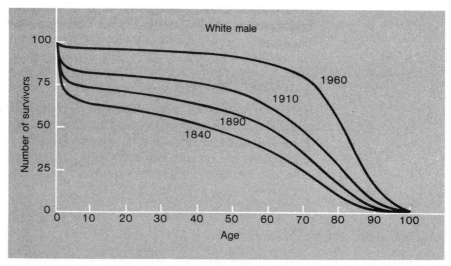

Figure 11.6. Secular trends in life expectancy for men. One of the major reasons for the change is that death rates for infants and young children have dropped dramatically in the last century, so more and more men are living to retirement age. Medical advances have also made it possible for more men who reach adulthood to live into their seventies and eighties, as well. (*Source:* Jacobson, 1964, p. 42.)

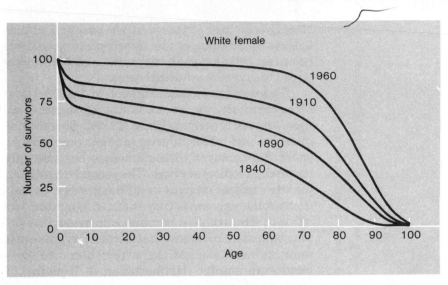

Figure 11.7. Secular trends in life expectancy for women. Just as with men, the biggest change is in the number of women who survive infancy and childhood. Women also live longer than men born in the same year. (*Source:* Jacobson, 1964, p. 42.)

cy, too. Each year a larger percentage of our population is elderly, putting a strain on all of the services that older people use, like medical care, social security, housing, and the like. This problem is likely to become more acute when the baby-boom generation, born in the late 1940s and early 1950s, reaches retirement age early in the twenty-first century.

Health Care Utilization

Long lives are not necessarily healthy lives, and a long life is not always entirely a blessing. A man who might have died in childhood of whooping cough if he had been born in 1840 may today live to age 70 only to suffer from **emphysema** (chronic obstructive lung disease) or lung cancer. Consequently, if we want to know more about levels of health, we need to have more information than just life expectancy.

One way of measuring health is to look at the kinds of health care services that are used by different groups of people. Actually, this is a way to study *ill* health rather than *good* health, but it has the advantage of using information that has already been collected, for example, in hospital records or health surveys.

Health care usage data show that there are both age and sex differences in the kinds of medical services used. Men show higher death rates at all ages and greater numbers of chronic conditions. Women, on the other hand, show more acute conditions and hospitalizations.

Nearly one third of the women's hospitalizations were for delivering babies, which changes our interpretation somewhat. Nonetheless, the basic fact is that women use more medical services during most of their lives but have lower death rates.

There are two disadvantages to this method of studying health. Most obviously, we are not studying *health* at all, we're studying illness, and fairly serious illness at that. Everyday discomforts like colds, allergies, and minor injuries are not considered at all. A person might suffer from many of these ailments—be quite unhealthy—but still not use many medical services. The second drawback is that different people use medical services in different ways. Some people may go to see a physician as soon as they notice a symptom, while others will put it off until the symptom becomes a more serious problem. In fact, there are some data to suggest that women pay more attention to their symptoms and seek medical aid earlier than men do—even when their ailments are similar (Hetherington & Hopkins, 1969). Dissatisfaction with studies of ill health have stimulated researchers to find other, better ways of studying good health.

Healthy Functioning

One of the most successful ways of actually measuring health is to estimate how much a person's normal behavior is impaired or not impaired. One scale used for this purpose was devised as part of the Duke University longitudinal study of aging (Dovenmuehle, Busse, & Newman, 1970).

The **physical functioning rating (PFR)** is a six-point scale that describes how well a person is able to carry out normal social and industrial (work-related) activities. If a person has no disease or physical limitation, she would be given a score of zero. A person with some form of disease who nevertheless could perform any activity she wanted would get a score of 1, while increasing degrees of physical limitation are given higher scores. For example, someone with arthritis who was unable to attend church or club meetings but who could still enjoy visiting with friends at home would get a score of 3 (21 to 50 percent limitation). On the other hand, a person whose sight or hearing was so poor that he couldn't cope with such visits would get a score of 5 (over 80 percent limitation).

You will not be surprised to learn that PFR scores tend to get worse in old age. When the subjects in the Duke study were divided into those under 70 years of age and those over 70, the younger participants had more favorable scores. Other research using the PFR has shown that women have more favorable scores than men, well-to-do people have more favorable scores than impoverished people, and whites have more favorable scores than blacks (and presumably other minority groups).

The chief advantage of scoring systems like the PFR is that they come quite close to actually measuring health—how good people feel in their daily activities. A second advantage is that they let us compare the health status of people who have different diseases or chronic conditions. This is very useful in research, of course, but it can also be helpful for those who are planning social or health services for older adults.

THREATS TO HEALTH

Since it would be impossible to discuss all of the possible threats to health in adults, we have chosen to approach this topic by looking at just two of the most important ones. In the first instance, we have chosen a significant health problem (in fact, the leading cause of death in people over age 35—cardiovascular disease) and will consider two risk factors associated with it. In the second case, we have chosen a set of social risk factors to see what impact they have on health.

The Risk of Cardiovascular Disease

Cardiovascular disease is the general name for an entire family of disorders involving the heart and blood vessels. The best known of these disorders is the "heart attack." Most heart attacks occur because the heart muscle itself fails to receive enough oxygen and nutrients from the bloodstream, usually because of some damage to the arteries that supply blood to the heart. Another cardiovascular disease is the stroke or, as it is sometimes called, a blood clot in the brain. When a stroke occurs, blood flow to the brain is interrupted, and without nourishment the brain cells die. Depending upon where in the brain the stroke occurs, the patient may suffer paralysis, loss of speech, loss of sensation, or other symptoms.

Hypertension.   Physicians have known for many years that both heart attacks and strokes are much more common among people who have high blood pressure than among those who do not. Unfortunately, high blood pressure (technically known as **hypertension**) is quite a common disorder in this country. Figure 11.8 shows that nearly half of the older black men in this country have hypertension; and so do a third of the black women and white men and about a quarter of the white women. Until recently, rising blood pressure was thought to be part of the normal aging process. Today, though, hypertension is considered a serious disease regardless of the age of the patient.

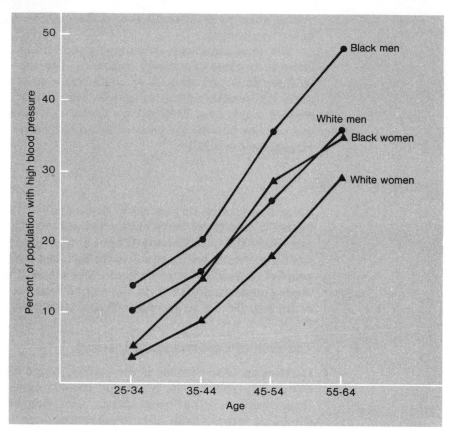

Figure 11.8.   Incidence of high blood pressure (hypertension) as a function of age. Overall, men are more likely than women, and blacks are more likely than whites, to have high blood pressure. For all groups, hypertension increases with age. (*Source:* Stamler, Schoenberger, Shekelle, & Stamler, 1974, p. 4.)

Hypertension is an unusual disease, in one sense, because it has no symptoms. In fact, many people are hypertensive without knowing it. Nonetheless, it is extremely important for people with high blood pressure to receive proper treatment. The treatment itself is usually quite straightforward: a reduction of salt intake, weight control, regular exercise, and (in some cases) taking prescribed medication. Because most people with the disease have no symptoms (and sometimes because the drugs have unpleasant side effects), many people with hypertension fail to follow this regimen. A large study undertaken by the Veterans Administration in the 1960s shows just how important it is for high blood pressure to be treated. In this study (Veterans Administration Cooperative Study Group on Antihypertensive Agents, 1970), the researchers compared patients whose blood pressure was kept down by treatment with other patients whose blood pressure remained high (either because they failed to follow the advice of their doctors or for other reasons). The dramatic results of this study are shown in Figure 11.9. The group of patients whose blood pressure was under control shows a very low rate of heart problems; the group that was not treated shows very high rates. Clearly, controlling high blood pressure can help prevent heart disease.

Type A Behavior.   Another risk factor for cardiovascular disease was identified through the research of Meyer Friedman and Ray Rosenman (1974), two cardiologists (physicians specializing in heart disease). Their research began when, just out of curiosity, they asked a group of businessmen what *they* thought was the cause of heart attacks in

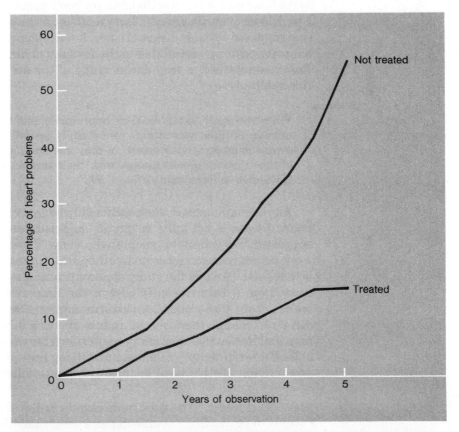

Figure 11.9.   Effects of treatment upon the health of high blood pressure patients. The risk of developing heart problems is far lower in people whose hypertension is treated than it is in those in which it is untreated. (*Source:* Veterans Administration Cooperative Study Group on Antihypertensive Agents: *Effects of Treatment on Morbidity in Hypertension II.* c 1970, American Medical Association.)

their friends. More than 70 percent thought that "excessive competitive drive and meeting deadlines," was the outstanding characteristic of their own colleagues who had heart trouble. Friedman and Rosenman were about to dismiss this as an old wives' tale, when they asked the same question of a group of doctors. The doctors said the same thing. Starting from this simple observation, Friedman and Rosenman developed a description of an entire lifestyle characterized by what they call **Type A behavior.** The central trait in this lifestyle is the sense of time urgency, of too much to be done in too little time. There are other aspects of Type A behavior (listed in Table 11.1), but the sense of being chronically late or of being constantly behind schedule is the most important part.

At the time this theory was first put forward, most physicians believed (and many still do) that the primary cause of heart disease was a high level of **cholesterol** (a fatty acid) in the blood. If Type A behavior was supposed to cause heart disease, it was important to show that the behavior pattern was related to the levels of cholesterol. Friedman and Rosenman devised a very clever study of tax accountants to examine this relationship:

> When the April 15 tax deadline approached, and the sense of time urgency of these accountants rose sharply, so did the level of their serum cholesterol. Conversely, in May and early June, when their sense of time urgency almost disappeared, their serum cholesterol fell (Friedman & Rosenman, 1974, p. 59).

As you might expect, the relationship between Type A behavior and heart disease is not quite as simple as Friedman and Rosenman first suggested. For example, people who show Type A behavior in their work do not necessarily do so in other situations where time pressures do not exist. (And as the study of accountants shows, some people may show Type A behavior only part of the time even at work.) Still, research about these behavior patterns suggests that anything a person can do to change them should reduce the risk of heart disease. Friedman and Rosenman offer many suggestions for ways to do this, but they all boil down to simply relaxing and letting time go by. That's probably good advice, but it's hard for most people to follow.

More Good News.   The good news about cardiovascular disease is that it seems to be declining somewhat as a major health hazard for adults. Some of this decline has to do with better medical care for people who have suffered heart attacks and strokes. The rest of it, though, has to do with changes in personal habits (like reducing Type A behavior), adherence to treatment for hypertension, and concern about diet (espe-

TABLE 11.1
Characteristics of the Type A Behavior Pattern

You possess the Type A behavior pattern if:

1. You have (a) a habit of explosively accentuating various key words in your ordinary speech . . . and (b) a tendency to utter the last few words of your sentences far more rapidly than the opening words.

2. You *always* move, walk, and eat rapidly.

3. You feel an impatience with the rate at which most events take place.

4. You indulge in *polyphasic* thought or performance, frequently striving to think of or do two or more things simultaneously. . . .

5. You find it *always* difficult to refrain from talking about or bringing the theme of any conversation around to those subjects that especially interest and intrigue you, and when unable to accomplish this maneuver, you pretend to listen but really remain preoccupied with your own thoughts.

6. You almost always feel vaguely guilty when you relax and do absolutely nothing for several hours to several days.

7. You no longer observe the more important or interesting or lovely objects that you encounter in your milieu. . . .

8. You do not have any time to spare to become the things worth *being,* because you are so preoccupied with getting the things worth *having.*

9. You attempt to schedule more and more in less and less time, and in doing so make fewer and fewer allowances for unforeseen contingencies. . . .

10. On meeting another severely afflicted Type A person, instead of feeling compassion for his affliction you find yourself compelled to challenge him.

11. You resort to certain characteristic gestures or nervous tics. . . .

12. You believe that whatever success you have enjoyed has been due in good part to your ability to get things done faster than your fellow man, as if you are afraid to stop doing everything faster and faster.

13. You find yourself increasingly and ineluctably committed to translating and evaluating not only your own but also the activities of others in terms of numbers.

SOURCE: From *Type A behavior and your heart,* by Meyer Friedman and Ray Rosenman. © 1974 by Meyer Friedman. Reprinted by permission of Alfred A. Knopf, Inc.

cially cholesterol), exercise, and smoking (which accounts for approximately a quarter of a million deaths each year). It is reassuring to hear that the risk of some diseases really can be significantly reduced.

The Risks of Social Change

Now we want to look at a different set of risks—events that happen in the social realm that may have some impact on general health and daily life.

Retirement.   One big change that occurs in the lives of older persons who have been employed outside the home is ending their employment through retirement. We will be talking about some of the psychological consequences of retirement in Chapter 13. The question we want to ask here is whether or not it has any impact on health.

The answer seems to be fairly clear-cut: Among adults who are physically healthy when they retire, retirement itself is *not* associated with any loss of health (Palmore, 1981; Myers, 1965). So the classic image of the newly retired man who is dying of boredom and gets physically sick as a result seems to be false. In fact, it is far more common for people to retire *because* they are in ill health than it is for people to become sick because they have retired.

In this case, retirement appears to have little effect on health because it is an *anticipated* life change. Many of the adjustments required can be planned ahead of time, which greatly reduces the impact.

Change of Residence.   Another potentially difficult situation for older people is moving from one residence to another. Sometimes this is occasioned by other events, like the death or disability of a spouse, and sometimes by preference for living closer to family or in a more favorable climate.

In one large study of older people, Schooler (1975) identified those who had and those who had not moved in the preceding three years. In general, those who had moved reported some declines in general health and morale, but these effects were not very large. It was anticipating moving—doing the planning and preparation—that had the biggest impact on health and on morale. Not surprisingly, when the new residence was less desirable than the old one, the health declines were the most marked.

Sometimes changes in residence are not entirely voluntary. Several studies (reviewed by Lawton, 1977) have shown that elderly people relocated from one institution to another show declines in health and increases in rate of mortality. In one such study (Marlowe, 1973), it seemed that moving was a make-or-break affair. Some of the old people did well in their new surroundings, but some deteriorated or even died.

Taken together, the evidence suggests that changing residences is a real threat to the health of older people, whether they initiate the change themselves or it is initiated by others. Sometimes a relatively poor environment may actually be less hazardous to the elderly than a move to a better place.

Death of a Spouse.   Perhaps the most disruptive social change for adults is the death of a spouse. Both men and women who have been widowed generally are more likely to be institutionalized (Palmore, 1976b) and have higher mortality and suicide rates. There is also a tendency for widows and widowers to report more psychosomatic symptoms than married people of the same age (Palmore, Cleveland, Nowlin, Ramm, & Siegler, 1979).

At the same time, there does not appear to be a large change in *physical* health associated with the death of a spouse. Dorothy Heyman and Daniel Gianturco (1974) used longitudinal data from the Duke University study to compare physical functioning ratings before and after the loss of a spouse. There was no significant change in the ratings after the loss, nor were there any differences between men and women on these scores. Furthermore, most of the people in this study seemed to keep up their normal activities (things like visiting family and friends or attending church) at about the same rate.

Good and Bad News about Social Risks.   It is surprising to realize that retirement and loss of a spouse, which we consider to be major life changes, seem to have less effect on health than moving, which seems comparatively minor. In the last section of this chapter, we are going to look more carefully at life changes and how they affect both illness and wellness.

PROMOTING HEALTH

We have been alternating good news and bad news in this chapter; and since we started off with some bad news, it's only fitting that we end with some good news. In this section we want to focus on things that can be done to avoid illness, promote wellness and development, and postpone or minimize the effects of aging.

Life Change

During our lives, each of us experiences events that demand we change our habits, adjust to new conditions, make new friends, or change our lifestyles. Marriage, divorce, the birth of a child, the death of a relative, or a promotion at work are all examples of these life changes. For the past several years Thomas Holmes and his colleagues have investigated the impact of these life changes upon health (Holmes & Rahe, 1967; Holmes & Masuda, 1973).

Holmes theorizes that each life change introduces some stress into your life. That is, you have to cope with the change and adapt your behavior to new conditions. The greater the number and severity of these events, the greater the amount of stress, which is in varying degrees psychological, physical, and physiological. While each person

can tolerate a moderate amount of stress, greater amounts may interfere with normal psychological, physical, and physiological functioning.

To test out these ideas, Holmes and Rahe (1967) devised a questionnaire called the Social Readjustment Rating Scale, which is reproduced
in the project at the end of the chapter. Each item on the questionnaire
has been assigned a number of **life change units,** which reflects how
much adaptation and coping it requires. The sum of the life change
units for all the events that have happened to a person in the last year
is the score on this instrument.

In one of the early studies, Holmes gave this questionnaire to a
group of 88 young doctors. They were asked to report any health problems they experienced, as well as fill out the Social Readjustment Rating Scale. In Figure 11.10 you can see the relationship between life
change scores and health: Those with major life crises were very likely
to experience health problems.

You should notice, however, that the amount and type of life change
that occurs does not predict what *kind* of health change will occur. In
Holmes's study, health changes included everything from infectious
diseases to broken legs. All the score seems to predict is that *some* adverse change in health status is likely to occur.

The Social Readjustment Rating Scale includes items that are both
negative (getting fired) and positive (outstanding personal achievement), because Holmes and his co-workers believe that any
change—good or bad—requires adjustment. Other researchers, like
Irwin Sarason (Sarason, Johnson, & Seigel, 1978) have taken a slightly
different approach by asking each subject whether each event was positive or negative. In one study of college students, Sarason found that
only the events rated as negative were associated with health problems. On the other hand, having many positive events did not seem to
improve health.

Research results like these can be applied to real-life situations.
Suppose a woman has a new baby. Her Social Readjustment Rating
Scale might look like this:

13. Pregnancy	40
19. New family member	39
5. Major change in sleeping habits	16
7. Major change in eating habits	15
9. Revision of personal habits (a diet)	24
Total	134

We might suggest that she refrain from moving (20 life change units)
or beginning work (26 units) or school (26 units) for the time being. Of
course, adults don't always have control over their life events, but the

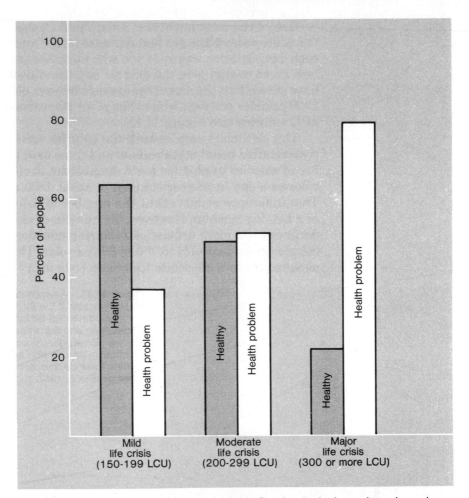

Figure 11.10. Impact of life crises upon health. People who had experienced a major life crisis (defined by Holmes and Rahe as anything over 300 points on the total score on their scale) were very likely to have a health problem. Those with lower scores on the life change scale had lesser chances of having a health problem. (*Source:* Holmes, T. H., & M. Masuda, p. 175. Copyright 1973 by the American Association for the Advancement of Science).

idea of not overdosing on change can be a helpful one for avoiding problems.

Nutrition

We have already emphasized the need for good nutrition prenatally and during the first two decades of life. You won't be surprised, then, to learn that nutrition also plays an important part in the health and development of adults.

One of the most important nutritional changes that occurs during the adult years is the gradual decrease in the number of calories eaten each day. Calories, as any of you who have dieted must know, measure how much energy is in the food we eat. Careful studies of adult males have shown that the diet of the average 28-year-old man contains about 2700 calories per day, while that of an 80-year-old man is only about 2100 calories (see Figure 11.11).

This decline is seen in both the calories used for basic bodily processes (called **basal metabolism**) and those used for activity. The number of calories needed for basic metabolism declines from about 1550 calories a day in 28-year-old men to about 1350 a day in 80-year-olds. That difference equals about the number of calories in a piece of pie or a hot dog in a bun. However, the number of calories used in activity declines even more dramatically during adulthood—from about 1150 calories in 28-year-olds to 750 in 80-year-olds. That 400 calorie drop is about equal to a chocolate ice cream soda every day.

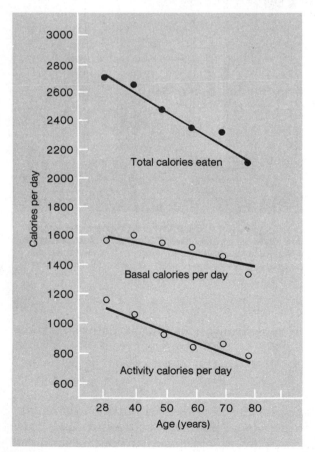

Figure 11.11. Average diet of adult men, as a function of age. If the total calories you eat exceeds the amount needed for basic bodily needs (basal metabolism) and the amount used up in exercise, you will gain weight. Since both activity and basal metabolism decline with age (typically), older adults require fewer calories to maintain their weight. (*Source:* Shock, 1972, p. 18.)

When dietary intake goes down, the supply of specific nutrients goes down, too. A diet with fewer calories is likely to provide fewer vitamins and minerals and less protein than one with more calories. The drop in the *quality* of nutrition may be just as important as the drop in the *quantity* of food eaten.

To give just one example, the diets of many elderly people are mildly deficient in the mineral potassium. T. G. Judge (1972), a nutritionist, was interested in whether this deficiency had any impact on the elderly. Judge gave a nonverbal reasoning test to two groups of elderly people both before and after they were given a vitamin supplement. For half the group, this supplement included potassium; for the other half, it did not (this is sometimes called a **placebo**). Both groups of subjects improved their scores the second time they took the test, but the group that had received potassium improved significantly more.

This study does not show that all elderly people need to take potassium supplements, nor that potassium increases IQ. It *does* show, though, that even minor nutritional deficiencies may have a noticeable effect on some kinds of behavior.

A decrease in the amount and quality of food is not the only nutritional problem faced by the aging. On the contrary, there are a large number of factors that make eating well increasingly difficult for them. We have summarized these for you in Table 11.2.

In spite of the importance of nutrition for the elderly, little is actually known about the nutritional needs of older people. For example,

TABLE 11.2
Factors That Determine Eating Habits in the Elderly

Loss of teeth or denture problems. Denture wearer must chew food four times as long to get the same effect as a person with natural teeth.

Decrease in salivation may make chewing more difficult.

Diminished sense of smell and taste (which may lead to oversalting of food, a problem for those with high blood pressure).

Loss of neuromuscular coordination (inability to feed self easily).

Chronic diseases.

Food preferences and habits.

Decreased physical activity, which limits caloric needs and may lead to weight problems.

Decreased physical activity, which makes it more difficult to shop and prepare foods.

Decreased basal metabolism rate, which supports basic bodily functions.

Long-term dietetic habits.

Income, which may limit availability of different foods.

Emotional upsets and problems, especially widowhood and widowerhood.

Lack of adequate food storage and cooking facilities.

the United States government has suggested nutritional requirements for infants, children, and adults, but not for the elderly. Furthermore, relatively little is known about the long-term effects of diet—both good and poor—on the behavior of older people or on the aging process itself. This is an area where good research, both basic and applied, still remains to be done.

Good Health Practices

Avoiding stress, eating nutritious foods, and exercising regularly have all been shown to improve health and to partially counteract the effects of aging. But just how much good do these good habits really do? How much difference does it make to keep yourself relaxed, well nourished, and physically fit? If you do all of those things, will you really feel any better or live any longer than your friends who are nervous, overweight, and flabby?

Indeed you will. Studies by Nedra Belloc and her co-workers (Belloc, 1973; Belloc & Breslow, 1972) have shown that these and other health practices are clearly related to expected life duration. Belloc began by compiling a list of seven desirable health practices, which we've noted in Table 11.3. Each of the items on the list has been shown individually to reduce the death rate among adults.

Belloc was also interested in whether combining these good practices would reduce the death rate. She tested this possibility by using data that had been collected in a large-scale (6928 persons) health survey of Alameda County, California. She got information from the survey concerning all of the health habits and from the county records concerning all of the deaths. The results of this analysis are shown in Figure 11.12.

TABLE 11.3
Good Health Practices

1. Usually sleep seven or eight hours.
2. Eat breakfast almost every day.
3. Eat between meals once in a while, rarely, or never.
4. Weight for a man between 5 percent under and 20 percent over desirable weight for height. Weight for a woman not more than 10 percent over desirable weight for height.
5. Often or sometimes engage in active sports, swimming, or take long walks, or often garden or do physical exercises.
6. Drink not more than four drinks at a time.
7. Never smoke cigarettes.

SOURCE: Belloc & Breslow, 1972, p. 415.

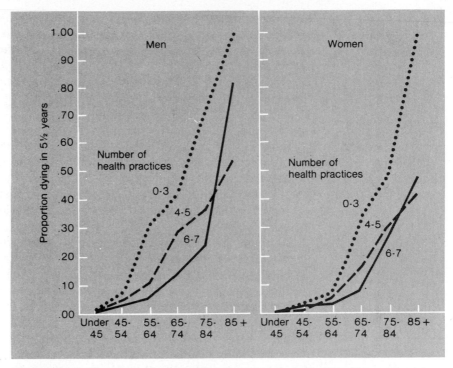

Figure 11.12. The effect of good health practices upon death rates. The more good health habits a person has, the smaller is his or her chance of dying. This effect is much more dramatic among older groups, which may give the impression that you can get away with poor health habits when you are young. Probably, though, the effect is at least partly cumulative, so it is wise to adopt these good practices as soon as possible. (*Source:* Belloc, 1973, p. 75.)

For both men and women, the highest death rates were found for those who had the smallest number of good health practices. This effect was particularly dramatic for the older subjects. But at any age, the more good habits, the longer the life.

AGING VERSUS DISEASE

The more we have learned about aging, the clearer it has become that changes resulting *only* from the aging process are few in number. Though we made a long list of the ways people get smaller, slower, weaker, lesser, and fewer, we have also made a long list of changes that are the result of other causes, like hypertension, stress, Type A behavior, or social changes.

Of course, we think this distinction between aging and disease is an important one for understanding developmental psychology, but it is also important when making decisions for individuals. It is clear that we need to be very careful not to assume that some infirmity is a natural result of aging unless we have carefully eliminated all of the unnatural causes.

SUMMARY

1. Most of the bodily changes that are associated with aging can be described as making you smaller, slower, weaker, lesser, and fewer.
2. The body does continue to grow; and the basic bodily functions, including sexual activity, continue throughout the entire life span.
3. Many of the changes associated with aging are also characteristic of adults in bed rest or astronauts in weightlessness. Some of the changes may thus be the result of disuse rather than aging.
4. Some theories of aging focus on changes in cells, while others emphasize changes in specific organs or in the functioning of the entire system.
5. The average life span has increased over the past century or so, but the total life span still rarely exceeds 90 to 100 years.
6. Data about ill health show that men have higher death rates and more chronic conditions, while women have more acute conditions and are hospitalized more frequently.
7. Ratings of physical functioning show that health declines with age. They also show sex, social class, and racial differences.
8. Hypertension is a risk factor for cardiovascular diseases like heart attacks and strokes. When treated, the degree of risk drops considerably.
9. Type A behavior is also a risk factor for heart disease. Changing this pattern is desirable but often difficult.
10. Social events like retirement, moving, and widowhood can have impact on health. Surprisingly, moving is often more stressful than retiring or losing a spouse.
11. High levels of life change seem to predispose people to health problems. This is probably more true of negative changes.
12. The need for calories from food declines over the life span, which may make it harder to obtain necessary nutrients. Some behavioral difficulties among the elderly may be caused by poor nutrition.
13. Adhering to good health habits seems to reduce both the number of illnesses and the mortality rate; this is particularly true among men.

14. Since it is difficult to distinguish between aging and disease, it is important to rule out the latter before deciding that some ailment is caused by the former.

KEY TERMS

Basal metabolism   The amount of energy (calories) needed by the body for its basic functions.

Cardiovascular disease   Diseases of the heart *(cardio)* and circulatory system *(vascular)*, including what is commonly called "heart attack" and stroke.

Cholesterol   Fatty acid in the blood believed to be related to heart disease.

Climacteric   The general name for changes that occur in the reproductive system as a result of aging. Includes the female menopause.

Emphysema   Chronic obstructive lung disease.

Homeostasis   The internal steady state of the human body. If this balance is upset, the body must respond and compensate or illness or injury will result.

Hypertension   High blood pressure.

Immunological response   Chemical responses made by the body when it is invaded by some external agent such as a cold or flu virus.

Life change units   Amount of life change reflected on the Social Readjustment Rating Scale.

Menopause   The cessation of menstrual periods in women.

Osteoporosis   Weakening of bones caused by loss of calcium. It is particularly common in women following menopause.

Physical functioning rating (PFR)   Ratings that reflect the impairment, or lack of impairment, in daily social and work activities. Scores can range from 0 (for no impairment) to 5 (for more than 80 percent impairment).

Placebo   The substance given a control group to show the effects of a drug used in an experiment.

Type A behavior   A lifestyle characterized by a sense of time urgency and competitiveness.

SUGGESTED READINGS

Bortz, W. M. II. Disuse and aging. *Journal of the American Medical Association,* 1982 (Sept.), *248,* 1203–1208.
This brief paper is a fascinating analysis of the effect of lack of exercise or other kinds of disuse on the aging of the body.

The Diagram Group. *Man's body: An owner's manual.* New York: Paddington Press, 1976. (Also published by Bantam Books, 1977.)
This is a companion volume to *Woman's body* (below) and is excellent. It is loaded with diagrams, pictures, and graphs on subjects from conception to aging.

The Diagram Group. *Woman's body: An owner's manual.* New York: Paddington Press, 1977. (Also published by Bantam Books, 1978.)
This is a good book about adult bodies aimed particularly at women. It lacks

some of the emotional content of *Our bodies, ourselves,* but it is still very informative.

Kart, C. S., Metress, E. S., & Metress, J. F. *Aging and health: Biologic and social perspective.* Reading, Mass.: Addison-Wesley, 1978.
This is a complete summary of the many physiological and health changes that occur in old age. It does an unusually good job of showing the connections between health and behavior in real-life situations.

PROJECT 11.1
Calculating Your Life Change Score

Earlier in the chapter we described Holmes and Rahe's Social Readjustment Rating Scale. Students always seem to like calculating their own life change score, so we have given the items in this scale in the accompanying table. Check off all those changes that have occurred in your life in *the past year,* and then add up the points to get a total score.

Social Readjustment Rating Scale

Item	Life change units	Check changes in the past year
1. Marriage	50	
2. Trouble with boss	23	
3. Detention in jail or other institution	63	
4. Death of spouse	100	
5. Major change in sleeping habits	16	48
6. Death of a close family member	63	
7. Major change in eating habits	15	
8. Foreclosure of mortgage or loan	30	
9. Revision of personal habits	24	
10. Death of close friend	37	
11. Minor violations of the law	11	
12. Outstanding personal achievement	28	28
13. Pregnancy	40	
14. Minor change in health or behavior of family member	44	44
15. Sexual difficulties	39	29
16. In-law troubles	29	15
17. Change in family get-togethers	15	
18. Change in financial state	38	39
19. New family member	39	
20. Change in address or residence	20	
21. Son or daughter leaving home	29	
22. Marital separation	65	
23. Change in church activities	19	
24. Marital reconciliation	45	
25. Being fired	47	

26. Divorcing	73	_____
27. Changing line of work	36	_____
28. Change in arguments with spouse	35	*35.*
29. Change in responsibilities at work	29	_____
30. Beginning or ceasing work	26	_____
31. Change in working hours or conditions	20	*20*
32. Change in recreation	19	*19*
33. Taking mortgage greater than $10,000	31	_____
34. Taking loan less than $10,000	17	_____
35. Major personal injury or illness	53	_____
36. Major business readjustment	39	_____
37. Change in social activities	18	*18*
38. Change in living conditions	25	_____
39. Retirement	45	_____
40. Vacation	13	*13*
41. Changing schools	20	_____
42. Beginning or ceasing formal schooling	26	_____

SOURCE: Holmes & Rahe, 1967.

A score of 0–149 describes no life crisis.
A score of 150–199 describes a mild life crisis.
A score of 200–299 describes a moderate life crisis.
A score of 300 or more describes a major life crisis.

Compare your score to these categories. If your score is high, are there ways in which you could reduce the adaptational requirements of your life pattern? Are there anticipated changes you could postpone in order to prevent your score from rising further?

If all members of the class complete this scale, it may be informative to calculate an average score and the range of scores. It may also be of interest to have each student (anonymously, of course) indicate whether he or she has experienced some major illness in the past year. Are those students with high life change scores more likely to report a recent illness? Do the results replicate those shown in Figure 11.10? If not, what might account for the differences in results?

Chapter 12
Growth and Change
in Adult Intelligence

(12)

My grandmother was an intelligent and articulate woman who supported herself for nearly 20 years as a department store saleswoman. Her specialty was silverware, and she was able to keep track of hundreds of different patterns and items in her head. The year she turned 71, though, she broke her hip and had to give up her job. Around this time we noticed that her memory, which had seemed so remarkable at the store, didn't seem to be so remarkable anymore. In fact, she confused the names of her grandchildren, forgot to pay bills, misplaced her belongings, and repeated her favorite anecdotes over and over. [SM]

What was the real cause of this decline? Was it a health problem, a normal aging process, or perhaps even a result of leaving her job? In this chapter, we will try to answer some of these questions. As before, we'll organize our discussion around the three definitions of intelligence: power, structure, and style.

COGNITIVE POWER IN ADULTS

In earlier chapters we have looked at cognitive power in terms of individual differences: Do people with high scores continue to have high scores on tests, and do they do well on activities (like schoolwork) that should be related to intelligence? Strangely, there is relatively little research about the stability of IQ and other intellectual measures in the adult years (there are some data about other activities, and we will look at that shortly). Instead, most of the research concerned with cognitive power in adults asks whether mental abilities decline with advancing age.

Age Changes in Mental Abilities

Our cultural stereotypes of absentminded and even senile senior citizens suggest that large declines in mental abilities occur. Like most stereotypes, though, when examined thoroughly, this one turns out to be less clear-cut than it first seems. Let's approach this question—whether intelligence declines with age—as if it were a detective story and see if we can fit together the clues that will help us arrive at an answer.

Clue 1: Cross-sectional Studies. Most of the data we have about changes in adult mental abilities come from cross-sectional studies, in which separate groups of people of different ages are tested and average group scores compared. In Figure 12.1 you can see the results of a cross-sectional study of scores on the WAIS, given to subjects who ranged in age from 16 to over 75 (Matarazzo, 1972).

These data make the answer to our original question look quite simple. Intelligence seems to increase until about age 22, stay the same from 22 to about 30, and then decline steadily from age 30 on. The decline becomes rapid after the late sixties. Similar results have been

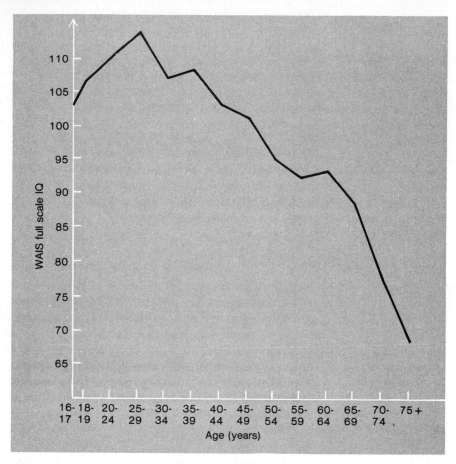

Figure 12.1. Cross-sectional study of adult intelligence. The full-scale (total) scores on the WAIS increase through the late twenties, then show a steady decline through the rest of the adult years. (*Source:* Matarazzo, 1972.)

found using other groups of subjects and using group IQ tests as well as the WAIS, and the conclusion looks quite firm: The older you become, the less intelligent you become. This conclusion certainly matches the cultural stereotype about the aging process, which makes it that much harder to refute. But all the same, it is incorrect.

Clue 2: Different Kinds of Mental Abilities.   We can show you why it is incorrect by using exactly the same data but showing them to you in a slightly different way. In Figure 12.2, we have taken the results from the same study as we did in Figure 12.1, only this time we're showing you the Performance IQ and the Verbal IQ scores separately.

There is certainly a dramatic difference in the patterns shown by the two types of scores. The Performance test scores seem to follow the

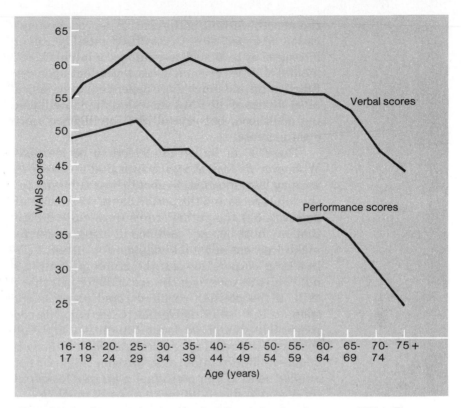

Figure 12.2. Cross-sectional study of adult verbal and performance abilities. The performance scores show the same pattern of age differences as we saw in Figure 12.1, but the verbal scores remain high for all but the oldest subjects. (*Source:* Matarazzo, 1972.)

pattern we saw for the total scores; that is, they seem to rise until about age 22, level off through age 30, and then decline steadily. Verbal scores, on the other hand, do *not* show a decline after age 30. In fact, Verbal scores on the WAIS do not begin to decline significantly until after age 62.

These two patterns of development have been found using other tests of intellectual abilities, too. One of the best known is a battery of short tests called the Primary Mental Abilities test, or **PMA.** Although it is based on the original theories of Leon Thurstone (1938), this test has been studied most recently by Raymond B. Cattell and John Horn (Cattell, 1963, 1971; Horn & Cattell, 1966). Subtests of the PMA are characterized by these researchers as measuring either **fluid intelligence** or **crystallized intelligence.**

Fluid intelligence, according to this theory, is measured by tests like response speed, memory span, and nonverbal reasoning. These tasks, like those on the Performance half of the WAIS, are dependent upon the smooth working of the central nervous system more than upon education or experience. Crystallized intelligence, on the other hand, is measured by tests such as reading comprehension or vocabulary. These mental abilities are much less dependent upon central nervous system functioning and much more dependent upon education and experience. Most studies of the PMA show that fluid intelligence scores decline during adulthood, but crystallized intelligence scores remain steady or even increase.

There is an important lesson to be learned from these results. Whenever we look at *total* scores that are made up of several subtests, we may lose information about those subtests. In this particular case, the total scores and the performance scores had similar developmental patterns, but the verbal scores were quite different. This also means that we must be very cautious in using research results like these to make decisions about individuals. For instance, if a personnel manager in a large corporation saw the graph in Figure 12.1, she might decide not to hire anyone over the age of 30 for jobs that required intellectual skill. If the position required rapid response speed, a long memory span, or the use of nonverbal reasoning, this conclusion might seem reasonable (though we doubt it really is). On the other hand, if the position required reading comprehension, a large vocabulary, and a store of general information, older persons might be superior candidates for employment. If the personnel manager looks only at group data for total scores, she could make a costly mistake.

Clue 3: Longitudinal Studies.   If we stopped here, you could conclude that there is some loss of ability, although not in all areas. Even this conclusion may be partly wrong.

We hope that most of you have begun to wonder why we are using data from *cross-sectional* studies when this is clearly a question requiring *longitudinal* data. All the cross-sectional studies can tell us is that older people get lower scores—they can't tell us whether individuals have actually declined over time. It may be that older people have always performed at a lower level—they have certainly had different educational and life experiences than people born more recently.

The reason we are using cross-sectional data is that there is not very much longitudinal data available. A longitudinal study of adult intelligence could take 30 or 40 years, and most of our mental tests are barely that old. It should be no surprise, then, that there are no single studies that really cover the entire adult life span. But there have been several studies that followed groups for 5, 10, or even 20 years. By putting these together, we can get a good idea of what real longitudinal data would look like.

One of the best studies of this kind is a 14-year longitudinal project done by K. Warner Schaie and his colleagues (Schaie and Strother,

1968; Schaie and Labouvie-Vief, 1974). In 1956, Schaie administered the PMA test to a large group of subjects who ranged in age from 20 to 70. Seven years later (in 1963) and seven years after that (in 1970), he retested as many as possible of the original participants—161 people in all. Schaie divided this large group of subjects into smaller groups on the basis of their age at the beginning of the study: One group averaged 25 years, another 33 years, and so forth up to a group that averaged 67 years at the start of the study. Each of these groups is called a **cohort,** and the test scores for each cohort can be viewed as a small longitudinal study of a particular 14-year "slice" of adulthood. By combining these "slices," we can get some idea about the entire course of adulthood.

Some of the results of this study are shown in Figure 12.3, for a measure of crystallized ability, and in Figure 12.4, for a measure of fluid ability. Each of the short lines on these graphs represents the average scores of one cohort over the 14-year course of the study. On the test of crystallized thinking (Figure 12.3), the younger cohorts seem to be improving while the older ones are staying steady or declining. On the test of fluid thinking (Figure 12.4), scores seem to stay the same or decline for all cohorts.

So far, the longitudinal data seem to say just about what the cross-sectional data did: Older people tend to get lower scores. So you would think that if we drew a graph of cross-sectional results and a graph of the longitudinal results, the two would look the same. Surprisingly, this is not the case.

Let us look at Schaie's study again to see why not. Suppose we smoothed out the longitudinal graphs we have just looked at. Then we

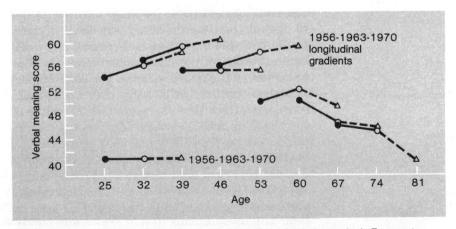

Figure 12.3. Longitudinal study of a crystallized ability (verbal meaning). For most cohorts, scores on the PMA vocabulary test increase as the people get older. Only for the oldest subjects (those over 60 when first tested) is any age-related decline evident. (*Source:* Schaie & Labouvie-Vief, 1974.)

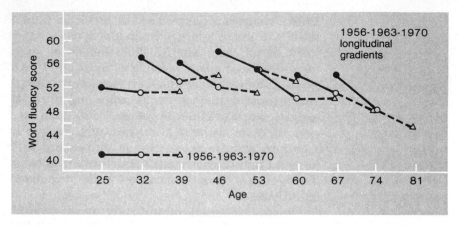

Figure 12.4.   Longitudinal study of a fluid ability (word fluency). The scores for all age groups on this task decline as they get older, with the oldest cohorts showing the most dramatic drops. (*Source:* Schaie & Labouvie-Vief, 1974.)

could take the same set of data and organize it as a cross-sectional study (easy to do, since Schaie tested people of many ages on each occasion) (Schaie & Strother, 1968). If we draw the cross-sectional graph and compare it to the longitudinal graph, we get something like what is shown in Figure 12.5. The scores of individuals seem to increase up through the late adult years (as shown in the upper line for the longitudinal data), while the scores of groups born at different times seem to go down over the same period (as shown in the lower line for the cross-sectional data). How can both of these things be true?

The answer to this part of the puzzle requires you to think about the differences between the cohorts who were compared in the cross-sectional analysis. We know, obviously, that they were of different ages at the time the study was done. If you think about it, people of different ages may have had remarkably different life experiences. Some examples of these life experiences are shown in Figure 12.6. At the bottom of the figure we show you some important historical events of the last century (we're sorry they are rather grim). At the top we have drawn lines that represent the life spans of the different groups of subjects in Schaie's study. Members of cohort A, the oldest in the study, were born in 1889, and they spent their childhoods during the nineteenth century. Those in cohort C, the youngest in the study, were 25 years old when first tested. They were born in 1931 and grew up during the Great Depression and the beginning of World War II. The intermediate group of subjects (cohort B) were born in 1910 and spent their childhood during World War I and the Roaring Twenties.

The point is that there are *many* differences between the cohorts: Subjects in cohort A are more likely to have grown up in a rural area, less likely to have had good medical care, less likely to have gone to

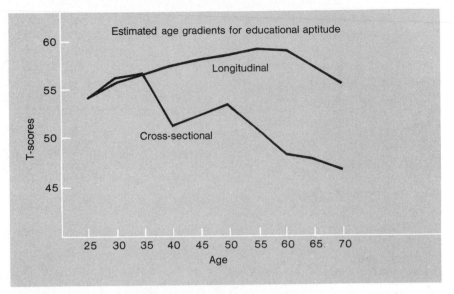

Figure 12.5. Comparison of longitudinal and cross-sectional results from a single study. The longitudinal part of this analysis indicates that scores on a test of educational aptitude continue to increase through age 60 and drop only slightly after that. The cross-sectional analysis, on the other hand, shows a decline beginning around age 35. (*Source:* Schaie & Strother, 1968.)

high school, and more likely to have been in a large family than those in cohorts B or C. As we saw back in Chapter 4, any one of these differences could account for the differences we see in their mental test scores. In fact, most mental abilities show the pattern we have seen here: Longitudinal data show less decline with age and a later start for that decline than cross-sectional studies do. Even so, there is some decline in abilities near the end of the life span, and our last puzzle piece may help to explain that decline.

Clue 4: Terminal Drop.   Several researchers, including Klaus and Ruth Riegel (1972) and Erdman Palmore and William Cleveland (1976), have argued that there is little or no decline in most intellectual abilities during the entire life span *until* about five years before death, when there is a sort of **terminal drop** in skill. Since each successive older cohort includes more and more people who are within five years of death, it makes it look as if the entire group is declining. What's more, neither cross-sectional nor longitudinal studies avoid this problem.

The way to check this possibility is to backtrack from the time of death for each subject in a longitudinal study and see whether his score stayed fairly steady until some point before death. Palmore and Cleveland (1976) did just this for a group of 178 deceased men who

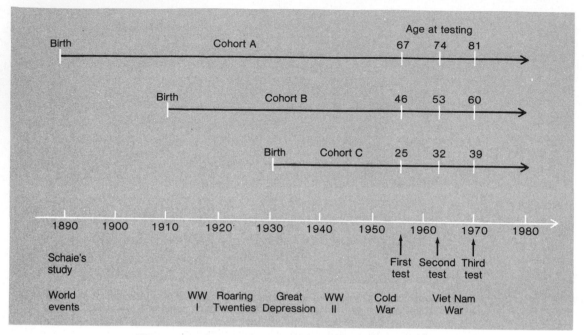

Figure 12.6.   Life experiences of different cohorts. The people who were already elderly at the time Schaie's study began (cohort A) have lived through quite different world events than the youngest subjects (cohort C) have. Cohorts often also differ on things like education and standard of living. Any of these factors could be related to apparent age differences found in cross-sectional studies.

had been part of the Duke University longitudinal study of aging. During the study, the men had had physical checkups regularly and had been given the WAIS as well. *None* of the physical measures showed any indication of terminal drop, but the IQ score *did.* That is, regardless of how old the men were, when they reached a point a few years before their death, their scores went down. Palmore and Cleveland suggest that the reason for this result may be that the WAIS is sensitive to the relatively small drops in many separate physiological and neurological functions, none of which are abruptly declining themselves. Taken together, though, all these small decrements may affect the organized mental functioning that is measured by the WAIS.

Putting the Clues Together.   After looking at all the data, how shall we answer our original question: Do mental abilities decline with age? The answer is a very qualified "yes." Nearly all mental tests show lower scores for the very oldest subjects, but the amount of decline and the age at which that decline begins differ according to the kind of skill *and* the cohort of the subjects. As the number of very old people (those over 75) increases in our society, we can expect even more interest in this important question.

Mental Abilities and Employment

We have seen that children's and adolescents' IQ test scores are good predictors of school achievement. Since youngsters are required to attend school, a test that predicts school achievement is very useful. Most adults, though, are *not* in school, and predicting their academic performance is not as useful. What most adults do do is *work,* so a useful test of adult abilities would be one that could predict occupational choices and job success. Do adult IQ tests do this?

Intelligence and Job Choice. One way to answer this question is to look at the IQ scores of people who have chosen (or been selected for) different occupations. Thomas and Margaret Harrell (1945) conducted a study like this during World War II, when all army recruits were required to take an IQ test. In Table 12.1 you can see the IQ scores obtained by men according to their civilian occupations.

In a general way, these results indicate that IQ is a fairly good predictor of job choice: Men with higher IQs have jobs with more status and prestige, and those with lower IQs have jobs with less status and prestige. But notice, too, that this finding is partly a result of the ways people get into high status jobs: They must have special education or training. This requirement acts to put a lower limit on the IQ of people

TABLE 12.1

Average IQ Scores for White Army Enlisted Men according to Their Civilian Jobs

Civilian occupation	Average IQ	Range
Accountant	128.1	94–157
Teacher	122.8	76–155
Draftsman	122.0	74–155
Bookkeeper	120.0	70–157
Clerk, general	117.5	68–155
Manager	116.0	60–151
Radio repairman	115.3	56–151
Salesman	115.1	60–153
Manager, retail store	114.0	52–151
Stock clerk	111.8	54–151
Salesclerk	109.2	42–149
Auto serviceman	104.2	30–141
Carpenter (construction)	102.1	42–147
Cook and baker	97.2	20–147
Farmhand	91.4	24–141

SOURCE: Adapted from: Harrell, T. W., & Harrell, M. S., 1945, pp. 229–239.

who choose such careers. In other words, the average IQ for jobs like accountant and teacher is high because people with low IQs are not permitted to enter these occupations.

The column labeled "Range" in Table 12.1 shows the highest and lowest scores found for each occupation in this study. The *high* scores are remarkably similar for all occupations, from accountant down to farmhand, but the *low* scores differ from one job to another. What this implies is that people with high IQ scores have a wide selection of occupations from which to choose, while those with low IQ scores have a much narrower range. In other words, job choice is related to IQ for some people (those with low scores) but not for others (those with higher scores).

Intelligence and Job Success.   Even if job choice is based on intelligence, what about success on the job? Are the best teachers (or accountants or salesmen or electricians) the ones with the highest IQ scores? There have been scores of studies on this topic: Some have found a strong relationship between mental ability and success, some have found no relationship, and a few have even found that high IQ scores are associated with poor performance! However, if we divide these studies according to the kinds of jobs they considered (as suggested by Brody & Brody, 1976), we can make sense of the contradictory findings.

For jobs that have entrance requirements like advanced training and education, IQ is *not* related to success. Brilliant people are not, on the average, better teachers, engineers, doctors, or lawyers than less outstanding folks. The most probable explanation is that everyone who is allowed to enter these occupations is competent enough to do well. Differences in performance (like differences in college success among those who score high on entrance examinations) are likely due to factors like personality, motivation, creativity, or artistic talent.

For jobs that do not have entrance requirements, the specific job requirements seem to determine whether IQ is a good predictor of performance. If the job has intellectual content (such as secretarial or bookkeeping work), then people with higher IQs tend to be more skillful and accurate. On the other hand, if the job lacks intellectual content (as it does for factory workers or package wrappers), then higher IQs are not associated with better performance.

Do high IQ workers ever do worse on the job? Are some people really *overqualified* for dull and routine work? There does not seem to be any evidence that high IQ workers perform poorly on tasks like assembly-line work, but it does appear that their rates of tardiness, absenteeism, and job turnover are higher on jobs of this type. They can do the work satisfactorily, but they don't like it and don't keep on doing it if they can find other jobs.

Intelligence and Job Complexity. So far, we have considered intelligence to be a predictor, and job choice and success to be outcomes. Ask the question the other way now: How do jobs influence intelligence?

Melvin Kohn (1980) has defined an aspect of jobs that he calls **substantive complexity.** According to Kohn, substantive complexity is "the degree to which the work, in its very substance, requires thought and independent judgment" (Kohn, 1980, p. 197). Jobs that require making many decisions, especially those that have ill-defined decision rules, are high in substantive complexity. For example, a police officer's job is substantively more complex than a fire fighter's job for two reasons: It requires work with ideas and people more than with objects, and it involves decision making in more kinds of situations.

Kohn has done several studies linking the substantive complexity of jobs with what he calls the **intellectual flexibility** of workers in those jobs. By intellectual flexibility he means actual performance during an interview, things like the handling of perceptual and projective (personality) tests, the tendency to agree to things said by the interviewer, and so forth. Intellectual flexibility seems to be a fairly consistent trait among adults, but Kohn has shown that the substantive complexity of a job has a sizable influence on this measure of general cognitive power. That is, the more complex a person's present job is (at least among the men in a large survey study), the higher is his intellectual flexibility. Interestingly, the complexity of jobs held in the past is *not* a good predictor of this cognitive ability.

Some Cautions

We want to be sure to call to your attention some limitations on the kinds of studies we have been discussing, especially those concerned with employment. Most of the studies reported here (with the exception of Kohn's work on substantive complexity) are relatively old: Many were done during World War II, and some are products of the 1930s. More important, these studies had only one kind of subject: healthy, young, white American males. Today's job market includes many millions of workers who are women or members of minority groups. It is by no means obvious that the reported relationships between IQ and job choice and success would hold true for these groups of people.

Finally, these studies were done before the federal government enacted legislation such as the Equal Employment Opportunity Act. Job selection today is expected to be more on the basis of merit and less on the basis of family ties and influence than it was previously. Just as entrance requirements may change relationships between mental ability and job success, *changes* in those entrance requirements may change those relationships again. Studies from the past are interesting theoretically and historically and can give us many clues about the

BOX 12.1

Mental Tests and Employment

During the 1950s and 1960s most job seekers could expect to be given a test of general intelligence as part of the application process. This practice came under criticism for two reasons. First, as we have already seen, intelligence test scores are often not related to success on the job. Second, and probably more important, certain groups of people—especially racial minorities—tend to score poorly on such tests and saw them as a roadblock to obtaining better jobs.

In response to these criticisms, the federal government issued regulations in 1970 and 1971 designed to ensure the fair use of testing in job selection. The basic rule is a simple one: If an employer proposes using a test, he must show that scores on the test are related to job performance. Because traditional mental tests do not meet this criterion, industrial psychologists have looked for other ways to assess abilities that will be related to job performance.

INTERVIEWS

During an interview, a company representative talks individually with a job candidate. The hope is that the interviewer will be able to judge attributes like sincerity, general intelligence, and integrity from a short conversation. Needless to say, there is little evidence to suggest that information from interviews is any more related to job performance than test results are. Besides, there is *more* chance for an employer to discriminate against a minority group member, a female, or a handicapped person in an interview than in a traditional test.

WORK SAMPLING

It seems logical that the best predictor of performance on the job would be a task that is very much like the job, and that is the idea behind work sampling. Work samples can be as simple as typing or filing tests or as complicated as something called an "in-basket" test. The job candidate is given a stack of memos, letters, routine forms, and the like

that she might really have to deal with on the job. Her job is to take action on each of them, and her decisions are rated according to a preset scoring procedure. One study of the use of work samples to choose mechanics (Campion, 1972) found that performance on the samples was a better predictor of job performance than traditional tests were and, moreover, that the employees felt the procedure was fairer.

ASSESSMENT CENTERS

Another strategy for selecting employees, especially managers and executives, has been to use a combination of interview, testing, and work samples in a program called an "assessment center." A job applicant may spend from one to five days at such a center, so you can see that this is a very expensive alternative to paper-and-pencil testing. The research results suggest that the expense may be worthwhile. In one study of a large manufacturing company (Hinrichs, 1975), ratings made during an assessment center were compared with the corporate status of 30 managers made eight years later. The correlation between the assessments and job success was about .58. While this is a sizable correlation (about the same size as the relationship between childhood IQ and school achievement), it still means that many other factors enter into determining who will succeed in a job.

Interestingly, most studies of predicting job success do not take age in to account. Since verbal (and other crystallized) skills are generally increasing during the adult years and performance (and other fluid) skills are usually decreasing, we might expect that the accuracy of things like work samples might differ according to age.

In short, it appears that employers are turning away from tests of general cognitive power as predictors of job success and turning toward measures of specific job-related skills—which probably reflect cognitive styles and structure.

kinds of questions we should be asking today, but their results should most certainly not be the basis for public policy in the 1980s.

COGNITIVE STRUCTURE IN ADULTS

Up until now, we have discussed cognitive structure primarily in terms of Piaget's theory. This theory, though, does not have a great deal to say about cognition in adults. The final stage described is formal operations, which may begin as early as age 11 or 12 and is surely in place by the early twenties.

It seems to us that there are two questions that remain to be answered about cognitive structure in adulthood. First, are there any age changes in the abilities associated with cognitive structures? We have seen that there are some decrements in cognitive power late in the life span, and we need to ask whether this is also true of Piagetian-type tasks. Second, we need to ask whether cognitive *development* really ends with formal operations or whether there are additional *stages* in development during adulthood.

Age Changes in Cognitive Structures

We can begin to answer the first question by looking at studies in which researchers have given Piagetian tasks to adults of various ages and compared their performance to that of children.

Concrete and Formal Operations.   One study of this kind was conducted by Diane Papalia (1972). The participants in this research ranged in age from 6 to 74 years, and they were given several tasks, including conservation of number, substance, weight (all indicative of concrete operations), and volume (usually considered a formal operational task). Papalia's results are shown in Figure 12.7. As you can see, number conservation was the easiest task—it was done successfully by everyone over 7 years old. Volume conservation—the formal operations task—was clearly the most difficult. Although both younger (18 to 19 years) and older (55 to 64) subjects did well on this task, the elderly (over 65) did very poorly indeed.

Another cross-sectional study, this time using the "Twenty Questions" game, showed a similar result. Douglas and Nancy Denney (1973) played this game with groups of middle-aged (26- to 46-year-old) and elderly (75- to 90-year-old) women. The elderly women were much *less* likely to ask constraint questions (those that showed use of hierarchical categories) and much *more* likely to ask hypothesis questions (those that amounted to guessing one item after another), as you can see in Figure 12.8.

These cross-sectional studies have the same limitation as the ones

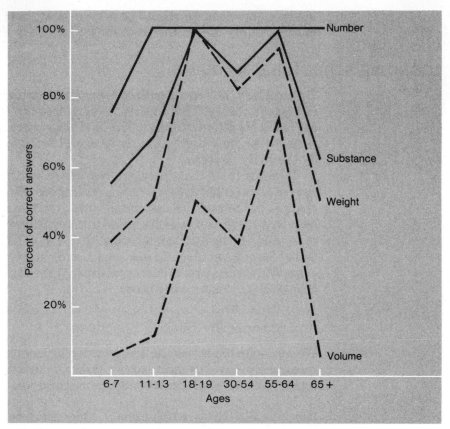

Figure 12.7. Conservation abilities over the life span. Conservation of volume—a formal operations task—is the hardest conservation task over the entire life span, but it is especially difficult for the elderly. (*Source:* Papalia, 1972.)

we looked at earlier about mental test performance: We cannot tell whether the older subjects *used* to perform more maturely but have stopped or whether they *never* could do the tasks at all. Since formal operational tasks are presumed to be related to education and since older cohorts are likely to have had less education than younger ones, the differences found in studies like Papalia's and Denney and Denney's may reflect educational differences more than age differences.

Unfortunately, we know of no longitudinal studies of these Piagetian-type tasks that will help us untangle these explanations. The closest we can come is a longitudinal study of problem solving done by D. Arenberg (1974). The subjects in this study initially ranged in age from 24 to 87 years; they were tested twice, six years apart. The cross-sectional comparisons showed that subjects over the age of 60 made significantly more errors than those below 60. On the other hand, the longitudinal data analysis revealed a decline only in individuals who were over 70. You will remember this same pattern of results on the Primary Mental Abilities Test: Longitudinal data show old-age decreases that are smaller and that occur later than those based on cross-sectional data.

Preoperational Thought.   At first glance, it seems rather foolish to think that any adults would be using preoperational levels of thought. However, we have just seen that there is evidence that some adults are *not* using concrete operations, and we need to explore whether they are using preoperational cognitive structures instead.

In Chapter 4 we described a study by Nancy Denney in which young preschoolers grouped objects into designs, while older children used groupings based on common features, such as size, color, or shape. This same study has also been done using middle-aged and elderly adults as subjects (Denney & Lennon, 1972). Middle-aged subjects almost universally used groupings based on categories, while elderly subjects frequently made the same kinds of designs that were made by the youngest children in the earlier study.

There is something unsettling about the idea of elderly people thinking like 2-year-olds. We'd like to know whether they are using

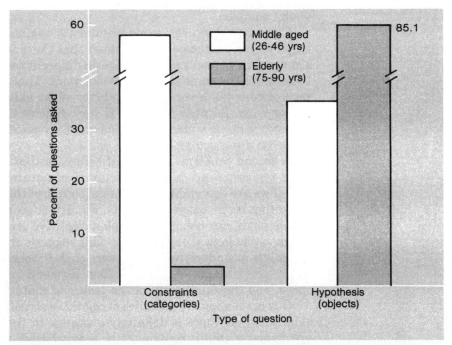

Figure 12.8. The "Twenty Questions" game played by middle-aged and elderly women. The elderly women used very few constraint questions but very many hypothesis queries. (*Source:* Denney & Denney, 1973, p. 277.)

this kind of classification because it is the only kind they are *able* to do (that is, poor competence) or because they prefer to for some reason (that is, poor performance). Nancy Denney (1974) explored this distinction in another study in which she *demonstrated* classification by similarity to a group of elderly people who had used design groupings in a previous trial. When she gave the subjects the cardboard shapes again, the ones who had seen the demonstration (often called *modeling*) changed their behavior sharply and sorted the pieces according to size and shape. The ones who had not seen a demonstration continued to sort the shapes in other ways. Judith Hornblum and Willis Overton (1976) performed a similar study using tests of area and volume conservation. They found that subjects who received training learned very quickly, often in just one trial, and were able to show conservation on other similar tasks as well.

Does Development Go Backward?   One very convenient way to sum up the changes we have described is to think of older adults *regressing*—going backward—in their cognitive development. Two pieces of evidence support this conclusion: Abilities that develop latest, like formal operations and the conservation of volume, seem to be most often missing among elderly subjects; and some behavior of the elderly, like the sorting of shapes and colors, looks very much like the behavior of very young children.

There are, however, some arguments against this interpretation. First, we have stressed several times that there is relatively little consistency in a person's performance on different tasks that are supposed to measure the same stage of development. That is, the ability to conserve area is not a very good predictor of the ability to conserve quantity or mass. Because of this, it is very difficult to tell whether or not a person is doing worse overall in concrete operational thought or just worse on a particular task.

A second problem, mentioned before, is that studies that seem to show regression are all cross-sectional in nature, so we can never be sure if we are describing changes that occur within individuals or only those that occur between cohorts. Finally, it seems clear that elderly people often *can* use more complex cognitive strategies than they *do* use in psychological experiments. This suggests that change may occur much less in underlying competence than it does in the variables that affect performance—variables like memory, motivation, response speed, and the familiarity of the task and materials.

Our conclusion from studies of cognitive structure in adults and the elderly is that there is definitely a change in the kinds of skills that are displayed, but it remains to be seen whether these changes reflect only performance declines or some combination of both competence and performance declines.

Is There a Fifth Stage of Cognitive Development?

Although Piaget admits that adults may become increasingly skillful at the use of logical thought processes after achieving the stage of formal operations, he does not think that any new *kinds* of thought develop after this time. In other words, an adult might reason more quickly or accurately as he gains maturity and experience, but he does not reason any differently.

Many theorists and researchers have been critical of this aspect of Piaget's theory, and some have proposed a fifth stage of cognition to account for differences they believe occur after the mastery of formal operations.

Problem Finding.   One suggestion, made by Patricia Kennedy Arlin (1975, 1977), is that the fifth stage be labeled **problem finding.** You might think of problem finding skills as being the natural extension of divergent thinking skills. In divergent thinking, people put together ideas in new ways, or think of new uses for objects, or think of a variety of meanings for words or phrases. In problem finding, people put together ideas in ways that create new *problems,* rather than new *answers.* In fact, in doing her studies, Arlin used a set of objects similar to those used in studies of creativity and insightful problem solving. However, instead of asking what they could be *used* for, she asked what kinds of *problems* they suggested.

Unfortunately, the studies that have explored this theory have had conflicting results: Some found that problem finding was more advanced than formal operations, while others found that the two were not related. Whether or not this particular theory is supported by data, the idea of there being other kinds of adult thought not included in Piaget's theory is an important addition to developmental psychology.

Dialectical Operations.   Another extension of Piaget's theory was advocated by the late Klaus Riegel (1973). He argued that the problem with Piaget's theory is that formal thought is *not* the most mature kind of thought. According to Riegel, *mature* thought is characterized by the acceptance that things can be both true and not true at the same time. He used the word **dialectical,** borrowed from philosophy, to describe this contradictory state of affairs. In fact, Riegel believed that every stage of cognitive development could be described in dialectical terms. For example, the person using concrete operations must deal with the fact that two lumps of clay are simultaneously the *same* (in amount or mass) and *different* (in shape). The person using formal operations must understand that two pendulums may look different (one with a heavy weight at the end and one with a light weight), but they will still perform in the same way (swing at the same speed). In terms of the cognitive themes we have used to describe Piaget's theory, Riegel is focusing on the themes of constancies and classification. Where Piaget emphasized that the child has to *resolve* these contradictions by building new cognitive structures, Riegel emphasizes that the child—and the adult—have to *accept* them.

Riegel's theory of dialectical operations has been very influential among life span psychologists, especially those in Europe. Even those psychologists, though, who do not accept it find the theory a useful reminder that many individuals use concrete operations skillfully and flexibly in their lives, and their cognitive achievements should not be belittled.

COGNITIVE STYLE IN ADULTS

Of course, Riegel is not the only psychologist who recognizes that there are many ways of thinking. Most of the researchers and theorists concerned with styles of thought in adults have focused on one of three ways of describing them: perceptual, categorizational, or creative.

Perceptual Styles

Reflectivity versus Impulsivity.   Adults, like children, can be categorized as either having a reflective or an impulsive style. As you will remember, reflective people are those who take a long time to respond to a test item but usually get it correct, while impulsive people give quick responses that are more frequently incorrect. It is a little like the difference between the tortoise (reflective) and the hare (impulsive), and some authors (like Botwinick, 1973) have suggested that older adults prefer to be tortoises. The notion is that the elderly may be slower (and we have seen that there is certainly a biological basis for that finding) but that they would be correspondingly more accurate.

Nancy Denney and Judith List (1979) explored this commonsense idea using the Matching Familiar Figures test. Each item on this test consists of one standard figure and six similar alternatives, from which the subject must pick the one that is identical to the standard. As expected, the latency of responses (that is, the amount of time it took for the subject to answer) was longer for older subjects than it was for younger ones. However, contrary to the tortoise-and-hare theory, the older subjects did not make *fewer* errors; they made *more* (shown in Figure 12.9). Even when Denney and List reanalyzed their data—taking into account the subjects' age, sex, education, occupation, and retirement—they got the same results: Older subjects were both slower *and* less accurate than younger ones.

One of the problems of this definition of perceptual style is that it assumes that speed and accuracy will always go together—faster will be less accurate and slower will be more accurate. Since this is appar-

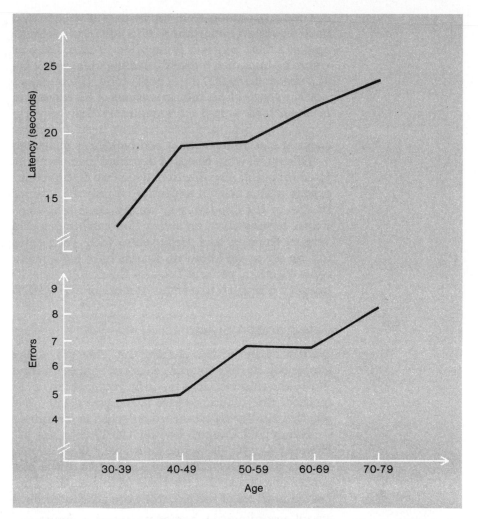

Figure 12.9. Adult performance on the Matching Familiar Figures Test. On this test of reflectivity versus impulsivity, older adults show slower responding (longer latencies) and more errors. This suggests that slow responding indicates a decay in ability, rather than just an attempt to avoid errors. (*Source:* Denney & List, 1979.)

ently not true among older adults (nor among some younger people, for that matter), we need to be very careful in applying this theory to their cognitive behaviors. We can't help wishing that there were some longitudinal data about the development of response speed and accuracy over the adult years; maybe by the next edition of this book, there will be.

Mental Imagery.   Another mental style that seems to be important in adult thought is the use of mental images (Shepard, 1978). Mental images are simply the pictures that we see in our mind's eye, and there are many anecdotes from the history of science that suggest that they have played an important part in advancing scientific theories. For example, Albert Einstein is reported to have done mental experiments where he imagined himself traveling alongside a beam of light moving at a speed of 186,000 miles per second. His famous theory of relativity was the result of his interpretations of his mental experiences. In fact, Einstein later stated quite explicitly that he very rarely thought in words at all. Similar anecdotes have been told about discoveries in the areas of electromagnetism and biological molecular structures.

Of course, what Shepard describes as mental imagery is closely related to spatial visualization, which we discussed in Chapter 9. Not everyone who is skillful at spatial visualization, though, can use mental images in the creative way we are describing here. It is almost as if we are talking about an ability that combines spatial thinking with divergent thinking and perhaps also with Arlin's stage of problem finding. So far as we know, no studies have been made to link these concepts together, perhaps because the really remarkable use of mental imagery is limited to a small number of extraordinarily gifted people.

Categorization Styles

We saw earlier in this chapter that elderly people sometimes classify simple objects (like colored geometric shapes) in ways that are very similar to the classifications made by young children. Since categorization methods are sometimes used to indicate cognitive style, we might ask whether similar results are found when more complex stimuli are used.

Nancy and Douglas Denney (1982) used the 42 pictures from the "Twenty Questions" game in a study of categorization. The experimenter asked each subject to choose two of the pictures that went together and to explain the basis of this choice. The procedure was repeated until all of the pictures were accounted for. Each response was scored according to whether it showed a similarity relationship (two red items, two heavy items, two cooking utensils) or a complementary relationship (hat and coat, cow and barn). Since there were many ways that these 42 pictures could be paired, the researchers were interested only in the reasons for the choices, not in which pictures were actually named.

You can see on the left side of Figure 12.10 that older people in this study were more likely to use complementary relationships, while younger ones were more likely to use similarity relationships. On the right side of Figure 12.10 are the results of the game of "Twenty Questions" played by these same subjects. Classification by similarity is associated with asking constraint questions, while classification by complementary relationships is associated with using hypothesis questions.

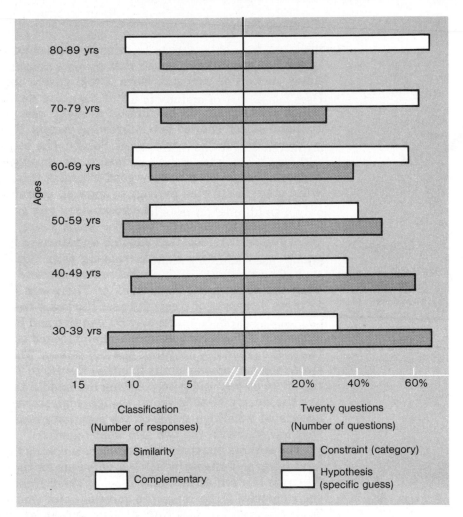

Figure 12.10. The relationship between classification and questioning strategies among adults. Older subjects tend to make fewer classifications that are based on similarity and to ask more hypothesis questions than younger people. (*Source:* Denney & Denney, 1982.)

Other studies of classification have asked adults to put pictures and objects into groups, rather than just asking about pairs. The advantage of this strategy is that the researcher can look at more characteristics of the categories used, such as how many objects are in each group, how abstract the groupings are, and the proportion of items that are successfully grouped. Studied like this (for example, Kogan, 1974) have found almost the same results that Denney and Denney did: Older subjects depend more upon the relationships between objects, and less upon the similarities between them, in making their categories.

Creative Styles

We are delighted to include creativity in this chapter, because it is one of the few cognitive variables that shows a consistent *rise* during the adult years. For example, Horn (1981) gave a test called "Common Uses" as a part of a study of adult cognitive development. This test, which asks the subject to think of as many uses as possible for some common object, showed two interesting results. First, scores did show an increase over the adult years. Second, the scores were correlated with age-related increases in crystallized intelligence. Horn's result suggests that people who show good divergent thinking skills are somewhat more likely than average to show an overall increase (although only a small one) on tests like vocabulary and general information.

Increases in creativity over the adult years have been found by other researchers, too. Gail Jaquish and Richard Ripple (1981), for example, used auditory stimuli (ranging from thunderstorm noises to electronically synthesized cymbal rolls) and asked adults to write down what the noises made them think of. There was a pattern of increase in three measures of creativity over the years from 18 to 60, followed by lower scores for subjects over 60. Jaquish and Ripple also gave these subjects a self-esteem questionnaire and looked at the relationship between the creativity measures and self-esteem. There were no links between the two among adults in either the 18- to 25-year-old group nor the 26- to 39-year-old group. Among the middle adults (40 to 60 years) and the elderly (60 to 84 years), though, high scores on self-esteem were associated with high scores on the creativity measures (which means that low scores on the two also went together).

The authors interpret this finding as meaning that older adults may have lower self-esteem (which was only true for the oldest subjects) and that this low self-esteem may prevent them from expressing some of their creative ideas. Since the questionnaire was given *after* the creativity assessment, we would be inclined to think that perhaps elderly people who had done well on the task may have felt better about themselves and gotten higher scores on self-esteem because of it. Whichever is correct, studies like this one are an important start at looking at the links between cognitive styles and personality traits.

POWER, STRUCTURE, AND STYLE

Information Processing by Experts

All of the tests for determining cognitive style in adults use materials and procedures that are somewhat artificial. Cognitive psychologists, on the other hand, have often focused on the ways in which people use their mental processes on real-life tasks. One method used to do this is to compare experts and novices on tasks like playing chess or solving physics problems. These studies have focused on expertise rather than on age—that is, they have compared people who differ in their training and skill, rather than those who differ in age. So although these studies are not strictly developmental, they do give us some hints about the ways that more mature thinkers may differ from less mature ones.

A study of three chess players done by William Chase and Herbert Simon (1973) will give you the flavor of some of this research (and perhaps remind you of the study by Chi [1978] on young chess players that we mentioned in Chapter 4). Chase and Simon compared a chess master, a "class A" chess expert (who had won his ranking in organized play), and a beginner (who had played fewer than 100 hours of chess). In one of their experiments, they placed chess pieces on a board in a configuration that might be found during a game and let each subject look at it for 5 seconds. When asked to recall the location of the pieces, the chess master was clearly superior, with the expert and novice less accurate. When the same pieces were put on the board in *random* order, though, there was no difference in recall among the three.

Then Chase and Simon wanted to know if this difference was primarily *perceptual,* that is, if it concerned how the players *saw* the board; or if it was primarily *conceptual,* that is, if it concerned how the players *thought* about the board. To find out, they videotaped the players doing a much simpler task, simply looking at pieces on one chess board and reproducing the arrangement on another board. Although memory was not involved, they found an interesting difference between the three players. The master (and, to a lesser extent, the expert) would look at the sample board, then quickly place several pieces that were grouped together. Cognitive psychologists refer to this as *"chunking"* and generally interpret such behavior to mean that these pieces were somehow mentally organized together.

Similar studies have been done comparing physicists and physics students on the way they solve physics problems (Larkin, McDermott, Simon, & Simon, 1980). Here again, the secret of expertise seems to be in the chunking together of information. If you have ever taken a course in physics, you know that most problems require you to read some information, then choose appropriate equations to describe the situation, and solve for the unknown quantity. Sometimes the information does not directly fit the equations, and intermediate calculations are necessary before the problem can be solved. Physicists seem to be able to do those intermediate calculations much more automatically than beginners do and to use characteristics of the problem to pick the appropriate equations more quickly.

From the descriptions of both kinds of experts, the process seems to combine aspects of conceptualization (putting things together in groups to remember them) and spatial visualization (using physical or logical relationships to make the groupings). It may be that this represents a high-level integration of left- and right-brain activities. That is, a chess master may chunk together five or six pieces (an analytical, left-brain activity) but recognize and remember them in a holistic way (an intuitive, right-brain activity).

Of course, the kinds of specific problem-solving abilities required for chess playing and physics are probably no more common to everyday life for most of us than are classification rules for pictures. However, research like this suggests that the study of experts—and how they think—may provide models of cognitive development that are not captured by more simple experimental methods.

BOX 12.2

Intelligence, Experience, and Leadership

When we think about people who are leaders, we often get a mental picture of someone who is older, smarter, and wiser than ourselves. Studies of leadership, though, have usually found that there is almost no relationship between skill as a leader and traditional measures of intelligence (Stogdill, 1974) or of experience (Fiedler, 1967).

Some recent research by psychologist Fred Fiedler and his colleagues suggests that both intelligence and experience may be important—but just how important depends upon how stressful the work situation is and what kind of task is to be accomplished. In a series of studies (summarized by Fiedler, 1982) in various military organizations, the researchers obtained measures of intelligence (from paper-and-pencil tests), experience (from the amount of time spent in the service), performance (as rated by superiors), and stress (the extent to which the subject got along with his own boss).

Overall, these variables were not related to one another. Men with high and low intelligence were equally likely to give good performance, as were men with more and less experience, or more and less stress with their bosses. However, when you look separately at those men who have high stress with their bosses, the picture changes.

In high stress situations, there was no association between intelligence and performance, but there was between *experience* and performance. In other words, in difficult situations, it was helpful to "know the ropes." In low stress situations, the findings were just the reverse: Experience was not related to good performance, but *intelligence* was. That is, when things are going well, intelligence is very useful in leadership.

Of course, there are other kinds of stress besides not getting along with the boss. Some jobs, like fire fighting, are stressful most of the time. A study of fire fighters' performance under high and low stress conditions (Frost, Fiedler, & Anderson, in press) also found the experienced officers performed best under situations of stress.

None of this is really very surprising. We noted earlier that many jobs don't have much intellectual content, and this seems to be true of leadership jobs as well as follower jobs. If you have ever had a supervisory job, you probably found that at least as much energy went into handling people as went into handling the job itself. Tests of intelligence—at least the ones we have now—do not predict success in handling people.

Unexercised and Optimally Exercised Abilities

We would like to end this chapter by looking at a model of mental development that may seem more biological than psychological. You have probably noticed that a large number of studies of adult cognition have been done by Nancy Denney and her colleagues, and this model is her attempt to integrate many of these research results (Denney, 1982).

Denney's theory is based on the comparison of two different levels of performance on most abilities. The first is the level of performance that could be accomplished by a normal healthy person living in a normal healthy environment, without any special training or unusual experience with the task. The second is the level of performance of that same normal healthy person, but this time with the optimal amount of training and experience. Denney refers to these as **unexercised** and **optimally exercised** abilities, and the normal life course of each of these is shown in general terms in Figure 12.11.

What we think is especially exciting about this theory is that it not only describes changes on specific mental tests, it also describes several other sets of data that we have looked at in this chapter and the last.

Physical Abilities.   We saw in Chapter 11 that several physical abilities (such as running speed, strength, and endurance) display much the pattern shown in Figure 12.11. For most people, the curve looks like the lower line (and the word *unexercised* may be particularly appropri-

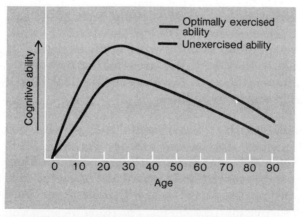

Figure 12.11. Denney's theory of unexercised and optimally exercised abilities in adulthood. The shape of these curves may vary for some abilities, but the relationship between exercised and unexercised abilities should remain the same. (*Source:* Denney, 1982.)

ate here!); while for athletes and other people in top physical condition, the curve looks like the upper line. In fact, when Denney explains her theory, she uses running speed as an example of an ability described by these curves.

Longitudinal and Cross-sectional Data.   We noted several times earlier in this chapter that longitudinal data seem to show better performance and later (and smaller) declines with age than cross-sectional data. In fact, if you were to go back and look at Figure 12.5, you'll see it looks very much like the graph of Denney's theory. Why do cross-sectional data look like unexercised abilities and longitudinal data look like optimally exercised ones?

The answer is probably found in a methodological problem we have not yet discussed. The people who stay in longitudinal studies tend to differ from those in cross-sectional studies in some potentially important ways. For one thing, they did not die or become disabled (if they had, they wouldn't still be in the study), nor did they lose interest in being in the study or move away. Several researchers have shown that longitudinal participants (compared to dropouts) are healthier, better educated, and financially better off. We suspect, then, that longitudinal participants are optimally exercised in several ways. This fact, along with the cohort differences we discussed earlier, is probably what makes Denney's theory fit these data.

Differential Ability Data.   If you will go back and look at Figure 12.2, you'll see another graph that looks very much like Denney's theory. This was the graph that compared Verbal and Performance IQ scores over the adult years. Most adults probably do not exercise the abilities that are measured by the Performance tests, which include putting pictures in order to tell a story and completing jigsaw puzzles. Verbal skills, on the other hand, are practiced every day, and the level of these skills over the adult years does, in fact, look like Denney's graph of optimally exercised abilities.

Task Difficulty.   Some mental and physical tasks are more difficult than others, and Denney's theory lets us look at the effects of task difficulty at different parts of the age span. In Figure 12.12 we have redrawn the curves for exercised and unexercised abilities and have also shown you two sets of tasks with items of varying difficulty—swimming and solving math problems. The thing we want you to see in this graph is that exercising an ability has two effects: First, it makes it possible to do more difficult tasks; and second, it makes it possible to do them for longer portions of the life span.

Aside from the fact that it helps us to understand several different phenomena, we think this theory of mental development has another

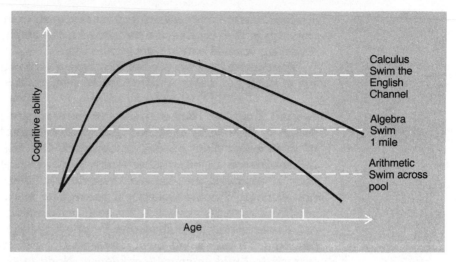

Figure 12.12. Denney's theory applied to tasks that differ in difficulty. Exercising an ability makes it possible to do more difficult tasks and to do them for a longer portion of the life span. (*Source:* Denney, 1982.)

important contribution to make. It describes the way in which experience—which includes training, practice, education, and the like—builds upon innate abilities to produce individual patterns of skills and abilities.

What Is Optimal Exercise?

Of course, this entire theory only makes sense if we can demonstrate that providing optimal exercise actually does increase abilities and lengthen the portion of the life span where they can be displayed. There have been several different kinds of exercise studied, some based on direct training of skills and some based on indirect training.

Direct Training.   Earlier in this chapter we mentioned one study (Denney, 1974) that showed how direct training through modeling could change the classification strategies used by elderly subjects. Another study by Nancy Denney, done with Frances Jones and Susan Krigel (1979), compared several ways of modifying the questioning strategies used by adults and young children playing the game of "Twenty Questions." One training method emphasized *classifying* the pictures into groups. A second method emphasized *using information* obtained with each question; and the third emphasized actually *using constraint questions.* For both the younger and adult subjects (all of whom had failed to use constraint questions during a pretest), the instruction on exactly how to use constraint questions was the most effective training. In a second experiment, these same authors compared the usefulness of *de-*

scribing constraint questions and *modeling* an example of such a question. Again the results were the same for the children and the elderly: Modeling worked better than explaining.

The conclusion from studies like these seems to be that direct training of skills can make a difference on performance.

Indirect Training.   Some researchers have suggested that poor performance by the elderly on some cognitive tasks might be caused by levels of motivation, time needed to complete the task, or the subject's self-confidence. In yet another study, Nancy Denney (1980) systematically investigated the effects of these factors upon performance in the now famous "Twenty Questions" game. She increased motivation by providing monetary rewards for good performance, she gave subjects extra time to plan their strategies for playing the game, and she administered some easy items from another test (which the subjects all got correct) to build their self-confidence. None of these manipulations (which qualify as experience if not exactly training) made a significant difference in the number of questions it took the subjects to guess the correct object.

Another way of investigating indirect training has to do with the way problems are chosen for an experiment, rather than what kind of instructions the subjects are given. Nancy Denney and Ann Palmer (1981) compared subjects' responses to the traditional "Twenty Questions" game (which we would think she would be tired of by now!) with their responses to more realistic and lifelike problems. Here's an example of one of the problems they used:

> Now let's say that one evening you go to the refrigerator and you notice that it is not cold inside, but rather, it's warm. What would you do? (Denney & Palmer, 1981, p. 325)

Answers to these problems were scored on the basis of how many solutions were suggested and how active a part the subject took in the solution. For this problem, calling a repair person scored two points, while trying to fix it himself (by checking the fuse box, for instance) scored three points. The assumption in this study was that the real-life problems would represent exercised abilities, while the "Twenty Questions" game would represent unexercised ones.

In fact, the results (which we have shown you in Figure 12.13) suggest that this is true. Scores on the real-life problems increase through ages 50 to 59 and then decline only slightly. Scores on the "Twenty Questions" game, on the other hand, peak in a younger age group (30 to 39) and decrease considerably after that.

Taken together, these studies suggest that with unexercised tasks, changing the circumstances of testing or providing indirect training

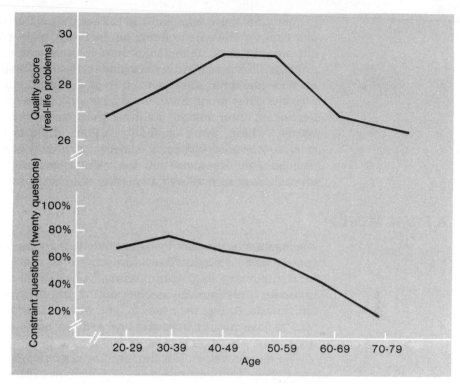

Figure 12.13. Adult performance on real-life problems compared to the game of "Twenty Questions." Although these two tasks were scored in different ways, it is difficult to make a direct comparison. However, it appears that practical problem solving shows a smaller decline among the elderly than laboratory problem solving does. (*Source:* Denney & Palmer, 1981.)

has little effect on performance. However, changing the *task* to an exercised one makes a big difference.

General Training. Finally, we can ask whether or not there is any general mental exercise that helps to keep mental abilities at high levels over the life span (like a cognitive sit up, perhaps). One answer comes from the study by Horn (1981) of creativity and intelligence. His results seemed to show that adults who exhibited high levels of divergent thinking also had continuing gains on tests like vocabulary and general knowledge, that are measures of crystallized intelligence. It's easy to imagine divergent thinking—generating new possibilities and ideas—as being exercise for the mind.

Another answer comes from studies that have looked at differences between elderly people (members of the same cohort) with differing levels of education. June Blum and Lissy Jarvik (1974), for instance, gathered a group of 54 octogenarians—people over 80 years of age. They divided the group into those who had attended high school (32 people) and those who had not (22 people). All of them had been out of school for 60 years or more; but even so, the people with high school educations scored higher than those with only elementary school backgrounds. The investigators also had test scores for these same individuals obtained when they were in their sixties. Looking at the two tests together, they found that the subjects with more education showed less *decline* in their mental abilities than those with less education. Of course, there were probably other differences between these groups—the ones with more education probably had held more intellectual jobs, for instance—but the results certainly suggest that early mental exercise is related to mental abilities throughout the life span.

A FINAL WORD

We began this chapter by asking about the cause of a specific mental decline (SM's grandmother). The answer to that question seems to be (as it is on many final examinations) "all of the above." Mental abilities in adults, and especially in older adults, are the product of many different factors. Aging, poor health, and lack of mental exercise all play a part in determining how, and how well, an adult can use her cognitive abilities.

We should also notice that studies of adult intelligence show much less division into our categories of power, structure, and style than did studies of children and youth. Research on cognitive power, especially using the PMA, seems to overlap research on problem solving and formal operations. Studies of cognitive styles and of information processing are related to the optimal exercise of Denney's theory and perhaps also to cerebral specialization. While there is still no single point of view to explain *all* about cognitive development, we are beginning to bridge the gaps.

SUMMARY

1. Data from cross-sectional studies on traditional IQ tests show that intelligence begins to decline at about age 30.
2. Different mental abilities (verbal versus performance IQ or fluid versus crystallized intelligence) show different patterns of age changes, with verbal abilities and general knowledge showing later and smaller declines than nonverbal abilities.
3. Studies that use longitudinal comparisons show fewer and later declines than those that use cross-sectional comparisons.
4. Some of the decline among very old people may be due to terminal drop, a somewhat sudden decrease in abilities that precedes death.
5. Scores on mental tests are related to job choices, but people with high scores have many more available alternatives than those with low scores.

6. Scores on mental tests are related to job performance only for careers with few entrance requirements that have some intellectual content.

7. Having an intellectually challenging job (that is, one high on substantive complexity) seems to help increase intellectual flexibility among adults.

8. Cross-sectional studies of performance on Piagetian tasks show the same deficits in the elderly as studies of cognitive power.

9. Although some older subjects show preoperational reasoning in experiments, they can often be quickly taught to use more advanced reasoning. This suggests that experiments may not adequately tap competence in these areas.

10. Several theorists have suggested that there may be a fifth stage of cognitive development, but the research results so far have failed to demonstrate one.

11. Older adults seem to show a perceptual style—slow responses *and* errors—which is not described by the theory of reflectivity/impulsivity.

12. Mental imagery is probably an important cognitive style among adults, but little is known about its development.

13. Studies of categorization styles have shown that older subjects use relationship categories rather than similarity categories.

14. Creativity, as measured by divergent thinking tests, seems to increase over the adult years; and higher levels of creativity are associated with continued gains in general mental ability.

15. Information-processing studies of expert chess players and physicists show that they make extensive use of chunking in memory and recall and that their skills may involve spatial skills as well as analytical ones.

16. Denney's theory of exercised and unexercised abilities describes mental development in adulthood and helps to explain other research results as well.

17. Direct training on cognitive tasks seems to serve as appropriate exercise to improve performance.

18. Indirect training is less successful as a method of exercising mental abilities. However, when tasks are chosen that are highly familiar to subjects so that we can assume they have been naturally exercised, performance is improved.

KEY TERMS

Cohort   A group of individuals born at about the same time. Members of different cohorts always differ in age, and they may also differ in specific and historic experiences.

Crystallized intelligence   Mental abilities that depend upon education and experience. Most verbal skills, such as vocabulary and comprehension, are crystallized skills.

Dialectical operations   Fifth stage of intellectual development, according to Riegel, that involves accepting that objects and events can have contradictory properties.

Fluid intelligence   Mental abilities that depend more upon the integrity of the central nervous system and less upon training or experience.

Intellectual flexibility   General mental ability as revealed in a person-to-person situation like an interview.

Optimally exercised ability   The level of ability shown by a person who has received special training in an area or who has extensive experience. Optimally exercised abilities show smaller and later declines with age than do unexercised abilities.

PMA (Primary Mental Abilities   Test) Test of adult mental abilities, based on the work of Thurstone and often interpreted in terms of fluid and crystallized intelligence.

Problem finding   Fifth stage of intellectual development, suggested by Arlin, in which individuals increase their ability to see what problems are suggested by a set of materials or circumstances.

Substantive complexity   The degree to which a job requires thought and independent judgment. Jobs that deal with people or with data are usually (though not always) more substantively complex than those that deal with objects.

Terminal drop   A rapid decline that occurs shortly before death. WAIS scores have been demonstrated to show terminal drop.

Unexercised ability   The level of ability that we expect to find in a normal healthy person living in a normal environment.

SUGGESTED READINGS

Baltes, P. B., & Schaie, K. W. Aging and IQ: The myth of the twilight years. *Psychology Today,* 1974, 7 (No. 10), 35–40.
This is a nontechnical but reasonably complete account of the work done by Schaie and Baltes comparing longitudinal and cross-sectional research designs. Not all psychologists agree that old-age declines in IQ are myths, but these authors make a convincing case.

Denney, N. W. Aging and cognitive changes. In B. B. Wolman (Ed.), *Handbook of developmental psychology.* Englewood Cliffs, N.J.: Prentice-Hall, 1982.
This is an excellent review of cognitive changes in the later years combined with a clear description of her theory about these changes (which we discussed at some length in this chapter). It is not suitable for casual reading, but if you are seriously interested in knowing more about the topic, this is the place to begin.

Hebb, D. O. On watching myself get old. *Psychology Today,* 1978, *12,* 15–23.
This is a wonderful, personal paper by one of the most distinguished psychologists today. Not only does he tell about all of the changes that have occurred in his thought processes, he links it up with some of his own important theoretical work.

PROJECT 12.1
Thinking in the Elderly

In this project, we would like you to use two of the experimental tasks that have been used in many studies of thinking in people of varying ages, "Twenty Questions" and sorting.

Subjects

You will need to interview an elderly person to collect data for this project. The person should be over 65, in reasonably good health (although possibly bedridden), and not suffering any mental problems (like continual confusion). We think this project is especially interesting if you work together as a class and get some elderly people who are living independently and others who are living in group settings, like retirement homes or nursing homes.

If you already know the person you are going to interview, you need only explain that you are doing a class project and want to ask them to work some problems for you. If you don't know the person, arrange for someone to introduce you. If the person is a resident in some group facility, it is important that you tell someone in charge there what you are doing and reassure them that this is only a class project. Your instructor may even ask you to get formal permission—you should check about this before you begin.

Materials

For the "Twenty Questions" game you will need to put together a card (9 × 12 or larger) with pictures of at least 24 common objects. If you are artistic, you can draw them yourself; otherwise, you can cut them out of children's picture books, catalogs, or whatever. You should pick items that can be put together in categories (several kinds of toys, machines, kitchen utensils, perhaps) and that your subject will be sure to know. Different breeds of cat, for example, might be too specialized for the person you are going to interview.

For the sorting task, you will need to cut shapes from sturdy construction paper or cardboard: three shapes (circle, square, triangle) in each of three colors (red, blue, yellow) in each of two sizes (small and big). That's 18 pieces altogether.

Procedure

After you have chatted for a few minutes with the subject, show him the card with the pictures on it and read the following instructions:

"I am thinking of one of these pictures and it is your job to try to determine which picture it is. The way you do this is by asking questions—any question at all as long as I can answer it either 'yes' or 'no.' So go ahead and ask a question and try to discover which picture I'm thinking about in the fewest number of questions possible" (Denney & Denney, 1982, p. 191).

Write down each question that the subject uses, word for word if you can. After you are finished, get out the colored shapes and read this set of directions:

"Now I'd like you to sort out these pieces for me in whatever way seems best. Put them into groups so that the pieces in each group go together. You can make as many or as few groups as you want, just so the pieces in each group belong together."

When the subject finishes, write down the groupings. When you are finished, be sure to thank the person for his help.

Report

First, classify each question used in the "Twenty Questions" game as being a *constraint* question (asking about a category) or a *hypothesis* (asking about a specific item). Then, look at the way in which the person sorted the geometric shapes—is it based on *similarity* (color, shape, size) or on *complementarity* (designs or other arrangements).

In your report, try to answer the following questions:

1. What strategy did your subject use in the game of "Twenty Questions"? Did he use this consistently and systematically?
2. How many questions did it take for the subject to guess the correct item? How many questions do you think it would take you?
3. What strategy did the subject use in the sorting task? Did he use this consistently and systematically? How many groups did he use?
4. Are your subjects' responses consistent with the results reported by Denney & Denney (1982)? That is, if he used constraint questions did he also sort on the basis of similarity, or if he used hypothesis questions did he also sort on the basis of complementary relationships? If you are working with your classmates, how many of the subjects showed one of these patterns?
5. If you are comparing those who live independently with those in a group residence, is there any difference between these two groups? Is one group more likely to use constraint questions, or to guess the "Twenty Questions" item in few tries, or to use grouping based on similarity? If you find such differences, how would you account for them?
6. Do you think these two tasks represent exercised or unexercised problems for your subject? Do you think this had any effect on his performance?

Chapter 13
The Self and Personality
in Adulthood

DEVELOPMENTAL PATTERNS IN ADULT ROLES
Changes in Family Roles during Adulthood
Work Roles in Adulthood
Blending Work and Family Roles
Sex Roles in Adulthood
PERSONALITY IN ADULTHOOD: CONTINUITY AND CHANGE
Consistencies in Personality in Adulthood
Changes in Personality in Adulthood
PERSONALITY IN ADULTHOOD: A SYNTHESIS AND A FINAL LOOK
SUMMARY
KEY TERMS
SUGGESTED READINGS
PROJECT

Yesterday was my forty-third birthday. As usual I got up and ran my daily 5 miles, then went to the university for a morning's work. I met with colleagues to plan for a large research project we are beginning, turned out a mountain of memos to everyone, and left the secretaries with a heap of typing. (As I left, I said to one of them: "You'll be sorry I came in today!") At noon I went with a group of colleagues to a twice-weekly aerobic dance class (got to keep that "aging" body in shape), and conferred briefly with Sandy Mitchell about this book. Later I had lunch with two other colleague-friends, stood in line for tickets to the evening's play-off game of the Seattle SuperSonics (of which I am an unrepentant, dyed-in-the-wool fan), talked to my father on the phone, and had an unexpected visit from my 21-year-old son and his steady girl friend, who brought flowers for my birthday (amazing!). Finally, I went out to dinner and to the basketball game with a friend I have known all my life (and watched the Sonics lose by two points in the last 5 seconds of the game).

I confess that in some ways this was not a typical day. It was more full and complicated than many days. In fact, the really striking thing about it is how many different roles were involved: colleague, employer, coauthor, student, daughter, mother, friend, and fan. There was also a highly ambiguous but interesting role with my son's girl friend—one I think I have not yet mastered.[HB]

We have talked about roles before. The shift from preschooler to school-age child is a change in role as well as a change in cognitive level. The development of intimate relationships in the early twenties involves both a new set of skills and the acquisition of the major new roles of *partner* or *spouse* or *husband* or *wife*.

Indeed, the transition from teenager to adult involves the accumulation of a large number of new roles, including work roles, family roles, and even redefined sex roles. Over the adult years, those roles undergo some further changes, changes that are shared by many people in our society. Since a person's identity is partially defined by the collection of roles she occupies, we can understand the changes in the self that take place during adulthood by looking at the ways those roles change with age.

However, the self—the personality—is more than just roles. There are also persisting temperamental qualities and differences in the ways people handle the tasks they must confront. There may also be systematic *changes* in personality over the adult years as well, such as increasing maturity or greater personality integration.

These issues should be familiar ones by now. We are asking whether there are developmental changes over adulthood and whether at the same time there are individual differences in the way adult tasks are handled.

The questions are complicated and the research evidence is sparse. Psychologists have studied personality in adulthood, and sociologists have studied roles in adulthood, but neither group has talked much about the *developmental* patterns. Still, the information is accumulating, and we know quite a lot more than we did even four years ago when we last wrote about this topic. Let us begin by looking at what we know about role changes during adulthood and then turn to continuities and changes in personality.

DEVELOPMENTAL PATTERNS IN ADULT ROLES

Each of us occupies many roles—a point we tried to illustrate at the beginning of the chapter. It is oversimplifying things, of course, to divide these roles into sets, since they interact in complex ways, but let us nonetheless divide our discussion into three areas: **family roles, work roles,** and **sex roles.** This grouping does not include all the roles occupied by adults (where does *fan* or even *friend* fit, for example?). But these three sets of roles all appear to show systematic change over the adult years.

Changes in Family Roles during Adulthood

Evelyn Duvall (1957, 1977) was one of the first to propose that a family had a life cycle of its own that was more than merely the sum of the life cycles of the individual members. She divided the family life cycle into eight stages, which we presented in abbreviated form in Table 1.6 in Chapter 1 and which we have repeated in Table 13.1. Most stages

TABLE 13.1
Stages of the Family Life Cycle

I.	Married couples, without children	Typically this period lasts about two years.
II.	New parents	This stage is defined as the period from the birth of the first child until that child is 30 months old.
III.	Preschool children	The oldest child is between 30 months and 6 years.
IV.	School children	Oldest child is between 6 and 12.
V.	Adolescent children	Oldest child is between 13 and about 18 or 20, depending on when the oldest child leaves home.
VI.	Children leaving home	Sometimes called the *launching-center* period of family life. This lasts from the time the first child leaves home until the last one departs.
VII.	Last child gone	Sometimes called the *postparental* period or the *empty nest* period. This period lasts from the departure of the last child until retirement from work.
VIII.	Aging family	In Duvall's system, this period lasts from retirement to the death of both spouses, on average a period of 10 to 15 years.

involve the addition or loss of family members by birth or death or by departure from the family unit. Some involve a change in role of members within the group, such as when the eldest child goes off to school or becomes a teenager.

As an adult moves from one of these stages to the next, new roles are acquired or shed. A woman becomes not only wife but mother, a man becomes not only husband but father. The process is not merely one of adding new roles but of adapting to changes in the old roles at the same time. Being a wife *and* mother is not just the sum of two unconnected roles, for example, since the spousal roles change with the birth of the first child, too. The couple spends less uninterrupted time together, and their activities together change as well. The parenting role, too, is not static. It changes in predictable ways as the children get older. As we pointed out in Chapter 10, being a parent of an adolescent requires a delicate new dance involving steady withdrawal of constraints combined with an equally steady application of support and affection.

When the last child has gone from home, the spousal roles undergo still more changes, as the husband and wife find themselves once again with time for one another, but under new circumstances and with a long history behind them.

How do these family-role changes affect adult life?

Family Roles and Marital Satisfaction.   The most consistent finding is that both marital satisfaction and overall life satisfaction appear to be predictably related to an adult's family life-cycle stage. The relationship is a curvilinear one. Satisfaction is at a high point immediately after marriage (Duvall's first stage). But as soon as the first child is born, marital satisfaction goes down and continues to be low through the teenage years of the oldest child. The low point is at the end of the child-rearing period, while the children are leaving home. The postparental period, however, seems to be a happier one for many couples. Figure 13.1 shows data from one of the classic studies (Rollins and Feldman, 1970) of a group of 400 middle-class men and women. Other researchers have found the same pattern in studies of working-class families (Gove & Peterson, 1980; Hoffman & Manis, 1978; Glenn & McLanahan, 1982). Not all researchers find that the level of satisfaction rises quite as high in the postparental period as Rollins and Feldman first showed, but nearly everyone does show some curve in the line.

What might cause such a pattern of lowered satisfaction during the child-rearing period? One obvious possibility is that it is simply the number of different roles a person has to occupy that creates problems (Rollins & Cannon, 1974; Rollins & Galligan, 1978). Adding one child to a family immediately doubles the number of roles. If this way of looking at the situation is correct, then having children spread out in age

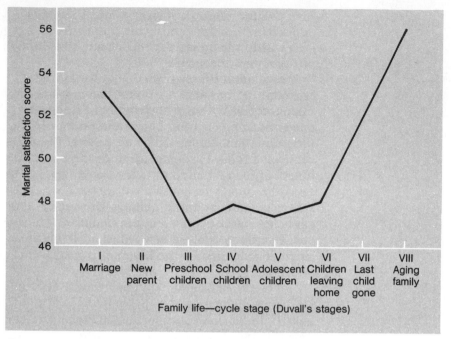

Figure 13.1. Rollins and Feldman asked men and women at various stages in the family life cycle about their satisfaction with their marriages. As you can see, those adults with children at home reported lower marital satisfaction than those in the newlywed or postparental stages. This is cross-sectional research, however, so we must be cautious about assuming that every couple experiences this pattern. (*Source:* Rollins & Feldman, 1970.)

ought to make it tougher, too, since being a parent of a teenager is a different role from being the parent of a 6-year-old or an infant.

Hoffman and Manis (1978) have provided us with some results that support such a speculation. They grouped their 2000 subjects into categories that took into account the age of the younger children as well as the older children, which led to the pattern of reported marital satisfaction in Figure 13.2. The most intriguing finding here is that while marital satisfaction was generally lower when children were present, having all your children in the same approximate stage at the same time seemed to make things easier. When all the children were preschoolers or all of them were elementary-school age but not yet pubertal adolescents, marital satisfaction was high. When the children bridged several different stages, and thus required different parental roles, satisfaction was lower.

Another possible explanation for the curvilinear relationship between family life cycle and marital satisfaction is that couples with younger children are typically also at a time in their lives when their income is low and job pressure is high. One or both parents may still

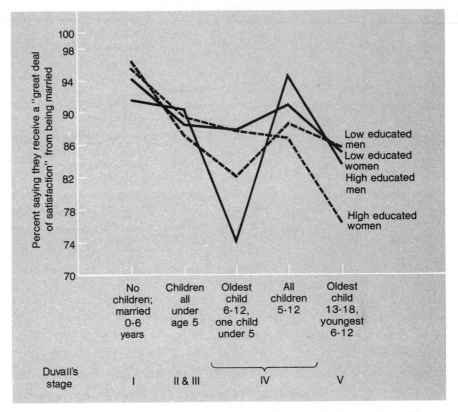

Figure 13.2. In a study similar to the Rollins and Feldman study (Figure 13.1), although covering a narrower range of the family life cycle, Hoffman and Manis divided the families according to the ages of all children rather than merely the oldest child. These data suggest that having all your children in the same stage, rather than spread across stages, is associated with greater marital satisfaction. (*Source:* Hoffman & Manis, 1978, p. 194–195.)

be in school when the first child is born, and during the children's preschool and early school years parents may have their energies and time devoted to the early stages of a career. The period with school-age children is also a time crunch, often especially for fathers whose role as financial provider consumes more time at that stage than at other periods of the family life cycle (Harry, 1976).

If either a financial crunch or a time crunch is part of the explanation for the lowered satisfaction during child-rearing years, we ought to find that couples who suffer less from these problems should show more satisfaction, or at least a smaller drop in morale, when children are born. That is precisely what Estes and Wilensky (1978) found in a study of family morale among employed and unemployed professional people. As you can see in Figure 13.3, those who had young children but had few financial problems actually showed higher morale

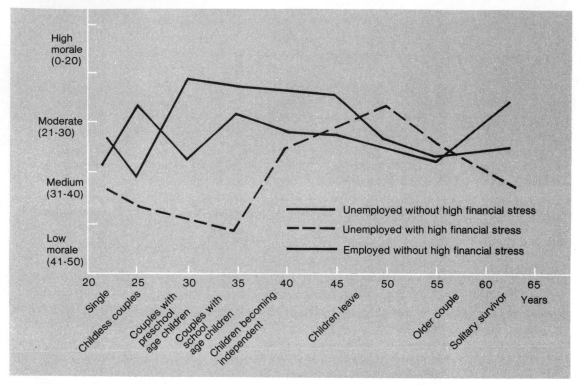

Figure 13.3.   The figure shows the morale of employed and unemployed professional people at various stages of the family life cycle. Those professionals who were employed (and thus possibly not experiencing the financial strain of having a family with young children) did *not* show the typical decline in morale associated with the arrival of children. (*Source:* Estes & Wilensky, 1978, p. 286.)

than those without children. The pattern for families experiencing financial problems, however, was the typical curvilinear one.

There is no need for us to choose between role conflict and time- or money-crunch explanations of the impact of children on marital satisfaction. No doubt both are true. Rearing children inescapably increases the number of roles an adult must fulfill, but whether a particular adult will experience this increase as stressful or difficult will depend on the availability of other resources and the time demands of the conflicting roles, especially job roles.

The Pleasures of Child Rearing.   In emphasizing the relationship between the presence of children and *reductions* in marital satisfaction or morale, there is a very real risk that we will give the impression that having children is an unmitigated disaster. That is very far from the case. Go back and take another look at Figure 13.2, only this time look at the actual percentage of adults who say they are very satisfied with their marriages. While the number is lower among couples with children, 80 to 90 percent are still saying they receive a great deal of satisfaction. In this same study, Hoffman and Manis found that more than 80 percent of the subjects said their lives had changed in positive or neutral ways after the birth of the first child. Many reported that children brought husband and wife closer together because rearing children was a common task with shared joys. They described a sense of fulfillment, a pleasure in being needed, and a feeling of having achieved adulthood. The sense of fulfillment was particularly evident among those whose oldest children were teenagers. Perhaps at that age it is easier to see your successes with your children.

Clearly the major child-rearing years are a mixed blessing to most parents. There is the stress of the accumulation of and conflict among roles at a time of financial strain. For most parents, though, there is also satisfaction and joy in seeing the children develop.

The Postparental Stages. If you are 20 years old, looking forward toward your adult life, the years of childbearing and child rearing may

Figure 13.4. The joys of parenthood! Although many adults report a drop in marital satisfaction after the arrival of children, nearly all parents also say that children bring pleasure and shared enjoyment into their lives.

loom large. But in fact they represent a smaller percentage of the total adulthood than many of us suppose. In the United States, the average age for women when their last child marries is now about 52 (Borland, 1982), and for men it is about 55. With life expectancies increasing, the average couple can expect to live together without their children for 13 to 15 years after the last child has permanently left home. In 1900, this postparental period was only 2 to 3 years, so there has been a major shift in the past century.

Folklore would have it that the postparental period is a time of distress, especially for women. Suddenly the role of *mother* is withdrawn. If a woman had defined herself primarily through her child-rearing role, we might expect to see a new identity crisis—the so-called *empty-nest syndrome.* This expectation is *not* confirmed. There is little evidence that the postparental period is a stressful or disturbing one for most adults (Borland, 1982), male or female. As we mentioned in Chapter 11, there is no notable increase in physical symptoms or emotional disturbance among women during this age period other than the relatively limited symptoms associated with menopause. Among married couples, sexual activity often remains high (Palmore, 1981), and overall marital satisfaction is also frequently quite high (look back at Figure 13.1).

We do not want to paint a picture of inevitable harmony for this period of adult life, just as we did not wish to exaggerate a bleak picture of the early parental years. Some recent findings from a study by Clifford Swensen and his colleagues (Swensen, Eskew, & Kohlhepp, 1981) suggest that the higher levels of marital satisfaction among couples in this period comes about mostly because marital problems and conflict have markedly declined. But at the same time, among the subjects in this study, expressions of love—affection, support, morale boosting, and the like—were also less common between couples in this stage than among those at earlier stages.

Interestingly, however, Swensen found that among postparental couples, those whose sense of self was primarily focused on stereotypic role relationships (a pattern Jane Loevinger calls the **conformist stage** of ego development) showed a greater decline of loving expressions than did those whose values were internalized and less based on norms and roles. Loevinger calls this latter approach the **conscientious stage** of ego development, but it also sounds a great deal like Kohlberg's postconformist moral development or Selman's final stage of social perspective taking. The basic point is that whether the postparental period is characterized by an improved or enriched marital relationship may depend in part on whether the husband and wife have, individually or jointly, moved into more mature levels of ego development.

Grandparenthood. The stage left out of the Duvall family life stages is being a grandparent. About three-quarters of adults over 65 in the United States have living grandchildren, and the majority of these actually see their grandchildren quite often—as often as every week' or two (Troll, 1980). Whether this is a significant and satisfying role for the adult and for the grandchildren seems to depend partly on how old the grandparent is. Grandchildren seem to like their grandparents better when they are in their fifties, sixties, or seventies. Very young grandparents (in their forties) and very old grandparents (eighties or older) are less preferred (Troll, 1980). For the adult, filling the role of grandparent in your forties—which is out of phase to some degree—is also less pleasurable, and older grandparents may find young children physically trying.

Despite the apparent time involvement in the role of grandparent, however, it does not seem to be the central factor in determining how satisfied an older person is with his or her life. High morale and life satisfaction in older adults is more related to the quality of friendships than to the quality of relationships with either children or grandchildren (Palmore, 1980; Wood and Robertson, 1978)—something we will touch on again in the next chapter.

Normal and Atypical Family Life Cycles. Most of you will have noticed that everything we have said so far about the family life cycle assumes a typical family in which the couple marries, has children, and stays married. With divorce rates rising and the number of childless couples increasing, this typical pattern probably represents less than half of the total adult population.

Figure 13.5 may give you some sense of the other combinations that occur. The figure is based on estimates by Glick (1980) for 1975 data. If we were to use 1983 data, the percentage of divorces would probably be higher than the 40 percent we have shown in the figure. Glick also has found that about 40 percent of all current marriages involve at least one partner who has been married before—compared to only 30 percent in 1970. Quite obviously the typical pattern is becoming less and less common.

We know next to nothing about the effects of such variations in the family life cycles on the developmental patterns of adults. We will talk about one such variation, *non*marriage, in Box 13.1. However, there are many other combinations that deserve further study. Weingarten (1980) has found that remarried adults describe themselves as being about as happy with their marriages and with their lives as do first-married couples. But they are also more likely to feel that children have a negative impact on their marriage than do first-married adults.

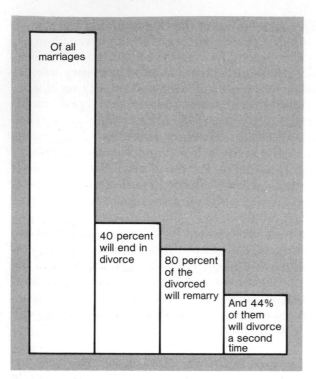

Figure 13.5. These figures are based on current estimates by Paul Glick. They show that approximately 40 percent of all marriages beginning today will end in divorce, but most of those who divorce will remarry. (*Source:* Glick, 1980.)

Unfortunately, neither Glick nor Weingarten has looked at the impact of remarriage on the *developmental* patterns for adults. Divorcing and remarrying change the family-role sequence markedly, and we know essentially nothing about the effect of such variations over time. Do adults who have remarried—and had a second, younger family—experience the same increase in life satisfaction in their late forties or fifties? How do "blended" families (those with children from previous marriages of both husband and wife) affect relationships between parents and offspring during the years of late adulthood? How do patterns of marriage, divorce, and remarriage affect personal growth or identity over adulthood? All of these questions will need to be examined in future research on adult family life.

Work Roles in Adulthood

The vast majority of adult men and a growing majority of adult women in this country are employed outside the home. Whether the jobs are unskilled, skilled, managerial, or professional, work plays an important part in nearly all of our adult lives. The study of work and of work roles has traditionally been a part of industrial and organizational psychology and of sociology, not a part of developmental psychology. Nonetheless, we think there are systematic changes over the life span in the work roles of adults that deserve attention from a developmental perspective.

Patterns of Working.   Many of you may think that when you leave college you will select a job or an occupational field and stick with that job or field for the rest of your working life. In reality, such a pattern—like the typical family life cycle—is becoming nearly extinct. Alvin Toffler (1970) estimates that most adults will change jobs 5 to 10 times in their working lives. Sometimes this is merely shifting to another employer; often it involves an entirely new job.

A second myth about working patterns is that men are likely to be continuously employed while women move in and out of the work force. While it is true that *more* women show mixtures of work and nonwork than do men, a pattern of continuous work is the most common for both sexes, as you can see in Table 13.2. These findings are from a study by Mary Corcoran (1978) of a group of 5000 American families. For women in this group, the second most common pattern after continuous employment is a combination of nonwork followed by employment (Pattern B). Presumably most of these are women who married relatively early and did not work until their children were past infancy. For men, the second most common pattern includes one period of nonwork, which may be for further schooling or because of loss of a job.

These research results tell us that there are many patterns of adult work, but they do not tell us whether some sequences or patterns are more optimal than others for the mental or emotional health of the adult. Bernice Neugarten (1979) has argued for many years that there is a price to be paid for being "off pattern" in your educational, job, or family sequences. For example, men and women who marry unusually early experience an increase in educational and marital problems, as we pointed out in earlier chapters. Being unusually late in marriage or childbearing may also bear some costs. Alice Rossi (1980), in a small study of a group of women in their late forties who still had teenage

TABLE 13.2
Percentages of Adult Men and Women
in Five Different Work/Nonwork Patterns over Their Adult Lives

Work pattern	White men	White women	Black men	Black women
Pattern A: continuous work	55%	36%	61%	42%
Pattern B: nonwork/work	11	29	15	42
Pattern C: work/nonwork/work	29	15	22	5
Pattern D: nonwork/work/nonwork/work	3	8	1	7
Pattern E: at least five periods of alternating work and nonwork	3	12	1	4

SOURCE: From Corcoran, 1978, as adapted by Giele, 1982, p. 125.

BOX 13.1

The Single Adult

Our description of adult life in terms of stages in the family life cycle is obviously based on the assumption that all adults marry. Of course, that is not the case. For the unmarried, the pattern may be quite different.

The group of adults labeled as *unmarried* is actually made up of many different types, including the once-married, but now widowed or divorced, and the never-married. Among the never-married, there are also subcategories, depending on whether the singleness is voluntary or involuntary, temporary or stable (Stein, 1978). These different reasons for singleness undoubtedly affect both life style and life course, but since most researchers have not divided the never-married group into subtypes, we must be content for now with a more global look at singleness. Mostly we want to talk about the never-married, rather than the divorced or widowed.

One of the things we know about never-married adults is that their numbers are increasing. Glick (1979) estimates that 8 to 9 percent of those adults presently in their twenties will be single for their lifetimes. Thirty years ago, the equivalent number was only 4 to 5 percent.

A second general statement we can make about single adults is that more of them are men than women. This is true at every age up until 65, when women's greater life expectancy means that more unmarried women than men are still alive.

Third, being single is not as healthy as being married. This is particularly true of *mental* health, as you can see in the accompanying figure, which shows data from a recent study of single adults by Leonard Cargan and Matthew Melko (1982). They found that married adults had more *physical* ailments than did single adults, but many fewer emotional problems. In particular, single adults are markedly more lonely than are married adults. In the same vein, Leonard Pearlin (Pearlin & Johnson, 1977) has found that singleness is particularly difficult when an adult is faced with some kind of stress,

such as financial worries or social isolation. Single adults are much more likely to respond to such stresses with depression than are equivalently stressed married adults.

Note, though, that it is the *divorced* adults who show these patterns most clearly. We will be talking further about divorce and its effects in Chapter 14. For now it is important to notice that not all single adults are alike in their responses.

When we look at the data more closely, though, we find that most of the statements we have just made about greater emotional problems for single adults than married adults are far more true for men than for women. In fact, a number of authors have gone so far as to suggest that singleness is good for women but bad for men (Cargan & Melko, 1982). That is probably too strong a statement, but it is at least partially correct.

Women who remain single tend to be well educated, with high IQ scores and white-collar jobs. They are also less likely to experience emotional disturbances than are married women (Gove, 1972; Spreitzer & Riley, 1974). In contrast, single men are likely to have more average IQs and to be less well educated than single women. They are *more* likely to show some form of emotional disturbance than are married men. Spreitzer and Riley (1974) also found that single men were likely to have had very poor relationships with all the members of their families: mothers, fathers, sisters, and brothers. In this study, at least twice as many single men had poor relationships as had good ones. Among the single women in this study, on the other hand, good to adequate relationships with family members were more common, although many single women reported difficulties in their relationships with their mothers.

The picture that emerges is that singlehood is a more positive state for women than for men. Among men, there is a hint that singleness reflects a failure of intimacy.

Women who remain single, however, seem to be far healthier than their single male counterparts in a number of respects. Could it be that more single women are *voluntarily* single, such as women who choose to focus their energies on a career (Hennig & Jardim, 1976) rather than on a family? This possibility fits with the fact that single women are better educated and brighter than the average.

Overall, the subgroup with the best mental health and the greatest happiness seems to be married men. The *least* healthy and happy are the single men, with married and single women falling somewhere in between. On some measures mar-

ried women look less healthy than their unmarried sisters, and on other measures the pattern is reversed. Regardless of the rank ordering of single and married women, though, it is clear that among single adults women are better off than men; and among married adults, men are better off than women. We can think of several possible explanations of this pattern, including the higher role conflict and lower status of the role of housewife/mother compared to the traditional male role of provider/worker. Whatever the explanation, the pattern is intriguing and worth further study.

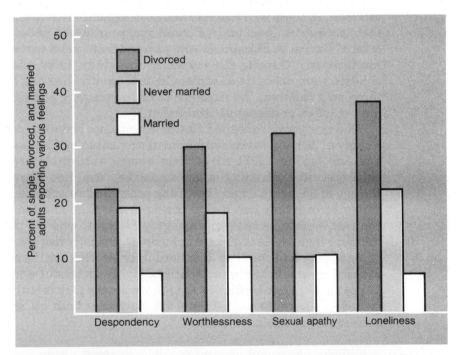

Box 13.1A. Cargan and Melko's results are typical of many studies that show that married adults are less depressed, less prone to emotional disturbance, and less lonely than are unmarried adults. It is clear, however, that among the unmarried, the divorced are worse off than those who never married. (*Source:* Cargan & Melko, 1980, p. 143.)

children at home, found that such women reported more dissatisfaction with their lives than did younger women with teenagers.

For women, one of the critical sequencing questions concerns the ordering of career and motherhood. Is it better (for career success, particularly) to have children while you are young and establish a career later, or is it better to pursue occupational goals first and have children later?

In view of the practical importance of this question for contemporary young adults, there is remarkably little information available. A number of studies suggest that work discontinuities for women do *not* lower a woman's professional attainment or earning power (women's earnings are lower than men's even when they work continuously; Giele, 1982). Nor—within limits—does it seem to matter which of the several work/family patterns a woman chooses. In one study of women with doctorates, for example (Perun and Bielby, 1980), those who had paused in their careers to marry (and have children in some cases) before attending graduate school had the same level of professional attainment as those who had married (and had children) after obtaining their doctorates. And both of these groups attained about the same level of success as did women who pursued family and career paths simultaneously. (Among the women in this study, those who had had children were not quite as successful as those who had not; but among those with children, the sequence of career training and childbearing did not affect professional attainment.)

One intriguing exception to this conclusion, however, comes from a study of 25 highly successful women executives by Margaret Hennig and Ann Jardim (1977). All of these women were either presidents or chief executive officers of large companies. *None* had married before the age of 35, and all had the strong sense that to achieve maximum career success they had had to postpone marriage and family life. In contrast, women in the same age group (cohort) who did not achieve the same high levels of success in business typically had married earlier, and many had children. It is hard to know whether the same delay of marriage would be characteristic of highly successful women today. Times have changed, after all. On the whole, the jury is still out on the impact of alternate work/family life pathways both on professional success and on life satisfaction.

Job Types.   A second way we can look at work experience over the adult years is to compare the types of jobs that are held by younger and older workers. In a study of a large California aircraft manufacturing firm, Karl Kunze (1974) found that he could identify a type of developmental sequence in the work role. A person's first job is at an entry level position, which requires little skill or training. This first job doesn't pay well, and it may require strength, speed, or endurance from the worker. The young worker is ideally suited for this job: He has little skill or experience and has a great deal of strength and stamina. A person's job later in life is farther up the job sequence (or the career ladder, as it is sometimes called). This job requires more skill, training, and experience. The pay is higher, and the job is less likely to require brute strength and more likely to require coordinated skill.

The age differences in job characteristics that Kunze describes may be more marked for blue-collar workers than for professionals (such as doctors, lawyers, university professors, or the like); but for most of us, there are changes in job demands and responsibilities over the adult work years. In particular, the older worker is more likely to be in a position of supervising younger workers. Daniel Levinson (1978, 1980), one of the major current theorists about adult life patterns, suggests that the role of **mentor**—guiding and supporting the career of a younger colleague—is an important one for older workers. It is one element in what Erikson calls **generativity,** the stage Erikson sees as crucial in the years of midlife. Young workers are making their own way, pushing upward in the system, striving for success. By midlife, however, they may find new satisfaction from being a model to younger workers, a mentor in Levinson's sense.

One of the characteristic differences Kunze found between young and old jobs is not developmental in nature: There is a strong cohort effect in the nature of the job itself. Modern technology has provided hundreds of new job categories in the last 30 years, the majority of which are performed by younger workers. Most computer designers, operators, and programmers, for example, are relatively young. So are many plastics workers, electronic technicians, and medical paraprofessional workers. Alvin Toffler, in his book *Future Shock* (1970), estimates that at least a quarter of you reading this book will find yourselves 25 years from now in a type of job that presently does not exist. If this continuous technological change persists, then young workers will continue to hold new jobs, while older workers will hold traditional jobs.

Job Performance and Satisfaction.   While the type of work varies with age, the *quality* of work does not. Productivity is just as high among older workers as among younger ones, for example (Schwab & Heneman, 1977; Meier & Kerr, 1977). Job *satisfaction,* though, increases with age. Robert Quinn and his associates (U.S. Department of Labor, 1974; Staines & Quinn, 1979) have consistently found that older workers are more satisfied with their work, as you can see in Figure 13.6. Note that the actual level of satisfaction was lower at every age in the 1977 survey than in 1973, but that the shape of the curve was highly similar at both time points.

Part of the increase in job satisfaction with age is probably ac-

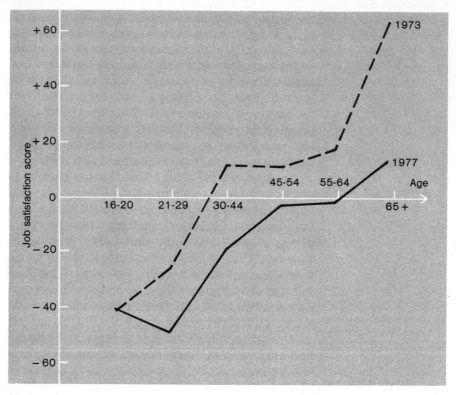

Figure 13.6. National surveys of worker satisfaction in 1973 and 1977 both show that satisfaction is greater among older workers, although the overall level of satisfaction is considerably lower in the 1977 findings. (*Source:* Staines & Quinn, 1979, p. 6.)

counted for by the characteristics of young jobs we described earlier. It is easier to be dissatisfied with a boring, low-level, poorly paying job than it is with a more stimulating, advanced, or better-paying one. It is also probably true that older workers have had time to try out various occupations and choose the one in which they feel the most comfortable.

Another possible explanation for the relatively low job satisfaction among young people is the pressure of supporting a family. Workers with young children—in Stages II and III in Duvall's system—have lower job satisfaction than do workers without young children (Hoffman & Manis, 1978; U.S. Department of Labor, 1974). This relationship is especially strong for less well educated workers whose jobs are likely to be the poorest paid. Since the majority of workers with young children are under 30, this may help to explain the pattern of results in Figure 13.6.

Retirement.   The final stage in the work cycle for most adults is retirement. In 1978, 53 percent of the men and 76 percent of the women between 60 and 69 were not working. For those over 70, the comparable figures were 86 percent and 95 percent (U.S. Bureau of Labor Statistics, 1978). The national trends show that men are retiring earlier than they were 20 years ago, while more women are working into and through their sixties. Some of the most complete information about the effects of retirement comes from the Duke longitudinal studies (Palmore, 1981), which we mentioned in Chapter 11. The researchers have followed a number of groups of men and women from late middle age through the period of retirement and old age. In this sample, the majority retired involuntarily, either because they had reached a mandatory retirement age for their job or because of disability or ill health. Only about 15 percent said they retired because they wanted to enjoy more leisure time.

Several common assumptions about the effects of retirement are contradicted by the results of the Duke studies. One of the most common beliefs is that most retired or elderly people are poor. It is true that *more* of the aged than the young are poor, but the difference is not huge. In 1975, 14 percent of adults 65 or older were living below the federal poverty line, compared to 12 percent of those younger than 65 (Administration on Aging, 1978). Furthermore, while most retired persons have lower incomes than they had while working, they also have lower expenses. Thus their incomes may be more adequate for their needs than a first glance at the figures suggests. We are not suggesting that poverty is not a real problem for many elderly adults. However, the pervasive assumption that *most* retired persons are poor is not supported by the facts.

A second common assumption is that the stress of retirement often leads to illness or early death. This, too, is not supported by the facts. As we pointed out in Chapter 11, results from the Duke longitudinal studies (Palmore, 1981) show that among those adults who were not already ill when they retired, retirement did not increase the probability of illness or death.

A third myth is that retired people will be less satisfied with their lives because of too much time on their hands, boredom setting in, or more conflict between husband and wife. On the whole, this seems not to be true either. Only 10 to 20 percent of retired adults report that their overall life satisfaction has declined. But neither does retirement offer a magic potion, guaranteeing improved morale or greater happiness. In the Duke studies, those who reported the greatest life satisfaction after retirement were generally those who had been satisfied with their lives *before* they retired. Those who thought of themselves as "middle-aged" rather than "old" were also more likely to be satisfied with their postretirement life.

There is some danger that we have painted an overly positive picture of the impact of retirement. There are clearly major changes involved in retirement, and they have some effect. Among men over 60, for example, those who are still employed report slightly higher self-esteem than those who are retired (Keith, Dobson, Goudy, & Powers, 1981), and retirement is usually accompanied by reductions in both income and activity level. For most adults, however, retirement does *not* bring with it either overall depression or the reverse.

Blending Work and Family Roles

We have talked about family roles and work roles separately, but it is clear that the two are combined in complex ways by most adults. This has an impact on children in the family, as well as on the adults, as described in Box 13.2.

For the adult, role conflict is increased when both husband and wife work and family roles must be filled simultaneously. However, given the way the wife-and-mother role is defined in our culture, the role conflict for the woman is typically greater. You can see this sex difference if you go back and look at Figure 1.2 in Chapter 1. The figure shows that both men and women with young children are less satisfied with their jobs than are workers without young children, but the effect is much greater for women than for men.

One obvious source of the heightened work dissatisfaction reported by mothers with young children could be plain old work overload. Husbands of working women do more child care and housework than do husbands of full-time housewives (Pleck, 1979), but working mothers frequently have two "jobs": For couples in which both the husband and wife work, the woman still does the majority of the housework and child care. For example, in a recent national survey, Pleck and Rustad (1980) found that husbands of employed women (working 30 hours a week or more) were spending an average of 3.8 hours per day on household work or child care, while their working wives were spending 6.9 hours per day. (These figures seem high to us, but the relative proportions of husband/wife work seem valid.)

Obviously, these are merely averages and mask a great deal of variation from one couple to another and variations over time in any given couple. When Suzanne Model (1981) interviewed 650 women about their husbands' participation in such household chores as cooking, cleaning, and grocery shopping, she found that regardless of whether the woman was working or not, husbands provided most household help when there were no children present (newlywed couples and retired couples) and least when there were children (where are they when you need them most?).

Whether or not women report that their efforts to combine work and family roles results in dissatisfaction or unhappiness, however, seems to depend on several other factors besides her husband's assistance, including the level of the woman's education and her style of

BOX 13.2

The Effect of Mothers' Employment on Children

It is no longer news that women with children are, increasingly, employed outside the home as well as in the home. Nationally, over 55 percent of married women with children of school age (6 to 18) were working in 1977. Among married women with children under age 6, 40 percent were employed in the same year (U.S. Bureau of the Census, 1978). Note that we have been describing *married* women. Among divorced or widowed or never-married women with young children, the number of workers is far higher. Between 60 and 70 percent of unmarried women with preschool-age children are working.

There is every sign that these numbers will continue to rise in the years ahead. Gordon and Kammeyer (1980), for example, found that in a sample of 700 married women they studied over a period of years, 72 percent had worked either part time or full time in the four years since the birth of their first child. Thirty years ago, only about 10 to 15 percent of women with such young children were employed, so this represents a massive change in our cultural patterns.

There are two basic reasons for mothers' working. By far the most important reason is for economic need (Gordon & Kammeyer, 1980). A secondary reason is for fulfillment or self-gratification. The latter reason is more common among well-educated women who work at high-level professions. Among working-class women financial need is THE reason for working.

These facts and figures tell us that for many of you reading this book, the question no longer is, "Shall I work or not while I have young children?" The current question is, "What are the effects of my employment on my child(ren), and how can I maximize the benefits and reduce any emotional costs?"

THE EFFECT OF MATERNAL EMPLOYMENT ON THE CHILD

There is a fair amount of research on the development of children of working mothers, so you would think we'd have really firm and clear answers. We need to be cautious, though, about such firm conclusions for at least two reasons. First, research in this area is extremely difficult to do well. Women who are able to manage financially without working, or who stay at home out of choice, are already different from women who work in a host of ways. So if we compare their children, we may well be comparing apples and oranges. The best way around this is to match the working and nonworking mothers in as many ways as possible—such as education, marital status, previous work history, number of children in the family, and so forth. It's very difficult to do this well.

A second reason for caution is that the work patterns are changing so fast that we are never really up-to-date. We know little, for example, about the effect of maternal employment on *infant* development because few women with infants worked until recently. Now they do so in large numbers, but the research has not caught up with the facts. Thus we can't say what the consequences are with any certainty.

With those cautions in mind, however, let us summarize the evidence.

Benefits to the Child. Children whose mothers work appear to reap several benefits. They are encouraged to develop greater independence, and they are given more responsibility at home. As a result, such children not only show more independent behavior, they also show a stronger achievement orientation in school (Hoffman, 1979). This pattern is particularly evident in working-class families.

A second benefit (at least from our point of view) is that both boys and girls whose mothers work seem to develop more egalitarian (more androgynous, perhaps) views of adult sex roles (Marantz & Mansfield, 1977). Daughters of employed mothers also show higher self-esteem.

A third finding is that infants and children whose mothers work show no signs of impaired attachment to their mothers or fathers (Belsky & Steinberg, 1978). Most of the research on this has focused on the effect of day care, rather than on the effect of the mother's employment. Of course, the two go together in most instances. What we do not know is whether working has any effect on the *mother's* attachment to the child. It is conceivable that mothers who return to work very early after the birth of a child may have a somewhat weaker attachment. At the moment, however, there are no research data one way or the other.

Possible Problems for the Child. Two potential problem areas have emerged from the research. First, for boys in working-class families (but not in middle-class families) there is some suspicion of

strain between father and son (Hoffman, 1979). It may be that in such families there is still a strong value on the man supporting his family. If the wife works, the son may see this as a failure on the part of the father.

A second hint of problems comes in two recent studies of toddlers, both of which showed that children of employed mothers have slightly lower IQs than do children of nonworking mothers (Schachter, 1981; Hock, 1980). This is a puzzling finding since studies of school-aged children show exactly the opposite—slightly higher levels of school performance and IQ among the children of working mothers. At the moment we do not have a good solution to this puzzle, but any hint of negative effects is obviously worth a much harder look.

Source: Doonesbury, by G. B. Trudeau.

We can offer two pieces of advice, based on our reading of the evidence:

You will hear it said that *quality time* is more important than quantity. It seems to be true; but 15 minutes a day, no matter how high the quality, is not enough time with a child. Full-time parental involvement does not seem to be required to raise secure, independent children. But some regular, predictable time is essential.

The quality of the alternative care you arrange for your young child is also critical. Stability of the care arrangement is important; children who are moved frequently from one care setting to another have more difficulty than those who remain in one setting. Attentive and loving caregivers are also important, as is the cognitive richness of the environment in which your child spends his day. You can check on these aspects of care by visiting and observing in any day care center or home day care setting you are considering for your child. Watch the ways in which the adults respond to the children, the number of children in the group, the number of adults available, the activities planned for the day. Shop around, just as you would for any service.

We are convinced that with thoughtful planning, it is entirely possible for both parents to work while their children are young without any negative effect on the child and with some potential benefits. But it is a complex, demanding life. Plan on being tired a lot!

coping with the role conflict or the role overload. As a general rule of thumb, working while raising a family is associated with lower life satisfaction or poorer marital adjustment primarily among poor or working-class women. For this group, with less flexible jobs and insufficient funds to hire help, the role overload can be substantial. There just isn't enough time to get everything done.

The way a woman solves the combined roles also affects her life satisfaction. Douglas Hall has found in several studies (1972, 1975) that those women who consciously redefine and restructure their family roles, giving up some tasks and sharing others, are likely to find the combined family/work roles least stressful. Those who try to do it all (today's "superwomen") are most likely to experience stress.

Both role conflict and role overload are involved in the problem of combining family and work roles. What women most often complain of is lack of time to do everything they would like to do. Obviously, a more equal sharing of the child rearing and household tasks by husbands and wives will alleviate part of this time pressure, although that would certainly increase the sense of pressure experienced by men. The clear, inescapable fact is that the two roles are each highly demanding of time and energy. There is no perfect way to combine them that will eliminate all stress or overload.

Sex Roles in Adulthood

In talking about family and work roles, we have repeatedly described somewhat different patterns for men and women. The obvious implication is that there are different adult roles assigned to men and women—a statement that will not come as startling news to anyone. Despite the obviousness of the difference, though, it is worth our while to spend at least a few paragraphs being more specific about such sex roles.

We pointed out in Chapter 6 that children as young as 5 or 6 have definite ideas about what men and women are like. Such generalized expectations (stereotypes) are just as common among adults. Most of us carry around a very specific set of sex stereotypes in our heads (Broverman et al., 1972). The male stereotype is centered around the concept of competence: Men are seen as more aggressive, independent, objective, competitive, direct, skilled in business, able to be leaders, active, and worldly. The female stereotype is centered around warmth and expressiveness: Women are seen as more gentle, quiet, need more security, are more aware of others' feelings, more talkative, and more able to express their tender feelings.

These stereotypes persist despite the fact that when we observe men and women in real situations, there are far more similarities than there are differences. Men are found to be more aggressive and assertive, but women are not more dependent or quiet nor less able to be leaders.

The *roles* we assign to men and women, though, match the stereotypes better than does actual behavior. Judith Worell (1981) suggests that the best way to think of a sex role (or any role for that matter) is as a *job description.* It is a set of "organized expectancies for behavior and activities that are considered to be appropriate and desirable for either males or females in a particular culture" (Worell, 1981, p. 315). In our culture, as in most cultures, the job assigned to women involves primary responsibility for child care, for family care, and for the affective stability of the family. The job assigned to men is primarily one of financial and physical support of the family.

In fact, either men or women could (and do) occupy either of these two jobs. Single parents (males or females) fill both jobs, and women who work outside the home also fill both jobs to at least some degree. In our culture, however, it is clear that the expected pattern is that women will do the female job and men will do the male job. Obviously, this role assignment matches (and strengthens) the sex stereotypes.

There are a thousand questions we could ask about such sex roles. But since our focus in this book is on developmental change, we want to deal primarily with one central issue: Do the roles, the job descriptions, for males and females change over the adult years, or do they remain constant?

There is less truly developmental research on this question than we would like, but the emerging answer seems to be that there is some systematic change: Male and female roles are most strongly differentiated from one another in the second stage of the family cycle, after the

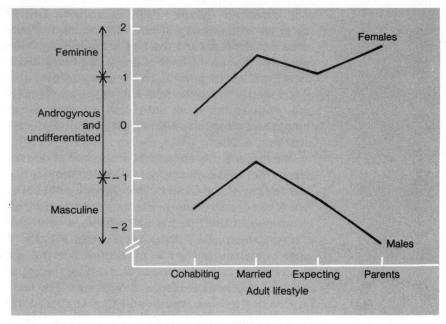

Figure 13.7. Sex role self-descriptions are most strongly differentiated (stereotyped) in families with children and least differentiated (most equal) for cohabiting females and married men without children. This finding is part of the growing evidence showing that sex roles undergo systematic changes over the adult life span. (*Source:* Abrahams, Feldman, & Nash, 1978, p. 398.)

birth of the first child. They are most similar to each other in midlife and beyond.

Sex Roles in Young Couples. A number of researchers have found that the advent of the first child polarizes the sex roles in the family. The husband becomes more powerful, more in control of family decision making, less involved in housework and other family activities (Hoffman & Manis, 1978; Abrahams, Feldman, & Nash, 1978; Feldman, Biringen, & Nash, 1981).

You can see one example of this effect in Figure 13.7, which shows results from a study by Barbara Abrahams and her colleagues (Abrahams, Feldman, & Nash, 1978). They measured the masculine, feminine, or androgynous self-perceptions of groups of young adults in four different living arrangements: living together but not married, married without children, married expecting a baby, and married with a child. You can see in the figure that couples with a child showed the most traditional self-perceptions: The men saw themselves as most masculine; the wives saw themselves as most feminine.

Sex Roles in Midlife. In contrast to the exaggeration of sex-role differences in the early stages of family formation, in midlife there are signs of a "crossover" in sex roles (Giele, 1982). George Vaillant (1978), in his longitudinal study of Harvard students, found that men became more feminine toward the end of middle age (late forties). For many men, this was an offshoot of becoming more involved with the lives of their families. In general, in the postparental and grandparent stages of the family life cycle, men show greater compassion and tenderness, and women show more autonomy. In some sense, then, the accepted female and male roles become more androgynous in midlife (Feldman, Biringen, & Nash, 1981).

We can see this change in a number of domains. We have already pointed out that men are more likely to provide household help in these later stages of the family cycle (Model, 1981), which is one manifestation of the change. Another is the major participation in the work force by women in their forties and fifties—a relatively recent change but a very pronounced pattern at present. Finally, we can see the same crossover theme in the role of mentor. Serving as role model and guide to a younger colleague requires many of the supportive, caring behaviors typically assigned to the female role. The fact that many men take on this new role at midlife and that the mentoring role is seen as an entirely appropriate one for a man in his forties or fifties is still further evidence that the sex role has changed.

We must enter a note of caution in interpreting these changes in sex roles over the life span. Nearly all of the research we have described so far is cross-sectional rather than longitudinal. That is, we have been comparing different groups of adults of differing ages, rather than following the same group over time. Any such comparison mixes up cohort differences and real developmental change. We do not know for sure whether each individual couple shifts from relative equality in sex roles in early marriage, to maximum role differentiation after the birth of the first child, and then back to greater equality 20 years later.

Even if these are real and common developmental changes, we don't know whether the timing of the changes varies depending on whether the wife works outside the home or not. We suspect that it does. John Scanzoni (1980), for example, describes three types of family sex-role structures based on the descriptions of family power relationships by a group of over 500 women in their twenties and early thirties: (1) wife as equal partner, (2) wife as junior partner, and (3) wife as complement. In the equal-partner couples, the wife is much more likely to work and to be well paid for her work. These couples seem to have worked out a more equal division of both power and labor, similar to what Hall calls a "structural role redefinition." In the wife-as-complement couples, on the other hand, the wife typically does not work. In these pairs maximum differentiation of male and female roles exists initially and persists. Whether the latter group will show a crossover pattern at midlife we simply do not know.

Our best conclusion at the moment is that there are some developmental patterns of changing sex roles, from maximum differentiation in the early stages of family life to greater role equivalence in later life. There are obviously wide individual differences, though, superimposed on that developmental progression.

PERSONALITY IN ADULTHOOD: CONTINUITY AND CHANGE

In talking about roles in adulthood, we have been talking primarily about externals—about the "jobs" each of us holds. However, personality goes beyond roles to include traits, skills, temperament, and style of response.

How much consistency is there in such aspects of personality over adulthood? Do most of us stay basically the same, despite changes in roles? Or are there inward changes that match the outward ones? Another possibility is that there may be sequential changes, or stages, that are shared by most adults regardless of the roles they fill.

It would be easy to contrast these several views as if only one of them could be correct: continuity *or* change. But the truth is that both continuity and change exist in adult personality. Jack Block states the case eloquently:

> NO personality psychologist contends that later experiences, later environmental contexts, and everyone's inevitable passage through the sequence of biologically and societally imposed stages of life do not have important influences on behavior and even on personality organization and reorganization. What is contended is that how experience registers, how environments are selected and modified, and how the stages of life are negotiated depends, importantly and coherently, on what the individual brings to these new encounters—the resources, the premises, the intentions, the awareness, the fears and the hopes, the forethoughts and the afterthoughts that are subsumed by what we call personality (Block, 1981, pp. 40–41).

As we look first at consistency in personality and then at changes and stages over the adult years, keep Block's point in mind. This is not an either/or proposition. Both forces are at work.

Consistencies in Personality in Adulthood

There are two ways to ask the question about consistencies in personality: (1) Are there some aspects of personality on which most or all people show consistencies? and (2) Are there some *people* who are more consistent (less changeable) than others? The answer to both questions seems to be "yes."

Dimensions of Personality Consistency.   There appear to be at least three underlying dimensions on which people show consistency over the teenage and adult years (Costa & McCrae, 1980):

Extraversion versus introversion. Compared to introverts, extraverts are consistently more oriented toward other people, are more gregarious, more active, more assertive, more excitement seeking, and more positive in their emotions. They have more friends and choose occupations involving people. Introverts are more solitary or socially isolated. This basic personal characteristic seems to be stable over both adolescence and adulthood.

Neuroticism. Adults who are high on this dimension (compared to those who are low in neuroticism) are typically more anxious, more often depressed, more self-conscious, impulsive, and hostile. They frequently describe themselves as unhappy with their lives, whatever their situation may be, and they are more likely to complain about their health, smoke more, drink more, and describe more sexual problems. Adults who are low on this dimension have fewer symptoms and are generally happy with themselves and their lives. Again, there is good evidence for consistency of this general trait or dimension over the adult years.

Openness to experience versus rigidity. Open adults, compared to more closed adults, are those who are willing to try new things, to take risks, to make big changes. These may well be people who have "crises," since they experience both the bad and the good more forcefully. (In fact, such open people sound a good deal like what Gail Sheehy calls "pathfinders" in her recent book [1981] on adult lives.) Rigid adults, in contrast, are more likely to stick with what has worked before, to stay in the same groove. We might think of adolescents who remain in Marcia's foreclosure status as rigid in this sense, while those who move into moratorium would be more open.

Evidence for the consistency of the open versus rigid dimension is the weakest of the three. However, the possible existence of this type of consistency is especially intriguing because it suggests that there may be some people for whom *change* is a consistent characteristic—a possibility we will return to shortly.

Notice that these three dimensions are *inner* qualities. Costa and McCrae are not suggesting that *behavior* is always consistent but that some aspects of underlying personality persist. A person with an introverted personality may behave in an appropriately gregarious manner at a party or be quite able to function effectively with co-workers. But his overall style, his preferences, will lead him to choose somewhat different activities or jobs and may affect the manner in which he relates to others.

David McClelland makes exactly the same point when he argues that consistency of personality exists at the level of what he calls "operants": "If you want to predict behavior successfully, be sure to include measures of motives, schemas, and traits—that is, of what people want to do, of what they understand the situation to be, and of traits or adaptive skills they can use in the situation" (McClelland, 1981, p. 108).

When we look at specific behaviors demanded by particular situations (which McClelland calls "respondents"), we see much less consistency over time. A person's interests or needs may persist, but the specific ways those interests or needs are expressed change over adulthood (just as a child or adult's central attachment may persist, while the manner of expression—the attachment *behaviors*—changes over time).

If we combine this view with what we have already said about role changes in adulthood, we can see that it is entirely possible for someone to experience changes in family, work, or sex roles but still show consistency in underlying style, motives, and needs. Thus social learning theorists like Walter Mischel (1968) are correct in stating that our behavior is strongly influenced by the environmental circumstances we find ourselves in and by the reinforcement contingencies in force. At the same time temperament and psychoanalytic theorists appear to be partly correct, too, in their contention that there are underlying continuities.

Consistent and Inconsistent People.   Despite all the evidence for personality continuity, it would be a mistake to assume that all adults are equally consistent. We are not. Some of us appear to be remarkably unchanging, while others change a great deal—in personality as well as behavior.

Jack Block has offered an especially provocative set of evidence to illustrate such individual differences (Block, 1981). He describes a group of adults who had been studied as adolescents, in their thirties, and again in their forties. Among these 70 men and 76 women were some who were remarkably consistent in basic personality over 25 years. Others were "unrecognizable in later years from their junior high school descriptions" (p. 36).

For some, consistency seemed to represent persisting integration and success. One group Block describes as "ego resilients" were consistently likable, had high self-esteem, independence, and intellectual efficiency. For others, consistency seemed to signify lack of growth. For still others, there was a shift from ineffective behavior to more mature strategies, illustrating the sort of change we might think of as growth.

Changes in Personality in Adulthood

It is exactly this kind of increasing maturity or psychological growth over time that most theories of personality change in adulthood emphasize. Some theorists see the change as a gradual process, while others see steps or stages. Both groups see at least the possibility of systematic change.

Gradual Change in Personality.　The most persuasive advocate of the gradual change position is George Vaillant (1977). Like Freud and Erikson, Vaillant believes that all adults have instinctual strivings and needs to be met as well as daily conflicts to resolve. To meet these needs and conflicts successfully we must develop increasingly adaptive **ego mechanisms,** frequently called **defense mechanisms.**

A defense mechanism (a concept first proposed by Freud) is fundamentally an unconscious method of fooling yourself, of protecting yourself against unwanted ideas, impulses, or feelings. We *all* use such techniques, so the issue is not whether an adult is defensive or not but whether the particular types of defense mechanisms she uses are adaptive and mature rather than immature.

Vaillant organized the common defense mechanisms into a developmental hierarchy, classifying each defense as *immature* (such as projection of your own feelings or thoughts onto someone else), *neurotic* (such as repression of feelings or thoughts, or rationalization), or *mature* (such as altruism, humor, or anticipation). He then searched for each of these types of defense in the responses of a group of Harvard men who had been part of a major longitudinal study called the Grant Study. These men were first seen when they were in college, and last seen when they were in their forties or fifties.

Within this group of men there was a gradual shift over the adult years from immature to more mature forms of defense mechanisms. For example, only 15 percent of the defenses displayed by these men while they were in college were of the most mature type. When they were in their forties, this had risen to about 35 percent. Even more interesting is the fact that those men whose adult lives were most successful—with lasting marriages, successful children, higher-level jobs, and good physical health—showed the largest gains in mature defense mechanisms. Those men whose adult lives were characterized by lower levels of outward success also showed the greatest persistence of immature patterns.

One of the elements in the lives of adults that seems to have a powerful influence on this maturing process is social class. Farrell and Rosenberg (1981), like Vaillant, have found that men in their forties, compared to men in their twenties, have more integrated personalities. Furthermore, this was *much* more true of middle-class men than of working-class men. In Farrell and Rosenberg's view, the working-class man is likely to present a "facade of integration." He has created a pattern of surface calm but may deny or repress basic conflicts and stresses built into his life.

The change toward greater integration that Vaillant is describing seems to occur in early and middle adulthood. Another type of change has been proposed for later adulthood and old age, a process Cumming and Henry (1961) called **disengagement.** Disengagement involves a gradual withdrawal of interest in and concern with the issues of the outer world, a reduction of social activity, and a greater preoccupation with inner thoughts and feelings. Cumming and Henry also argued that such disengagement is a normal, desirable developmental process. Their studies of older persons showed that those who had disengaged were happier than those who had not.

Evidence on this point from more recent research is decidedly mixed. There does seem to be a slight but steady decline in social contacts in the years from age 60 or 70 on (Palmore, 1981). However, most researchers find that those older adults who remain *more* involved socially are the most content with their lives. In the Duke longitudinal studies, for example, those adults who were more involved with friends and groups had better health and greater "affect balance" (emotional stability).

Studies of gradual change in personality over adulthood are scarce. Obviously, there is a great deal we do not know. For now, it appears plausible to think of a general movement from immaturity to maturity. It is also clear, however, that not all adults move along this pathway, and not all move at the same speed. What we need now, as Block has pointed out, is to understand why some adults change and grow while others do not.

Stages in Adult Personality Change.   Another way to think about changes in adult personality is in terms of steps or stages. Erikson first proposed this in 1954, and his thinking has influenced an entire generation of psychologists and sociologists.

For Better or For Worse   by Lynn Johnston

Figure 13.8. Maturity can be an elusive thing. Does anyone ever feel fully mature?
Source: Johnston, "For Better or Worse," copyright Universal Press Syndicate.

The fundamental assumption underlying all the stage theories is that there is a sequence of what Havighurst (1972) calls **developmental tasks** faced by each person over the course of adulthood. These tasks are partially defined by the changes in roles we have already described; but stage theorists generally assume that there are *inner* tasks as well, such as reassessments of identity or the development of the capacity for intimacy or generativity.

Daniel Levinson (1978, 1980, 1981) has offered one of the most forceful arguments for adult stages. He suggests that each adult moves through alternating periods of transition and relative stability. During the stable periods, we create a **life structure** that is made up of a network of roles and relationships. During the transitions, we reexamine that life structure and decide whether to change it or to maintain it. The ladder of adult stages that emerges from this formulation is shown in Figure 13.9.

Each of the transition periods is thought to have a particular content. For example, Levinson argues that the midlife transition—of which we have all read so much lately—includes three main tasks: (1) to reappraise the adult years and decide what has been worthwhile and what has been left out; (2) to "integrate the great polarities: young/old; destruction/creation; masculine/feminine; and attachment/separateness" (1980, p. 286). At this point in our lives, Levinson thinks we must each deal with the inevitability of our own aging and death, with the existence of both feminine and masculine qualities in each of us, and with our needs to be cared for as well as to care for others, to be dependent as well as independent. After grappling with these issues, the adult must (3) create a new life structure that will serve over the next period of years.

This entire process may be internal, with no external signs of crisis or turmoil. However, for many adults—perhaps those who are open (in Costa and McCrae's sense) or those who face an unusually large set of life changes at the same time—there may be drastic changes in marriage, jobs, or in other relationships.

Whether the changes are visible or not, Levinson is very clear about the fact that he thinks these stages or steps are universal:

> We energetically offer the following hypothesis: This sequence of eras and periods exists in all societies, throughout the human species, at the present stage in human evolution. The eras and periods are grounded in the nature of man as a biological, psychological and social organism, and in the nature of society as a complex enterprise extending over many generations (Levinson, 1978, p. 322).

Most stage theorists do not agree with Levinson that the stages are universal. But there is agreement that there is a set of tasks to be con-

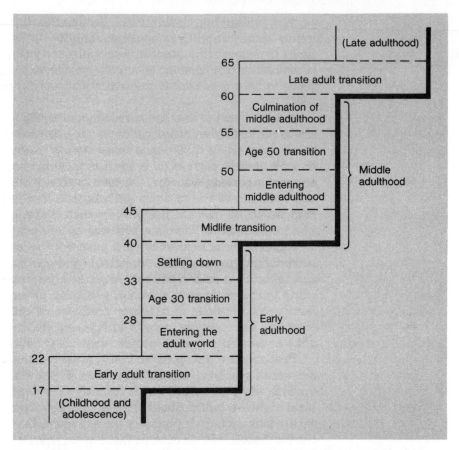

Figure 13.9. The developmental periods in early and middle adulthood proposed by Levinson. Note that there are periods of stability, such as "entering the adult world" and "settling down," punctuated by periods of transition. (*Source:* Levinson, 1978.)

fronted in adulthood, and that for most adults the confrontation occurs in a particular order at a roughly predictable pace.

PERSONALITY IN ADULTHOOD: A SYNTHESIS AND A FINAL LOOK

It may seem to you that we have spent a lot of time in this chapter saying, "On the one hand . . . and on the other hand. . . ." Both theory and research on developmental changes (or consistencies) in personality over adulthood are still in their infancy, so inevitably there are more opinions than facts. Still, let us try to pull the several strands together.

There are basically three different views about adult personality changes. The first is that there is little or no change at all. This position is held by people like Costa and McCrae, who argue that there are important underlying continuities, personality types if you will, that create lasting stability in adult personality. In fact, there is good evidence to support this position, especially for such aspects of behavior as sociability. The amount of contact we choose to have with others appears to be a predictable characteristic, well into old age (Palmore, 1981).

A second view is that there are sequences of changes, but that these are generated by external patterns such as changing family or work roles. Janet Giele (1982) calls these *timing models* of the life course. In such models, each of us is seen as moving simultaneously along a series of separate pathways. On each pathway there may be a predictable sequence of events, such as changes in family roles; but the speed with which we move is different on each pathway, and there is little or no coordination from one pathway to the next.

Again there is support for this position. Despite the continuities of personality type, there are predictable changes in adults' self-concepts and behavior in each of the role sequences (pathways) they occupy. For many purposes, in fact, a person's location along a sequence like the family-role sequence is a better predictor of behavior and attitudes than age. For example, people with young children behave and think alike in certain ways, no matter what their actual ages may be.

Proponents of this position insist, however, that there are no *stages*, no overall *synchrony* across sequences. If you think back to Chapters 4 and 9, when we talked about cognitive development from the structural view, we talked about themes and about stages. The distinction we are making here is precisely the same one. Do the themes, the separate pathways, add up in some fashion to create stages? Leonard Perlin (1980), Marjorie Fiske (1980), and others argue that they do not. Their studies of working-class adults do not suggest stages or synthesis. Rather, the adults appear to move along from day to day, or week to week, handling the crises or problems as they come along. Fiske, in fact, does not see much sign of personal growth at all in most of the subjects she studied.

The third view, in some ways the most optimistic of the three, is that adult personality development is a process of individual growth. Most theorists of this persuasion also think that this growth occurs in definable stages. Each stage is thought to involve a reanalysis and a reorganization, not unlike the sequence Marcia describes for the identity crisis in adolescence.

In its most extreme form—perhaps represented by Erikson, Gould, and Loevinger—the stages are seen as hierarchical. Each step builds on the conflicts and discoveries of the previous stage.

The strong appeal of this last view, at least to us, lies in its emphasis on personal growth over adulthood. Since both of us are in the period usually called midlife, we would like to think that the next 40 years will be made up of small bits of personal progress, rather than merely a long string of days or weeks survived as best as possible. However, the evidence for hierarchical, inner stages is not terribly impressive. Two sorts of counterevidence are particularly troubling.

First, there is the repeated indication that if there are stages, they do not occur in the same order for men and for women. For many women, the central identity crisis, involving decisions about occupation or independent values, seems to occur after intimacy and even generativity have been developed. For men, generativity and the development of nurturance and compassion are more delayed. The crossover theme we talked about in the discussion of sex roles is a perfect example of these different male and female pathways. In midlife, women become more independent and men become more affectionate and empathetic. If the sequences of stages were really hierarchical, it shouldn't work like this.

An even more striking type of counterevidence is the fact that many adults do not seem to mature or grow at all. Vaillant found this, as did Farrell and Rosenberg, and both Fiske and Pearlin have reported the same thing. Whatever definition of maturing or growth we may use—changes in defense mechanisms, or greater personality integration, or expressions of generativity, or whatever—it is clear that many adults do not show significant change at all, let alone stagelike reevaluations. In particular, working-class men and women are especially unlikely to describe stagelike changes or to show increased integration or maturity.

Taken together, these two kinds of evidence would seem to eliminate any possibility of a stage theory of adult personality. But many adults *do* describe changes that match Erikson's or Levinson's stages. How can we reconcile this perception of change by many adults with the other evidence?

Janet Giele (1982) has offered a synthesis that we think allows us to have our cake and eat it too.

> Evidently some people experience distinct stages of adult development while others do not. It is the degree of social complexity on the job or in other aspects of everyday life that appears critical. Those who must learn a great deal and adapt to many different roles seem to be the most concerned with trying to evolve an abstract self, conscience, or life structure that can integrate all these discrete events. By contrast, those with a simple job, limited by meager education and narrow contacts, are less apt to experience aging as a process that enhances autonomy or elaborates one's mental powers (Giele, 1982, p. 8).

In essence, Giele is saying that stages, or the sense of personal transformation, are a formal operational process, involving creation of a superordinate sense of self. Since most of us do not use such complex levels of thinking unless the situation demands it, those adults whose lives are predictable and controllable without such higher-order constructs will normally get along without them.

Most of us *do* go along day to day, coping with the crises and conflicts (as well as pleasures and joys) as they come along. When the level of complexity reaches some threshold, however—because we are occupying myriad roles or because of some unexpected change occurs, such as the death of a parent or an illness or injury—we may be pushed into reassessment and emerge with a somewhat different pattern. In James Marcia's terms (see Chapter 10), most adults remain in a foreclosure identity status; only those confronted by conflict or change will go through a new moratorium (disequilibrium) and move to a new identity.

We would add two further elements to Giele's synthesis. First, one's underlying personality type may affect the way an adult handles these transitional periods in life. As one example, those who are open rather than rigid, or low rather than high in neuroticism, may be more likely to show increasing maturity over adulthood. Similarly, those who have successfully moved through the adolescent identity crisis and mastered the earlier stages Erikson describes may be more able to respond to later crises with creative transformation.

Second, while we agree that there is a set of tasks, issues, or questions that are the common fodder of these life transitions, we believe that there is no *single* order in which those tasks can be faced and handled successfully.

Both of these points are still highly speculative. Over the next few years, as research on such questions expands, we will see how our ideas fare in the face of the evidence. And as we both age, we can add our own experience of consistency or growth to the mixture.

SUMMARY

1. We can look at identity and personality in adulthood both by examining developmental changes in roles and by looking at continuities and discontinuities in personality patterns over adulthood.
2. Family roles change in systematic ways as children are born, enter school, become adolescents, move away from home. Marital satisfaction is typically at its highest immediately after marriage and in the postparental period.
3. The decline in marital satisfaction during child-rearing years may be caused by multiplication of roles, producing role overload. Or it may occur because this is a period in which economic and work strain is also at a maximum for most adults.
4. Rearing children also brings notable pleasures to most adults.
5. Grandparenthood is another distinct role, one that appears to be

most comfortable if it occurs on time, when the adult is in his/her fifties, sixties, or seventies.

6. Typical family life cycles no longer occur in many adult lives, however, with the rise of divorce and remarriage and the increase of nonmarriage. Single women appear to be somewhat better adjusted than single men, but there is as yet too little research to say why this might be so.

7. Work roles also shape most adult lives. Continuous work during adulthood is the most common pattern for both men and women, although women are more likely to show work/nonwork patterns than men.

8. Jobs held during the early years of adulthood are qualitatively different from *old* jobs. *Young* jobs typically require less skill, more muscle, pay less well, and bring fewer satisfactions. Generally, job satisfaction increases during adulthood.

9. Retirement from working is less of an upheaval for most adults than previously believed. Retirement does not appear to increase sickness or lower life satisfaction, although it is frequently associated with lowered incomes and somewhat lowered self-esteem.

10. Combining work and family roles is a complex task for many couples, with the role overload greater for women than for men in most cases. On average, working women perform approximately two thirds of the child care and housework, even in two-parent households.

11. Sex roles ("jobs" assigned to men and women) change in at least two ways in adulthood: They become maximally differentiated (stereotyped, even) after the birth of children and then become more similar in midlife.

12. Personality in adolescence and adulthood appears to be consistent on at least three dimensions: extraversion versus introversion, neuroticism, and openness versus rigidity. Overt behaviors, however, show far less consistency than do these underlying personal styles.

13. Some adults appear to be more consistent in personality over adulthood than others. For some, inconsistency is a sign of growth or resolution of new identity crises.

14. When change occurs in personality in adulthood, it appears to happen in particular ways, such as increasing use of mature defense mechanisms or greater personality integration. Contrary to some theories, however, there does not appear to be a general tendency toward greater disengagement among the elderly.

15. Other theorists have proposed clearly differentiated sequences of stages, shared by all adults. *Some* adults appear to demonstrate such systematic change, but it is less common than stage theorists suggest.

16. Whether an adult goes through personality transformations of the kind suggested by stage theorists appears to be related to education, social class, and work demands. Adults confronted with complex jobs and roles may resolve the conflicts by creating new higher-level personal identities.

Conformist stage   One of several stages of ego development proposed by Jane Loevinger. Adults in this stage perceive others in basically stereotypic ways, emphasizing role relationships and responsibilities.

Conscientious stage   Another stage proposed by Jane Loevinger, coming after the conformist stage and characterized by more internalized values.

Defense mechanisms   Term used by Freud to describe unconscious methods for defending ourselves against anxiety or fear. Vaillant has organized these into a developmental hierarchy with mechanisms such as denial as primitive defenses, while humor and suppression are mature defenses.

Developmental tasks   Phrase used by Havighurst to describe specific sets of outer roles and inner (psychological) dilemmas normally confronted by each adult at particular points in the adult life cycle.

Disengagement   A progressive withdrawal from social encounters hypothesized by some theorists as a normal and healthy part of the years of old age.

Ego mechanisms   Another phrase used to describe defense mechanisms.

Extraversion   A dimension of personality found to be fairly consistent over adolescence and adulthood. Extraverts are outgoing, sociable, oriented to relationships with others.

Family roles   The jobs associated with membership in a marriage or family. These jobs change systematically as children are born and grow.

Generativity   Term used by Erikson to describe the central task of the years from the mid-twenties through the thirties and forties. The adult must contribute to the next generation in some way by raising children, assisting younger colleagues, or through creativity.

Introversion   The other end of the dimension of extraversion. An introverted person is more inwardly directed, less oriented toward and interested in relationships with others.

Life structure   Phrase used by Levinson to describe a relatively stable combination of roles and relationships created by an adult following a life transition.

Mentor   The role of leader/guide/nurturant supporter frequently filled by older workers in their relationship with selected younger workers.

Neuroticism   A dimension of personality on which stability has been noted from adolescence through adulthood. Adults high in neuroticism are likely to display many symptoms and to describe themselves as unhappy with their lives.

Openness to experience versus rigidity   A third dimension of personality that shows some stability over adulthood. Open adults are willing to try new experiences, to admit their faults and crises.

Sex roles   The set of jobs assigned to males and females in any given culture.

In our culture, the male sex role centers around basic competence and financial support of the family. The female sex role centers around nurturance and emotional support.

Work roles   The collection of behaviors expected from someone in an occupation. These roles change somewhat with age and vary depending on the occupation as well.

SUGGESTED READINGS

Giele, J. Z. Women's work and family roles. In J. Z. Giele (Ed.), *Women in the middle years*. New York: Wiley, 1982.

This chapter is more scholarly and somewhat tougher reading than the other selections in this list, but it is a splendid review of this material.

Gould, R. L. *Transformations: Growth and change in adult life*. New York: Simon & Schuster, 1978.

We have not talked about Gould's stage theory of adult development for lack of space, but many of you will find this book a wonderfully insightful look at some of the issues in your own lives.

Scarf, M. *Unfinished business. Pressure points in the lives of women*. New York: Doubleday, 1980.

Another book about women, also first-rate. Both men and women would profit from reading it.

Sheehy, G. *Pathfinders*. New York: Dutton, 1982.

By the author of *Passages,* this new book offers fascinating insights about a special subgroup of adults who go through profound personal transformations. There are many great case studies sprinkled through the book.

Vaillant, G. E. *Adaptation to life*. Boston: Little, Brown, 1977.

Of all the books on personality changes and continuities in adult life, this may well be the best. Not easy, but worth the effort.

PROJECT 13.1
Adult Roles

In this project, you are going to ask a number of adults to tell you how they divide up their energies and enthusiasm among the different roles that they play. You will need to locate two adults over 65 (one male, one female), two adults in their thirties or forties (one male, one female), and two adults in their college years or early twenties (one male and one female).

Materials

You will need a piece of paper with a 6-inch circle on it for each person you interview. The person will also need a pencil, a place to write, and about 15 minutes time. For each subject, you should also ask about present marital status and whether there are children present in their home. Be sure that each of your papers has this information clearly marked for future reference.

Directions

Read these instructions to the subject:

"I am doing a project about the ways that different people divide up their time and energies among the different activities they do. I would like you to divide this circle up into a pie, with each piece of the pie representing a role that you play in your life. For example, you might have one piece for your job, another piece for your marriage, and another for your household work or hobbies. You can use any categories you like, but please label each piece with the activity and the percent of your time and energy that you spend on it."

Analysis and Discussion

If you are reporting on only your own six interviews, compare those given by men and women and by the three age groups. Are there differences? Do they match what you expected, given the information in the chapter? How much more information would you want to have (how many more subjects, for example) before you were more confident about your conclusions?

If the results from an entire class are combined, several interesting analyses are possible, including (but not restricted to) the following:

1. Compare the activities of young, middle-aged, and old adults across the larger sample. In particular, look at the amount of time devoted to work and to family for the three age groups. Are they different?
2. Compare the roles described by men and women across ages or within each age. For this analysis, it probably makes a difference if the adult is married and has children, is married without children, or unmarried. You may thus end up with several categories for each gender. Are the age trends different for males and females, or for different marital-status groups?

Chapter 14
Attachments in Adulthood

(14)

Years ago, Freud was asked to define *maturity*. His answer was that maturity was to be found in the capacity of the adult to love and to work. In the last chapter we talked about the work of the adult—both the roles filled and the inner work of individual development. In this chapter we want to talk about love.

Ah, love. A splendid state. Each of you has undoubtedly been in love at least once (some of us many times), so you know the sense of involvement, preoccupation, passion, and joy that is part of what we usually mean by *being in love*. But loving goes beyond the first flush of attraction. As Freud meant it, and as we mean it, loving in adulthood includes relationships with a whole range of other people. Most of us have (or strive for) intimate and loving relationships with our partner, our parents, grandparents, siblings, our own children, and our friends.

We think it makes sense to talk about such loving relationships in terms of *attachments*. What we will be asking in this chapter, then, is what type of attachments adults have to each other, to their children, their parents, their friends, and how those attachments may or may not change with age. As usual, we will also be asking whether there are systematic individual differences in the patterns we can detect and the impact of those differences on adult development.

Regrettably, loving is not all sunsets and holding hands. Inevitably each of us faces the loss of loving as well, a process we can think of as *dis*attachment or *detachment*. Breaking up with a lover is one kind of detachment, as is divorce or the death of someone close to you. Losing a job or retiring are also kinds of detachment, as is the departure of your children from home out into their own lives. We can also think of our own death as the final detachment.

Describing these relationships in the language of attachment theory is somewhat unusual—although we have company (Kahn & Antonucci, 1980; Troll & Smith, 1976; Henderson, 1977). John Bowlby, who was one of the first theorists to talk about attachments between infants and their parents, specifically states that attachments continue to be formed and persist throughout the life span:

> During the course of healthy development attachment behaviour leads
> to the development of affectional bonds or attachments, initially
> between child and parent and later between adult and adult. The forms
> of behaviour and the bonds to which they lead are present and active
> throughout the life cycle (Bowlby, 1980, p. 39).

What we are assuming is that the relationship created between husband and wife or between friends is at least analogous to the attachment a child develops for its parents. Furthermore, we are assuming that the quality of that first attachment may well have repercussions for the relationships that the individual is able to create in adulthood.

Attachment Behavior and Attachment.   Before going on, it may be helpful to remind you of a distinction we made in Chapter 7 between **attachment** and **attachment behavior.** The attachment is the basic inner affectional bond between one person and another. When we watch people with one another, though, we do not see the attachment. What we see are the outer manifestations of that attachment, namely, attachment behavior. Attachment behaviors serve to create or maintain proximity to some other person.

Three points about attachment behavior are important when we look at adult attachments. First of all, older children and adults have much larger repertoires of attachment behaviors at their disposal. An infant cries, clings, cuddles, smiles, makes eye contact, shows all the "proximity promoting" behaviors we described in Chapter 7. An older child may call to his mother from another room or glance up from his play now and then. If we watch adults who are in what Michael Argyle (1972) calls "focused interaction" (face to face, as in a conversation), we see many of the same attachment behaviors we notice in an infant or between infants and their parents. The two people stand near each other—but not too near (3 to 5 feet is about right for most interactions). They make eye contact, at least at the start of the interaction, and they more or less look at each other during most of the conversation. If the two people are in love with one another, they maintain eye contact even longer and stand or sit closer together (Rubin, 1973). Most important, each person paces his or her part in the interaction according to what the other person is doing. When one is talking, the other is listening. This is very much the same sort of process that Ken Kaye has called "turn taking" between a mother and an infant, that Blehar and her associates described as "contingent pacing," and that we have consistently referred to as "dancing."

But adults are also able to use a whole range of much more abstract attachment behaviors that bridge physical distances, such as writing letters, phoning a friend, or even imagining the loved person. Adults may sometimes disguise their attachment behaviors as well— something we do not see in the young child.

I have a friend who can hardly bear to admit that he might need some help or support. I have learned to listen between the words if he calls. Does he sound depressed? Does he hint in any way that he's a little lonely or not feeling well? If I hear such a hint—highly disguised, always—I know that I need to offer some help, some time, some laughter. He will not *ask,* but the message is there to read if I listen. [HB]

A second key point is that attachment behaviors are much more likely to be visible when a person is under stress. We see this in 3-year-olds who cling to their mothers only when they face something strange or

Figure 14.1. These adults are in what Argyle calls "focused interaction." They are looking at each other, are 3 to 5 feet apart, and are giving all the nonverbal signals that suggest interest. If they were in love with one another, they would stand closer, or touch, and would gaze more continuously into each other's eyes.

frightening; we see it in adults who seek contact with others when they have experienced a loss or when they are tired or otherwise stressed. The point is that while attachments persist in adulthood (at least we assume they do), they may be displayed only part of the time. This makes the study of attachments in adults much more difficult than it is in children.

The third point to keep in mind is that it is tricky to move from observations of attachment behaviors to inferences about the quality of the attachment itself. In particular, we have to bear in mind that it is not the *quantity* of attachment behavior that is the signal for a strong or secure attachment, but the *quality* of that behavior—the relative amounts of positive and negative signals, the timing of the signals, the use of the key person as a safe base under conditions of stress. As an example, we are likely to learn far more about an adult's underlying attachments by seeing whom he calls when he is facing a crisis than we will by watching whom he smiles at or sits near at a business meeting.

Despite the difficulties inherent in studying attachments in adults, we think that this concept can help us create some orderliness out of the complex of relationships adults have with others.

THE ATTACHMENT TO A PARTNER OR SPOUSE

In Chapter 10 we talked about the formation of a central loving partnership (usually resulting in marriage) and about some of the factors that influence the stability of marriages. We didn't give much detail, though, about how marriages may change over time and what good marriages or bad marriages look like or feel like on the inside. Following our usual custom, let us look at the developmental changes first and then at the differences between stable or "vital" marriages and distressed marriages.

Changes in Marriages over Time

We have two somewhat conflicting sets of information about developmental changes in marital relationships. One set of research—mostly studies of happy marriages that have lasted over many years—tells us that the attachment remains strong over time but that the central emphasis of the relationship changes somewhat. A feeling of emotional security (trust, affection, caring, and concern) is a key to good relationships at every age but seems to become somewhat more important in older couples (those in their fifties, sixties, and seventies). In contrast, self-disclosure, honest communication, and sexual intimacy all are more important in maintaining a satisfying marriage among young couples (in their twenties) than they are for older couples (Reedy, Birren, & Schaie, 1981). Over the adult years, then, satisfying, loving relationships may become less emotionally intense and more focused on shared experiences, shared goals.

A second developmental theme in research on marriage, however, paints a somewhat different picture. The consistent finding from research on marital satisfaction, from both cross-sectional and longitudinal research, is that satisfaction declines over time. As we have already pointed out in Chapter 13 (go back and look at Figure 13.1 again), there is evidence that this trend turns around during the postparental period for those marriages that survive that long. Still, the overall pattern is of less and less satisfaction over the years of marriage, particularly the early years (Swensen, Eskew, & Kohlhepp, 1981).

We suggested in Chapter 13 that part of the reason for this decline may be the extra role strains involved in raising children. Another possibility is that spouses display fewer and fewer positive attachment behaviors to one another. Some recent findings from Clifford Swensen and his colleagues (1981) suggest that both of these elements may enter

(handwritten margin note: nevertheless)

Figure 14.2. Love does not always fade away. . . . Research shows that expressions of affection tend to decline even in long-lasting marriages, but this couple certainly shows that affection and caring can continue well into old age.

the equation. They asked a group of 776 adults to complete a questionnaire describing aspects of loving interaction between themselves and their spouse and aspects of marital problems they encountered. Figure 14.3 shows the results from this study comparing the responses of adults who were at different points in Duvall's family life cycle. Marriage problems were highest when there were toddlers or school-age children at home and at their lowest after the children left home—the same pattern we saw in the last chapter. But added to that was a steady

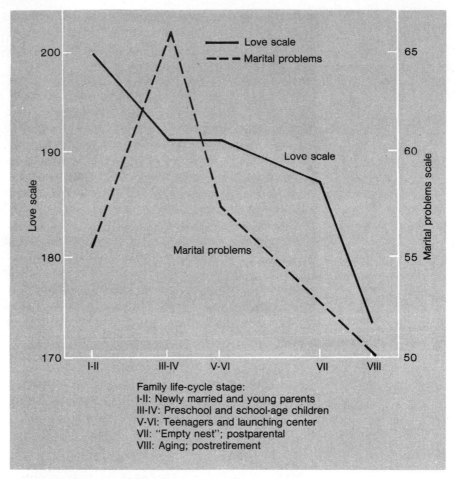

Figure 14.3. In this study, subjects described the expressions of love between themselves and their spouses and the marital problems they experienced. As you can see, both love and problems declined in later stages of marriage. This combination has sometimes been described as the devitalized marriage. (*Source:* Swensen, Eskew, & Kohlhepp, 1981, p. 848.)

decline in expressions of love between spouses. Swensen argues that the combination of these two trends describes a *devitalization* of marriage in middle age.

Combining these two batches of information about marriages in adulthood is no simple task, partly because the researchers have used very different groups of subjects and asked very different questions. When we study lasting, happy marriages, it looks like the underlying attachment remains strong but that it is expressed somewhat differently. When we study less selected groups of married couples, we find that satisfaction declines steadily over age and over length of marriage.

The most obvious synthesis of this information is to suggest that over time one of the key changes in marital relationships is that partners direct fewer positive attachment behaviors toward one another—fewer glances, fewer touches, less time spent physically near one another, and the like. In part, this seems to be an acceptable change since the passionate, sexually intimate part of marriage decreases somewhat in importance over the years of adulthood, while security and loyalty become more important. For many couples, though, the lessening of such loving gestures may create the impression that the spouse's fundamental attachment has weakened (which, in fact, it may well have done in some cases). The interactive pattern may then begin to resemble an *insecure attachment* rather than a secure one. Those relationships in which this problem becomes acute are likely to terminate in divorce; those couples who maintain an adequate level or pattern of loving expressions continue to be satisfied.

If we are correct in this speculative extension of attachment theory, we ought to find that satisfying marriages (secure attachments, in our terms) are typified by a pattern of attachment behaviors that include more positive ("come here") signals than are found in marriages that the participants describe as unhappy or distressed. In fact, a number of recent studies suggest that this is true.

Good versus Bad Marriages

Several clear themes emerge from the numerous studies comparing satisfying and dissatisfying or distressed and happy marriages:

1. *In satisfying marriages, couples exchange many more pleasing or positive behaviors and fewer negative behaviors* than is true for unsatisfying or distressed marriages. In the language of learning theory, satisfying marriages are characterized by a high rate of positive reinforcements.

For example, Birchler, Weiss, and Vincent (1975) compared a group of 12 distressed couples with a group of 12 happily married couples. Each member of each pair kept a daily record of pleasing and displeasing behaviors of the spouse over a period of 14 days. The nondistressed couples, on the average, reported about 30 pleases for every displease, while for the distressed couples the ratio was only about 4 to 1. Notice that in both groups there were more pleasing than displeasing events (we presume that if the displeasing behaviors became more numerous, the couple would be unlikely to stay together at all). However, the ratio is very different in the two groups.

These findings certainly show that the more loving things spouses do for each other the happier their marriage is likely to be. As we suggested earlier, though, it may not be the *actual* rate of positive attachment behaviors that is really critical. Rather, what the spouses *notice* about the partner's behavior may be more important. For example, Neil Jacobson and his colleagues (Jacobson, Waldron, & Moore, 1980) asked couples to rate their overall marital satisfaction each day for 15 consecutive days. The spouses also filled out a long checklist describing the positive and negative behavior of the partner during that day. What Jacobson found was that the dynamic was different in the distressed couples. For them, the thing that made a day good was a *low* level of *displeasing* events. For couples with good marriages, a good day was one with a high level of shared activities and pleasing events.

Distressed couples may also underestimate the number of actual positive exchanges that go on (Robinson & Price, 1980). They are so focused on the negative exchanges that the positive interactions have less impact.

Figure 14.4. Unpleasant encounters in a marriage, like this one, are more likely to be noticed and remembered by couples who are already experiencing marital difficulties than they are by usually happy couples.

2. *Happily married couples read each other's signals better than unhappily married couples.* Failing to notice positive exchanges is one sign of this, but the problem is more pervasive. A great deal of attachment behavior is nonverbal—mutual eye contact, smiles, movement of the body toward the other person, and so on. In distressed couples, these nonverbal signals are not "read" correctly.

This is nowhere more apparent than in the results of a splendidly clever study by John Gottman and Albert Porterfield (1981). They had couples try to communicate specific sentence meanings by using nonverbal signals. For example, the partner might be told to say "I'm cold, aren't you?" and to suggest which of three possible meanings was intended by using body language ("Are you cold too?" or "Please warm me up with some physical affection" or "Please turn up the heat"). The listener had to try to figure out which meaning was intended. Gottman and Porterfield then had *other* couples (strangers) watch videotapes of these exchanges to see if they could figure out what was meant.

What the researchers found was that in distressed couples, the husband was misreading the wife's cues. Since neutral watchers could figure out what the wife was sending, it was clear that the problem was in the receiver and not in the sender. In happily married couples, the partners read each other's signals somewhat *better* than strangers could, which suggests a sort of private language had been developed.

3. *Happily married couples solve their problems and disagreements in less aggressive and more intimate ways.*

Once again we can illustrate this with the results of a recent study. Marilyn Rands and her colleagues (Rands, Levinger, & Mellinger, 1981) had 244 young married couples describe the way they reacted and the kinds of things they said and their spouse said when they had a conflict. They also described the outcome of such conflicts (kiss and make up, compromise, continuing annoyance or escalation of the problem, among others). Each subject also rated his or her satisfaction with the marriage. Table 14.1 shows the main result: Those who used the most aggressive and least intimate forms of conflict resolution were least satisfied with their marriages.

TABLE 14.1
Amount of Marital Satisfaction Reported by Couples
Who Differ in Style of Marital Conflict Resolution

INITIAL STYLE OF HANDLING CONFLICT	STYLE OF RESOLVING CONFLICT	
	Intimate	*Nonintimate*
Low attack	+.59	+.14
High attack	+.03	−.72

SOURCE: Rands, Levinger, & Mellinger, 1981.

What do these various findings tell us about good marriages and about attachment to the spouse? Think back to what we said about the attachment process between the newborn infant and the parent. We described it as a process of learning to "dance" together smoothly, to read each other's signals, and to emit the sort of come hither signals that keep the other member of the pair involved in the interaction. Securely attached infants appear to have parents who manage the contingent pacing that is required.

We are struck by the similarity between this and the description of a satisfying marital relationship. The partners are emitting clear, frequent, positive signals and are reading the other person's signals well. When they find themselves disagreeing, they listen rather than try to force their own ideas on the other person. In other words, satisfied couples sound like securely attached pairs, while distressed couples sound like insecurely attached pairs. The fundamental attachment may be strong in both cases—as it is in infants. But the system works smoothly in one case and not in the other.

The fact that marital satisfaction typically declines when children enter the family unit suggests that for some pairs, the complexities of maintaining several concurrent attachment relationships strain the ability of the pair to maintain contingent pacing with one another.

The link in this chain of logic that is missing is the relationship between the security of early childhood attachments and the success or security of the marital attachment. Obviously, Erikson's theory leads us to expect such a link, as does Bowlby's. At the moment we know of no decent longitudinal data that would allow us to test this hypothesis. The basic assumption, though, is an intriguing one: Some people may be simply better at forming and maintaining attachments than others. If this is so, we should see evidence of it not only in continuity between childhood relationships and marriages, but also in all of an adult's relationships with others.

RELATIONSHIPS WITH OTHER FAMILY MEMBERS DURING ADULTHOOD

For many, if not most, adults the relationship with a partner or spouse is the central attachment in adulthood. Our sense of satisfaction with life is perhaps more influenced by the quality of this relationship than by any other. At the same time, though, we also maintain relationships with a great many others, including both friends and family. By *family* we mean the entire (genetic) kinship network: parents, brothers, sisters, cousins, grandparents, and our own children. We talked about the formation of the parents' attachment to newborn children in Chapter 7 and about parent-child relationships during adolescence in Chapter 10. Here we want to focus on adults' relation-

ships with their grown children and with their own parents and siblings.

Are there changes in our relationships with family members over
the life span? Are elderly adults more, or less, involved in family interactions? Do our contacts with our parents decline or increase over
time?

Frequency of Contact with Family Members in Adulthood

We can think of a number of arguments that might lead us to expect
that contact with parents, siblings, and other family members would
decline during one's twenties or thirties, when getting started in a job
and a family take up so much of your time. Surprisingly, the results
of a number of cross-sectional studies show that family contacts remain
essentially constant over the entire adult period (Troll & Bengston,
1979). Geoffrey Leigh's study (1982) is the most recent and complete,
so let us use his findings as an illustration.

Leigh interviewed a group of 800 adults in 1964 and another group
of nearly 500 adults in 1976. He asked each person how frequently she
or he saw, wrote to, or talked on the phone with parents, brothers and
sisters, cousins, and grown children (for those members of the sample
who were old enough to have grown children). He then looked at the
relationship between frequency of reported contact and the adult's
stage in Duvall's family life cycle, with the results shown in Figure
14.5. We've shown both the monthly and weekly contacts with parents,
siblings, and grown children.

The most striking thing about these results is how astonishingly stable the family contacts are over age groups. Virtually everyone reported that they had contact with their parents at least once a month.
There is a small decline in frequent (weekly) contacts during the early
stages of marriage and parenthood, but the overall pattern is one of
stable, high levels of contact.

Regular contact with family members seems to be maintained well
into old age, too. A national survey conducted by Louis Harris for the
National Council on the Aging (1975) showed that 81 percent of adults
over 65 said they had seen one or more of their children in the past
week; 73 percent said they had seen or talked to a grandchild within
the past week. These levels of contact were true even for the very oldest
adults in the survey, those over 80. Harris also created a measure of
social and family contact for this survey that included frequency of contact with close friends as well as family members and found *no* difference in this score across the age groups he surveyed—from 18 to past
80.

We should emphasize (again) that these are cross-sectional comparisons, not longitudinal ones. These results do not tell us that today's 20-

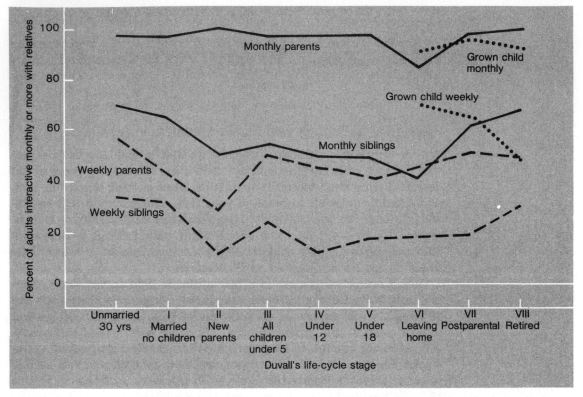

Figure 14.5. These cross-sectional data show that the amount of contact people have with their parents and brothers, sisters, and grown children changes very little over the life-cycle stages; it is high at all ages. (*Source:* Leigh, 1982, p. 202.)

or 30-year-olds will maintain a steady level of involvement with family members for the rest of their lives, nor that today's 70-year-olds did so. However, the consistency of the findings from this study, and from cross-sectional studies done in earlier decades, is impressive.

Why do we maintain contact with our families? Is it just habit, or duty? Or is this contact an expression of continuing attachment? Leigh's results suggest the latter. Most of the adults he interviewed said that they saw or wrote to their relatives because they felt close to them and enjoyed the contact. Giving or receiving assistance from relatives was another reason for contact, and physical proximity to one's relatives was also an important ingredient. Physical proximity seemed especially important, in fact, for siblings and cousins. These adults say they saw their brothers and sisters if they lived nearby but didn't see them or have much contact with them if they were farther away. That was not true of contact with parents, however, which was high even when the parents were not close by. Still, in this study, for all the groups the strongest basis for contact seemed to be pleasure in the company of family members. That sounds much more like attachment than habit.

Other evidence, though, suggests that habit or a sense of obligation may play a greater role in family contacts during the middle years (thirties and forties) than either earlier or later. Norman Shulman (1975), for example, found that 72 percent of adults in the 31 to 44 age group he studied listed obligation as one of the reasons they maintained relationships with relatives and friends, compared to only 21 percent of 18- to 30-year-olds or 19 percent of those over 45.

Type of Contact with Family Members

This change in the sense of obligation toward family members should not surprise us very much in view of the changes in the *content* of family contacts at various points in the family life cycle. In particular, if we look at who is giving help and who is receiving help, we see generational shifts.

Figure 14.6. Most adults will say that they see their families because it is enjoyable to do so—although there may be some flavor of duty or obligation, too.

The young adult with children of his own is obviously giving a great deal to his immediate family. However, we might expect that in his relationship with his own parents and grandparents he is much more on the receiving than on the giving end of financial and emotional support. At the other end of the life span we might also expect to see a balance in favor of receiving rather than giving aid. At this point in many parent-child relationships there is a kind of role reversal, with the aging parent no longer the nurturant partner. The middle-aged child now takes on the nurturing role, giving aid and support.

The generation caught in this squeeze is the middle-aged parents who have both grown children and elderly parents. This group is likely to give more than it receives in both directions. These changes in the nature of family exchanges are shown very clearly in an older study by Reuben Hill (1968) of three generations in a group of families. Each family in this study had a set of grandparents who were over 60 years of age, a set of parents (aged 40 to 60), and a set of married children (aged 20 to 40). Hill asked family members in all generations what kinds of help they gave to others in the family and what kinds of help they received. Figure 14.7 summarizes their answers.

The parents in these families—the middle generation—gave the most help, almost half of all the help that was given. The younger generation was on the receiving end of a great deal of the aid, especially financial help and help with child care. The grandparent generation, too, seemed to be mostly on the receiving end. In some sense, the generation in the middle acts as parents to both their own children and to their parents.

We think the picture emerging from Hill's study is probably generally accurate, but it is misleading in at least one respect. Although Hill's grandparent generation is described as being 60 or over, in fact most of them were in their seventies or eighties. Other evidence points to the fact that adults continue to give high levels of aid and support to their families through their sixties and into their early seventies. The switch in roles, with the elderly person assuming a more dependent role, if it occurs at all, seems to take place later than Hill's results suggest.

For example, Lee and Ellithorpe (1982) found that among adults over 60, age was an important predictor of giving family aid: The younger the adult the more aid she gave. Louis Harris (1975) found the same thing in his survey for the National Council on the Aging. For instance, 65 percent of those between 65 and 69 in this survey said they baby-sat with grandchildren at least occasionally; 53 percent of those between 70 and 79 baby-sat, while only 34 percent of those over 80 years old said they performed this service. Thus while there is a decline in aid and assistance given during the retirement years, most elderly adults continue to give significant assistance to their families well into their seventies and beyond.

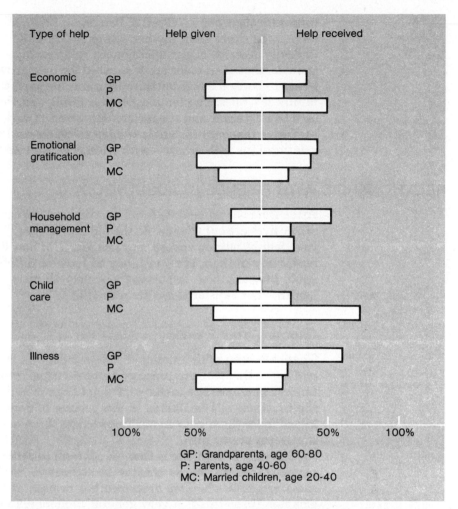

Figure 14.7. The middle generation of adult parents whose own parents are still living is the one that seems to bear the largest burden of giving aid, since they give more to both their own children and to their parents than they receive from either, as the results in this figure show. (*Source:* Ethel Shanas and Gordon F. Streib, Social structure and the family, 1965, p. 125. Reprinted by permission of Prentice-Hall, Inc., Englewood Cliffs, N.J.)

Sex Differences in Family Interactions

One footnote on the family interaction patterns deserves some mention, if only because it is consistent with what we know about friendship patterns as well: There is a small but consistent tendency for women to maintain closer ties with their families than for men to do so.

In the vast majority of cultures around the world, families are linked through women (Troll & Bengston, 1979). Mother-daughter ties seem to be closer than mother-son or father-child ties, and daughters typically describe closer affectionate relationships with their parents than do sons. If an older adult is cared for by a grown child, it is more likely to be by a daughter than by a son. In part, this may reflect the family sex roles. The female job in a family, as we discussed earlier, is to be nurturant and supportive. However, it may also reflect a more pervasive tendency for adult women to create and maintain intimate relationships with others—with friends as well as family.

RELATIONSHIPS WITH FRIENDS IN ADULTHOOD

Aside from our immediate families, the most important people in most of our lives are our friends. As the old saying goes, "You are stuck with your family, but you choose your friends." But how do you choose them, how many of them are you likely to have at different points in your adult life, and how important are they to your development, your health, your satisfaction with your life?

Choosing Your Friends

There has been a fair amount of research done on friendship formation and friendship patterns among adults. As usual, most of it is not longitudinal, and most researchers have not been primarily concerned with the functions of friendships in the process of development. Nonetheless, despite these gaps in our knowledge, there are a few conclusions that seem pretty firm.

The very firmest one is that we all tend to choose our friends from among those we see as similar to ourselves. We talked about this same principle when we described the process of finding partners in Chapter 10, so this is a very general tendency. Literally hundreds of studies by sociologists and social psychologists show that the more you think you are like someone, the more you will like him, and the more likely you are to become and to remain friends. Our friends are usually people our own age, the same sex, from the same educational or social-class background, with similar lifestyles and beliefs. There are obviously exceptions. A significant minority of adults have cross-sex friendships—perhaps 30 to 40 percent—and many of us have friends who are not from our own generation. But similarity is the usual rule.

Maintaining friendships, however, requires more than similarity. Marjorie Fiske Lowenthal and her colleagues (Lowenthal, Thurnher, & Chiriboga, 1975) asked a group of several hundred adults, of varying ages, what qualities their friendships actually had and what qualities

Figure 14.8. Most of us pick our best friends from among others who are the same approximate age, the same sex, and the same general family background.

they thought should ideally determine friendships. Aside from similarity, the subjects most often mentioned *reciprocity* as a key quality. They wanted their friends to be supportive, dependable, understanding, and accepting.

The importance of intimate, trusting, affection in friendships is underlined in the results of a 1979 survey by *Psychology Today*. To be sure, subscribers to this magazine are not typical of all adults (among other things, 70 percent of the respondents were women), and we cannot be sure that other groups would emphasize precisely the same qualities, but the findings are nonetheless intriguing. The qualities of friendships these adults thought were most important were keeping confidences, loyalty, warmth, affection, supportiveness, and frankness. In the language we used in Chapter 9, it is clear that most adults view friendship at Selman's Level 4—as a complex, mutually shared relationship.

Changes in Friendship Patterns over Adulthood

Unlike contacts with family members, which remain highly stable over the life span, there seem to be some systematic patterns of change in friendship over the adult years. The general pattern is to have more, and more intimate, friendships in your early twenties and again after 60 than in the middle years. The lowest point, especially for men, seems to be at midlife. In Lowenthal's study, for example, newlywed young adults (Duvall's Stage I) reported an average of 7.6 friends, 60-year-olds listed an average of 6.0 friends, while 50-year-olds listed only 4.7.

The same developmental pattern shows up in Farrell and Rosenberg's study (1981) of a group of men at various stages in the life cycle, as you can see in Figure 14.9. Young unmarried men reported the most friends; middle-aged men reported the least.

Two other things may strike you about the results in Figure 14.9. First, the actual number of friends the men said they had is much lower than the numbers Lowenthal and her colleagues found. Farrell and Rosenberg's subjects have only one or two friends, instead of five or six. There is so little research on adult friendship that we can't be sure which set of numbers is the more accurate, but there are bits and pieces that make it look as if the one-to-two level is accurate for men in midlife at least. Daniel Levinson, for example (1978), whose theory of adult development we described in the last chapter, found that friendships were quite rare among 35- to 45-year-old men he studied.

A second point about Farrell and Rosenberg's data is that working-class men described themselves as having fewer friends than did middle-class men, a finding reported in several other studies as well (Bell, 1981).

Not only do the sheer numbers of friends decline in midlife, friendships also seem to become less intimate during those years (Farrell & Rosenberg, 1981; Shulman, 1975). We see our friends less often, and we disclose less and share less. There are hints that friendships become deeper once again in the later years of adulthood, but the evidence is simply scarce.

What we've said so far makes it look as if friendships are quite unimportant in the middle years. But there seem to be some pluses, nonetheless. Among other things, as we get older the friendships that we retain are ones that have endured over a long time. [As I write this—at age 43—I am thinking about my own close friendships. The shortest one is of 10 years duration, and most have lasted 20 years or more. HB] To the extent that old friendships become more comfortable and easier, this is a plus. Shulman (1975) also has found that in midlife people's family and friendship network becomes more close-knit. That is, the people you are close to are more likely to know each other, too. Among young adults, looser-knit collections of friends are more the rule.

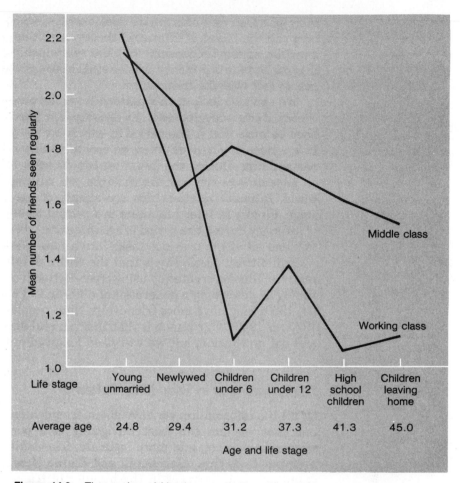

Figure 14.9. The number of friends reported by men at different life-cycle stages declined fairly steadily, at least up through the mid-forties. These findings do not tell us whether friendships increase later in life, although other data suggest that they do. *Source:* Farrell & Rosenberg, 1981, p. 195.

In sum, young adults' friendships are numerous, intimate, and typically organized into a loosely knit network. Many of the relationships are also of relatively short duration. In the midyears, adults have fewer friends, but these tend to be long-duration relationships, and the friends are likely to know each other. In late adulthood, friends become more numerous, and the relationships once again become more intimate.

The apparent decline in the number and intimacy of friendships in the middle years is striking and requires explanation. One obvious possibility is that these are the years in which both men and women are concentrating their energies on their own immediate families and on their jobs. One view of intimate relationships, which Farrell and Rosenberg call the "fund of intimacy" theory, says that each of us has only a certain amount of capacity for close relationships. If we are using up that capacity in our family (spouse and children), then there isn't much energy left over for friendships.

We can also look at this pattern from the perspective of Erikson's theory of adult development. Friendships are important in early adulthood because that is the period in which intimacy is the central task. It is a time in our lives when we create lasting friendships and form partnerships. During the following two decades, however, the focus is on *generativity*—on rearing children, on making your mark in the world. Intimate relationships are simply of less importance at this stage. Finally in later life, there is a partial return to the importance of intimacy during the period of *ego integrity*, when the adult attempts to blend all of the previous tasks into a new whole.

Still a third possibility is that the entire developmental pattern is really an illusion created by using cross-sectional comparisons. We may simply be describing a generational difference. People who grew up in the 1960s may have more friendships than people who grew up in the 1930s or 1940s. Our hunch is that this is a real developmental pattern and not an illusion, but we will need longitudinal studies to be sure.

Sex Differences in Friendship Patterns

Of all the information we have about friendships between adults, the one that we find the most intriguing is a persistent finding that women have more, and more intimate, friendships than men do. Not everyone finds this. Alan Booth and Elaine Hess (1974), for example, found no sex differences in the number of friends in a group of 800 adults, all aged 45 and older. However, nearly everyone else does find a sex difference either in the number or the intimacy of friendship patterns (Bell, 1981; Tognoli, 1980; Lowenthal, Thurnher, & Chiriboga, 1975; Powers & Bultena, 1976; Wright, 1982). We've summarized some of the differences in Table 14.2, but we can give you the flavor of the difference more fully by quoting two adults interviewed by Robert Bell:

A 42-year-old divorced woman:
> I love my women friends for their warmth and compassion. I can share anything about my life with them and they never pass judgment or condemn. They are very open and share much of their inner thoughts with me. These friends have helped me tremendously in my own personal growth and through great changes in my life. They are fun to be with and have a grand sense of humor. I would tell those women anything. There are no limitations on disclosure that I am aware of.

The special quality of these female friendships is the openness. I have never been able to talk and share my feelings and experiences in the same way with any man (p. 63).

A 38-year-old male executive:

I have three close friends I have known since we were boys and they live here in the city. There are some things I wouldn't tell them. For example, I wouldn't tell them much about my work because we have always been highly competitive. I certainly wouldn't tell them about my feelings of any uncertainties with life or various things I do. And I wouldn't talk about any problems I have with my wife or in fact anything about my marriage and sex life. But other than that I would tell them anything. [After a brief pause he laughed and said:] That doesn't leave a hell of a lot, does it? (p. 81–82)

Men's friendships appear to include more competitiveness and less self-disclosure. By most definitions they are less intimate. This difference seems to be present in the friendship patterns of children and adolescents as well, as we pointed out in earlier chapters. Compared to girls, 6- and 7-year-old boys play in larger groups, have fewer close chums, and are more competitive with their friends.

Some observers believe that men's friendships are more meaningful than women's, with levels of comradeship and sociability not seen among women. One anthropologist, Lionel Tiger (1969), even goes so far as to suggest that such a sex difference is biological in origin. Since men had to learn to band together and work cooperatively in order to survive, those who were especially skilled at creating group solidarity were most likely to survive and reproduce.

Tiger's position has little support. Certainly the fact that (in our society at least) women's friendships are closer, with greater solidarity than men's friendships, is not consistent with Tiger's view.

We do not want to suggest by this discussion that men have no

TABLE 14.2

Some of the Sex Differences in Friendship Patterns in Adulthood

Pattern	Men	Women
Percentage who say they would reveal themselves to their friends (Bell, 1981)	35%	60%
Mean number of close same-sex friends: Bell's data (1981)	3.2	4.7
Lowenthal et al. (1975)	5.2	6.3
Percentage who report cross-sex friends (Booth & Hess, 1974)	35%	24%
Usual number of friends in a close group (Bell, 1981)	3–4	2
Usual activity (Bell, 1981; Parlee, 1979)	doing things	talking

friends. Obviously, they do. In Farrell and Rosenberg's sample, nearly 70 percent of the middle-aged men had at least one friend they saw regularly. Powers and Bultena (1976), in a study of friendships and family contacts among elderly adults (70+), found that men actually had more frequent social contacts than women did. However, women appear to create and maintain close relationships over their life spans far more than men do. In Powers and Bultena's study, for example, 42 percent of the elderly men said they had *never* had an intimate friend, while this was true for only 30 percent of the women.

Unlike Tiger, we do not believe that this sex difference is biological. It seems far more likely that these friendship patterns are learned by both men and women. As Edward Powers and Gordon Bultena (1975) put it:

> From early childhood, American men learn patterns of behavior appropriate for their respective social networks. Through play, organized team sports, work, mass media, and war, men are taught the importance of cooperative behavior. The masculine sex role emphasizes aggressiveness and unemotional behavior . . . [they] are not expected to share intimate problems or anxieties. . . . Women, however, learn from experiences that emphasize expressive [rather than competitive] behavior. . . . Even in sports, women tend to be channeled into individual efforts such as tennis, swimming or gymnastics. The feminine sex role prescribes compassionate and expressive behavior, thereby freeing women to develop relationships in which they can more openly discuss intimate problems and needs (pp. 739–740).

Since precisely these elements of the male and female sex roles are changing in today's society, it will be interesting to see whether researchers 10 years from now find that men's friendships have become more intimate or that women's relationships have become less so. We hope that it is the former change that will occur.

DETACHMENTS IN ADULT LIFE: LETTING GO OF ATTACHMENTS

No matter how supportive our family relationships or how extensive our friendships, no one of us can escape the process of *de*tachment. Every love affair does not end happily; most of us will face the death of one or both of our parents before our own death; nearly half of us will be divorced; some of us will have to cope with the death of a spouse. In most of these cases, to a lesser or greater degree, we are severing or weakening an attachment bond.

One of our clinical psychology colleagues once described to us the process of detachment that must occur following a divorce—a process he had often observed in therapy with his clients. He said it is as if each partner is joined to the other with thousands of strands of fine wire or filament. When the couple separates, those strands must be cut, or wither, or be "reeled in" by each person until there are no longer any connecting links and no strands still left floating in the breeze. That is a very graphic description of the detachment process we are talking about.

A less dramatic kind of detachment can also occur when you find yourself physically separated from someone to whom you are strongly attached. The attachment may well remain strong, but you are suddenly unable to express that attachment with the usual range of attachment behaviors, and you must adjust to the separation. Having your children go away to college or marry would be one example of this kind of detachment, as would moving to another city and losing contact with good friends, or even getting fired or laid off from work. The strands of attachment are not broken, but many of them become difficult to express.

What we know about the way adults deal with either of these types of detachments suggests two general principles: First, our reactions to detachments appear to follow predictable patterns no matter what the detachment may be. Second, it is easier to deal with predictable or scheduled detachments than with unexpected or unscheduled ones.

Stages in Response to Detachment

John Bowlby (1961, 1980) has described four phases of mourning that he thinks occur in most, if not all, instances of detachment or loss. We have listed these in Table 14.3, alongside the five stages of dying described by Elizabeth Kübler-Ross (1969, 1975). Although Bowlby's stages are designed to describe the way we react to the loss of someone else (such as in widowhood) and Kübler-Ross was describing the way we react to our *own* impending death, the parallels between the two lists are striking. The common ingredients seem to be denial, anger, disorganization or depression, and finally integration or acceptance.

Kübler-Ross originally argued that these steps always occur in the sequence given and that every dying person who knows she is dying—regardless of her age—goes through these steps. Not everyone agrees that all five steps are visible in all dying patients (including Kübler-Ross in her more recent comments) or in all adults facing other losses (Schulz & Alderman, 1974). Bowlby argues that people may move back and forth from one "step" to another several times before moving on. However, there is remarkably general agreement that there is a *process* of mourning or detachment, that this process has distinguishable elements (Parkes, 1972, 1975), and that highly

TABLE 14.3

**Stages of Dying Proposed by Kübler-Ross
and Stages of Mourning Described by Bowlby**

Kübler-Ross	Bowlby
1. *Denial:* The individual's reaction is almost always "No, not me!"	1. *Numbing,* lasting from a few hours to weeks, followed by *intense distress and anger,* usually in brief bursts.
2. *Rage and anger:* The person feels it is unfair that others will live and he will not.	
3. *Bargaining:* The person accepts the inevitability of death but wants a chance for a bit more of life.	2. *Yearning and searching* for the lost figure, lasting months or even years.
4. *Depression:* The individual mourns but becomes quiet and prepared for death.	3. *Disorganization, and despair.*
5. *Acceptance:* The individual accepts that his time is close, without joy, but usually without great unhappiness either.	4. *Reorganization,* which may occur to a greater or a lesser degree.

SOURCE: Adapted from Kübler-Ross, 1975, p. 10; Bowlby, 1980, p. 85.

similar processes can be seen in many different types of detachment. Parkes describes such steps in widows, and Herrman (1974) sees parallel steps in the adjustment of adults to a failed marriage. Before the separation there may be bargaining and depression, after the separation there is anger and disorganization, and finally there is acceptance.

Because marital separation and divorce is such a common—and devastating—loss in adult life today, we have explored some of these steps and stages more fully in Box 14.1.

Scheduled versus Unscheduled Detachments

A second basic rule about detachments in adulthood is that they are a lot easier to handle if they are predictable rather than unpredictable. Leonard Pearlin (1980) makes this distinction when he talks about *scheduled* and *nonscheduled* events. Scheduled events are those predictable changes in roles that occur during the typical life cycle. Having your children leave home in their late teens or early twenties is a scheduled event, as is the death of your own parents when you are in your fifties or sixties. Unscheduled events, in contrast, are ones that are out of cycle, like having to retire early because of illness, or the death of a child, or a divorce, or the death of your parents or your spouse at an unexpectedly early time.

Bernice Neugarten (1979) makes a similar distinction between *on-time* and *off-time* life events. Marrying late or having your children late puts you off time, as does being widowed in your twenties or thirties or retiring at 50.

We have already pointed out that being off-time in family role stages seems to create some difficulties for adults (see Chapter 13). Neugarten and Pearlin also argue that off-time or unscheduled separations, losses, and detachments are also harder to handle. A few examples may make this point clear.

Pearlin and his colleagues interviewed 2300 adults, aged 18 to 65, about their work, family, and life experiences. Many of these adults were reinterviewed four years later, so for once we have some evidence about *change* in people's stability or distress. In the work arena, Pearlin found that the unscheduled loss of a job or an unexpected demotion was associated with an increase in anxiety or depression. *Scheduled* job losses, such as retirement, produced no such consequences.

Studies of widows show the same pattern. Older widows, for whom widowhood may be considered a scheduled event, generally show better or more rapid adjustment than do younger widows (Balkwell, 1981). There is also some indication that regardless of the widow's age, the *sudden* (and thus unexpected or unscheduled) death of a spouse is associated with longer and more severe grief reactions than is a more gradual, more anticipated death. When the widow is *both* young (under 45) and experiences a sudden rather than a gradual loss, the effect seems to be particularly bad (Balkwell, 1981). This combination obviously represents two types of unscheduledness, an off-time widowhood and a death that could not be predicted even days ahead of time.

The most reasonable explanation of the differential effect of scheduled and unscheduled losses is simply that when you know something difficult is going to happen—you know you are retiring or your children are leaving home or your spouse is in his sixties and has had a long illness—you are able to move through at least some of the stages of mourning or detachment ahead of time. You can do some of your "grief work" (disconnect some of the strands of attachment) in advance. The more accurately you can foresee the changes that are coming next, the better you can prepare for them.

Since many more kinds of losses are unscheduled for the young adult than for the older adult, we are likely to see bigger disruptions, greater problems in dealing with the detachment process in the 25-year-old than in the 65-year-old. But this does not necessarily mean that young adults are inherently less able to handle loss. We simply don't know whether each of us, over the course of our adult lives, becomes more skillful in handling the detachments we encounter. To our knowledge, no one has asked the question in quite this way. What is clear, however, is that detachment, at whatever age, is a disruptive process. You should not expect to get over a loss within a matter of days

BOX 14.1

Divorce: Its Effects on Adults and Their Children

Any one of you who reads a newspaper or news magazine regularly or listens to the news knows that the rate of divorce is at an all-time high. As we pointed out in Chapter 13, something between 40 and 50 percent of all marriages begun today are likely to end in divorce, and roughly 4 of out every 10 children born in the 70s will spend at least a part of their childhood in a one-parent family (Keniston, 1977). How does this major life change affect people?

Aside from the death of a spouse, divorce is the single most difficult detachment faced by most adults. In fact, many researchers find that divorce is *more disruptive* than widowhood (Bloom, Asher, & White, 1978; Nelson, 1982). As we saw in Chapter 13 (Box 13.1), divorced adults show significantly greater symptoms of distress and loneliness than do never-married adults. But although the magnitude of upheaval is greater, the sequence of response to divorce seems to be very similar to what we see in other detachments.

SHORT-TERM EFFECTS

For both parents and children the immediate effect of separation or divorce is disorganization. Mavis Hetherington and her colleagues (Hetherington, Cox, & Cox, 1975, 1978, 1979) devised a family disorganization scale that they used to describe a set of families they followed for two years after divorce. The scores on this scale are shown in the table. In these families, children become more disobedient, meals are not eaten together, discipline becomes erratic, and there are fewer displays of affection. The children are angry at their parents and long for things to be the way they were (Waller-

Family Disorganization Scores for Divorced Mothers and Those from Intact Families

Time since divorce	Divorced mothers' scores	Comparison scores for moms in intact families
Two months	20.31	13.17
One year	22.85	12.96
Two years	17.56	12.75

SOURCE: Hetherington, Cox, & Cox, 1975.

stein & Kelley, 1980)—two of the first stages of mourning Bowlby describes. Young children—those under age 5 or 6—may show regression to earlier forms of behavior or increased aggression or depression. Older children, too, may show depression or withdrawal. In sum, both parents and children are often profoundly unhappy in the months immediately following the divorce (Nock, 1981; Wallerstein & Kelley, 1980).

LONG-TERM OUTCOMES

Children. There is no *general* tendency for children from divorced families to be worse off in the long run than children in intact families, especially if we compare *unhappy* intact families with divorced families. Wallerstein and Kelley (1980), in their very sensitive study of 60 divorcing families, found that about a third of the children looked notably healthy and well-adjusted five years later and about a third looked disturbed, unhappy, or lonely. Which group a child fell into seemed to be primarily a function of the quality of the relationship the child maintained with the *absent* parent. Where both parents made

or weeks. If the basic attachment was complex and strong, then the detachment process is also likely to be complex, lengthy, and painful.

THE IMPORTANCE OF ATTACHMENTS IN ADULT LIFE

Most of what we have said so far about adult attachments has been descriptive. We have tracked both the continuities and the changes that take place over family cycle stages, or over age, in the number and

an effort to maintain loving and frequent contacts with the child, there seemed to be no lasting ill effect. But where the noncustodial parent was unavailable or psychologically withdrawn, problems often ensued.

Very long-term consequences for children are harder to trace. There seems to be a slight tendency for children whose parents divorced to divorce themselves in later life (Greenberg & Nay, 1982; Price-Bonham & Baslwick, 1980), although there are a number of studies that show no such long-term effects (Kukla & Weingarten, 1979; Nock, 1982). On the whole, children of divorced families do not seem to look very different as adults from children who grew up in intact families. However, *individual* children are likely to show lasting effects if the parents do not provide the needed emotional support.

Adults. For adults the long-term effects are more positive. Within about two years following the divorce the level of disruption seems to decline, the immediate emotional upheaval passes, the anger at the former spouse fades, and some type of resolution is achieved. Thus the several steps of response to detachment have been traversed.

How swiftly and how successfully one passes through this sequence seems to depend on several things, including the degree of financial stress experienced, how many children there are to care for, and the level of emotional support provided by friends and family (White & Bloom, 1981).

TO DIVORCE OR NOT TO DIVORCE

For as many as half of you reading this book, all this information will have poignant relevance at some time in the future, as you grapple with a decision about terminating your own marriage. Given what we have said, how might one decide the issue? The choice, in most cases, is between remaining in a stressful marriage (which *might* be improved with effort or counseling) and divorcing. Leonard Pearlin (1980), in his study of working-class and middle-class adults, found that his subjects reported *greater* distress when they remained in marriages that failed to live up to their expectations than they did after a divorce. Regrettably, we have little other evidence of this kind to help in your decision. If you do decide to divorce, there are two points you may want to keep in mind:

1. Divorce is highly stressful. If you choose this road, you should expect one to two years of disorganization and turmoil. However, the long-term possibilities for growth definitely exist, especially if you avail yourself of your entire supportive network.
2. The effect on any children you may have will be marked, especially during the same two-year period. Children do not get *better* because of a divorce. For them the loss of one parent is an acute detachment—as much or more stressful than living with both parents who are unhappy together. Thus divorce cannot be justified on the grounds that children will be better off, just as one cannot justify staying together on the same grounds. Both situations are hard on children. The key to softening the long-term effects on children seems to be to lessen the detachment with the missing parent by arranging for *frequent* contact—in person, by letter, by phone.

quality of relationships. An equally significant set of issues has to do with how important those relationships are for life satisfaction or for psychological growth in adulthood.

The phrase **social network** is currently in vogue as a description of the total set of personal relationships with family and friends maintained by each of us. Robert Kahn and Toni Antonucci (1980) have added a life-span developmental element to this concept when they describe a **convoy,** which is a social network that you carry through time.

It is clear from what we have already said about relationships with family and friends that most of us do indeed have convoys that accompany us on our adult lives. Our relationships with our families seem to be remarkably persistent, and many of us have friendships that last over decades.

What these networks, or convoys, provide is **social support,** which is made up of a complex combination of *affect, affirmation,* and *aid* (Kahn & Antonucci, 1980). Many expressions of social support can also be thought of as attachment behaviors. The verbal and nonverbal signals we use with our attachment objects are ways of communicating our affection, our respect, our loving of that person. But social support may also come in the form of financial aid, advice, or physical assistance, as we saw when we looked at the type of assistance family members give each other at different points in the life cycle.

The key question is not whether adults have networks or convoys (we do), but how important such networks may be for successful passage through the adult years. Research touching on this question is of two kinds. Some psychologists have looked at the impact of social networks on the overall well-being of the adult. Others have looked at the role of networks or convoys in helping adults handle stresses. In each case, it seems clear that one of the key elements differentiating those adults who surmount life's hurdles easily and those who do not is the quality of the social relationships they have created and maintained.

Social Networks and Life Quality

George Vaillant (1977), in his analysis of the results of the Grant study, has given us some particularly provocative bits of evidence about the impact of friendship and family relationships on life quality and maturity. As you may remember, a group of Harvard men were studied from the time they were undergraduates until they were in their late forties or early fifties. During the early interviews with the young men, the subjects were also asked about their childhoods and about the quality of their relationships with their parents. Vaillant identified one group who had had the least loving childhoods, whom he calls the "loveless," and another group with the best childhoods, whom he calls the "lucky." When he compared these two group 30 years later, he found four main differences:

1. The loveless did not play as adults; they didn't play games with their friends or engage in any kind of sport.
2. The loveless were mistrustful and dependent as adults. They were pessimistic, self-doubting, and passive all at the same time.
3. The loveless were more likely to show mental illness as adults. Only one tenth of the lucky showed any distinct emotional disturbance,

while half of the loveless were diagnosed as mentally ill at one time or another in their adult lives.

4. The loveless were less likely to have friends in middle life.

This last difference is particularly interesting to us. It suggests that poor relationships with parents—perhaps even insecure attachments, if we may stretch the point a bit—may predispose an adult to a continued impoverishment of supportive relationships, especially with friends.

A difference in friendship patterns also emerged when Vaillant divided his group into those whose adult lives had been most successful and those who had had the least success as adults. *Success* in this case included not only professional success but also physical health, social health, and psychological health. His comparison of these best and worst outcomes is in Table 14.4. The men with the best outcomes seem to be those who have positive, intimate, supportive networks: They married early and stayed married, they have friends, and they get along well with their children. The suggestion that emerges is that men who lack the skill to create such a network will experience lower levels of success or health in all facets of their lives.

Farrell and Rosenberg (1981) have found a similar pattern in their study: Men with more friends were also more successful in their work, but this was true only for middle-class men. Among working-class men, friendship seemed to be unrelated to work success.

TABLE 14.4
Comparison of Best and Worst Outcomes in Vaillant's Grant Study

Characteristic	Best outcomes	Worst outcomes
Poor childhood environment	17%	47%
Pessimism, self-doubt, passivity, and fear of sex at age 50	3%	50%
In college, personality integration put in the bottom fifth	0%	33%
Career choice reflected identification with father	60%	27%
Dominated by mother in adult life	0%	40%
Failure to marry by 30	3%	37%
Bleak friendship patterns at 50	0%	57%
Current job has little supervisory responsibility	20%	93%
Children admitted to father's college	47%	10%
Children's outcome described as good or excellent	66%	23%
Average yearly charitable contribution	$3,000	$500

SOURCE: From *Adaptation to life,* by George E. Vaillant, by permission of Little, Brown and Co. Copyright 1977 by George E. Vaillant. Originally appeared in *Psychology Today* magazine.

There is a real problem here in teasing out the causal relationships. Does an 18-year-old with few friends have lesser success later in his life *because* he lacks a supportive network? Vaillant thinks that in part he does. As evidence in favor of his position, he describes several cases in which young men from very unloving families nonetheless had very successful adult lives. In each case, the man was "healed" (to use Vaillant's word) by an especially intimate and supportive marriage.

Social encounters may also be important for overall well-being in older adults. Palmore (1979) found that adults with successful aging were much more likely to have extensive involvement with clubs and other social activities, compared to those with less successful aging. (In this case *successful aging* was defined as surviving to age 75 in good health and happiness.) Mancini (1980) has also found that competence in friendship relationships was related to morale among retired adults.

All of this evidence is consistent with our basic assumption that the quality and number of an adult's attachments have a pervasive influence on adult life. However, there are some intriguing pieces of counterevidence.

Most puzzling is a repeated finding that among older adults (50 and older), the frequency of contact with family members has *no* relationship to life satisfaction, morale, happiness, or longevity. In Palmore's study, successfully aging adults did not have more contacts with their families than unsuccessfully aging adults. And Gary Lee, in several studies (Lee & Ellithorpe, 1982; Lee & Ihinger-Tallman, 1980), could find no link between frequency of contact with children, grandchildren, or other family members and life satisfaction. In fact, older adults with no children at all seem to be just as happy as those who have extended families (Glenn & McLanahan, 1981).

These findings present us with a real paradox. Adults appear to maintain high levels of contact with their families and say they do so because they enjoy it and receive support and gratification from it. However, the *lack* of such contact—at least among older adults—does not bring about lower levels of satisfaction. In contrast, the lack of friendship does seem to be associated with poorer health and less life success.

Social Networks and Response to Stress

Unlike the evidence on life satisfaction, which as we have just seen is somewhat mixed, the role of social networks in helping adults face crises is very clear. An adult facing a major transition, a detachment, or other life crisis, who lacks supportive relationships, is more likely to become ill or depressed than is someone facing the same kinds of crises who has a more complete convoy (Kahn & Antonucci, 1980).

A few examples will help make the point. Cobb and Kasl (1977) studied a group of 200 blue-collar workers who had lost their jobs because
the company they worked for had gone out of business. As a group,
these men showed a variety of signs of physical and emotional illness
in the two years following the layoff. But those who had supportive social networks—spouse, friends, and family—showed many fewer symptoms.

We can see the same effect in a widely quoted study of elderly adults

Figure 14.10.   Men whose wives were their only really close confidant typically have an
especially hard time dealing with their spouses' deaths—an example of the importance
of social networks in helping adults cope with detachments and other stress.

by Lowenthal and Haven (1968). They found that those adults who had *at least one* confidant were far less likely to end up requiring institutionalization than were those adults who had no such support.

As a third example, we can see the importance of supportive relationships in the response of adults to treatment for alcoholism. Ward (1981) recently found that those alcoholics who had satisfying family relationships were more likely to maintain sobriety after treatment than were those whose families were not supportive.

Social Support and Adult Health: A Last Look

We find all of this research fascinating—perhaps because of its personal relevance to each of us—and we are frustrated at the gaps in our knowledge. We know far too little about the differing roles that may be played by friends and families in helping adults respond to transitions or crises. We know far too little about the role of attachments in supporting or promoting the sort of inner growth or development we talked about in the last chapter. Furthermore, we know almost nothing about any *developmental* changes in the importance or functions of convoys. Nonetheless, several conclusions seem at least plausible at this stage of our knowledge.

1. Quality of attachments is more important than quantity (Kahn & Antonucci, 1980). Most of the research on social networks has focused on the *number* of friends or the number of contacts you have with your family. Almost no one has looked at the quality of the interaction—whether the attachment is secure or insecure, whether the attachment behaviors are clear and contingently paced, whether the relationship is satisfying. But when researchers have looked at such aspects of relationships, the quality seems to be more predictive of life satisfaction or physical health or adjustment than is quantity (Connor, Powers, & Bultena, 1979; Kahn & Antonucci, 1980).
2. There is, however, a minimum number of genuinely central attachments required for health and development: That minimum is one. One confidant, one satisfying marital relationship, one friend seems to be the basic, irreducible requirement. Those who lack such a relationship are more prone to illness, die sooner, and show more emotional disturbance (Kahn & Antonucci, 1980).

   An interesting corollary of this point is that those adults who have only one such relationship are at greater risk of problems if they lose that single person through death. Thus husbands whose wives are their single close confidant (and this *is* more common in men than in women) are more greatly disturbed by their spouse's death than are women, most of whom have maintained other intimate relationships outside of marriage.

3. The type of support adults receive from family members is probably qualitatively different from the support received from friends. If we go back to the three basic elements of social support—affect, affirmation, and aid—perhaps we can think of the family (parents, grandparents, siblings) as the primary source of aid, while friends provide both affect and affirmation.

All of these conclusions require further study. For now, though, they may provide food for thought as you consider your own social network, your own convoy.

SUMMARY

1. We can think of the tasks of adulthood as consisting of working and loving. Loving includes relationships with family and friends, as well as with spouse or partner.
2. The language of attachment theory can be helpful in describing both the loving relationships and the inevitable detachments of adulthood, such as death of family or friends, divorce, or other losses.
3. We assume that attachments remain strong in adulthood, but that they are not always as visible because attachment behaviors have often become more distant or symbolic.
4. The central attachment for an adult is normally with a spouse or long-term partner. Over time, most marriages appear to become less satisfying, less vital. Those marriages that remain satisfying, however, are characterized by more positive encounters, better reading of the partner's signals, and less aggressive and more intimate conflict resolution.
5. Relationships with other family members—including both grown children, parents, siblings, and more distant relatives—remain strong throughout adulthood, with frequent contact. For most adults, such contacts appear to arise from pleasure, not from obligation.
6. Types of aid and assistance given to or received from family members changes over the family life cycle. The middle generation, with both adult children and aging parents, gives more aid than it receives. Other groups tend to receive more than they give.
7. Friends are another element in adult relationships. Friends are chosen primarily on the basis of similarity to oneself and are maintained because of continuing similarity and perceived reciprocity.
8. The largest number of friends and the most intimate friendships

appear to occur in early and late adulthood, with the lowest level at midlife. This may result from a focus of energy on the nuclear family and on work roles during those years.

9. A consistent sex difference in friendship patterns exists, with women reporting more intimate friendships at virtually every age studied.

10. Some detachments, as well as attachments, are inevitable in adult life. Regardless of the type of detachment—death of someone close, divorce, or one's own death, for example—there seem to be stages or steps in response to the loss, including anger, depression and disorganization, and finally acceptance or reintegration.

11. Unscheduled (unexpected or off-time) detachments are more difficult to handle than are predictable, scheduled losses, such as the death of an aging parent.

12. The existence of a supportive network or convoy appears to be helpful both in increasing an adult's life satisfaction and improving an adult's ability to cope with life's transitions or losses.

13. Such supportive networks are usually conceived of as providing social support, which is made up of affect, affirmation, and aid.

14. The quality of interactions among members of this network are probably more important for adult health and satisfaction than is the number of members.

15. The minimum number of close confidants, however, for healthy adulthood seems to be one.

KEY TERMS

Convoy Term used by Kahn and Antonucci to describe the social network that each of us carries through time. The membership in the convoy changes somewhat, but there is basic stability.

Social network The collection of friends and relatives from which each person receives social support.

Social support A combination of affect, affirmation, and aid received from one's social network or convoy.

SUGGESTED
READINGS

Kahn, R. L., & Antonucci, T. C. Convoys over the life course: Attachment, roles, and social support. In P. B. Baltes & O. G. Brim, Jr., (Eds.), *Life-span development and behavior* (Vol. 3). New York: Academic Press, 1980.
Although this paper was written for an audience of fellow professionals, it is extremely clear and fascinating. By far the best discussion of attachments in adulthood that we know of.
Kübler-Ross, E. *Death: The final stage of growth.* Englewood Cliffs, N.J.: Prentice-Hall, 1975.
In this volume, Kübler-Ross and others expand upon her earlier work on the stages of dying. Many of the selections are very personal and deeply moving.

Smelser, N. J., & Erikson, E. H. *Themes of work and love in adulthood.* Cambridge, Mass.: Harvard University Press, 1980.
This volume contains fascinating papers by many of the major figures in the study of adult development, including Daniel Levinson, Roger Gould, Janet Giele, Leonard Pearlin, and others. All the papers are highly readable. An excellent general source book.

PROJECT 14.1
Adult Attachments

This project parallels the project for Chapter 13, except that in this case we want you to ask your adult respondents to draw you a picture of their relationships rather than their roles. Again we would like you to locate two adults in each of three age groups: over 65, thirties to forties, and college age or early twenties. One of each pair should be male, one female. If you use the same respondents for this project that you used for the project in Chapter 13, it would allow some additional analyses and comparisons of great interest, though it is not essential.

Materials

For each subject, you will need a piece of paper with a set of three concentric circles (like a bull's-eye) on it. The smallest circle should be about 2 inches in diameter, the middle circle about 4 inches or 5 inches across, and the largest circle about 8 inches in diameter. At the very center place a small dot.

Each of these sheets of paper should also have a place where the respondent gives his/her age and gender.

Directions

Read these instructions to the subject:

"I am doing a project about the kinds of friendships and other close relationships people have. I would like you to fill in these circles with the initials of your friends or close family members. Think of yourself as the dot in the middle here (point to the dot). Put the initials of the people who are your very closest, most intimate confidants in this small circle (point to the smallest circle). In this next circle, put the initials of those family or friends with whom you are fairly close, but who are not your very closest confidants. And in this largest, outer circle, put the initials of family or friends with whom you may share certain activities or interests but who are not terribly close friends. You don't have to have initials in every circle; just put your own family and friends into the circles that you think best reflect your relationship with them."

(After the subject has finished, say:) "Now as a last step, would you put a small circle around each set of initials for someone in your own immediate family (spouse, children, parents, cousins, and so on)."

Analysis and Discussion

The analysis and discussion should parallel the issues we raised for the project in Chapter 13. Compare the number of people listed in the smallest circle and those in the middle circle, for males and females, and for the different age groups. Do your results correspond to the pattern we described in the chapter?

Part III Summary
The Developing Adult
and a Look at the Whole Life Span

In summarizing childhood and adolescence, we divided our discussion into two main sections: structural or developmental changes and individual differences. To be consistent, we will follow the same plan here, although, as you know by now, there is a good deal of dispute about whether it is appropriate to say that an adult *develops*. If we define development as Heinz Werner did, *as increasing differentiation and hierarchic integration* (Werner, 1948), then in many respects adults do not develop. Certainly there is *change* in adulthood. But some of that change is in the form of decline or loss of function, and some of it is day-to-day or year-to-year change that does not appear to lead to greater integration or greater differentiation. Still, as we have seen, there are major theorists who believe that adults do show genuine development in predictable sequences. So let us preserve this organization at least for the time being.

STAGES OF DEVELOPMENT IN ADULTHOOD

As we have seen, there are two general theoretical approaches to adulthood that emphasize stages. Erikson's concept of *normative life crises,* in particular, has been very influential. He describes three broad stages in adulthood, beginning with intimacy versus isolation in the twenties, to generativity versus stagnation in the thirties and perhaps early forties, and then integrity versus despair in the later decades of adulthood. The basic assumption here is that there is "an inherent ground plan" for all adults (to use Alice Rossi's nice phrase, 1980). Each task is thought to have a particular time in the life cycle, linked to physical age and to the role demands that are typical of that age. *Normal* development thus involves a series of predictable crises or dilemmas.

A similar developmental model of adulthood emerges from the sociological concept of the family life cycle. In the typical adult life course, there are specific and predictable role changes that are related primarily to the addition and subtraction of family relationships—marriage, addition of children, departure of children.

Obviously, using a family life-cycle model to structure the stages of adulthood requires the assumption that nearly every adult in fact experiences these changes in family relationships—an assumption that was much more true 20 years ago than it is today. Such a model seems to us to be less useful now when more and more adults are choosing not to marry or not to have children or are marrying and divorcing and creating myriad combinations of families.

You have probably also noticed that neither of these developmental models of adulthood includes much mention of physical changes. In childhood, many of the developmental stages can be linked directly to maturationally controlled body changes—changes in the role of the cortex at 1 to 2 months, full cortical development at 2 years, and pubertal changes at adolescence. Maturation does not end with puberty, of course. As we have mapped in Chapter 11, there are highly predictable and systematic changes in body functioning from 20 to 80, including the climacteric. Yet stage theories of adult development are generally *not* linked to these physical changes. The usual assumption has been that adult changes are psychological rather than physiological in origin. That's a debatable assumption, as we have pointed out before.

We can take a critical look at some of these questions by examining the summary table of adulthood (Table III.1). The divisions between the subperiods listed here are partially arbitrary; we could probably have listed the middle-adulthood period as beginning at 45 just as well as at 40, or we could have listed many more substages. The divisions we have chosen are fairly typical, though, and reflect some of the basic divisions suggested by developmental theorists such as Erikson or Levinson.

Early Adulthood: From 22 to 40

Once the transition to independent living has taken place (which is usually in the early twenties), with all its attendant strains and adaptations, the young adult moves into a long period of consolidation, from the early twenties until perhaps 40. This span of years is characterized by maximum physical and mental capacity, typically focused on work performance (especially in men). Training for a job usually occurs during this period, as does the time of most intense concentration on job success and advancement. Many other concerns take a back seat to job preoccupation. As we noted in Chapter 14, friendships seem to be least important during these years (again especially for men), and marital satisfaction is frequently at low ebb, especially if there are children in

Figure III.1. Many physical capacities are at their peak in the years of young adulthood, including running speed. If this young man continues to exercise, though, he can remain at a high plateau of physical skill well into middle adulthood.

TABLE III.1
Summary of Developmental Changes during Adulthood

Age	Physical development	Cognitive development	Social development
Early adulthood: 22–40	Maximum function in most body skills; maximum number of cells, taste buds, speed of response, work capacity, and so on. Peak of capacity usually thought to be age 25 or 30, although it is earlier for some functions and later for others.	Formal operations are in place for at least some adults; maximum mental performance for most adults is in this period, whether they are using optimally exercised or unexercised skills. Some decline in mental test measures that call for speed or on measures of fluid intelligence may occur at the very end of the period.	In the typical pattern, this period includes marriage, birth of all children (the first three to four stages of the family life cycle). Usually associated with high marital satisfaction initially and then a decline in satisfaction for the rest of the period. Work satisfaction typically low initially, but this rises steadily from 22 to 40. There is a strong emphasis on work achievement in these years, especially for men. Friendships are initially high and decline, reaching the lowest ebb at about 40. These years include Erikson's stages of intimacy and generativity.
Middle adulthood: 40–65	Continued loss of physical abilities in some areas, with cell loss accelerated. Degree of physical loss heavily influenced by optimal exercise of capacities. Climacteric occurs for both women and men, involving gradual loss of sexual hormones. In women, there is also a loss of reproductive capacity.	Continued gradual decline for *some* mental measures—those that tap fluid intelligence (speed particularly), but little or no decline in exercised or crystallized intelligence. Increase in creativity may occur for many adults during this period.	Erikson's stage of integrity versus despair. This is a period of high work satisfaction and high marital satisfaction after children have departed. However, it is also a period of generational squeeze with demands from both children and parents. Marriage may also show loss of loving expression. Friendship seems to increase in importance; and for both men and women there are signs of a crossover in achievement and affective emphases, leading to greater psychological androgyny in both sexes.

the family. Thus once the central intimate relationships have been formed, the adult's peak physical and mental capacities appear to be partially directed away from social relationships and concentrated on achievement, self-assertion, testing the limits of personal abilities.

For women, this period frequently has a different emphasis, since the bearing and rearing of children calls for affiliative and nurturant

Age	Physical development	Cognitive development	Social development
Late adulthood: 65–75	Further decline in function, such as loss of eyesight, hearing, oxygen uptake, taste buds, and hair loss. Degree of exercise of physical skills again influences rate of decline.	Mixed evidence, but seems to be some loss in most measures of cognitive function (less if exercised and less if practical skill). Structurally, we see loss of the most complex forms of thinking, but these may be retained for practical use.	Usually a maintenance of social contacts, particularly with family. Friends are important here, especially for maintaining life satisfaction. Little evidence of any withdrawal or disengagement. Retirement, which occurs during this time for most adults, appears to cause relatively little trauma for most.
Late, late adulthood: 75–?	Even in those individuals who remain physically active (exercised), there is now a notable loss of speed and function in many physical areas, although those older adults who retain good health show this less.	Cognitive decline is more notable in this period than in the 65 to 75 decade, although such decline is more evident in the five years just prior to death.	There appears to be some social disengagement, at least for some older adults, during this period, although most elderly adults continue to see their children and other family members with some regularity and spend time with friends.

qualities, as well as achievement. Still, for women as for men, this is a period in which friendships seem to be least significant, and even relationships with parents are temporarily less frequent. Nurturing is concentrated in the immediate family.

Middle Adulthood: From 40 to 65

All the major stage theories of adulthood mark the period around the fortieth year as a major transition point, a time in life that has come to be called the *midlife crisis*. As we pointed out in Chapter 13, there is real reason to doubt that a crisis is experienced by most adults at this age, but for many there are both role changes and physical changes at about this age that may require new adaptations, new integrations. Such a reexamination may then be followed by a long consolidation period characterized by new patterns of relationships.

First of all, for most adults the physical and intellectual peak has been passed by age 40 or 45. The decline from the peak is not immediate or rapid, but there does seem to be a slowing down of some mental processes and more measurable losses of physical capacities. Before you sink into pits of depression at the thought of being over the hill by age 40, let us remind you that there are *wide* individual differences in the peak achieved, in the rate of decline, and in the timing of the decline. A person's degree of physical fitness and mental activity seems to be a key element in the equation. To use Denney's phrase, we retain peak or near-peak use of "optimally exercised" skills far longer than we retain unexercised skills; so those adults who remain physically and mentally active in midlife may experience little or no decline.

The other strongly positive thing to be said about middle adulthood is that it seems to be socially the richest and most satisfying time for many adults. Work satisfaction is high; marital satisfaction seems to peak after the children have left home, friendship becomes strong and important once again, and the role of *mentor* may become significant as well. There are some negative signs, too, of course. Some research shows, for example, that while marital satisfaction is high, loving expressions have declined in the forties and fifties. Adults in this age period also encounter a kind of generational squeeze, with demands for support both from children and from aging parents. Despite these sources of strain, however, it seems fair to describe this period as one in which there is a renewed involvement in nurturing and in intimacy.

Such a return to intimacy seems to be more characteristic of men than of women. In fact, for many women the period from 40 to 65 is a time of increased emphasis on achievement concerns. The consequences of this crossing over of men's and women's traditional characteristics is to make both sexes in this age period more *androgynous*.

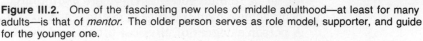

Figure III.2.   One of the fascinating new roles of middle adulthood—at least for many adults—is that of *mentor*. The older person serves as role model, supporter, and guide for the younger one.

This is true physically, since the hormone patterns of men and women in their fifties are more similar than they have been since early childhood. It is true psychologically as well. Men and women in this age group are more likely to express a balance between nurturance and achievement, between "agency" and "affiliation," to use Rossi's terms (1980).

Late Adulthood: From 65 to 75

Conventionally a transition is marked at 65, at the time of retirement from work. Obviously, this change in role does herald some other changes in people's lives, but the current evidence suggests that for most adults there is relatively little upheaval at the time of retirement. The adjustment is expected ("scheduled" in Pearlin's language), and some of the mental and physical preparation has already been done. Mostly what we see in this period is a continuation of the physical, mental, and social trends that were already evident in the 40 to 65 period. There is a further gradual loss of some physical and some mental functions, although such fluid intelligence abilities as conversational skills, vocabulary, and the like are often maintained at a very high level during these years.

These changes are gradual, but they may be more obvious to the observer (or to the individual herself) in the sixties and seventies than they were before. Eyesight normally becomes poorer (although this change starts in the forties); hearing also becomes poorer. The culmination of the gradual changes is often glasses or hearing aids—visible, outward signs of loss of function. Graying hair (or loss of hair) may also become more evident.

However, contrary to some earlier speculation about social and emotional disengagement during this period, there seems to be little or no decline in social activity, family involvement, or relationships with friends. The emphasis on intimacy and relationships that was evident in the forties and fifties is still evident in the seventies.

Late, Late Adulthood: From 75 to ?

We have marked another transition period at around 75, although there is no widely shared external or internal change that signals or triggers a transition at this age. The changes during the years after 65 are very gradual, but there is a good deal of evidence that the *old old* (those 75 or older) should be differentiated from the *young old* (those in their sixties and early seventies).

It is among the old old that we see signs of disengagement in the form of gradual withdrawal from active social involvements. There are also obvious losses in mental and physical functioning, even in those who have maintained maximal exercise. In a pattern that is reminiscent of the adage "last hired, first fired," those mental structures that are acquired the latest in childhood and adulthood are usually lost first in late old age (Denney, 1982). We rarely see formal operational thinking, for example; although if we do see it, it is almost always applied to practical, daily concerns.

It is important to emphasize that while the mental and physical skills of the 80-year-old adult are lower than they were in the same adult at 20 or 30 or even 40, they may still be quite adequate for the demands of his daily life, especially if the person remains in good physical health. More than any other single element, health is the factor that influences quality of life experience for older adults.

Some Possible Links across Physical, Mental, and Social Development in Adulthood

If you examine Table III.1 and reread what we have said about each of the stages of adulthood, you will probably be struck by the fact that physical and mental development seem to follow very similar patterns,

Figure III.3. There are few signs of social disengagement among adults from 65 to 75; but in late, late adulthood some adults show a gradual withdrawal from social contacts and concentrate more of their attention on their own inner processes.

with peak capacity in the twenties or thirties and gradual decline after that. Both patterns are also affected in very similar ways by exercise or use of the specific function: Exercise can prolong peak performance, raise the overall level of performance, and slow the rate of decline. These parallels certainly provide strong evidence for assuming a maturational basis for many changes in mental ability, as well as for the changes in physical performance.

Social development, however, does not seem to follow a similar path, and the possible links between social and physical or social and mental development are far less obvious. In fact, the picture one gets is of two somewhat distinct developmental threads, one physical and one social, which weave together at only a few points. It is in the realm of inner development—identity, personality, intimacy—that there are hints of development or growth. Older adults are generally *more* capable of sustaining an array of intimate relationships while simultaneously engaging in productive work. They are more nurturant, more altruistic, more generous. It is very difficult to see how changes of this kind can be explained by physical maturation or by changes in mental capacity, except that as Erikson suggests, the *sense* of physical or mental decline may be one of the triggers that leads an adult to reexamine values and make inner changes.

Exploration of the connections between physical and mental changes, on the one hand, and social/emotional changes, on the other, is one of the great research tasks for the next decades. Does the psychological androgyny in the fifties emerge in some way from the physiological changes of the climacteric? Do people who experience greater physical or mental loss early in adulthood have different inner experiences? We know that in older adults, the loss of health is a major predictor of life satisfaction (Palmore, 1980), but we need more, and more detailed, information at earlier ages.

INDIVIDUAL DIFFERENCES IN ADULT DEVELOPMENT

While the overall stagelike pattern of development in adulthood we have just given is a reasonable general description, the really striking thing about adulthood is how varying the patterns of change are from one person to the next. Personality differences (perhaps originating partially in basic genetically programmed temperament) flavor each person's development. This is not to suggest that there is perfect consistency over any one person's life span. There is not. A rotten, unloving childhood does not automatically warp a child for life, and a loving and supportive childhood does not guarantee happiness. Unsociable children may later develop valued and supportive friendships, and gregarious children may end up divorcing as adults. But within adulthood, as Costa and McCrae (1980) and McClelland (1981) have pointed out, there are dimensions of personality that affect the way an adult approaches the developmental changes outlined in Table III.1. As Palmore has found in the Duke longitudinal studies (1981), the best single predictor of satisfaction or sexual activity or social activity in late adulthood is a person's level of satisfaction or sexual activity or social activity in middle age. We take ourselves with us throughout adulthood.

Aside from personality, however, there are two dimensions of individual difference that stand out when we look at adult lives: sex differences and social-class differences. Of the two, the most consistent is social class.

Social-Class Differences in Adult Patterns

We want to overstate the case a bit to make the point: By almost any yardstick of adult satisfaction or happiness or growth, the better educated you are the better off you are.

Middle-class (better-educated) adults not only have higher IQs, they maintain intellectual skill and performance better into old age (Palmore, 1981).

Better-educated adults are healthier and live longer than less well-educated adults (Palmore & Stone, 1973). In women, active sexuality in old age is also more common among the better educated (Palmore, 1981).

Middle-class or better-educated adults have more stable marriages and greater reported happiness in marriage (Campbell, 1981; Lewis & Spanier, 1979). Figure III.4 shows some representative results documenting this generalization from a recent study by Anne Locksley (1982) involving a sample of over 2000 adults.

Better-educated and middle-class adults are, in general, more satisfied with their lives, happier, or more likely to show significant personal growth (Harris, 1975). In Farrell and Rosenberg's study (1981) of adult men (a study we referred to often in Chapters 13 and 14), for example, the least well educated men with the lower-paying jobs showed not growth but progressive alienation and disintegration by midlife. They also had fewer friends than did middle-class men at every stage of the family life cycle except during the newlywed period, as we showed in Figure 14.9. The general relationship between social class and happiness, taken from national survey data (Campbell, 1981), is shown in Figure III.5.

A modest exception to this overall pattern lies in the domain of work. Campbell (1981) has found in his national surveys that adult men with very low levels of education (eighth grade or less) are usually as satisfied with their work as are those who have been to college. Among the better educated, college graduates describe themselves as more satisfied than do those with less than college education, but the greatest

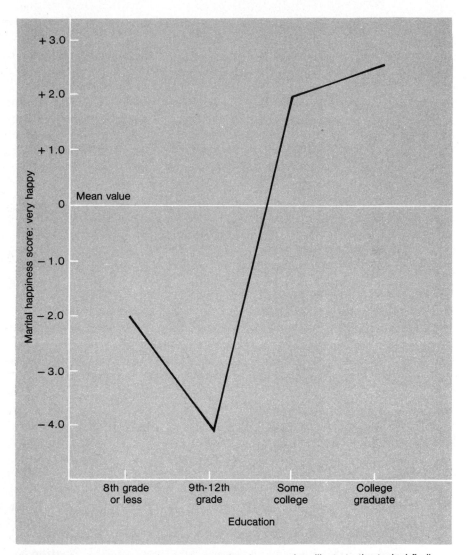

Figure III.4. These recent results from national survey data illustrate the typical finding that those adults with more education report greater marital happiness than do those with lower levels of education. (*Source:* Locksley, 1982.)

satisfaction is among the least educated. What *is* true of the college-educated worker, however, is that he sees his work as providing not only an income but also a challenge and a sense of accomplishment. Among less well educated workers, steady income is seen as the greatest value of work. Work thus appears to play a different role in the lives of the college educated than of the less well educated adult.

Despite this exception, the list of educational differences in adult experiences is somewhat startling. It suggests that one's education or

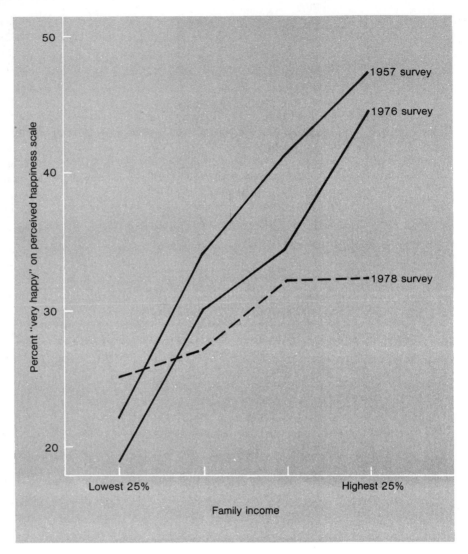

Figure III.5. Like marital happiness, overall perceived happiness with life is higher among adults with higher incomes (most of whom are also better educated). Note, however, that the 1978 survey data show this less vividly than do earlier surveys, which may mean that this pattern is changing somewhat. (*Source:* Campbell, 1981.)

social class may be one of the (if not the most) significant factors in shaping both the developmental pathway followed in adulthood and the level of satisfaction an adult is likely to feel. Why might this be true?

Money. The most obvious place to begin is with money. Better-educated adults earn more and are less likely to have their work careers interrupted with layoffs. As we pointed out in Chapter 13 (for example, Estes & Wilensky, 1978), money can provide a buffer against the stresses of multiple roles. Good child care can be afforded, as just one example. In later adulthood, money obviously buys some of the comforts that make retirement more satisfying.

Job Complexity.   We mentioned Melvin Kohn's work in Chapter 12 (1980). He has found that jobs that are "substantively complex" are more satisfying, lead to higher self-esteem, and stimulate the development of greater intellectual flexibility. Kohn finds that these relationships hold *within* social-class groups as well as between them. That is, less well educated adults with complex jobs are better off than those with simple jobs, and the same is true among the better educated. Since most substantively complex jobs require fairly high levels of education or training, more middle-class adults perform them.

Kohn's argument is reminiscent of Janet Giele's similar point (1982), which we mentioned in Chapter 13. She argues that those adults who experience complexity on the job or in an assortment of life roles are more likely to be forced to develop an abstract self or an integrated life structure. Job complexity may thus not only produce more maximally exercised cognitive skills and thus prolong good intellectual functioning, it may also promote the reflectiveness that leads to emotional and personal growth.

Differing Family Life Cycles.   Education is also correlated with age of marriage and with size and timing of family. Working-class (less well educated) adults marry sooner, have children sooner, and have larger families. All of this not only creates a differently timed set of life-cycle changes, it also piles up the maximum demand on financial and emotional resources in the twenties, when the level of employment, and thus income, is likely to be low. These extra strains may contribute to the higher divorce rate among the less well educated; certainly they contribute to lower marital satisfaction.

Health.   The poorer health of less well educated adults may also be a causal contributor to their lower levels of life satisfaction. As a group, the poor receive less (and less good) medical care. They are more likely to retire because of ill health rather than because of free choice— perhaps because their jobs more often involve physical labor. In later adulthood, poor physical health is the single best predictor of low life satisfaction.

We do not want to suggest by this long (and rather depressing) list that all adults with less than a college education are doomed to dreary and unsatisfying adult lives. That is clearly not the case. We are talking about average differences, and there are many exceptions. Among

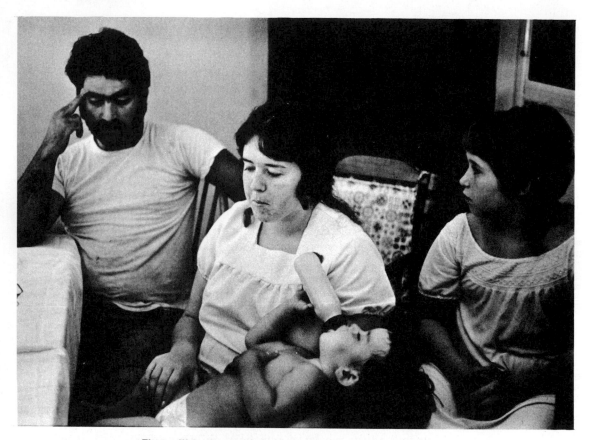

Figure III.6. Working-class men and women marry earlier, have their children earlier, and have more children than do middle-class couples. These differences cannot help but have a huge impact on their adult-life experiences.

other things, qualities of temperament and personality can override the effects of social class, just as immature personality can lead to very poor outcomes among very well educated adults (Vaillant, 1977). However, the accumulation of findings is striking. In our society, at least, educational experience in early adulthood appears to be a significant factor in establishing the adult life pathway for an individual.

Sex Differences in Adulthood

Next to the education differences, the sex differences—while visible—seem somewhat pale. We have summarized the known differences in Table III.2, and you'll see that many of the differences are continuations of patterns we have already described in adolescence and youth. Adult women have more intimate friendships, just as was true in childhood and adolescence; adult women are less skillful at spatial visualiza-

TABLE III.2
Summary of Sex Differences in Development during the Adult Years

Physical development

Life expectancy	Women live longer than men do.
Strength/speed, and so forth	The differences in heart and lung capacity and in strength and speed, evident in adolescence, continue through adulthood.
Climacteric	Both men and women experience changes in hormone patterns in the late forties and fifties, but for women this involves a loss of reproductive capacity, while men are able to father children well into old age.

Cognitive development

Spatial visualization	The difference shown in adolescence persists: Men are better at such tasks, on average, than women are.
Mathematical reasoning	Men are higher on most measures, as at earlier ages.
Verbal reasoning	Women are higher on most measures, as at earlier ages.
Cognitive structure	There is almost no information available about any differences among adults, except that in young adults more men show formal operations reasoning.

Social development

Aggression/dominance	Men continue to show higher levels of such behavior than do women, although there are hints that this difference declines somewhat in middle adulthood, as part of the crossover phenomenon.
Intimacy/friendships	Women appear to have more intimate friendships (and more friends) throughout adulthood, although men's friendships appear to become more intimate in middle adulthood than they were earlier. Women's emphasis on intimacy gives way somewhat in the middle years and is replaced by a greater emphasis on achievement.
Family roles	Women's family role includes more child care and more nurturing of both children and spouse than does men's family role. This is true even among women who work full time.
Work roles	Differences in work roles are declining as more women work continuously throughout adulthood, but men's work histories are still more predictable and continuous than women's are (on average), and work status appears to play a more central role in men's identity, especially in early adulthood.

tion and mathematical reasoning tasks and better at verbal reasoning, as was true in adolescence; adult men are more assertive, aggressive, and competitive than are adult women, just as was true from early childhood.

Beyond these continuing patterns, the major differences in the pathways of adult men and women seem to have to do with the centrality of relationships for women and the centrality of achievement for men (Scarf, 1980). This is partially a result of differing job descriptions (roles) for the two sexes. Women bear and primarily rear children, and their roles as wives and daughters also contain more expectation of nurturance and support than do the parallel roles of husband or son. It is also true, as we pointed out in Chapter 13, that while men's work patterns are likely to be fairly steady and predictable, women's patterns are more variable. Whereas Levinson (1978) envisions men's life course as a series of orderly "seasons," McGuigan (1980) envisions women's life course as "a braid of threads in which colors appear, disappear, and reappear" (p. xii). Given what we have just said about the long-range beneficial effect of such complexity on the development of cognitive complexity and on personal growth, one might argue that women have a greater likelihood of emerging into old age with integrity rather than despair. That is a hypothesis yet to be tested, but it is obviously one that is attractive to both of us!

Cohort Effects

We cannot leave this summary discussion of adulthood without one final word of caution. The theme should be familiar by now, since we sometimes feel as if we have said this on every page. Nonetheless it bears repeating. Not only is most of our knowledge of adult development based on cross-sectional rather than on longitudinal research, it is almost all based on studies of a particular generation of adults—those who grew up in the 1920s and 1930s or perhaps 1940s. These are adults who spent their childhoods during the Great Depression or the Second World War, at a time when sex-role definitions were much more differentiated, college education was far less common, and severe economic hardship was experienced by many. It is not at all obvious that the elements influencing the lives of those adults are going to be the same ones that are significant in the lives of the generation who grew up in the 1960s or 1970s or later. For example, a midlife crisis may be a common experience for one cohort, confronted by a particular set of converging life experiences. But it may be quite rare for your generation. You can see another example of a cohort difference in Figure III.2, which shows a smaller effect of social class on life satisfaction in recent surveys than in samples studied at earlier points. As people live longer and stay healthier longer, many of our conclusions about the characteristics of old age may need revision. So take what we said about adulthood as food for thought, but be sure to add the grain of salt.

THE DEVELOPING PERSON: A FINAL LOOK AT THE LIFE SPAN

In the three summary sections, we have tried to pull some of the separate threads together for you, but we have still left the person in three parts: child, adolescent, and adult. Some of the themes that link these three life periods together have appeared repeatedly through the book, and you can do much of the integration yourself. But let us say just a few words about two issues that seem particularly important.

Consistency and Inconsistency across the Life Span

We raised the question of life-span consistency in personal qualities in Chapter 1 as one of the issues that divide the several theories of development. We have mentioned it at regular intervals since. Just how fixed is development in childhood? Are the early years a *critical period* for the establishment of personality, of cognitive skill, even of physical health?

Before we look at the data, a word is in order about what we mean by *consistency*. There are two possible meanings: (1) Do people stay the same in some *absolute* sense; do their IQs, or their health, or their height remain the same over time? (2) Regardless of whether the absolute level of some characteristic remains the same, we can ask whether people stay in the same *relative* position with respect to others; is the teenager with the highest IQ the 50-year-old with the highest IQ? Is the healthiest child among the healthiest adults?

We have talked fairly frequently about the first of these two meanings of consistency, such as when we traced changes in IQ scores over adulthood or looked for systematic changes in personality integration or maturity in adults. Here we want to focus on the second of these two meanings.

The best way to answer questions about this kind of stability would be to study the same people for 70 or 80 years and see whether they stay in the same approximate rank order on variables such as IQ or health or personality characteristics. That's a tall order. (Among other things, the working life of the researchers is only about 40 years, so such a study would take at least two full generations of researchers to accomplish and then another generation to analyze the results.) Amazingly enough, we now have several studies that begin to approximate such an age span. The recent findings from the Berkeley and Oakland growth studies, for example, cover the period from about age 12 to about age 50 (Eichorn, Clausen, Haan, Honzik, & Mussen, 1981)—not perfect, but remarkable nonetheless. Since there are pieces of the life span covered by other studies, we can begin to patch together a few answers.

Consistency in Physical Development and Health.   Some aspects of physical functioning have very high consistency over the life span. Height, for example, is a highly predictable characteristic from early childhood onward. Tall children typically become tall adults, and among adults (barring accidents) the rank order of height remains essentially unchanged over time (Kareem Abdul-Jabbar is not likely to shrink enough to become shorter than very many other people).

Relative weight is much less consistent over the life span. While it is true that very fat children tend to be fat as adults and very thin children tend to be thin adults (Zack, Harlan, Leaverton, & Cornoni-Huntley, 1979), there are also many people who shift in relative weight from childhood to adulthood. In the Oakland and Berkeley Growth Studies (Bayer, Whissell-Buechy, & Honzik, 1981), height/weight ratio (a measure of fatness) in childhood was correlated with adult fatness at only about .30 (a very modest correlation), and adolescent fatness predicted adult fatness at about .40. Thus while there is some consistency, there is a lot of change as well (a heartening thought for those of us who plan to lose a few pounds).

Similarly, overall health is only modestly consistent from childhood to adulthood. In the Berkeley Growth Study, for example, the subjects' overall health had been rated by physicians in childhood, in adolescence, and again at about age 40. These three ratings were only very weakly related in women and almost completely unrelated among men. So children who were particularly physically robust or particularly sickly may or may not display good health as adults (Bayer, Whissell-Buechy, & Honzik, 1981).

Consistency in Intellectual Power over the Life Span.   Nearly all of what we know about consistency or inconsistency in intellectual performance over a lifetime is based on measures of global IQ, and nearly all of it comes from a few longitudinal studies. However, the results are quite consistent. In infancy, children's IQ scores are highly unstable; in childhood they are modestly stable, but many children show large IQ changes from one testing to the next (Honzik, Macfarlane, Allen, 1948; McCall, Appelbaum, & Hogarty, 1973). (A change of 15 points from one testing to the next is common; larger changes are also fairly frequent.)

Stability in IQ is much stronger from adolescence to adulthood. In the Berkeley and Oakland studies, the correlation between IQs at ages 17 to 18 and IQ measured at middle age (36 to 48) was .83 for males and .77 for females (Eichorn, Hunt, & Honzik, 1981). Such numbers describe a remarkably high level of consistency over a 20- to 30-year period, although there is still room for individual increases or declines. In fact, Dorothy Eichorn and her colleagues report that those adults who improved in IQ scores relative to others were likely to have married someone with a higher IQ; those who declined relative to the rest of the group frequently showed high levels of alcohol use or debilitative illness as adults. Thus while consistency of rank ordering of IQs from adolescence to adulthood is the general rule, there are specific conditions that can deflect a person from his or her expected trajectory.

Consistency in Personality over the Life Span. We have already talked in some detail about consistency in personality in the adult years (Chapter 13); there remains the question of consistency from childhood or adolescence to adulthood. Certainly if the temperament theorists are correct, we ought to find such relative stability.

In fact there is some, but there is more change than there is stability. If you see that a child is a bookworm, loves school, is fairly sociable, and is quite self-confident, chances are pretty good that the same child will turn out to be a grown-up who reads the newspaper regularly, has a college education, is still fairly self-confident, and has a wide circle of friends (Haan, 1981). If the child is a girl, you may be able to make some reasonable predictions about her dependency as an adult from knowing how dependent she was as a child; if the child is a boy, your predictions of adult aggressiveness (but not dependency) are likely to be fairly decent (Kagan & Moss, 1962). But the magnitude of the correlations on which we base these statements is not huge—on the order of .30 or .40. There is a *lot* of room for change.

Part of the difficulty in studying personality consistency over the full life span is simply finding measures at every age that accurately reflect basic personality or temperament qualities. We may well be underestimating the consistency that really exists because so many different kinds of measures have been used. It is clear, though, that children and adults respond to changing environments, changing roles, and changing demands with changes in behavior, or even with alterations of basic personality traits. Childhood patterns may predispose each of us to particular adult pathways, but they do not *determine* them in any absolute sense. That may be a distressing conclusion for those psychologists (and others) who would like development to be orderly and predictable. However, it is a comforting thought for those of you who came from less than splendid childhoods or who relish (as we do) the challenge of growth and change throughout life.

Internal and External Influences: Inner and Outer Changes

A second melody that we have played again and again in these pages is the theme of biological versus environmental influence. In each age period, we can find at least some physical changes that seem to be influential. But when we look at the role of biological change over the entire life span, we can see that there is an interesting ebb and flow of importance.

To illustrate this, we have put together a master chart (Figure III.7) that shows the level of change (development or decline) that we see in each of several domains in each age period. You should understand that this is our synthesis. Other researchers and authors would no doubt disagree with us about the number of *X*'s in each square, but we think there is fairly good agreement about the overall pattern we have shown.

If you look at the figure, you can see that during the first 15 to 20 years of life, many of the major changes we can see are linked to physical developments or to universally shared social demands such as school. These are *unavoidable* changes, marked by fairly clear transitions. These early years are easy to talk about and easy to organize into age periods because of the underlying importance of maturational change and because we have come to understand the sequence of cognitive changes that occur here as well.

However, most of the changes in the adult period—particularly in

Age	Changes in perceptual skill	Changes in language skill	Changes in cognitive skill	Changes in biological characteristics or physical skill	Changes in social interactions and family roles	Changes in sex roles	Changes in work roles
0-2 months	X	—	X	XXX	X	—	—
2-18 months	X	XX	XXX	XXX	XX	—	—
18 mos-6 yrs	—	XXX	XXX	X	XX	X	—
6-12 yrs	—	—	XXX	X	X	—	—
12-22 yrs	—	—	XX	XXX	XXX	XX	X
22-40 yrs	—	—	—	—	XXX	XXX	XXX
45-65 yrs	X	—	X	XX	XX	XXX	XX
65-75 yrs	X	—	XX	XXX	X	X	XXX
75 +	XX	—	XXX	XXX	XX	X	—

Figure III.7.   Master chart of development, showing those areas at each stage in which we think there is no major change (-), some change (x), substantial change (xx), and major or critical change (xxx). The areas of maximum change are highlighted at each age. Note the movement from physical to cognitive and back to physical changes in childhood and the return in importance of physical change in late adulthood. In early and middle adulthood, changes in family and work roles, and in patterns of social interaction, seem to be of greater significance.

early and middle adulthood—do not appear to be linked either to physical change or to orderly cognitive sequences. There appears to be some inner change taking place, at least for some people. But many more of the changes we see are associated with systematic variations in such externals as work roles, family roles, and sex roles.

In the years past 65 or 75, physical and cognitive change (decline, in this case) again appears to be a major force in shaping development, except that there is far wider variation from one adult to the next in pattern of change than was true among children. For these reasons, the transitions of adulthood occur less often at shared chronological ages than is true of the transitions of childhood.

You should keep in mind that Figure III.7 reflects ignorance as well as knowledge. One of the many research tasks over the next decades will be to explore the role of biological change in shaping the adult years. We may well discover that more is going on than we now know. What is clear is that what we perceive as development over the life span is invariably a complex blend of inner and outer change, biological and environmental influence.

Bibliography

Abrahams, B., Feldman, S. S., & Nash, S. C. Sex role self-concept and sex role attitudes: Enduring personality characteristics or adaptations to changing life situations? *Developmental Psychology,* 1978, *14,* 393–400. (**13**)

Acredolo, L. P., & Hake, J. L. Infant perception. In B. B. Wolman (Ed.), *Handbook of developmental psychology.* Englewood Cliffs, N.J.: Prentice-Hall, 1982. (**2**)

Adams, B. N. Mate selection in the United States: A theoretical summarization. In W. R. Burr, R. Hill, F. I. Nye, & I. L. Reiss (Eds.), *Contemporary theories about the family* (Vol. 1). New York: Free Press, 1979. (**10**)

Administration on Aging. *Statistical notes,* No. 2 (August), 1978. (**13**)

Ainsworth, M. D. S., Bell, S. M., & Stayton, D. J. Individual differences in the development of some attachment behaviors. *Merrill-Palmer Quarterly,* 1972, *18,* 123–143. (**2, Sum I**)

Ainsworth, M. D. S., Blehar, M. C., Waters, E., & Wall, S. *Patterns of attachment.* Hillsdale, N.J.: Erlbaum, 1978. (**1, 7**)

Ainsworth, M. D. S., & Wittig, B. A. Attachment and exploratory behavior of one-year-olds in a strange situation. In B. M. Foss (Ed.), *Determinants of infant behavior* (Vol. 4). New York: Methuen, 1969. (**7**)

Aleksandrowicz, M. K., & Aleksandrowicz, D. R. Obstetrical pain-relieving drugs as predicators of infant behavior variability. *Child Development,* 1974, *45,* 935–945. (**2**)

Alexander, J. F. Defensive and supportive communications in normal and deviant families. *Journal of Consulting and Clinical Psychology,* 1973, *40,* 223–231. (**10**)

Anglin, J. *Word, object, and conceptual development.* New York: Norton, 1977. (**5**)

Anthony, E. J. The behavior disorders of childhood. In P. H. Mussen (Ed.), *Carmichael's manual of child psychology* (Vol. 2, 3d ed.). New York: Wiley, 1970. (**Sum II**)

Apgar, V. A. A proposal for a new method of evaluation of the newborn infant. *Anesthesia and Analgesia,* 1953, *32,* 260–267. (**2**)

Apter, A., Galatzer, A., Beth-Halachmi, N., & Laron, Z. Self-image in adolescents with delayed puberty and growth retardation. *Journal of Youth and Adolescence,* 1981, *10,* 501–506. (**8**)

Arenberg, D. A longitudinal study of problem solving in adults. *Journal of Gerontology,* 1974, *29,* 650–658. (**12**)

Arend, R., Gove, F. L., & Sroufe, L. A. Continuity of individual adaptation from infancy to kindergarten. A predictive study of ego-resiliency and curiosity in preschoolers. *Child Development,* 1979, *50,* 950–959. (**6**)

Argyle, M. Nonverbal communication in human social interaction. In R. Hinde (Ed.), *Non-verbal communication.* New York: Cambridge University Press, 1972. (**14**)

Arlin, P. K. Cognitive development in adulthood: A fifth stage? *Developmental Psychology,* 1975, *11,* 602–605. (**12**)

————. Piagetian operations in problem finding. *Developmental Psychology,* 1977, *13,* 297–298. (**12**)

Asher, S. R., Oden, S. L., & Gottman, J. M. Children's friendships in school settings. In L. G. Katz (Ed.), *Current topics in early childhood education* (Vol. 1). Norwood, N.J.: Ablex, 1977. (**7**)

Ausubel, D. P., Montemayor, R., & Svajian, P. *Theory and problems of adolescent development* (2d ed.). New York: Grune & Stratton, 1977. (**10**)

Bear, D. M. *An age-irrelevant concept of development.* Paper presented at the annual meetings of the American Psychological Association, New York, 1966.

Balkwell, C. Transition to widowhood: A review of the literature. *Family Relations,* 1981, *30,* 117–128. (**14**)

Bamberger, J. Growing up prodigies: The midlife crisis. In D. H. Feldman (Ed.), *Developmental approaches to giftedness and creativity.* San Francisco: Jossey-Bass, 1982. **(9)**

Bandura, A. *Social learning theory.* Englewood Cliffs, N.J.: Prentice-Hall, 1977*a*. **(1)**

———. Self-efficacy: Toward a unifying theory of behavioral change. *Psychological Review,* 1977*b, 84,* 191–215. **(6)**

———. Self-efficacy mechanism in human agency. *American Psychologist,* 1982, *37,* 122–147. **(6)**

Baratz, J. C. Teaching reading in an urban Negro school system. In J. C. Baratz & R. Schuy (Eds.), *Teaching black children to read.* Washington, D.C.: Center for Applied Linguistics, 1969. **(5)**

Barnard, K. E., & Bee, H. L. *Parent interaction with full-term and pre-term infants.* Paper presented at the International Conference on Infant Studies, Austin, Texas, 1982. **(7)**

Barnard, K. E., & Eyres, S. *Child health assessment, part 2. Results of the first twelve months of life.* Washington, D.C.: U.S. Government Printing Office, 1979. **(2)**

Barrett, M. D. Distinguishing between prototypes: The early acquisition of the meaning of object names. In S. Kuczaj II, (Ed.), *Language development (Vol. 1): Syntax and semantics.* Hillsdale, N.J.: Erlbaum, 1982. **(5)**

Bates, E., Bretherton, I., Beeghly-Smith, M., & McNew, S. Social bases of language development: A reassessment. In H. W. Reese & L. P. Lipsitt (Eds.), *Advances in child development and behavior* (Vol. 16). New York: Academic Press, 1982. **(Sum I)**

Batter, B. S., & Davidson, C. V. Wariness of strangers: Reality or artifact? *Journal of Child Psychology and Psychiatry,* 1979, *20,* 93–109. **(7)**

Bauer, D. M. *An age-irrelevant concept of development.* Paper presented at the annual meetings of the American Psychological Association, New York, 1966. **(1)**

Baumrind, D. Socialization and instrumental competence in young children. In W. W. Hartup (Ed.), *The young child: Reviews of research* (Vol. 2). Washington, D.C.: National Association for the Education of Young Children, 1972. **(6)**

———. Early socialization and adolescent competence. In S. E. Dragastin & G. H. Elder, Jr., (Eds.), *Adolescence in the life cycle.* New York: Halsted, 1975. **(10)**

Bayer, L. M., Whissell-Buechy, D., & Honzik, M. Health in the middle years. In D. H. Eichorn, J. A. Clausen, N. Haan, M. P. Honzik, & P. H. Mussen (Eds.), *Present and past in middle life.* New York: Academic Press, 1981. **(Sum III)**

Bayley, N. Comparisons of mental and motor test scores for ages 1–15 months by sex, birth, order, race, geographical location, and education of parents. *Child Development,* 1965, *36,* 379–411. **(4)**

———. *Bayley scales of infant development: Birth to two years.* New York: Psychological Corporation, 1969. **(4)**

Bee, H. L., Barnard, K. E., Eyres, S. J., Gray, C. A., Hammond, M. A., Spietz, A. L., Snyder, C., & Clark, B. Prediction of IQ and language skill from perinatal status, child performance, family characteristics, and mother–infant interaction. *Child Development,* 1982, *53,* 1134–1156. **(Sum I)**

Beischer, N. A., & Mackay, E. V. *Obstetrics and the newborn for midwives and medical students.* Philadelphia: Saunders, 1976. **(2)**

Bell, R. R. *Worlds of friendship.* Beverly Hills, Calif.: Sage, 1981. **(14)**

Belle, D. Depression and low income, female-headed families. In E. Corfman (Ed.), *Families today: A research sampler on families and children* (Vol. 1). Washington, D.C.: U.S. Government Printing Office, 1979. **(13)**

Belloc, N. B. Relationship of health practices and mortality. *Preventive Medicine,* 1973, *2,* 67–81. **(11)**

Belloc, N. B., & Breslow, L. Relationship of physical health status and health practices. *Preventive Medicine,* 1972, *1,* 409–421. **(11)**

Belsky, J., & Steinberg, L. D. The effects of day care: A critical review. *Child Development,* 1978, *49,* 929–949. **(13)**

Bem, S. L. The measurement of psychological androgyny. *Journal of Consulting and Clinical Psychology,* 1974, *42,* 155–162. **(10)**

Berg, W. K., & Berg, K. M. Psychophysiological development in infancy: State, sensory function, and attention. In J. D. Osofsky (Ed.), *Handbook of infant development.* New York: Wiley, 1979. (2)

Berndt, T. J. Developmental changes in conformity to peers and parents. *Developmental Psychology,* 1979, *15,* 608–616. (10)

———. Age changes and changes over time in prosocial intentions and behavior between friends. *Developmental Psychology,* 1981*a,* *17,* 408–416. (7)

———. Effects of friendship on prosocial intentions behavior. *Child Development,* 1981*b, 52,* 636–643. (7)

Bertenthal, B. I., & Fischer, K. W. Development of self-recognition in the infant. *Developmental Psychology,* 1978, *14,* 44–50. (6)

Best, D. L., Williams, J. E., Cloud, J. M., Davis, S. W., Robertson, L. S., Edwards, J. R., Giles, H., & Fowles, J. Development of sex-trait stereotypes among young children in the United States, England, and Ireland. *Child Development,* 1977, *48,* 1375–1384. (6)

Binet, A., & Simon, T. Methodes nouvelles pour le diagnostic du niveau intellectual des anormaux. *L'Annee Psychologigue,* 1905, *11,* 191–244. (4)

Birchler, G. R., Weiss, R. L., & Vincent, J. P. Multidimensional analyses of social reinforcement exchange between maritally distressed and non-distressed spouse and stranger dyads. *Journal of Personality and Social Psychology,* 1975, *31,* 348–360. (14)

Bissell, J. S. Planned variation in Head Start and Follow Through. In J. C. Stanley (Ed.), *Compensatory education for children, ages 2 to 8.* Baltimore: Johns Hopkins University Press, 1973. (4)

Blehar, M. C., Leiberman, A. F., & Ainsworth, M. D. S. Early face-to-face interaction and its relation to later mother–infant attachment. *Child Development,* 1977, *48,* 182–194. (7, **Sum I**)

Block, J. Some enduring and consequential structures of personality. In A. I. Rabin, J. Aronoff, A. M. Barclay, & R. A. Zucker (Eds.), *Further explorations in personality.* New York: Wiley, 1981. (13)

Bloom, B. L., Asher, S. J., & White, S. W. Marital disruption as a stressor: A review and analysis. *Psychological Bulletin,* 1978, *85,* 867–894. (14)

Blum, J. E., & Jarvik, L. F. Intellectual performance of octogenarians as a function of education and initial ability. *Human Development,* 1974, *17,* 364–375. (12)

Booth, A., & Hess, E. Cross-sex friendship. *Journal of Marriage and the Family,* 1974, *36,* 38–47. (14)

Borke, H. Piaget's mountains revisited: Changes in the egocentric landscape. *Developmental Psychology,* 1975, *11,* 240–243. (4)

Borland, D. C. A cohort analysis approach to the empty-nest syndrome among three ethnic groups of women: A theoretical position. *Journal of Marriage and the Family,* 1982, *44,* 117–129. (13)

Bortz, W. M., II. Disuse and aging. *Journal of the American Medical Association,* 1982, *248* (September), 1203–1208. (11)

The Boston Women's Health Book Collective. *Our bodies, ourselves: A book by and for women* (2d ed.). New York: Simon & Schuster, 1977. (2)

Botwinick, J. *Aging and behavior.* New York: Springer-Verlag, 1973. (12)

Bower, T. G. R. Slant perception and shape consistency in infants. *Science,* 1966, *151,* 832–834. (3)

———. Infant perception of the third dimension and object concept development. In L. B. Cohen & P. Salapatek (Eds.), *Infant perception: From sensation to cognition* (Vol. 2). New York: Academic Press, 1975. (3)

———. *The perceptual world of the child.* Cambridge, Mass.: Harvard University Press, 1977. (3)

Bowerman, C. E., & Kinch, J. W. Changes in family and peer orientation of children between the fourth and tenth grades. *Social Forces,* 1959, *37,* 206–211. (10)

Bowlby, J. Process of mourning. *International Journal of Psycho-Analysis,* 1961, *42,* 317–340. (14)

———. *Attachment and loss (Vol. 1). Attachment.* New York: Basic Books, 1969. (7)

———. *Attachment and loss (Vol. 2). Separation,*

anxiety, and anger. New York: Basic Books, 1973. **(7)**

————. *Attachment and loss (Vol. 3). Loss, sadness, and depression.* New York: Basic Books, 1980. **(7, 14)**

Bradley, R. H., & Caldwell, B. M. Screening the environment. *American Journal of Orthopsychiatry,* 1978, *48,* 114–129. **(Sum I)**

Braine, M. D. S. The ontogeny of English phrase structure: The first phase. *Language,* 1963, *39,* 1–13. **(5)**

Brazelton, T. B. *Infants and mothers: Differences in development.* New York: Dell, 1969. **(2)**

————. *Neonatal behavioral assessment scale.* Philadelphia: Lippincott, 1973. **(2)**

Bretherton, I., Stolberg, U., & Kreye, M. Engaging strangers in proximal interaction: Infants' social initiative. *Developmental Psychology,* 1981, *17,* 746–755. **(7)**

Broderick, C. B. Adult sexual development. In B. B. Wolman (Ed.), *Handbook of developmental psychology.* Englewood Cliffs, N.J.: Prentice-Hall, 1982. **(11)**

Brody, E. B., & Brody, N. *Intelligence: Nature, determinants and consequences.* New York: Academic Press, 1976. **(12)**

Bromwich, R. M. Focus on material behavior in infant intervention. *American Journal of Orthopsychiatry,* 1976, *46,* 439–446. **(7)**

Bronfenbrenner, U. *The ecology of human development.* Cambridge, Mass.: Harvard University Press, 1979. **(1)**

Bronson, G. W. The postnatal growth of visual capacity. *Child Development,* 1974, *45,* 873–890. **(3)**

Brooks-Gunn, J., & Matthews, W. S. *He and she. How children develop their sex-role identity.* Englewood Cliffs, N.J.: Prentice-Hall, 1979. **(7)**

Broverman, I. K., Broverman, D. M., Clarkson, F. E., Rosenkrantz, P. S., & Vogel, S. R. Sex-role stereotypes and clinical judgments of mental health. *Journal of Consulting and Clinical Psychology,* 1970, *34,* 1–7. **(6)**

Broverman, I. K., Vogel, S. R., Broverman, D. M., Clarkson, F. E., & Rosenkrantz, P. S. Sex-role stereotypes: A current appraisal. *Journal of Social Issues,* 1972, *28,* 59–78. **(6, 10, 13)**

Brown, A. L., Bransford, J. D., Ferrara, R. A., & Campione, J. C. Learning, remembering, and understanding. In J. H. Flavell & E. M. Markman (Eds.), *Carmichael's manual of child psychology* (Vol. 1). New York: Wiley, 1983. **(9)**

Brown, A. L., & Day, J. D. Macrorules for summarizing texts: The development of expertise. *Journal of Verbal Learning and Verbal Behavior,* in press. **(9)**

Brown, A. L., & Smiley, S. S. Rating the importance of structural units of prose passages: A problem of metacognitive development. *Child Development,* 1977, *48,* 1–8. **(9)**

Brown, R. *Social psychology.* New York: Free Press, 1965. **(5)**

————. *A first language: The early stages.* Cambridge, Mass.: Harvard University Press, 1973. **(5)**

————. Introduction. In C. E. Snow and C. A. Ferguson (Eds.), *Talking to children.* New York: Cambridge University Press, 1977. **(5)**

Brown, R., & Bellugi, U. Three processes in the acquisition of syntax. *Harvard Educational Review,* 1964, *34,* 133–151. **(5)**

Brown, R., Cazden, C., & Bellugi, U. The child's grammar from I to III. In J. P. Hill (Ed.), *Minnesota symposia on child psychology* (Vol. 2). Minneapolis: University of Minnesota Press, 1969. **(5)**

Bryant, P. E., & Trabasso, T. Transitive inferences and memory in young children. *Nature,* 1971, *232,* 456–458. **(4)**

Bureau of the Census. *Marital status and living arrangements: March 1979.* Current Population Reports, Series P-20, #349. U.S. Department of Commerce, Bureau of the Census. Washington, D.C.: U.S. Government Printing Office, 1980. **(10)**

Burnett, S. A., Lane, D. M., & Dratt, L. M. Spatial ability and handedness. *Intelligence,* 1982, *6,* 57–68. **(9, Sum II)**

Buss, A. H., & Plomin, R. A. *Temperament theory of personality development.* New York: Wiley, 1975. **(1, 6)**

Byrne, D., & Nelson, D. Attraction as a linear function of positive reinforcements. *Journal of Personality and Social Psychology,* 1965, *1,* 659–663. **(10)**

Caldwell, B. M., Wright, C. M., Honig, A. S., & Tannenbaum, J. Infant day care and attachment. *American Journal of Orthopsychiatry,* 1970, *40,* 397–412. **(7)**

Campbell, A. *The sense of well-being in America.* New York: McGraw-Hill, 1981. **(Sum III)**

Campbell, S. B. Mother–infant interaction as a function of maternal ratings of temperament. *Child Psychiatry and Human Development,* 1979, *10,* 67–76. **(6)**

Campbell, S. B. G., & Taylor, P. M. Bonding and attachment: Theoretical issues. In P. M. Taylor (Ed.), *Parent–infant relationships.* New York: Grune & Stratton, 1980. **(7)**

Campion, J. E. Work sampling for personnel selection. *Journal of Applied Psychology,* 1972, *56,* 40–44. **(12)**

Campos, J. J., Langer, A., & Krowitz, A. Cardiac responses on the visual cliff in prelocomotor human infants. *Science,* 1970, *170,* 196–197. **(3)**

Cargan, L., & Melko, M. *Singles. Myths and realities.* Beverly Hills, Calif.: Sage, 1982. **(13)**

Carlsson, S. G., Fagerberg, H., Horneman, G., Hwang, C-P, Larsson, K., Rodholm, M., Schaller, J., Danielsson, B., & Bundewall, C. Effects of various amounts of contact between mother and child on the mother's nursing behavior: A follow-up study. *Infant Behavior and Development,* 1979, *2,* 209–214. **(7)**

Caron, A. J., & Caron, R. F. Processing of relational information as an index of infant risk. In S. L. Friedman & M. Sigman (Eds.), *Preterm birth and psychological development.* New York: Academic Press, 1981. **(3)**

Carr, J. *Young children with Down's syndrome: Their development, upbringing, and effect on their families.* London: Butterworth, 1975. **(3)**

Cattell, R. B. Theory of fluid and crystallized intelligence: A critical experiment. *Journal of Educational Psychology,* 1963, *54,* 1–22. **(12)**

———. *Abilities: Their structure, growth, and action.* Boston: Houghton Mifflin, 1971. **(12)**

Chase, W. G., & Simon, H. A. The mind's eye in chess. In W. G. Chase (Ed.), *Visual information processing.* New York: Academic Press, 1973. **(12)**

Chess, S., & Thomas, A. Infant bonding: Mystique and reality. *American Journal of Orthopsychiatry,* 1982, *52,* 213–222. **(7)**

Chi, M. T. Knowledge structure and memory development. In R. S. Siegler (Ed.), *Children's thinking: What develops?* Hillsdale, N.J.: Erlbaum, 1978. **(4)**

Chilman, C. S. Social and psychological research concerning adolescent childbearing: 1970–1980. *Journal of Marriage and the Family,* 1980, *42,* 793–806. **(10)**

Chomsky, N. *Aspects of a theory of syntax.* Cambridge, Mass.: M.I.T. Press, 1965. **(5)**

Chumlea, W. C. Physical growth in adolescence. In B. B. Wolman (Ed.), *Handbook of developmental psychology.* Englewood Cliffs, N.J.: Prentice-Hall, 1982. **(8)**

Clark, E. V. What's in a word? On the child's acquisition of semantics in his first language. In E. Moore (Ed.), *Cognitive development and the acquisition of language.* New York: Academic Press, 1973. **(5)**

———. Knowledge, context, and strategy in the acquisition of meaning. In D. P. Date (Ed.), *Georgetown University round table on language and linguistics, 1975.* Washington, D.C.: Georgetown University Press, 1975. **(5)**

———. Strategies and the mapping problem in first language acquisition. In J. Macnamara (Ed.), *Language learning and thought.* New York: Academic Press, 1977. **(5)**

Clarke, A. D. B. Learning and human development—The 42nd Maudsley lecture. *British Journal of Psychiatry,* 1968, *114,* 161–177. **(Sum I)**

Clarke, A. M., & Clarke, A. D. B. *Early experience: Myth and evidence.* New York: Free Press, 1976. **(Sum I)**

Clarke-Stewart, K. A. Interactions between mothers and their young children: Characteristics and consequences. *Monographs of the Society for Research in Child Development,* 1973, *38,* (Whole No. 153). **(5)**

———. And daddy makes three: The father's impact on mother and young child. *Child Development,* 1978, *49,* 466–478. **(7)**

Clarke-Stewart, K. A., & Hevey, C. M. Longitudinal relations in repeated observations of mother–child interaction from 1 to 2½ years. *Developmental Psychology*, 1981, *19*, 127–145. (**7**)

Clarke-Stewart, K. A., Vander Stoep, L. P., & Killian, G. A. Analysis and replication of mother–child relations at two years of age. *Child Development*, 1979, *50*, 777–793. (**4, 5, Sum I**)

Clifton, R. Heart rate conditioning in the newborn infant. *Journal of Experimental Child Psychology*. 1974, *13*, 43–57. (**2**)

Coates, S. *Preschool embedded figures tests*. Palo Alto, Calif.: Consulting Psychologists Press, 1972. (**3**)

Cobb, S., & Kasl, S. *Termination: The consequences of job loss* (Publication No. 77–224). Washington, D.C.: DHEW (NIOSH), 1977. (**14**)

Cohen, L. B., DeLoache, J. S., & Strauss, M. S. Infant visual perception. In J. D. Osofsky (Ed.), *Handbook of infant development*. New York: Wiley, 1979. (**3**)

College Entrance Examination Board. *On further examination: Report of the advisory panel on the Scholastic Aptitude Test score decline*. New York: College Entrance Examination Board, 1977. (**9**)

Colombo, J. The critical period concept: Research, methodology, and theoretical issues. *Psychological Bulletin*, 1982, *91*, 260–275. (**Sum I**)

Comstock, G. New emphases in research on the effects of television and film violence. In E. L. Palmer & A. Dorr (Eds.), *Children and the faces of television*. New York: Academic Press, 1980. (**6**)

Connor, K. A., Powers, E. A., & Bultena, G. L. Social interaction and life satisfaction: An empirical assessment of late-life patterns. *Journal of Gerontology*, 1979, *34*, 116–121. (**14**)

Coopersmith, S. *The antecedents of self esteem*. San Francisco: Freeman, 1967. (**6**)

Corcoran, M. Work experience, work interruption, and wages. In G. J. Duncan & J. N. Morgan (Eds.), *Five thousand American families—Patterns of economic progress*. Ann Arbor, Michigan: University of Michigan, Institute for Social Research, 1978. (**13**)

Corso, J. F. Auditory perception and communication. In J. E. Birren & K. W. Schaie (Eds.), *Handbook of the psychology of aging*. New York: Van Nostrand Reinhold, 1977. (**11**)

Costa, P. T., Jr., & McCrae, R. R. Still stable after all these years: Personality as a key to some issues in adulthood and old age. In P. B. Baltes and O. G. Brim, Jr., (Eds.), *Life-span development and behavior*. New York: Academic Press, 1980. (**13, Sum III**)

Costanzo, P. R., & Shaw, M. E. Conformity as a function of age level. *Child Development*, 1966, *37*, 967–975. (**10**)

Cottrell, L. S. The analysis of situational fields in social psychology. *American Sociological Review*, 1942, *7*, 370–382. (**1**)

Cox, R. D. *Youth into maturity: A study of men and women in the first ten years after college*. New York: Mental Health Materials Center, 1970. (**10**)

Crockenberg, S. B. Infant irritability, mother responsiveness, and social support influences on the security of infant–mother attachment. *Child Development*, 1981, *52*, 857–865. (**6, 7**)

Cumming, E., & Henry, W. E. *Growing old*. New York: Basic Books, 1961. (**13**)

Cureton, T. K. *The physiological effects of exercise programs on adults*. Springfield, Ill.: Thomas, 1969. (**11**)

Curtiss, S. *Genie: A psycholinguistic study of a modern day "wild child."* New York: Academic Press, 1977. (**5**)

Dale, P. S. *Language development: Structure and function* (2d ed.). New York: Holt, Rinehart and Winston, 1976. (**5**)

Danner, F. W., & Day, M. C. Eliciting formal operations. *Child Development*, 1977, *48*, 1600–1606. (**9**)

Davidson, E. S., Yasuna, A., & Tower, A. The effect of television cartoons on sex-role stereotyping in young girls. *Child Development*, 1979, *50*, 597–600. (**6**)

DeCasper, A., & Fifer, W. Of human bonding: Newborns prefer their mothers' voices. *Science*, 1980, *208*, 1174–1176. (**3**)

de Chateau, P. Effects of hospital practices on synchrony in the development of the infant–parent relationship. In P. M. Taylor

(Ed.), *Parent–infant relationships.* New York: Grune & Stratton, 1980. **(7)**

Denney, D. R., & Denney, N. W. The use of classification for problem solving: A comparison of middle and old age. *Developmental Psychology,* 1973, *9,* 275–278. **(12)**

Denney, N. W. Free classification in preschool children. *Child Development,* 1972, *43,* 1161–1170. **(1, 4)**

———. Classification abilities in the elderly. *Journal of Gerontology,* 1974a, *29,* 309–314. **(1)**

———. Classification criteria in middle and old age. *Developmental Psychology,* 1974b, *10,* 901–906. **(12)**

———. The effect of the manipulation of peripheral, non-cognitive variables on problem-solving performance among the elderly. *Human Development,* 1980, *23,* 268–277. **(12)**

———. Aging and cognitive changes. In B. B. Wolman (Ed.), *Handbook of developmental psychology.* Englewood Cliffs, N.J.: Prentice-Hall, 1982. **(12, Sum III)**

Denney, N. W., & Denney, D. R. The relationship between classification and questioning strategies among adults. *Journal of Gerontology,* 1982, *37,* 190–196. **(12)**

Denney, N. W., Jones, F. W., & Krigel, S. W. Modifying the questioning strategies of young children and elderly adults. *Human Development,* 1979, *22,* 23–36. **(12)**

Denney, N. W., & Lennon, M. L. Classification: A comparison of middle and old age. *Developmental Psychology,* 1972, *7,* 210–213. **(1, 12)**

Denney, N. W., & List, J. A. Adult age differences in performance on the Matching Familiar Figures test. *Human Development,* 1979, *22,* 137–144. **(12)**

Denney, N. W., & Palmer, A. M. Adult age differences on traditional and practical problem-solving measures. *Journal of Gerontology,* 1981, *36,* 323–328. **(12)**

Dennis, W. Causes of retardation among institutional children: Iran. *Journal of Genetic Psychology,* 1960, *96,* 47–59. **(3)**

Derwing, B. L. Is the child really a "little linguist"? In J. Macnamara (Ed.), *Language*

learning and thought. New York: Academic Press, 1977. **(5)**

DeVries, R. Relationship among Piagetian, psychometric and achievement measures. *Child Development,* 1974, *45,* 746–756. **(4)**

The Diagram Group. *Man's body: An owner's manual.* New York: Paddington Press, 1976. **(11)**

———. *Child's body: A parent's manual.* New York: Paddington Press, 1977a. **(3)**

———. *Woman's body: An owner's manual.* New York: Paddington Press, 1977b. **(11)**

Dicks-Mireaux, M. J. Mental development of infants with Down's syndrome. *American Journal of Mental Deficiency,* 1972, *77,* 26–32. **(3)**

Dobson, V., & Teller, D. Y. Visual acuity in human infants: A review and comparison of behavioral and electrophysiological studies. *Vision Research,* 1978, *18,* 1469–1483. **(3)**

Dollard, J., Doob, L. W., Miller, N. E., Mowrer, O. H., & Sears, R. R. *Frustration and aggression.* New Haven, Conn.: Yale University Press, 1939. **(7)**

Dominick, J. R., & Greenberg, B. S. Attitudes toward violence: The interaction of television exposure, family attitudes, and social class. In G. A. Comstock & E. A. Rubenstein (Eds.), *Television and social behavior (Vol. 3): Television and adolescent aggressiveness.* Washington, D.C.: U.S. Government Printing Office, 1972. **(6)**

Dovenmuehle, R. H., Busse, E. W., & Newman, G. Physical problems of older people. In E. Palmore (Ed.), *Normal aging.* Durham, N.C.: Duke University Press, 1970. **(11)**

Dreyer, P. H. Sexuality during adolescence. In B. B. Wolman (Ed.), *Handbook of developmental psychology.* Englewood Cliffs, N.J.: Prentice-Hall, 1982. **(8)**

Drillien, C. M. Development and progress of prematurely born children in the preschool period. *Archives of Disease in Childhood,* 1948, *23,* 69–83. **(3)**

Dunphy, D. C. The social structure of urban adolescent peer groups. *Sociometry,* 1963, *26,* 230–246. **(10)**

Duvall, E. M. *Marriage and family development.* Philadelphia: Lippincott, 1957. **(13)**

———. *Family development* (2d ed.). New York: Lippincott, 1962. **(1)**

———. *Marriage and family development* (5th ed.). Philadelphia: Lippincott, 1977. **(13)**

Dworkin, B. R. Instrumental learning for the treatment of disease. *Health Psychology,* 1982, *1,* 45–60. **(8)**

Easterbrooks, M. A., & Lamb, M. E. The relationship between quality of infant–mother attachment and infant competence in initial encounters with peers. *Child Development,* 1979, *50,* 380–387. **(6)**

Eaton, W. O., & Von Bargen, D. Asynchronous development of gender understanding in preschool children. *Child Development,* 1981, *52,* 1020–1027. **(6)**

Eckerman, C. O., & Whatley, J. L. Toys and social interaction between infant peers. *Child Development,* 1977, *48,* 1645–1656. **(7)**

Edwards, B. *Drawing on the right side of the brain.* Los Angeles: Tarcher (Boston: Houghton Mifflin), 1979. **(9)**

Edwards, C. P., & Lewis, M. Young children's concepts of social relations: Social functions and social objects. In M. Lewis & L. A. Rosenblum (Eds.), *The child and its family.* New York: Plenum, 1979. **(6)**

Egeland, B., & Sroufe, L. A. Attachment and maltreatment. *Child Development,* 1981, *52,* 44–52. **(7)**

Eichorn, D. H., Clausen, J. A., Haan, N., Honzik, M. P., & Mussen, P. H. *Present and past in middle life.* New York: Academic Press, 1981. **(Sum III)**

Eichorn, D. H., Hunt, J. V., & Honzik, M. P. Experience, personality, and IQ: Adolescence to middle age. In D. H. Eichorn, J. A. Clausen, N. Haan, M. P. Honzik, & P. H. Mussen (Eds.), *Present and past in middle life.* New York: Academic Press, 1981. **(Sum III)**

Eisenberg-Berg, N., & Hand, M. The relationship of preschoolers' reasoning about prosocial moral conflicts to prosocial behavior. *Child Development,* 1979, *59,* 356–363. **(9)**

Elardo, R., Bradley, R., & Caldwell, B. The relation of infants' home environments to mental test performance from six to thirty-six months: A longitudinal analysis. *Child Development,* 1975, *46,* 71–76. **(4)**

———. A longitudinal study of the relation of infants' home environments to language development at age three. *Child Development,* 1977, *48,* 595–603. **(5)**

Emde, R., Baensbauer, T., & Harmon, R. Emotional expression in infancy: A biobehavioral study. *Psychological Issues,* 1976, *10* (1, Whole No. 37). **(7)**

Emmerich, W., & Shepard, K. Development of sex-differentiated preferences during late childhood and adolescence. *Developmental Psychology,* 1982, *18,* 408–417. **(10)**

Engle, M., Nechlin, H., & Arkin, A. M. Aspects of mothering: Correlates of the cognitive development of black male infants in the second year of life. In A. Davids (Ed.), *Child personality and psychopathology: Current topics* (Vol. 2). New York: Wiley, 1975. **(5)**

Enright, R. D., Lapsley, D. K., Drivas, A. E., & Fehr, L. A. Parental influences on the development of adolescent autonomy and identity. *Journal of Youth and Adolescence,* 1980, *9,* 529–545. **(10)**

Erikson, E. H. *Childhood and society.* New York: Norton, 1950, 1963. **(1)**

———. *Identity and the life cycle.* New York: International Universities Press, 1959 (Reissued by Norton, 1980).

Estes, R. J., & Wilensky, H. L. Life cycle squeeze and the morale curve. *Social Problems,* 1978, *25* (No. 3), 277–292. **(13, Sum III)**

Eveleth, P. B., & Tanner, J. M. *Worldwide variation in human growth.* New York: Cambridge University Press, 1976. **(8)**

Fagan, J. F., III, & McGrath, S. K. Infant recognition memory and later intelligence. *Intelligence,* 1981, *5,* 121–130. **(4)**

Fantz, R. L. A method for studying early visual development. *Perceptual and Motor Skills,* 1956, *6,* 13–15. **(3)**

———. Pattern vision in newborn infants. *Science,* 1963, *140,* 296–297.

Fantz, R. L., Fagan, J. F., III, & Miranda, S. B. Early visual selectivity. In L. B. Cohen & P. Salapatek (Eds.), *Infants' perception: From sensation to cognition* (Vol. 1). New York: Academic Press, 1975. **(3)**

Farber, S. L. *Identical twins reared apart.* New York: Basic Books, 1981. **(4)**

Farran, D., & Ramey, C. Infant day care and attachment behaviors toward mothers and teachers. *Child Development,* 1977, *48,* 1112–1116. **(7)**

Farrell, M. P., & Rosenberg, S. D. *Men at midlife.* Boston: Auburn House, 1981. **(13, 14, Sum III)**

Faust, M. S. Somatic development of adolescent girls. *Monographs of the Society for Research in Child Development,* 1977, *42* (Whole No. 169.) **(3)**

Feldman, S. S., Biringen, Z. C., & Nash, S. C. Fluctuations in sex-related self-attributions as a function of stage of family life-cycle. *Developmental Psychology,* 1981, *17,* 24–35. **(13)**

Feshbach, S. Aggression. In P. H. Mussen (Ed.), *Carmichael's manual of child psychology* (Vol. 2, 3d ed.). New York: Wiley, 1970. **(7)**

Fiedler, F. E. *A theory of leadership effectiveness.* New York: McGraw-Hill, 1967. **(12)**

————. *Are leaders an intelligent form of life?* Technical report 82-2, F. Fiedler, July 1982. **(12)**

Field, T. M. Maternal stimulation during infant feeding. *Developmental Psychology,* 1977*a,* *13,* 539–540. **(2)**

————. Effects of early separation, interactive deficits, and experimental manipulations on infant–mother face-to-face interaction. *Child Development,* 1977*b,* *48,* 763–771. **(7)**

Fischer, J. L. Transitions in relationship style from adolescence to young adulthood. *Journal of Youth and Adolescence,* 1981, *10,* 11–23. **(10)**

Fiske, M. Changing hierarchies of commitment in adulthood. In N. J. Smelser & E. H. Erikson (Eds.), *Themes of work and love in adulthood.* Cambridge, Mass.: Harvard University Press, 1980. **(13)**

Flavell, J. H. Developmental studies of mediated memory. In H. W. Reese & L. P. Lipsitt (Eds.), *Advances in child development and behavior* (Vol. 5). New York: Academic Press, 1970. **(4)**

Flavell, J. H., Friedrichs, A. G., & Hoyt, J. D. Developmental changes in memorization processes. *Cognitive Psychology,* 1970, *1,* 324–340. **(4)**

Fox, L. H. Programs for the gifted and talented: An overview. In A. H. Passow (Ed.), *The gifted and the talented: Their education and development.* The seventy-eighth yearbook of the National Society for the Study of Education. Chicago: University of Chicago Press, 1979. **(9)**

Fraiberg, S. Blind infants and their mothers: An examination of the sign system. In M. Lewis & L. A. Rosenblum (Eds.), *The effects of the infant on its caregiver.* New York: Wiley, 1974. **(7)**

————. The development of human attachments in infants blind from birth. *Merrill-Palmer Quarterly,* 1975, *21,* 315–334. **(7)**

Fremer, J., & Chandler, M. O. Special studies. In W. H. Angoff (Ed.), *The College Board Admissions Testing Program: A technical report on research and development activities relating to the Scholastic Aptitude Test and Achievement Tests.* New York: College Entrance Examination Board, 1971. **(9)**

Freud, S. Three contributions to the theory of sex. *The basic writings of Sigmund Freud* (A. A. Brill, Trans.). New York: Random House (Modern Library), 1905. **(1)**

————. *A general introduction to psychoanalysis* (J. Riviere, Trans.). New York: Washington Square Press, 1965 (originally published 1920). **(1)**

Friedman, M., & Rosenman, R. H. *Type A behavior and your heart.* New York: Knopf, 1974. **(11)**

Friedrich-Cofer, L. K., Huston-Stein, A., Kipnis, D. M., Susman, E. J., & Cleweet, A. S. Environmental enhancement of prosocial television content: Effects on interpersonal behavior, imaginative play, and self-regulation in a natural setting. *Developmental Psychology,* 1979, *15,* 637–646. **(7)**

Frost, D., Fiedler, F., & Anderson, J. Role of personal courage in effective leadership. *Human Relations,* in press. **(12)**

Frueh, T., & McGhee, P. E. Traditional sex role development and amount of time spent watching television. *Developmental Psychology,* 1975, *11,* 109. **(6)**

Gallup, G. G., Jr., McClure, M. K., Hill, S. D., & Bundy, R. A. Capacity for self-recognition in differentially reared chimpanzees. *The Psychological Record,* 1971, *21,* 69–74. **(6)**

Garbarino, J., & Sherman, D. High-risk neighborhoods and high-risk families: The human ecology of child maltreatment. *Child Development,* 1980, *51,* 188–198. **(7)**

Gardner, B. T., & Gardner, R. A. Two comparative psychologists look at language acquisition. In K. Nelson (Ed.), *Children's language* (Vol. 2). New York: Gardner Press, 1980. **(5)**

Gardner, H. What we know (and don't know) about the two halves of the brain. *Harvard Magazine,* 1978, *80* (No. 4), 24–27. **(9)**

Gelman, R., & Gallistel, C. R. *The child's understanding of number.* Cambridge, Mass.: Harvard University Press, 1978. **(4)**

Gelman, R., & Shatz, M. Appropriate speech adjustments: The operation of conversational constraints on talk to two-year-olds. In M. Lewis & L. A. Rosenblum (Eds.), *Interaction, conversation, and the development of language.* New York: Wiley, 1977. **(5)**

Gerbner, G. Violence in television drama: Trends and symbolic functions. In G. A. Comstock & E. A. Rubenstein (Eds.), *Television and social behavior* (Vol. 1). Washington, D.C.: U.S. Government Printing Office, 1972. **(6)**

Gerbner, G., Gross, L., Morgan, M., & Signorielli, N. The "mainstreaming" of America: Violence profile no. 11. *Journal of Communications,* 1980, *30,* 10–29. **(6)**

Gesell, A. *The mental growth of the preschool child.* New York: Macmillan, 1925. **(1)**

Gesell, A., & Thompson, H. Learning and growth in identical twins: An experimental study by the method of co-twin control. *Genetic Psychology Monographs,* 1929, *6,* 1–123. **(3)**

Getzels, J. W., & Jackson, P. W. *Creativity and intelligence: Explorations with gifted students.* New York: Wiley, 1962. **(9)**

Gewirtz, J. L., & Boyd, E. F. Does maternal responding imply reduced infant crying? A critique of the 1972 Bell and Ainsworth report. *Child Development,* 1977, *48,* 1200–1207. **(2)**

Gibson, E. J. *Principles of perceptual learning and development.* Englewood Cliffs, N.J.: Prentice-Hall, 1969. **(3)**

Gibson, E. J., & Walk, R. D. The "visual cliff." *Scientific American,* 1960, *202,* 80–92. **(3)**

Giele, J. Z. Women in adulthood: Unanswered questions. In J. Z. Giele (Ed.), *Women in the middle years. Current knowledge and directions for research and policy.* New York: Wiley, 1982. **(Sum III)**

————. Women's work and family roles. In J. Z. Giele (Ed.), *Women in the middle years. Current knowledge and directions for research and policy.* New York: Wiley, 1982. **(13)**

Gilligan, C. Why should a woman be more like a man? *Psychology Today,* 1982, *16* (No. 6), 68–77. **(9, 10)**

Glenn, N. D., & McLanahan, S. The effects of offspring on the psychological well-being of older adults. *Journal of Marriage and the Family,* 1981, *43,* 409–421. **(14)**

————. Children and marital happiness: A further specification of the relationship. *Journal of Marriage and the Family,* 1982, *44* 63–72. **(13)**

Glick, P. C. Remarriage: Some recent changes and variations. *Journal of Family Issues,* 1980, *1,* 455–478. **(13)**

Gold, D., & Andres, D. Developmental comparisons between 10-year-old children with employed and nonemployed mothers. *Child Development,* 1978, *49,* 75–84. **(13)**

Goldberg, S., Perlmutter, M., & Myers, N. Recall of related and unrelated lists by two-year-olds. *Journal of Experimental Child Psychology,* 1974, *18,* 1–8. **(4)**

Golden, M., Birns, B., Bridger, W., & Moss, A. Social class differentiation in cognitive development among black preschool children. *Child Development,* 1971, *42,* 37–46. **(4, Sum I)**

Goldman, R. Aging of the excretory system: Kidney and bladder. In C. E. Finch & L. Hayflick (Eds.), *Handbook of the biology of aging.* New York: Van Nostrand Reinhold, 1977. **(11)**

Goldsmith, H. H., & Gottesman, I. I. Origins of variation in behavioral style: A longitudinal study of temperament in young twins. *Child Development,* 1981, *52,* 91–103. **(6)**

Goleman, D. Leaving home: Is there a right time to go? *Psychology Today,* 1980, *14* (No. 3., August), 52–61. **(10)**

Goodenough, F. L. *Anger in young children.* Minneapolis: University of Minnesota Press, 1931. **(7)**

Gordon, H. A., & Kammeyer, K. C. W. The gainful employment of women with small children. *Journal of Marriage and the Family,* 1980, *42,* 327–336. **(13)**

Gottman, J. M., & Parkhurst, J. T. A developmental theory of friendship and acquaintanceship processes. In A. Collins (Ed.), *Minnesota symposia on child psychology* (Vol. 13). Hillsdale, N.J.: Erlbaum, 1980. **(7)**

Gottman, J. M., & Porterfield, A. L. Communicative competence in the nonverbal behavior of married couples. *Journal of Marriage and the Family,* 1981, *43,* 817–824. **(14)**

Gould, R. *Transformations: Growth and change in adult life.* New York: Simon & Schuster, 1978. **(1, 10, 13)**

———. Transformations during early and middle adult years. In N. J. Smelser & E. H. Erikson (Eds.), *Themes of work and love in adulthood.* Cambridge, Mass.: Harvard University Press, 1980. **(10)**

Gove, W. R. The relationship between sex roles, marital status, and mental illness. *Social Forces,* 1972, *51,* 34–44. **(13)**

Gove, W. R., & Peterson, C. An update of the literature on personal and marital adjustment: The effect of children and the employment of wives. *Marriage and Family Review,* 1980, *3,* 63–96. **(13)**

Gratch, G. Recent studies based on Piaget's view of object concept development. In L. B. Cohen & P. Salapatek (Eds.), *Infant perception: From sensation to cognition* (Vol. 2). New York: Academic Press, 1975. **(4)**

———. The development of thought and language in infancy. In J. D. Osofsky (Ed.), *Handbook of infant development.* New York: Wiley, 1979. **(3)**

Gray, S. W., & Klaus, R. A. An experimental preschool program for culturally deprived children. *Child Development,* 1965, *36,* 887–898. **(4)**

Greenberg, E. F., & Nay, W. R. The inter-generational transmission of marital instability reconsidered. *Journal of Marriage and the Family,* 1982, *44,* 335–347. **(14)**

Greenberg, J., & Kuczaj, S. A., II. Towards a theory of substantive word-meaning acquisition. In S. A. Kuczaj II (Ed.), *Language development (Vol. 1): Syntax and semantics.* Hillsdale, N.J.: Erlbaum, 1982. **(5)**

Greenberg, M., & Morris, N. Engrossment: The newborn's impact upon the father. *American Journal of Orthopsychiatry,* 1974, *44,* 520–531. **(7)**

Grossmann, K., Thane, K., & Grossmann, K. E. Maternal tactual contact of the newborn after various postpartum conditions of mother–infant contact. *Developmental Psychology,* 1981, *17,* 158–169. **(7)**

Grumbach, M. M., & Van Wyk, J. J. Disorders of sex differentiation. In R. H. Williams (Ed.), *Textbook of endocrinology* (5th ed.). Philadelphia: Saunders, 1974. **(2)**

Guilford, J. P. The structure of intellect. *Psychological Bulletin,* 1956, *52,* 267–293. **(4)**

Haan, N. Common dimensions of personality development: Early adolescence to middle life. In D. H. Eichorn, J. A. Clausen, N. Haan, M. P. Honzik, & P. H. Mussen (Eds.), *Present and past in middle life.* New York: Academic Press, 1981. **(Sum III)**

Haan, N. Adolescents and young adults as producers of their own development. In R. M. Lerner & N. A. Busch-Rossnagel (Eds.), *Individuals as producers of their own development.* New York: Academic Press, 1981. **(Sum II)**

Hall, D. T. A model of coping with role conflict: The role behavior of college educated women. *Administrative Science Quarterly,* 1972, *17,* 471–486. **(13)**

———. Pressures from work, self, and home in the life stages of married women. *Journal of Vocational Behavior,* 1975, *6,* 121–132. **(13)**

Hammar, S. L. Adolescence. In D. W. Smith, E. L. Bierman, & N. M. Robinson (Eds.), *The biological ages of man from conception through old age.* Philadelphia: Saunders, 1978. **(8)**

Hanson, R. A. Consistency and stability of home environmental measure related to IQ. *Child Development,* 1975, *46,* 470–480. **(4)**

Hardy-Brown, K., Plomin, R., & DeFries, J. C. Genetic and environmental influences on the rate of communicative development in the first year of life. *Developmental Psychology,* 1981, *17,* 704–717. **(5)**

Harrell, T. W., & Harrell, M. S. Army general classification test scores for civilian occupations. *Educational and Psychological Measurement,* 1945, *5,* 229–239. **(12)**

Harris, L. *The myth and reality of aging in America.* Washington, D.C.: National Council on the Aging, 1975. **(14, Sum III)**

Harry, J. Evolving sources of happiness for men over the life cycle: A structural analysis. *Journal of Marriage and the Family,* 1976, *38,* 289–296. **(13)**

Hartford, T. C. Patterns of alcohol use among adolescents. *Psychiatric Opinion,* 1975, *12,* 17–21. **(8)**

Hartup, W. W. Peer interaction and social organization. In P. H. Mussen (Ed.), *Carmichael's manual of child psychology* (Vol. 2, 3d ed.). New York: Wiley, 1970. **(7)**

————. Aggression in childhood. Developmental perspectives. *American Psychologist,* 1974, *29,* 336–341. **(7)**

————. The origins of friendships. In M. Lewis & L. A. Rosenblum (Eds.), *Friendship and peer relations.* New York: Wiley, 1975. **(7)**

Havighurst, R. *Developmental tasks and education.* New York: McKay, 1972. **(13)**

Heber, F. R. Sociocultural mental retardation: A longitudinal study. In D. Forgays (Ed.), *Primary prevention of psychopathology* (Vol. 2). Hanover, N.H.: University Press of New England, 1978. **(Sum I)**

Heider, F. *The psychology of interpersonal relations.* New York: Wiley, 1958. **(10)**

Henderson, S. The social network, support and neurosis. The function of attachment in adult life. *British Journal of Psychiatry,* 1977, *131,* 185–191. **(14)**

Hennig, M., & Jardim, A. *The managerial woman.* Garden City, N.Y.: Doubleday (Anchor Books), 1976. **(13)**

Herrman, S. J. Divorce: A grief process. *Perspectives in Psychiatric Care,* 1974, *12,* 108–112. **(14)**

Hershenson, J. Visual discrimination in the human newborn. *Journal of Comparative and Physiological Psychology,* 1964, *58,* 270–276. **(3)**

Hess, B. B., & Waring, J. M. Changing patterns of aging and family bonds in later life. *The Family Coordinator,* 1978, *27,* 303–314. **(14)**

Hetherington, E. M., Cox, M., & Cox, R. *Beyond father absence: Conceptualization of the effects of divorce.* Paper presented at the biennial meetings of the Society for Research in Child Development, Denver, 1975. **(14)**

————. The aftermath of divorce. In M. H. Stevens, Jr., & M. Mathews (Eds.), *Mother/child, father/child relationships.* Washington, D.C.: National Association for the Education of Young Children, 1978. **(6, 14)**

————. *Family interaction and the social, emotional, and cognitive development of preschool children following divorce.* Paper presented at the biennial meetings of the Society for Research in Child Development, San Francisco, 1979. **(6, 14)**

Hetherington, R. W., & Hopkins, C. E. Symptom sensitivity: Its social and cultural correlates. *Health Survey Research,* 1969, *4,* 63–75. **(11)**

High/Scope Foundation Research report: Can preschool education make a lasting difference? Results of follow-up through eighth grade for the Ypsilanti Perry Preschool Project. *Bulletin of the High/Scope Foundation,* Fall 1977 (4), 1–8. **(4)**

Hill, R. Decision making and the family life cycle. In B. L. Neugarten (Ed.), *Middle age and aging: A reader in social psychology.* Chicago: University of Chicago Press, 1968. **(14)**

Hinrichs, J. R. An eight year follow-up of a management assessment center. *Journal of Applied Psychology,* 1975, *63,* 596–601. **(12)**

Hock, E. Working and nonworking mothers and their infants: A comparative study of maternal caregiving characteristics and infant social behavior. *Merrill-Palmer Quarterly,* 1980, *26,* 79–101. **(13)**

Hodgson, J. W., & Fischer, J. L. Sex differences in identity and intimacy development in college youth. *Journal of Youth and Adolescence,* 1979, *8,* 37–50. **(10)**

Hoffman, L. W. Maternal employment: 1979. *American Psychologist,* 1979, *34,* 859–865. **(13)**

Hoffman, L. W., & Manis, J. D. Influences of children on marital interaction and parental satisfactions and dissatisfactions. In R. M. Lerner & G. B. Spanier (Eds.), *Child influences on marital and family interaction. A life-span perspective.* New York: Academic Press, 1978. **(13)**

Hogan, R. The gifted adolescent. In J. Adelson (Ed.), *Handbook of adolescent psychology.* New York: Wiley, 1980. **(9)**

Hogan, R., Viernstein, M. C., McGinn, P. V., Daurio, S., & Bohannon, W. Verbal giftedness and sociopolitical intelligence. *Journal of Youth and Adolescence,* 1977, *6,* 107–116. **(9)**

Holm, V. A. Childhood. In D. W. Smith, E. L. Bierman, & N. M. Robinson (Eds.), *The biologic ages of man from conception through old age.* Philadelphia: Saunders, 1978. **(3)**

Holmes, T. H., & Masuda, M. Life change and illness susceptibility. In J. P. Scott & E. C. Senay (Eds.), *Separation and depression: Clinical and research aspects.* Washington, D.C.: American Association for the Advancement of Science, 1973. **(11)**

Holmes, T. H., & Rahe, R. H. The Social Readjustment Rating Scale. *Journal of Psychosomatic Research,* 1967, *11,* 213–218. **(11)**

Honig, A. S., & Oski, F. A. Developmental scores of iron deficient infants and the effects of therapy. *Infant Behavior and Development,* 1978, *1,* 168–176. **(3)**

Honzik, M. P., Macfarlane, J. W., & Allen, L. The stability of mental test performance between two and eighteen years. *Journal of Experimental Education,* 1948, *17,* 309–324. **(Sum III)**

Horn, J. L. The theory of fluid and crystallized intelligence in relation to apprehension, memory, speediness, laterality, and physiological functioning through the "vital years" of adulthood. In F. I. M. Craik & S. E. Trehub (Eds.), *Aging and cognitive processes.* New York: Plenum, 1981. **(12)**

Horn, J. L., & Cattell, R. B. Refinement and test of theory of fluid and crystallized ability intelligences. *Journal of Educational Psychology,* 1966, *57,* 253–270. **(12)**

Hornblum, J. N., & Overton, W. F. Area and volume conservation among the elderly: Assessment and training. *Developmental Psychology,* 1976, *12,* 68–74. **(12)**

Hoving, K. L., Spencer, T., Robb., K., & Schulte, D. Developmental changes in visual information processing. In P. A. Ornstein (Ed.), *Memory development in children.* Hillsdale, N.J.: Erlbaum, 1978. **(4)**

Hsia, D. Y. *Human developmental genetics.* Chicago: Year Book Medical Publishers, 1968. **(2)**

Huba, G. J., & Bentler, P. M. The role of peer and adult models for drug taking at different stages in adolescence. *Journal of Youth and Adolescence,* 1980, *9,* 449–465. **(8)**

————. A developmental theory of drug use: Derivation and assessment of a causal modeling approach. In P. B. Baltes & O. G. Brim, Jr., (Eds.), *Life-span development and behavior* (Vol. 4). New York: Academic Press, 1982. **(8)**

Hubel, D. H., & Weisel, T. N. Reception fields of cells in striate cortex of very young, visually inexperienced kittens. *Journal of Neurophysiology,* 1963, *26,* 996–1022. **(3)**

Hulka, B. S. Effect of exogenous estrogen on postmenopausal women: The epidemiologic evidence. *Obstetrical and Gynecological Survey,* 1980, *35,* Supplement (June), 389–399. **(11)**

Hunt, J. V. Predicting intellectual disorders in childhood for preterm infants with birthweights below 1501 gm. In S. L. Friedman & M. Sigman (Eds.), *Preterm birth and psychological development.* New York: Academic Press, 1981. **(2)**

Hunt, M. *Sexual behavior in the 1970s.* New York: Playboy Press, 1974. **(11)**

Huston-Stein, A., & Higgins-Trenk, A. Development of females from childhood through adulthood: Career and feminine role orientations. In P. B. Baltes (Ed.), *Life-span development and behavior* (Vol. 1). New York: Academic Press, 1978. **(10)**

Inhelder, B., & Piaget, J. *The growth of logical thinking from childhood to adolescence.* New York: Basic Books, 1958. **(4, 9)**

Jacobson, J. L. The role of inanimate objects in early peer interaction. *Child Development,* 1981, *52,* 618–626. **(7)**

Jacobson, N. S., Waldron, H., & Moore, D. Toward a behavioral profile of marital distress.

Journal of Consulting and Clinical Psychology, 1980, *48,* 696–703. **(14)**

Jacobson, P. H. Cohort survival for generations since 1940. *Milbank Memorial Fund Quarterly,* 1964, *42*(3), 36–53. **(11)**

Jaquette, D. S. A case study of social-cognitive development in a naturalistic setting. In R. L. Selman (Ed.), *The growth of interpersonal understanding: Developmental and clinical analyses.* New York: Academic Press, 1980. **(9)**

Jaquish, G. A., & Ripple, R. E. Cognitive creative abilities and self-esteem across the adult life-span. *Human Development,* 1981, *24,* 110–119. **(12)**

Jaquish, G. A., & Savin-Williams, R. C. Biological and ecological factors in the expression of adolescent self-esteem. *Journal of Youth and Adolescence,* 1981, *10,* 473–486. **(8)**

Jencks, C., Smith, M., Acland, H., Bane, M. J., Cohen, D. K., Gintis, H., Heyns, B., & Michelson, S. *Inequality: A reassessment of the effect of family and schooling in America.* New York: Basic Books, 1972. **(4)**

Jensen, A. R. *Bias in mental testing.* New York: Free Press, 1980. **(4)**

Jones, K. L., Smith, D. W., Ulleland, C. N., & Streissguth, A. P. Patterns of malformation in offspring of chronic alcoholic mothers. *Lancet,* 1973, *1,* 1267–1271. **(2)**

Jones, M. C. The later careers of boys who were early- or late-maturing. *Child Development,* 1957, *28,* 115–128. **(8)**

———. Psychological correlates of somatic development. *Child Development,* 1965, *36,* 899–911. **(8)**

Josselson, R., Greenberger, E., & McConochie, D. Phenomenological aspects of psychosocial maturity in adolescence. *Journal of Youth and Adolescence,* 1977*a,* 6, 25–56. **(10)**

———. Phenomenological aspects of psychosocial maturity at adolescence. Part II. Girls. *Journal of Youth and Adolescence,* 1977*b,* 6, 127–144. **(10)**

Judge, T. G. Potassium metabolism in the elderly. In L. A. Carlson (Ed.), *Nutrition in old age.* X Symposia of the Swedish Nutrition Foundation. Uppsala: Almqvist & Wiksell, 1972. **(11)**

Justice, B., & Justice, R. *The abusing family.* New York: Human Sciences Press, 1976. **(7)**

Kacerguis, M. A., & Adams, G. R. Erikson stage resolution: The relationship between identity and intimacy. *Journal of Youth and Adolescence,* 1980, *9,* 117–126. **(10)**

Kagan, J. Reflection-impulsivity and reading ability in primary grade children. *Child Development,* 1965, *36,* 609–628. **(3)**

———. *Change and continuity in infancy.* New York: Wiley, 1971. **(3)**

———. Family experience and the child's development. *American Psychologist,* 1979, *34,* 886–891. **(Sum I)**

Kagan, J., Kearsley, R. B., & Zelazo, P. R. *Infancy. Its place in human development.* Cambridge, Mass.: Harvard University Press, 1978. **(7)**

Kagan, J. & Kogan, N. Individuality and cognitive performance. In P. H. Mussen (Ed.), *Carmichael's manual of child psychology* (3d ed.). New York: Wiley, 1970. **(4)**

Kagan, J., Lapidus, D. R., & Moore, N. Infant antecedents of cognitive functioning: A longitudinal study. *Child Development,* 1978, *49,* 1005–1023. **(3)**

Kagan, J., & Moss, H. A. *Birth to maturity.* New York: Wiley, 1962. **(1, Sum III)**

Kagan, J., Rosman, B. L., Day, D., Albert, J., & Phillips, W. Information processing in the child: Significance of analytic and reflective attitudes. *Psychological Monographs,* 1964, *78* (Whole No. 578). **(4)**

Kahn, R. L., & Antonucci, T. C. Convoys over the life course: Attachment, roles, and social support. In P. B. Baltes & O. G. Brim, Jr. (Eds.), *Life-span development and behavior* (Vol. 3). New York: Academic Press, 1980. **(14)**

Kamin, L. J. *The science and politics of IQ.* Hillsdale, N.J.: Erlbaum, 1974. **(4)**

Kandel, D. B., & Faust, R. Sequence and stages in patterns of adolescent drug use. *Archives of General Psychiatry,* 1975, *32,* 923–932. **(8)**

Kaplan, E., & Kaplan, G. The prelinguistic child. In J. Elliot (Ed.), *Human development and cognitive processes.* New York: Holt, Rinehart and Winston, 1971. **(5)**

Karmel, B. Z., & Maisel, E. B. A neuronal activity model for infant visual attention. In L. B. Cohen & P. Salapatek (Eds.), *Infant perception: From sensation to cognition* (Vol. 1). New York: Academic Press, 1975. **(3)**

Kart, C. S., Metress, E. S., & Metress, J. F. *Aging and health: Biologic and social perspective.* Reading, Mass.: Addison-Wesley, 1978. **(11)**

Kasch, F. W. The effects of exercise on the aging process. *The Physician and Sports Medicine,* 1976 (June), 64–68. **(11)**

Katchadourian, H. *The Biology of adolescence.* San Francisco: Freeman, 1977. **(8)**

Keating, D. P. Precocious cognitive development at the level of formal operations. *Child Development,* 1975, *46,* 276–280. **(Sum II)**

———. Thinking processes in adolescence. In J. Adelson (Ed.), *Handbook of adolescent psychology.* New York: Wiley, 1980. **(Sum II)**

Keating, D. P., & Bobbitt, B. L. Individual and developmental differences in cognitive-processing components of mental ability. *Child Development,* 1978, *49,* 155–167. **(4)**

Keating, D. P., & Schaefer, R. A. Ability and sex differences in the acquisition of formal operations. *Developmental Psychology,* 1975, *11,* 531–532. **(Sum II)**

Keeney, T. J., Cannizzo, S. R., & Flavell, J. H. Spontaneous and induced verbal rehearsal in a recall task. *Child Development,* 1967, *38,* 935–966. **(4)**

Keith, P. M., Dobson, C. D., Goudy, W. J., & Powers, E. A. Older men. Occupational status, household involvement, and well-being. *Journal of Family Issues,* 1981, *2,* 336–349. **(13)**

Kempe, R. S., & Kempe, H. *Child abuse.* Cambridge, Mass.: Harvard University Press, 1978. **(7)**

Keniston, K. Youth: A "new" stage in life. *American Scholar,* Autumn 1970, 631–654. **(8, Sum II)**

———. *All our children. The American family under pressure.* New York: Harcourt Brace Jovanovich, 1977. **(14)**

Kennedy, W. Z., Van de Reit, V., & White, C. C., Jr. A normative sample of intelligence and achievement of Negro elementary school children in the southeastern United States. *Monographs of the Society for Research in*

Child Development, 1963, *28* (Whole No. 90). **(4)**

Kennell, J. H., Jerauld, R., Wolfe, H., Chesler, D., Kreger, N. C., McAlpine, W., Steffa, M., & Klaus, M. H. Maternal behavior one year after early and extended post-partum contact. *Developmental Medicine and Child Neurology,* 1974, *16,* 172–179. **(7)**

Kessner, D. M. *Infant death: An analysis by maternal risk and health care.* Washington, D.C.: National Academy of Sciences, 1973. **(2)**

Kinsbourne, M. Hemispheric specialization and the growth of human understanding. *American Psychologist,* 1982, *37,* 411–420. **(9)**

Kinsey, A. C., Pomeroy, W. B., & Martin, C. E. *Sexual behavior in the human male.* Philadelphia: Saunders, 1948. **(11)**

Kinsey, A. C., Pomeroy, W. B., Martin, C. E., & Gebhard, P. H. *Sexual behavior of the human female.* Philadelphia: Saunders, 1953. **(11)**

Klaus, M. H., & Kennell, J. M. *Maternal-infant bonding.* St. Louis: Mosby, 1976. **(1, 7)**

Klaus, R. A., & Gray, S. W. The early training project for disadvantaged children: A report after five years. *Monographs of the Society for Research in Child Development,* 1968, *33* (Whole No. 120). **(4)**

Klein, M., & Stern, L. Low birth weight and the battered child syndrome. *American Journal of Diseases of Children,* 1971, *122,* 15–18. **(7)**

Kogan, N. Creativity and cognitive style: A life span perspective. In P. Baltes & K. W. Schaie (Eds.), *Life span developmental psychology: Personality and socialization.* New York: Academic Press, 1973. **(4)**

———. Categorization and conceptualizing styles in younger and older adults. *Human Development,* 1974, *17,* 218–230. **(12)**

———. *Cognitive styles in infancy and early childhood.* Hillsdale, N.J.: Erlbaum, 1976. **(4)**

Kohlberg, L. Development of moral character and moral ideology. In M. L. Hoffman & L. W. Hoffman (Eds.), *Review of child development research (Vol. 1).* New York: Russell Sage Foundation, 1964. **(9)**

———. Stage and sequence: The cognitive-developmental approach to socialization. In D. Goslin (Ed.), *Handbook of social-*

ization theory and research. Skokie, Ill.: Rand McNally, 1969. **(9)**

————. Education for justice: A modern statement of the platonic view. In N. F. Sizer & T. R. Sizer (Eds.), *Moral education: Five lectures.* Cambridge, Mass.: Harvard University Press, 1970. **(9)**

————. Stages and aging in moral development: Some speculations. *Gerontologist,* 1973, *13,* 497–502. **(1)**

————. The cognitive developmental approach to moral education. *Phi Delta Kappan,* June 1975, 670–677. **(9)**

————. Revisions in the theory and practice of moral development. In W. Damon (Ed.), *Moral development. New directions for child development.* San Francisco: Jossey-Bass, 1978. **(9)**

Kohlberg, L., & Elfenbein, D. The development of moral judgments concerning capital punishment. *American Journal of Orthopsychiatry,* 1975, *45,* 614–640. **(9)**

Kohlberg, L., LaCrosse, J., & Ricks, D. The predictability of adult mental health from childhood behavior. In B. B. Wolman (Ed.), *Manual of child psychopathology.* New York: McGraw-Hill, 1972. **(Sum I)**

Kohn, M. L. Job complexity and adult personality. In N. J. Smelser & E. H. Erikson (Eds.), *Themes of work and love in adulthood.* Cambridge, Mass.: Harvard University Press, 1980. **(12, Sum III)**

Konstadt, N., & Forman, E. Field dependence and external directedness. *Journal of Personality and Social Psychology,* 1965, *1,* 490–493. **(9)**

Kopp, C. B. Perspectives on infant motor system development. In M. H. Bornstein & W. Kessen (Eds.), *Psychological development from infancy: Image to intention.* Hillsdale, N.J.: Erlbaum, 1979. **(3)**

Kopp, C. B., & Parmelee, A. H. Prenatal and perinatal influences on infant behavior. In J. D. Osofsky (Ed.), *Handbook of infant development.* New York: Wiley, 1979. **(2)**

Kübler-Ross, E. *On death and dying.* New York: Macmillan, 1969. **(14)**

————. *Death: The final stage of growth.* Englewood Cliffs, N.J.: Prentice-Hall, 1975. **(14)**

Kuczaj, S. A., II. The acquisition of regular and irregular past tense forms. *Journal of Verbal Learning and Verbal Behavior,* 1977, *16,* 589–600. **(5)**

————. Children's judgments of grammatical and ungrammatical irregular past tense verbs. *Child Development,* 1978, *49,* 319–326. **(5)**

————. Evidence for a language learning strategy: On the relative ease of acquisition of prefixes and suffixes. *Child Development,* 1979, *50,* 1–13. **(5)**

————. On the nature of syntactic development. In S. A. Kuczaj II (Ed.), *Language development (Vol. 1): Syntax and semantics.* Hillsdale, N. J.: Erlbaum, 1982. **(5)**

Kuhn, D., Nash, S. C., & Brucken, L. Sex role concepts of two- and three-year-olds. *Child Development,* 1978, *49,* 445–451. **(6)**

Kukla, R. A., & Weingarten, H. The long-term effects of parental divorce in childhood on adult adjustment. *Journal of Social Issues,* 1979, *35,* 50–78. **(14)**

Kunze, K. R. Age and occupations at Lockheed-California: Versatility of older workers. *Industrial Gerontology,* 1974, *1,* 57–64. **(13)**

Labov, W. *Language in the inner city: Studies in the black English vernacular.* Philadelphia: University of Pennsylvania Press, 1972. **(5)**

Ladd, G. W. Effectiveness of social learning methods for enhancing children's social interaction and peer acceptance. *Child Development,* 1981, *52,* 171–178. **(6)**

Lamb, M. E. *The role of the father in child development.* New York: Wiley, 1976. **(7)**

————. Father–infant interaction in the first year of life. *Child Development,* 1977, *48,* 167–181. **(7)**

Lamb, M. E., Easterbrooks, M. A., & Holden, G. W. Reinforcement and punishment among preschoolers: Characteristics, effects, and correlates. *Child Development,* 1980, *51,* 1230–1236. **(6)**

Lamb, M. E., Frodi, A. M., Hwang, C-P, Frodi, M., & Steinberg, J. Mother– and father–infant interaction involving play and holding in traditional and nontraditional Swedish families. *Developmental Psychology,* 1982, *18,* 215–221. **(7)**

Langer, E., & Rodin, J. The effects of choice and enhanced personal responsibility for the aged: A field experiment in an institutional setting. *Journal of Personality and Social Psychology,* 1976, *34,* 191–198. **(1)**

Larkin, J., McDermott, J., Simon, D. P., & Simon, H. A. Expert and novice performance in solving physics problems. *Science,* 1980, *208,* 1335–1342. **(12)**

La Rue, A., & Jarvik, L. F. Old age and biobehavioral changes. In B. B. Wolman (Ed.), *Handbook of developmental psychology.* Englewood Cliffs, N.J.: Prentice-Hall, 1982. **(11)**

LaVoie, J. C. Ego identity formation in middle adolescence. *Journal of Youth and Adolescence,* 1976, *5,* 371–385. **(10)**

Lawton, M. P. The impact of the environment on aging and behavior. In J. E. Birren & K. W. Schaie (Eds.), *Handbook of the psychology of aging.* New York: Van Nostrand Reinhold, 1977. **(11)**

Leadbeater, B. J., & Dionne, J-P. The adolescent's use of formal operational thinking in solving problems related to identity resolution. *Adolescence,* 1981, *16,* 111–121. **(Sum II)**

Leboyer, F. *Birth without violence.* New York: Knopf, 1975. **(2)**

Lee, G. R. Age at marriage and marital satisfaction: A multivariate analysis with implications for marital stability. *Journal of Marriage and the Family,* 1977, *39,* 493–504. **(10)**

Lee, G. R., & Ellithorpe, E. Intergenerational exchange and subjective well-being among the elderly. *Journal of Marriage and the Family,* 1982, *44,* 217–224. **(13, 14)**

Lee, G. R., & Ihinger-Tallman, M. Sibling interaction and morale: The effects of family relations on older people. *Research on Aging,* 1980, *2,* 367–391. **(14)**

Leigh, G. K. Kinship interaction over the family life span. *Journal of Marriage and the Family,* 1982, *44,* 197–208. **(14)**

Lenneberg, E. H. *Biological foundations of language.* New York: Wiley, 1967. **(5)**

Lesser, G. S., Fifer, G., & Clark, D. H. Mental abilities of children from different social class and cultural groups. *Monographs of the Society for Research in Child Development,* 1964, *30* (Whole No. 102). **(4)**

Levinson, D. J. *The seasons of a man's life.* New York: Knopf, 1978. **(13, 14)**

————. Toward a conception of the adult life course. In N. J. Smelser & E. H. Erikson (Eds.), *Themes of work and love in adulthood.* Cambridge, Mass.: Harvard University Press, 1980. **(13)**

————. Exploration in biography: Evolution of the individual life structure in adulthood. In A. I. Rabin, J. Aronoff, A. M. Barclay, & R. A. Zucker (Eds.), *Further explorations in personality.* New York: Wiley, 1981. **(13)**

Lewin, R. Starved brains. *Psychology Today,* 1975, *9,* 29–33. **(3)**

Lewis, M. State as an infant-environment interaction: An analysis of mother–infant behavior as a function of sex. *Merrill-Palmer Quarterly,* 1972, *18,* 95–121. **(5)**

————. Self-knowledge: A social cognitive perspective on gender identity and sex-role development. In M. E. Lamb & L. R. Sherrod (Eds.), *Infant social cognitions: Empirical and theoretical considerations.* Hillsdale, N. J.: Erlbaum, 1981. **(6)**

Lewis, M., & Brooks, J. Self-knowledge and emotional development. In M. Lewis & L. A. Rosenblum (Eds.), *The development of affect.* New York: Plenum, 1978. **(6)**

Lewis, M., & Brooks-Gunn, J. Toward a theory of social cognition: The development of self. *New Directions for Child Development,* 1979*a, 4,* 1–20. **(6)**

————. Toward a theory of social cognition: The development of the self. In I. C. Uzgiris (Ed.), *Social interaction and communication during infancy.* San Francisco: Jossey-Bass, 1979*b*. **(4)**

————. Visual attention at three months as a predictor of cognitive functioning at two years of age. *Intelligence,* 1981, *5,* 131–140. **(4)**

Lewis, R. A. Social influences on marital choice. In S. E. Dragastin & G. H. Elder, Jr. (Eds.), *Adolescence in the life cycle.* New York: Halsted Press, 1975. **(10)**

Lewis, R. A., & Spanier, G. B. Theorizing about the quality and stability of marriage. In W.

R. Burr, R. Hill, F. I. Nye, & I. L. Reiss (Eds.), *Contemporary theories about the family* (Vol. 1). New York: Free Press, 1979. **(10)**

Lieberman, A. F. Preschoolers' competence with a peer: Relations with attachment and peer experience. *Child Development,* 1977, *48,* 1277–1287. **(6)**

Liebert, R. M., & Schwartzberg, N. S. Effects of mass media. In M. R. Rosenzweig & L. W. Porter (Eds.), *Annual review of psychology* (Vol. 28). Palo Alto, Calif.: Annual Reviews, 1977. **(6)**

Light, R. J. Abused and neglected children in America: A study of alternative policies. *Harvard Educational Review,* 1973, *43,* 556–598. **(7)**

Lipsitt, L. P. Learning processes in human newborns. *Merrill-Palmer Quarterly,* 1966, *12,* 45–71. **(2)**

Lipsitt, L. P., & Kaye, H. Conditioned sucking in the human newborn. *Psychonomic Science,* 1964, *1,* 29–30. (2)

Livson, N., & Peskin, H. Perspectives on adolescence from longitudinal research. In J. Adelson (Ed.), *Handbook of adolescent psychology.* New York: Wiley, 1980. **(Sum II)**

Ljung, B. O., Bergsten-Brucefors, A., & Lindgren, G. The secular trend in physical growth in Sweden. *Annals of Human Biology,* 1974, *1,* 245–256. **(8)**

Locksley, A. Social class and marital attitudes and behavior. *Journal of Marriage and the Family,* 1982, *44,* 427–440. **(Sum III)**

Loehlin, J. C., Lindzey, G., & Spuhler, J. N. *Race differences in intelligence.* San Francisco: Freeman, 1975. **(4)**

Loehlin, J. C., & Nichols, R. C. *Heredity, environment and personality.* Austin, Texas: University of Texas Press, 1976. **(4)**

Loevinger, J. *Ego development.* San Francisco: Jossey-Bass, 1976. **(1)**

Lomax, E. M. R., Kagan, J., & Rosenkrantz, B. G. *Science and patterns of child care.* San Francisco: Freeman, 1978. **(Sum I)**

Londerville, S., & Main, M. Security of attachment, compliance, and maternal training methods in the second year of life. *Developmental Psychology,* 1981, *17,* 289–299. **(7)**

Lounsbury, M. L., & Bates, J. E. The cries of infants of differing levels of perceived temperamental difficultness: Acoustic properties and effects on listeners. *Child Development,* 1982, *53,* 677–686. **(5)**

Lovaas, O. I. *Language acquisition programs for nonlinguistic children.* New York: Irvington, 1976. **(5)**

Lowenthal, M. F., Thurnher, M., & Chiriboga, D. *Four stages of life.* San Francisco: Jossey-Bass, 1975. **(14)**

Lowenthal, M. P., & Haven, C. Interaction and adaptation: Intimacy as a critical variable. *American Sociological Review,* 1968, *33,* 20–30. **(14)**

Lytton, H. Do parents create, or respond to, differences in twins? *Developmental Psychology,* 1977, *12,* 456–459. **(4)**

McCall, R. B. *Infants: The new knowledge.* Cambridge, Mass.: Harvard University Press, 1979. **(2)**

————. Nature-nurture and the two realms of development: A proposed integration with respect to mental development. *Child Development,* 1981, *52,* 1–12. **(Sum I)**

McCall, R. B., Appelbaum, M. I., & Hogarty, P. S. Developmental changes in mental performance. *Monographs of the Society for Research in Child Development,* 1973, *38* (Whole No. 150). **(4, Sum III)**

McCarthy, J. D., & Hoge, D. R. Analysis of age effects in longitudinal studies of adolescent self-esteem. *Developmental Psychology,* 1982, *18,* 372–379. **(Sum II)**

McClelland, D. C. Is personality consistent? In A. I. Rabin, J. Aronoff, A. M. Barclay, & R. A. Zucker (Eds.), *Further explorations in personality.* New York: Wiley, 1981. **(13, Sum III)**

Maccoby, E. E., & Jacklin, C. N. *The psychology of sex differences.* Stanford, CA: Stanford University Press, 1974. **(5, 7)**

————. Sex differences in aggression: A rejoinder and reprise. *Child Development,* 1980, *51,* 964–980. **(7, Sum I)**

McDevitt, S. C., & Carey, W. B. Stability of ratings vs. perceptions of temperament from early infancy to 1–3 years. *American Journal of Orthopsychiatry,* 1981, *51,* 342–345. **(6)**

Macfarlane, A. *The psychology of childbirth.*

Cambridge, Mass.: Harvard University Press, 1977. **(2)**

Macfarlane, J. W., Allen, J. W., Allen, L., & Honzik, M. P. A development study of the behavior problems of normal children between twenty-two months and fourteen years. *University of California Publications in Child Development* (Vol. 2). Berkeley, Calif.: University of California Press, 1954. **(1)**

McGraw, M. D. *Growth: A study of Johnny and Jimmy.* Englewood Cliffs, N. J.: Prentice-Hall, 1935. **(3)**

McGuigan, D. G. Exploring women's lives: An introduction. In D. G. McGuigan (Ed.), *Women's lives: New theory, research & policy.* Ann Arbor, Mich.: University of Michigan, Center for Continuing Education of Women, 1980. **(Sum III)**

Mackey, W. C. Parameters of the smile as a social signal. *The Journal of Genetic Psychology,* 1976, *129,* 125–130. **(1)**

Macklin, E. D. Nontraditional family forms: A decade of research. *Journal of Marriage and the Family,* 1980, *42,* 905–922. **(13)**

McNeill, D. *The acquisition of language: The study of developmental psycholinguistics.* New York: Harper & Row, 1970. **(5)**

Madden, J., Levenstein, P., & Levenstein, S. Longitudinal IQ outcomes of the mother–child home program. *Child Development,* 1976, *47,* 1015–1025. **(Sum I)**

Main, M., Tomasini, L., & Tolan, W. Differences among mothers of infants judged to differ in security. *Developmental Psychology,* 1979, *15,* 472–473. **(7)**

Main, M., & Weston, D. R. The quality of the toddler's relationship to mother and to father: Related to conflict behavior and the readiness to establish new relationships. *Child Development,* 1981, *52,* 932–940. **(7)**

Malina, R. M. *Late maturation in female athletes—A biosocial interpretation.* Paper presented at the biennial meetings of the Society for Research in Child Development, Boston, Mass: 1981. **(8)**

———. Motor development in the early years. In S. G. Moore & C. R. Cooper (Eds.), *The young child: Reviews of research* (Vol. 3). Washington, D. C.: National Association for the Education of Young Children, 1982. **(3)**

Mancini, J. A. Friend interaction, competence, and morale in old age. *Research on Aging,* 1980, *2,* 416–431. **(14)**

Marano, H. Breast-feeding. New evidence: It's far more than nutrition. *Medical World News,* 1979, *20,* 62–78. **(2)**

Marantz, S. A., & Mansfield, A. F. Maternal employment and the development of sex-role stereotyping in five- to eleven-year-old girls. *Child Development,* 1977, *48,* 668–673. **(13)**

Marcia, J. E. Development and validation of ego identity status. *Journal of Personality and Social Psychology,* 1966, *3,* 551–558. **(10)**

———. Identity six years after: A follow-up study. *Journal of Youth and Adolescence,* 1976, *5,* 145–160. **(10)**

———. Identity in adolescence. In J. Adelson (Ed.), *Handbook of adolescent psychology.* New York: Wiley, 1980. **(10)**

Marcus, D. E., & Overton, W. F. The development of cognitive gender constancy and sex role preferences. *Child Development,* 1978, *49,* 434–444. **(6)**

Marlow, R. A. *Effects of environment on elderly state hospital relocatees.* Paper presented at annual meeting of the Pacific Sociological Association, Scottsdale, Ariz., May 1973. **(11)**

Marsland, D. W., Wood, M., & Mayo, F. A data bank for patient care, curriculum, and research in family practice: 526,196 patient problems. *Journal of Family Practice,* 1976, *3,* 24. **(8)**

Martorano, S. C. A developmental analysis of performance on Piaget's formal operations tasks. *Developmental Psychology,* 1977, *13,* 666–672. **(9)**

Massad, C. M. Sex role identity and adjustment during adolescence. *Child Development,* 1981, *52,* 1290–1298. **(10)**

Masters, J. C., & Furman, W. Popularity, individual friendship selection, and specific peer interaction among children. *Developmental Psychology,* 1981, *17,* 344–350. **(7)**

Matarazzo, J. D. *Wechsler's measurement and appraisal of adult intelligence* (5th ed.). Baltimore: Williams & Wilkins, 1972. **(12)**

Matheny, A. P., Jr. Bayley's infant behavior record: Behavioral components and twin analyses. *Child Development,* 1980, *51,* 1157–1167. **(6)**

Matheny, A. P., Jr., Wilson, R. S., Dolan, A. B., & Kranz, J. Z. Behavioral contrasts in twinships: Stability and patterns of differences in childhood. *Child Development,* 1981, *52,* 579–588. **(6)**

Mayer, J. Obesity during childhood. In M. Winick (Ed.), *Childhood obesity.* New York: Wiley, 1975. **(8)**

Mead, G. H. *Mind, self, and society.* Chicago: University of Chicago Press, 1934. **(1)**

Meece, J. L., Parsons, J. E., Kaczala, C. M., Goff, S. B., & Futterman, R. Sex differences in math achievement: Toward a model of academic choice. *Psychological Bulletin,* 1982, *91,* 324–348. **(Sum II)**

Meier, E. L., & Kerr, E. A. Capabilities of middle-aged and older workers: A survey of the literature. *Industrial Gerontology,* 1977, *4,* 147–156. **(13)**

Meilman, P. W. Cross-sectional age changes in ego identity status during adolescence. *Developmental Psychology,* 1979, *15,* 230–231. **(10)**

Mervis, C. B., & Mervis, C. A. Leopards are kitty-cats: Object labeling by mothers for their thirteen-month-olds. *Child Development,* 1982, *53,* 267–273. **(5)**

Miller, C., Younger, B., & Morse, P. The categorization of male and female voices in infancy. *Infant Behavior and Development,* 1982, *5,* 143–159. **(3)**

Mischel, W. *Personality assessment.* New York: Wiley, 1968. **(13)**

Model, S. Housework by husbands. Determinants and implications. *Journal of Family Issues,* 1981, *2,* 225–237. **(13)**

Montemayor, R., & Eisen, M. The development of self-conceptions from childhood to adolescence. *Developmental Psychology,* 1977, *13,* 314–319. **(6, 10)**

Morse, P. A., & Cowan, N. Infant auditory and speech perception. In T. M. Field, A. Huston, H. C. Quay, L. Troll, & G. E. Finley (Eds.), *Review of human development.* New York: Wiley, 1982. **(3)**

Morton, T. L., Alexander, J. F., & Altman, I. Communication and relationship definition. In G. R. Miller (Ed.), *Annual review of communication research, (Vol. 5): Interpersonal communication.* Beverly Hills, Calif.: Sage, 1976. **(10)**

Mosher, F. A., & Hornsby, J. R. On asking questions. In J. S. Bruner, R. R. Olver, & P. M. Greenfield (Eds.), *Studies in cognitive growth.* New York: Wiley, 1966. **(9)**

Mueller, E., & Brenner, J. The origins of social skills and interaction among playgroup toddlers. *Child Development,* 1977, *48,* 854–861. **(7)**

Munday, L. A. *Declining admissions test scores.* ACT Research Report No. 71. Iowa City, Iowa: The American College Testing Program, 1976. **(9)**

Munro, G., & Adams, G. R. Ego-identity formation in college students and working youth. *Developmental Psychology,* 1977, *13,* 523–524. **(10)**

Munsinger, H., & Douglass, A., II. The syntactic abilities of identical twins, fraternal twins, and their siblings. *Child Development,* 1976, *47,* 40–50. **(5)**

Murray, A. D., Dolby, R. M., Nation, R. L., & Thomas, D. B. Effects of epidural anesthetic on newborns and their mothers. *Child Development,* 1981, *52,* 71–82. **(2)**

Mussen, P., Conger, J., Kagan, J., & Geiwitz, J. *Psychological development: A life-span approach.* New York: Harper & Row, 1979. **(11)**

Myers, R. Factors in interpreting mortality after retirement. *Journal of American Statistical Association,* 1965, *49,* 499–509. **(11)**

Nathanson, C. A., & Lorenz, G. Women and health: The social dimensions of biomedical data. In J. Z. Giele (Ed.), *Women in the middle years: Current knowledge and directions for research and policy.* New York: Wiley, 1982. **(11)**

National Center for Health Statistics. Births, marriages, divorces, and deaths for 1977. Provisional statistics. *Monthly Vital Statistics Report, 26,* 1978. **(10)**

National Institute on Drug Abuse. *National survey on drug abuse: Main findings 1979.* U.S. Department of Health and Human Services, 1979. **(8)**

National Research Council, Food and Nutrition

Board, *Recommended dietary allowances* (8th rev. ed.). Washington, D.C.: National Academy of Sciences, 1974. **(2)**

Neimark, E. D. Intellectual development during adolescence. In F. D. Horowitz (Ed.), *Review of child development research* (Vol. 4). Chicago: University of Chicago Press, 1975. **(Sum II)**

————. Adolescent thought: Transition to formal operations. In B. B. Wolman (Ed.), *Handbook of developmental psychology.* Englewood Cliffs, N.J.: Prentice-Hall, 1982. **(9)**

Nelson, G. Coping with the loss of father. Family reaction to death or divorce. *Journal of Family Issues,* 1982, *3,* 41–60. **(14)**

Nelson, K. Structure and strategy in learning to talk. *Monographs of the Society for Research in Child Development,* 1973, *38* (Whole #149). **(5)**

————. Individual differences in language development: Implications for development and language. *Developmental Psychology,* 1981, *17,* 170–187. **(5)**

Nelson, K., Rescorla, L., Gruendel, J., & Benedict, H. *Early lexicons: Ewhat doi they mean?* Paper presented at the Biennial Meeting of the Society for Research in Child Development, New Orleans, 1977. **(5)**

Nelson, K. E. Facilitating children's syntax acquisition. *Developmental Psychology,* 1977, *13,* 101–107. **(5)**

Neugarten, B. L. Time, age, and the life cycle. *American Journal of Psychiatry,* 1979, *136,* 887–894. **(13, 14)**

Newcomb, T. M. The prediction of interpersonal attraction. *American Psychologist,* 1956, *11,* 575–586. **(10)**

Newman, H. H., Freeman, F. N., & Holzinger, K. J. *Twins: A study of heredity and environment.* Chicago: University of Chicago Press, 1937. **(4)**

Nichols, P. L. *Minimal brain dysfunction: Association with perinatal complications.* Paper given at the biennial meetings of the Society for Research in Child Development, New Orleans, 1977. **(2)**

Nilsson, L. *A child is born.* New York: Dell (Delacorte Press), 1977. **(2)**

Nock, S. L. Family life-cycle transitions: Longi-

tudinal effects on family members. *Journal of Marriage and the Family,* 1981, *43,* 703–714. **(14)**

————. Enduring effects of marital disruption and subsequent living arrangements. *Journal of Family Issues,* 1982, *3,* 25–40. **(14)**

Novak, L. Total body potassium, fat-free mass, and cell mass in males and females between 18 and 85 years. *Journal of Gerontology,* 1972, *27,* 438–443. **(11)**

O'Connor, S., Vietze, P. M., Sandler, H. M., Sherrod, K. B., & Altemeier, W. A. Quality of parenting and the mother–infant relationship following rooming-in. In P. M. Taylor (Ed.), *Parent–infant relationships.* New York: Grune & Stratton, 1980. **(7)**

Oden, S. Peer relationship development in childhood. In L. G. Katz (Ed.), *Current topics in early childhood education* (Vol. 4). Norwood, N.J.: Ablex, 1982. **(7)**

O'Neill, C. *Starving for attention.* New York: Continuum, 1982. **(8)**

Orlofsky, J., Marcia, J., & Lesser, I. Ego identity status and the intimacy vs. isolation crisis in young adulthood. *Journal of Personality and Social Psychology,* 1973, *27,* 211–219. **(10)**

Ornstein, P. A., Naus, M. J., & Liberty, C. Rehearsal and organizational processes in children's memory. *Child Development,* 1975, *46,* 818–830. **(4)**

Otto, L. B. Antecedents and consequences of marital timing. In W. R. Burr, R. Hill, F. I. Nye, & I. L. Reiss (Eds.), *Contemporary theories about the family* (Vol. 1). New York: Free Press, 1979. **(10)**

Palmore, E. Total chance of institutionalization among the aged. *Gerontologist,* 1976, *16,* 504–507. **(11)**

————. Predictors of successful aging. *Gerontologist,* 1979, *19,* 427–431. **(14)**

————. *Social patterns in normal aging: Findings from the Duke longitudinal study.* Durham, N.C.: Duke University Press, 1981. **(11, 13, 14, Sum III)**

Palmore, E., & Cleveland, W. Aging, terminal decline, and terminal drop. *Journal of Gerontology,* 1976, *31,* 76–81. **(12)**

Palmore, E., Cleveland, W., Nowlin, J., Ramm, D., & Siegler, I. Stress and adaptation in later life. *Journal of Gerontology,* 1979, *31,* 841–845. **(11)**

Palmore, E., & Stone, V. Predictors of longevity. *Gerontologist,* 1973, *13,* 88–90. **(Sum III)**

Papalia, D. E. The status of several conservation abilities across the life span. *Human Development,* 1972, *15,* 229–243. **(12)**

Parke, R. D., & O'Leary, S. E. Father–mother–infant interaction in the newborn period: Some findings, some observations and some unresolved issues. In K. Riegel & J. K. Meacham (Eds.), *The developing individual in a changing world* (Vol. 2). *Social and environmental issues.* The Hague: Mouton, 1976. **(7)**

Parke, R. D., O'Leary, S. E., & West, S. Mother–father–newborn interaction: Effects of maternal medication, labor and sex of infant. *Proceedings of the American Psychological Association,* 1972, 85–86. **(7)**

Parke, R. D., & Sawin, D. B. *Infant characteristics and behavior as elicitors of maternal and paternal responsivity in the newborn period.* Paper presented to the Society for Research in Child Development, Denver, April 1975. **(7)**

Parke, R. D., & Tinsley, B. R. The father's role in infancy: Determinants of involvement in caregiving and play. In M. E. Lamb (Ed.), *The role of the father in child development* (2d ed.). New York: Wiley, 1981. **(7)**

Parkes, C. M. *Bereavement—Studies of grief in adult life.* New York: International Universities Press, 1972. **(14)**

———. Determinants of outcome following bereavement. *Omega: Journal of Death and Dying,* 1975, *6,* 303–323. **(14)**

Parlee, M. B. The friendship bond. *Psychology Today,* 1979 (October), *14,* 43–54, 113. **(14)**

Pastalan, L. A., Mautz, R. K., & Merril, J. The simulation of age related losses: A new approach to the study of environmental barriers. In W. F. E. Preiser (Ed.), *Environmental design research* (Vol. 1). Stroudsburg, Pa.: Dowden, Hutchinson & Ross, 1973. **(11)**

Pastor, D. L. The quality of mother–infant attachment and its relationship to toddlers' initial sociability with peers. *Developmental Psychology,* 1981, *17,* 326–335. **(6)**

Patterson, G. R. *Families. Applications of social learning to family life.* Champaign, Ill.: Research Press, 1975. **(6)**

Pearlin, L. I. Life strains and psychological distress among adults. In N. J. Smelser & E. H. Erikson (Eds.), *Themes of work and love in adulthood.* Cambridge, Mass.: Harvard University Press, 1980. **(13, 14)**

Pearlin, L. I., & Johnson, J. S. Marital status, life-strains and depression. *American Sociological Review,* 1977, *42,* 704–715. **(13)**

Pederson, E., Faucher, T. A., & Eaton, W. W. A new perspective on the effects of first-grade teachers on children's subsequent adult status. *Harvard Educational Review,* 1978, *48,* 1–31. (4)

Perun, P. J., & Bielby, D. D. V. Structure and dynamics of the individual life course. In K. W. Back (Ed.), *Life course: Integrative theories and exemplary populations.* AAAS Selected Symposium 41. Boulder, Colo.: Westview Press, 1980. **(13)**

Peskin, H. Pubertal onset and ego functioning. *Journal of Abnormal Psychology,* 1967, *72,* 1–15. **(8)**

———. Influence of the developmental schedule of puberty on learning and ego functioning. *Journal of Youth and Adolescence,* 1973, *2,* 272–290. **(8)**

Petersen, A. C. Physical androgyny and cognitive functioning in adolescence. *Developmental Psychology,* 1976, *12,* 524–533. **(Sum II)**

Petersen, A. C., & Taylor, B. The biological approach to adolescence: Biological change and psychological adaptation. In J. Adelson (Ed.), *Handbook of adolescent psychology.* New York: Wiley, 1980. **(8)**

Peterson, G. H., Mehl, L. E., & Leiderman, P. H. The role of some birth-related variables in father attachment. *American Journal of Orthopsychiatry,* 1979, *49,* 330–338. **(7)**

Pfeiffer, E., & Davis, G. C. Determinants of sexual behavior in middle and old age. In E. Palmore (Ed.), *Normal aging II.* Durham, N.C.: Duke University Press, 1974. **(11)**

Phillips, J. R. Syntax and vocabulary of mothers' speech to young children: Age and sex comparisons. *Child Development,* 1973, *44,* 182–185. **(5)**

Piaget, J. *The origins of intelligence in children.* New York: International Universities Press, 1952*a.* (1)

――. *The child's concept of number.* New York: Norton, 1952*b.* (4)

――. *The construction of reality in the child.* New York: Basic Books, 1954. (3, 4)

――. Piaget's theory. In P. H. Mussen (Ed.), *Carmichael's manual of child psychology* (3d ed.). New York: Wiley, 1970. (4)

――. *The grasp of consciousness. Action and concept in the young child.* Cambridge, Mass.: Harvard University Press, 1976. (1)

――. *The development of thought. Equilibration of cognitive structures.* New York: Viking Press, 1977. (1)

Piaget, J., & Inhelder, B. *The psychology of the child.* New York: Basic Books, 1969. (1)

Pines, M. The civilizing of Genie. *Psychology Today,* 1981 (September), *15,* 28–34. (5)

Pleck, J. Married men: Work and family. In E. Corfman (Ed.), *Families today: A research sampler on families and children* (Vol. 1). Washington, D.C.: U.S. Government Printing Office, 1979. (13)

Pleck, J., & Rustad, M. *Husbands' and wives' time in family work and paid work in the 1975–1976 study of time use.* Wellesley, Mass.: Wellesley College Research Center on Women, 1980. (13)

Plomin, R., & Foch, T. T. Sex differences and individual differences. *Child Development,* 1981, *52,* 383–385. (Sum I)

Plomin, R., & Rowe, D. C. Genetic and environmental etiology of social behavior in infancy. *Developmental Psychology,* 1979, *15,* 62–72. (6)

Podd, M. H. Ego identity status and morality: The relationship between the two constructs. *Developmental Psychology,* 1972, *6,* 497–507. (Sum II)

Power, C., & Reimer, J. Moral atmosphere: An educational bridge between moral judgment and action. In W. Damon (Ed.), *Moral development.* San Francisco: Jossey-Bass, 1978. (1)

Powers, E. A., & Bultena, G. L. Sex differences in intimate friendships of old age. *Journal of Marriage and the Family,* 1976, *38,* 739–747. (14)

Prader, A., Tanner, J. M., & Von Harnack, G. A. Catch-up growth following illness or starvation. *Journal of Pediatrics,* 1963, *62,* 646–659. (3)

Prechtl, H., & Beintema, D. *The neurological examination of the full term newborn infant. Clinics in developmental medicine, no. 12.* London: Spastics Society with Heinemann Medical, 1964. (2)

Price-Bonham, S., & Balswick, J. O. The noninstitutions: Divorce, desertion, and remarriage. *Journal of Marriage and the Family,* 1980, *42,* 959–972. (14)

Quinlan, D. M., & Blatt, S. J. Field articulation and performance under stress: Differential predictions in surgical and psychiatric nursing training. *Journal of Consulting and Clinical Psychology,* 1972, *39,* 517. (9)

Ramey, C. T., Farran, D. C., & Campbell, F. A. Predicting IQ from mother–infant interactions. *Child Development,* 1979, *50,* 804–814. (4)

Ramey, C. T., & Haskins, R. A modification of intelligence through early experience. *Intelligence,* 1981, *5,* 5–20. (Sum I)

Rands, M., Levinger, G., & Mellinger, G. D. Patterns of conflict resolution and marital satisfaction. *Journal of Family Issues,* 1981, *2,* 297–321. (14)

Rapoport, D. The controversial Leboyer method. *The Female Patient,* 1978, *3,* 84–86. (2)

Rappoport, L. *Personality development: The chronology of experience.* Glenview, Ill.: Scott, Foresman, 1972. (6)

Reedy, M. N., Birren, J. E., & Schaie, K. W. Age and sex differences in satisfying love relationships across the adult life span. *Human Development,* 1981, *24,* 52–66. (14)

Reisman, J. M., & Shorr, S. I. Friendship claims and expectations among children and adults. *Child Development,* 1978, *49,* 913–916. (7, 10)

Reiss, I. *The social context of sexual permissiveness.* New York: Holt, Rinehart and Winston, 1967. (8)

Reynolds, N. J., & Risley, T. R. The role of social and material reinforcers in increasing talking of a disadvantaged preschool child. *Journal of Applied Behavior Analysis,* 1968, *1,* 253–262. (5)

Richardson, S. *Ecology of malnutrition: Non-nutritionmal factors influencing intellectual and behavioral development.* Pan American Health Organization Scientific Publication #251, 1972. **(2)**

Riegel, K. F. Dialectic operations: The final period of cognitive development. *Human Development,* 1973, *16,* 346–370. **(12)**

———. Adult life crises. A dialectic interpretation of development. In N. Datan & L. H. Ginsberg (Eds.), *Lifespan developmental psychology. Normative life crises.* New York: Academic Press, 1975. **(Sum I)**

Riegel, K. F., & Riegel, R. M. Development, drop, and death. *Developmental Psychology,* 1972, *6,* 306–319. **(12)**

Ringler, N. M., Trause, M. A., & Klaus, M. H. Mother's speech to her two-year-old, its effects on speech and language comprehension at 5 years. *Pediatric Research,* 1976, *10,* 307. **(7)**

Rivers, C., Barnett, R., & Baruch, G. *Beyond sugar and spice. How women grow, learn, and thrive.* New York: Putnam, 1979. **(10)**

Roberts, D. F., & Bachen, C. M. Mass communication effects. *Annual Review of Psychology,* 1981, *32,* 347–356. **(6)**

Robinson, E. A., & Price, M. G. Pleasurable behavior in marital interaction: An observational study. *Journal of Consulting and Clinical Psychology,* 1980, *48,* 117–118. **(14)**

Robinson, N. M., & Robinson, H. B. The optimal match: Devising the best compromise for the highly gifted student. In D. H. Feldman (Ed.), *Developmental approaches to giftedness and creativity.* San Francisco: Jossey-Bass, 1982. **(9)**

Roche, A. F. Secular trends in human growth, maturation, and development. *Monographs of the Society for Research in Child Development,* 1979, *44* (Whole No. 179). **(8)**

Roedell, W. C. Social development in intellectually advanced children. In H. B. Robinson (chair), *Intellectually advanced children: Preliminary findings of a longitudinal study.* Symposium presented at the Annual Convention of the American Psychological Association, Toronto, August 30, 1978. **(4)**

Roedell, W. C., Jackson, N. E., & Robinson, H. B. *Gifted young children.* New York: Teachers College Press, 1980. **(4)**

Roffwarg, H. P., Muzio, J. N., & Dement, W. C. Ontogenetic development of the human sleep-dream cycle. *Science,* 1966, *152,* 604–619. **(2)**

Rollins, B. C., & Cannon, K. F. Marital satisfaction over the family life cycle: A reevaluation. *Journal of Marriage and the Family,* 1974, *36,* 271–282. **(13)**

Rollins, B. C., & Feldman, H. Marital satisfaction over the family life cycle. *Journal of Marriage and the Family,* 1970, *32,* 20–27. **(13)**

———. Marital satisfaction over the family life cycle. *Journal of Marriage and the Family,* 1974, *36,* 294–302. **(1)**

Rollins, B. C., & Galligan, R. The developing child and marital satisfaction of parents. In R. M. Lerner & G. B. Spanier (Eds.), *Child influences on marital and family interaction. A life-span perspective.* New York: Academic Press, 1978. **(13)**

Rosenkrantz, P., Vogel, S., Bee, H., Broverman, I., & Broverman, D. M. Sex-role stereotypes and self-conceptions of college students. *Journal of Consulting and Clinical Psychology,* 1968, *32,* 287–295. **(6)**

Rosenthall, R., & Jacobson, L. *Pygmalion in the classroom: Teacher expectations and pupils' intellectual development.* New York: Holt, Rinehart and Winston, 1968. **(4)**

Rosett, H. L., Ouellette, E. M., & Weiner, L. A pilot prospective study of the fetal alcohol syndrome at the Boston City Hospital. Part I: Maternal drinking. In F. A. Seixas & S. Eggleston (Eds.), Work in progress on alcoholism. *Annals of the New York Academy of Science,* 1976, *273,* 118–122. **(2)**

Ross, G., Kagan, J., Zelazo, P., & Kotelchuck, M. Separation protest in infants in home and laboratory. *Developmental Psychology,* 1975, *11,* 256–257. **(7)**

Rossi, A. S. Life-span theories and women's lives. *Signs: Journal of Women in Culture and Society,* 1980a, *6,* 4–32. **(Sum III)**

———. Aging and parenthood in the middle years. In P. B. Baltes & O. G. Brim, Jr. (Eds.),

Life-span development and behavior. New York: Academic Press, 1980*b*. **(13)**

Rossi, A. S., & Rossi, P. E. Body time and social time: Mood patterns by menstrual cycle phase and day of the week. In J. E. Parsons (Ed.), *The psychobiology of sex differences and sex roles.* New York: Hemisphere, 1980. **(8)**

Rothbart, M. K. Measurement of temperament in infancy. *Child Development,* 1981, *52,* 569–578. **(6)**

Rothbart, M. K., & Derryberry, D. Development of individual differences in temperament. In M. E. Lamb & A. L. Brown (Eds.), *Advances in developmental psychology,* (Vol. 1). Hillsdale, N.J.: Erlbaum, 1981. **(6)**

Rowe, I., & Marcia, J. E. Ego identity status, formal operations, and moral development. *Journal of Youth and Adolescence,* 1980, *9,* 87–99. **(Sum II)**

Rubin, Z. *Liking and loving. An invitation to social psychology.* New York: Holt, Rinehart and Winston, 1973. **(14)**

————. *Children's friendships.* Cambridge, Mass.: Harvard University Press, 1980. **(7)**

Ruble, D. N., Balaban, T., & Cooper, J. Gender constancy and the effects of sex-typed televised toy commercials. *Child Development,* 1981, *52,* 667–673. **(6)**

Ruble, D. N., & Brooks-Gunn, J. The experience of menarche. *Child Development,* 1982, *53,* 1557–1566. **(8)**

Rutter, M. Family, area and school influences in the genesis of conduct disorders. In L. Hersov, M. Berber, & D. Shaffer (Eds.), *Aggression and antisocial behavior in childhood and adolescence.* Elmsford, N.Y.: Pergamon, 1978. **(6, Sum I)**

————. Maternal deprivation, 1972–1978: New findings, new concepts, new approaches. *Child Development,* 1979, *50,* 283–305. **(Sum I)**

————. Social-emotional consequences of day care for preschool children. In E. F. Zigler & E. W. Gordon (Eds.), *Day care. Scientific and social policy issues.* Boston, Mass.: Auburn House, 1982. **(7)**

Sacks, E. Intelligence scores as a function of experimentally established social relationships between child and examiner. *Journal of Abnormal and Social Psychology,* 1952, *46,* 354–358. **(4)**

Salapatek, P. Pattern perception in early infancy. In L. B. Cohen & P. Salapatek (Eds.), *Infant perception: From sensation to cognition* (Vol. 1). New York: Academic Press, 1975. **(3)**

Salapatek, P., & Kessen, W. Visual scanning of triangles by the human newborn. *Journal of Experimental Child Psychology,* 1966, *3,* 155–167. **(2)**

Sameroff, A. J., & Chandler, M. J. Reproductive risk and the continuum of caretaking casualty. In F. D. Horowitz (Ed.), *Review of child development research* (Vol. 4). Chicago: University of Chicago Press, 1975. **(2, Sum I)**

Sangiuliano, I. *In her time.* New York: Morrow, 1978. **(10)**

Sarason, I., Johnson, H., & Seigel, M. Assessing the impact of life changes: Development of the life experiences survey. *Journal of Consulting and Clinical Psychology,* 1978, *46,* 932–946. **(11)**

Sattler, J. M. *Assessment of children's intelligence.* Philadelphia: Saunders, 1974. **(4)**

Savage-Rumbaugh, E. S., & Rumbaugh, D. M. Language analogue project, phase II: Theory and tactics. In K. E. Nelson (Ed.), *Children's language* (Vol. 2). New York: Gardner Press, 1980. **(5)**

Scanzoni, J. Contemporary marriage types. *Journal of Family Issues,* 1980, *1,* 125–140. **(13)**

Scarf, M. *Unfinished business. Pressure points in the lives of women.* Garden City, N.Y.: Doubleday, 1980. **(13, Sum III)**

Scarr, S., & Weinberg, R. A. Intellectual similarities within families of both adopted and biological children. *Intelligence,* 1977, *1,* 170–191. **(4)**

Scarr-Salapatek, S. An evolutionary perspective on infant intelligence: Species patterns and individual variations. In M. Lewis (Ed.), *Origins of intelligence.* New York: Plenum, 1976. **(Sum I)**

Schachter, F. F. *Everyday mother talk to toddlers.* New York: Academic Press, 1979. **(5)**

————. Toddlers with employed mothers. *Child Development,* 1981, *52,* 958–964. **(13)**

Schachter, F. F., Shore, E., Hodapp, R., Chalfin, S., & Bundy, C. Do girls talk earlier? MLU in toddlers. *Developmental Psychology,* 1978, *14,* 388–392. **(5)**

Schaie, K. W., & Labouvie-Vief, G. Generational versus ontogenetic components of change in adult cognitive behavior: A fourteen-year cross-sequential study. *Developmental Psychology,* 1974, *10,* 305–320. **(12)**

Schaie, K. W., & Strother, C. R. A cross-sequential study of age changes in cognitive behavior. *Psychological Bulletin,* 1968, *70,* 671–680. **(12)**

Schooler, K. K. Response of the elderly to environment: A stress-theoretic perspective. In P. G. Windley & G. Ernst (Eds.), *Theory development in environment and aging.* Washington, D.C.: Gerontological Society, 1975. **(11)**

Schrader, W. B. The predictive validity of college board admissions tests. In W. H. Angoff (Ed.), *The College Board Admissions Testing Program: A technical report on research and development activities relating to the Scholastic Aptitude Test and Achievement Tests.* New York: College Entrance Examination Board, 1971. **(9)**

Schulz, R., & Alderman, D. Clinical research and the "stages of dying." *Omega,* 1974, *5,* 137–144. **(14)**

Schwab, D. P., & Heneman, H. G., III. Effects of age and experience on productivity. *Industrial Gerontology,* 1977, *4,* 113–117. **(13)**

Scollon, R. *Conversations with a one-year-old.* Honolulu: University of Hawaii Press, 1976. **(5)**

Sears, R. R., Maccoby, E. E., & Levin, H. *Patterns of child rearing.* New York: Harper & Row, 1957. **(1, 6)**

Sells, C. J. Infancy—The first two years. In D. W. Smith, E. L. Bierman, & N. M. Robinson (Eds.), *The biologic ages of man from conception through old age.* Philadelphia: Saunders, 1978. **(3)**

Selman, R. L. *The growth of interpersonal understanding: Developmental and clinical analyses.* New York: Academic Press, 1980. **(9, 10)**

Sharabany, R., Gershoni, R., & Hoffman, J. E. Girlfriend, boyfriend: Age and sex differences in intimate friendship. *Developmental Psychology,* 1981, *17,* 800–808. **(10)**

Shatz, M., & Gelman, R. The development of communication skills: Modifications in the speech of young children as a function of the listener. *Monographs of the Society for Research in Child Development,* 1973, *38* (Whole No. 153). **(4)**

Sheehy, G. *Pathfinders.* New York: Dutton, 1982. **(13)**

Sheldon, W. H. *The varieties of human physique.* New York: Harper & Row, 1940. **(3)**

Shepard, R. N. The mental image. *American Psychologist,* 1978, *33,* 125–137. **(12)**

Sheridan, M. D. Final report of a prospective study of children whose mothers had rubella in early pregnancy. *British Medical Journal,* 1964, *2,* 536–539. **(2)**

Shock, N. W. Energy metabolism, caloric intake and physical activity in the aging. In L. A. Carlson (Ed.), *Nutrition in old age.* X Symposia of the Swedish Nutrition Foundation. Uppsala: Almqvist & Wiksell, 1972. **(11)**

———. Biological theories of aging. In J. E. Birren & K. W. Schaie (Eds.), *Handbook of the psychology of aging.* New York: Van Nostrand Reinhold, 1977. **(11)**

Shulman, N. Life-cycle variations in patterns of close relationships. *Journal of Marriage and the Family,* 1975, *37,* 813–823. **(14)**

Siegel, O. Personality development in adolescence. In B. B. Wolman (Ed.), *Handbook of developmental psychology.* Englewood Cliffs, N.J.: Prentice-Hall, 1982. **(8, Sum II)**

Siegler, R. S., & Richards, D. D. The development of intelligence. In R. J. Sternberg (Ed.), *Handbook of human intelligence.* New York: Cambridge University Press, 1982. **(4)**

Sigel, I. E., & Olmsted, P. Modification of cognitive skills among lower-class black children. In J. Hellmuth (Ed.), *The disadvantaged child* (Vol. 1). New York: Brunner-Mazel, 1970. **(4)**

Silvestre, D., & Fresno, N. Reactions to prenatal diagnosis: Analysis of 87 interviews. *American Journal of Orthopsychiatry,* 1980, *50,* 610–617. **(2)**

Sinclair, D. *Human growth after birth.* New York: Oxford University Press, 1978. **(3)**

Sizonenko, P. C., & Paunier, L. Hormonal changes in puberty (III): Correlation of plasma dehydroepiandrosterone, testosterone, FSH, and LH with stages of puberty and bone age in normal boys and girls and in patients with Addison's disease and hypogonadism or with premature or late adrenarche. *Journal of Clinical Endocrinology and Metabolism,* 1975, *41,* 894–904. **(8)**

Skinner, B. F. *Verbal behavior.* Englewood Cliffs, N.J.: Prentice-Hall, 1957. **(5)**

Slaby, R. G., & Frey, K. S. Development of gender constancy and selective attention to same-sex models. *Child Development,* 1975, *46,* 849–856. **(4, 6)**

Slaby, R. G., Quarfoth, G. R., & McConnachie, G. A. Television violence and its sponsors. *Journal of Communication,* 1976, *26,* 88–96. **(6)**

Smelser, N. J., & Erikson, E. H. (Eds.). *Themes of work and love in adulthood.* Cambridge, Mass.: Harvard University Press, 1980. **(14)**

Smith, D. W. Growth. In D. W. Smith, E. L. Bierman, & N. M. Robinson (Eds.), *The biologic ages of man from conception through old age.* Philadelphia: Saunders, 1978. **(3, 11)**

Smith, D. W., & Stenchever, M. A. Prenatal life and the pregnant woman. In D. W. Smith, E. L. Bierman, & N. M. Robinson (Eds.), *The biologic ages of man: From conception through old age.* Philadelphia: Saunders, 1978. **(2)**

Snow, C. E., & Ferguson, C. A. (Eds.) *Talking to children.* New York: Cambridge University Press, 1977. **(5)**

Snyder, C., Eyres, S. J., & Barnard, K. New findings about mothers' antenatal expectations and their relationship to infant development. *MCN,* 1979, *4,* 354–357. **(2)**

Sorenson, J. R., Swazey, J. P., & Scotch, N. A. Reproductive pasts, reproductive futures: Genetic counseling and its effectiveness. *Birth Defects: Original Article Series,* 1981, *17* (No. 4), 1981. **(2)**

Spanier, G. B., & Lewis, R. A. Marital quality: A review of the seventies. *Journal of Marriage and the Family,* 1980, *42,* 825–840. **(10)**

Spelke, E. S., & Owsley, C. J. Intermodal exploration and knowledge in infancy. *Infant Behavior and Development,* 1979, *2,* 13–27. **(3)**

Spence, J. T., & Helmreich, R. L. *Masculinity and femininity.* Austin, Texas: University of Texas Press, 1978. **(10)**

Spivack, G., & Shure, M. B. *Social adjustment of young children.* San Francisco: Jossey-Bass, 1974. **(4)**

Spreitzer, E., & Riley, L. E. Factors associated with singlehood. *Journal of Marriage and the Family,* 1974, *36,* 533–542. **(13)**

Sroufe, L. A. Wariness of strangers and the study of infant development. *Child Development,* 1977, *48,* 731–746. **(7)**

———. Attachment and the roots of competence. *Human Nature,* 1978, *1,* 50–56. **(6, 7)**

———. The coherence of individual development: Early care, attachment, and subsequent developmental issues. *American Psychologist,* 1979, *34,* 834–841. **(7, Sum I)**

Sroufe, L. A., & Egeland, B. *Forms of child maltreatment.* Paper presented at the biennial meetings of the Society for Research in Child Development, Boston, 1981. **(6)**

Sroufe, L. A., & Waters, E. Attachment as an organizational construct. *Child Development,* 1977, *48,* 1184–1199. **(7)**

Stadel, B. V., & Weiss, N. S. Characteristics of menopausal women: A survey of King and Pierce counties in Washington, 1973–1974. *American Journal of Epidemiology,* 1975, *102,* 209–216. **(11)**

Stahlke, H. F. W. On asking the question: Can apes learn language? In K. E. Nelson (Ed.), *Children's language* (Vol. 2). New York: Gardner Press, 1980. **(5)**

Staines, G. L., & Quinn, R. P. American workers evaluate the quality of their jobs. *Monthly Labor Review,* 1979 (January), 3–12. **(13)**

Stamler, J. S., Schoenberger, J. A., Shekelle, R. B., & Stamler, R. Hypertension: The problem and the challenge. In *The hypertension handbook.* West Point, Pa.: Merck, Sharp & Dohme, 1974. **(11)**

Stanley, J. S., Keating, D. P., & Fox, L. H. (Eds.), *Mathematical talent: Discovery, description, and development.* Baltimore: Johns Hopkins University Press, 1974. **(9)**

Staub, E. A child in distress: The effects of focusing responsibility on children on their attempts to help. *Developmental Psychology,* 1970, *2,* 152–154. **(7)**

———. To rear a prosocial child: Reasoning, learning by doing, and learning by teaching others. In D. J. DePalma & J. M. Foley (Eds.), *Moral development. Current theory and research.* Hillsdale, N.J.: Erlbaum, 1975. **(7)**

———. *Positive social behavior and morality* (Vol. 2). New York: Academic Press, 1979. **(7)**

Stechler, G., & Halton, A. Prenatal influences on human development. In B. B. Wolman (Ed.), *Handbook of developmental psychology.* Englewood Cliffs, N.J.: Prentice-Hall, 1982. **(3)**

Stein, P. J. The lifestyles and life chances of the never-married. *Marriage and Family Review,* 1978, *1,* (4), 1–11. **(13)**

Stein, Z., Susser, M., Saenger, G., & Morolla, F. *Famine and human development: The Dutch hunger winter of 1944–1945.* New York: Oxford University Press, 1975. **(2, 8)**

Steinberg, L. D. Transformations in family relations at puberty. *Developmental Psychology,* 1981, *17,* 833–840. **(10, Sum II)**

Steiner, J. E. Human facial expressions in response to taste and smell stimulation. In H. W. Reese & L. P. Lipsitt (Eds.), *Advances in child development and behavior* (Vol. 13). New York: Academic Press, 1979. **(3)**

Stenchever, M. A. Prenatal life and the pregnant woman: The pregnant woman. In D. W. Smith, E. L. Bierman, & N. M. Robinson (Eds.), *The biologic ages of man from conception through old age.* Philadelphia: Saunders, 1978*a.* **(8)**

———. Perinatal life for mother and baby: Labor and delivery. In D. W. Smith, E. L. Bierman, & N. M. Robinson (Eds.), *The biologic ages of man from conception through old age.* Philadelphia: Saunders, 1978*b.* **(8)**

Stern, D. *The first relationship: Infant and mother.* Cambridge, Mass.: Harvard University Press, 1977. **(7)**

Sternberg, R. J. Who's intelligent? *Psychology Today,* 1982, *16*(4), 30–39. **(4)**

Sternberg, R. J., Conway, B. E., Ketron, J. L., & Bernstein, M. People's conceptions of intelligence. *Journal of Personality and Social Psychology,* 1981, *41,* 37–55. **(4)**

Sternglanz, S. H., & Serbin, L. A. Sex role stereotyping in children's television programs. *Developmental Psychology,* 1974, *10,* 710–715. **(6)**

Stogdill, R. M. *Handbook of leadership.* New York: Free Press, 1974. **(12)**

Strauss, M. E., Starr, R. H., Jr., Ostrea, E. M., Jr., Chavez, C. J., & Stryker, J. C. Behavioral concomitants to prenatal addiction to narcotics. *Journal of Pediatrics,* 1976, *89,* 842–846. **(2)**

Strayer, F. F. Social ecology of the preschool peer group. In A. Collins (Ed.), *Minnesota symposia on child psychology* (Vol. 13). Hillsdale, N.J.: Erlbaum, 1980. **(7)**

Strayer, F. F., & Strayer, J. An ethological analysis of social agonism and dominance relations among preschool children. *Child Development,* 1976, *47,* 980–989. **(7)**

Streissguth, A. P., Martin, D. C., Martin, J. C., & Barr, H. M. The Seattle longitudinal prospective study on alcohol and pregnancy. *Neurobehavioral Toxicology and Teratology,* 1981, *3,* 223–233. **(2)**

Sullivan, K., & Sullivan, A. Adolescent-parent separation. *Developmental Psychology,* 1980, *16,* 93–99. **(10)**

Svejda, M. J., Campos, J. J., & Emde, R. N. Mother–infant "bonding": Failure to generalize. *Child Development,* 1980, *51,* 775–779. **(7)**

Swensen, C. H., Eskew, R. W., Kohlhepp, K. A. Stage of family life cycle, ego development, and the marriage relationship. *Journal of Marriage and the Family,* 1981, *43,* 841–853. **(13, 14)**

Talbert, G. B. Aging of the reproductive system. In C. E. Finch & L. Hayflick (Eds.), *Handbook of the biology of aging.* New York: Van Nostrand Reinhold, 1977. **(11)**

Tannenbaum, A. J. Pre-Sputnik to post-Watergate concern about the gifted. In A. H. Passow (Ed.), *The gifted and the talented: Their education and development.* The seventy-eighth yearbook of the National Society for the Study of Education. Chicago: University of Chicago Press, 1979. **(9)**

Tanner, J. M. *Growth at adolescence.* Springfield, Ill: Thomas, 1962. **(8)**

————. Physical growth. In P. H. Mussen (Ed.), *Carmichael's manual of child psychology* (Vol. 1, 3d ed.). New York: Wiley, 1970. **(3, Sum II)**

————. *Fetus into man: Physical growth from conception to maturity.* Cambridge, Mass.: Harvard University Press, 1978. **(8)**

Tanner, J. M., Whitehouse, R. H., Marshall, W. A., Healy, M. J. R., & Goldstein, H. *Assessment of skeletal maturity and prediction of adult height.* New York: Academic Press, 1975. **(8)**

Tanner, J. M., Whitehouse, R. H., & Takaishi, M. Standards from birth to maturity for height, weight, height velocity and weight velocity: British children, 1965. *Archives of Disease in Childhood,* 1966, *41,* 613–635. **(3)**

Teeple, J. Physical growth and maturation. In M. V. Ridenour (Ed.), *Motor development: Issues and applications.* Princeton, N.J.: Princeton Book Company, 1978. **(3)**

Terman, L. M., & Merrill, M. *Measuring intelligence: A guide to the new revised Stanford-Binet test of intelligence.* Boston: Houghton Mifflin, 1937. **(4)**

————. *Stanford-Binet Intelligence Scale. Manual for the third revision.* Boston: Houghton Mifflin, 1960. **(4)**

Terrace, H. S., Petitto, L. A., Sanders, R. J., & Bever, T. G. On the grammatical capacity of apes. In K. E. Nelson (Ed.), *Children's language* (Vol. 2). New York: Gardner Press, 1980. **(5)**

Thomas, A., & Chess, S. *Temperament and development.* New York: Brunner/Mazel, 1977. **(1, 6)**

Thomas, A., Chess, S., & Birch, H. G. The origin of personality. *Scientific American,* 1970, *223,* 102–109. **(4)**

Thompson, S. K. Gender labels and early sex role development. *Child Development,* 1975, *46,* 339–347. **(6)**

Thurstone, L. L. *Primary mental abilities.* Chicago: University of Chicago Press, 1938. **(12)**

Tieger, T. On the biological basis of sex differences in aggression. *Child Development,* 1980, *51,* 943–963. **(7)**

Tierney, J. Getting older. *The Seattle Post-Intelligencer,* 1982, July 4–6. **(11)**

Tiger, L. *Men in groups.* New York: Random House, 1969. **(14)**

Toffler, A. *Future shock.* New York: Random House, 1970. **(13)**

Tognoli, J. Male friendship and intimacy across the life span. *Family Relations,* 1980, *29,* 273–280. **(14)**

Tomlinson-Keasey, C. Formal operations in females from eleven to fifty-four years of age. *Developmental Psychology,* 1972, *6,* 364. **(Sum II)**

Tomlinson-Keasey, C., & Keasey, C. The mediating role of cognitive development in moral judgment. *Child Development,* 1974, *45,* 291–298. **(9)**

Tonna, E. A. Aging of skeletal-dental systems and supporting tissues. In C. E. Finch & L. Hayflick (Eds.), *Handbook of the biology of aging.* New York: Van Nostrand Reinhold, 1977. **(11)**

Torgersen, A. M., & Kringlen, E. Genetic aspects of temperamental differences in twins. *Journal of American Academy of Child Psychiatry,* 1978, *17,* 433–444. **(6)**

Troll, L. Grandparenting. In L. W. Poon (Ed.), *Aging in the 1980s. Psychological issues.* Washington, D.C.: American Psychological Association, 1980. **(13)**

Troll, L., & Bengston, V. Generations in the family. In W. R. Burr, R. Hill, F. I. Nye, & I. L. Reiss (Eds.), *Contemporary theories about the family* (Vol. 1). New York: Free Press, 1979. **(14)**

Troll, L. E., & Smith, J. Attachment through the life span: Some questions about dyadic bonds among adults. *Human Development,* 1976, *19,* 156–170. **(10, 14)**

Tulkin, S. R., & Covitz, F. E. *Mother–infant interaction and intellectual functioning at age six.* Paper presented at the biennial meeting of the Society for Research in Child Development, Denver, 1975. **(4)**

Udry, J. R. *The social context of marriage* (2d ed.). Philadelphia: Lippincott, 1971. **(10)**

Ullian, D. Z. The child's construction of gender: Anatomy as destiny. In E. K. Shapiro & E. Weber (Eds.), *Cognitive and affective growth.* Hillsdale, N.J.: Erlbaum, 1981. **(6)**

Undergraduate admissions: The realities of institutional policies, practices and procedures (American Association of Collegiate Registrars and Admissions Officers and the College Board). New York: College Entrance Examination Board, 1980. **(9)**

U.S. Bureau of the Census. *Statistical abstract of the United States: 1978* (99th ed.). Washington, D.C.: U.S. Government Printing Office, 1978. **(13)**

———. Fertility of American Women: June 1979. *Current population reports, population characteristics,* Series P-20, No. 358, 1980. **(8)**

U.S. Department of Labor. Job satisfaction: Is there a trend? *Manpower Research Monograph No. 30.* Washington, D.C.: U.S. Government Printing Office, 1974. **(13)**

Urberg, K. A., & Labouvie-Vief, G. Conceptualizations of sex roles: A life-span developmental study. *Developmental Psychology,* 1976, *12,* 15–23. **(10)**

Vaillant, G. E. *Adaptation to life: How the best and the brightest came of age.* Boston: Little, Brown, 1977. **(1, 14, Sum III)**

———. *Adaptation to life: How the best and the brightest came of age.* Boston: Little, Brown, 1978. **(13)**

Vaughn, B., Egeland, B., Sroufe, L. A., & Waters, E. Individual differences in infant–mother attachment at twelve and eighteen months: Stability and change in families under stress. *Child Development,* 1979, *50,* 971–975. **(7)**

Vaughn, B. E., & Waters, E. Attention structure, sociometric status, and dominance: Interrelations, behavioral correlates, and relationships to social competence. *Developmental Psychology,* 1981, *17,* 275–288. **(7)**

Vener, A., & Stewart, C. Adolescent sexual behavior in middle America revisited: 1970–1973. *Journal of Marriage and the Family,* 1974, *36,* 728–735. **(8)**

Veterans Administration Cooperative Study Group on Antihypertensive Agents. Effects of treatment on morbidity in hypertension (II). Results in patients with diastolic blood pressure averaging 90 through 114 mm Hg. *Journal of the American Medical Association,* 1970, *213,* 1143–1152. **(11)**

Vigersky, R. A. (Ed.), *Anorexia nervosa.* New York: Raven Press, 1977. **(8)**

Vygotsky, L. S. *Thought and language.* Cambridge, Mass.: M.I.T. Press, 1962. **(1)**

Waber, D. P. Sex differences in mental abilities, hemispheric lateralization, and rate of physical growth at adolescence. *Developmental Psychology,* 1977, *13,* 29–38. **(9, Sum II)**

Wachs, T. D. Proximal experience and early cognitive-intellectual development: The physical environment. *Merrill-Palmer Quarterly,* 1979, *25,* 3–41. **(Sum I)**

Waddington, C. H. *The strategy of the genes.* London: Allen & Unwin, 1957. **(Sum I)**

Walker, L. J., & Richards, B. S. Stimulating transitions in moral reasoning as a function of stage of cognitive development. *Developmental Psychology,* 1979, *15,* 95–103. **(9)**

Walker, R. N. Body build and behavior in young children: I. Body and nursery school teachers' ratings. *Monographs of the Society for Research in Child Development,* 1962, *27* (Whole No. 84). **(3)**

Wallach, M. A., & Kogan, N. *Modes of thinking in young children: A study of the creativity-intelligence distinction.* New York: Holt, Rinehart and Winston, 1965. **(4)**

Wallerstein, J. S., & Kelly, J. B. *Surviving the breakup. How children and parents cope with divorce.* New York: Basic Books, 1980. **(6, 14)**

Walster, E., & Walster, G. W. *A new look at love.* Reading, Mass.: Addison-Wesley, 1978. **(10)**

Walters, R. H., & Brown, M. Studies of reinforcement of aggression. III. Transfer of responses to an interpersonal situation. *Child Development,* 1963, *34,* 563–571. **(1)**

Ward, D. A. The influence of family relationships on social and psychological functioning: A followup study. *Journal of Marriage and the Family,* 1981, *43,* 807–815. **(14)**

Waterman, A. S., Geary, P. S., & Waterman, C. K. A longitudinal study of changes in ego identity status from the freshman to the senior year at college. *Developmental Psychology,* 1974, *10,* 387–392. **(10)**

Waterman, A. S., & Goldman, J. A. A longitudinal study of ego identity development at a liberal arts college. *Journal of Youth and Adolescence,* 1976, *5,* 361–369. **(10)**

Waterman, A. S., & Waterman, C. K. A longitudinal study of changes in ego identity status during the freshman year at college. *Developmental Psychology,* 1971, *5,* 167–173. **(10)**

Waterman, C. K., & Nevid, J. S. Sex differences in the resolution of the identity crisis. *Journal of Youth and Adolescence,* 1977, *6,* 337–342. **(10)**

Waters, E. The reliability and stability of individual differences in infant-mother attachment. *Child Development,* 1978, *49,* 483–494. **(7)**

Waters, E., Vaughn, B. E., & Egeland, B. R. Individual differences in infant–mother attachment relationships at age one: Antecedents in neonatal behavior in an urban, economically disadvantaged sample. *Child Development,* 1980, *51,* 208–216. **(7)**

Waters, E., Wippman, J., & Sroufe, L. A. Attachment, positive affect, and competence in the peer group. *Child Development,* 1979, *50,* 821–829. **(6)**

Webb, R. A. (Ed.) *Social development in childhood.* Baltimore: Johns Hopkins University Press, 1978. **(4)**

Wechsler, D. *The measurement and appraisal of adult intelligence.* Baltimore: Williams & Wilkins, 1958. **(9)**

———. *Wechsler Preschool and Primary Scale of Intelligence, manual.* New York: Psychological Corporation, 1967. **(4)**

———. *Manual for the Wechsler Intelligence Scale for Children—Revised.* New York: Psychological Corporation, 1974. **(4)**

Weikart, D. P. Relationship of curriculum, teaching, and learning in preschool education. In J. C. Stanley (Ed.), *Preschool programs for the disadvantaged.* Baltimore: Johns Hopkins University Press, 1972. **(4)**

Weingarten, H. Remarriage and well-being: National survey evidence of social and psychological effects. *Journal of Family Issues,* 1980, *1,* 533–560. **(13)**

Weiss, R. S. The fund of sociability. *Trans-Action,* 1969, *6,* 36. **(7)**

Wells, K. Gender-role identity and psychological adjustment in adolescence. *Journal of Youth and Adolescence,* 1980, *9,* 59–73. **(10)**

Werker, J. F., Gilbert, J. H. V., Humphrey, K., & Tees, R. C. Developmental aspects of cross-language speech perception. *Child Development,* 1981, *52,* 349–355. **(5)**

Werner, H. *Comparative psychology of mental development.* Chicago: Follett, 1948. **(1, Sum III)**

Weymouth, F. W. Visual acuity of children. In M. J. Hirsch & R. E. Wick (Eds.), *Vision of children: An optometric symposium.* Radnors, Pa.: Chilton, 1963. **(3)**

White, B. L. An experimental approach to the effects of experience on early human behavior. In J. P. Hill (Ed.), *Minnesota symposia on child psychology.* Minneapolis: The University of Minnesota Press, 1967. **(3)**

White, S. W., & Bloom, B. L. Factors related to the adjustment of divorcing men. *Family Relations,* 1981, *30,* 349–360. **(14)**

Whiting, B. B., & Whiting, J. W. M. Altruistic and egoistic behavior in six cultures. In L. Nater & T. W. Maretzki (Eds.), *Cultural illness and health: Essays in human adaptation.* Washington, D.C.: American Anthropological Association, 1973. **(7)**

———. *Children of six cultures.* Cambridge, Mass.: Harvard University Press, 1975. **(7)**

Williams, J. E., Bennett, S. M., & Best, D. L. Awareness and expression of sex stereotypes in young children. *Developmental Psychology,* 1975, *11,* 635–642. **(6)**

Wilson, R. S. Twins and siblings: Concordance for school-age mental development. *Child Development,* 1977, *48,* 211–216. **(4)**

———. Synchronies in mental development: An epigenetic perspective. *Science,* 1978, *202,* 939–948. **(4)**

Winch, R. F. Complementary needs and related notions about voluntary mate selection. In R. F. Winch & G. B. Spanier (Eds.), *Selected studies in marriage and the family.* New York: Holt, Rinehart and Winston, 1974. **(10)**

Witkin, H. A. *The role of cognitive style in academic performance and in teacher-student relations.* (RB-73-11) Princeton, N.J.: Educational Testing Service, 1973. **(4)**

Witkin, H. A., Dyk, R. B., Faterson, H. F., Goodenough, D. R., & Karp, S. A. *Psychological differentiation.* New York: Wiley, 1962. **(3, 4)**

Witkin, H. A., Moore, C. A., Goodenough, D. R., & Cox, P. W. Field-dependent and field-independent cognitive styles and their educational implications. *Review of Educational Research,* 1977, *47,* 1–64. **(9)**

Wolff, P. H. Mother–infant relations at birth. In J. G. Howels (Ed.), *Modern perspectives in international child psychiatry.* New York: Brunner/Mazel, 1971, 20–97. **(2)**

Wood, V., & Robertson, J. F. Friendship and kinship interaction: Differential effect on the morale of the elderly. *Journal of Marriage and the Family,* 1978, *40,* 367–375. **(13)**

Worden, P. E. Effects of sorting on subsequent recall of unrelated items: A developmental study. *Child Development,* 1975, *46,* 687–695. **(4)**

Worell, J. Life-span sex roles: Development, continuity, and change. In R. M. Lerner & N. A. Busch-Rossnagel (Eds.), *Individuals as producers of their own development. A life-span perspective.* New York: Academic Press, 1981. **(13)**

Wright, P. H. Men's friendships, women's friendships and the alleged inferiority of the latter. *Sex Roles,* 1982, *8,* 1–20. **(14)**

Wright, P. H., & Keple, T. W. Friends and parents of a sample of high school juniors: An exploratory study of relationship intensity and interpersonal rewards. *Journal of Marriage and the Family,* 1981, *43,* 559–570. **(10)**

Yarrow, L. J., Rubenstein, J. L., Pedersen, F. A. *Infant and environment.* New York: Halsted Press, 1975. **(1)**

Young, H. B., & Ferguson, L. R. *Puberty to manhood in Italy and America.* New York: Academic Press, 1981. **(8)**

Zack, P. M., Harlan, W. R., Leaverton, P. E., & Cornoni-Huntley, J. A longitudinal study of body fatness in childhood and adolescence. *Journal of Pediatrics,* 1979, *95,* 126–130. **(8, Sum III)**

Zahn-Waxler, C., Radke-Yarrow, M., & King, R. A. Child rearing and children's prosocial initiations toward victims of distress. *Child Development,* 1979, *50,* 319–330. **(7)**

Zajonc, R. B. Birth order and intelligence: Dumber by the dozen. *Psychology Today,* 1975, *8,* 37–43. **(4)**

Zelnik, M., & Kantner, J. F. First pregnancies to women aged 15–19: 1976 and 1971. *Family Planning Perspectives,* 1978, *10,* 11–19. **(8)**

Zelnik, M., Kantner, J. F., & Ford, K. *Sex and pregnancy in adolescence.* Beverly Hills, Calif.: Sage, 1981. **(8)**

Zeskind, P. S., & Lester, B. M. Acoustic features and auditory perceptions of the cries of newborns with prenatal and perinatal complications. *Child Development,* 1978, *49,* 580–589. **(5)**

Zeskind, P. S., & Ramey, C. T. Fetal malnutrition: An experimental study of its consequences on infant development in two caregiving environments. *Child Development,* 1978, *49,* 1155–1162. **(Sum I)**

———. Preventing intellectual and interactional sequelae of fetal malnutrition: A longitudinal, transactional, and synergistic approach to development. *Child Development,* 1981, *52,* 213–218. **(2, Sum I)**

Zigler, E., & Butterfield, E. C. Motivational aspects of changes in IQ test performance of culturally deprived nursery school children. *Child Development,* 1968, *39,* 1–14. **(4)**

Index